Communications
in Computer and Information Science 390

T0211751

Emmanouel Garoufallou   Jane Greenberg (Eds.)

Metadata and Semantics Research

7th Research Conference, MTSR 2013
Thessaloniki, Greece, November 19-22, 2013
Proceedings

 Springer

Volume Editors

Emmanouel Garoufallou
Alexander Technological Educational Institute
of Thessaloniki, Greece
E-mail: mgarou@libd.teithe.gr

Jane Greenberg
University of North Carolina
at Chapel Hill, NC, USA
E-mail: janeg@email.unc.edu

ISSN 1865-0929   e-ISSN 1865-0937
ISBN 978-3-319-03436-2   e-ISBN 978-3-319-03437-9
DOI 10.1007/978-3-319-03437-9
Springer Cham Heidelberg New York Dordrecht London

Library of Congress Control Number: 2013951846

CR Subject Classification (1998): H.3, H.2, I.7, I.2.4, I.2.7, H.4, K.3, K.4, H.5

Typesetting: Camera-ready by author, data conversion by Scientific Publishing Services, Chennai, India

Printed on acid-free paper

Springer is part of Springer Science+Business Media (www.springer.com)

Preface

Metadata and semantics are integral to any information system and significant to the sphere of Web data. Research focusing on metadata and semantics is crucial for advancing our understanding and knowledge of metadata; and, more profoundly for being able to effectively discover, use, archive, and repurpose information. In response to this need, researchers are actively examining methods for generating, reusing, and interchanging metadata. Integrated with these developments is research on the application of computational methods, linked data, and data analytics. A growing body of work also targets conceptual and theoretical designs providing foundational frameworks for metadata and semantic applications. There is no doubt that metadata weaves its way into nearly every aspect of our information ecosystem, and there is great motivation for advancing the current state of metadata and semantics. To this end, it is vital that scholars and practitioners convene and share their work.

Since 2005, the Metadata and Semantics Research Conference (MTSR) has served as a significant venue for dissemination and sharing of metadata- and semantic-driven research and practices. This year, 2013, marked the seventh MTSR Conference, drawing scholars and researchers investigating and advancing our knowledge on a wide range of metadata- and semantic-driven topics. MTSR has grown in numbers and submission rates over the last decade, marking it as a leading, international research conference. Continuing the successful mission of previous MTSR Conferences (MTSR 2005, MTSR 2007, MTSR 2009, MTSR 2010, MTSR 2011 and MTSR 2012), MTSR 2013 aimed to bring together scholars and practitioners who share a common interest in the interdisciplinary field of metadata, linked data, and ontologies.

The MTSR 2013 program and the contents of these proceedings show a rich diversity of research and practices, drawing on problems from metadata and semantically focused tools and technologies, linked data, cross-language semantics, ontologies, metadata models, and semantic system and metadata standards. The general session of the conference included 18 papers covering a broad spectrum of topics, proving the interdisciplinary field of metadata, and was divided into three main themes: platforms for research data sets, system architecture and data management; metadata and ontology validation, evaluation, mapping and interoperability; and content management. Metadata as a research topic is maturing, and the conference also supported the following five tracks: Metadata and Semantics for Open Repositories, Research Information Systems and Data Infrastructures; Metadata and Semantics for Cultural Collections and Applications; Metadata and Semantics for Agriculture, Food and Environment; Big Data and Digital Libraries in Health, Science and Technology; and European and National Projects, and Project Networking. Each track had a rich selection of papers, giving broader diversity to MTSR, and enabling deeper exploration of significant topics.

All the papers underwent a thorough and rigorous peer-review process. The review and selection this year was highly competitive and only papers containing significant research results, innovative methods, or novel and best practices were accepted for publication. Only 29 of 89 submissions were accepted as full papers, representing 32.5% of the total number of submissions. Additional contributions covering noteworthy and important results in special tracks or project reports were accepted, totaling 42 accepted contributions.

This year's conference included two outstanding keynote speakers. Dr. Stefan Gradmann, a professor arts department of KU Leuven (Belgium) and director of university library, addressed semantic research drawing from his work with Europeana. The title of his presentation was, "Towards a Semantic Research Library: Digital Humanities Research, Europeana and the Linked Data Paradigm". Dr. Michail Salampasis, associate professor from our conference host institution, the Department of Informatics of the Alexander TEI of Thessaloniki, presented new potential, intersecting search and linked data. The title of his talk was, "Rethinking the Search Experience: What Could Professional Search Systems Do Better?"

This year's conference, also, hosted the "Special Workshop of Project Networking," the "European and National projects" and a number of additional workshops and tutorials. Furthermore, the MUMIA (Multilingual and Multifaceted Interactive Information Access) group hosted a full day Interdisciplinary WG meeting, "Using Metadata and Semantics for Integrating Information Retrieval and Natural Language Processing technologies," including professionals from across Europe. All of these activities energized the creation of synergies amongst conference attendants, professionals and project partners and representatives.

It is fitting that MTSR 2013 was held in Thessaloniki, the second-largest city in Greece, and a true mecca for knowledge and the emergence of new ideas from antiquity to current times. The Alexander Technological Educational Institute of Thessaloniki (ATEITH) was both honored and inspired to host MTSR. The ATEITH and the conference organizers were committed to supporting an engaging conference environment enabling thoughtful discussion and advancing approaches to addressing metadata challenges.

We conclude this preface by thanking the many people who contributed their time and energy to MTSR 2013, and made possible this year's conference. We also thank all the organizations that supported the conference.

We extend a sincere thank you to the members of the Program Committees (track committees included), the Steering Committee, and the Organization Committees (both general and local) as well as the conference reviewers.

September 2013   Emmanouel Garoufallou
                                                             Jane Greenberg

Organization

Program Chairs

Garoufallou Emmanouel
(Chair)
    Alexander Technological Educational Institute of Thessaloniki, Greece

Greenberg Jane (Co-chair)
    University of North Carolina at Chapel Hill, USA

Organization Chairs

Siatri Rania
    Alexander Technological Educational Institute of Thessaloniki, Greece

Manghi Paolo
    Institute of Information Science and Techologies (ISTI), National Research Council, Italy

Houssos Nikos
    National Documentation Center (EKT), Greece

Hartley R.J.
    Manchester Metropolitan University, UK

Special Track Chair

Balatsoukas Panos
    University of Manchester, UK

Conference Steering Committee

Sicilia Miguel-Angel
    University of Alcalá, Spain

Manouselis Nikos
    Agro-Know Technologies, Greece

Sartori Fabio
    Università degli Studi di Milano-Bicocca, Italy

Dodero Juan Manuel
    University of Cádiz, Spain

Local Organizing Committee

Plakotari Dora
    Alexander Technological Educational Institute of Thessaloniki, Greece

Theodoridou Christina
    Alexander Technological Educational Institute of Thessaloniki, Greece

Hatzilia Margarita
    Alexander Technological Educational Institute of Thessaloniki, Greece

Christianoudis Ioannis
    Alexander Technological Educational Institute of Thessaloniki, Greece

Koutsomiha Damiana	American Farm School, Greece
Gaitanou Panorea	Ionian University, Greece
Ioannidis Giannis	Alexander Technological Educational Institute of Thessaloniki, Greece
Rousidis Dimitris	University of Alcalá, Spain
Mouskeftaropoulou Elena	Alexander Technological Educational Institute of Thessaloniki, Greece
Noulas Nikolaos	Alexander Technological Educational Institute of Thessaloniki, Greece
Paraskeuopoulos Kostas	Alexander Technological Educational Institute of Thessaloniki, Greece

Program Committee

Akerkar Rajendra	Western Norway Research Institute, Norway
Altun Arif	Hacetepe University, Turkey
Athanasiadis Ioannis N.	Democritus University of Thrace, Greece
Balatsoukas Panos	University of Manchester, UK
Bartol Tomaz	University of Ljubljana, Slovenia
Caracciolo Caterina	Food and Agriculture Organization of the United Nations, Italy
Cechinel Christian	Federal University of Pampa, Brazil
Chebotko Artem	University of Texas - Pan American, USA
Closs Sissi	Karlsruhe University of Applied Sciences, Germany
Costopoulou Constantina	Agricultural University of Athens, Greece
Cunningham Sally Jo	Waikato University, New Zealand
Escribano Otero Juan José	Universidad Europea de Madrid, Spain
Dogdu Erdogan	TOBB Teknoloji ve Ekonomi University, Turkey
Dodero Juan Manuel	University of Cádiz, Spain
Foulonneau Muriel	Tudor Public Research Centre, Luxemburg
Gaitanou Panorea	Ionian University, Greece
Garoufallou Emmanouel	Alexander Technological Educational Institute of Thessaloniki, Greece
Gergatsoulis Manolis	Ionian University, Greece
Greenberg Jane	University of North Carolina at Chapel Hill, USA
Hartley R.J.	Manchester Metropolitan University, UK
Houssos Nikos	National Documentation Center (EKT), Greece
Iglesias Carlos A.	Universidad Politecnica de Madrid, Spain
Jaiswal Pankaj	Oregon State University, USA
Jorg Brigitte	UKOL, UK
Kanellopoulos Dimitris	University of Patras, Greece
Kapidakis Sarantos	Ionian University, Greece
Kop Christian	University of Klangenfurt, Austria

Manghi Paolo · Institute of Information Science and Technologies (ISTI), National Research Council, Italy
Manouselis Nikos · Agro-Know Technologies, Greece
Moen William · University of North Texas, USA
O'Brien Ann · Loughborough University, UK
Ochoa Xavier · Centro de Tecnologias de Informacion Guayaquil, Equador
Okur Mehmet C. · Yaşar University, Turkey
Colomo-Palacios Ricardo · Universidad Carlos III, Spain
Palmonari Matteo · University of Milano-Bicocca, Italy
Papaleo Laura · University of Genova, Italy
Papatheodorou Christos · Ionian University, Greece
Poulos Marios · Ionian University, Greece
Prabhakar T.V. · Indian Institute of Technology Kanpur, India
Sanchez Salvador · University of Alcalá, Spain
Sartori Fabio · Università degli Studi di Milano-Bicocca, Italy
Senkul Pinar · METU, Turkey
Sgouropoulou Cleo · Technological Educational Institute, Athens, Greece
Sicilia Miguel-Ángel · University of Alcalá, Spain
Sugimoto Shigeo · University of Tsukuba, Japan
Ternier Stefaan · Open University of The Netherlands, The Netherlands
Tonkin Emma · University of Bath, UK
Zschocke Thomas · United Nations University, Germany

Referees

Rousidis Dimitris
David King
Antonopoulou Stavroula
Nikolaos Korfiatis
Christoph Schindler
Maltesh Motebennur
Koutsomiha Damiana

Athena Salaba
Mouskeftaropoulou Ele
Vangelis Banos
Sfakakis Michalis
Siatri Rania
Zafeiriou Georgia

Track on Big Data and Digital Libraries in Health, Science and Technology

Special Track Chairs

Garoufallou Emmanouel (Chair) · Alexander Technological Educational Institute of Thessaloniki, Greece
Balatsoukas Panos (Co-chair) · University of Manchester, UK

Program Committee

Chen Bin	Stanford University, USA
Couch Philip	University of Manchester, UK
Grabar Natalia	Université Lille 3, France
Grant Maria	University of Salford, UK
Hartley R.J.	Manchester Metropolitan University, UK
Jansen Ludger	University of Rostock, Germany
Kuo Alex	University of Victoria, Canada
McCusker James	Yale University, and Rensselaer Polytechnic Institute, USA
Nykanen Pirkko	University of Tampere, Finland
O'Brien Ann	Loughborough University, UK
Rubin Eitan	Ben-Gurion University of the Negev, Israel
O'Sullivan Dympna	City University, UK
Sicilia Miguel-Angel	University of Alcalá, Spain
Urquhart Christine	Aberystwyth University, UK
Wang Fusheng	Emory University, USA
Weller Peter	City University, UK

Track on European and National Projects, and Project Networking

Special Track Chair

Garoufallou Emmanouel	Alexander Technological Educational Institute of Thessaloniki, Greece

Program Committee

Antonopoulou Stavroula	American Farm School
Balatsoukas Panos	University of Manchester, UK
Gaitanou Panorea	Ionian University, Greece
Greenberg Jane	University of North Carolina at Chapel Hill, USA
Hartley R.J.	Manchester Metropolitan University, UK
Houssos Nikos	National Documentation Center (EKT), Greece
Koutsomiha Damiana	American Farm School, Greece
Manghi Paolo	Institute of Information Science and Techologies (ISTI), National Research Council, Italy
Mouskeftaropoulou Elena	Alexander Technological Educational Institute of Thessaloniki, Greece
Rousidis Dimitris	University of Alcalá, Spain
Siatri Rania	Alexander Technological Educational Institute of Thessaloniki, Greece
Sicilia Miguel-Angel	University of Alcalá, Spain

Track on Metadata and Semantics for Open Repositories, Research Information Systems and Data Infrastructures

Special Track Chairs

Subirats Imma	Food and Agriculture Organization of the United Nations, Italy
Houssos Nikos	National Documentation Center, Greece

Program Committee

Baker Thomas	DC, USA
Besemer Hugo	Wageningen UR Library, The Netherlands
Dunshire Gordon	University of Strathclyde, UK
Elbadawi Ibrahim Ahmed	Federal Government, United Arab Emirates
Grosser Stephanie	US Agency for International Development, USA
Gur Siddeswara	University of Queensland, Australia
Luzi Daniela	Institute for Population and Social Policy Research - Italian National Research Council (IRPPS-CNR), Italy
Jack Kris	Mendeley, UK
Jeffery Keith	Keith G Jeffery Consultants, UK
Jörg Brigitte	UKOLN, University of Bath, UK
Koskela Rebecca	University of New Mexico, USA
Manghi Paolo	Institute of Information Science and Techologies (ISTI), National Research Council, Italy
Manola Natalia	University of Athens, Greece
Matthews Brian	Science and Technology Facilities Council, UK
Qin Jian	Syracuse University, USA
Schöpfel Joachim	University of Lille, France
Shin Edwin	MediaShelf, USA
Stathopoulos Panagiotis	National Documentation Center (EKT), Greece
Tzitzikas Yannis	University of Crete and ICS-FORTH, Greece
Zeng Marcia	Kent State University, USA
Vila Daniel	Polytechnic University of Madrid, Spain
Wang Zhong	Sun Yat-sen University, China

Track on Metadata and Semantics for Cultural Collections and Applications

Special Track Chairs

Gergatsoulis Manolis	Ionian University, Greece

Program Committee

Bountouri Lina	General State Archives, Greece
Dekkers Makx	Independent consultant, Spain
Francesco Giuliana	De Cultural Heritage and Technical Assistance Division, Council of Europe
Gradmann Stefan	Leuven University, Belgium
Isaac Antoine	Vrije Universiteit Amsterdam, The Netherlands
Lourdi Irene	University of Athens, Greece
Masci Maria Emilia	Scuola Normale Superiore di Pisa, Italy
Meghini Carlo	National Research Council of Italy (ISTI-CNR), Italy
Papatheodorou Christos	Ionian University and Digital Curation Unit, IMIS, Athena RC, Greece
Sfakakis Michalis	National Documentation Center (EKT), Greece
Stead Stephen	Paveprime Ltd., UK
Tsinaraki Chrisa	Technical University of Crete, Greece
Tudhope Douglas	University of Glamorgan, UK

Track on Metadata and Semantics for Agriculture, Food and Environment

Program Chairs

Athanasiadis Ioannis N.	Democritus University of Thrace, Greece
Manouselis Nikos	Agro-Know Technologies, Greece
Pane Juan	Universidad Nacional de Asunción, Paraguay, Universidad de Trento, Italy

Special Track Steering Committee

Keizer Johannes	Food and Agriculture Organization of the United Nations, Italy
Rizzoli Andrea E.	IDSIA, Switzerland
Janssen Sander	Alterra, Wageningen UR, The Netherlands

Program Committee

Baez Marcos	University of Trento, Italy
Brewster Christopher	Aston Business School, Aston University, UK
Caracciolo Caterina	Food and Agriculture Organization of the United Nations, Italy
Drakos Andreas	Agro-Know Technologies, Greece
Ebner Hannes	Metasolutions, Sweden
Hénaff Diane	Le INRA RD 10, France
Houssos Nikos	National Documentation Center (EKT), Greece
Konstantopoulos Stasinos	NCSR Demokritos, Greece
Lezcano Leonardo	University of Alcalá, Spain

Table of Contents

General Session

Platforms for Research Data Sets, System Architecture and Data Management

Change and a Future for Metadata 1
  Jane Greenberg and Emmanouel Garoufallou

Rethinking the Search Experience: What Professional Search Systems
Could Do Better? 6
  Michail Salampasis

Advancing the DFC Semantic Technology Platform via HIVE
Innovation 14
  Mike C. Conway, Jane Greenberg, Reagan Moore,
  Mary Whitton, and Le Zhang

Metadata, Domain Specific Languages and Visualisations as Internal
Artifacts Driving an Agile Knowledge Engineering Methodology 22
  Angelos Yannopoulos, Yannis Christodoulou, Effie Bountris,
  Katia Savrami, and Maria Douza

OAIzer: Configurable OAI Exports over Relational Databases 35
  Sandro La Bruzzo, Paolo Manghi, and Alessia Bardi

CMSs, Linked Data and Semantics: A Linked Data Mashup over
Drupal for Personalized Search 48
  Aikaterini K. Kalou, Dimitrios A. Koutsomitropoulos, and
  Georgia D. Solomou

Linking Search Results, Bibliographical Ontologies and Linked Open
Data Resources 60
  Fabio Ricci, Javier Belmonte, Eliane Blumer, and René Schneider

A Simple Approach towards SKOSification of Digital Repositories 67
  Enayat Rajabi, Miguel-Angel Sicilia, and Salvador Sánchez-Alonso

Metadata and Ontology validation, Evaluation, Mapping and Interoperability

Cross-Language Ontology Alignment Utilizing Machine Translation
Models 75
    Antonis Koukourikos, Pythagoras Karampiperis, and
    Giannis Stoitsis

Using Metadata to Facilitate Understanding and Certification of
Assertions about the Preservation Properties of a Preservation
System 87
    Jemel H. Ward, Hao Xu, Mike C. Conway, Terrell G. Russell, and
    Antoine de Torcy

Tools and Techniques for Assessing Metadata Quality 99
    Effie Tsiflidou and Nikos Manouselis

Applying the Nominal Group Technique for Metadata Training of
Domain Experts 111
    Nikos Palavitsinis, Nikos Manouselis, and
    Charalampos Karagiannidis

Encoding Provenance Metadata for Social Science Datasets 123
    Carl Lagoze, Jeremy Willliams, and Lars Vilhuber

Perceived Helpfulness of Dublin Core Semantics: An Empirical Study ... 135
    Mohammad Yasser Chuttur

Content Management

A Semantic Model for Personal Consent Management 146
    Ozgu Can

Storing Metadata as QR Codes in Multimedia Streams 152
    Athanasios Zigomitros and Constantinos Patsakis

Semantic Mapping in CLARIN Component Metadata 163
    Matej Durco and Menzo Windhouwer

Using Metadata Standards to Improve National and IMF DATA 169
    Nalini Umashankar

Leveraging Semantics to Represent and Compute Quantitative Indexes:
The RDFIndex Approach 175
    Jose María Álvarez-Rodríguez, José Emilio Labra-Gayo, and
    Patricia Ordoñez de Pablos

Track on Big Data and Digital Libraries in Health, Science and Technology

The Semantics of Negation Detection in Archaeological Grey
Literature   188
   Andreas Vlachidis and Douglas Tudhope

A Preliminary Approach on Ontology-Based Visual Query Formulation
for Big Data   201
   Ahmet Soylu, Martin G. Skjæveland, Martin Giese,
   Ian Horrocks, Ernesto Jimenez-Ruiz, Evgeny Kharlamov, and
   Dmitriy Zheleznyakov

Personalized Vaccination Using Ontology Based Profiling   213
   Ozgu Can, Emine Sezer, Okan Bursa, and Murat Osman Unalir

Big Data for Enhanced Learning Analytics: A Case for Large-Scale
Comparative Assessments   225
   Nikolaos Korfiatis

1-5 Stars: Metadata on the Openness Level of Open Data Sets
in Europe   234
   Sébastien Martin, Muriel Foulonneau, and Slim Turki

Metadata Requirements for Repositories in Health Informatics
Research: Evidence from the Analysis of Social Media Citations   246
   Dimitris Rousidis, Emmanouel Garoufallou, Panos Balatsoukas,
   Kostas Paraskeuopoulos, Stella Asderi, and Damiana Koutsomiha

Track on European and National Projects, and Project Networking

Semantic Accessibility to E-learning Web Services   258
   Juan Manuel Dodero, Manuel Palomo-Duarte, Iván Ruiz-Rube, and
   Ignacio Traverso

Exploring the Potential for Mapping Schema.org Microdata and the
Web of Linked Data   266
   Alberto Nogales, Miguel-Angel Sicilia,
   Elena García-Barriocanal, and Salvador Sánchez-Alonso

Track on Metadata and Semantics for Open Repositories, Research Information Systems and Data Infrastructures

Semantically Enhanced Interactions between Heterogeneous Data
Life-Cycles: Analyzing Educational Lexica in a Virtual Research
Environment   277
    Basil Ell, Christoph Schindler, and Marc Rittberger

Integrating Heterogeneous and Distributed Information about Marine
Species through a Top Level Ontology   289
    Yannis Tzitzikas, Carlo Allocca, Chryssoula Bekiari,
    Yannis Marketakis, Pavlos Fafalios, Martin Doerr,
    Nikos Minadakis, Theodore Patkos, and Leonardo Candela

A Semantic Approach for the Annotation of Figures: Application to
High-Energy Physics   302
    Piotr Praczyk and Javier Nogueras-Iso

Towards a Stepwise Method for Unifying and Reconciling Corporate
Names in Public Contracts Metadata: The CORFU Technique   315
    Jose María Álvarez-Rodríguez, Patricia Ordoñez de Pablos,
    Michail Vafopoulos, and José Emilio Labra-Gayo

Merging Controlled Vocabularies through Semantic Alignment Based
on Linked Data   330
    Ioannis Papadakis and Konstantinos Kyprianos

Transient and Persistent RDF Views over Relational Databases in the
Context of Digital Repositories   342
    Nikolaos Konstantinou, Dimitrios-Emmanuel Spanos, and
    Nikolas Mitrou

Document Mark-Up for Different Users and Purposes   355
    David King and David R. Morse

Track on Metadata and Semantics for Cultural Collections and Applications

Federating Natural History Museums in Natural Europe   361
    Konstantinos Makris, Giannis Skevakis, Varvara Kalokyri,
    Polyxeni Arapi, Stavros Christodoulakis, John Stoitsis,
    Nikos Manolis, and Sarah Leon Rojas

Toward Common Ontologies of Facets of the Archival Access Portal   373
    Tarvo Kärberg

A Meta - model Agreement for Architectural Heritage   384
    Michail Agathos and Sarantos Kapidakis

Highlights of Library Data Models in the Era of Linked Open Data   396
    Sofia Zapounidou, Michalis Sfakakis, and Christos Papatheodorou

Track on Metadata and Semantics for Agriculture, Food and Environment

agriOpenLink: Towards Adaptive Agricultural Processes Enabled by
Open Interfaces, Linked Data and Services   408
    Slobodanka Dana Kathrin Tomic, Anna Fensel, Christian Aschauer,
    Klemens Gregor Schulmeister, Thomas Riegler, Franz Handler,
    Marcel Otte, and Wolfgang Auer

Issues in Harvesting Resources from Agricultural Repositories   414
    Devika P. Madalli

Preliminary Work towards Publishing Vocabularies for Germplasm and
Soil Data as Linked Data   423
    Valeria Pesce, Guntram Geser, Caterina Caracciolo,
    Johannes Keizer, and Giovanni L'Abate

Ontology-Based Representation of Scientific Laws on Beef Production
and Consumption   430
    Piotr Kulicki, Robert Trypuz, Rafał Trójczak, Jerzy Wierzbicki, and
    Alicja Woźniak

Semantic Shared Spaces for Task Allocation in a Robotic Fleet for
Precision Agriculture   440
    Domagoj Drenjanac, Lukas Klausner, Eva Kühn, and
    Slobodanka Dana Kathrin Tomic

Author Index   447

Change and a Future for Metadata

Jane Greenberg[1] and Emmanouel Garoufallou[2]

[1] The University of North Carolina at Chapel Hill, Chapel Hill, NC, USA
janeg@email.unc.edu
[2] Alexander Technological Educational Institute of Thessaloniki, Greece
mgarou@libd.teithe.gr

Abstract. Future predictions generally resolve some place between a desired outcome and a predetermined path set by fixed circumstances. This essay explores the future of metadata, recognizing the impossibility of creating a precise road map comingled with the fact that researchers and practitioners do, in fact, have some capacity to impact future plans. We address the unprecedented time in which we live, shaped by the latest networked and technological capacities. Observations presented address the future province of metadata, a role for metadata in addressing grand challenges, and emerging synergistic environments. The conclusion summarizes these observations and confirms the significance of metadata.

Keywords: Metadata research, grand challenges, community scholarship, synergistic environments, semantic web, linked data, Research Data Alliance (RDA), e-science, e-research.

1   Introduction

We are living in unprecedented times with networked and digital technologies integrated into nearly every aspect of our daily lives. The impact is profound on education, government, research, and our social being. Metadata is an essential part of this change. Metadata helps to connect humans and machines and enables knowledge sharing across domains and oceans. This evolution invites us to ask about the future of metadata.

What is the future of metadata? Will metadata systems and standards become common everyday components of daily tasks and operations? Nothing is impossible; and there is always the chance the metadata could become as common as a cup of coffee to start the day. In this case, the burgeoning community of metadata researchers may no longer have problems to study and solve. It is much more likely that technological advances will solve some existing problems and introduce new areas of study. In other words, metadata solutions will become common-place for accomplishing various tasks that currently require extensive resources; and, in parallel, new metadata-specific problems will emerge.

As time progresses, we will likely experience a future where metadata generation is better understood and easily incorporated into our information workflows.

E. Garoufallou and J. Greenberg (Eds.): MTSR 2013, CCIS 390, pp. 1–5, 2013.

While some problems will be solved, new technologies will undoubtedly impact information practices and introduce a set of different problems. Human and machine metadata driven solutions may help address some of these challenges. In the following sections of this paper we consider a future province of metadata, a role for metadata in addressing grand challenges, and the emergence new synergistic environments.

2   The Future Province of Metadata

The future province of metadata is grand. There is no shortage of metadata innovation as demonstrated by the Semantic web, linked data, and services supported by schema.org. New technologies and applications relying on metadata are weaving their way into our everyday social-technological fabric. Perhaps the latest rage to hit the scene is Big Data—a topic we hear about nearly every day in the popular press, and which requires metadata.

Metadata has by all accounts joined a range of vernaculars, beyond the information intensive environs. One very recent factor is the high profile case in the United States, with Edward Snowden exposing the U.S. National Security Administration's infringement on individual rights and exploitation of phone record metadata [1]. In turning to cultural and societal benefits, metadata, has reached an important status, recognized as an essential component if not the 'glue' for global and multinational cultural efforts, such as Europeana, "an internet portal that acts as an interface to millions of books, paintings, films, museum objects and archival records that have been digitised throughout Europe," [2] and the Digital Public Library of America (DPLA), which "brings together the riches of America's libraries, archives, and museums, and makes them freely available to the world" [3].

Perhaps, the most telling phenomena revealing metadata's grand province are the array of digital communication technologies (smart phones, iPads, and other mobile devices) that people use daily. Even during recreational activities or exercise routines humans connect to devices that measure heart rate, caloric activities, and speed. In practical terms, these devices are collecting data, frequently numeric data points. The gathered data is useless without the associated metadata that documents 'when the data was captured', 'what is it for', 'who is it about', and other scenarios characteristics indicative of *property/value* documentation; or, in more popularized metadata lingo, *element/descriptor*. The overriding conclusion is that the daily production of reams of digital data requires metadata to be effectively used. Metadata is this realm is being generated via human, automatic, or combinatory means. The need for metadata will, if anything, increase to meet growing adoption and use of digital technologies; and it will be an essential component for addressing grand challenges.

3   Addressing Grand Challenges: A Place for Metadata

Today, approximately 60% of the world's population neither connects to nor uses the Internet via ways that seem common place for many in progressive, developed countries [4]. The information divide is, unfortunately, a reflection of the human condition.

Our world is still very much plagued by devastating problems. At the top of the list we have hunger and disease, environmental problems posed by climate change, and the severe shortage of clean drinking water. Metadata, alone, will not solve these problems, but metadata is essential part of the solution. Capturing, logging, and describing research data is part of the research process. Metadata is needed for data synthesis, research documentation, and disseminating results. Metadata in this context is a component to the toolkit for addressing grand challenges. A forthcoming issue of the *International Journal of Metadata, Semantics and Ontologies* (IJMSO), co-edited by Garoufallou and Papatheodorou [5], chronicles metadata for e-science and scientific data management, providing in depth coverage of metadata in this context.

On a global level, the recent launch of the Research Data Alliance (RDA) [6] may hold a significant place. RDA, a global network developed to facilitate data sharing and exchange, underscores the significance of data for solving grand challenges [7]. The RDA Council recently recognized and endorsed the Metadata Standards Directory working group; one of six confirmed international working groups. Metadata WG will develop collaborative, open directory of metadata standards applicable for scientific data. A RDA Metadata Interest Group also serves as an open forum for an array of metadata issues. Directly focusing on world challenges, a group of RDA members have also proposed Agricultural Data Interoperability Interest Group. This initiative was inspired by the desire for global interoperability among all 'wheat data,' a goal that is crucial to addressing world hunger.

The benefits of metadata for description, discovery and access to information are well known. It is also known that metadata functionalities support a full array of needs associated with the information life-cycle, from information generation to use and reuse, preservation, archiving, managing, provenance tracking, and other activities [8]. Metadata, undoubtedly, has a significant role to play in advancing knowledge and finding solutions to grand challenges. The place and dependency on metadata for addressing such challenges further impacts the development of a synergistic environment bringing together members from an array of disciplines and domains.

4   Synergistic Environments

Synergy connotes a vibrant and enthusiastic collaborative environment. Metadata researchers can not only hope for participating in lively environments, but truly have no choice if they are committed to advancing the current state of knowledge. A seemingly mundane topic, metadata, like library cataloging, has had its share of critics [9, 10]. Those engaged in metadata development and implementation are quite aware that metadata cannot be studied in a vacuum. In fact, even the study 'of' metadata 'for' metadata (meta-metadata) integrates with social and computational areas of study. Indeed, any metadata examination intersects with a domain and discipline.

As explored in above section three, metadata has a future in addressing grand challenges. Our world, unfortunately, has no shortage of significant problems; and, metadata is an essential ingredient for documenting, accessing, preserving, and using data to address the data deluge [11]. Clearly, not every problem can be classed as a grand challenge. Even so, there are many truly important endeavors of study where metadata can help with daily activities and workflows, and there are an array of new disciplines and topics defining these synergies.

Over the last decade, a range of new disciplines and areas of study have emerged. Examples include medical and bioinformatics, digital humanities, eco-informatics (for ecology), information economics, and personal information management. Although these areas can intersect with grand challenges, there are less weighty issues that invite metadata study; and by virtue of domain intersections, research partnerships define a synergistic environment. Key metadata-related areas of R&D include:

- Semantic technologies, ontologies, linked data,
- Naming and identification (e.g., the implementation of Open Researcher & Contributor ID (ORCID)),
- Metadata modeling (e.g., RDF, FRBR, METS),
- Metadata workflows (when and where to capture metadata during the life-cycle),
- Metadata generation techniques (automatic and human oriented metadata, how to best integrate the approaches?), and
- Data citation/metadata for data.

It is impossible to capture to full scope of metadata related study in a single paper; moreover, outline the long-term impact of R&D efforts in these areas. Despite the impossible task, it is clear that the above listed topics must be pursued in some domain or area. Any research effort forms a unique synergy; and this path represents a future driving phenomenon for advancing metadata knowledge and application. At times the metadata expert is pursued by the by the disciplinary scholar or practitioner (e.g., the art historian or scientist); and during other times, the metadata researcher pursue the discipline, explaining how their expert knowledge may complement and improve current practice. These unifications produce a source of energy that is greater than the sum of the individual activities and define the emerging synergistic environment that not only houses, but compels the discipline of metadata research.

5   Conclusion

Predicting or suggesting an impending change specific to metadata research presents an opportunity to ponder and experiment with ideas. The future of metadata is bright and exciting, and there are many paths to pursue. As discussed above, the future province of metadata extensive. Metadata has a role in addressing grand challenges; and pursuing metadata, will, no doubt, help in the forming of new synergistic environment. Although it is impossible to create a precise road map, metadata researchers and practitioners have the capacity to shape a future where metadata can be common place and also serve as a golden key solving problems and easing challenges.

References

1. Black, I.: NSA Spying Scandal: What We Have Learned (2013),
   http://Theguardian.com,
   http://www.theguardian.com/world/2013/jun/10/
   nsa-spying-scandal-what-we-have-learned
2. Europeana, http://www.europeana.eu/
3. Digital Public Library of America [about page], http://dp.la/info/
4. Internet Usage and World Population Statistics are for, The reporting notes 34.4% of the total world population connects to the internet. Connectivity has likely increased since this reporting (June 30, 2012), http://www.internetworldstats.com/stats.htm
5. Garoufallou, E., Papatheodorou, C. (eds.): Metadata for e-Science and e-Research (Special Issue). International Journal of Metadata, Semantics and Ontologies 9(1) (2014) (in press)
6. Research Data Alliance (RDA), https://rd-alliance.org/
7. Research Data Alliance About, https://rd-alliance.org/about.html
8. Greenberg, J.: Metadata and Digital Information. In: Encyclopedia of Library and Information Science, 3rd edn., pp. 3610–3623. Marcel Dekker, Inc., New York (2010)
9. Doctorow, C.: Metacrap: Putting the torch to seven straw-men of the meta-utopia (2001), http://www.well.com/~doctorow/metacrap.htm
10. Dimitrova, N.: Is It Time for a Moratorium on Metadata? IEEE Multimedia 11(4), 10–17 (2004)
11. Greenberg, J., White, H., Carrier, C., Scherle, R.: A Metadata Best Practice for a Scientific Data Repository. Journal of Library Metadata 9(3), 194–212 (2009)

Rethinking the Search Experience: What Professional Search Systems Could Do Better?

Michail Salampasis

Department of Informatics, Technology Educational Institute of Thessaloniki, Greece
msa@it.teithe.gr

Abstract. This paper presents the traditional Information Retrieval (IR) model which is implemented in current search engines that support web search. Professional search is defined and the parameters that differentiate professional search from web search are discussed. Then, another model that provides an increased design space for developing Integrated Professional Search (IPS) systems is presented. The framework the model suggests facilitates loosely coupled IPS systems in which each of their search tools have little or no knowledge of the details of other search tools or components. The paper also describes, as a case study of an IPS, the architecture and the main functionalities of a patent search system. The integration of a search tool into this search system is discussed to demonstrate how analysing search experience facilitates straightforward integration and the effective use of integrated search tools.

1   Introduction

The tremendous power and speed of current web search engines to respond, almost instantaneously to millions of user queries on a daily basis is one of the greatest successes of the past decade. Also, the great success of web search engines has produced a generation of digital natives for whom search is a query box and ten blue links and these 10 hits in Google are the truth [1].

On the other hand search technologies are used for **professional search** (e.g. bibliographic, patent, medical, engineering, scientific literature search) for more than 40 years as an important method for information access [2]. Despite the tremendous success of web search technologies, there is a significant skepticism from professional searchers and a very conservative attitude towards adopting search methods, tools and technologies beyond the ones which dominate their domain [3]. An example is patent search where professional search experts typically use the Boolean search syntax and quite complex intellectual classification schemes [4]. Of course there are good reasons for this.

A patent search professional often carries out search tasks for which high recall is important. Additionally s/he would like to be able to reason about how the results have been produced, the effect of any query re-formulation action in getting a new set of results, or how the results of a set of query submission actions can be easily and accurately reproduced on a different occasion (the latter is particularly important if

E. Garoufallou and J. Greenberg (Eds.): MTSR 2013, CCIS 390, pp. 6–13, 2013.
© Springer International Publishing Switzerland 2013

the patent searcher is required to prove the sufficiency of the search in court at a later stage). Classification schemes and metadata are heavily used because it is widely recognized that once the work of assigning patent documents into classification schemes is done, the search can be more efficient and language independent.

Generally speaking, apart from the differences in the patent search domain presented above, there are a number of important parameters and characteristics that differentiate professional search (that is search in the workplace or search for a professional reason or aim) from web search such as: lengthy search sessions (even days) which may be suspended and resumed, the notion of relevance can be different, many different sources will be searched separately, and focus is on specific domain knowledge in contrast to public search engines which are not focused on expert knowledge.

The current status of Information Retrieval (IR) and search engine technologies is that they are able to reply to shorter queries (1-3 terms) at the document level and they can also respond to factoid queries ("what is the population of Thessaloniki?") at the sentence level. However, professional information needs are quite different and much more demanding many times. Again if we look at the patent domain, information needs would include general inquiries such as "how much is my patent worth if I sell it?" or "shall my company invest 10 million EUR in plastic packaging business?"

The above discussion reveals the challenge of how to should design next generation systems for professional search in a way that: a) will exploit the accumulated successes of IR research and development, and b) at the same time will be able to support professionals to satisfy their complex information needs.

A first issue in designing next generation systems for professional search is to rethink the search experience beyond the query box and a list of search results. In fact, users working in complex information workplaces use multiple tools, interfaces, and engage in rich and complex interactions to achieve their goals. This view expresses a user-centered and highly interactive approach to information seeking. To address this view better the model of Integrated Search Systems is presented. Finally a patent search system (PerFedPat) which is based on this key objective is analyzed. The key objective is to integrate a set of tools and to enable effective support of the different tasks, stages and the cognitive states of the user during the patent search process.

2   Integrated Professional Search Systems

The complexity of the tasks which need to be performed by professional searchers, which usually include not only retrieval but also information analysis, usually require association, pipelining and possibly integration of information as well as synchronization and coordination of multiple and potentially concurrent search views produced from different datasets, search tools and user interfaces. Many facets of search technology (e.g. exploratory search, aggregated search, federated search, task-based search, Information Retrieval (IR) over query sessions, cognitive IR approaches, Human Computer IR) aim to at least partially address some of these demands.

The current trend in professional search is towards Integrated Professional Search Systems [5][6][7][8]. Although it is relatively easy to differentiate professional search from 'public search' with a number of characteristics (some of them briefly outlined in Section 1), the concept of an *integrated* search system is not clear. Most definitions found in the Information Retrieval (IR) literature converge to use the term "integrated" to define search systems that simultaneously access a number of different data sources providing a single point of search. This view is much more compatible with the Federated Search view that allows the simultaneous search of multiple resources [9].

One objective of this paper is to present a general framework for understanding and developing integrated professional search systems, therefore it should be made clear from the beginning that in our framework and definition of *integrated professional search systems,* the term integrated is used beyond the way that it is used in Federated (or aggregated) search. It is primarily used as a method for integrating multiple search tools that can be used (in parallel or in a pipeline) from the professional searcher during a potentially lengthy search session. Some of these tools may serve for example the need of retrieving information from distributed data sets as it happens in federated search, or to expand and suggest a query but other tools may operate at runtime to deliver to the searcher's desktop multiple information flows and views. As a result our definition of integrated professional search systems primarily describes a rich information seeking environment for different types of searches, utilizing multiple search tools and exploiting a diverse set of IR and Natural Language Processing (NLP) technologies (Figure 1).

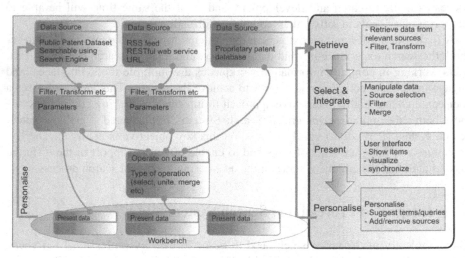

Fig. 1. A high level overview of an Integrated Search System

The architecture depicted in Figure 1 suggests a different process model for information search when it is compared with the IR/web basic processes model [10] (Figure 2). Despite the fact that many different IR technologies are used in the various sub-processes, and many exciting developments have been achieved that increased the efficiency and the effectiveness of the model shown in Figure 2, from an architectural point of view, it is important to observe that the relationships and dependencies between the different technologies, the core services which are used and the workflows and interactions which are executed in a search system during an information seeking process are not well defined.

For example, many search systems today combine a faceted search module based on static or dynamically extracted metadata [11]. The faceted search tool and views can be combined with the "traditional" ranked result list. This simple and very common design of combining multiple search views is not captured in the basic IR model presented in Figure 2. This is an important drawback. The IR research community has achieved tremendous progress in developing new indexing and ranking algorithms and tools in various areas of information processing and retrieval, however there was little attention paid on how these results can come together to design next generation search systems. This view is reinforced by the fact that using and managing information workflows between autonomous (and possibly distributed) IR tools/services is the main design method used by different groups working in managing languages resources [12] or professional search systems [13].

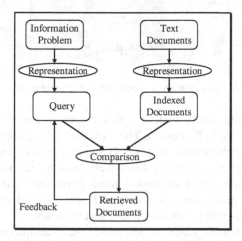

Fig. 2. Basic Information Retrieval Processes

3   Case Study: An Integrated Systems for Patent Search

The **PerFedPat**[1] system is a federated patent search system based on ezDL [14], [15] a system for developing interactive search applications. PerFedPat provides core services and operations for being able to search, using a federated method, multiple on-line patent resources (currently Esp@cenet, Google patents, Patentscope and the MAREC collection), thus providing access to multiple patent sources while hiding complexity from the end user who uses a common query tool for querying all patent datasets at the same time. Wrappers are used which convert PerFedPat's internal query model into the queries that each remote service can accept. "Translated" queries are routed to remote search systems and their returned results are internally re-ranked

---

[1] www.perfedpat.eu

and merged as a single list presented to the patent searcher. Except patent resources there are other resources already supported by ezDL, most of them offering access to online bibliographic search services. Based on this architecture PerFedPat aims to become a pluggable system which puts together the following components: retrieval, selection, integration, presentation and adaptation (Figure 3).

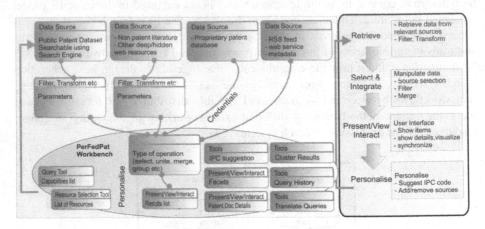

Fig. 3. PerFedPat architecture and component overview

One innovative feature of PerFedPat is that it enables the use of multiple search tools which are integrated in PerFedPat. The tools that a designer will decide to integrate into a patent search system, do not only have to do with existing IR technologies, but probably more with the context in which a patent search is conducted and the professional searcher's behavior and task at hand. Furthermore, it is also very important to understand a search process and how a specific tool can attain a specific objective of this process and therefore increase its efficiency.

Currently the search tools which are integrated are a) an International Patent Classification (IPC) selection tool b) a tool for faceted search producing different facets of the results retrieved based on existing metadata in patents, c) a tool producing clustered views of patent search results d) a MT tool for translating queries. The first tool aims to support a specific objective during prior art search, i.e. to narrow the search by identifying relevant IPC codes and the effectiveness of the IPC selection tool method has been evaluated [16]. In this paper what it is emphasized more is the design principle and the process which has been used to integrate this and the other tools in PerFedPat.

From the perspective of the general model for integrated search systems what is also important to mention is that the integration of the IPC suggestion tool was implemented sending *http requests* to an external server providing the IPC selection services. The server hosting the IPC selection tool receives the requests and sends a response back about the IPC codes suggested. It is important also to mention that for the IPC tool to operate there is a need to access certain metadata that are produced using Distributed IR core services (resource representation) and are managed locally by the IPC selection server. This data could also exist in the original PerFedPat server and could be sent on request to different tools which need to access such data. It is therefore important to mention that interoperability at the process level is achieved, however this process level interoperability is not based on full exchange of metadata but some form of regular updates may be necessary.

To achieve effective integration of the IPC suggestion tool, it is very important to understand a search process and how a specific tool can attain a specific objective of this process and therefore increase its efficiency. For example, Lupu and Hanbury [17] in a recent review of patent retrieval present a typical Prior Art Search use case, analyzed in different sub-processes, performed by a patent examiner (pp. 15) to model and better understand prior art search. The IPC suggestion tool supports sub-process 3 which is "defining a text query, potentially by Boolean operators and specific field filters". So given a query, the IPC suggestion tool selects the most appropriate IPCs and in this way support better focused filtered search based on the automatically selected IPCs.

In PerFedPat there are more search tools integrated in similar way (tools for faceted search, clustered views of results etc). From information seeking process perspective, the integration of different search tools in addition to the basic ranked list of patent documents returned from the DIR retrieval engine, allows different views of patent information to coexist.

This process-oriented integration provides some useful services to the PerFedPat patent search system but synchronization between the tools is required so one event or action in one tool can update the views produced from the other tools. For example selecting an IPC code may affect the results presented in the faceted search tool. This synchronization of multiple search tools and their UIs is a major challenge in re-thinking the user experience.

4   Conclusion

A framework for developing Integrated Professional Search (IPS) systems is very much needed. The framework should not only provide the context to better classify and characterize what IPS systems are, but it should be also used to increase the design space of IPS systems by enabling straightforward integration of multiple search tools. To increase the benefits for users using integrated systems from professional search we must rethink the user experience when designing these systems. Primarily they should be designed with a focus to support the users in the different stages of solving their information needs. To make this design feasible, a different interaction model is needed which enables the coordinated use of multiple search tools and UIs in a parallel or pipeline way.

Also, without any doubt the development of integrated professional search systems will greatly benefit if communication and coordination protocols are well defined to allow interoperability between different IR tools in a service oriented paradigm. The exact methodology (message exchange, process oriented, workflow management, etc.) which will be used to develop such protocols remains an open issue, probably the task of a standardization activity. However we believe that it is an interesting way to develop search systems but it can also become an attractive business model for research groups building different types of IR technologies and tools or for SMEs developing search solutions.

Of course we do not ignore the major concern of the communication overhead and the other efficiency costs which occur in the development of search systems based on interoperable components. However, we believe that the scalability which has been practically demonstrated over the last ten years, together with carefully crafted protocols and workflows, indicates that this is a feasible path towards the design of next generation professionals search systems. In fact we consider this movement of "Open Search Tools" as a paradigm which can couple to the movement of Open Data and could eventually lead to Information Seeking Environments which will emphasise information finding and understanding rather than only information retrieval.

Acknowledgements. The research leading partially to these results has received funding from the European Union Seventh Framework Programme (FP7/2007-2013) under grant agreement n° 275522 (PerFedPat).

References

1. Lagemaat, W.G.: The future of information tools and technology – Our joint effort. World Patent Information 35(2), 93–94 (2013)
2. Adams, S.: The text, the full text and nothing but the text: Part 1 – Standards for creating textual information in patent documents and general search implications☆. World Patent Information 32(1), 22–29 (2010)
3. Krier, M., Zaccà, F.: Automatic categorisation applications at the European patent office. World Patent Information 24(3), 187–196 (2002)
4. Dirnberger, D.: A guide to efficient keyword, sequence and classification search strategies for biopharmaceutical drug-centric patent landscape searches - A human recombinant insulin patent landscape case study. World Patent Information 33(2), 128–143 (2011)
5. Kohn, A., Bry, F., Manta, A.: Professional Search: Requirements, Prototype and Preliminary Experience Report. In: Iadis International Conference WWW (2008)
6. Lund, H., Lauridsen, H., Hansen, J.H.: Summa – integrated search. Zuletzt Abgerufen 13, 1–13 (2010)
7. Masiakowski, P., Wang, S.: Integration of software tools in patent analysis. World Patent Information 35(2), 97–104 (2013)
8. Salampasis, M., Fuhr, N., Hanbury, A., Lupu, M., Larsen, B., Strindberg, H.: Integrating IR technologies for professional search. In: Serdyukov, P., Braslavski, P., Kuznetsov, S.O., Kamps, J., Rüger, S., Agichtein, E., Segalovich, I., Yilmaz, E. (eds.) ECIR 2013. LNCS, vol. 7814, pp. 882–885. Springer, Heidelberg (2013)
9. Shokouhi, M., Si, L.: Federated Search. Foundations and Trends in Information Retrieval 5(1), 1–102 (2011)
10. Broder, A.: A taxonomy of web search. ACM Sigir Forum 36(2), 3–10 (2002)
11. Kitsos, I., Fafalios, P., Marketakis, Y.: Enriching Web Searching with Real-Time Entity Mining. Organization, 1–15
12. Bel, N.: Platform for Automatic, Normalized Annotation and Cost- Effective Acquisition of Language Resources for Human Language Technologies. PANACEA. Procesamiento del Lenguaje Natural 45, 327–328 (2010)

13. Hanbury, A., Müller, H.: Khresmoi – multimodal multilingual medical information search. In: MIE Village of the Future (2012)
14. Fuhr, N., Klas, C.-P., Schaefer, A., Mutschke, P.: Daffodil: An Integrated Desktop for Supporting High-Level Search Activities in Federated Digital Libraries. In: Agosti, M., Thanos, C. (eds.) ECDL 2002. LNCS, vol. 2458, pp. 597–612. Springer, Heidelberg (2002)
15. Fuhr, N.: An Infrastructure for Supporting the Evaluation of Interactive Information Retrieval, p. 4503 (October 2011)
16. Salampasis, M., Paltoglou, G., Giahanou, A.: Report on the CLEF-IP 2012 Experiments: Search of Topically Organized Patents. In: CLEF (Online Working Notes/Labs/Workshop) (2012)
17. Mihai, L., Allan, H.: Patent Retrieval. Foundations and Trends in Information Retrieval 7(1) (2013)

Advancing the DFC Semantic Technology Platform via HIVE Innovation

Mike C. Conway[1], Jane Greenberg[2], Reagan Moore[1],
Mary Whitton[1], and Le Zhang[2]

[1] The University of North Carolina at Chapel Hill, Chapel Hill, NC, USA
michael_conway@unc.edu, {rwmoore,whitton}@renci.org
[2] Metadata Research Center, School of Library and Information Science, University
of North Carolina at Chapel Hill, Chapel Hill, NC, USA
janeg@email.unc.edu, lezha@live.unc.edu

Abstract. The DataNet Federation Consortium (DFC) is developing data grids for multidisciplinary research. As the DFC grid grows in size and number of disciplines, it becomes critical to address metadata management and findability challenges. The HIVE project is being integrated into the iRODS in the DFC architecture to provide a scaleable linked open data approach to scientific data sharing.

Keywords: HIVE, iRODS, semantic web, linked open data, SKOS.

1   Introduction

National and global cyberinfrastructure initiatives must manage large data collections across their entire life-cycle, enabling research and scientific discovery [1]. Data findability and access are crucial to these goals. As scientific research becomes multidisciplinary in nature, and data increase in volume and diversity, the data management challenges involved also become metadata management challenges [2]. Additionally, as infrastructure evolves through multiple efforts, such as the U.S. DataNet implementations and European Unions's INSPIRE initiative, data management challenges further reveal metadata interoperability challenges [3,4].

Semantic systems, specifically linked open data (LOD) vocabularies, can address these challenges and advance cyberinfrastructure development [5]. Open, shared semantics introduce new capabilities that ought to be explored with scientific data. Semantic systems enhance findability by defining standard vocabularies used within a community. Researchers within the community can then reference data sets using a consensus naming convention. Semantic systems enhance interoperability because they provide a way to translate between the vocabularies used by different communities. The DataNet Federation Consortium (DFC) recognizes LOD capabilities and team members are exploring open semantics via HIVE, a technology that supports the dynamic integration of linked data vocabularies encoded in the Simple Knowledge Organization System (SKOS) [6].

E. Garoufallou and J. Greenberg (Eds.): MTSR 2013, CCIS 390, pp. 14–21, 2013.
© Springer International Publishing Switzerland 2013

The DFC is extensively interdisciplinary, hosting data documenting ocean observations, hydrologic science, engineering education and archives, plant genome sequences, and social science research. There is no single semantic system that covers the wide variety of disciplines being integrated into the DFC, particularly at the granular level that data requires [7]. Creating a single vocabulary to enhance interoperability among the expanse of DFC datasets is prohibitively expensive, and neither practical nor feasible. DFC's approach is to instead leverage the universe of existing semantic systems that are already developed and maintained by other agencies. HIVE technology supports this goal by providing a simple means for integrating multiple disciplinary-specific vocabularies, on a basic level [8], and is being pursued as part of the DFC R&D efforts within the iRODS data grid.

This paper reports on this DFC/HIVE initiative. The paper is organized as follows: Section 2 reviews the relationship between semantics and data; section 3 provides an overview of HIVE; section 4 introduces the DFC and the iRODS platform (software technology) on which this system relies; section 5 reveals the DFC's semantic needs; section 6 reports project implementation progress; and section 7 presents a conclusion and identifies next steps.

2 Semantics and Data

Semantics systems used in the information/database community vary in scope, structure, domain and other aspects. The diversity is reflected in varied naming conventions referenced as ontologies, taxonomies, authority control lists, vocabularies, lexicons and the like [9]. Notwithstanding differences, these semantic systems all support similar functions, chiefly they aim to facilitate discovery, link related resources, and add context to a collection. Semantic systems also support interoperability, enabling the sharing, cross- searching and exchange of information that is being represented.

Semantic systems are crucial for data management. Historical examples commonly link back to Linnaean taxonomy, or delve as far back as Aristotle's naming of specimens in his *Historia Animalium* (History of Animals) [10], and his contribution to binomial means "two names" convention for naming specimens, a practice replicated in many scientific domains. The development and sharing of semantic systems in science thrives today, due to digital innovation and networked technologies. Examples include the National Center for Biological Ontologies (NCBO) [11], for registering scientific ontologies the collective effort to develop the Gene Ontology–GO [12], and the Marine Metadata Initiative, which creates, published, and makes accessible semantic systems, in an open format [13]. These developments provide infrastructure that can be leveraged to improve interoperability and the sharing and exchange of data. The DFC is advancing its semantic technology platform via integration of the HIVE system with the iRODS data management system.

3 An Overview of HIVE

HIVE is an acronym for Helping Interdisciplinary Vocabulary Engineering. As part of the HIVE project, a framework was developed to allow curators to manage multiple controlled vocabularies defined in SKOS [14]. The HIVE system includes support for importing SKOS vocabularies through an administrative toolkit. This import takes a SKOS vocabulary, and populates a `Sesame/Elmo` triple store. HIVE provides an easy API to interactively query and navigate across and within loaded vocabularies from a user interface [15].

As vocabularies are imported into HIVE, they are indexed to support concept retrieval, using the Lucene search engine. This index allows a curator to find appropriate terms across selected vocabularies using concepts specified as a free text search query, and then to select and navigate based on matching concepts.

HIVE also supports automatic term suggestion for documents using the `KEA++` and `MAUI` algorithms [16,17]. These machine learning algorithms are trained with a sample set of documents indexed by a human working with a designated vocabulary. The training enables the use of these learned patterns during the dynamic indexing activities, although candidate terms are drawn from the SKOS vocabulary, or multiple vocabularies, based on novel document content. This term suggestion process is applied at the time that a document is uploaded into a repository, allowing users to view suggested terms, and to select the terms that best apply. The DFC project is exploring automatic term extraction as a policy applied within the iRODS grid, and this is discussed in the next steps section.

HIVE provides a framework to manage open vocabularies, and includes the functionality to integrate multiple vocabularies into the metadata workflow aiding researchers and curators, providing consistent and enhancing findability in multidisciplinary research environment.

4 DFC and iRODS Technology

The DataNet Federation Consortium (DFC) is one of five DataNet projects under the National Science Foundation DataNet initiative. The stated goal of the DFC is to "..assemble national data infrastructure that enables collaborative research, through federation of existing data management infrastructure..." [18] The DFC is based on the iRODS data grid, which provides the interoperability mechanisms needed to federate existing data management systems with a national collaboration environment. Federation requires the encapsulation of three types of domain knowledge:

- knowledge required to access community resources and discover and retrieve relevant input data sets;
- knowledge needed to execute a data-driven research analysis;
- knowledge needed to manage research results in compliance with NSF data management plans.

Given these three types of knowledge, it becomes possible to support reproducible data-driven research. All of these types of knowledge encapsulation require the ability to manage domain vocabularies. Each domain uses different terms to describe the contents of data repositories, different terms to describe the operations performed in an analysis, and different terms for describing research results. The DFC offers an opportunity to investigate and prototype findability and interoperability solutions across deployed research infrastructure.

iRODS is an open-source, policy managed data grid, developed by the Data Intensive Cyber Environments group (DICE). iRODS is an acronym for the Integrated Rule-Oriented Data System [19]. The iRODS software manages a central metadata catalog of distributed data collections. iRODS virtualizes collections of data, presenting a uniform, abstract view across multiple physical storage architectures. An iRODS grid can exist on distributed storage nodes, and grids can be federated between organizations [20].

Central to iRODS is the concept of policy managed data. iRODS has a concept of microservices, which are defined as "... small, well-defined procedures/functions that perform a certain task... " [21]. These microservices can be chained together by rules to create complex actions. iRODS provides a rule engine that runs at each remote storage location. Policy Enforcement Points (PEPs) are defined within the software middleware that can trigger rule execution based on events within the grid. Administrators can thus define policies to control data management, which are enforced by the grid, and which can be verified by assessing the state of the catalog [22].

Through the iRODS catalog (ICAT), it is possible to manage and query for user defined metadata. The user defined metadata is stored as Attribute-Value-Unit (AVU) triples, and these arbitrary triples can be associated with collections and data objects contained by the grid. These AVUs are rudimentary and free-form, with no ability to express rich or linked relationships. On the other hand, these AVUs benefit from the policy management and preservation capabilities of iRODS. Layering the capabilities of the HIVE system above the facilities of iRODS adds metadata richness and expressivity to the native iRODS metadata approach.

5   DFC Semantic Needs

As iRODS and the DFC represent a policy managed, open architecture for scientific data management, any approaches to findability must follow a similar open approach. As new policies may be required by the inclusion of new scientific domains, new metadata vocabularies may also be required. HIVE is particularly attractive in that it operates as a 'container', neutral to the vocabularies it contains, able to be augmented with new vocabularies, and able to work across multiple vocabularies.

SKOS, and more broadly, RDF, with a resource centric approach, map well to the DFC architecture. iRODS maintains a global logical namespace over DFC collections. In effect, these collections and files are dereferenceable resources. Attaching SKOS vocabulary terms to these target collections and files can be accomplished with no alteration to the DFC architecture, since they are easily stored as Attribute-Value-Unit (AVUs) attached to DFC files and collections. This delineation of responsibilities is key, as iRODS archives have historically grown up to hundreds of millions of data objects [23]. Maintaining metadata and processing rich queries on such large repositories is a daunting challenge. Using an architecture where iRODS serves as a canonical metadata store, and indexes are generated and replicated as ephemeral entities is key to the DFC approach. It is important to maintain a clear separation of concerns between all of the elements of this solution.

Maintenance and storage of metadata in iRODS is simple and well understood. SKOS defines a fairly rich metadata schema in a format that is approachable and realistic. HIVE maintains dynamic access to libraries of controlled vocabularies, providing researchers and curators an user- friendly application to annotate and classify DFC collections. Triple store implementations via Jena, enables the storage and manipulation RDF data, and inferencing and querying. All of these separate, well-defined operations and the marriage of policy-managed preservation with linked open data approaches are showing promise in the first iteration of this integration.

Improving findability through semantic metadata presents a classic information organization versus information retrieval dilemma. HIVE is attractive for DFC because it is oriented towards easy annotation by researchers and curators. HIVE translates easily to the DFC web interfaces, allowing search and exploration of appropriate terms across multiple configured vocabularies, without requiring any knowledge of, or exposure of the semantic nature of the underlying data. In addition, HIVE supports automatic term suggestion using the KEA++ and MAUI frameworks. This term suggestion approach has been shown to provide consistent and accurate and useful annotations with reduced effort on researchers and curators [24]. Algorithmic term extraction approaches are especially appealing in the policy-managed DFC environment, and such metadata extraction is easily supported by the iRODS software as part of the data curation lifecycle.

6   Implementation Progress

The DFC has demonstrated iRODS/HIVE integration using a working system that implements three primary system components. These are:

- Interface integration to allow navigating and searching vocabularies stored in HIVE, and applying selected terms to the DFC grid;
- Indexing services to extract vocabulary metadata that was stored in the DFC grid, in order to populate a triple store with vocabulary and DFC metadata;
- Creation of a search service, and integration of search of the indexed semantic metadata, via SPARQL, into the user interface, allowing search and linking to the underlying DFC data associated with the SPARQL query results.

The HIVE service is integrated into the iRODS iDrop web interface, providing a metadata tab in the user interface when viewing grid data. This 'concept browser' view provides an intuitive way to navigate around the SKOS vocabulary, by moving to narrower, broader, or related terms in the selected set of

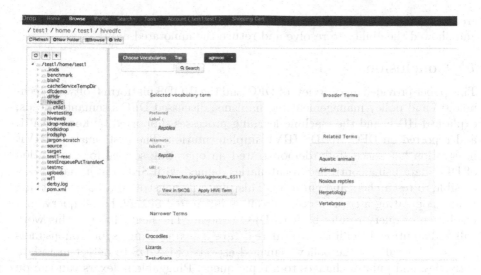

Fig. 1. HIVE Concept Browser in iDrop

vocabularies. When desired terms are located, they may be applied, resulting in the recording of AVU metadata within the DFC grid, essentially as a serialized RDF triple. The concept browser, through the HIVE API, masks the semantic nature of this data, and instead represents links between concepts in a pivot table arrangement, rather than a hierarchical tree. Comparisons between tree representations of controlled vocabularies and this concept browser arrangement are an interesting area for future study.

Once the metadata is serialized into the DFC grid, an indexing process extracts relevant metadata to populate an external triple store. Currently, the first phase uses a batch indexing mode, where the DFC master catalog is queried to locate such RDF triples. During this sweep operation, a Jena triple store is populated with the SKOS vocabularies, and the application of these vocabularies to iRODS logical resources (files and collections), along with other catalog metadata, expressed in an iRODS OWL schema. This iRODS system metadata can include characteristics of files and collections, such as ownership, access control relationships, provenance, and collection membership. Note here that sharing relationships between researchers can be extracted to FOAF, and developing this social dimension is an interesting future research topic.

To complete the first phase, the SPARQL query language, as implemented by Jena, was used to demonstrate metadata search based on SKOS vocabulary terms, including the ability to find collections annotated with a given term, as well as the ability to find collections related to a given term. This demonstrates the enhanced findability that results from semantic metadata, and highlights the potential utility of the HIVE + iRODS approach for richer queries. The search facility was implemented as a RESTful web service, and integrated into the search toolbar of the iDrop web interface. The search results included dereferenceable links that corresponded to the iRODS URI for the files or collections, and showed the ability to resolve and return the annotated data.

7   Conclusion

This paper provided an overview of DFC and the iRODS platform (software technology) and policy management mechanisms, discussed DFC's semantic needs, explained HIVE and the machine learning processes supported by Kea++/MAUI, and reported on DFC/iRODS HIVE implementation. The first phase of HIVE integration has successfully demonstrated an operating service for annotation of DFC data using controlled vocabularies defined with SKOS in a manner accessible to researchers and curators. This phase demonstrated a batch indexing mode, populating a triple store, as well as integrated SPARQL based query, and resolution of query results back to DFC content. The next phase of this work will add additional facilities for near-real-time indexing using asynchronous messaging. This will use the policy-managed aspects of iRODS to detect metadata activities, and publish changes to a topic queue. Pluggable indexers can run on an external message bus, allowing other metadata tools to be easily integrated.

As phase two of this work begins, we will add automatic extraction of terms to documents deposited into DFC working with Kea++ and MAUI and generating AVU metadata that serialize the detected SKOS terms. These terms will be indexed, and used for searching. It is hypothesized that users of DFC search can then rate returned documents based on appropriateness, allowing the gradual improvement of metadata quality through actual use. The automatic term extraction approach lowers the cost of metadata annotation, enables greater interoperability across the full DFC and with other datagrids, and can improve findability of data. This marrying of automatic term extraction and interactive rating of metadata quality will be added to the iDrop web interface in the next phase. Planned assessments will allow us to study and improve this work, and contribute new functionalities to operating research grid.

HIVE code is open source. The GForge repository at the Renaissance Computing Institute (RENCI) holds the HIVE and HIVE-iRODS integration libraries at https://code.renci.org/gf/project/irodshive/. The iDrop browser implementation is available at https://code.renci.org/gf/project/irodsidrop/, with the HIVE integration on the git branch 1131-hive-integration.

Acknowledgments. The work in this paper is supported, in part, by the U.S. National Science Foundation (OCI 0940841).

References

1. Moore, R.W., Whitton, M.: Data Intensive Cyber Environments Center: Six Month Report. University of North Carolina at Chapel Hill: dfc quarterly report (2012), http://datafed.org/dev/wp-content/uploads/2012/04/DFC-quarter-2_7kag1.pdf
2. Willis, C., Greenberg, J., White, H.: Analysis and Synthesis of Metadata Goals for Scientific Data. Journal of the American Society for Information Science and Technology 63(8), 1505–1520 (2012)

3. Lee, J.W., Zhang, J.T., Zimmerman, A.S., Lucia, A.: Datanet: an emerging cyberin-frastructure for sharing, reusing and preserving digital data for scientific discovery and learning. Aiche Journal 55, 2757–2764 (2009)
4. Portele, E. (ed.): GIGAS Technical Note - Data Harmonisation and Semantic Interoperability. Project co-funded by the European Commission within the Seventh Framework Programme,
   http://inspire-forum.jrc.ec.europa.eu/pg/pages/view/9782/
5. Janowicz, K., Schade, S., Bröring, A., Keßler, C., Maué, P., Stasch, C.: Semantic enablement for spatial data infrastructures. Transactions in GIS 14(2), 111–129 (2010)
6. Greenberg, J., Rowell, C., Rajavi, K., Conway, M., Lander, H.: HIVEing Across U.S. DataNets. In: Research Data Management Implementations Workshop, March 13-15. NSF/Coalition for Academic Scientific Computation (CASC), Arlington, VA (2013), http://tinyurl.com/d85kywg
7. Greenberg, J., Moore, R.W., Whitton, M.: Advancing Interoperability and Interdisciplinarity Across Datanets. NSF Supplement Proposal (2012)
8. Greenberg, J., Losee, R., Pérez Agüera, J.R., Scherle, R., White, H., Willis, C.: HIVE: Helping Interdisciplinary Vocabulary Engineering. Bulletin of the American Society for Information Science and Technology 37(4), 23–26 (2011)
9. Rowell, C., Greenberg, J.: Advancing Interoperability of NSF DataNet Partners Through Controlled Vocabularie, July 7-8, 2013. DataOne Users Group meeting. Chapel Hill, North Carolina (2012)
10. Historia animalium, vol. 2. Loeb Classical Library (1993)
11. National Center for Biological Ontologies: Bioportal,
    http://bioportal.bioontology.org/
12. Gene ontology, http://www.geneontology.org/
13. Marine Metadata Initiative: Vocabularies: Dictionaries, Ontologies, and More,
    https://marinemetadata.org/guides/vocabs
14. Greenberg, et al.: Ibid (2011)
15. Greenberg: (2009) presentation at,
    http://www.cendi.gov/presentations/
    11-17-09_cendi_nfais_Greenberg_UNC.pdf
16. Kea, http://www.nzdl.org/Kea/download.html
17. MAUI, https://code.google.com/p/maui-indexer/
18. Moore, R.W., et al.: DataNet Federation Consortium Vision and Rationale [Project Proposal] (2012),
    http://datafed.org/dev/wp-content/uploads/2012/04/DFCproposal.pdf
19. Rajasekar, A., Moore, R.W.: iRODS Primer: Integrated Rule-Oriented Data System Synthesis Lectures on Information Concepts, Retrieval, and Services. Morgan and Claypool Publishers (2010),
    http://www.morganclaypool.com/doi/abs/10.2200/
    S00233ED1V01Y200912ICR012?journalCode=icr
20. iRODS White Paper, https://www.irods.org/pubs/DICE_RODs-paper.pdf
21. iRODS Microservices Overview,
    https://www.irods.org/index.php/Micro-Services
22. Moore, Rajasekar, Marciano (2007),
    https://www.irods.org/pubs/DICE_DigcCur-Trusted-Rep-07.pdf
23. iRODS Fact Sheet,
    https://www.irods.org/pubs/iRODS_Fact_Sheet-0907c.pdf
24. White, H., Willis, C., Greenberg, J.: The HIVE impact: Contributing to Consistency via Automatic Indexing. In: iConference 2012, Toronto, ON, Canada, February 7-10 (2012), doi:10.1145/2132176.2132297

Metadata, Domain Specific Languages and Visualisations as Internal Artifacts Driving an Agile Knowledge Engineering Methodology

Angelos Yannopoulos, Yannis Christodoulou,
Effie Bountris, Katia Savrami, and Maria Douza

Department of Electrical and Computer Engineering,
National Technical University of Athens, Athens, Greece

Abstract. We introduce M(krDSL), an agile Knowledge Engineering methodology. It addresses the Knowledge Acquisition bottleneck. The point of differentiation of M(krDSL) from previous practice involves knowledge engineers and domain experts collaborating extremely closely: "The domain expert constructs the model. The model is independently useful as a communication tool." We introduce two additional layers of abstraction between human domain experts and operational software: a shared Knowledge Model of the domain, and Visualisation mockups/prototypes. Tools of the methodology include: DSLs and graphical representations; Qualitative analysis of the DSLs; Semantic Metadata for Test Driven Design; and analysis of concurrently evolving Visualisation output mockups/prototypes. In our experience, following this methodology helped us escape from situations where we had completely ceased to be able to make any modelling progress at all, while even at times when we were able to make easy progress in our KE tasks, M(krDSL) gave us a high degree of confidence in the correct prioritisation and correct results of our work.

1 Introduction and Background

We introduce M(krDSL), an agile methodology for constructing a formal <u>Knowledge Model (KM)</u>. We first overview relevant <u>Knowledge Engineering (KE)</u> issues; we then describe the methodology in general; finally, the specific techniques of the M(krDSL) toolbox are described. M(krDSL) was the methodological basis of the European R&D project ANSWER[1].

---

[1] This work was supported in part by the EC FP7, in the context of the ANSWER project, under grant agreement no 216489 (www.answer-project.org). The ANSWER project's work on Semantics was initially based on the DILIGENT methodology. The project was intended from its conception to focus on an internal language layer, here documented as a krDSL, but, initially, the interplay between KE and the krDSL was only a hypothesis. The project's methodological innovations evolved as the project team accumulated useful experiences. M(krDSL) systematises the completed project's most useful lessons.

E. Garoufallou and J. Greenberg (Eds.): MTSR 2013, CCIS 390, pp. 22–34, 2013.
© Springer International Publishing Switzerland 2013

Mainstream adoption of KE is progressing at a measured rather than revolutionary pace, but today examples including Linked Data [1], Semantic Wikis [2] and integrated semantic capabilities in mainstream products such as Oracle 11g [3] attest to the significant progress that is being made. As a result, increasing attention is being paid to KE from a Software Engineering (SE) point of view. For instance, many methodologies for constructing ontologies have been proposed, such as Common-KADS [4], METHONTOLOGY [5], DILIGENT [6], HCOME [7], UPON [8], RapidOWL [9], XD [10]. Two important trends seen in the more recent KE methodologies are collaboration and agility. M(krDSL) focuses on the latter of these – agility. Our purpose is to enrich the knowledge engineer's toolbox with a number of novel techniques that we have found to be useful in practice. In particular, M(krDSL) addresses the "Knowledge Acquisition (KA) bottleneck" [20-22].

It is often the case that KE faces problems that are familiar from SE [11], e.g. initially imprecise requirements, difficulty in prioritising requirements, difficulty of end-users understanding the issues the engineers need to address. An agile process requires an appropriate methodology as well as appropriate technology, e.g. the KM under construction must be amenable to iterative development, providing demonstrable value in each iteration. Interestingly, flexible systems addressing KA often also offer an inherent agility, e.g. Ripple-Down Rules (RDR) in the context of situated cognition [12], or use of procedural knowledge for collaboration support [13]: these approaches support the evolution of the underlying KE requirements, and are highly amenable to a test-first approach.

We can define a KM as per [14]: (1) an ontology, (2) a knowledge base, (3) domain-independent problem-solving methods, and (4) mappings relating (1) and (2) to (3). However, additional artifacts internally support the KE process. For instance, KA techniques such as laddering, concept sorting and reperatory grids rely on informally constructed concept graphs, or physical cards that can be sorted or clustered [15],[12]; other internal (to the KE process) artifacts are: storyboards; application lexicons; lists of Competency Questions (CQs), contextual statements, and use cases [8]; and documentation of reasoning requirements.

2   Methodology

The techniques of M(krDSL) support and function effectively in the context of an agile approach such as the Crystal Clear methodology [16]: KE is performed by a small, collocated team, with the deep involvement of a domain expert (who is permanently available and regularly present) and availability of all relevant skills including ontology engineering, visualisation development, integration with relevant tools, and software engineering. The team aims to produce a working prototype as early as possible, and thereafter focuses on incrementally adding functionality that offers as much real value as possible in the shortest possible iterations. Regular revisions – refactoring at the technical level, and conceptual re-assessment at the knowledge level – are essential. Human communication between team members is most important: formal documentation follows. The defining feature of M(krDSL) is that:

"The domain expert constructs the model.
The model is independently useful as a communication tool."

This approach is inspired by pair programming that is extended to pairs with different roles, e.g. a developer and business analyst. In M(krDSL), the technical correctness of the model (e.g. its formality and consistency) depends on the knowledge engineer, but the conceptual definitions are made directly by the domain expert, as these roles collaborate on creating the model. Indeed, the KM being constructed is no longer exclusively a technical model. Rather, we introduce two additional layers of abstraction[2] between human domain experts and operational software[3] (the new layers are printed in italics):

> domain experts → knowledge & software engineers → informal or semi-formal documentation such as CQs, cards, stories, etc → *shared KM of the domain: Knowledge Representation DSLs (krDSL)* → *visualisation mockups/prototypes based on the krDSL* → technical model of the domain knowledge (or "TDM") → integration of problem solving methods that can handle the domain model → integration into a software tool

A krDSL is a domain representation language that the domain expert can understand and use as a way to document domain-specific ideas, and that the knowledge engineer can use as a concrete specification of the conceptualisation that is to be captured and formalised by the technical domain model (TDM). As an example, consider music notation: to a musician, it is a written language documenting a composer's compositional choices; but to a music-technologist, it has specific technical semantics (pitch, duration, etc). Technically, a krDSL is a language with a formal, machine processable definition of its vocabulary, grammar and syntax, but deferring the formalisation of its semantics to the TDM.

In the "old" (i.e., state of the art) case, knowledge is "acquired" by constructing the technical model of the domain from the informal or semi-formal documentation (and based on personal interactions) [17-19]. The technical model is e.g. an ontology and knowledge base that the technical team members develop. It is normal that the domain experts will not understand the TDM in depth – they should understand e.g. the domain taxonomy, but they cannot be expected to understand e.g. non-trivial Description Logic property restrictions. This limits collaboration within the team to the level

---

[2] The relationships shown are conceptual rather than temporal. They hold throughout the development and operation lifecycle of a knowledge-based application, organised e.g. as in [17]. They show knowledge being transformed from implicit expertise, through the modelling effort, into actionable software.

[3] Feedback should also be a pervasive feature in the team's activity. At all times, feedback from every layer of abstraction should be taken into account at every other layer. This is not a mere platitude. In terms of software engineering, it is a pre-requisite for constant, reflective improvement (in the sense of [16]). It is also essential technically, so as to ensure that, as discussed below, the krDSL corresponds accurately to the underlying technical model. Therefore, feedback should be based on intuitive processes such as discussion and regular reviews of results and ongoing work; and also on formal processes, including detailed technical testing with, if possible, complete coverage.

where KA is performed based on intuitive tools and resulting in informal/semi-formal representations.

In the "new" (i.e., proposed) case, we add the krDSL layer. The result is that both the semantics and the representation of the knowledge captured by the KM are fully accessible to domain experts, who can therefore collaborate on creating and refining the KM. Indeed, in our experience it is most effective if the domain experts lead the process of creating and refining the krDSL, thus collaborating on creating and refining the underlying TDM. The KM comprises both the krDSL and the underlying TDM – the former is the KM's visual representation, the latter is its technical formalisation.

We also add, before reaching the technical model, a layer of visualisation mock-ups/prototypes based on the krDSL. This level is not mandatory, but it is very useful, as discussed below. This layer contains visual tools that assist users to understand the information that has been input using the krDSL, e.g. displaying icons, representing semantic metadata, over frames in a video editing suite, so as to notify the film editor of the film director's intentions when shooting a scene in a movie.

Although the krDSL can be text-based, we are particularly interested in the value of using graphical languages (e.g. diagrams or symbolic notation representations). As examples, we can consider the following already-existing languages to be usable as krDSL's: mathematical notation; music notation; improvised pseudocode; certain types of diagrams of scientific conceptualisations, e.g. of chemical compounds, of electrical circuits, or of data structures; chess notation.

M(krDSL) is effective because it enables three powerful tools to be applied to KA: (1) DSLs and graphical representations, (2) Semantic Metadata for Test Driven Design (TDD), and (3) Visualisation output mockups/prototypes. We next discuss each of these tools in detail.

3   Methodology Components

3.1   DSLs and Graphical Representations

A Domain Specific Language (DSL) [23],[25],[26] is a machine-processable language (e.g. programming language or specification language) designed specifically to express solutions to problems in a particular domain. Example DSLs include HTML, dot/GraphViz and BPMN. As discussed in [23] (with relevant elaboration in [24]) every DSL corresponds to a Semantic Model (SM): the SM is instantiated from information captured using the DSL, and programme execution is based on this SM instantiation. "A SM is a notion very similar to that of a Domain Model", "you can build a DSL and SM together, using the discussions with domain experts both to refine the expressions of the DSL and the structure of the Domain Model" [23], but KE and KMs are often not regarded as relevant for DSLs, e.g. "In the context of a DSL, a SM is a representation, such as an in-memory object model, of the same subject that the DSL describes. [...] Other ways of representing [DSLs include] a data structure, with the [appropriate] behavior [...] coming from functions that act upon that data, [...]

a model held in a relational database, [... and] there are occasions when an AST [abstract syntax tree] is an effective SM for a DSL" [23].

DSLs are an old technique and industrial experience demonstrates their many advantages [23],[25-28]. These advantages include usability, separation of concerns, maintainability of DSL programmes, and others. Critically, for our priorities, they also include collaboration: a DSL can normally be understood and used both by software engineers and domain experts. In particular, pair programming (in its "extended" form where different "roles" programme together) using DSLs is a very powerful approach [26-28]; e.g. a team consisting of a lawyer, an economist and a software engineer can collaboratively translate a contract into executable code that enforces the contract, and every team member can read the executable code side-by-side with the contract (legal document) and directly verify the correspondence [26]. "Many teams practiced what we have come to call ultimate pair programming, where an expert developer and a domain expert shared a keyboard and mouse. This is the best of XP where the customer actually becomes a co-developer" [27].

A fundamental idea in M(krDSL) is to use the krDSL *development process* as a tool within the KM development process. This is most useful in cases where domain modelling is very difficult, especially when a direct attempt to model the domain might fail outright. A related challenge is when there is no way to assess whether a domain model is successful: even if it is sufficient with respect to a given set of CQs, does it really capture deeper knowledge about the domain, so that it will be capable of being expanded or generalised? DSLs are known to be, in general terms, useful in supporting domain modelling: "Involving domain experts in a DSL is very similar to involving domain experts in building a model. I've often found great benefit by building a model together with domain experts" [23]. M(krDSL) systematically applies this technique in the context of KE and the KA bottleneck, and structures the process of developing a krDSL in a way that amplifies the design, modelling and verification questions pertaining to the construction of the KM. This is achieved using Semantic Metadata for TDD and Visualisation output mockups/prototypes, as discussed in the following Sections, as well as by Qualitative analysis of the krDSL, as discussed below. DSLs are used as a tool for communication between domain experts and knowledge engineers, for explicitly representing domain modelling choices, for magnifying and exposing potential problems of the technical knowledge modelling process (so that they can be solved early), and as a part of the KM itself (the DSL functions as the KM's visual representation and the TDM as the KM's underlying formalisation).

Qualitative analysis of the krDSL facilitates the development of a KM that will be expandable and generalisable, and it also improves the team's ability to assess the KM under development. The krDSL has its own structural features, especially its own vocabulary and syntax, and we can analyse the correspondence between these features and the language's semantics, which are formalised in the underlying TDM. In particular, syntactic patterns can be identified, and an intuitive understanding can be developed concerning which aspects of the domain can easily be modelled relying on the structure that is already available. The semantics of the krDSL will be stricter than those of a natural language description; by studying a sample written in the krDSL, and considering its exact meaning as documented by the team's knowledge engineers, the domain experts can make explicit distinctions between available domain modelling choices. Finally, the krDSL leads the team to address the most important and the hardest problems first.

The ideas of situated cognition [12] and conversational KA [22] highlight the benefit of allowing a representation of knowledge to emerge organically through a knowledge-intensive process, in interaction with domain experts. The development of a krDSL for the domain focuses such a collaboration on a formal artifact that can be incrementally developed, directly tested, and is fully understood by domain experts. A very effective technique is to concurrently design and implement the krDSL and prototypes of useful tools for the domain experts, such as visualisations as discussed below (Section 3.3). The domain experts are able to provide exceedingly nuanced guidance to the definition of the TDM, as they control the actionable krDSL/tool-prototype pair, mapping knowledge representation to expected interpretation. The TDM (together with appropriately coupled problem-solving methods) is a hidden intermediate step on the path from krDSL to the output of the tool prototype. The TDM thus operates as an information "bottleneck"[4] between input and output interfaces where domain knowledge is manifested in an easily understandable and verifiable representation.

The domain experts are engaged in a natural-feeling process of terminology definition, by creating terms for the krDSL's that they can use directly. More importantly, they develop an "operational" understanding of the model they are constructing, since they use it as actionable input for useful (prototype) tools.

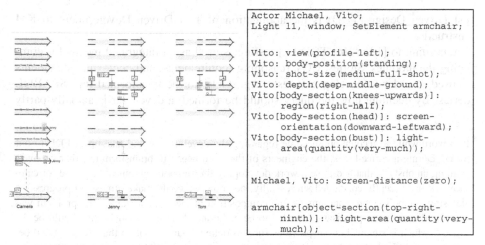

Fig. 1. Using a krDSL as a krDSL – graphical and text-based representations

The result of this process is the development of a krDSL and a TDM that formalises it. Together, these two artifacts comprise the KM that the methodology produces: the krDSL is the visual, readable representation of the KM, the TDM is the technical formalisation of the same information. The TDM is very "intuitively close" to the

---

[4] This structure is intuitively similar in conception to "learning internal representations" in [29],[30].

krDSL: for instance, the domain experts can understand the semantics of the TDM by reading the krDSL – this has been actively ensured, and tested, through the development process. The KM evolves organically thanks to this harmony between intuition and formalisation. Thus, we have achieved the core aim of the methodology: "The domain expert constructs the model. The model is independently useful as a communication tool".

Figure 1 shows two example krDSL's that we developed in our work on Director-Notation (DN) [32-41], addressing the domain of Film Directing. On the left is a sample of DN itself (a symbolic notation); on the right is a sample of our text-only Frame Description Language (FDL). The graphical DSL makes it easier to qualitatively analyse the modelling choices that it embodies. For instance, in DN, we can analyse our modelling choices in terms of spatial layout (different dimensions with different semantics – y axis: time, x axis: thematic areas), symbol structure (large symbols composed of smaller ones – this corresponds to attributes / data properties), symbol relevance to eachother (symbols are placed nearby for a reason; technically this translates into relationships / class properties), compromises that we make (e.g. symbols that we understand to be related, but which are separated in the diagram – this indicates e.g. reasoning requirements, for filling in the semantics that are not asserted).[5]

3.2   Semantic Metadata for TDD

Test Driven Design (TDD) is the application of Test Driven Development to KM construction.

According to [10]: "[In] TDD [...] testing is used as an integrated means for completing the modules. Stories, CQs, reasoning requirements, and contextual statements are used in order to develop unit tests, e.g., CQs can be transformed into SPARQL queries. By deciding how the query should be formed, a developer is actually partly

---

[5] It is worthwhile to recount an anecdote regarding the development and take-up of FDL in our work. During a coffee-break, the engineers of the team began to brainstorm together on overcoming an obstacle that had arisen: work developing the symbolic graphical language for camerawork had recently concluded successfully, but now we could make almost no progress on devising symbolic representations for the composition of the camera frame. The problem was that the domain conceptualisation needed to be elaborated before its visualisation could be designed (which is simple, but our previous success delayed our realisation that the work had become more difficult now). In desperation, the engineers started scribbling prolog-like statements as shorthand notes of concepts and relationships that might need to be represented. The surprise came when the film directors, literally looking over the engineers' shoulders, started asking questions about these notes. The engineers said "please don't worry about this, it's like programming, you won't understand it", and the film directors replied "but we do understand it – what we're asking is why you did it this way, since it would be better to...". Thus, the value of a text-based DSL for collaboration was discovered by chance, when the domain experts fully understood what was originally thought to be a technical representation. Eventually, the text-based DSL, developed by the whole team together, enabled us to develop the graphical one. Very similar experiences have been reported in [28],[42], which we discovered later.

designing the model, hence, the notion 'test-driven' design. [TDD] enforces the task-oriented approach of the method, i.e., the principle that modules should realize exactly what is required [...]." M(krDSL) embraces and extends TDD as defined in [10].

In our work on DN [32-41] (also see Figure 1), the krDSL is of high intrinsic value. When an end-user documents domain-specific information using it, all provided information can be extracted and re-purposed as semantic metadata (which is useful in applications such as visualisation, content-based search, automatic cost estimation, and others). This provided an immediate link to TDD: we can specify intended inputs and corresponding outputs, then incrementally evolve the system to pass the test. It is important that the tests are derived from an application that exploits the KM, rather than artificially exercising the KM directly based on inputs and outputs corresponding to CQs.

In M(krDSL), TDD is applied to KA, not simply to the technical modelling process as described in e.g. XD [10]. The intended inputs and corresponding outputs of each test must be specified at two distinct levels: as a technical representation, and as a visual or conceptual representation. Thus, we specify a test in terms of how the domain expert will define the specific problem instance as input for a software application, as well as in terms of how the system will internally represent this input; and in terms of the visual (or other) output that will be provided by the application, as well as in terms of how the system will internally represent this output.

By defining how the inputs should be expressed and how the outputs should be structured, the domain expert is contributing to the modelling process itself, because the krDSL and visualisation tools are themselves being developing in parallel to the modelling process, and they serve to define the TDM. By re-casting the domain expert's krDSL input as a SPARQL query or other technical testing form, the knowledge engineer is both partly developing the TDM according to the logic of [10] quoted above, and also partly developing the mapping from the krDSL to the TDM. Thus, all design levels, from KA to TDM development, are being addressed.

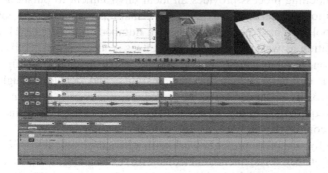

Fig. 2. Prototype tool that displays visualisations including metadata for the Film Directing domain

Figure 2 shows a screenshot of the Bones Dailies application, in a prototype version that has been expanded to show film notation (using DN [32-41]), visualisation (an automatically generated animation corresponding to the DN), and semantic metadata (extracted from the DN). In the corresponding use case, the notation has been authored by the film director, but this is a post-production tool, being used by a film editor (a different domain expert). A reasoner extracts implicit information from the director's DN (e.g. identifying that a scene is a dialogue scene) and displays it over the appropriate frames in the film editor's interface. The film editor can thus easily visualise the content that she has to work with.

Before adding new features to DN or the application, we create a test – if we represent x in DN, we expect y to appear in Bones Dailies – and proceed according to TDD.

3.3   Visualisation Output Mockups/Prototypes

The principle of situated cognition, as framed constructively in [12], gives us the following insight: *"Any rule or knowledge statement a person provides will apply to the current situation, but will be over-general, as it will not identify all the features that distinguish this context from all possible contexts." "A concept used in a rule or knowledge statement, will point to some feature in the data, but this feature may not have a well-defined meaning which applies outside the context."* This suggests that the KA process will be greatly enhanced if we create a practical context that highlights different situations in the application domain corresponding to necessary differences within the model being constructed. The principle is that people do not *"explain the process of how they reach a conclusion; rather they create explanations to justify their decision in the particular context of the decision"* [12]. Therefore, a KM can be iteratively constructed by exploring the context in which the knowledge represented thus far has emerged: distinctions in the context will be discovered that require refinements to components of the current model, which in turn will be discovered to be only partially applicable.

Iterative development of <u>Knowledge Visualisation (KV)</u> tools in parallel to the M(krDSL) modelling process provides an ideal environment to pursue KA based on situated cognition. KV basically involves the visual representation of knowledge, but full-fledged tools can be expected to possess a number of qualities [31]: capture and depict information as well as insights, experiences, concepts, perspectives – of more than one person, in interrelation; use systematic visual metaphor(s); support interaction, including editing, updating for new insights, and debate through the visual medium; be broadly understandable; be capable of uncovering new knowledge. KV provides the required capability, as discussed above, to iteratively refine the consideration of the context in which knowledge statements are made.

The reason for which we prefer to work with a visual/graphical krDSL, as stated in Section 2, is that such a system simultaneously serves as a DSL and as a visualisation. An interesting argument can be based on the idea of "cognitive effectiveness" of visual notations [42]: Cognitive effectiveness can not be assessed without understanding the domain – so, in order to assess the visual notation, we must develop our understanding of the domain. Nevertheless, in practice humans are extremely capable at understanding visual systems intuitively – in fact, they can often assess cognitive effectiveness better than we would expect from their level of explicit understanding of the domain. Therefore, working to assess a visual notation that is under development can be exploited as a KA tool: the process of iterative development of the notation, and assessment of its cognitive effectiveness, helps the researcher to intuitively access, and thereafter elicit, tacit knowledge of the domain that she possess but has not yet made explicit.

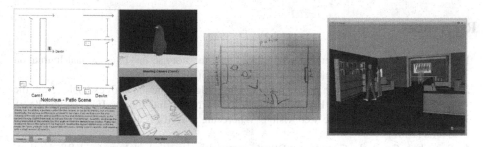

Fig. 3. Visualisations and mockups for the Film Directing domain

Figure 3 shows a selection of the visualisations that we worked with for DN. On the left, a simple "penguin" character was animated over a floorplan rather than in a 3D environment, and shown from a top-view as well as from the camera's view (a tutorial using this setup was eventually created for teaching the basics of DN, but originally the setup was used in internal discussions of DN and its semantics). In the middle, a hand-drawn floorplan is shown. On the right, we present a screenshot of the output of the prototype system for producing accurate animations showing the film documented in DN by the film director. These visualisations evolved gradually, through many revisions and changes, in parallel with the development of DN and of the underlying DN ontology. We worked to define the semantics of DN by working on the visualisations themselves. Some important questions that arose as to the semantics of DN, that were addressed early and understood clearly thanks to the parallel development of visualisations, include the following examples: Should we allow the film director to specify that an actor moves through an object or wall? Do the trajectories of the camera and actors, when specified as sequences of line segments, have rounded corners? At what height is the camera by default? Should we model the size of objects with simple bounding boxes or is this an oversimplification?

4   Conclusions and Future Work

M(krDSL) is an agile KE methodology that exploits DSLs, semantic metadata in the context of TDD, and visualisation techniques for overcoming the KA bottleneck. Applying M(krDSL) not only produces an effective KM, but also a krDSL that allows domain experts to express their conceptualisation in a convenient form (the krDSL and corresponding TDM comprise the domain KM). M(krDSL) is founded theoretically on the concepts of agile software development, situated cognition, conversational KA, cognitive effectiveness of visual notations, and knowledge visualisation.

In our ongoing and future research, we plan to systematically analyse the progress of our completed work using M(krDSL) and compare to KE work that we performed without the methodology, in order to deliver a numerical measurement showing the impact of the methodology. We also aim to experiment with and document specific application areas where M(krDSL) can be of particular value.

References

1. Bizer, C., Heath, T., Berners-Lee, T.: Linked data-the story so far. International Journal on Semantic Web and Information Systems (IJSWIS) 5(3), 1–22 (2009)
2. Boulos, M.N.K.: Semantic Wikis: A comprehensible introduction with examples from the health sciences. Journal of Emerging Technologies in Web Intelligence 1(1), 94–96 (2009)
3. Cardoso, J.: The semantic web vision: Where are we? IEEE Intelligent Systems 22(5), 84–88 (2007)
4. Schreiber, G., et al.: CommonKADS: A comprehensive methodology for KBS development. IEEE Expert 9(6), 28–37 (1994)
5. Blázquez, J., et al.: Building ontologies at the knowledge level using the ontology design environment. In: 11th Banff Knowledge Acquisition for Knowledge-Based Systems Workshop (KAW 1998), Banff, Alberta, Canada, April 18-23 (1998)
6. Pinto, H.S., Staab, S., Tempich, C.: DILIGENT: Towards a fine-grained methodology for Distributed, Loosely-controlled and evolving Engineering of Ontologies. In: ECAI, vol. 16 (2004)
7. Kotis, K., Vouros, G.A.: Human-centered ontology engineering: The HCOME methodology. Knowledge and Information Systems 10(1), 109–131 (2006)
8. De Nicola, A., Missikoff, M., Navigli, R.: A software engineering approach to ontology building. Information Systems 34(2), 258–275 (2009)
9. Auer, S., Herre, H.: RapidOWL—An Agile Knowledge Engineering Methodology. In: Virbitskaite, I., Voronkov, A. (eds.) PSI 2006. LNCS, vol. 4378, pp. 424–430. Springer, Heidelberg (2007)
10. Presutti, V., et al.: Pattern-Based Ontology Design. Ontology Engineering in a Networked World, pp. 35–64. Springer, Heidelberg (2012)
11. Knublauch, H.: Extreme programming of knowledge-based systems. In: Research Institute for Applied Knowledge Processing (FAW), Conference Proceedings from eXtreme Programming and Agile Processes in Software Engineering (XP 2002), Alghero, Sardinia, Italy (2002)
12. Compton, P.: Situated cognition and knowledge acquisition research. International Journal of Human-Computer Studies 71(2), 184–190 (2013)
13. Wickler, G., Tate, A., Hansberger, J.: Using shared procedural knowl-edge for virtual collaboration support in emergency management. IEEE Intelligent Systems (2013)
14. Musen, M.A.: The knowledge acquisition workshops: A remarkable convergence of ideas. International Journal of Human-Computer Studies (2012)
15. Schreiber, G.: Knowledge engineering and management: the Common KADS methodology. The MIT Press (2000)
16. Cockburn, A.: Crystal clear: a human-powered methodology for small teams. Addison-Wesley Professional (2005)
17. Sure, Y., Staab, S., Studer, R.: Ontology engineering methodology. In: Handbook on Ontologies, pp. 135–152. Springer, Heidelberg (2009)

18. Sure, Y., Angele, J., Staab, S.: OntoEdit: Guiding ontology development by methodology and inferencing. In: Meersman, R., Tari, Z. (eds.) CoopIS 2002, DOA 2002, and ODBASE 2002. LNCS, vol. 2519, pp. 1205–1222. Springer, Heidelberg (2002)
19. Dombeu, F., Vincent, J., Huisman, M.: Semantic-Driven e-Government: Ap-plication of Uschold and King Ontology Building Methodology for Semantic Ontology Models Development. arXiv preprint arXiv:1111.1941 (2011)
20. Waterman, D.A.: A guide to expert systems. Addison-Wesley, Reading (1986)
21. Wagner, C.: End-users as expert system developers. Journal of End User Computing 12(3), 3–13 (2000)
22. Wagner, C.: Breaking the knowledge acquisition bottleneck through conversational knowledge management. Information Resources Management Journal (IRMJ) 19(1), 70–83 (2006)
23. Fowler, M.: Domain-specific languages. Pearson Education (2010)
24. Fowler, M.: Patterns of enterprise application architecture. Addison-Wesley Longman Publishing Co., Inc. (2002)
25. Völter, M.: DSL Engineering: Designing, Implementing and Using Domain-specific Languages. CreateSpace Independent Publishing Platform (2013)
26. Jones, S.P., Eber, J.-M., Seward, J.: Composing contracts: an ad-venture in financial engineering (functional pearl). ACM SIGPLAN Notices 35(9) (2000)
27. Thomas, D., Barry, B.M.: Model driven development: the case for domain oriented programming. In: Companion of the 18th Annual ACM SIGPLAN Conference on Object-Oriented Programming, Systems, Languages, and Applications. ACM (2003)
28. Flouris, G., Cigni, R.: Groovy Solutions for Data Flows. Presentation Given at Groovy & Grails eXchange, London, December 16-17 (2010)
29. Rumelhart, D.E., Hinton, G.E., Williams, R.J.: Learning internal representations by error propagation. No. ICS-8506. San Diego La Jolla Inst for Cognitive Science, California Univ. (1985)
30. Kramer, M.A.: Nonlinear principal component analysis using autoassociative neural networks. AIChE Journal 37(2), 233–243 (1991)
31. Eppler, M.J.: What is an effective knowledge visualization? Insights from a review of seminal concepts. In: Knowledge Visualization Currents, pp. 3–12. Springer, London (2013)
32. Yannopoulos, A.: DirectorNotation: Artistic and technological system for professional film directing. Journal on Computing and Cultural Heritage (JOCCH) 6(1), 2 (2013)
33. Yannopoulos, A., et al.: ANSWER: Documentation, formal conceptualisation and annotation of new media. In: Adjunct Proceedings of EuroITV 2009, Leuven, Belgium, June 3-5 (2009)
34. Beales, R., et al.: Automated 3d previs for modern production. In: International Broadcasting Convention (IBC) 2009, Amsterdam, September 10-15 (2009)
35. Chakravarthy, A., et al.: ANSWER: a semantic approach to film direction. In: Fourth International Conference on Internet and Web Applications and Services, ICIW 2009. IEEE (2009)
36. Chakravarthy, A., et al.: A Notation Based Approach To Film Pre-vis. In: 2010 Conference on Visual Media Production (CVMP). IEEE (2010)
37. Mavrogeorgi, N., et al.: Reasoner system for video creation having as input a conceptual video description. In: 2011 IEEE Workshop on Computational Intelligence for Visual Intelligence (CIVI). IEEE (2011)
38. Jung, Y., et al.: Storyboarding and pre-visualization with x3d. In: Proceedings of the 15th International Conference on Web 3D Technology. ACM (2010)

39. Mavrogeorgi, N., Christodoulou, Y., Kalogirou, P.: Semi-automatic Film-Direction Technique in Internet-Based Interactive Entertainment. In: Third International Conference on Internet and Web Applications and Services, ICIW 2008. IEEE (2008)
40. Nikoletta, M., Christodoulou, Y.: Complete, cinematic and expressive presentation in computer game. In: Proceedings of the 1st International Conference on Pervasive Technologies Related to Assistive Environments. ACM (2008)
41. Christodoulou, Y., Mavrogeorgi, N., Kalogirou, P.: Use of Ontologies for Knowledge Representation of a Film Scene. In: Third International Conference on Internet and Web Applications and Services, ICIW 2008. IEEE (2008)
42. http://www.se-radio.net/?s=dsl (retrieved August 20, 2013)
43. Moody, D.: "The "physics" of notations: toward a scientific basis for constructing visual notations in software engineering. IEEE Transactions on Software Engineering 35(6), 756–779 (2009)

OAIzer: Configurable OAI Exports
over Relational Databases

Sandro La Bruzzo[1], Paolo Manghi[1], and Alessia Bardi[1,2]

[1] Consiglio Nazionale delle Ricerche
Istituto di Scienza e Tecnologie dell'Informazione "A. Faedo"
name.surname@isti.cnr.it
[2] Dipartimento di Ingegneria dell'Informazione, Università di Pisa
alessia.bardi@for.unipi.it

Abstract. Modern Digital Library Systems (DLSs) typically support information spaces of interconnected objects, whose graph-like document models surpass the traditional DL payload-metadata document models. Examples are repositories for enhanced publications, CRIS systems, cultural heritage archives. To enable interoperability, DLSs expose their objects and interlinks with other objects as "export packages", via standard exchange formats (e.g. XML, RDF encodings) and OAI-ORE or OAI-PMH protocols. This paper presents OAIzer, a tool for the easy configuration and automatic deploy of OAI interfaces over an RDBMS-based DLS. Starting from the given relational representation of a document model, OAIzer provides DLS developers with user interfaces for drafting the intended structure of export packages and the automated deploy of OAI endpoints capable of exporting such packages.

1 Introduction

A Digital Library System (DLS) [1] offers to a user community functionalities for the management, access and dissemination of information objects whose structure is defined by a data model called *document model*. In the past, DLSs typically adopted document models representing *flat* collections of information objects with a file-metadata structure, where metadata information describes files for the purpose of discovery, visualisation, and consumption. Today, the new trends of e-Research and e-Science are pushing for DLSs capable of storing *graph-like* collections of information objects with an entity-relationship structure. Typically, such *graph document models* represent file-metadata pairs of different typologies (logical entities) together with the semantic relationships between them (logical associations). Examples of such information spaces are provided by enhanced publication tools [2], scholarly communication infrastructures [3,4], Cultural Heritage infrastructures [5,6,7]. The adoption of graph document models and the realisation of DLSs capable of managing the relative graphs of information objects introduced a number of challenges at all levels, concerning the way such object graphs are physically stored, displayed, and exported to enable interoperability.

E. Garoufallou and J. Greenberg (Eds.): MTSR 2013, CCIS 390, pp. 35–47, 2013.

DLSs may export their objects in several ways, though two standards defined by the OAI initiative are often cited: OAI-PMH (Open Archives Initiative Protocol for Metadata Harvesting) [8] and OAI-ORE (Open Archives Initiative Object Reuse and Exchange) [9]. Informally, the former provides bulk access to sets of XML object representations, while the latter offers access by identifier to one given XML/RDF object representation. In the case of graph-shaped information spaces, such representations (hereafter *export packages*) are encodings of "interlinked sets of objects"; e.g. an XML/RDF file representing a publication together with all its related datasets. In fact, OAI APIs are implemented given: (*i*) the export package *structure*, identified as a sub-part (hereafter *logical view*) of the graph document model, (*ii*) the relative export *format* (e.g. XML, RDF) and *schema* (e.g. LIDO, EAD, DC), and (*iii*) the OAI protocol of interest.

Several DLSs are today still implementing their graph-shaped information spaces over Relational Database Management Systems (RDBMSs): logical entities and relationships of the document model are implemented as interconnected relational tables (see Section 3 for real-cases of such DLSs). In this work we shall focus on the specific problem of realizing OAI protocol APIs for RDBMS-based DLSs. To this aim, DLS developers must cope with the well-known RDBMS's "impedance mismatch" issue and reverse-engineer which sub-set of the relational database corresponds to the logical view of the given export packages. Only then, they can implement from scratch the code required to query the database and generate/export the export packages according to the specifications. The costs of realization and maintenance of such code are often not affordable by responsible organizations. Realization is complicated by the fact that document model views are defined at the logical level and must be found a correspondence into the relative relational database implementation. Maintenance actions may be expensive when any change to the document model, to the views or to the physical relational schema is required. This paper presents OAIzer, a tool capable of connecting to any JDBC-compatible RDBMS and providing DLS developers with user interfaces for drafting logical views and selecting the desired OAI protocol. Once views and protocol are provided, the tool deploys an OAI HTTP address for each view and the code required to respond to OAI access requests by generating export packages according to the given structure. The tool generates export packages according to a pre-defined XML format capable of encoding the structure of any views, and offers the possibility to add XSLT files to further customise their OAI outputs. OAIzer avoids the workload of realizing view-specific OAI interfaces from scratch and reduces maintenance costs since new OAI exports can be always generated with minor administrative costs whenever structural changes are required.

Outline. Section 2 introduces concepts and terminology, and defines the problem to be addressed. Section 3 describes the issues to be tackled in order to construct and expose export packages from a relational database via OAI-PMH and OAI-ORE. Section 4 presents the general-purpose solution realized by OAIzer. Finally, Section 5 concludes the paper and discusses future avenues.

2   Graph Document Models, Views, and Export Packages

A document model is a formal definition of the structure and semantics of DLS content in terms of entities and relationships. An entity type typically describes properties of objects in terms of name, cardinality and value type. A relationship type usually has a semantic label expressing the nature of the association and the types of entities allowed as sources and targets of the relationship. Figure 1 shows a document model defining three types of entities (Article, File, and Data) and relationships between them, together with an example of object graph.

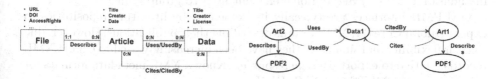

Fig. 1. Example of graph document model and relative object graph

Object graphs conforming to graph document models may be exported according to a variety of strategies, depending on which entities and relationships have to be exposed to third party consumers. In order to make the export process systematic and independent from the current content of the DLSs such strategies are often based on the expected structure (graph document model) of the object graph. Logically this can be done by specifying *views* of the document model, which are rooted sub-graphs identifying the *perspective* of the export, i.e. the entity of the root object, and the *context* of the root object, i.e. the transitive closure of entities and relationships to be exported with the root object. Figure 2 illustrates two views of the graph document model in Figure 1, relative to Article and Data root entities, together with examples of the corresponding *export packages*, i.e. the object sub-graphs to be exported.

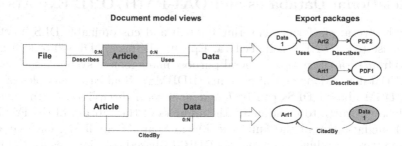

Fig. 2. Example of document model views and export packages

In order to exchange and re-use export packages, interoperability issues must be tackled. The Open Archives Initiative [10] defines two standard protocols for data interoperability and information reuse: OAI-PMH Open Archives Initiative

Protocol for Metadata Harvesting [8] and OAI-ORE Open Archives Initiative Object Reuse and Exchange [9]. OAI-PMH is meant for bulk export of sets of XML records; OAI-ORE is meant for the export of web-interpretable XML/RDF representations of so-called *aggregations*.

OAI-PMH supports an application-independent interoperability framework based on metadata harvesting. Its data model has four main elements: (*i*) *Resource:* an object described by one or more metadata records; (*ii*) *Metadata record:* XML data describing a resource. Each metadata record has its metadata format, often referred to as the XML Schema; (*iii*) *Item:* container of metadata records describing one resource. Each item must have at least one Dublin Core metadata record; (*iv*) *Set:* optional element used to group items.

OAI-PMH interfaces are typically implemented by literature repositories to expose Dublin Core [11] XML records describing their publications. However, due to their flexibility and simplicity they have been increasingly used to export XML records relative to export package resources. Known XML metadata formats for this purpose are METS and XML-DIDL.

OAI-ORE defines standards for the description and exchange of Web resources called aggregations. An aggregation is a Web resource with its own identity, accessible via a URL, created to represent a group of interlinked Web resources. The data model of OAI-ORE includes the following entities: (*ii*) *Aggregated resource:* resource that belongs to an aggregation, that is the ORE representation of an information object in a compound object; (*iii*) *Resource map:* serializable description of an aggregation, whose suggested formats are XML/RDF or ATOM feeds. A resource map lists the aggregated resources and may contain properties about the aggregation and its aggregated resources, e.g. relationships among aggregated and external resources; (*iv*) *Proxy:* resource that allows to assert relationships among aggregated resources in the context of a specific aggregation.

In the context of DLSs, metadata records can be encoded as ORE aggregated resources and export packages can be encoded as ORE aggregations, exportable via resource map serializations.

3   Relational Databases and OAI-PMH/ORE Exports

Although several platforms delivering built-in and customizable DLS functionalities exist (e.g. D-NET [12], Fedora, Eprints, DSpace), DLSs are still often realized from scratch on top of general-purpose management systems, such as Relational Database Management Systems (RDBMS). Real-case examples of very large RDBMS-based DLSs can be found in several disciplines. In the field of social history, worth to mention are the archives of the Library of the Friedrich Ebert Foundation[1] and the Fundação Mário Soares.[2] Similarly, cinemateques and filmographic archives often opt for RDBMS-based solutions, as for the Danish Film Institute[3] and Filmoteca Española.[4] Other examples, in life-science

---

[1] FES Library: http://library.fes.de/index_en.htm
[2] Fundação Mário Soares: http://www.fmsoares.pt/
[3] DFI: http://www.dfi.dk/Service/English/Films-and-industry.aspx
[4] Filmoteca Española: http://www.mcu.es/cine/MC/FE/index.html

and palaeontology, are the archives EuropePMC[5] and Invertebrate Paleontology Knowledgebase.[6]

Going for RDBMS-based solutions gives more freedom to the developers, who are not bound to platform restrictions (e.g. DSpace and Eprints document models), and does not entail any learning curve (e.g. Fedora data model and tools), but requires all DLS functionality to be implemented. The implementation of OAI-PMH or OAI-ORE interfaces starting from one or more views of the graph document model implementation is one of such functionalities. Figure 3 illustrates this scenario. Typically developers are provided by designers with a graph document model – i.e. a conceptual model given in terms of entities, their attributes, and relationships between entities – and a specification of the end-user functionalities to be implemented. Based on such inputs, developers implement a relational database. Figure 4 shows how the document model in Fig. 1 can be represented in terms of relations. According to well-known best practices, entities and attributes are represented by relational tables and properties, while relationships are encoded via primary and foreign keys mechanisms. In particular, one-to-many relationships are encoded by adding a foreign key reference to the source table of the relationship, while many-to-many references are encoded by adding an "intermediate" table whose records contain the foreign keys to the records to be associated. These are general modelling guidelines, but specificities of the scenario (i.e. size of tables, cardinality of properties, sub-classing) and preferences of developers may result in substantially different relational database encodings for the same document model.

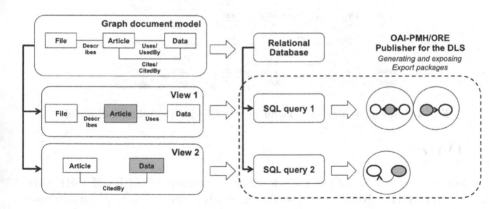

Fig. 3. Implementing OAI publisher modules over RDBMSs

In a second stage, having to implement OAI-PMH/ORE APIs, developers will be provided with the views of the document model to be considered for the export, i.e. *view1* and *view2* in Figure 3. Developers face an "impedance

---

[5] europePMC: http://europepmc.org
[6] IPKB: http://dl.acm.org/citation.cfm?id=2232837

mismatch" problem, having to identify the subsets of the relational database corresponding to logical views. Typically, mapping a relational database into the original conceptual model is a semi-automated (often manual) operation based on the intuition – see database reverse engineering literature, from initial [13] to recent [14]). The technical challenge is to write the SQL query and the transformation code necessary to extract content from such database portions and properly package it to create corresponding export packages. If we consider *view1* in the example, rooted in the entity Article, the corresponding portion of the database will include tables *Article*, *Data*, *File*, and *Uses*. The SQL query will create one export package for each record in *Article*, including the records in *Data* which are reachable by *Uses* and those in *File* which refer to the record *Article*. The transformation code will encode export packages in a on-the-wire exchange format of interest, e.g. XML, HTML, RDF, JSON, and w.r.t. a given export schema, e.g. METS, XML-DIDL, LIDO, EAD. Finally, further code will have to be written to deliver export packages via the desired OAI protocol and to either generate the requested export packages on-the-fly or materialize them in-synch with the database content. Realizing such OAI export modules is an expensive operation, driven by view-specific requirements and subject to the relational implementation of the graph document model. Moreover, maintaining such code may also represent a challenge, since any modifications to the graph document model, the relative physical representation, or to the export views requires the adaptation of the export modules.

File			
fileID	URL	...	isDescribedBy
PDF1	"http one"	...	Art1
PDF2	"http two"	...	Art2

Article		
artID	Title	...
Art1	"Title one"	...
Art2	"Title two"	...

Data		
dataID	Title	...
data1	"Title 3"	...

Cites	
artID	dataID
Art1	Data1

Uses	
artID	dataID
Art2	Data1

Fig. 4. Implementation of a document model with the relational model

4   OAIzer

OAIzer is a tool that facilitates DLS developers at defining OAI-PMH/ORE publishers over relational databases. To this aim, the tool connects to a given database to extract the graph of relational tables and offers graphical user interfaces to semi-automatically reconstruct the document model via reverse engineering of the database structure. The document model identifies the main entities and the relative relationships and keeps track of bindings with the local relational database implementation. A second interface allows the developer to define the views of interest, by selecting a root and following paths to other entities. Once the view is constructed, the developer finalizes the configuration by selecting the OAI protocol of interest. View definition and OAI protocol are used by OAIzer to generate the code necessary to build export packages w.r.t. the current database content and to deploy the required OAI HTTP access point. The architecture of the tool is illustrated in Figure 5 and described in the following sections.

4.1 Re-construction of the Graph Document Model

Developers using OAIzer first have to specify the JDBC configuration settings of their relational database. Once connected, the tool downloads the database schema from the Relation Catalogue and builds an internal representation of the graph document model. The first analysis builds a graph which contains an entity for each table (using the table name) and a one-to-many relationship for each foreign key (using the attribute name). This action instantiates the function $impl$ which returns for each triple $E, R, \bar{E}$ the kind of the relationship R: one-to-many, one-to-one, many-to-one, or many-to-many. The graph document model resulting from the database in Figure 4 is represented in Figure 6, where, for example, $impl(Files, DescribedBy, Articles) = N : 1$ (many-to-one) and $impl(Articles, DescribedBy, Files) = 0 : N$ (optional one-to-many).

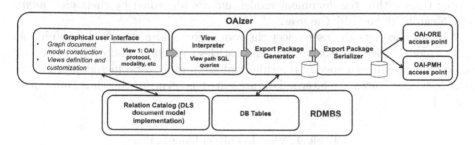

Fig. 5. OAIzer: the architecture

OAIzer prompts the user with a user interface that graphically represents the current document model and highlights those entities which are "worth" further human analysis since they may be representing many-to-many relationships. Such entities are those with two (or more) outgoing one-to-many relationships, hence candidate to become themselves many-to-many relationships. In the example, this is the case for the entities *Uses* and *Cites*. Figure 6 shows the graph document model once the user has selected the entity *Uses* to promote it as a relationship (with the table name). This action updates the function $impl$ by removing the entries $impl(Articles, artID, Uses)$ and $impl(Uses, dataID, Data)$ and adding the definitions $impl(Articles, Uses, Data) = N : M$ and $impl(Data, Uses, Articles) = N : M$ (many-to-many).

4.2 Definition of Views

Once the developer has finalised the graph document model with the proper enrichments, OAIzer provides a graphical user interface for the construction of

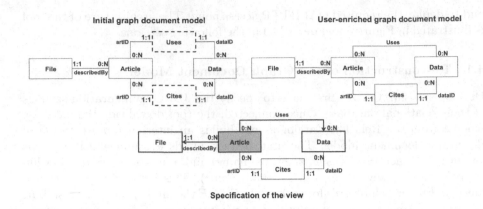

Fig. 6. Graph document model: semi-automatic reconstruction

logical views over the model. Views define the structure of the export packages as rooted trees within the document model and are identified by their *view name*, which can be defined by the user.

The interface lets the user select the root entity and navigate the graph document model to select relationships and entities to include in the view. For each entity it is possible to specify the subset of attributes to be included in the export packages. Views are internally represented as terms of the *view language* in Table 1.

Table 1. View Definition Language

$VIEW$	$::=$ $Root\ NODE$	Root node entity
$NODE$	$::=$ $Entity\ E(A)\{EDGES\}$	Node entity E with attributes A possibly with EDGES to other node entities
$EDGES$	$::=$ $Rel\ R\{NODE\}; EDGES \mid \epsilon$	Sequence of relationships R to node entity NODE
A	$::= p_1, \dots, p_k$	Attributes from current node entity

$$view1 \ = \ Root\ Article$$
$$\{Rel\ describedBy\ \{Entity\ Files\}\}$$
$$\{Rel\ Uses\ \{Entity\ Data\}\}$$

For example, the bottom of Table 1 shows the encoding of the view corresponding to the document model navigation and selection at the bottom of Figure 6, in turn corresponding to *view 1* defined in Figure 3.

4.3   Interpretation of Views and Construction of Export Packages

OAIzer uses views as specifications of the export package structure. In particular, given a view and the internal representation of the graph document model, the tool generates the SQL queries and the transformation code necessary to construct the view export packages from the current database (see Fig.5). OAIzer has been designed to offer two ways to construct export packages: *materialization* and *on-demand*. According to the former modality, not yet available in the current implementation, all export packages relative to the view are generated and prepared for export in advance. Developers can manually generate further snapshots of their views to synchronize them with database updates. According to the latter, export packages are generated on-the-fly from the database to serve given OAI protocol calls. The trade-off between the two approaches is between response time and synchronisation with database content and it is up to the developers to make the right choice, based on the database size, the complexity of the views, and the available hardware resources.

Table 2. Generating "view-path SQL queries"

$$P ::= E(A).R.P \mid \text{View-paths language} \quad genSQL(P) = \text{SELECT } \mathcal{S}(P)$$
$$E(A) \qquad\qquad\qquad\qquad\qquad\qquad \text{FROM } \mathcal{F}(P)$$

$$\mathcal{S}(P) = \begin{cases} E(A), \ \mathcal{S}(\bar{P}) & \text{if } P = E(A).R.\bar{P} \\ E(A) & \text{if } P = E(A) \end{cases}$$

$$\mathcal{F}(P) = \begin{cases} \text{E LEFT OUTER JOIN (F(P))} & \text{if } (impl(E,R,\bar{E}) = N:1 \\ \quad \text{ON E.R} = \text{PKey}(\bar{E}) & \quad And\ (P = \bar{E}(\bar{A}).\bar{R}.\bar{P}) \\ \text{E LEFT OUTER JOIN (F(P))} & \text{if } (impl(E,R,\bar{E}) = 1:N \\ \quad \text{ON } \bar{E}.\text{R} = \text{PKey(E)} & \quad And\ (P = \bar{E}(\bar{A}).\bar{R}.\bar{P}) \\ \text{E LEFT OUTER JOIN} & \text{if } (impl(E,R,\bar{E}) = N:M \\ \quad \text{(R LEFT OUTER JOIN (F(P))} & \quad And\ (P = \bar{E}(\bar{A}).\bar{R}.\bar{P}) \\ \quad\quad \text{ON FKey}_{\bar{E}}(\text{R}) = \text{PKey}(\bar{E})\ ) & \\ \quad\quad \text{ON FKey}_{E}(\text{R}) = \text{PKey(E)} & \\ \bar{E} & \text{if } P = \bar{E}(\bar{A}) \end{cases}$$

The OAIzer *View Interpreter* module takes as input a view definition and a graph document model representation. For each path P in the view (from the root entity to a leaf entity), the module generates the "view-path SQL query" necessary to identify the relative labelled-tree paths for all export packages. The query is generated with the algorithm in Table 2, where P is the language of paths in a view and $genSQL$ is the function that, with the supplementary functions $\mathcal{S}$ and $\mathcal{F}$, generates the SQL query relative to a given path P. The function $\mathcal{F}$ generates the FROM clause exploiting the graph document model function *impl* and the functions $PKey(E)$ and $FKey_{\bar{E}}(E)$, which respectively return the primary key of a table E and the foreign key towards a table $\bar{E}$ in the table E.

The OAIzer *Export Package Generator* module takes in input a view and the relative "view-path SQL queries". It can be configured to construct export packages via materialization or on-demand:

Materialization. In materialization mode all export packages are created in memory as *labelled-tree data structures*. In such data structures, nodes and edges correspond to records with properties A from tables/entities $E(A)$ and relationships R in the view, respectively. This is done by executing the SQL query returning all records r in the root table E, projecting the properties A, and generating the labelled-tree with root node r. All nodes also include by default the primary key of the records; such values will be used to identify the export package (i.e. the root primary key) and to identify its subparts (i.e. node primary keys). Secondly, the module executes the "view-path SQL queries", keeps the relative tables of results in memory, and processes their records to complete the export package labeled-trees with all their paths. This action is quite straightforward, since each record r from the SQL query $genSQL(E_1(A_1).R_1 \ldots R_{n-1}.E_n(A_n))$ has a structure $r(A_1), \ldots, r(A_n)$ and can be directly mapped onto a corresponding path $r_1(A_1).R_1. \ldots .R_{n-1}.r_n(A_n)$ of the labelled-tree whose root is $r(A_1)$. Paths are added to the trees in such a way that only the new sub-part of the paths are added to the trees. Materializing all export packages of a view by SQL navigation of database tables is a potentially expensive operation in terms of query execution time and memory space. The solution optimises execution time by dynamically generating the minimal set of required SQL queries. To limit the occupation of memory space it is possible to opt for the "on-demand mode".

On-demand. The OAIzer *Export Package Generator* module executes the same actions required for the materialization approach, but executes only the "view-path SQL queries" required to create the requested export package.

4.4   OAI Protocols and Serialisation of Export Packages

Once export packages have been generated as labelled-trees in memory, the next step is serializing them onto an exchange format to serve the given OAI protocol requests. This action is performed by the OAIzer module *Export Package Serializer*, whose behaviour differs for OAI-PMH and OAI-ORE.

The OAI-PMH Export Package Serializer has been designed and it is currently under implementation. OAIzer deploys an OAI-PMH HTTP access point at the address: `http://<host>/<view_name>/oai?`. To serve protocol requests, the Export Package Serializer generates for each export package a proprietary XML record whose format (the OAIzer XML schema) respects the OAI-PMH record structure: the *header* section contains an OAI-item identifier which corresponds to the primary key value for the record in the root of the labelled-tree and a time stamp which corresponds to the data of creation of the export package; the *metadata* section encodes the tree nodes, i.e. entity type and set of attribute-value pairs, and tree edges, i.e. relationships. The records are returned when the OAI metadata format prefix `oaizer` is specified in the verbs `ListRecords`, `GetRecord`, and `ListIdentifiers`. Optionally, developers can add export metadata formats for the same view, by providing a unique metadata prefix name (e.g. `oai_dc` for full compatibility with the protocol) and uploading an XSLT mapping from the `oaizer` metadata format to the given metadata format (e.g. Dublin Core). The first release of the OAI-PMH Export Package Serializer will not support OAI sets, but the feature is planned for further releases.

The goal of the OAI-ORE access point is to provide access to web resources. In our context web resources are the metadata records managed by the DLS. OAIzer deploys an HTTP access point at the address: `http://<host>/<view_name>/ore`. The OAI-ORE Export Package Serializer generates for each export package one ORE aggregation encoded as an RDF/XML Resource Map. The Map is returned in response to the call `http://<host>/<view_name>/ore/aggregation/<record_identifier>` and internally encodes the export package labelled-tree, where the nodes are the ORE aggregated resources and relationships are encoded via ORE proxies. The aggregated resources are instead identified by addresses of the form `http://<host>/<view_name>/ore/resource/<record_identifier>` and are encoded as XML files describing the individual records and matching the OAIzer format.

4.5   Demo and Evaluation of OAIzer

A demo of OAIzer is available at: `http://demo.oaizer.research-infrastru -ctures.eu`. The instance has been configured to work over a Postgres database implementing the entity-relationship diagram in figure 1. The database contains 100,000 entries of class File, 50,000 entries of class Article, 25,000 entries of class Data and 150.000 relationships. The tool has been evaluated over the database by implementing the view *view1* in figure 3 to export packages via OAI-ORE, on-demand mode. Results are calculated as averages of 100 requests of different view instances: (*i*) average time for the creation of one *labelled-tree data structure* in memory: 107 ms; (*ii*) average memory space occupied by one *labelled-tree data structure*: 15 KB; (*iii*) average disk space occupied by one serialized *labelled-tree data structure*: 1.1 KB; (*iii*) average response time for one OAI-ORE request: 1,183 ms.

For the materialization mode, we expect the memory indicator will increase linearly with the number of export packages to generate. The response time indicator is instead expected to have lower values because in this case the response time does not include the time for the on-the-fly generation of export packages.

5   Conclusion

We presented the architecture of OAIzer, a tool for the customization of OAI-PMH and OAI-ORE exports over existing relational databases. OAIzer finds its best application in scenarios where existing DLSs, supporting information spaces of graphs of objects, are suddenly demanded to provide OAI interfaces to export views of their content, namely export packages. The tool connects to a JDBC-compatible relational database and exploits its Relation Catalogue to construct the graph document model. The tool then enables developers to define the views, i.e. the structure of export packages, and to select the OAI protocol of interest. Developers can further customize the tool to transform export packages into their preferred metadata formats.

A first implementation of OAIzer has been realised to deliver some of the designed functionalities, namely: (*i*) graphical UI for the visualization of the graph document model, (*ii*) a graphical UI for the definition of the view, (*iii*) creation of export packages with the on-demand modality, (*iv*) serialization of export packages via OAI-ORE. An extension of the current system is currently on going to realise also the missing features, namely the materialization mode and serialization for OAI-PMH.

Acknowledgements. This work is co-funded by the European Commission with the projects OpenAIRE (FP7-INFRA-2009-1, Grant Agreement no. 246686) and OpenAIREplus (FP7-INFRA-2011-2, Grant Agreement no. 283595).

References

1. Candela, L., Castelli, D., Pagano, P., Thanos, C., Ioannidis, Y.E., Koutrika, G., Ross, S., Schek, H.J., Schuldt, H.: Setting the foundations of digital libraries: The delos manifesto. D-Lib Magazine 13(3/4) (2007)
2. Woutersen-Windhouwer, S., Brandsma, R., Hogenaar, A.: Enhanced Publications: Linking Publications and Research Data in Digital Repositories. Amsterdam University Press (2009)
3. Johansson, Å., Ottosson, M.O.: A national current research information system for sweden. In: e-Infrastructures for Research and Innovation: Linking Information Systems to Improve Scientific Knowledge Production. Agentura Action M (2012)
4. Manghi, P., Bolikowski, L., Manola, N., Shirrwagen, J., Smith, T.: Openaireplus: the european scholarly communication data infrastructure. D-Lib Magazine 18(9-10) (September/October 2012)
5. Isaac, A., Clayphan, R., Haslhofer, B.: Europeana: Moving to linked open data. Information Standards Quarterly 24(2-3) (September 2012)
6. Bardi, A., Manghi, P., Zoppi, F.: Aggregative data infrastructures for the cultural heritage. In: Dodero, J.M., Palomo-Duarte, M., Karampiperis, P. (eds.) MTSR 2012. CCIS, vol. 343, pp. 239–251. Springer, Heidelberg (2012)
7. Artini, M., et al.: Data interoperability and curation: The european film gateway experience. In: Agosti, M., Esposito, F., Ferilli, S., Ferro, N. (eds.) IRCDL 2012. CCIS, vol. 354, pp. 33–44. Springer, Heidelberg (2013)
8. Lagoze, C., Van de Sompel, H.: The OAI Protocol for Metadata Harvesting, http://www.openarchives.org/OAI/openarchivesprotocol.html
9. Lagoze, C., Van de Sompel, H.: The OAI Protocol for Object Reuse and Exchange, http://www.openarchives.org/ore/

10. Lagoze, C., Van de Sompel, H.: The open archives initiative: building a low-barrier interoperability framework. In: Proceedings of the First ACM/IEEE-CS Joint Conference on Digital Libraries, pp. 54–62. ACM Press (2001)
11. Dublin Core Metadata Initiative: Dublin Core Metadata element set, version 1.1: Reference description, http://dublincore.org/documents/dces/
12. Manghi, P., Mikulicic, M., Candela, L., Castelli, D., Pagano, P.: Realizing and Maintaining Aggregative Digital Library Systems: D-NET Software Toolkit and OAIster System. D-Lib Magazine 16(3/4) (March/April 2010)
13. Hainaut, J.L., Tonneau, C., Joris, M., Chandelon, M.: Transformation-based database reverse engineering. In: Elmasri, R.A., Kouramajian, V., Thalheim, B. (eds.) ER 1993. LNCS, vol. 823, pp. 364–375. Springer, Heidelberg (1994)
14. Cleve, A., Noughi, N., Hainaut, J.-L.: Dynamic program analysis for database reverse engineering. In: Lämmel, R., Saraiva, J., Visser, J. (eds.) GTTSE 2011. LNCS, vol. 7680, pp. 297–321. Springer, Heidelberg (2013)

CMSs, Linked Data and Semantics: A Linked Data Mashup over Drupal for Personalized Search

Aikaterini K. Kalou, Dimitrios A. Koutsomitropoulos, and Georgia D. Solomou

High Performance Information Systems Laboratory (HPCLab),
Computer Engineering and Informatics Dpt., School of Engineering,
University of Patras, Building B, 26500 Patras-Rio, Greece
{kaloukat,kotsomit,solomou}@hpclab.ceid.upatras.gr

Abstract. Semantic mashups are a representative paradigm of Web applications which highlight the novelties and added-value of Semantic Web technologies, especially Linked Data. However, Semantic Web applications are often lacking desirable features related to their 'Web' part. On the other hand, in the world of traditional web-CMSs, issues like front-end intuitiveness, dynamic content rendering and streamlined user management have been already dealt with, elaborated and resolved. Instead of reinventing the wheel, in this paper we propose an example of how these features can be successfully integrated within a semantic mashup. In particular, we re-engineer our own semantic book mashup by taking advantage of the Drupal infrastructure. This mashup enriches data from various Web APIs with semantics in order to produce personalized book recommendations and to integrate them into the Linked Open Data (LOD) cloud. It is shown that this approach not only leaves reasoning expressiveness and effective ontology management uncompromised, but comes to their benefit.

1 Introduction

Traditional mashups [7] are Web applications that aggregate data or functionality from various online third-party sources, especially Web APIs. With the prevalence of the Semantic Web, mashups are 'transformed' to semantic mashups which consume data from interlinked data sources on the cloud. Nevertheless, a semantic mashup can be considered as any mashup that employs semantic web technologies and ideas in any part of its design, architecture, functionality or presentation levels.

The Linked Open Data (LOD) project [10] has successfully brought a great amount of data to the Web. The availability of interlinked data sets encourages developers to reuse content on the Web and alleviates them from the need to discover various data sources. In the case of semantic mashups, contribution to the LOD effort can come by appropriately combining data from Web APIs with semantics and then providing them as Linked Data.

As is often the case with any Semantic Web application, semantic mashup development usually puts too much effort in the bottoms-up construction of elaborate, knowledge intensive set-ups. This kind of applications often dwells on high-end reasoning services, efficient rule processing and scalability over voluminous data, thus hardly leaving any room for traditional Web development.

E. Garoufallou and J. Greenberg (Eds.): MTSR 2013, CCIS 390, pp. 48–59, 2013.
© Springer International Publishing Switzerland 2013

This gap can be bridged by traditional web content management systems (CMSs) which offer an up-to-date and tailored web infrastructure and leave more room for the designer to concentrate on successful content production and delivery, rather than technical details. As they form the spearhead of Web 2.0, it might then feel natural to employ them as a basis for Semantic Web applications, but this presents a series of challenges that it is not always straightforward to overcome.

In this paper, we therefore propose how such applications and CMSs can be integrated, by presenting Books@HPClab, a semantic mashup application, which we purposely establish on top of the Drupal CMS. Books@HPClab [6, 13] has been initially developed from scratch and offers personalization features to users searching for books from various data sources. The key concept of this mashup is that it gathers information from Amazon and Half eBay Web APIs, enriches them with semantics according to an ontology (*BookShop* ontology) and then employs OWL 2 reasoning to infer matching preferences. The triplified book metadata are also linked to other resources, thus becoming more reusable and effectively more sharable on the LOD cloud.

The following text is organized as follows: in Section 2, we start by discussing the desirable properties of CMSs that make them suitable as a basis for developing Semantic Web applications. In Section 3, we describe in detail the BookShop ontology. Furthermore, in Section 4, we explain how we proceeded with the actual integration and discuss how we addressed the problems arising in this process, putting particular focus on the data workflow, reasoner integration and provision of Linked Data. Next, in Section 5, we briefly illustrate the features and the functionality of our application, now completely re-engineered over Drupal, by outlining an indicative application scenario. Finally, Section 6 summarizes our conclusions and future work.

2   CMS as a Semantic Web Infrastructure

A typical CMS generally comes with the ability to help and facilitate the user, even the non-technical one, in various ways. It always ensures a set of core features [12] such as:

— *Front-end Interface*: The developer community of all available CMSs invests significantly in the layout, appearance and structure of the content that is created and delivered by a CMS. Therefore, content remains completely separate from appearance. To this end, users of CMSs can select from a great variety of well-designed templates.
— *User management*: CMSs offer also considerable advantages in regard to user administration and access issues. It can be easily controlled whether users are allowed to register on a web application as well as what kind of privileges they can have, by providing access layers and defining sections of the web application as public or private. Moreover, CMSs allow for assigning roles to users so as to involve them in the workflow of web content production.
— *Dynamic content management*: Usually a CMS relies on an RDBMS to efficiently store and manage data and settings, which are then used to display page content.

So, the installation of a CMS always involves setting-up a database schema in the corresponding SQL server. The database schema actually used, varies depending on the CMS.

— *Modular design*: CMSs follow architecture styles such as *Model-View-Controller* (MVC) or *Presentation-Abstraction-Control* (PAC) that permit the organization of code in such a way that business logic and data presentation remain separate. This enables the integration of small, standalone applications, called *modules*, which accomplish a wide variety of tasks. These artifacts can be easily and simply installed/uninstalled and enabled/disabled in the core of CMSs. Modularity is one of the most powerful features and the one that saves the most development effort.

— *Caching*: It is also important that most CMSs offer cache capabilities to users/developers. Thus, CMS-based web applications can have fast response times by caching frequently requested content and reducing their overhead.

Features such as these, that contemporary CMSs unsparingly offer, are exactly the ones sometimes neglected by Semantic Web applications. In the case of our work, we chose to integrate Books@HPClab within the core of Drupal CMS [14]. Regardless of Drupal's semantic character, other significant advantages such as flexibility and scalability make it stand out from the large pool of CMSs. Besides, Drupal has been used before as a basis for offering Linked Data services [4]. Finally, Drupal can be viewed not only as a CMS, but also as a content management *framework*, by accommodating development of any type of web application.

3   Ontology Design

Taking into account the kind of metadata offered by Amazon and Half eBay responses, we designed the core ontology BookShop shown partially in Figure 1. BookShop contains five main classes *Book*, *Author*, *Offer*, *User* and *Modality*.

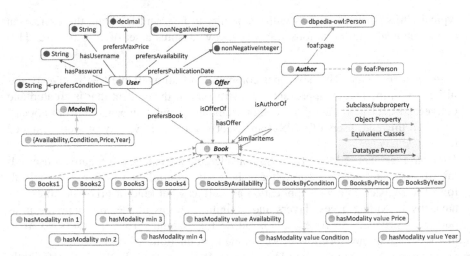

Fig. 1. BookShop Ontology

In our ontology, the class *User* is meant to express user profiles. We capture the preferences of each user in this class, such as preferable condition, preferable minimum availability, preferable minimum publication year and preferable maximum price (preference criteria). All this data about users are represented as datatype properties.

The class *Book* represents all book items that are gathered from Amazon and Half eBay sales markets. A reasoner is responsible for entailing which books match what criteria in the current user profile and classifies them accordingly (*BooksByAvailability*, *BooksBycondition*, *BooksByPrice*, *BooksByYear*). The kind of a matched criterion is represented by the members of the *Modality* class. Given the cardinality restrictions on the *hasModality* property, the books are finally classified depending on the number of satisfied preference criteria (*Books...Books4*). For example, the *Books1* class contains all the books that match at least one of the preference criteria.

4   System Design and Integration

In this section, we present the overall design of our application and its interaction with all necessary external and embedded components. We also describe thoroughly the main issues we had to put up with and how we addressed each one of them.

4.1   Architecture and Integration Challenges

The modular philosophy of a CMS allows us to extend its capabilities with ready-made modules and to reuse them for our purposes. To this end, we utilize the *AmazonStore module*[1] that offers an attractive wrapper and front-end for the Amazon Web API. We have extended this module so as to include support for eBay as well. We also make use of the *WebForm module*[2], which supports form-based data collection and is used as the initiating point for constructing user profiles. The architecture of our re-engineered mashup is illustrated in Figure 2.

In order to re-engineer our semantic mashup on top of Drupal so as to leverage all CMSs' core features mentioned in Section 2, we encountered a series of challenges, originating from the fact that CMSs are usually not semantics-aware. Although latest versions of Drupal offer some inherent semantic features [3], in our implementation we needed to put a strong focus on reasoning, ontology management as well as data interlinking, which is beyond Drupal's state-of-the-art (or any other CMS's for that matter). All these issues are analysed in the following subsections and summarized below:

— *User profile construction and maintenance*: Managing users as well as their profiles are common issues that have already been addressed within a web CMS. In the context of our application, the issue is how we can map and maintain the relational user profiles in terms of OWL 2 expressions (see section 4.2).

---

[1] http://drupal.org/project/amazon_store
[2] http://drupal.org/project/webform

— *Synchronizing relational and ontology back-ends*: Semantic Web applications deal
with content that needs to be semantically expressed. The manipulation of semantic
data should be consistent with web content management and delivery policies
which are based on robust relational back-ends in the context of a web-CMS (see
Section 4.2).
— *Reasoner integration*: Once embedded within a CMS, a Semantic Web application
must pay special attention to the efficient and interoperable communication with a
reasoning service (see Section 4.3).
— *Data linking*: A semantic mashup, which aggregates a significant amount of ontological data, can be a worthy contribution to the LOD cloud, even though it is
implemented within a CMS framework (see Section 4.4).

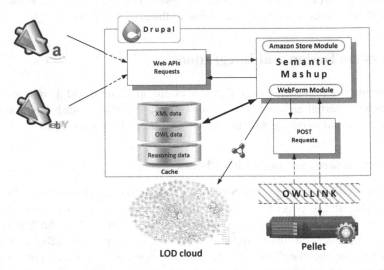

Fig. 2. Architecture and communication flow for integrating Semantic Mashup with Drupal

4.2   Data Collection and Storage

In the context of our application, with the term *data*, we mean the conjunction of user
profiles, externally collected information and ontological data before and after the
reasoning process. In this sub-section, we review in detail the data collection and
storage workflow, and all the existing Drupal modules that we have exploited to this
end.

Regarding user profile construction, user preferences are collected using web
forms, designed with the aid of the WebForm module. A unique ID is assigned to
each user. In addition to user preferences, each user has to set his unique password
and username, as well as his e-mail address so as to get notifications from the application. All this user-related information is stored in tables of the relational database.

In order to perform reasoning however, these preferences have to be translated into
semantically rich expressions, which form the ontological profile of each user.

In our case, we retrieve user preferences from the database and then we construct the profile on-the-fly, by mapping preferences to a set of OWL 2 expressions.

In order to collect book data from Amazon and Half eBay, we have extended the existing functionality of AmazonStore module by adding communication ability with the Half eBay Web API. Whenever a user types a keyword and sends a *searching call*, the searching process starts to query data from Amazon Web Services (AWS), and especially from the *US E-Commerce Service (ECS)* via functions available by the AmazonStore module. In general, a request to Amazon may have many thousands of results. Returning all these items at once may be inefficient and impractical. To this end, it is defined that Amazon operations return paginated results, 10 results per page.

Once our application completes the search process at Amazon, it starts searching Half eBay: for each book returned by Amazon, we find additional offers that may be available at Half eBay. We use the *eBay shopping Web Services* and particularly, the *FindHalfProducts* operation. The interaction with the eBay shopping API is based on the REST-protocol and the exchange of URL requests and XML files-responses. By augmenting the data storage policy of AmazonStore module, we save the Amazon XML results, enriched with additional book-offers from Half eBay, in the *XML data cache* (see Figure 2).

Next, search results need to be transformed into the OWL word in order to enable inferences. This conversion adheres to our BookShop ontology schema and is achieved via XSLT. The transformed ontological data are cached in the *OWL data cache*. In order to achieve personalization, OWL data as well as the ontological user profile are sent to the remote reasoning service. Finally, the inferred knowledge is stored at the *reasoning cache*.

An algorithm (shown in Table 1) is responsible for synchronizing between the caches, which, apart from checking for repeating queries, additionally expunges reasoning cache whenever a user updates his profile. Note that the cache can be flushed after a configurable amount of time (in this case, 24 hours). A profile update initiated by a user causes the removal from cache of all reasoning results related to the particular profile u, i.e. $\mathcal{R} \rightarrow \mathcal{R} / \{r_{*,u}\}$, where * denotes all o_q.

Table 1. Algorithm for the synchronization of data storage

$\mathcal{B}$: XML book data cache, b_q: XML book data for query q $\mathcal{O}$: Ontological book data cache, o_q: ontological book data for query q $\mathcal{R}$: Reasoner results cache, $r_{o_q,u}$: reasoner results for o_q and user profile u	
if $\{b_q\} \not\subseteq \mathcal{B}$ **then** $b_q \rightarrow$ **get_amazon_data** (q) $b_q \rightarrow$ **get_ebay_data** (q) $\mathcal{B} \rightarrow \mathcal{B} \cup \{b_q\}$ $o_q \rightarrow$ **triplify** (b_q) $\mathcal{O} \rightarrow \mathcal{O} \cup \{o_q\}$ $r_{o_q,u} \rightarrow$ **invoke_reasoner** (o_q, u) $\mathcal{R} \rightarrow \mathcal{R} \cup \{r_{o_q,u}\}$ **return** $r_{o_q,u}$	**if** $\{b_q\} \subseteq \mathcal{B}$, $\{o_q\} \subseteq \mathcal{O}$ and $r_{o_q,u} \not\subseteq \mathcal{R}$ //since b_q is in $\mathcal{B}$, o_q will always be in $\mathcal{O}$ **then** $r_{o_q,u} \rightarrow$ **invoke_reasoner** (o_q, u) $\mathcal{R} \rightarrow \mathcal{R} \cup \{r_{o_q,u}\}$ **return** $r_{o_q,u}$ **if** $\{b_q\} \subseteq \mathcal{B}$, $\{o_q\} \subseteq \mathcal{O}$ and $r_{o_q,u} \subseteq \mathcal{R}$ **then return** $r_{o_q,u}$

The adoption of the database caching and data replication strategy allows CMS modules to remain oblivious to the ontology data and lets them to operate on their own data cache. This caching idea, which is also carried over to reasoning results, actually improves the effective reasoning throughput by keeping reasoner engagement to a minimum.

4.3   Reasoner Integration

Most OWL 2 reasoners (like, Pellet, FaCT++ and HermiT) are traditionally deployed directly in-memory and interaction is performed by means of a java-based API. Although a PHP-to-Java bridge[3] is available, there are many reasons why one may want to keep reasoning services logically and/or physically separated [8]. Among them, the need for interoperability and independence from the actual programming language are of particular importance for integration with a CMS.

In our implementation, we use OWLlink [9] as the reasoner communication protocol of choice and its implementation, the OWLlink API [11] that helps us deploy a true 3-tier architecture. OWLlink offers a consistent way of transmitting data to and receiving responses from the most popular Semantic Web reasoners, in a REST-like manner and over HTTP. Potential communication overhead that may be introduced with this approach can be alleviated by freeing up resources as a consequence of delegating computationally hard reasoning tasks to another tier [8]. Moreover, Drupal offers us generic function implementations that can be used to wrap and construct HTTP requests, like `drupal_http_request`. Messages are encoded in XML format and Pellet is used as the inference engine of choice.

The interaction between the OWLlink server and our client-application consists of four main request-response messages. Firstly, we allocate a Knowledge Base (KB) within the OWLlink server by sending a `CreateKB` request. The unique user id is assigned as an identifier to the KB, in order to logically separate knowledge bases under the same reasoner. In the same message, we embed a `LoadOntologies` request so as to load the BookShop ontology schema into the given KB by reading the ontology file.

Next, we add the ontological user profile and the OWL data results for a specific query by sending two distinct `Tell` requests to the OWLlink server. At this point user preferences are fetched from the DB and are used to construct the ontological user profile on the fly, which amounts to a set of OWL 2 restrictions (see Table 2). Both user profile and OWL data are encoded in OWL/XML syntax. In order to get the inferred knowledge from the reasoner, we send a `GetFlattenedInstances` request. Its purpose is to retrieve all books that satisfy up to four preference criteria (instances of *Books1*, *Books2*, *Books3* and *Books4* classes). The `direct=true` parameter ensures that the above sets will be mutually disjoint, i.e. they will include only unique book instances. Finally the KB is destroyed by issuing a `ReleaseKB` request within the same message.

---

[3] `http://php-java-bridge.sourceforge.net/pjb/`

Table 2. Interaction with OWLlink server

	No. 1	No. 2	No. 3	No. 4
Request	CreateKB kb=[*User_ID*] LoadOntologies IRI=[*BookShop ontology*] ·	Tell *preferences* BooksByPrice ≡ ∃hasOffer.(∃offerP rice.[≤*user_pref*]) BooksByCondi-tion... BooksByAvailabili-ty... BooksByYear...	Tell data OWL Book data from cache (query results)	GetFlat-tenedInstances direct="true" class IRI={*Books1, Books2, Books3, Books4*} ReleaseKB kb=[*User_ID*]
Response	ResponseMessage OK	ResponseMessage OK	ResponseMessage OK	SetofIndividu-als {*1..4*} NamedIndividu-als IRI=[*Book re-source URL*]

Table 2 summarizes all the messages that are exchanged between our application and the OWLlink server.

4.4 Linked Data Service

Usually, LOD can be considered as a significant data source and a Semantic Web tool can consume them in order to construct a mashup application. The reverse is also desirable and in the case of Books@HPCLab, we interlink aggregated data with other available web resources, thus contributing to the LOD cloud.

In order to publish Linked Data, we follow the Linked Data principles, as they are explicitly described in [5]. In order to identify real-world entities, either people or abstract concepts, we assign HTTP URIs to them. To encompass the book items, we mint HTTP URIs using the following pattern that is based on the application's name-space: First, each book item is uniquely identified by a single URI, describing the item itself. Then, we assign to each book another URI that describes the item and has an HTML representation, appropriate for consumption by humans. Next, another URI is given to the book item in order to describe it and provides an RDF/XML represen-tation for machine readbility.

Following this URI pattern, for the case where a book item has ASIN number 0890425558, we end up with the three next URIs:

— http://levantes.hpclab.ceid.upatras.gr:8000/bookmashup/resour ce/0890425558
— http://levantes.hpclab.ceid.upatras.gr:8000/bookmashup/item/0 890425558 (HTML)
— http://levantes.hpclab.ceid.upatras.gr:8000/bookmashup/data/0 890425558 (RDF)

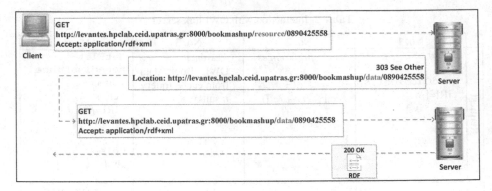

Fig. 3. A complete example of content negotiation

Moreover, these HTTP URIs are dereferenceable by using HTTP content negotiation (HTTP *303 See Other* redirects, see Fig. 3).

To associate our data with other data sets on the Web, we interlink our entities with others by adding RDF external links. More precisely, in the case of book offers, relationship links are added so as to point to the bookstore origin. We also inject DBpedia HTTP URIs into author RDF descriptions originally available from the Web APIs. The following figure (Fig. 4) depicts an excerpt of published RDF data with the external RDF links.

Fig. 4. Interlinking data set of Books@HPClab with external data sets

5   A Usage Scenario

When a user visits our app for the first time, he has to register by filling a form with his username and e-mail. An administrator then enables the account and a password is sent to the user at the specified mail address.

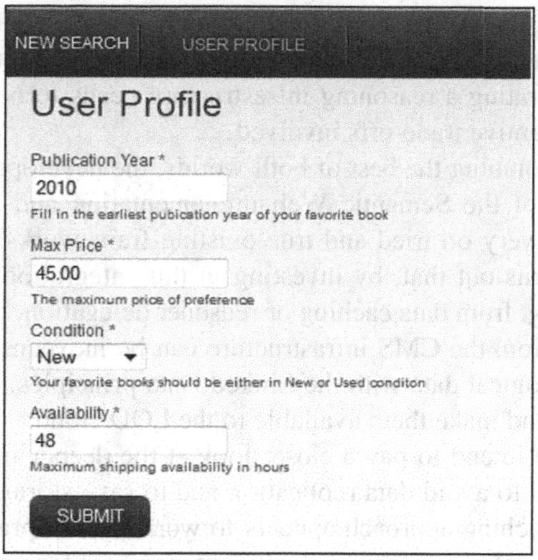

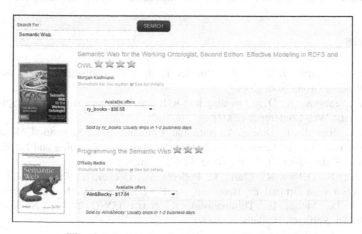

Fig. 5. Collecting user preferences

After successful authorization, logged users can set their profile using the WebForm module. The form fields correspond to user preferences and include: book condition ("new" or "used"), maximum book price, earliest publication year and maximum availability (Fig. 5). A user can update his profile at any time. Note also that if a user does not define preferences, the application behaves as a standard book mashup and the reasoner is never engaged.

Fig. 6. Result list and preference ranking (stars)

6   Conclusions and Future Work

Integration of Semantic Web applications with a CMS is not always straightforward. In order to achieve a seamless alignment, a series of issues has first to be resolved, and in this paper we have indicated exactly how this can be achieved in the case of our semantic mashup. Primarily, the semantic-oblivious nature of most CMSs calls for the explicit manipulation of semantically enriched data, which can be far from trivial, especially when their robust relational back-end is to be taken advantage of. Additionally, incorporating a reasoning infrastructure needs to be carefully designed as there may be substantive trade-offs involved.

Nevertheless, by combing the best of both worlds, the developer can genuinely focus on the internals of the Semantic Web implementation and assign web content management and delivery on tried and true existing frameworks, instead of wasting time and effort. It turns out that, by investing in this integration, even the semantic aspects can benefit e.g. from data caching or reasoner delegation, thus making a virtue of necessity. In addition, the CMS infrastructure can be inexpensively utilized in order to align our ontological data with the Linked Data principles, associate them with additional resources and make them available to the LOD cloud.

As a next step, we intend to pay a closer look at the deeper integration with relational data in a means to avoid data replication and to save storage space in the database. Although our caching approach appears to work well in practice, it is not clear whether the separate cache maintenance really compensates for on-the-fly transformations or how does it compare with virtualized graph access as in D2RQ [2]. The RESTful style of reasoner communication also allows for investigating potential alternatives with a view on scalability, like rule-based triple stores [13]. To this end, an assessment of our system's performance and efficiency is in order. We also intend to wrap additional RESTful web service functionality around our semantic mashup as a means for other applications to consume and exchange Linked Data without manual intervention. Finally, we plan to package our prototype as a totally independent CMS module, thus allowing its smooth installation and reuse by other developers.

References

1. Berrueta, D., Phipps, J. (eds.): Best Practice Recipes for Publishing RDF Vocabularies. W3C Working Group Note (2008)
2. Bizer, C., Seaborne, A.: D2RQ-treating non-RDF databases as virtual RDF graphs. In: 3rd Int. Semantic Web Conference (2004)
3. Bratsas, C., Bamidis, P., Dimou, A., Antoniou, I., Ioannidis, L.: Semantic CMS and Wikis as Platforms for Linked Learning. In: 2nd Int. Workshop on Learning and Education with the Web of Data – 24th Int. World Wide Web Conference (2012)
4. Corlosquet, S., Delbru, R., Clark, T., Polleres, A., Decker, S.: Produce and Consume Linked Data with Drupal! In: Bernstein, A., Karger, D.R., Heath, T., Feigenbaum, L., Maynard, D., Motta, E., Thirunarayan, K. (eds.) ISWC 2009. LNCS, vol. 5823, pp. 763–778. Springer, Heidelberg (2009)

5. Heath, T., Bizer, B.: Linked Data: Evolving the Web into a Global Data Space, 1st edn. Synthesis Lectures on the Semantic Web: Theory and Technology, vol. 1, pp. 1–136. Morgan & Claypool (2011)
6. Kalou, K., Pomonis, T., Koutsomitropoulos, D., Papatheodorou, T.S.: Intelligent Book Mashup: Using Semantic Web Ontologies and Rules for User Personalisation. In: 4th IEEE Int. Conference on Semantic Computing - Int. Workshop on Semantic Web and Reasoning for Cultural Heritage and Digital Libraries, pp. 536–541. IEEE (2010)
7. Koschmider, A., Torres, V., Pelechano, V.: Elucidating the Mashup Hype: Definition, Challenges, Methodical Guide and Tools for Mashups. In: 2nd Workshop on Mashups, Enterprise Mashups and Lightweight Composition on the Web (2009)
8. Koutsomitropoulos, D., Solomou, G., Pomonis, T., Aggelopoulos, P., Papatheodorou, T.S.: Developing Distributed Reasoning-based Applications for the Semantic Web. In: 24th IEEE Int. Conference on Advanced Information and Networking - Int. Symposium on Mining and Web, pp. 593–598. IEEE (2010)
9. Liebig, T., Luther, M., Noppens, O., Wessel, M.: OWLlink. Semantic Web Journal 2, 23–32 (2011)
10. Linked Open Data Project, http://linkeddata.org/
11. Noppens, O., Luther, M., Liebig, T.: The OWLlink API-Teaching OWL Components a Common Protocol. In: 7th Workshop on OWL: Experiences and Directions. CEUR Workshop Proceedings, vol. 614 (2010)
12. Patel, S.K., Rathod, V.R., Prajapati, J.B.: Performance Analysis of Content Management Systems-Joomla, Drupal and WordPress. International Journal of Computer Applications 21, 39–43 (2011)
13. Solomou, G., Kalou, K., Koutsomitropoulos, D., Papatheodorou, T.S.: A Mashup Personalization Service based on Semantic Web Rules and Linked Data. In: 7th Int. Conference on Signal Image Technology and Internet Information Systems, pp. 89–96. IEEE (2011)
14. Tomlinson, T.: Beginning Drupal 7. Apress (2010)

Linking Search Results, Bibliographical Ontologies and Linked Open Data Resources

Fabio Ricci, Javier Belmonte, Eliane Blumer, and René Schneider

Haute Ecole de Gestion de Genève, 7 route de Drize, CH-1227 Carouge
{fabio.fr.ricci,javier.belmonte,eliane.blumer,
rene.schneider}@hesge.ch

Abstract. This paper describes a lightweight approach to build an environment for scientific research that connects user-selected information resources with domain specific ontologies and the linked open data cloud. Search results are converted into RDF triples to match with ontology subjects in order to derive relevant subjects and to find related documents in external repositories data that are stored in the Linked Open Data Cloud. With the help of this deterministic algorithm for analyzing and ranking search subjects, the explicit searching process, as effectuated by the user, is implicitly supported by the LOD-technology.

Keywords: Innovative Scientific Search, Metadata Reusability, Linked Open Data Technologies.

1   Introduction

Libraries have always been interested in developing meta data descriptions for the documents they take care of. In recent years, more and more of these taxonomies and the thesauri developed for this purpose are converted into ontologies or ontology-like repositories (i.e. the data is expressed as ontologies are) that can be used to support scientific search in user created search environments [1]. Users can expand or narrow their search results with the help of the ontology terms that are presented in the faceted browsing menu and improve their search. Yet, this search process has to be triggered by the user who generally seems to prefer to use simple and fast search environments that are easy to understand and do not need prior explanations. Alternatively, the search topic, search results and the ontological terms can be combined and connected in a kind of black box. In this context we follow the berrypicking metaphor described by Bates in [2] where searching is not seen as a linear process, but a meandering way finding process. In our system RODIN (=ROue D'INformation, i.e. information wheel), we developed an interface that enables the user to explicitly perform scientific search by picking search terms from ontologies and search results. Due to the complexity of the system, we tried to find a solution that makes parts of the berrypicking process implicit by the help of Linked Open Data Technology, as described in the following paper.

E. Garoufallou and J. Greenberg (Eds.): MTSR 2013, CCIS 390, pp. 60–66, 2013.
© Springer International Publishing Switzerland 2013

2 Context

2.1 Prior Work

RODIN is a personalizable information portal that relies on the Posh Portal (http://sourceforge.net/projects/posh Portaneo) for widget administration. Widgets operations are carried on by our ad-hoc developed object oriented framework, which easily allows the integration of new information sources into widgets. The user selects data sources and runs a distributed search with the results being displayed in each widget and stored in a database in a homogenized format for fast reuse. This framework has been extended by adding the following components: a) ontological facets, i.e. RDF thesauri based on the SKOS (=Simple Knowledge Organization System) [3] model, b) a SOLR (=Searching On Lucene with Index Replication) index machine for fast information processing concerning widget results using the vector space model document metrics, result similarity functions, term distance measures representing the vector space distance between all documents, term matching inside RDF thesauri and ranking methods, c) an interactive graphical visualization of the SKOS part of DBPedia [4] and STW (=Standard Thesaurus Wirtschaftswissenschaften, i.e. the standard thesaurus for economic sciences) graph, d) thesauri based on SKOS enabling navigable auto complete suggestions.

Afterwards and as described in this paper, this architecture was enhanced by an RDF engine that enriches RODIN search results with external LOD documents relying on shared subjects as described in detail in the following part. One reason for this extension lied in a shift of the data layer from a relational database to a triple store, enhancing the compatibility of the results with current further LOD sources. Search results as well as subjects and result-related information are stored as RDF generic resources and made available (querieable) through a further LOD interface called dbRODIN (with db for database). We called this operation "RDFization". The other purpose is in enhancing the number of the attached thesauri and enhancing the power of the filtering functionality while augmenting the usability of the same system.

2.2 Related Work

Compared to other work done in this domain, RODIN tries to find new ways to build bibliographical search engines by subscribing to the view of the web of data, similar to the Europeana approach [5] without necessarily relying on the FRBR (= Functional Requirements for Bibliographical records) concept [6]. RODIN tries to balance the information seeking and management process between the user and the machine as well as between internal and external information resources. This means that only part of the information seeking process is in the hand of the user and some parts are taken over by the retrieval engine. Only a very specific part of the information processed is kept in internal representations or repositories. The balance has to be found between keeping large parts of the search space external and without prior processing such as indexing or harvesting [7] and by adequately building own information repositories that are linkable to other open data available online.

3   Linking Documents, Ontologies and Linked Open Data

3.1   Rodin Architecture

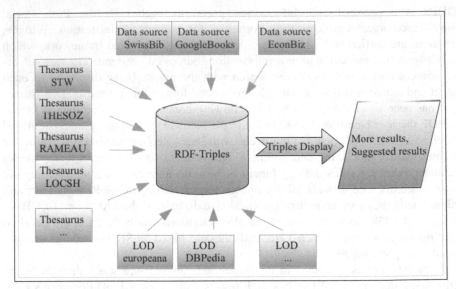

Fig. 1. RODIN general architecture based on widget data, thesauri and LOD sources

As stated before, RODIN (see Fig. 1.) integrates already a number of information sources as widgets (e.g. Google Books, SwissBib, and EconBiz) and several RDF thesauri (e.g. DBPedia, STW, THESOZ (= Thesaurus for the Social Sciences), RAMEAU (=Répertoire d'autorité-matière encyclopédique et alphabétique unifié, i.e. the French standard for subject headings), and LCSH (= Library of Congress Subject Headings)) for the semantic expansion of search related terms.

A significant enhancement of RODIN's result delivery coverage comes from an added RDF processing component, which accesses further related documents from LOD data sources based on shared subjects extracted from widget result documents. This added RDF module transforms widget result information and subjects into an own homogenous RDF store. All further operations, semantic expansion and ranking of subjects, and imported LOD documents are performed on the basis of the information in the RDF store. During result RDFization, widget result documents are processed as follows:

1. Subject expansion: Every subject provided from a specific widget document is expanded with respect to configured RODIN ontological sources (thesauri) as activated by the user, which produces SKOS related subjects in the same language as the search term to be added to the subjects of the widget documents. Every related subject is stored in RODIN's RDF store.

2. Document expansion: Based on every original and related subject, documents in the same language as detected on the search term are retrieved from the LOD data sources and homogenized inside RODIN's RDF store.
3. RDF mirror: Besides the presented RDF process we created in RODIN the RDF mirror of its search data as well as the search results and the expanded data - called dbRODIN – offering a DBPedia like RDF graph navigator and an LOD SPARQL (=Simple Protocol and RDF Query Language) endpoint for public search results access and RDF download [8][9]. In this way RODIN gets its own LOD cloud which can be made accessible for shared use in the linked open data space.

3.2   RDFization and Linking of Documents

Figure 2 illustrates the steps in RODIN's RDFization process. In Step 1 a reference corpus for later subject ranking is built out of the search term and matched against the connected RDF thesauri (Example a). The same action is performed on the subjects of each widget result document: delivered subjects are matched against the RDF thesauri to gather further related subjects (steps 3 and 4, Example b). All subjects in 3 and 4 are ranked in step 5 with respect to their vector space distance to the reference corpus (Example c). Using the ranked subjects of step 5, we search for documents inside the LOD sources (steps 6a, 6b), afterwards we homogenize the triples delivered by the LOD source (since we do not yet have multigraph processing RDF engines) on the given subjects and add them to RODIN's RDF store (Example d). Note that fetching LOD records delivers not only documents but also further related subjects. The latter

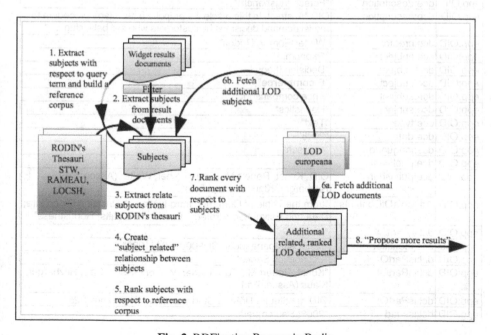

Fig. 2. RDFization Process in Rodin

will be added to RODIN's store as well. The quality or added value of suggested LOD documents relies strongly on how precisely subjects can be extracted from widget results. Missing subjects in widget result meta data force RODIN to "guess" subjects using the result title – this being a source of "noise" inside the illustrated RDFization process.

The final step consists in ranking all the subjects again. All documents (widget documents and LOD documents) are re-ranked with respect to their (ranked) subjects (step 7). The order obtained (top ranked first) is used to display all found documents in RODIN's unified view from the most ranked to the least ranked document. The following series of examples relies on the search term "digital economy" and shall be taken to follow the RDFization process in all his steps.

— Example a: Title is "digital economy and e-commerce technology", derived subjects are: "digital, economy, e-commerce".
— Example b: The reference corpus for "digital economy" built in RODIN is "digital economy, e-health, business intelligence system".
— Examplec: Ranked subject with respect to reference corpus are: "digital, economy, e-commerce, editorial, data protection, open source".
— Example d: Homogenized LOD triplets on subject "e-commerce" are shown in table 1 – (shortened example).

Table 1. Homogenized external LOD triples on subject "e-commerce" (excerpt)

epp:OID	dce:title	"Buying Online: Sequential Decision Making by Shopbot Visitors"
epp:OID	dce:description	"Forschungsbericht"
epp:OID:	dce:description	OID "Abstract: In this article we propose a two stage procedure to model demand decisions by customers who are balancing …"
epp:OID	dce:creator	"Winter-Ebmer, Rudolf"
epp:OID	dce:subject	"Ökonomie"
epp:OID	dce:subject	"Decision theory"
epp:OID	dce:subject	**"E-commerce"**
epp:OID	dce:subject	"Price comparison"
epp:OID	dce:subject	"Heuristics"
epp:OID	dce:type	"Text"
epp:OID	dce:date	"2008"
epp:OID	dce:language	"englisch"
epp:OID	dce:publisher	"Wien"
epp:OID	dce:publisher	OID "Kunst, Robert M. (Ed.) ; Fisher, Walter (Assoc. Ed.) ; Ritzberger, Klaus (Assoc. Ed.)"
epp:OID	dct:tableOfContents	"from the Table of Contents: Introduction; A Decision Procedure; Data and Estimation Strategy; Empirical Results; Robustness"
epp:OID	dct:extent	"24 pp."
epp:OID	dce:identifier	"oai:at.europana-local: SHI/000000471088"
epp:OID	dct:isPartOf	"Economics Series"
epp:OID	dct:isPartOf	"Kunst, Robert M. (Ed.); Fisher, Walter (Assoc. Ed.); Ritzberger, Klaus (Assoc. Ed.)"
epp:OID	dct:isPartOf	OID "Institut für Höhere Studien; Reihe Ökonomie; 225"
epp:OID	dct:issued	"2008, September"

3.3   Creating the LOD Store in dbRODIN

Since triples are used to connote resources, it is important to assign unique identifiers for each created RDF resource generated from search results and their expansions. In dbRODIN resources we find objects concerning works, articles, publishers; it is therefore mandatory to generate for each of these resources unique identifiers as they are imported from an external LOD source as well as from a widget. In dbRODIN, unique identifiers are generated by compressing the resource description (eliminating punctuation) and by limiting the resulting id length. The corresponding dbRODIN RDF store contains only RODIN's graphs. The combination of the "rodin" namespace and the unique id guarantees uniqueness inside dbRODIN graph. Finally, in order to assure compatibility for any further processing of dbRODIN's triples outside the own data store, triples components have to be shaped using adequate common vocabularies. In dbRODIN, we use – besides a few own "rodin" terms – standard vocabularies like DublinCore (http://purl.org/dc/elements/1.1/), dcterms (http://purl.org/dc/terms/), bibo (http://bibliontology.com/bibo/bibo.php), bio (http://vocab.org/bio/0.1/), foaf (http://xmlns.com/foaf/0.1/), rdf (http://www.w3.org/1999/02/22-rdf-syntax-ns#), and rdfs (http://www.w3.org/2000/01/rdf-schema).

3.4   Personal Result Filters

RODIN users can benefit from a final result biasing on their specific scientific interests (e.g. economical experts or medical doctors) they have. Using a simple vector space distance algorithm and two freely definable sets of words – a positive and a negative "resonance" set – defining which terms should have a higher resonance and which ones should be less important, the user gets finally results with a higher resonance first, while less important ones are ranked lower in the result list, according to the preferences and rejections defined before.

4   Conclusions

In this paper we described an approach to extend and re-rank search results by connecting RDFized search results with subjects derived from bibliographical ontologies as well as external documents from the Linked Open Data cloud. This approach integrates smoothly three layers of information: web documents from priory selected information resources, semantically rich information from thesauri that were converted into a semantic web compatible format as well as external data that found no prior consideration in the search process but semantically match to the original search structure. The newly added documents built the basis for opening the scientific perspective and may also be of value for suggesting cooperation in scientifically based social networks.

The system generates its own LOD space for public access and offers the benefit of sharing enriched search results from information specialists in an "LOD-way". Personal search filters re-rank relevant results e.g. with respect to the professional group the user is belonging to. Through its LOD interface, RODIN opens up to the linked open data community by sharing searches and results done by information professionals and scientists.

References

1. Belmonte, J., Blumer, E., Ricci, F., Schneider, R.: RODIN – An E-Science Tool for Managing Information in the Web of Documents and the Web of Knowledge. In: Kurbanoğlu, S., Al, U., Erdoğan, P.L., Tonta, Y., Uçak, N. (eds.) IMCW 2012. CCIS, vol. 317, pp. 4–12. Springer, Heidelberg (2012)
2. Bates, M.J.: The design of browsing and berrypicking techniques for the online search interface. Online Review 13, 407–424 (1989)
3. Miles, A., Brickley, D., Matthews, B., Wilson, M.: SKOS Core Vocabulary Specification. In: International Conference on Dublin Core and Metadata Applications, pp. 3–10 (2005)
4. Auer, S., Bizer, C., Kobilarov, G., Lehmann, J., Cyganiak, R., Ives, Z.G.: DBpedia: A Nucleus for a Web of Open Data. In: Aberer, K., Choi, K.-S., Noy, N., Allemang, D., Lee, K.-I., Nixon, L.J.B., Golbeck, J., Mika, P., Maynard, D., Mizoguchi, R., Schreiber, G., Cudré-Mauroux, P. (eds.) ASWC 2007 and ISWC 2007. LNCS, vol. 4825, pp. 722–735. Springer, Heidelberg (2007)
5. Aloia, N., Concordia, C., Meghini, C.: The Europeana Linked Open Data Pilot Server. In: Agosti, M., Esposito, F., Ferilli, S., Ferro, N. (eds.) IRCDL 2012. CCIS, vol. 354, pp. 241–248. Springer, Heidelberg (2013)
6. Howarth, L.C.: FRBR and Linked Data: Connecting FRBR and Linked Data. Cataloging & Classification Quarterly 50(5-7), 763–776 (2012)
7. Introna, L., Nissenbaum, H.: Defining the Web: the politics of search engines. Computer 33(1), 54–62 (2000)
8. Sheth, A., Krishnaprasad, T.: Semantics-empowered Web 3.0, Managing Enterprise, Social, Sensor, and Cloud based Data and Services for Advanced Applications. Synthesis Lectures on Data Management 4(6), 1–175 (2012)
9. Fensel, D., Facca, F.M., Simperl, E., Toma, I.: Semantic Web Services. Springer, Berlin (2011)

A Simple Approach towards SKOSification
of Digital Repositories

Enayat Rajabi, Miguel-Angel Sicilia, and Salvador Sánchez-Alonso

Information Engineering Research Unit, Computer Science Department,
University of Alcalá, Ctra. Barcelona km. 33.6, 28871 Alcalá de Henares, Spain
{enayat.rajabi,msicilia,salvador.sanchez}@uah.es

Abstract. Many knowledge organizations and digital repositories have leveraged different software to manage their taxonomies and thesauri. However,
some of them do not have enough technical knowledge or experts to create
complex structure e.g., OWL. On the other side, SKOS, as a simple language
for classifying the knowledge organization systems e.g., thesauri, allows data to
be distributed and composed on the Web of Data in a structured way. This short
paper presents an approach to expose taxonomies, classification schemes and
other types of vocabularies as SKOS by developing a mapping tool. It also visualizes the output in a graphical user interface in order to explore the vocabularies along with their relationships as well.

Keywords: Vocabularies, Taxonomies, SKOS, Excel, Visualization, Linked
Data.

1   Introduction

Large numbers of digital repositories have applied different types of information in
recent years to classify their content based upon well-known knowledge systems [1].
Furthermore, many institutions use vocabulary management mechanisms in order to
manage vocabularies and terminologies along with their relationships. On the other
side, Simple Knowledge Organization System (SKOS) [2] is a W3C standard that
builds on the RDF [3], RDFS, and complex ontology language (OWL) [4] specifications for providing a standard model to represent taxonomies, controlled vocabularies,
and thesauri. It is intended to express Knowledge Organization Systems (KOS) and
allow concepts to be composed on the Web of Data. SKOS can be also used either as
a flat list of terms or as a complex navigational structure, because it defines a simple
structure including classes, subclasses, and properties along with relationships to other concepts [5]. Repositories can also utilize the SKOS to store a term along with its
definition, notes, labels and a variety of other properties [1].

Another advantage of SKOS is connecting concepts to a wider range of data on the
Web by making use of RDF ability, regardless of using the SKOS ontology [6].
Moreover, terminologies can be easily linked to valuable datasets in Linked Open
Data Cloud e.g., DBpedia[7]. The published concepts also become accessible via

E. Garoufallou and J. Greenberg (Eds.): MTSR 2013, CCIS 390, pp. 67–74, 2013.

SPARQL Endpoints [8] and can be queried by users as well. However, the SKOS is simpler than the OWL, although it is described as vocabulary taken from RDF and OWL [9]. The OWL represents complex structures to generate rich metadata and support inference tools. Furthermore, constructing classification and taxonomies is demanding in terms of expertise, effort, and cost. In many cases, these efforts are superfluous to requirements of data publishers. Hence, the SKOS is easier to use, and harder to misuse than OWL, as it provides an ideal entry point for those wishing to apply the Semantic Web for knowledge organization [10].

This paper presents an approach to expose vocabularies and terminologies as Linked Data format, by importing data either as an OWL file with complex structure or as an Excel file with simple structure. The developed tool in this study is also integrated with a visualization tool to browse the imported data in a user-friendly GUI.

The rest of the paper is organized as follows. Section 2 describes briefly the existing SKOS tools and software. In Section 3, we propose our tool in order to expose vocabularies and terminologies as Linked Data. A case study according to the proposed approach is presented in Section 4. Finally, conclusion is provided in Section 5.

2   Background

A wide acceptance of SKOS led to building a number of related tools. In consequence, we briefly state existing tools and approaches those are mostly involved in this context.

In terms of semantic tools and applications, Semantic Computing Research Group (SeCo) [11] has investigated some machine-processable approaches and developed some related tools for representing data in structured way. Hive system [12], as an open source volunteer project under the Apache Software Foundation [13], facilitates easy data summarization, ad-hoc queries, and the analysis of large datasets. STAR (Semantic Technologies for Archaeological Resources) [14] is also another project which aimed to develop new methods for linking digital archive databases, vocabularies, core ontology and natural language processing techniques.

In terms of vocabulary management, there exist a wide variety of tools and solutions described as follows. TemaTres [15] is an open source vocabulary server applied to exploit terminologies and taxonomies as SKOS. The SKOSed [16], as a plug-in for the Protégé ontology editor [17], also helps users to edit vocabularies and thesauri represented as SKOS. ThManager[18] is another open-source tool for facilitating the creation and visualization of the SKOS vocabularies. The MONDECA SKOS Reader[1] is also a SKOS tool in which users can easily navigate and browse a SKOS thesaurus published as an accessible SKOS file. iQvoc[2] is an open source tool for managing vocabularies that can import and export SKOS. Another system, which is appropriate for editing SKOS vocabularies, is PoolParty [19] which is a commercial system for managing any type of thesauri via easy-to-use GUI. TopQuadrant's Enterprise Vocabulary Net (EVN)[3] is also a commercial web-based collaborative system built around the

---

[1] http://labs.mondeca.com/skosReader.html
[2] http://iqvoc.net/
[3] http://www.topquadrant.com/

SKOS data model for the management of controlled vocabularies. Zoghlami et al. [20] also developed a web based tool which allows creating, sharing and transferring knowledge organization systems based upon the SKOS. Several conversion tools (e.g. XL2XML tool[4]) have been built up to generate the SKOS output from Excel files; however none of them support relationship between concepts (e.g. *broader* and *narrower*). Our tool, as will be discussed later, exposes the Excel sheets including terms, properties, and their relationships as Linked Data. Furthermore, it converts the OWL files to the SKOS format.

3   The Proposed Approach

The following figure summarizes the proposed approach for exposing the vocabularies. As the figure depicts, the input (OWL or Excel file) were read by the tool in the first step and converted to a relational database afterwards. All the terminologies and vocabularies along with their relationships were inserted into the database. In consequence, we used an open source tool to expose the data as Linked Data format in order to represent them as SKOS. Finally, we integrated the approach with a visualization tool in order to browse the terminologies and their relationships as well. We will explain the proposed approach in the following sections in details.

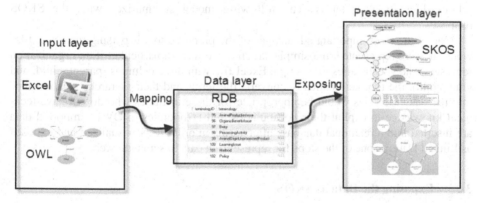

Fig. 1. Architecture of the proposed tool

3.1   Mapping Ontologies to Relational Database

Several knowledge organizations and institutes represent their data, thesauri, and taxonomies in different formats, while some others have not already exposed them as structural format. Some other repositories e.g., Organic-Edunet represent their vocabularies in the OWL format. We unified different formats of terminologies to a relational database as the following schema (Figure 2) in order to expose them as SKOS.

---

[4] https://twiki.auscope.org/wiki/Grid/ExcelToRdfTool

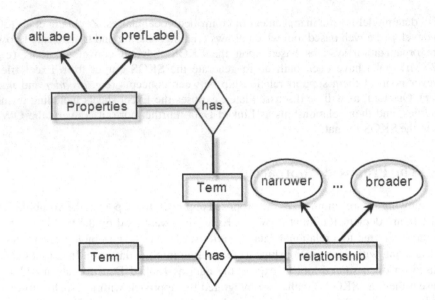

Fig. 2. The SKOS model

As the figure illustrates, each term has some properties along with different labels and relationships to other terms. The following model summarizes what the SKOS proposes.

One of the most important advantages of the proposed tool is parsing the Excel files when they are represented in a simple structural format. In particular, if an organization represents the vocabularies in a simple Excel file with three columns (parent, child, and grandchild), the tool automatically converts the terms and their hierarchy relationships into the database. This would be appropriate for those institutes who do not have technical knowledge to exploit their vocabularies and taxonomies in OWL. Imported data are inserted into a relational database afterwards, in order to be visualized and exposed as Linked Data, as one of the steps for representing data in semantic web.

3.2   Exposing the Data as SKOS

One of the approaches for exposing information as Linked Data is mapping the content which exists in a relational database to RDF. We used D2RQ service [21], as an open source tool for mapping the relational database to SKOS. Term labels, translations (if they are represented in the input file), and relationships (e.g. *narrower* and *broader*) were part of information mapped to the SKOS format. Furthermore, the D2RQ made the terminologies accessible through a SPARQL endpoint in order to be available for the queries provided by users.

3.3   Visualizing the Mapped Terminologies

The D2RQ allows users to explore the data and link them to other datasets on the Web of Data. However, the relationships between terminologies can be visualized in a user friendly browser. To this end, we applied an open source software, Radial Browser [22] to browse the data in a graphical user interface. The Radial Browser displays complex concept network structures in an intuitive manner and visualizes conceptual structures and anything else that can be expressed as nodes and links.

4   Case Study

We used the Organic-Edunet ontology as our case study in order to map the terminologies along with their relationships to the SKOS. The Organic-Edunet is a learning repository that provides access to digital learning resources on Organic Agriculture and Agroecology, facilitates access, usage, and exploitation of such content [6]. This collection currently contains the metadata of almost 11000 resources[5]. The Organic-Edunet ontology is a conceptual model useful for classifying learning materials on the Organic Agriculture domain. It is also the core element for the advanced searching functionality (called "Semantic Search") that is provided by the portal and allows users to get better results when searching for learning materials on this domain [23].

We imported the Organic-Edunet ontology, represented in an OWL file, into a relational database. As a result, around 61 terminologies along with 110 relationships extracted from the ontology. In particular, all the "*super-class*" and "*sub-class*" relationships in the ontology were converted to "*broader*" and "*narrower*" in the database. The mapping tool also supported multilinguality to convert different languages

Export this metadata as:

Property	Value
dcterms:identifier	OETaxonomy:Science
skos:narrower	< http://localhost:2020/page/terminology/8182 >
skos:narrower	< http://localhost:2020/page/terminology/8530 >
skos:narrower	< http://localhost:2020/page/terminology/8656 >
skos:prefLabel	Product @en
rdf:type	skos:concept

Fig. 3. SKOS exposure of OE ontology model

---

[5] http://organic-edunet.eu

of each term into the database. In consequence, we ran the D2RQ service on top of the database and mapped the data to the SKOS based upon its instructions [2].

Figure 3 illustrates the Linked Data version of the Organic-Edunet ontology. The exposed SKOS was also available via SPARQL endpoint to manipulate RDF graph content on the Web of Data.

Finally, we used the Radial Browser [22] to visualize the terminologies and their relationships. To this aim, the tool exported automatically the related data from the database into a XML file in order to illustrate them in a graphical user interface, as depicted in Figure 4.

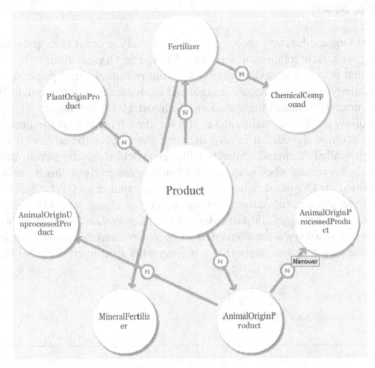

Fig. 4. Terminologies relationships in Radial Browser

5   Conclusions

Linking repositories concepts to useful dataset on the Web of Data enables navigation, improves resource seeking, and makes the repository information discoverable to all kind of users. Furthermore, enriching thesauri and terminologies by linking them to the provenance of data can be achieved by linking them to huge datasets e.g., DBpedia, as users can discover more valuable information in the target dataset.

In this paper we developed a tool for exposing terminologies and vocabularies as Linked Data by expressing them as SKOS which is a simple language for managing knowledge organization systems. The digital repositories that cannot provide their vocabularies in complex structural formats, can particularly import their data in a simple Excel file with regards to the hierarchical structure and expose them as Linked Data format using the presented tool. The OWL format has been also supported by the developed software and mapped to the SKOS.

Moreover, repositories federations can integrate different terminologies and vocabularies by shaping them in one unified approach, as there may exist several structural formats in the client repositories such as OWL.

Acknowledgment. The work presented in this paper has been part-funded by the European Commission under the ICT Policy Support Programme with project No. 297229 "Open Discovery Space (ODS)" and project No. 27099 "Organic.Lingua".

References

1. Solomou, G., Papatheodorou, T.: The Use of SKOS Vocabularies in Digital Repositories: The DSpace Case. In: 2010 IEEE Fourth International Conference on Semantic Computing (ICSC), pp. 542–547 (2010)
2. SKOS Simple Knowledge Organization System Namespace Document 30 July 2008 Edition, http://www.w3.org/TR/2008/
WD-skos-reference-20080829/skos.html (accessed: May 13, 2013)
3. Klyne, G., Carroll, J.J.: Resource Description Framework (RDF): Concepts and Abstract Syntax. W3C Recommendation (2004)
4. OWL 2 Web Ontology Language Document Overview, 2nd edn.,
http://www.w3.org/TR/owl2-overview/ (accessed: May 19, 2013)
5. Nagy, H., Pellegrini, T., Mader, C.: Exploring structural differences in thesauri for SKOS-based applications. In: Proceedings of the 7th International Conference on Semantic Systems, New York, NY, USA, pp. 187–190 (2011)
6. Improve your taxonomy management using the W3C SKOS standard (May 10, 2011), http://www.ibm.com/developerworks/xml/library/
x-skostaxonomy/ (accessed: May 14, 2013)
7. The Linking Open Data cloud diagram, http://lod-cloud.net/ (accessed: May 14, 2013)
8. SPARQL endpoint - semanticweb.org,
http://semanticweb.org/wiki/SPARQL_endpoint (accessed: May 14, 2013)
9. Jupp, S., Bechhofer, S., Stevens, R.: SKOS with OWL: Don't be Full-ish! In: Proceedings of the Fifth OWLED Workshop on OWL: Experiences and Directions, Collocated with the 7th International Semantic Web Conference (ISWC 2008), Karlsruhe, Germany, October 26-27. CEUR-WS.org (2008),
https://www.escholar.manchester.ac.uk/uk-ac-man-scw:2h72 (accessed: May 14, 2013)
10. Simple Knowledge Organization System - Wikipedia, the free encyclopedia,
http://en.wikipedia.org/wiki/Simple_Knowledge_
Organization_System (accessed: May 19, 2013)
11. Semantic Computing Research Group (SeCo), http://www.seco.tkk.fi/ (accessed: August 15, 2013)
12. Hive project, http://hive.apache.org/ (accessed: August 15, 2013)

13. The Apache Software Foundation, http://www.apache.org/ (accessed: August 15, 2013)
14. Keith, M., Binding, C., Tudhope, D.: A STAR is born: some emerging Semantic Technologies for Archaeological Resources. In: Proceedings Computer Applications and Quantitative Methods in Archaeology, Budapest, Hungary (2008)
15. TemaTres Controlled Vocabulary server, http://www.vocabularyserver.com/ (accessed: May 19, 2013)
16. skoseditor - SKOSEd - Thesaurus editor for the Semantic Web - Google Project Hosting, http://code.google.com/p/skoseditor/ (accessed: May 19, 2013)
17. The Protégé Ontology Editor and Knowledge Acquisition System, http://protege.stanford.edu/ (accessed: May 19, 2013)
18. ThManager - KOS editor, http://thmanager.sourceforge.net/ (accessed: May 19, 2013)
19. PoolParty Semantic Information Management, http://www.poolparty.biz/ (accessed: May 19, 2013)
20. Zoghlami, K., Kerherve, B., Gerbe, O.: Using a SKOS Engine to Create, Share and Transfer Terminology Data Sets. In: 2011 Seventh International Conference on Signal-Image Technology and Internet-Based Systems (SITIS), pp. 46–53 (2011)
21. Bizer, C.: D2RQ - treating non-RDF databases as virtual RDF graphs. In: Proceedings of the 3rd International Semantic Web Conference, ISWC 2004 (2004)
22. moritz.stefaner.eu - Relation browser, http://moritz.stefaner.eu/projects/relation-browser/ (accessed: May 05, 2013)
23. Organic.Edunet Metadata Application Profile - Organic.Edunet, http://wiki.organic-edunet.eu/index.php/ Organic.Edunet_Metadata_Application_Profile (accessed: May 12, 2013)

Cross-Language Ontology Alignment Utilizing Machine Translation Models

Antonis Koukourikos[1], Pythagoras Karampiperis[1], and Giannis Stoitsis[2,3]

[1] Software and Knowledge Engineering Laboratory, Institute of Informatics and Telecommunications, National Center for Scientific Research "Demokritos"Agia Paraskevi Attikis, P.O. Box 60228, 15310 Athens, Greece
[2] Agro-Know Technologies, Grammou 17 Str., Vrilissia Attikis, 15235 Athens, Greece
[3] Computer Science Department, Universidad de Alcala, 28871 Alcala de Henares, Madrid, Spain

Abstract. In the context of ontology alignment, linguistic analysis is a prominent solution, used by various proposed methodologies. When mapping ontologies that use the same language, the existent approaches have been shown to produce significant results, being able to handle complex descriptions of the enclosed concepts and properties. In order to expand the applied linguistic methods in a cross-language context, i.e. to align ontologies that use different languages, it is essential to automate the process of finding lexical correspondences, beyond simple term translation, between the entity descriptions provided by the involved ontologies. The present paper proposes a machine learning approach to obtain the optimal from a set of translation provided by different automated machine translation services, in order to use it as the basis for aligning ontology pairs that provide complex descriptions expressed in different languages.

Keywords: Ontology Alignment, Cross-language Alignment, Automated Machine Translation, Machine Learning.

1 Introduction

The progress on the availability and structuring of online information has made available huge amounts of disjoint information for multiple domains. The usability and effectiveness of this information is greatly increased if the contributions of different content providers is associated and used in liaison with each other. Therefore, the problem of managing the heterogeneity between various information resources in order to integrate seamlessly and efficiently the underlying knowledge is of particular interest.

In the context of the Semantic Web, ontologies are a common medium for describing the domain of interest and providing a contextualization of the different terms used for specifying the characteristics of the involved entities. Ontology matching is one of the prominent technologies used for integrating such descriptions on the conceptual level However, information and knowledge resources are not always

E. Garoufallou and J. Greenberg (Eds.): MTSR 2013, CCIS 390, pp. 75–86, 2013.
© Springer International Publishing Switzerland 2013

associated with an ontology. Classifications of different complexity and formalization are employed in different repositories. One major issue that further complicates the process of combining this information has to do with the variability on the languages used for labelling and describing concepts and properties of these ontologies.

The present papers builds on existing methods for monolingual ontology mapping and examines the efficiency of using automatic machine translation techniques for producing an ontological pair consisting of ontologies that now use the same language. In order to determine the impact of translation quality, we propose a machine learning mechanism for selecting the optimal translation for a specific label/ description from a set of available translations. We then examine the results both in terms of the quality of the alignment, as well as, the relative impact of selecting the best from a set of available translations instead of monolithically using a specific MT system.

The rest of the paper is structured as follows: We provide a brief overview of popular techniques for ontology alignment and efforts for cross-language ontology mapping. Afterwards, we present our method for aligning a pair of ontologies that use descriptions in different languages. Next, the MT Selector, our machine-learning approach for selecting an optimal translation from a set of available ones, is presented. We proceed with the description of our experimental setup and report on the acquired results. Finally, we conclude with some observations and the immediate steps for further improving and validating our approach.

2   Lexical-Based Ontology Alignment

The purpose of ontology matching is, in a broad context, to define correspondences and mappings between concepts, as the latter are expressed in different conceptualization schemas. Several formalizations of the above statement have been proposed [1, 2, 3]. In [4] it is stated:

Let O1 and O2 distinct ontologies. An alignment between these ontologies is a set of correspondences between entities belonging to the two ontologies. A correspondence is a quadruple of the form:<id,e1,e2,r>, where:

- id is a unique identifier for the correspondence
- e1 is an entity of the first ontology O1
- e2 is an entity of the second ontology O2
- r is the type of relation between e1 and e2

The relation between the matched entities can be equivalence, generalisation/specialisation and others, depending on the nature of the problem that is being examined.

There are various techniques used for performing ontology matching. A common method is the application of linguistic analysis within the ontology in order to compute similarities on the textual level. Another strategy for ontology matching is the examination of structural properties of the ontologies to be merged. The graph structure derived from the ontology, commonly via is-a/ part-of relationships between concepts, provides a means for examining the similarity between two ontologies based on the connections between their concepts. Instance-based approaches, where the objects described by the ontologies are available and annotated with ontological terms, are also of particular interest. Similarity between instances can lead to suggestion of similarities between the underlying concepts. Finally, external knowledge information, such as thesauri, dictionaries and taxonomies, are frequently employed in ontology matching in order to provide further information about the semantics of the concepts and relations in the ontologies to be matched.

In practice, these approaches are not mutually exclusive, as ontology alignment systems can use combinations of them or employ selection strategies to invoke a matcher based on features specific to the matching task at hand. Some prominent recent alignment systems and their approaches are described below.

SAMBO [5] is used for matching (and merging) biomedical ontologies. It supports the merging of ontologies expressed in OWL format. The system combines different matchers, each one computing a similarity value in the [0, 1] space. The terminological matcher examines similarities between the textual descriptions of concepts and restrictions of the ontologies, using the n-gram and edit distance metrics and a linguistic algorithm that compares the lists of words of which the descriptions terms are composed and discovers the common words. A structural matcher relies on the position of concepts relative to already aligned concepts and iteratively aligns additional entities based on their structural association (is-a/part-of connections with entities aligned during a previous iteration). SAMBO also examines the similarity of terms in the ontologies with an external domain-specific resource (UMLS) and employs a learning matcher that classifies documents with respect to their relation with ontology concepts and associates the entities that encapsulated the same documents.

RiMOM [6] uses a multi-strategy ontology matching approach. The matching methods that are employed are (a) linguistic similarity and (b) structural similarity. The linguistic similarity adopts the edit distance and vector instance metrics, while the structural similarity is examined by a modified similarity flooding [7] implementation. For each matching task, RiMOM quantifies the similarity characteristics be-tween the examined ontologies and dynamically selects the suitable strategy for per-forming the task.

The ASMOV [8] system handles pairs of ontologies expressed in OWL. The process employed by ASMOV includes two distinct phases. The similarity calculation phase activates linguistic, structural and extensional matchers in order to iteratively compute similarity measures for each pair of entities comprised by the elements of the ontologies to be matched. The measures are then aggregated into a single, weighted average value. From this phase, a preliminary alignment is produced by selecting the maximum similarity value for each entity. During the semantic verification phase, this alignment is iteratively refined via the elimination of the correspondences that are not verified by assertions in the ontologies.

BLOOMS [9] is an alignment system that discovers schema-level links between Linked Open Data datasets by bootstrapping already present information from the LOD cloud. After a light-weight linguistic processing, it feeds the textual descriptions of concepts in two ontologies to the Wikipedia search Web Service. The Wikipedia categories to which the search results belong to are inserted into a tree structure that is expanded with the subcategories of the aforementioned categories, until the tree reaches the fourth level. The trees belonging to the "forests" of the two input ontologies are compared in pairs and an overlap value is assigned to each tree pair. Based on this value, BLOOMS defines equivalence and specialization relations between the concepts of the ontologies.

The aforementioned systems have produced significant results in the context of classification schema matching. However, it is important to note that the majority of the systems handle monolingual ontology matching, that is, they perform their mapping methods on ontological pairs expressed in the same language. Several efforts have been made to support and exploit linguistic enrichment of ontological concepts [10, 11, 12]. Rich lexical information can be used in the same fashion from monolingual approaches by using shallow analysis techniques over labels/ descriptions in the same language. Furthermore, [13] proposes a system for aligning cross-languages ontologies using MT systems, but rely on a specific translation system, while the overall impact of inaccuracies of the translation is not strictly measured.

3   Method

Our approach relies on the acquisition of a translated version for one of the two ontologies to be aligned. To achieve this, we employ different translation systems in order to obtain the best possible (optimal) translation of a textual snippet, based on the text's features.

The overall process comprises the following steps:

```
Let O and O' be the ontologies to be aligned, with O regarded as
the base ontology.
For each label/ description T in O'
Calculate lexical features of T.
Assign the translation of T' to the most suitable machine trans-
lation service
Obtain the optimal translation for T'.
Produce the translated version of O', tO'
Align O and tO'
```

The next section discusses the process for analysing the textual description available in the ontology O' and selecting the optimal translation from a set of translation provided by different MT modules.

4   Automatic Selection of Machine Translation Models

The goal of MT Selector, the Machine Translation Selection service, is to provide an optimal translation of a text segment, by analysing the textual information, identifying certain characteristics and assigning the translation to a translation service better suited to these characteristics.

We define the selection process as a classification task that will be carried out using standard machine learning techniques. In this context, the classes represent the available Machine Translation services that are accessible via the MT Selector. The data for classification is the incoming translation tasks, that is, a segment of text of varying size and structure and a language pair, denoting the source language (the language in which the text is written) and the target language (the language to which the text will be translated). The features used for constructing the decision tree of the MT Selector Classifier are of purely linguistic and statistical nature.

4.1   MT Selector Service Architecture

The following figure depicts the high-level architecture of the MT Selector Service. The service is accessible via a set of ReST function calls. The functions pass the necessary information to the MT Selector Classification module, which (a) analyses the input text and constructs the feature vector for the specific translation task; (b) classifies the task with respect to its suitability for one of the underlying translation services; and (c) delegates the translation task to the appropriate service.

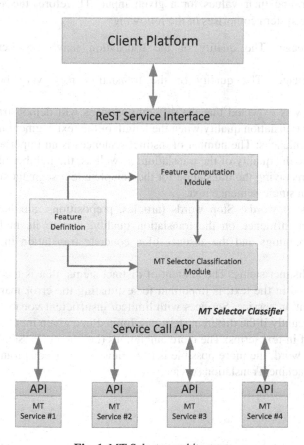

Fig. 1. MT Selector architecture

The diagram emphasises the distinction between loosely and tightly connected components within the MT Selector system. The modules internal to the MT Selector Classifier are connected via standard data sharing techniques (asynchronous database access, file-system sharing, object construction and function calls). In contrast, the communication with any possible client application and with the underlying Machine Translation services is realised via calls to Web Services that follow a strictly defined API.

The following subsections describe the individual components that comprise the MT Selector.

4.2   Feature Definition

The Feature Definition is a static, locally stored structure that provides the definitions for the lexical features taken into account by the system. In the current version of the system, it is a simple text file that follows the ARFF format [14]. Taken into account that the MT Selector should exhibit relatively quick response times, the current selection of features was done keeping in mind the complexity of linguistic analysis that is needed to determine their values for a given input. Therefore, the set of features examined by the system comprises of the following:

- Source language: The quality of the translation may vary between source languages.
- Target Language: The quality of the translation may vary between target languages.
- Text size: It was expected that the different services will demonstrate significant variations on translation quality when the length of the text segment increases.
- Number of sentences: The number of distinct sentences is an important metric as it may influence the quality of the translation, as well as, the number of calls that are required for receiving the translation for the complete text segment since some services work on single-sentence text.
- Number of stop words: Stop words (articles, prepositions, auxiliary verbs etc.) have a direct influence on the translation quality, due to its multiple context-dependent meanings and the absence of a concrete translation in different languages.
- Number of distinct stems: The amount of distinct stems, that is the base forms of the words used in the text, is important for estimating the error margins of a Machine Translation service. Services with limited/ insufficient vocabularies may not suffer significantly if the different stems are limited in a given input text.
- Ambiguity of in-text terms: The more ambiguous (i.e. the more "senses", meanings it bears) is a word, the more possible is to retrieve an erroneous translation for the word by a Machine Translation service.

4.3 Feature Computation

The Feature Computation Module (FCM) is responsible for performing the linguistic analysis tasks in order to determine the values of each feature for a given text segment. Since it is essential for the service to exhibit acceptable responsiveness for real-time use, the linguistic processing is held to relatively quick processes. Table 1 summarises the technologies that comprise the FCM and are used to extract the values of each feature from a text segment.

Table 1. Technologies used for calculating FCM features

Feature	Technologies Used	Description
Source Language	-	Given as input
Target Language	-	Given as input
Text Size	Word Count, Character Count	A simple module that returns the amount of characters and words in a text segment
Number of sentences	Sentence splitting	Based on existing libraries, the MT Selector incorporates a module that splits the input text into distinct sentences
Amount of stop-words	Word count	Pre-defined stop-words are detected and counted
Number of stems	Tokenization, Stemming, Hashing	Every word in the text segment is stemmed and the frequency of each stem is stored in a hash table
Term ambiguity	Stemming, WordNet, Custom Vocabularies	Lookup in WordNet and Custom Vocabularies for determining the number of different senses that a given word bears.

At the current version of the system, the source and target languages of a translation task are defined explicitly. If a need for language detection arises, it is straightforward to incorporate such modules without changes in the internal logic of the other components.

The size of the text in terms of characters is easily calculated. In the case of word count, the core functionality of the module is fixed; however, the module will use a different set of word separating characters for the different languages.

The MT Selector Sentence Splitter is implemented using standard Java libraries for tokenization.

For determining the number of stems, the input text will be tokenized and each token will be stemmed using the relevant modules provided by the Stanford Parser [15, 16].

In this system version, Term Ambiguity is defined as the number of different senses for a specific term given by the WordNet [17] database. This module can be significantly extended to consult additional, domain-specific vocabularies, in order to determine the ambiguity of a term more accurately.

4.4   Classification Module

The MT Selector Classification Module (SCM) is based on the widely used and tested Weka suite of Data Mining tools [18]. The current version of the system uses a Naïve Bayes Classifier and the decision tree is using the feature vectors provided by the FCM, exported in the ARFF data format.

5   Experimental Setup

5.1   AMT Services Integration

The MT Selector is designed so as to allow the introduction of different translation mechanisms with minimal effort. To this end, we defined a simple API that each service must satisfy in order to be called by the selection service.

In the current implementation of the MT Selector, the following automatic machine translations services were integrated:

Microsoft Translator. Microsoft Translator [19] provides a set of web service APIs that allows the use of the service in external applications, services and web sites. We used the REST-based API provided by the service, with predetermined source and target languages (Greek and English respectively).

```
http://api.microsofttranslator.com/V2/Http.svc/Translate?appId=&
text="+data+"&from="+srcLang+"&to="+trgLang+"&contentType=text/p
lain&category="+category
```

Fig. 2. Exemplary call of the Microsoft Translator service

iTranslate4. iTranslate4 [20] is an EU project that has developed a machine translation service for any pair of European languages. Again, we used the provided API for translating Greek-to-English documents.

```
HttpGet getRequest = new
HttpGet("http://itranslate4.eu/api/Translate?auth="+MotherBoard.
itran-
slate4Key+"&src="+srcLang+"&trg="+trgLang+"&dat="+data+"&dom="+co
ntext);
HttpResponse response = httpClient.execute(getRequest);

HttpEntity responseEntity = response.getEntity();
textResponse = EntityUtils.toString(responseEntity);

ObjectMapper mapper = new ObjectMapper();
JsonNode rootNode = map-
per.readTree(mapper.getJsonFactory().createJsonParser(textRespon
se));
textTranslated = rootNode.findValue("text").toString();
```

Fig. 3. Exemplary call of the iTranslate4 service

5.2   Training Process

The initial training session for the MT Selector used multilingual documents available from Europarl Parallel Corpus [21]. We used 500 documents of variable size and put them through basic cleaning in order to obtain the cleaned textual information. For the purposes of the experiment, we used the versions of the documents in English and Greek.

For each text file, we called the integrated MT services and obtained the respective translation text. In order to determine the best of these translations, we applied the BLEU and TER metrics, comparing our results with the translation provided by Europarl.

Table 2 summarizes the results for each translation service over the examined corpus.

Table 2. Edit Distance results for the services incorporated in MT Selector

Translation Service	BLEU	TER
Microsoft Translator	0.296	0.613
iTranslate4	0.301	0.621

5.3   Alignment Process

The next step of our experiment was to compare the results on aligning a pair of ontologies using labels/ descriptions in different languages, using the translations of each service and compare them with the matching achieved when using the MT Selector to dynamically select the optimal translation, as chosen by the classification module.

The input ontologies for the system were an English version of the Music ontology [22] and a Greek translation (manually constructed) of the BBC Playcount data, which used the Programmes ontology [23]. The Music Ontology provides the main concepts and properties for describing musical works, performances and recordings. The BBC Playcount data ontology is used for describing programmes and broadcasts. It is linked to the Musicbrainz linked data, which uses the Music ontology. This linkage is used to provide the golden standard for our experiments.

In order to provide proper text to the translation service, the labels within the ontologies underwent some basic manipulation. Basic heuristics, like splitting labels when capital letters are encountered mid-word or when an underscore is encountered, were applied and the labels were transformed to proper textual segments.

For performing the alignment of the base and the translated ontology, we used a combination of simple lexical and structural mapping algorithms, both using the Alignment API [24] for specifying alignments, and we merged the results of the individual tools. The lexical mapping algorithm examines the similarity of names and labels between the ontologies, while the structural mapping algorithm examines the graph similarities in parts of the ontologies and deduces equivalence mappings based on the results of the lexical similarity for some of the examined nodes.

6   Experimental Results

The present section summarizes the accuracy of the achieved matching for each run of the alignment process. Table 3 presents the results when using the Microsoft Translator service, while Table 4 presents the results when using the iTranslate4 service.

Table 3. Results from experiment using exclusively the Microsoft Translator service

Mappings using Microsoft Translator	
Correct Matches	0.68
Incorrect Matches	0.15
Ambiguous	0.17

Table 4. Results from experiment using exclusively the iTranslate4 service

Mappings using iTranslate4	
Correct Matches	0.71
Incorrect Matches	0.11
Ambiguous	0.18

Table 5 shows the alignment results when using the translated ontology as it was derived from the MT Selector process.

Table 5. Results from experiment using the MT Selector

Mappings using MT Selector	
Correct Matches	0.82
Incorrect Matches	0.09
Ambiguous	0.09

7   Conclusions and Future Work

The acquired results indicate that the impact of the translation quality is not insignificant when using the examined approach for mapping cross-language ontologies. A significant advantage is the reduction of unresolved mappings. It is, thus, interesting to exploit the proposed mechanism of selecting the optimal translation for ontological labels and descriptions in order to extend monolingual alignment approaches to a cross-language setting.

The presented system leaves plenty of room for introducing improvements and extensions to the original concept. The changes can be both in the process of translation and the process of selection. We aim to introduce a further set of MT services in the MT Selector, and perform a thorough analysis of the classification results in order to refine the feature selection part of our methodology. Another important aspect is the incorporation of external resources and domain-specific information, using multilingual thesauri and multilingual linguistic resources.

Another important experiment is the evaluation of different alignment algorithms in order to determine the impact of translation quality on their performance. It is expected that algorithms that better exploit structural and contextual information will be less affected by the quality of translation.

Acknowledgments. Part of the research leading to these results has received funding from the European Union 7th Framework Programme under grant agreement n° 318497 (SemaGrow - Data Intensive Techniques to Boost the Real – Time Performance of Global Agricultural Data Infrastructures). Furthermore, some of the work presented in this paper has been funded with support by the European Commission, and more specifically the CIP-ICT-PSP- 270999 project "Organic.Lingua: Demonstrating the potential of a multilingual Web portal for Sustainable Agricultural & Environmental Education".

References

1. Kalfoglou, Y., Schorlemmer, M.: Ontology mapping: the state of the art. The Knowledge Engineering Review 18(1), 1–31 (2003)
2. Shvaiko, P., Euzenat, J.: A survey of schema-based matching approaches. In: Spaccapietra, S. (ed.) Journal on Data Semantics IV. LNCS, vol. 3730, pp. 146–171. Springer, Heidelberg (2005)
3. Zimmermann, A., Krötzsch, M., Euzenat, J., Hitzler, P.: Formalizing ontology alignment and its operations with category theory. In: Proceedings of the 4th International Conference on Formal Ontology in Information Systems (FOIS), pp. 277–288 (2006)

4. Euzenat, J., Shvaiko, P.: Ontology Matching. Springer (2007)
5. Lambrix, P., Tan, H.: SAMBO – a system for aligning and merging biomedical ontologies. Journal of Web Semantics 49(1), 196–206 (2006)
6. Li, J., Tang, J., Li, Y., Luo, Q.: Rimom: A dynamic multistrategy ontology alignment framework. IEEE Transactions on Knowledge and Data Engineering 21(8), 1218–1232 (2009)
7. Melnik, S., Garcia-Molina, H., Rahm, E.: Similarity flooding: a versatile graph matching algorithm. In: Proceedings of the 18th International Conference on Data Engineering (ICDE), pp. 117–128 (2002)
8. Jean-Mary, Y.R., Shironoshita, E.P., Kabuka, M.R.: Ontology matching with semantic verification. Journal of Web Semantics 7(3), 235–251 (2009)
9. Jain, P., Hitzler, P., Sheth, A.P., Verma, K., Yeh, P.Z.: Ontology Alignment for Linked Open Data. In: Patel-Schneider, P.F., Pan, Y., Hitzler, P., Mika, P., Zhang, L., Pan, J.Z., Horrocks, I., Glimm, B. (eds.) ISWC 2010, Part I. LNCS, vol. 6496, pp. 402–417. Springer, Heidelberg (2010)
10. Pazienza, M.T., Stellato, A.: Exploiting Linguistic Resources for Building Linguistically Motivated Ontologies in the Semantic Web. In: Proceedings of the OntoLex Workshop, Interfacing Ontologies and Lexical Resources for Semantic Web Technologies (2006)
11. Peters, W., Montiel-ponsoda, E., Aguado De Cea, G.: Localizing Ontologies in OWL. In: Proceedings of the OntoLex 2007 Workshop (Held in Conjunction with ISWC 2007) (2007)
12. Espinoza, M., Gómez-Pérez, A., Mena, E.: Enriching an Ontology with Multilingual Information. In: Bechhofer, S., Hauswirth, M., Hoffmann, J., Koubarakis, M. (eds.) ESWC 2008. LNCS, vol. 5021, pp. 333–347. Springer, Heidelberg (2008)
13. Fu, B., Brennan, R., O'Sullivan, D.: Cross-Lingual Ontology Mapping and Its Use on the Multilingual Semantic Web. In: Proceedings of the 1st Workshop on the Multilingual Semantic Web, at the 19th International World Wide Web Conference (WWW 2010), Raleigh, USA (2010)
14. Weka-ARFF, http://weka.wikispaces.com/ARFF (last accessed February 2013)
15. Klein, D., Manning, C.D.: Accurate Unlexicalized Parsing. In: Proceedings of the 41st Meeting of the Association for Computational Linguistics, pp. 423–430 (2003)
16. de Marneffe, M.-C., MacCartney, B., Manning, C.D.: Generating Typed Dependency Parses from Phrase Structure Parses. In: LREC 2006 (2006)
17. Princeton University "aAbout WordNet". WordNet. Princeton University, http://wordnet.princeton.edu (last accessed February 2013)
18. Hall, M., Frank, E., Holmes, G., Pfahringer, B., Reutemann, P., Witten, I.H.: The WEKA Data Mining Software: An Update. SIGKDD Explorations 11(1) (2009)
19. Microsoft Translator, http://www.microsoft.com/en-us/translator (last accessed February 2013)
20. iTranslate4.eu, http://itranslate4.eu/project/ (last accessed August 2013)
21. Koehn, P.: Europarl: A Parallel Corpus for Statistical Machine Translation, MT Summit (2005)
22. Music Ontology Specification, http://musicontology.com/ (last accessed August 2013)
23. BBC-Ontologies-The Programmes Ontology, http://purl.org/ontology/po/ (last accessed August 2013)
24. Alignment API, http://alignapi.gforge.inria.fr/ (last accessed August 2013)

Using Metadata to Facilitate Understanding and Certification of Assertions about the Preservation Properties of a Preservation System

Jewel H. Ward[1], Hao Xu[2], Mike C. Conway[2], Terrell G. Russell[3], and Antoine de Torcy[3]

[1] The University of North Carolina at Chapel Hill, Chapel Hill, NC, USA
jewel_ward@unc.edu
[2] Data Intensive Cyber Environments Center (DICE), Chapel Hill, NC, USA
xuh@email.unc.edu, michael_conway@unc.edu
[3] Renaissance Computing Institute (RENCI), Chapel Hill, NC, USA
tgr@renci.org, adetorcy@email.unc.edu

Abstract. Developers of preservation repositories need to provide internal audit mechanisms to verify their assertions about how the recommendations outlined in the Open Archival Information System (OAIS) Reference Model are applied. They must also verify the consistent application of preservation policies to both the digital objects and the preservation system itself. We developed a method for mapping between the OAIS Reference Model Functional Model to a data grid implementation, which facilitates such tasks. We have done a preliminary gap analysis to determine the current state of computer task-oriented functions and procedures in support of preservation, and constructed a method for abstracting state transition systems from preservation policies. Our approach facilitates certifying properties of a preservation repository and bridges the gap between computer code and abstract preservation repository standards such as the OAIS Reference Model.

Keywords: preservation repository, OAIS Reference Model, trusted digital repository, state transition system, metadata, policy, rule-oriented programming.

1   Introduction

There exists a pressing need for the developers of preservation repositories to be able to provide internal audit mechanisms to verify their assertions about how the recommendations outlined in the Open Archival Information System (OAIS) Reference Model [1,2] are applied, as well as to verify the consistent application of preservation policies both to the objects in the repository and the system itself [3-5]. Currently, librarians, archivists, computer scientists and other preservation experts are in the process of standardizing the requirements to "certify the certifiers" of a Trusted Digital Repository (TDR) [6], which is a repository with "a mission to provide reliable, long-term access to managed digital resources to its designated community, now and into the future" [7].

E. Garoufallou and J. Greenberg (Eds.): MTSR 2013, CCIS 390, pp. 87–98, 2013.

Moore has proposed that a theory of digital preservation is possible [8]. He described this theory as a set of preservation processes that can be controlled by management policies, and a set of preservation metadata that record the operation of a preservation system. The preservation metadata may then be reviewed via a set of assessment criteria to prove that the preservation environment is working correctly, and, therefore, can be characterized as "trustworthy". This paper proposes an approach using Moore's theory that is based on a formalism, which allows us to make assertions about the "trusted" nature of a repository.

We propose a method for facilitating the ability to certify assertions about a preservation repository, which is composed of two parts. The first involves mapping the task-oriented computer functions and procedures to the OAIS Functional Model in order to understand if and how the mapping can be done at all. This is "metadata-as-a-preservation-task". The second involves using state transition systems to connect the computer code within a preservation repository to data management policies, by mapping machine-level events to state transitions, and data management policies to criteria for deciding legitimate sequences of state transitions. This is "metadata-as-states". The audit trail of the metadata generated can be thought of as a structured log of state transition events from a data grid.

Our method bridges the gap between computer code and human-readable standards. This method may be applied to any repository system and provides a foundation for translating the Functional Model of the OAIS Reference Model Recommendation to any preservation implementation. Our research is inspired by previous work to define the attributes of a trusted digital repository [5, 7]. These authors included as an attribute the ability to certify that a preservation system is actually doing what the managers claim it is doing, and work is progressing towards "certifying certifiers" [9]. Our method described in this paper addresses the certification challenge.

2   Background

In this section, we will briefly discuss metadata, human-readable and machine-readable policies, and a description of the preservation system to which we will apply our approach. Some knowledge of the OAIS Reference Model Functional Model is assumed.

2.1   Metadata

Information professionals define metadata simply as "data about data" [10] or "information about information" [11]. They use metadata to make it simpler to manage, retrieve, or use an information resource by describing, locating, or explaining what an information resource is. Practitioners and researchers in Information and Library Science are generally referring to descriptive, structural, and administrative metadata when they use the term. They use these types of metadata to refer to organized schemas such as the Dublin Core Metadata Element Set [12] or MARC XML [13], which operate as cataloging functions.

Computer scientists include digital exhaust, i.e., the trail a user leaves behind when using various technological tools, as metadata [14]. They may use the date, time, Internet Protocol numbers, or event data that triggers actions within the computer code as metadata, in order to mine for the desired relevant information. Thus, metadata may be data in and of itself.

The authors of the OAIS Reference Model [1,2] outlined the seven primary areas of a preservation repository in the Composition of Functional Entities. They are: common services, ingest, data management, access, administration, preservation planning, and archival storage. This recommendation provides a powerful description of the best practices for repository design that should be present in order to preserve digital material for the indefinite long-term. We have identified each of these Functional Entities as "metadata" — similar to a schema — against which we can map task-oriented computer functions and procedures, as well as events and actions triggered within the computer code.

2.2   Human- vs Machine-Readable Policies

The authors of the Oxford English Dictionary [15] define "policy" as "a course or principle of action adopted or proposed by an organization or individual". Within the context of a preservation repository, a policy may be both human-readable and machine-readable. A human-readable policy is one that describes a high-level policy such as trustworthiness, legal retention requirements, or confidentiality [16, 17]. A machine-actionable rule is one that maps control to procedure execution. One example of the former is "the repository shall comply with Access Policies" [17]. The same policy may be implemented at the machine level within a preservation repository as code as follows.

```
acAclPolicy { msiAclPolicy("STRICT"); } #code
```

Our work was motivated by previous work at high-level policy specification and binding through the Arch prototype [3]. The authors posited that an important conceptual exercise to further define a bridge between high-level policy and computer-actionable rules within a preservation system would be a mapping of events in an archive to the policies that pertain to that particular event at an abstract level.

Previous work in this area has examined how to implement natural language policies at the machine-level [18]. Moore and Smith mapped the RLG/NARA [19] trusted digital repository certification checklist to a set of data management policies. They wanted to examine how to enforce these data management polices as automated rules that control preservation services, so that they could audit the repository for a defined set of policies. They were able to demonstrate a self-consistent preservation environment with enforceable and auditable assessment criteria.

Most designers of policy implementations take a top-down approach, where natural language policies such as the OAIS and ISO 16363 are implemented manually and at a high level [2, 16, 20]. Our approach is rare, as we examine and implement policy implementation from the "bottom up", at the machine-level [21].

2.3   Preservation System

A data grid [22] is a system with a "virtualized" data collection that organizes data distributed across multiple locations into shareable collections using a client-server or peer-to-peer model.

The integrated Rule-Oriented Data System (iRODS) is an example of a data grid with an Adaptive Middleware Architecture (AMA) that implements explicit policy enforcement. The developers designed it with three main features: a networking model that manages the interactions between distributed storage and clients; a metadata catalog (iCAT) in which state information from remote operations is maintained along with data provenance attributes; and, a Rule Engine for executing policies as computer actionable rules. It provides the facilities necessary to enforce institutional procedures, automate administrative tasks, and validate assessment criteria [23].

We can customize data management functions by turning human-readable policies into machine actionable policies called, "rules" [24]. These rules are composed of task-oriented C-code programs called "microservices". The microservices of interest here are those that generate state information that is managed via the metadata catalog [23]. Rules composed of one or more microservices of this type can be applied at policy enforcement points located in the middleware when a preservation function is invoked. If the properties of the collection must be validated, then the authors of iRODS tailored it so that the validation will occur through either a parsing of the audit trails or queries on the metadata catalog. In theory, they designed it so that creating or selecting the appropriate microservices may implement any desired procedure. If an iRODS manager would like to enforce a policy, then he or she may do so via the development of appropriate rules (e.g., "code") that use particular microservices. Hedges, Blanke, and Hasan [25] noted that it is possible to design sets of rules that will be executed when a certain action occurs, such as ingest or the update of an object.

Currently, iRODS provides 70 policy enforcement points that may be triggered "pre-action", "action", or "post-action" [23]. For example, when a repository manager ingests a file, ten policy enforcement points are triggered, including: check whether the client request comes from an allowed host, check whether public access is being requested, check access control lists, select the storage resource, select a physical path name for the file, and so forth. A given client action may trigger multiple enforcement points, so that an iRODS user may apply multiple policies on each action. In an iRODS based environment these system-level events may be storage events, events triggered by microservice calls, or time-dependent events.

We chose to use this system because it provides us with the means to map task-oriented functions and procedures to the OAIS Reference Model -- i.e., the Composite of Functional Entities -- so that we can understand the preservation capabilities of a system. The generated state information is then logged pre-action, action, and post action as metadata via rules, which provides us with the relevant event information to facilitate certifying our assertions about the preservation capabilities of the system.

3   Mapping a Data Grid Implementation to the OAIS Functional Model

In this section, we describe a method for mapping various aspects of a data grid implementation to the OAIS Reference Model Functional Model.

In the first subsection, we briefly explain an ongoing related project where we map task-oriented functions and procedures to the OAIS Reference Model Functional Model. Second, we discuss a method for abstracting state transition systems from data management policies. Third, we use metadata to map machine-level events, actions, and rules into a state transition system. Finally, we use metadata to map machine-level events, actions, and rules into the OAIS Reference Model Functional Entities. As we will demonstrate, this combined approach provides a method to facilitate certifying the trustworthiness of a preservation repository.

3.1   Mapping Task-Oriented Functions and Procedures to the OAIS Functional Model

Task-oriented functions and procedures are building blocks of a data grid. In order to map a data grid to the overall OAIS Reference Model Functional Model, we must map these building blocks to each of the seven Functional Entities. We need to understand what existing code supports current preservation repository standards before we can apply our method to a data grid. We also wanted to understand the distribution of task-oriented procedures and functions within the preservation system, when compared to the standard recommended design of an archival system (the OAIS).

We mapped 255 task-oriented procedures and functions ("microservices") from the iRODS data grid to one or more of the seven sections of the OAIS Reference Model Composite of Functional Entities [1,2] and found 308 instances (Table 1). We calculated the percentage as the sum of the number of instances per OAIS Functional Entity divided by the total number of microservices. Six instances did not fit with any of the Functional Entities.

Table 1. Distribution of microservices across the OAIS Composite of Functional Entities

OAIS Functional Entity	# Instances per Microservice	# Instances per Microservice / # Microservices
Common Services	101	39.6%
Administration	67	26.3%
Data Management	45	17.6%
Ingest	37	14.5%
Access	28	11.0%
Archival Storage	24	9.4%
None	6	2.4%
Preservation Planning	0	0%

We were not surprised to learn that most machine-level procedures and functions are related to the general running of the preservation system via Common Services and Administration, rather than to the preservation of the objects in the repository; i.e., Archival Storage, None, and Preservation Planning (which is a human, not a machine function). We noted that there is not a one-to-one mapping between each of the 255 microservices and the seven Functional Entities.

The results of this study provide a gap analysis that allow us to determine where task-oriented functions and procedures for preservation management exist and are absent. This provides a vetted documented standard for what is currently available in the preservation system that supports the recommendations of the OAIS Reference Model. Any missing policy building block may either be added into the installed list of tasks and procedures, or augmented outside the system by human implemented policies or other software.

3.2   Method for Abstracting a State Transition System from Data Management Policies

A state transition system captures the states of data objects and collections as well as their transitions. Data management policies define which sequences of state transitions are compliant and which are not. In a non-deterministic state transition system, data management policies can be used to dictate which state transition to take. Despite the non-determinism, a state transition system encodes the formal structural requirements of a given set of data management policies.

Multiple iterations of refinement are necessary to obtain the level of granularity that accurately models such requirements. For example, in the most general case, we have three state transitions for data objects: Submission Information Package (SIP) to Archival Information Package (AIP), AIP to AIP, and AIP to Dissemination Information Package (DIP). However, a specific set of data management policies may specify multiple steps for a high-level state transition. For example, for ingest, as defined by the OAIS Reference Model Functional Model and shown in Fig. 1, below, we need to refine the state transition from SIP to AIP into multiple state transitions.

These refinements will yield a formal structure for data management policies. The significance of such a formal structure is that it provides us with criteria for designing metadata to capture states needed for certifying assertions about the preservation properties of a system. For example, a SIP turning into an AIP without going through a required state would be considered non-conforming to the data management policies. Such information is captured in the metadata, without which we can neither prove nor disprove conformity. In other words, the state transition system thus obtained specifies which metadata are necessary if the preservation properties are going to be certified.

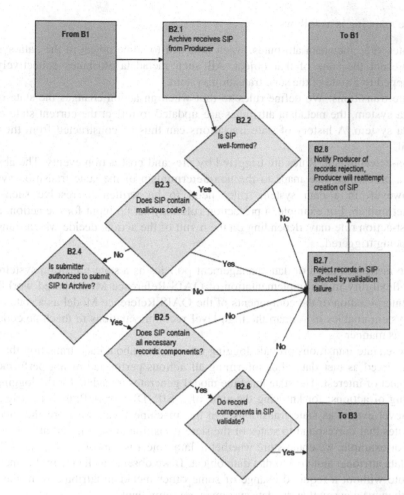

Fig. 1. Section B Transfer and Validation:Validation [26]. These steps are based on the OAIS Reference Model, Composite of Functional Entities, Ingest.

3.3   Using Metadata to Map Machine-Level Events, Actions, and Rules into a State Transition System

A data system consists of actions that change the various states of the system, events that trigger rules, and rules that consist of actions. To map such a data system to a state transition system, we need to identify all states and all possible actions of the data system. Furthermore, we need to identify the non-determinism in the data system. For this, we need to identify all events that trigger rules. We further require a set of metadata attributes in the data system that corresponds to the states of the state transition system.

The mapping is as follows:

- States: The metadata attributes, when attached to some object in the data system, represent the state of that object. All such metadata attributes collectively are mapped to a state of the state transition system.
- State transitions: We define rules so that when an action changes the state of the data system, the metadata attributes are updated to reflect the current state of the data system. A history of state transitions can thus be constructed from the audit trail.
- Non-determinism: Rules are triggered by pre- and post-action events. The absence of a predefined rule maps to the non-determinism of the state transition system. However, in a data system, rules need to be written to resolve such non-determinism. For example, a pre-action rule may set up input for the action, and a post-action rule may, depending on the result of the action, decide which transition is being triggered.

The instrumentation of data management policies as a state transition system provides flexibility in the implementation of OAIS Reference Model-based workflows. This interpretation of the components of the OAIS Reference Model as a state transition system enables us to map the high-level recommendations to machine code in a rigorous manner.

These state transitions provide logging information about each transition that may be preserved as metadata, thus informing all actions performed or not performed on the object of interest. The state machine model generates metadata for the logging and auditing of actions; for knowing the state of a SIP, DIP, or AIP; and, for triggering high-level events as state transitions. On the machine level, we store the metadata attributes that correspond to states of the state transition system in the metadata catalog. For example, we could store whether a data object is part of a SIP or an AIP as a metadata attribute attached to that data object. If we observe a change in this metadata attribute without a required change of some other metadata attribute from the audit trail, then we can say that the data system is not compliant.

3.4   Using Metadata to Map Machine-Level Events, Actions, and Rules into OAIS Functional Entities

If there is not a one-to-one mapping between actions and state transitions, we need additional metadata to distinguish between the intentions of these actions. For example, a move of a data object from one server to another may be mapped to one of the following state transitions.

- SIP to AIP: if the move is from a staging area to archival storage
- AIP to AIP: if it is from archival storage to archival storage
- AIP to DIP: if it is from archival storage to an access area

In this instance, we could attach metadata for each area of the data grid, identifying each of the Functional Entities from the OAIS Reference Model [1,2]. Using these metadata, the same underlying mechanism is repurposed for different preservation tasks. Combined with customized policies, we call each repurposed instance a "policy domain".

We apply the concept of a policy domain to Ingest. Figure 2 is a state transition diagram of the Ingest function, adapted from records management, as seen in Figure 1. Each circle represents a state. Each arrow represents a state transition. Each text label represents a policy enforcement point. Each state defined in the circle maps to section 4.1.5 "the repository shall have an ingest process which verifies each SIP for completeness and correctness" from the Audit and Certification of a Trusted Digital Repository [17], as represented in the Fedora and the Preservation of University Records Project [26], Figure 1. Both of these are based on the OAIS Reference Model Functional Model, Composite of Functional Entities, Ingest [1,2]. Although we show five policy enforcement points in this example, there may be additional policy enforcement points depending on the scenario.

Viewing the OAIS Reference Model as a state transition system has revealed important events within an archive based on state changes, and has disclosed preservation metadata requirements based on state tracking. This has provided a grounded representation of the history of an object based on identified state transitions.

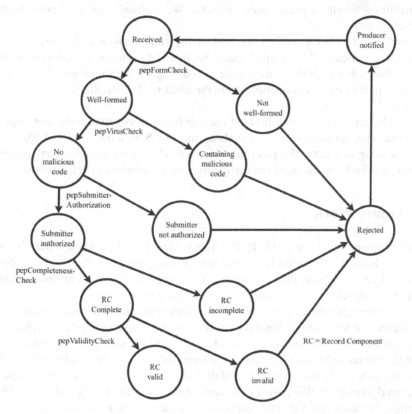

Fig. 2. Example Ingest Showing the State Machine and Policy Enforcement Points, Based on Figure 1 [26]

Basing policy domains on the above formalism enables the development of assessment criteria that evaluate the recorded state of each object and allow automated validation of the properties such as authenticity, integrity, chain of custody, and trustworthiness [7,17]. Our approach makes the assessment of the preservation state of the archive amenable to formal, automated validation via state transition events metadata.

4   Conclusion

We described mapping a data grid implementation to the OAIS Reference Model Functional Model so that we could compare an existing preservation system to current preservation standards and to create a method to facilitate certifying the properties of a preservation system.

First, we examined the "state of the state" by performing a preliminary gap analysis where we mapped task-oriented functions and procedures to the OAIS Reference Model Functional Model. We wanted to understand what existing code supports current preservation repository standards and the distribution of task-oriented procedures and functions within a preservation system. We defined this as "metadata-as-a-preservation-task".

Second, we detailed a method for abstracting state transition systems from data management policies. We mapped states to metadata attributes and synchronized those attributes to reflect the current state of a data grid. We illustrated that we could construct a history of state transitions from the audit trail. We defined this as "metadata-as-states".

In conclusion, this approach bridged the gap between concrete computer code and human-readable, abstract standards such as the OAIS Reference Model Functional Model by using metadata. We posit that this method may be applied to any preservation system in order to facilitate the certification of a trustworthy digital repository.

5   Future Work

The information objects in an OAIS Reference Model implementation may be combined, transformed, or divided into other information packages. We need to incorporate these transformations into our model. We would like to capture both the static and dynamic aspects of an instance of the OAIS Reference Model.

Further research related to mapping task-oriented functions and procedures to the OAIS Reference Model Functional Model will involve examining other machine code and procedures and functions against ISO 16363 [16], as well as comparing rules to the OAIS Reference Model Composite of Functional Entities. We will conduct follow up interviews with the data managers and data scientists who manage the repository.

We need to map iRODS policy enforcement points to the OAIS Reference Model semantics. For example, the static aspect determines the structure of an archive at a specific point in time. If we examine the dynamic aspect, then we will need to observe and capture how that structure changes over time. We would like to classify the policies required for particular types of repositories, so that the policies may be added at install as a module. Currently, the iRODS standard install comes with a default generic policy set appropriate for a distributed file system.

Acknowledgements. This research is partially supported by NSF grant #0940841 "DataNet Federation Consortium" and NSF grant #1032732 "SDCI Data Improvement: Improvement and Sustainability of iRODS Data Grid Software for Multi-Disciplinary Community Driven Application".

References

1. CCSDS. Reference Model for an Open Archival Information System (OAIS) (CCSDS 650.0-M-2). Magenta Book. National Aeronautics and Space Administration (NASA), Washington, DC (June 2012)
2. ISO/IEC 14721, Space data and information transfer systems – Open archival information system – Reference model (2003),
   http://www.iso.org/iso/catalogue_detail.htm?csnumber=24683
3. Conway, M.C., Ward, J.H., de Torcy, A., Xu, H., Rajasekar, A., Moore, R.W.: Policy-based Preservation Environments: Policy Composition and Enforcement in iRODS. Paper at the Society of American Archivists (SAA) 4th Annual Research Forum, Washington, D.C, August 12 (2010)
4. Nicholson, D., Dobreva, M.: Beyond OAIS: towards a reliable and consistent digital preservation implementation framework. Paper at the 16th International Conference on Digital Signal Processing, DSP 2009, July 5-7, Santorini, Greece (2009)
5. Waters, D., Garrett, J.: Preserving Digital Information. Report of the Task Force on Archiving of Digital Information. CLIR, Washington, DC (May 1996)
6. CCSDS. Requirements for bodies providing audit and certification of candidate trustworthy digital repositories recommended practice (CCSDS 652.1-M-1). Magenta Book. National Aeronautics and Space Administration (NASA), Washington, DC (November 2011)
7. Research Libraries Group. Trusted digital repositories: attributes and responsibilities an RLG-OCLC report. Research Libraries Group, Mountain View, CA (2002),
   http://www.oclc.org/content/dam/research/activities/
   trustedrep/repositories.pdf?urlm=161690 (retrieved July 13, 2013)
8. Moore, R.: Towards a Theory of Digital Preservation. International Journal of Digital Curation 3(1), 63–75 (2008)
9. ISO/IEC 17021, Conformity assessment – Requirements for bodies providing audit and certification of management systems (2011),
   http://www.iso.org/iso/iso_catalogue/catalogue_tc/
   catalogue_detail.htm?csnumber=56676 (retrieved December 30, 2011)
10. Greenberg, J.: A quantitative categorical analysis of metadata elements in image-applicable metadata schemas. Journal of the American Society for Information Science 52(11), 917–924 (2001)
11. NISO. Understanding Metadata. NISO Press, Bethesda (2001),
    http://www.niso.org/standards/resources/
    UnderstandingMetadata.pdf (retrieved July 13, 2013)
12. DCMI, Dublin Core Metadata Element Set (DCMES), Version 1.1 (2013),
    http://dublincore.org/documents/dces/ (retrieved July 17, 2013)

13. Library of Congress, MARC 21 XML Schema (2012),
    http://www.loc.gov/standards/marcxml/ (retrieved July 13, 2013)
14. Solove, D.J.: "I've got nothing to hide" and other misunderstandings of privacy. San Diego
    Law Review 44, 745–772 (2007)
15. Policy [Def. 1]. Oxford English Dictionary (2013),
    http://oxforddictionaries.com/definition/english/policy
    (retrieved July 15, 2013)
16. ISO/IEC 16363, Space data and information transfer systems – Audit and certification of
    trustworthy digital repositories (2012),
    http://www.iso.org/iso/iso_catalogue/catalogue_tc/
    catalogue_detail.htm?csnumber=56510
17. CCSDS. Audit and certification of trustworthy digital repositories recommended practice
    (CCSDS 652.0-M-1). Magenta Book. National Aeronautics and Space Administration
    (NASA), Washington, DC (September 2011)
18. Moore, R., Smith, M.: Automated Validation of Trusted Digital Repository Assessment
    Criteria. Journal of Digital Information 8(2) (2007),
    http://journals.tdl.org/jodi/article/view/198/181
    (retrieved March 2, 2010)
19. Research Libraries Group. An audit checklist for the certification of trusted digital reposi-
    tories, draft for public comment. Research Libraries Group, Mountain View, CA (2005),
    http://cdm267701.cdmhost.com/cdm/singleitem/collection/
    p267701coll33/id/408/rec/5 (retrieved August 20, 2013)
20. Marks, S.: Document Checklist. Trusted Digital Repository Documents (2012),
    http://spotdocs.scholarsportal.info/display/OAIS/
    Document+Checklist (retrieved August 20, 2013)
21. Rosenthal, D.S.H., Robertson, T., Lipkis, T., Reich, V., Morabito, S.: Requirements for
    digital preservation systems a bottom-up approach. D-Lib Magazine 11(11) (2005),
    http://www.dlib.org/dlib/november05/rosenthal/
    11rosenthal.html (retrieved August 20, 2013)
22. Berman, F., Fox, G.C., Hey, A.J.G.: Grid Computing. Wiley, West Sussex (2003)
23. Ward, J.H., Wan, M., Schroeder, W., Rajasekar, A., de Torcy, A., Russell, T., Xu, H.,
    Moore, R.W.: The integrated rule-oriented data system (iRODS) micro-service workbook.
    Data Intensive Cyberinfrastructure Foundation, La Jolla (2011)
24. Rajasekar, A., Moore, R., Wan, M., Schroeder, W.: Policy-based Distributed Data Man-
    agement Systems. Journal of Digital Information 11(1) (2010),
    http://journals.tdl.org/jodi/article/view/756
25. Hedges, M., Blanke, T., Hasan, A.: Rule-based curation and preservation of data: a data
    grid approach using iRODS. Future Generation Computer Systems 25, 446–452 (2009),
    http://www.sciencedirect.com/science/article/
    pii/S0167739X08001660
26. Fedora and the Preservation of University Records Project, 2.1 Ingest Guide, Version 1.0
    (tufts:central:dca:UA069:UA069.004.001.00006). Tufts University, Digital Collections
    and Archives, Tufts Digital Library (2006),
    http://repository01.lib.tufts.edu:8080/fedora/get/
    tufts:UA069.004.001.00006/bdef:TuftsPDF/getPDF

Tools and Techniques for Assessing Metadata Quality

Effie Tsiflidou and Nikos Manouselis

Agro-Know Technologies, Greece
effie@agroknow.gr, nikosm@ieee.org

Abstract. A significant amount of digital repository research and development activity is taking place worldwide. The quality of the metadata is considered really important for the main functionalities of a digital reportiory. In this paper we carry out a priliminary analysis of tools that can be used for the valid assessment of metadata records in a repository. More specifically, three different tools are studied and used to assess various quality metrics of metadata records. Then, an example quality assessment is presented for specific case study: the ProdInra open access repository. Finally, some conclusions are made and directions for the future work are identified.

Keywords: metadata quantitative analysis, metadata quality metrics, digital repositories, Google Refine, MINT.

1   Introduction

A significant amount of digital repository research and development activity is taking place worldwide. As Heery and Anderson (2005) also identify, digital content is deposited in a repository that possibly manages content, but typically manages metadata to offer a minimum set of basic services - for example, add, get, search and access control. Metadata are consider to be a key enabler to offer high quality services and search mechanisms on top of the digital repositories (Najjar et al., 2003; Shreeves et al., 2005; Yen and Park, 2006; Manouselis et al., 2010; Palavitsinis et al., 2012). Taking into consideration the aforementioned literature it is clear that high metadata quality should be one of the priorities within the development of a digital repository or content delivery services. One of the main concerns regarding the quality assessment of metadata in a digital repository is the fact that the process can be a time consuming and usually requires manual inspections of metadata records. There are several automatic approaches that are valuable but require the use of software tools (Vogias et al., 2013).

The main goal of this study is to present a benchmark of tools to support the metadata quality assessment. The tools presented are Google Refine[1], MINT[2] and a toolkit Agro-Know is currently developing called the AK Metadata Analytics Tool (Vogias et al., 2013). More specifically, in the paper we start by presenting some background

---

[1] http://code.google.com/p/google-refine/
[2] http://mint.image.ece.ntua.gr/

E. Garoufallou and J. Greenberg (Eds.): MTSR 2013, CCIS 390, pp. 99–110, 2013.
© Springer International Publishing Switzerland 2013

on the topic of the metadata quality and identify a number of metrics to be used for metadata analysis. Then we explain the methodology we have followed and the results of the tools' assessment. In the next section the case study of the metadata analysis of the ProdInra[3] repository with the tools used is presented. Concluding there is a discussion with the main outcomes of this study.

2   Background on Metadata Quality and Metrics

2.1   What Is Metadata Quality

The quality of the metadata records in a digital repository is considered really important for its main functionality that is to provide access to the resources. Additionally, other functionalities of the digital repository can be affected, such as out-dated information about the resources' URI preventing the accessibility to the resource (Ochoa et al., 2009).

According to (Ochoa et al., 2006) metadata quality refers to the quality of the information entered by indexers (human or automated) about a resource and stored in a metadata record. There are different approaches regarding the metadata quality of digital repositories. One case is to manually review a statistical sample of the records by comparing the values with those provided by metadata experts or with the use of visualization tools to help metadata experts in the task. Another approach is to collect statistical information from the metadata instances in the repositories to evaluate the usage of the metadata standard or to compare statistics on the metadata values in the repository and the values that are actually used in real searches (Najjar et al., 2004).

Many studies show that there is a significant problem with the quality of metadata in many digital collections, libraries and repositories (Heery and Anderson, 2005; Guy et al., 2004; Robertson, 2005). Greenberg & Robertson (2002) point out that accurate, consistent, sufficient, and thus reliable metadata is a powerful tool that enables the user to discover and retrieve relevant materials quickly and easily and to assess whether they may be suitable for reuse. Palavitsinis et al, (in press) underline the need of quality approaches assuring the metadata quality and study different approaches proposed in the literature. Additionally, in another study (Palavitsinis et al., in press-b) the authors developed a process that tries to address the way in which metadata quality can be improved in digital repositories.

2.2   Definitions of Metrics

The main goal of the present study is to evaluate certain tools in terms of their usability for the assessment of metadata quality. The quality metrics used in the present study for assessing metadata quality were based on previous studies of Bruce and Hillman (2004), Ochoa et al. (2006) and Vogias et al. (2013). In table 1 all the metrics and their definitions are presented.

---

[3] http://prodinra.inra.fr/

Table 1. Metrics used in the current study

Metric	Reference	Definition
Completeness	Bruce & Hillman (2004)	The percentage of records in which an element is used.
Element frequency	Ochoa et al. (2006)	This metric provides information about the number of values used in a metadata element
Entropy	Ochoa et al.(2006)	The entropy provides information about the amount of information that is included in an element.
Vocabularies Values distribution	Ochoa et al. (2006)	The metric is being used to study the frequency distribution of specific vocabulary values in controlled elements
Metadata multi-linguality for the free text elements (Language Attribution)	Vogias et al. (2013)	This metric is used to study the language attribute (eg. Lang=en) value usage frequency in free text metadata elements such as Title, Description and Keyword

3   Tools Assessment

The main purpose of this study is to define the tool or the tools for estimating metadata quality based on the quality metrics as these were presented on the previous chapter. In first place we decided to select two widely known, among data managers, tools, (a) Google Refine and (b) MINT and additionally (c) the metadata analysis tool that has been deployed by (Vogias et al. 2013). The reason for selecting Google Refine and MINT is because of their popularity among Information Scientists and digital repositories curators. The metadata analysis tool, called in this paper as AK metadata analysis tool, has been selected due to its specific functionalities that focus on the metadata analysis of digital repositories. The assessment was driven by the above-mentioned Quality Metrics testing whether these can be measured by each tool or not. One first remark during the assessment process was the fact that not all the metrics could be directly evaluated by some of the tools, but some additional tools and techniques need to take place. For that reason we have named each case correspondingly direct and indirect.

Table 2 demonstrates the results of this analysis. According to this, metadata Completeness and Entropy can be directly estimated using the AK metadata Analytics Tool. Element Frequency and Language Attribution are estimated using both AK Metadata Analytics Tool and MINT statistics. Last but not least, Vocabularies values distribution can be measured using all three tools. Additionally, in Google Refine can be indirectly estimated the metadata Completeness, Element Frequency and Language Attribution, while in MINT the metadata Completeness.

Table 2. Representative Results of the Tool Assessment

Metrics	AK-Metadata Analytics Tool	Google Refine	MINT statistics
Completeness	Yes	Indirect	Indirect
Element Frequency	Yes	Indirect	Yes
Entropy	Yes	No	No
Vocabularies values distribution	Yes	Yes	Yes
Language Attribution	Yes	Indirect	Yes

3.1   Google Refine

Google Refine is a tool for "working with messy data, cleaning it up, transforming it from one format into another, extending it with web services, and linking it to databases" [1]. Google Refine is a desktop application that needs to be downloaded and installed locally. However, it runs as a small web server on the computer pointing at the web browser at that web server in order to use it.

In this paper we study the possible use of Google Refine for evaluating the metadata quality of digital collections using specific metadata schemas (such as IEEE LOM and DC-based schemas). Google refine gives the opportunity either to upload data from computer files or giving a web address. Data can be in various formats like csv, xml/rdf, json etc. In the current study we have uploaded both an OAI PMH target and dump xml files. The OAI target belongs to the Traglor[4] educational repository following the IEEE LOM AP.

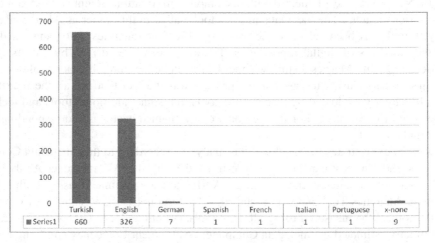

Fig. 1. Languages of the resources in the Traglor collection, counted using Google Refine

---

[4] http://traglor.cu.edu.tr/

What came as an outcome from the assessment regarding the Quality Metrics is that Google Refine can be used to measure the "Vocabularies Values Distribution" and the language attributes per element simply by applying the facet mode on the element evaluated (see fig 1). On the other hand, counting other metrics approved to be more complicated, and thus we marked them as indirect measurement. In Google Refine metadata completeness, metadata frequency, language attribute can be estimated indirectly. All these indirect measured metrics require exporting the collection in an excel file, rendering in that way excel as the actual tool of the metadata analysis.

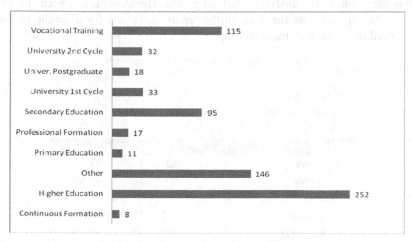

Fig. 2. Vocabulary values distribution in Traglor collection using Google Refine

3.2   MINT

MINT services compose a web based platform that was designed and developed to facilitate aggregation initiatives for cultural heritage content and metadata in Europe, by the National Technical University of Athens[5]. MINT has been adopted by various European Digital Libraries in the context of European funded projects, like the CARARE[6], ATHENA[7], EUROPEANA[8] and others. MINT aims to support a variety of aggregation workflows, such as the ingestion, mapping and aggregation of metadata records, and proceeds to implement a variety of remediation approaches for the resulting repository. The platform offers a user and organization management system that allows the deployment and operation of different aggregation schemes (thematic or cross-domain, international, national or regional) and corresponding access rights. Registered organizations can upload (http, ftp, oai-pmh) their metadata records in xml or csv serialization in order to manage, aggregate and publish their collections.

---

[5] http://www.ntua.gr/
[6] http://www.carare.eu/
[7] http://www.athenaeurope.org/
[8] http://www.europeana.eu/portal/

One of the services supplied in the platform is the data set statistics of the imported collection. MINT statistics count the element frequency, the number of the distinct values, and the average entry length (see Fig. 3). Thus, among the quality metrics that MINT can directly measure are the metadata frequency (see Fig. 4 and Fig. 3), Language attribution per element (fig. 5) and Vocabulary values distribution (Fig. 4). Additionally MINT can be used to measure Metadata Completeness. This metric is counted indirectly, comparing the "count" number to the total number of resources.

Although MINT offers a nice tool to measure the aforementioned quality metrics, exporting the results of the analysis is not supported. Therefore, if one needs to get the results in other applications for some further analysis, or just for a simple reporting s/he will need to "manually" them pick-up.

element	count	distinct	length
🗁 openarchives:lom			
⊡ @xsi:schemaLocation	363	1	74.0
🗁 ltsc:general			
🗁 ltsc:identifier			
⊡ ltsc:catalog	363	1	3.0
⊡ ltsc:entry	363	363	58.70248
🗁 ltsc:title			
🗁 ltsc:string	1497	1360	24.219105
⊡ @language	1497	10	2.005344

Fig. 3. MINT data set statistics

Value	Frequency
drill and practice	340
enquiry-oriented activity	15
exploration	8
project	1

Value	Frequency
en	363
et	362
ru	358
lv	357
hu	11
no	11

Fig. 4. Vocabulary values distribution on MINT

Fig. 5. Language Attribution per element on MINT

3.3   AK Metadata Analytics Tool

AK Metadata Analytics Tool has been deployed by (Vogias et al., 2013). The tool was developed using JAVA and its purpose is to analyze XML documents and export the results to a human readable format (CSV). As a first step, it performs a per repository analysis and as a second step it performs the analysis of the repositories at the aggregation level. The metrics that are being calculated are the element Frequency, metadata Completeness, Element Entropy and Vocabularies values distribution. Additionally, an attribute based value analysis (attribute value frequency) is also implemented that can be used to study the multilinguality of the free text metadata elements. The AK Metadata Analytics Tool is a JAVA program that needs to be installed locally in the computer and run on a command prompt. Although it lacks in terms of usability in comparison to the previous tools that both are web based and user friendly applications, once learned it is much easier to calculate metrics and get the results.

Table 3. Language element distribution for UVED repository

Element Used	Attribute	Frequency
Description	Fre	298
Description	Eng	15
Educational description	Fre	24
Installation remarks	Fre	271
Keyword	Fre	1072
Keyword	Eng	1071
Title	Fre	298
Title	Eng	16
Typical Age Range	Fre	12

Table 4. Metadata completeness (%) for the UVED collection

Element Name	Completeness(%)
Context	100
Intended end user role	100
Learning Resource Type	100
Typical Age Range	4,026845
Identifier	100
Keyword	100
Language	100
Title	100
Contribute Entity	98,99329
Metametadata Identifier	93,95973
Metametadata Language	98,99329
Rights Cost	100
Format	100
Location	100

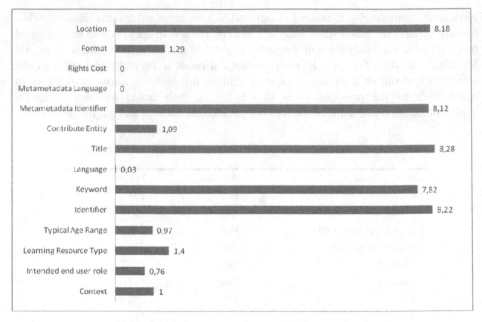

Fig. 6. Average entropy for the UVED metadata

4   Case Study: The ProdInra Collection

4.1   The Data Set

ProdInra[9] is an open archive and also a database designed to store references of scientific research works of INRA. INRA is the French National Institute for Agricultural Research[10]. In the context of the current study the subset of agro-ecology has been analyzed. The collection has main interest in research publications related to organic agriculture, like theses, journals, articles and reports.

In first place, using the OAI-PMH target we harvested the XML records of the agro-ecology subset. The total number of the records was 2.407 and the metadata format followed is the Organic Edunet IEEE LOM Application Profile[11] (OE IEEE LOM AP). For the analysis we have used AK-Metadata Analytics Tools and MINT statistics. Metadata completeness, Elements Frequency, metadata Multi-linguality for the free text elements (Language Attribute) and metadata Entropy were calculated using the AK-Metadata Analytics Tool, while Vocabularies distribution were estimated in the MINT statistics.

---

[9] http://prodinra.inra.fr/
[10] http://www.inra.fr
[11] http://wiki.organic-lingua.eu/
    Organic.Edunet_Metadata_Application_Profile

4.2   Results

In the current study we have used metadata Completeness metric in order to assess the compliance of the evaluated repository towards the OE IEEE LOM AP and more specifically towards the obligation of the elements. Therefore, in first place we are interested in the completeness of the mandatory elements (M) and secondly of the recommended elements (R). The analysis showed that almost all the mandatory elements are 100% complete, with the description element being completed 60.98%. On the other hand most of the recommended were 100% completed (see Table 5).

Table 5. Average Completeness and Frequency values for a selected set of elements on ProdInra collection

Element Name	Obligation	Frequency	Completeness(%)
lom.educational.context.value	R	2277.0	94.59
lom.educational.intendedenduserrole.value	R	2407.0	100.0
lom.educational.learningresourcetype.value	R	2407.0	100.0
lom.general.description.string	M	2110.0	60.98
lom.general.identifier.catalog	M	2407.0	100.0
lom.general.identifier.entry	M	2407.0	100.0
lom.general.keyword.string	R	39050.0	100.0
lom.general.language	R	2407.0	100.0
lom.general.title.string	M	3080.0	100.0
lom.lifecycle.contribute.entity	R	10186.0	100.0
lom.lifecycle.contribute.role.value	R	10186.0	100.0
lom.rights.copyrightandotherrestrictions.value	M	2407.0	100.0
lom.technical.format	R	2519.0	100.0
lom.technical.location	M	2407.0	100.0

According to the language attribute analysis ProdInra agro-ecology collection provides metadata in several languages, such as English, French, Spanish, Portuguese, Italian and others. In keywords and descriptions the language attribute used mostly is English, while in Titles is the French language.

The analysis of the elements Entropy aimed to measure the diversity of the information hold on the metadata. An element that holds high values of entropy means that there is a variety on the element values, therefore this elements holds mere information. Entropy can be really useful to extract conclusions about the use of vocabulary elements. For instance a high value of the technical format element shows that the variety of the different types of resources (text, videos, audio etc.).

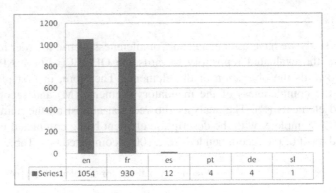

Fig. 7. Description language attribute for ProdInra collection

Table 6. Average entropy for ProdInra collection

Element Name	Entropy
lom.educational.context.value	0.0
lom.educational.difficulty.value	0.373
lom.educational.intendedenduserrole.value	0.0
lom.educational.learningresourcetype.value	0.0
lom.general.description.string	10.045
lom.general.identifier.catalog	0.0
lom.general.identifier.entry	11.233
lom.general.keyword.string	12.052
lom.general.language	1.041
lom.general.title.string	11.511
lom.lifecycle.contribute.entity	3.378
lom.lifecycle.contribute.role.value	1.052
lom.rights.copyrightandotherrestrictions.value	0.0
lom.technical.format	0.038
lom.technical.location	11.233

In the current work we have studied the contribute.role and technical.format vocabulary elements. Taking into consideration that ProdInra collection holds mostly research papers then we can estimate that authors, editors and publishers are expected to be the most frequent used values. Additionally, the technical format values provide information regarding the type of resources accessible through the collection.

Statistics for the Element ⊡ltsc:value	
Value	Frequency
author	7612
unknown	2033
publisher	404
editor	126
subject matter expert	10
validator	1

Statistics for the Element ⊡ltsc:format	
Value	Frequency
application/pdf	2510
application/octet-stream	6
text/html	2
image/jpeg	1

Fig. 8. Contribute.role vocabulary values distribution

Fig. 9. Format vocabulary values distribution

5   Conclusions and Directions for Future Research

This paper presented the process of a statistical evaluation analysis of the metadata elements of a digital repository. In first place we have selected the tools that were used to support the analysis and then we defined the quality metrics to be used. Following, we set the first experiment that was assessing the tools according to the quality metrics that have been defined. The aim of this assessment was to present the different uses of the evaluated tools for measuring different metadata quality metrics. Based on the results as these were presented on Table 2 we decided to use both Ak-Metadata Analytics tool and the MINT statistics. With the first one the metadata completeness, elements Frequency, elements entropy and the Language attribute were analyzed, while we used the MINT statistics to present the Vocabularies values distribution.

The aim of the present study was to define the tools and techniques that can be used for the assessment of metadata quality in terms of statistical analysis. Next steps of the current work will be the use of the presented tools and techniques in order to evaluate large scaled web2.0 data sets in terms of their metadata quality.

Disclaimer: The content of this publication does not reflect the official opinion of the European Union. Responsibility for the information and views expressed in the publication lies entirely with the author(s).

Acknowledgements. The work presented in this paper has been funded with support by the European Commission, and more specifically the project "Organic Lingua" of the ICT PSP Programme. All authors have been supported with funding by Agro-Know Technologies during the implementation of this work, in the context of the above mentioned EU project.

References

1. Currier, S., Barton, J., O'Beirne, R., Ryan, B.: Quality assurance for digital learning object repositories: issues for the metadata creation process. Association for Learning Technology Journal 12(1), 5–20 (2004)
2. Margaritopoulos, T., Margaritopoulos, M., Mavridis, I., Manitsaris, A.: A conceptual framework for metadata quality assessment. Universitätsverlag Göttingen, 104 (2008)
3. Palavitsinis, N., Manouselis, N., Sanchez Alonso, S.: Evaluation of a Metadata Application Profile for Learning Resources on Organic Agriculture. In: Sartori, F., Sicilia, M.Á., Manouselis, N. (eds.) MTSR 2009. CCIS, vol. 46, pp. 270–281. Springer, Heidelberg (2009)
4. Heery, R., Anderson, S.: Digital repositories review. UKOLN and Arts and Humanities Data Service, Bath (2005),
   http://www.jisc.ac.uk/uploaded_documents/
   digital-repositories-review-2005.pdf (retrieved November 15, 2007)
5. Greenberg, J., Robertson, W.: Semantic web construction: an inquiry of authors' views on collaborative metadata generation. In: Proceedings of the International Conference on Dublin Core and Metadata for e-Communities 2002, pp. 45–52 (2002)
6. Vogias, K., Hatzakis, I., Manouselis, N., Szegedi, P.: Extraction and Visualization of Metadata Analytics for Multimedia Learning Repositories: the case of Terena TF-media network. In: Proceedings of the LACRO 2013 Workshop (2013)
7. Najjar, J., Ternier, S., Duval, E.: The actual use of metadata in ARIADNE: an empirical analysis. In: Proceedings of the 3rd Annual ARIADNE Conference, pp. 1–6 (October 2003)
8. Bui, Y., Park, J.R.: An assessment of metadata quality: A case study of the national science digital library metadata repository (2006)
9. Ochoa, X., Duval, E.: Quality Metrics for learning object Metadata. In: Proceedings of World Conference on Educational Multimedia, Hypermedia and Telecommunications 2006, pp. 1004–1011 (2006)
10. Ochoa, X., Duval, E.: Quantitative analysis of learning object repositories. IEEE Transactions on Learning Technologies 2(3), 226–238 (2009)
11. Ochoa, X., Duval, E.: Automatic evaluation of metadata quality in digital repositories. International Journal on Digital Libraries 10(2-3), 67–91 (2009)
12. Palavitsinis, N., Manouselis, N., Sanchez, S.: Metadata Quality in Learning Object Repositories: A Case Study. The Electronic Library (in press)
13. Palavitsinis, N., Manouselis, N., Sanchez, S.: Metadata Quality in Digital Repositories: Empirical Results from the Cross-Domain Transfer of a Quality Assurance Process. Journal of the American Society for Information Science and Technology (in press-b)

Applying the Nominal Group Technique for Metadata Training of Domain Experts

Nikos Palavitsinis[1,2], Nikos Manouselis[2], and Charalampos Karagiannidis[3]

[1] University of Alcala de Henares, 28871 Alcalá de Henares, Madrid, Spain
palavitsinis@uah.es
[2] Agro-Know Technologies, 17 Grammou Str, Vrilissia, Athens, Greece, 15235
{palavitsinis,nikosm}@agroknow.gr
[3] University of Thessaly, Department of Special Education, Volos, Greece
karagian@uth.gr

Abstract. Low metadata quality is a problem faced by most digital repositories, affecting resource discoverability and the overall quality of services and search mechanisms that are supported by these repositories. Metadata training of human annotators presents itself as a major challenge to contribute towards higher metadata quality for the digital resources hosted in repositories. This paper discusses the positive results of previous approaches to metadata training in the cases of a educational, cultural and scientific/research repositories, and it attempts to improve them by using the Nominal Group technique.

Keywords: metadata, training, domain experts, evaluation.

1   Introduction

A large number of studies indicate that the quality of metadata is problematic in various repositories that host different types of digital content, ranging from the educational domain, to the research and cultural domains (Najjar et al., 2003; Stvilia et al., 2004; Shreeves et al., 2005; Yen & Park, 2006; Stvilia et al., 2007; Ochoa et al., 2011; Goovaerts & Leinders, 2012). Therefore metadata quality problems are inherent in repositories hosting any type of content. Although different annotators may produce different types of errors depending on their background and metadata knowledge (Cechinel et al., 2009), still the existence of any error in metadata is of the same importance for the services deployed over them. Drawing from the above, the need for addressing the problematic perception of metadata elements applies to all the types of content, repositories and annotators.

Taking this into account, this paper proposes an approach that is based on the Nominal Group technique (Van de Ven & Delbecq, 1972) for working with annotators on metadata concepts and application profile elements. This improvement in metadata understanding is expected to help the annotators to provide metadata of higher quality in the long term. To this direction, this paper presents results from a series of metadata understanding sessions held through a period of three years, and builds upon them to present an improved version which was deployed in a recent

E. Garoufallou and J. Greenberg (Eds.): MTSR 2013, CCIS 390, pp. 111–122, 2013.

metadata understanding session. The study concludes by building on, and extending these results to suggest an improved version of the metadata understanding session.

The remainder of this paper is structured as follows: Chapter 2 presents the background work that contributed to this paper whereas chapter 3 presents the improved Metadata Understanding Session process. Chapter 4 discusses the findings of the experiment whereas chapter 5 contributes a revised version of the MUS enhanced with aspects of an existing design-thinking process that is already tested in the environmental domain. Finally, chapter 6 outlines the main conclusions of the paper and provides directions for future research.

2   Background

In previous experiments, we applied the Metadata Quality Assurances Certification Process (MQACP) (Palavitsinis et al., *in press-a*) in the case of educational, cultural and research collections. This process is designed to support the metadata annotators through the various stages of a repository lifecycle, aiming to improve the metadata understanding and metadata creation processes. In the first step of the MQACP, a Metadata Understanding Session (MUS) is organized with domain experts coming from content providers to allow for the better understanding of the metadata application profile used in a specific repository. During these sessions, the domain experts are presented with a metadata application profile along with some examples of use and at the same time are asked to provide their input related to the following questions:

-    Is this element easy to understand?
-    Is this element useful for describing digital resources?
-    How important is the information contained in this element for you?

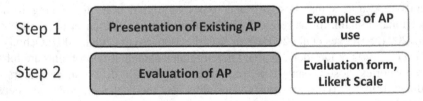

Fig. 1. Metadata Understanding Session Process

Each question is answered by choosing one value from a 5-point Likert Scale in the first two questions and by answering in terms of being mandatory, recommended or optional in the last one. Looking at results from previous experiments we see that the average perceived easiness in the case of domain experts of the research/scientific domain is relatively high as was the average perceived usefulness for the examined elements with enough room for improvement.

Table 1. Metadata understanding session results from (Palavitsinis *et al., in press-b*)

Domain	Base Schema/ Standard	Average Easiness	Average Usefulness	# of Elements	Experts Involved
Educational	IEEE LOM	3.7	3.4	57	17
Cultural	Dublin Core – ESE	3.9	4.1	29	11
Scientific	Dublin Core	4.1	4.2	35	16

In general, in all three cases, average scores are relatively high. However, if we exclude some common and easier to understand elements such as title and description the situation changes significantly. All the other elements, including also domain-specific ones that are of high value when deploying search mechanisms over the content itself, are rated even lower, showing problems in terms of understanding and perceived usefulness.

Table 2. Metadata understanding session results on non-common elements of the respective application profiles

Domain	Average Easiness	Diff	Average Usefulness	Diff
Educational	3.5	-0.2	3.1	-0.3
Cultural	3.8	-0.1	4.1	-0.1
Scientific	4	-0.1	4	-0.2

Looking at these results, our goal was to improve the specific process within the MQACP, so that a deeper understanding of the metadata and the metadata creation process can be provided to the domain experts that participate in these sessions. To this direction, we built on the literature related to working with groups of people in terms of maximizing the learning outcomes from this process and selected to apply the Nominal Group technique that is a structured process which taps the experiences and skills of participants. The process described by Delp at al., (1977) is as follows:

- A question is posed to the group,
- Each member writes down as many responses as possible,
- The group leader asks each member in turn to state an idea from his or her list and writes it on a flip chart placed before the group. No discussion is permitted until all ideas have been listed,
- Each item is then briefly discussed in an interacting group format,
- The participants indicate their preference for important items by rank-ordering, a process which may be repeated with intervening discussion and argument.

The outcome of the process is the mathematical aggregation of each member's preferences to give the group's ranking of responses to the question. Also looking into relevant literature related to teamwork and group dynamics (Jablin, 1981; VanGundy, 1988; Richardson & Andersen, 1995 and Andersen & Richardson, 1997) we developed a new approach for the metadata understanding session that based on the literature would address the following issues:

- Alignment of the perception of domain experts on metadata,
- Creation of consensus about the use of specific metadata elements,
- Generation of commitment among the metadata annotators to use the metadata elements that were decided within the group, in the long term,
- Efficient use of the time at our disposal,
- Balance between the level of guidance and the freedom level for the participants within the process itself.

3   Metadata Understanding Session Process

In order to enhance the domain expert experience in terms of the metadata and allow for their understanding which can in turn yield higher quality metadata, we introduced a set of steps prior to the presentation and evaluation of the application profile. These steps aim to help the domain experts work with metadata in a seamless way, focusing on the actual usefulness of describing a digital resource with metadata. To this end, we structured the process shown in Figure 2.

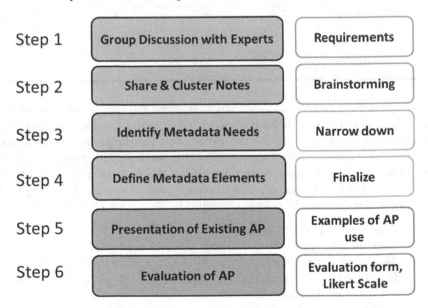

Fig. 2. Enhanced Metadata Understanding Session Process

- **Step 1**: The experts are presented with the challenge to think of attributes that would describe a digital resource related to their profession or professional activities. During this step, the experts note down some attributes that they consider useful for describing digital resources,
- **Step 2**: The experts share their notes on a common space, elaborating on the reason behind their choice and following that, once all the notes are shared, the group of experts is asked to cluster all the different attributes in groups, based on their similarity or relation,
- **Step 3**: The experts are asked to choose only the attributes they deem necessary for their needs, leaving out the ones that are too generic or considered useless by the majority,
- **Step 4**: The experts are asked to label the attributes with a name, label the clusters in which they have grouped them and finalize the schema with all the attributes.
- **Step 5**: The experts are presented with an existing application profile that describes digital objects containing specific examples of the element usage,
- **Step 6**: The experts are provided with an evaluation form containing all the presented elements along with the questions that were also used in the original approach to the Metadata Understanding Session.

The rationale behind this attempt is to allow the experts to work with metadata in a more abstract way helping them understand the basics of metadata annotation without intimidating them with technical terms or complex structures of metadata. In this way, once they are presented with an existing application profile in steps 5 and 6 and are asked to evaluate it, the results would hypothetically be better than in previous metadata understanding sessions since they would have some prior experience with the basics of metadata.

4   Findings

To test the new approach, we organized a MUS within a summer school on new technologies on agriculture and the environment. Our goal in this session was to evaluate the elements of a metadata application profile describing job profiles in the agricultural and environmental domain. The group that attended the specific session comprised of fifteen (15) domain experts from the agricultural and wider environmental field, including farmers (5), biologists (5) and chemists (5). The process followed in this session was one described in the previous section using the form presented in Figure 3 to collect the evaluations on the application profile presented.

The results from the metadata understanding session were far from encouraging. More specifically, out of a total of 30 elements, 24 were rated with an easiness to understand of 3.5 or more out of 5, whereas 14 of them (less than half) were considered useful with a score of 3.5 and above. The biggest problem was that from a total of fifteen experts, eleven of them understood the overall application profile at a

NO	ELEMENT	Is this attribute easy to understand?					Do you think it's useful for describing job profiles?					How necessary is it to have it?		
1	Identifier													
1.1	Catalog	1	2	3	4	5	1	2	3	4	5	1	2	3
1.2	Entry	1	2	3	4	5	1	2	3	4	5	1	2	3
2	Organization													
2.1	Name	1	2	3	4	5	1	2	3	4	5	1	2	3
2.2	Telephone	1	2	3	4	5	1	2	3	4	5	1	2	3
2.3	Address	1	2	3	4	5	1	2	3	4	5	1	2	3
2.4	Country	1	2	3	4	5	1	2	3	4	5	1	2	3
2.5	Email	1	2	3	4	5	1	2	3	4	5	1	2	3
2.6	Url	1	2	3	4	5	1	2	3	4	5	1	2	3
2.7	Type	1	2	3	4	5	1	2	3	4	5	1	2	3
2.8	Size	1	2	3	4	5	1	2	3	4	5	1	2	3
2.9	Coverage	1	2	3	4	5	1	2	3	4	5	1	2	3
2.10	Region	1	2	3	4	5	1	2	3	4	5	1	2	3

Fig. 3. Evaluation Form for Job Profiles Application Profile

satisfying degree so that they could provide their evaluation whereas the remaining seven, did not complete the evaluation questionnaire at all. In addition to that, from the eleven people that turned in their evaluations, only seven of them provided evaluations for all the elements.

Table 3. Results from the metadata understanding session

NO	ELEMENT	Easiness to understand	Usefulness	NO	ELEMENT	Easiness to understand	Usefulness
1	Identifier			4	Relation		
1.1	Catalog	3.0	3.2	4.1	Resource		
1.2	Entry	3.0	3.2	4.1.1	Identifier		
2	Organization			4.1.1.1	Catalog	3.9	3.4
2.1	Name	4.9	4.3	4.1.1.2	Entry	3.8	3.6
2.2	Telephone	4.9	4.1	4.2	Source	3.5	3.0
2.3	Address	4.9	4.0	4.3	Scale	3.7	3.2
2.4	Country	4.9	4.2	4.4	Operator	3.6	3.3
2.5	Email	4.9	4.3	5	Classification		
2.6	URL	4.4	3.3	5.1	Taxon Path		
2.7	Type	4.0	3.5	5.1.1	Source	3.5	3.0
2.8	Size	4.2	3.1	5.1.2	Taxon		
2.9	Coverage	4.4	3.9	5.1.2.1	Id	3.3	3.7
2.10	Region	4.8	3.4	5.1.2.2	Entry	3.4	3.7
3	Job Description			6	Meta-Metadata		
3.1	Title	4.7	4.2	6.1	Contribute		
3.2	Description	4.8	4.9	6.1.1	Role	4.0	3.3
3.3	Target Group	4.5	4.0	6.1.2	User	3.6	2.9
3.4	No. of employees	4.6	3.3	6.1.3	Date	3.4	2.7
				6.2	Schema	3.4	2.9
				6.3	Language	4.0	3.6
				6.4	Status	3.6	3.0

Looking at the results yielded in the previous experiments again, we see that with the introduction of the extra steps in the process, no significant improvement was made. More specifically, the results in the case of job profiles in terms of easiness were not higher than in the case of scientific/research repositories. Similarly, the usefulness was higher than in the case of educational repositories but still lower than in the other two cases.

Table 4. Comparison of results from previous MUSs with the last one

Domain	Average Easiness	Average Usefulness	# of Elements	Experts Involved
Educational	3.7	3.4	57	17
Cultural	3.9	4.1	29	11
Scientific/Research	4.1	4.2	35	16
Job Profiles	4.1	3.5	30	15

5   Creative Metadata Understanding Session

One lesson learned from the previous Metadata Understanding Sessions was that the reference to terms such as metadata or related technical terms is problematic for domain experts. To this end, in the new approach to the MUS, any reference to such terms is avoided to make sure that the participants that are mostly domain experts are not confused. To this end, in the description of the phases, both here and during the actual workshop, the terms that follow are replaced with terms that are generic and understandable:

-    Metadata element: Attribute
-    Element value/vocabulary: Value
-    Metadata Schema: Set of attributes

In addition, we adapted an existing approach developed by Agro-Know Technologies (the AK Creativity Package), used with communities of domain experts to generate ideas on environmental issues. To this end, we increased the steps of the process and grouped them in broader categories to map in a more efficient way the components of an application profile on which we wanted to train the domain experts.

In Figure 4, an overview of the Creative MUS approach is presented, with the main phases and the sub-phases in which they are broken down. Roughly, the first phase is intended to serve as an introduction to metadata where the domain experts discuss amongst them related to their needs whereas in the second phase, the discussion becomes more specific focusing on specific elements. In the third phase, the discussion revolves around vocabularies, allowing the experts to gain a better understanding of the elements through the values they take. Finally, in the last step, the existing application profile that we need to the experts to work with is presented to them and their evaluations are collected.

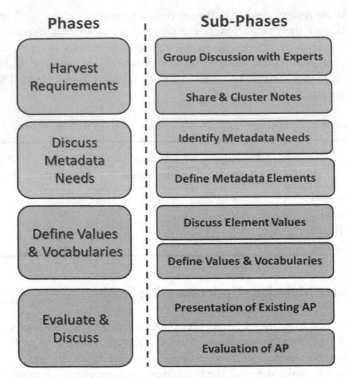

Fig. 4. Overview of Creative MUS process

5.1   Harvest Requirements

During this phase, the participants of the Metadata Understanding Session try to collect requirements related to the metadata that they would need in order to describe a digital resource. To do so, the process used, discusses about metadata in an indirect way, so as not to confuse participants with technical terms.

Group Discussion with Experts
The participants are posed with a question, related to their needs when describing or searching for digital content on their subject. More specifically, they are asked to write on a post-it and share with the group, the attributes of a digital resource they would provide for a resource they would create themselves. In the same sense, they are also asked which attributes they would like to be able to use when searching through this content, in a search engine or portal. The two questions posed to the group are the following:

-    Which attributes of the digital object you create would you consider important for a person that wants to use it? Title? Description? Other attributes?
-    When searching for digital content online, which attributes of a digital object would you consider important when searching? Its size? Its title? Other?

To manage and direct the discussion, a facilitator is appointed who provides the questions above to the participants and makes sure that the timing is kept. Once the questions are given to the group, each participant is given ten (10) minutes to think the questions on their own and take notes.

Share and Cluster Notes

Once all the participants have their notes, they are asked to share on a common space, the attributes they came up with, explaining the rationale to the group. All the notes are put on the wall with no specific order, and the participants take turns to provide their view on the questions posed in the beginning. During this phase, the facilitator may also coordinate a discussion among the participants, as there can be different opinions related to the attributes that each participant chooses. To continue with, the notes are collected on the wall and the participants are asked to approach and try to create clusters of similar attributes, that is connect similar of them, others that might refer to metadata elements that may belong under the same category, etc. Coming out of this part, the participants have to have a group of clusters that correspond more or less to the high level metadata categories of a metadata standard, i.e. the General, Lifecycle, Educational, etc. categories of the IEEE LOM standard. The purpose of this exercise is to give to the participants the perception of the actual organization of the data that may "follow" a digital object that is the metadata record itself.

5.2   Discuss Metadata Needs

During this phase, the group is introduced to the needs of organizing the information that will describe the digital object into a coherent schema of information so that the provision of this information during the creation of a new digital object is made easier to understand and carry out. No reference to metadata is made yet, to avoid confusion with the technical terms involved.

Identify Metadata Needs

The participants are asked to revisit the clusters of attributes that they created and decide on the ones that are necessary for the description of the digital object. They are asked to keep the ones that are either really important or less important for them, excluding only the ones that are of minor importance for them. The process of deciding on the retention of the attributes or not, is carried out by the group with no intervention of the facilitator other than answer any trivial questions about the expected outcomes of the process.

Define Metadata Elements

Having kept the attributes that the participants deem as necessary, the facilitator asks them to title the clusters of attributes with one word, so that they provide a concrete title for each one. The same exercise is carried out for each attribute. In this case, next to the post-its describing the attribute, a new post-it is placed with one or two words that represent the title for this attribute and consequently the metadata element that will be created from it. This part of the process is completed with the participants having a final attribute set arranged in categories.

5.3   Define Values and Vocabularies

During this phase, the participants of the Metadata Understanding Session are starting to familiarize themselves with the process of structuring a metadata application profile by defining the values that each element can take, whether it's a free-text field or a field that contains a vocabulary, ontology, etc.

Discuss Element Values
The facilitator asks the participants to place the attributes that they have decided upon on a new space and use post-its again to define the type of values that these attributes would take. The participants are split into groups corresponding to one or two categories of elements as these are decided previously. Each group is given twenty (20) minutes to think on the values that these attributes would take. Once they are finished, the groups come together and each group shares their view of the possible values. Answers here may include specific values such as "user, teacher, author", etc. or ranges of values, i.e. "10-100" or even specific ontologies that the participants know of. As the groups share their views on the values, other groups are allowed to add upon what they hear so that they enrich the notes taken and also contribute themselves to other element categories.

Define Values and Vocabularies
Finishing with the sharing of the possible element values, the participants are asked to decide on the final value of each attribute in the cases where more than one possibility is discussed within the groups. Finishing with this phase, the participants have defined the set of attributes they need to describe a digital object, they have clustered them into groups of attributes with a specific title and they have also defined the possible values of all attributes in all groups.

5.4   Evaluate and Discuss

During this phase, the time has come to expose the participants to a completed metadata application profile that is already used to describe digital objects. The presentation of this application profile follows, to allow the participants to make the connection between what they have defined and what is presented.

Presentation of Existing AP
During this phase the actual application profile is presented, element by element providing also examples of use for each one. The participants already have a form in their hands, where they are asked to rate each element that is presented using a 5 point Likert scale, in terms of the following (1 being the lowest):

-     Is this element easy to understand?
-     Is this element useful for describing digital resources?
-     How important is this element?

Evaluation of Existing AP
During this phase that is almost parallel to the previous, the participants complete their evaluations of the elements as these are presented and a discussion follows that is facilitated by the workshop facilitator, related to the similarities and differences between the attributes/elements defined by the participants and the ones proposed by the actual application profile.

Following the principle of strict time management that the "Guided Brainstorming" technique dictates, we limit the work of the domain experts in each phase to the following times provided in Table 5. The facilitator of the Creative MUS has to make sure that the groups working with the metadata concepts finish with each assignment given to them on time so that the process moves along quickly.

Table 5. Timing of the Creative MUS

Phase	Proposed Time
1. Harvest Requirements	**40'**
1.1 Group Discussion with Experts	20'
1.2 Share & Cluster Notes	20'
2. Discuss Metadata Needs	**30'**
2.1 Identify Metadata Needs	15'
2.2 Define Metadata Elements	15'
3. Define Values & Vocabularies	**35'**
3.1 Discuss Element Values	20'
3.2 Define Values & Vocabularies	15'
4. Evaluate & Discuss	**45'**
4.1 Presentation of Application Profile	30'
4.2 Evaluation of Application Profile	15'
TOTAL	**150'**

6   Conclusions

In this paper we showcased the results from a series of Metadata Understanding Sessions based on different approaches, showing similar results in terms of the understanding of a group of domain experts related to metadata. Although the results using the proposed approaches were satisfying, there's still enough room for improving them. To achieve this, based on these findings, we revised the proposed MUS into a Creative MUS, that incorporates brainstorming techniques and team work principles as these were proven effective in a different application context, oriented to generating ideas in the environmental domain.

One of the positive aspects of this process is that it is "domain agnostic", i.e. that it can be applied in different domains so that experts of different fields can enhance their understanding about metadata. The proposed approach aims to form the basis for the development of a comprehensive metadata training curriculum, which will incorporate innovative learning techniques targeting a better understanding of metadata from domain experts and therefore higher quality in the resulting metadata records. Future work will also focus more on the theoretical background of the brainstorming techniques adopted and research into other alternatives that can be used for the same purpose. Furthermore, the approach will be tested with real users to assess its effectiveness in comparison to previous approaches deployed. An interesting prospect for this research would be to adapt it to allow for its application online, for communities of users that contribute content online and seek metadata training without the need for physical presence.

References

1. Andersen, D.F., Richardson, G.P.: Scripts for group model-building. System Dynamics Review 13(2), 107–129 (1997)
2. Cechinel, C., Sánchez-Alonso, S., Sicilia, M.Á.: Empirical analysis of errors on human-generated learning objects metadata. In: Sartori, F., Sicilia, M.Á., Manouselis, N. (eds.) MTSR 2009. CCIS, vol. 46, pp. 60–70. Springer, Heidelberg (2009)
3. Delp, P., Thesen, A., Motiwalla, J., Seshardi, N.: Systems tools for project planning. International Development Institute, Bloomington (1977)
4. Gallagher, M., Hares, T., Spencer, J., Bradshaw, C., Webb, I.: he nominal group technique: a research tool for general practice? Fam. Pract. 10(1), 76–81 (1993)
5. Goovaerts, M., Leinders, D.: Metadata quality evaluation of a repository based on a sample technique. In: Dodero, J.M., Palomo-Duarte, M., Karampiperis, P. (eds.) MTSR 2012. CCIS, vol. 343, pp. 181–189. Springer, Heidelberg (2012)
6. Jablin, F.M.: Cultivating imagination: Factors that enhance and inhibit creativity in brainstorming groups. Human Communication Research 7, 245–258 (1981)
7. Najjar, J., Ternier, S., Duval, E.: The Actual Use of Metadata in ARIADNE: An Empirical Analysis. In: ARIADNE 3rd Conference (2003)
8. Ochoa, X., Klerkx, J., Vandeputte, B., Duval, E.: On the use of Learning Object Metadata: the GLOBE experience. In: Kloos, C.D., Gillet, D., Crespo García, R.M., Wild, F., Wolpers, M. (eds.) EC-TEL 2011. LNCS, vol. 6964, pp. 271–284. Springer, Heidelberg (2011)
9. Palavitsinis, N., Manouselis, N., Sanchez, S.: Metadata Quality in Learning Object Repositories: A Case Study. The Electronic Library (in press-a)
10. Palavitsinis, N., Manouselis, N., Sanchez, S.: Metadata Quality in Digital Repositories: Empirical Results from the Cross-Domain Transfer of a Quality Assurance Process. Journal of the American Society for Information Science and Technology (in press-b)
11. Richardson, G.P., Andersen, D.F.: Teamwork in Group Model Building. System Dynamics Review 11(2), 113–137 (1995)
12. Shreeves, S., Knutson, E., Stvilia, B., Palmer, C., Twidale, M., Cole, T.: Is 'quality' metadata 'shareable' metadata? The implications of local metadata practices for federated collections. In: Proceedings of the Association of College and Research Libraries (ACRL) 12th National Conference, Minneapolis, MN (2005)
13. Stvilia, B., Gasser, L., Twidale, M., Shreeves, S., Cole, T.: Metadata quality for federated collections. In: Proceedings of ICIQ 2004 - 9th International Conference on Information Quality, Boston, MA, pp. 111–125 (2004)
14. Stvilia, B., Gasser, L., Twidale, M.: A framework for information quality assessment. Journal of the American Society for Information Science and Technology 58(12), 1720–1733 (2007)
15. VanGundy, A.B.: Techniques of Structured Problem Solving, 2nd edn. Van Nostrand Reinhold Company, New York (1988)
16. Van de Ven, A.H., Delbecq, A.L.: The nominal group as a research instrument for exploratory health studies. American Journal of Public Health 62(3), 337–342 (1972)
17. Vennix, J.: Group model-building: tackling messy problems. System Dynamics Review 15, 379–401 (1999)
18. Yen, B., Park, J.: An assessment of metadata quality: A case study of the national science digital library metadata repository. In: Moukdad, H. (ed.) CAIS/ACSI 2006 Information Science Revisited: Approaches to Innovation (2006)

Encoding Provenance Metadata
for Social Science Datasets

Carl Lagoze[1], Jeremy Willliams[2], and Lars Vilhuber[3]

[1] School of Information, University of Michigan, Ann Arbor, MI
clagoze@umich.edu
[2] Cornell Institute for Social and Economic Research, Cornell University, Ithaca, NY
jw568@cornell.edu
[3] School of Industrial and Labor Relations, Cornell University, Ithaca, NY
lars.vilhuber@cornell.edu

Abstract. Recording provenance is a key requirement for data-centric scholarship, allowing researchers to evaluate the integrity of source data sets and reproduce, and thereby, validate results. Provenance has become even more critical in the web environment in which data from distributed sources and of varying integrity can be combined and derived. Recent work by the W3C on the PROV model provides the foundation for semantically-rich, interoperable, and web-compatible provenance metadata. We apply that model to complex, but characteristic, provenance examples of social science data, describe scenarios that make scholarly use of those provenance descriptions, and propose a manner for encoding this provenance metadata within the widely-used DDI metadata standard.

Keywords: Metadata, Provenance, DDI, eSocial Science.

1   Introduction

Quantitative social science has, for decades, been at the forefront of data-centric research methodologies [1]. An important foundation of this has been an international network of highly-curated and metadata-rich archives of social science data such as ICPSR (Inter-University Consortium for Political and Social Research) and the UK Data Archive.   This curated data, combined with the ever-increasing volume of social data on the web, offers exciting new research directions for scholars in economics, sociology, demographics, environmental science, health, and other fields.

However, the maturation of cyberinfrastructure for e-social science faces a number of hurdles, some of which are common across all eScholarship efforts, and some of which are exacerbated by or unique to the characteristics of social science data. One of these hurdles, which we described in [2], is the issue of confidentiality; a significant segment of these data are confidential because they associate the identities of the subjects of study (e.g., people, corporations, etc.) with private information such as income level, health history, etc. Notably, the data are not the only problem, because the metadata may also be subject to disclosure limitation. This may include statutory

E. Garoufallou and J. Greenberg (Eds.): MTSR 2013, CCIS 390, pp. 123–134, 2013.

disclosure restrictions on statistical features of the underlying data, such as extreme values, and even prohibitions on the disclosure of variables names themselves. In [2], we described a method for encoding disclosure attributes in DDI metadata [3].

In this paper, we address the issue of encoding provenance of social science data. A number of characteristics of social science data including the divide between inter-related private and publicly accessible data and metadata, complex multithreaded relationships among these data and metadata, and the existence of partially-ordered version sequences make it difficult to understand and trace the origins data that are the basis of a particular study. This places unacceptable barriers to the essential scholarly tasks of testing research results for validity and reproducibility, creating a substantial risk of breach of the scientific integrity of the research process itself.

Recent work undertaken under the auspices of the World Wide Web Consortium (W3C) provides the foundation for a semantically-rich and practical solution for encoding provenance. The PROV documents "define a model, corresponding serializations and other supporting definitions to enable the inter-operable interchange of provenance information in heterogeneous environments such as the web" [4].

In this paper, we report the results of our experiments with the PROV model for encoding real-world provenance scenarios associated with existing social science data. We also propose a preliminary method for encoding that provenance information within the metadata specification developed by the Data Documentation Initiative (DDI) [3], which is emerging as the de facto standard for most social science data. We show that, with some refinements, the PROV model is indeed suitable for this task, and thereby lays the groundwork for implementing user-facing provenance applications that could enrich the quality and integrity of data-centric social science.

The work reported here is one thread of an NSF Census Research Network award [5]. A primary goal of this project is to design and implement tools that bridge the existing gap between private and public data and metadata, that are usable to researchers with and without secure access, and that make proper curation and citation of these data possible. One facet of this larger project, which provides a development context for the work reported in this paper, is an evolving prototype and implementation of the Comprehensive Extensible Data Documentation and Access Repository (CED^{2}AR). This is a metadata repository system that allows researchers to search, browse, access, and cite confidential data and metadata, and the provenance thereof, through either a web-based user interface or programmatically through a search API.

2   The Provenance Problem

As defined by [6], which provides an excellent survey of the data provenance land-scape, "data provenance, one kind of metadata, pertains to the derivation history of a data product starting from its original sources ". As they state, this provenance meta-data is fundamental to the scientific process because "from it, one can ascertain the quality of the data base and its ancestral data and derivations, track back sources of errors, allow automated reenactment of derivations to update the data, and provide attribution of data sources".

Prior to the emergence of the Web, data and the means for encoding their prove-nance were generally siloed in specific applications and domains [7]. The web context has fundamentally changed this partitioned environment by providing accessibility to data from multiple sources, in heterogeneous formats, and of varying integrity and quality [8]. This has increased the importance of semantically-rich and interoperable provenance metadata for understanding the lineage of and integrity of the "mash-ups" that are facilitated by web data [9]. The development of the PROV model, which builds on earlier work on the Open Provenance Model (OPM) [10], leverages devel-opments by the semantic web community, such as RDF and OWL, to provide both the semantics and interoperable encoding that are necessary to express provenance in the web environment.

3   Applying the PROV Model to Social Science Scenarios

The W3C PROV Model is fully described in a family of documents [4] that cover the data model, ontology, expressions and various syntaxes, and access and searching. The model is based in the notions of *entities* that are physical, digital, and conceptual things in the world; *activities* that are dynamic aspects of the world that change and create entities; and *agents* that are responsible for activities. In addition to these three building blocks, the PROV model describes a set of relationships that can exist be-tween them that express attribution,. delegation, derivation, etc. Space limitations prohibit further explication of the model and paper assumes that the reader has a working familiarity with PROV.

In our earlier paper [4], we informally described the provenance of the production cycle of two frequently-used social science data products; Longitudinal Business Database (LBD) and the Longitudinal Employer-Household Dynamics (LEHD) data-base. In this section, we formalize these descriptions using PROV classes and proper-ties. The diagrams that follow are simplified for legibility and do not represent the full graph as it would be constructed in a production-quality system. Our diagramming convention follows that used throughout the W3C PROV documentation; oval nodes denote entities, rectangular nodes denote activities, and pentagonal nodes denote agents. We pair each diagram with a declaration of its component entities, activities, and agents expressed in PROV-N, a functional notation meant for human consump-tion [11]. Although our work includes an encoding of relationships among these ob-jects in the same notation, space limitations of this paper prohibit the inclusion of these full descriptions.

The Census Bureau's Longitudinal Business Database (LBD) is at the center of a complex provenance graph that is illustrated in Fig. 1. The LBD is derived entirely from the Business Register (BR), which is itself derived from tax records provided on a flow base to the Census Bureau by the Internal Revenue Service (IRS). The metho-dology to construct the LBD from snapshots of the BR is described in [12], and it is being continually maintained (updated yearly) at the Census Bureau. Derivative prod-ucts of the LBD are the Business Dynamics Statistics (BDS), an aggregation of the LBD, and the Synthetic LBD, a confidentiality-protected synthetic microdata version of the LBD. However, the LBD and its derivative products are not the only statistical data products derived from the BR. The BR serves as the enumeration frame for the quinquennial Economic Censuses (EC), and together with the post-censal data collected through those censuses, serves as the sampling frame for the annual surveys, e.g., the Annual Survey of Manufactures (ASM). Aggregations of the ASM and EC are published by the Census Bureau, confidential versions are available within the Census RDCs. Furthermore, the BR serves as direct input to the County Business Patterns (CBP) and related Business Patterns through aggregation and disclosure protection mechanisms.

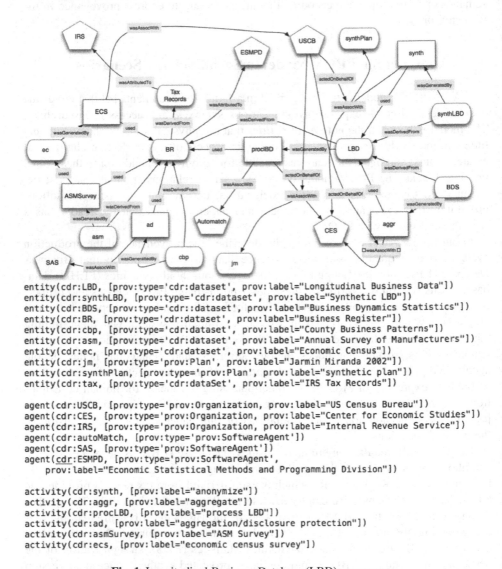

```
entity(cdr:LBD, [prov:type='cdr:dataset', prov:label="Longitudinal Business Data"])
entity(cdr:synthLBD, [prov:type='cdr:dataset', prov:label="Synthetic LBD"])
entity(cdr:BDS, [prov:type='cdr::dataset', prov:label="Business Dynamics Statistics"])
entity(cdr:BR, [prov:type='cdr:dataset', prov:label="Business Register"])
entity(cdr:cbp, [prov:type='cdr:dataset', prov:label="County Business Patterns"])
entity(cdr:asm, [prov:type='cdr:dataset', prov:label="Annual Survey of Manufacturers"])
entity(cdr:ec, [prov:type='cdr:dataset', prov:label="Economic Census"])
entity(cdr:jm, [prov:type='prov:Plan', prov:label="Jarmin Miranda 2002"])
entity(cdr:synthPlan, [prov:type='prov:Plan', prov:label="synthetic plan"])
entity(cdr:tax, [prov:type='cdr:dataSet', prov:label="IRS Tax Records"])

agent(cdr:USCB, [prov:type='prov:Organization, prov:label="US Census Bureau"])
agent(cdr:CES, [prov:type='prov:Organization, prov:label="Center for Economic Studies"])
agent(cdr:IRS, [prov:type='prov:Organization, prov:label="Internal Revenue Service"])
agent(cdr:autoMatch, [prov:type='prov:SoftwareAgent'])
agent(cdr:SAS, [prov:type='prov:SoftwareAgent'])
agent(cdr:ESMPD, [prov:type='prov:SoftwareAgent',
    prov:label="Economic Statistical Methods and Programming Division"])

activity(cdr:synth, [prov:label="anonymize"])
activity(cdr:aggr, [prov:label="aggregate"])
activity(cdr:procLBD, [prov:label="process LBD"])
activity(cdr:ad, [prov:label="aggregation/disclosure protection"])
activity(cdr:asmSurvey, [prov:label="ASM Survey"])
activity(cdr:ecs, [prov:label="economic census survey"])
```

Fig. 1. Longitudinal Business Database (LBD) provenance

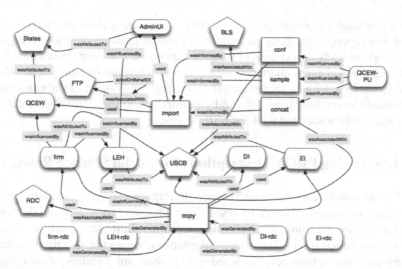

```
agent(cdr:States, [prov:type='prov:Organization, prov:label="State Agencies"])
agent(cdr:FTP, [prov:type='prov:SoftwareAgent')
agent(cdr:USCB, [prov:type='prov:Organization, prov:label="US Census Bureau"])
agent(cdr:BLS, [prov:type='prov:Organization, prov:label="Bureau of Labor Statistics"])
agent(cdr:RDC, [prov:type='prov:Organization, prov:label="Research Data Center"])

entity(cdr:AdminUI, [prov:type='cdr:dataset', prov:label="State Admin Unemploy Insur"])
entity(cdr:QCEW, [prov:type='cdr:dataset', prov:label="State Census of Employ & Wages"])
entity(cdr:firm, [prov:type='cdr:dataset', prov:label="Firm/Estab Characteristics"])
entity(cdr:LEH, [prov:type='cdr:dataset', prov:label="Longitudinal Employ History"])
entity(cdr:DI, [prov:type='cdr:dataset', prov:label="Demographic Info"])
entity(cdr:EI, [prov:type='cdr:dataset', prov:label="Ebterprise Info"])
entity(cdr:QCEW-PU, [prov:type='cdr:dataset', prov:label="QCEW Public Use"])
entity(cdr:firm-rdc, [prov:type='cdr:dataset', prov:label="Firm/Estab Characteristics"])
entity(cdr:LEH-rdc, [prov:type='cdr:dataset', prov:label="Longitudinal Employ History"])
entity(cdr:DI-rdc, [prov:type='cdr:dataset', prov:label="Demographic Info"])
entity(cdr:EI-rdc, [prov:type='cdr:dataset', prov:label="Ebterprise Info"])

activity(cdr:import, [prov:label="import state data"])
activity(cdr:conf, [prov:label="confidentiality protection"])
activity(cdr:sample, [prov:label="sample frames"])
activity(cdr:concat, [prov:label="concatenate quarterly QCEW"])
activity(cdr:copy, [prov:label="copy census data to RDC"])
```

Fig. 2. LEHD/QWI Provenance

A similar complex set of relationships exists for the Longitudinal Employer-Household Dynamics (LEHD) Infrastructure files, illustrated in Fig. 2. Published since 2003, the Quarterly Workforce Indicators (QWI) are derived from a complex set of combined firm-, job- and person-level files. The key inputs are administrative files from the Unemployment Insurance (UI) system, which are managed by each of the states of the union. The states also maintain an establishment-level set of related files, typically referred to as the Quarterly Census of Employment and Wages (QCEW). A snapshot is sent to the Census Bureau every quarter, where they are combined with historical data from previous quarters, additional demographic information matched from sources at the Census Bureau, and enterprise information from, among other sources, the Business Register. The resulting establishment-level flow statistics are further aggregated by geographic areas, using disclosure protection methods (noise infusion and suppression). Longitudinal linking and imputation of workplace geography for workers leads to revisions of historical quarters. The entire collection of time series is republished every quarter. Each revision of each file in this system, whether internal or published, has a unique identifier. A snapshot is made of the entire system approximately every four years for use by researchers in the Census Research Data Center, and can be associated with a specific release,

4   Leveraging PROV Descriptions for Social Science Research

These formal, machine-readable provenance descriptions serve as the foundation for sophisticated provenance queries by researchers who want to understand the foundations of data they are using. The following scenarios illustrate the utility of queries upon the provenance graph. Due to space limitations, we do not specify the nature of the query mechanism used here (as noted in [13] there are a variety of querying mechanisms for PROV), however in our implementation we are using SPARQL on RDF graphs generated from the PROV descriptions.

4.1   Scenario 1

An analyst investigating employment trends is making use of the public use version of the Quarterly Census of Employment and Wages (QCEW-PU). She hears from a fellow researcher that some of the data within the QCEW were derived from data collected from the states. Furthermore, she has read about computational problems in Florida during 1995 that affect the integrity of the data collected by that state. She needs to use the June 1999 version of the QCEW-PU and wants to see whether the troublesome Florida data might underlie this synthesized data.

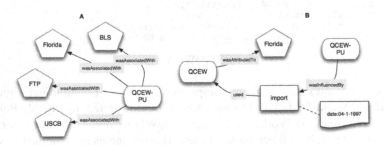

Fig. 3. Discovering the agents directly or indirectly responsible for a data set (left pane A) and the metadata of an activity for which a specific agent is responsible (right pane B)

As illustrated in Fig. 3 the analyst can first query the provenance system to discover the agents are involved in the provenance chain of the QCEW-PU data set. Upon doing this she sees that the state of Florida is included among a set of agents (left pane A). She zeroes in on the metadata of the activity (import) associated with linkage to

Florida data. Examining that metadata she sees that the import from Florida occurred on April 1, 1997 (right pane B), outside the time period when there were problems with the data from Florida. Relieved, she continues with her research.

4.2 Scenario 2

A university data archive wants to make data about long-term business trends available to its researchers. The LBD is such a dataset, but is encumbered with confidentiality restrictions that prevent the archive from acquiring the data themselves. The data archivist wants to explore related datasets that are publicly available, and what processes were used to generate them, in order to house them and make them accessible for university use. PROV supports, not only broad queries as demonstrated by the previous scenario, but deep queries into a particular process. In this case the provenance query focuses upon the process by which the Longitudinal Business Database is synthesized into a publicly accessible version.

The query issued by the archivist to the provenance system facilitates the exploration of the data production process by returning the entities that were derived from the LBD, the activities that generated those entities, any events that were connected to those entities, and any plans that were associated. In this case, the plan reveals documentation that will provide further detail to inform the archivist. A diagram of the resulting graph is given in Fig. 4.

While some details are needed for the sake of clarity (from this and other graph diagrams in this paper), the diagram in Fig. 4 shows a bit more of the capabilities of PROV for diving into the details of a particular activity in terms of derivation and generation events, as well as more detailed associations and documentation via plans.

4.3 Scenario 3

Updates to LEHD files occur quarterly, including updates to previous quarter's inputs. A researcher wants to examine the history of these updates in order to understand the nature of longitudinal data. She wishes to ask the following questions. What process updates existing data with improved data from previous quarters? How do these relate to the annually updated Business Dynamics Statistics?

PROV provides a sub-class of `Entity` called `prov:Bundle` that is in itself an entity and that an entire provenance graph. This can be extremely useful when trying to understand recurring data production processes and their results. If a new PROV graph is produced along with the other metadata that documents the data derivation process, a graph of graphs is possible, enabling the dimension of time to be queried across cycles. This scenario requires such a feature to capture the differences that took place over the quarterly updates to the various files within the provenance graph. The diagram in Fig. 5 represents two quarterly updates of the LEHD.

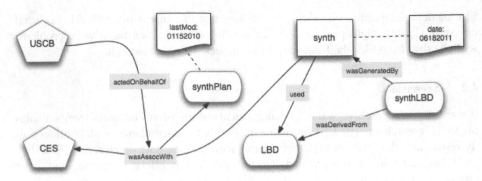

Fig. 4. Discovering the provenance chain of the synthetic LBD data set, including events, plans, and agents and their metadata

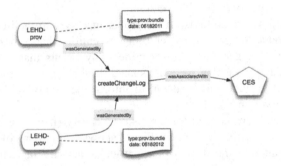

Fig. 5. The prov:Entity subclass, Bundle, is shown. In this case, an activity that creates a change log is discovered for two succeeding quarterly data processing cycles.

The diagram in Fig. 5 is limited to only two quarters of activity for the sake of illustration. At the scale of decades and centuries of provenance chains, this would be a truly valuable resource to the researcher.

5   Extending PROV Semantics

We found the PROV ontology to be a suitable way of expressing complex provenance chains for the LEHD and LBD. As shown by the scenarios above, the semantics defined by its classes and relations are sufficient for both broad descriptions of database production paths and detailed querying of these paths. We are confident that these two provenance graphs and associated exploration scenarios are adequate exemplars for others in the social science domain, but plan to continue experiments with other data.

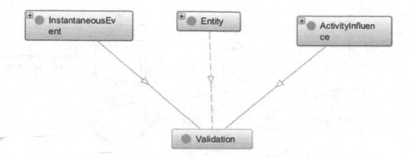

Fig. 6. The inheritance of the proposed Validation class

We did find in our experiments an area for which the ontology and data model might be specialized for our domain and possibly others. That is, the processes related to *validation*, which plays an important role in the documentation of derived datasets. Querying for actions influenced by validation or events related to validation is arguably a central requirement for social science research, specifically as a means of reporting on measures taken to ensure non-disclosure of confidential data in the production cycle. According to the PROV documentation, the `Plan` class is intended to serve the role of indicating validity throughout the model, and can be used "to validate the execution as represented in the provenance record, to manage expectation failures, or to provide explanations." [14] We found that, for our examples, this way of representing validation is indirect resulting in more complex queries that are slower to perform. We propose an alternative; provide a `Validation` class with related properties within the ontology.

If the ontology were extended to include validation semantics, it could be defined as a specialized `Activity` that provides additional information about how a particular `Entity` was confirmed to be valid. An instance of `Validation` would provide additional descriptions about a `prov:wasValidatedBy` relation linking a `prov:Entity` that was validated to the `prov:Activity` that validated it.

Fig. 6 illustrates the relationship of the proposed `Validation` class to other aspects of the PROV ontology. Our proposal is similar to the manner in which the notion of `PROV:Invalidation` is positioned within the ontology. That is, it inherits both from the `InstantaneousEvent` and `ActivityInfluence` classes. As defined in [14], an `prov:InstantaneousEvent` "happens in the world and marks a change in the world, in its activities and in its entities." A `prov:ActivityInfluence` is the "capacity of an activity to have an effect on the character, development, or behavior of another." While `prov:Invalidation` indicates the negative change of validity status, in our case, `Validation` would indicate a positive change of validity status of a given entity or activity.

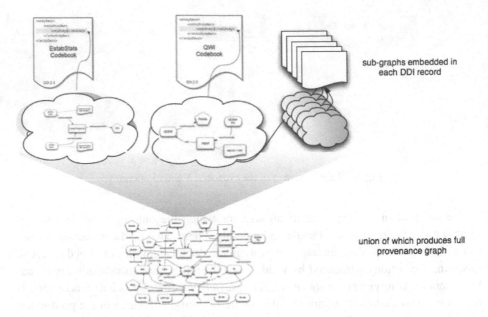

Fig. 7. Storing provenance subgraphs related to a given resource within the <relStudy> element in the corresponding DDI metadata. That subgraph would link, by resource, to other subgraphs located in other codebooks and facilitate dynamic generation of the entire provenance graph.

6   Integrating DDI and PROV

As mentioned earlier, DDI (Data Documentation Initiative) [3] has emerged as the standard for encoding metadata for social science data sets. Currently, there are two threads of development in the DDI community. The 2.X branch, commonly known as DDI-Codebook, primarily focuses on bibliographic information about an individual data set and the structure of its variables. The 3.X branch, commonly known as DDI-Lifecycle, is designed to document a study and its resulting data sets over the entire lifecycle from conception through publication and subsequent reuse. Some of the semantics of DDI-Lifecycle overlap and sometimes conflict with the PROV semantics described in this paper. We argue that rather than encoding provenance in a manner unique to DDI, a better strategy might be to work within the simpler DDI-Codebook context and embed PROV metadata within the individual data set-specific DDI records.

We specify here an easily implemented manner for embedding this information, which we plan to implement. We note that there is an active effort within the DDI community to develop an RDF encoding for DDI metadata that could easily accommodate RDF-encoding provenance metadata [15–17]. As that effort matures, we anticipate that our experiments with provenance and social science data will be a valuable contribution.

For now, the `<relStdy>` element in DDI 2.5 provides a useful place to encode provenance data specific to the respective data set. The solution is schema-conformant if the PROV metadata is wrapped within a `CDATA` tag. As illustrated in Fig. 7 our proposal for doing this is fully modular. Only the metadata related to the specific data set is stored in its respective DDI record, which then links to the PROV metadata stored in other DDI records. The full provenance graph can then be reconstructed dynamically by combining these individual subgraphs.

7   Future Work and Conclusions

Data provenance is an essential aspect of the scholarly process. Researchers need to have access to, explore, and query the lineage of the data that they use for their current research in order to understand and evaluate their integrity, promote reproducibility of the results, and evaluate suitability for future research. This has become especially critical in the web environment where data are sourced not only from established archives, but from many mixed credentialed providers.

In this paper, we have described our initial experiments with the PROV data model, an emerging standard for expressing and encoding provenance, the development of which was sponsored by the W3C. PROV is semantically-expressive and extensible making it a useful platform for encoding provenance in an interoperable and machine-actionable manner. Our experiments described here using PROV to encode some complex, but real, examples from social science research indicate the utility of the model.

Over the next year we plan to build on this work in the following threads. First and foremost, just because it is possible to encode provenance does not mean that is practical. Our modeling efforts described here took a considerable amount of human effort and encoding of tacit knowledge. We plan to work with our partners in the social science data community, especially researchers at ICPSR, who are investigating automatic means of recording provenance within the context of work on DDI-Lifecycle. Second, the utility of these provenance descriptions depends on their comprehensibility by the eventual user. We look forward to contributing our special knowledge of social science researchers and data provenance requirements to general work in the provenance community on visualization of provenance graphs. Finally, as we mentioned earlier in this paper, confidentiality and cloaking of data and metadata are essential within the social science domain. In this vein, we are planning to integrate our confidentiality and provenance work to make it possible for researchers to understand and explore provenance information regardless of their security status via selectively cloaking sensitive aspects of the provenance chain, while exposing all other possible data.

References

[1] Daw, M., Procter, R., Lin, Y., Hewitt, T., Ji, W., Voss, A., Baird, K., Turner, A., Birkin, M., Miller, K., Dutton, W., Jirotka, M., Schroeder, R., de la Flor, G., Edwards, P., Allan, R., Yang, X., Crouchley, R.: Developing an e-Infrastructure for Social Science. In: Proceedings of e-Social Science 2007 (2007)

[2] Lagoze, C., Block, W., Williams, J., Abowd, J.M., Vilhuber, L.: Data Management of Confidential Data. In: International Data Curation Conference (2013)

[3] Vardigan, M., Heus, P., Thomas, W.: Data Documentation Initiative: Toward a Standard for the Social Sciences. The International Journal of Digital Curation 3(1) (2008)

[4] Groth, P., Moreau, L.: PROV-Overview: An Overview of the PROV Family of Documents. W3C (2013)

[5] National Science Foundation, NSF Award Search: Award#1131848 - NCRN-MN: Cornell Census-NSF Research Node: Integrated Research Support, Training and Data Documentation (2011)

[6] Simmhan, Y., Plale, B., Gannon, D.: A survey of data provenance in e-science. ACM Sigmod Record (2005)

[7] Cheney, J., Chong, S., Foster, N., Seltzer, M., Vansummeren, S.: Provenance. In: Proceeding of the 24th ACM SIGPLAN Conference Companion on Object Oriented Programming Systems Languages and Applications - OOPSLA 2009, p. 957 (2009)

[8] Groth, P., Gil, Y., Cheney, J., Miles, S.: Requirements for Provenance on the Web. International Journal of Digital Curation 7(1), 39–56 (2012)

[9] McGuinness, D.L., Fox, P., Pinheiro da Silva, P., Zednik, S., Del Rio, N., Ding, L., West, P., Chang, C.: Annotating and embedding provenance in science data repositories to enable next generation science applications. AGU Fall Meeting Abstracts 1 (2008)

[10] Moreau, L., Freire, J., Futrelle, J., McGrath, R., Myers, J., Paulson, P.: The Open Provenance Model. University of Southampton, pp. 1–30 (August 2007)

[11] Moreau, L., Missier, P.: PROV-N: The Provenance Notation. W3C (2013)

[12] Jarmin, R., Miranda, J.: The Longtitudinal Business Database (2002)

[13] Klyne, G., Groth, P.: Provenance Access and Query. W3C (2013)

[14] Lebo, T., Sahoo, S., McGuinness, D.L.: PROV-O: The PROV Ontology. W3C (2013)

[15] Kramer, S., Leahey, A., Southall, H., Vampras, J., Wackerow, J.: Using RDF to describe and link social science data to related resources on the Web: leveraging the Data Documentation Initiative (DDI) model. Data Documentation Initiative (September 01, 2012)

[16] Bosch, T., Cyganiak, R., Wackerow, J., Zapilko, B.: Leveraging the DDI Model for Linked Statistical Data in the Social, Behavioural, and Economic Sciences. In: International Conference on Dublin Core and Metadata Applications; DC-2012–The Kuching Proceedings (September 2012)

[17] Bosch, T., Cyganiak, R., Gregory, A., Wackerow, J.: DDI-RDF Discovery Vocabulary: A Metadata Vocabulary for Documenting Research and Survey Data. In: Linked Data on the Web Workshop (2013)

Perceived Helpfulness of Dublin Core Semantics:
An Empirical Study

Mohammad Yasser Chuttur

University of Mauritius, Reduit, Mauritius
y.chuttur@uom.ac.mu

Abstract. In an experimental study, 120 participants randomly assigned to two groups were asked to rate the helpfulness of the Dublin Core elements definitions and guidelines while creating metadata records. In contrast to previous studies, findings reveal that participants had problems understanding definitions for the whole element set specified by Dublin Core. This study also reveals that careful attention should be given to the clarity of guidelines as well to ensure correct application of Dublin Core elements.

Keywords: Dublin Core, creating metadata record, best practice guideline, dc element definition.

1 Introduction

The use of a metadata scheme is central to the creation of metadata records. A metadata scheme establishes the meaning (semantics) of metadata elements that can be used to represent properties or characteristics of a resource; it may also provide content rules that serve as the guidelines for selecting values for each element; and it may also specify a syntax that establishes how element-value pairs are to be constructed (Taylor, 2004). It follows that the quality of metadata records is directly dependent on the clarity and efficiency of the scheme semantics.

Simple Dublin Core specifies fifteen elements as part of the Dublin Core Metadata Element Set version 1.1 (DCMES). Referred to as the de-facto standard for representing resources on the web (Weibel & Koch, 2000) and endorsed as a standard by the European Committee for Standardisation (CEN), the National Information Standards Organization (NISO), and the International Organization for Standardization (ISO), many projects make use of the fifteen elements specified by simple Dublin Core to represent their resources (Dalton, 2007; Palmer, Zavalina & Mustatoff, 2007). Given that the Online Archive Initiative (OAI) requires repositories and digital libraries to use Dublin Core to represent their collections, it is expected that more institutions will be adopting the scheme (Shreeves, Riley, & Hagendorn, 2007) emphasizing the need for research in the clarity and efficiency of Dublin Core semantics.

E. Garoufallou and J. Greenberg (Eds.): MTSR 2013, CCIS 390, pp. 135–145, 2013.

2   Dublin Core Semantics

The Dublin Core Metadata Initiative (DCMI) claims that the semantics of simple Dublin Core, (i.e., the elements and their definitions) are universally understood because they were "established by an international, cross-disciplinary group of professionals from librarianship, computer science, text encoding, the museum community, and other related fields of scholarship and practice" (Hillman, 2005). In addition, simple Dublin Core was developed as a metadata scheme that would be accessible to individuals with or without any metadata training. This is articulated in its goal for simplicity of creation and maintenance (Hillman, 2005):

> *The Dublin Core element set has been kept as small and simple as possible to allow a non-specialist to create simple descriptive records for information resources easily and inexpensively, while providing for effective retrieval of those resources in the networked environment.*

It is therefore expected that metadata creators who use Dublin Core would find the semantics supplied by the underlying scheme helpful when creating metadata records and that the resultant records would effectively serve the intended purpose. In other words, records created using DC would be free from any errors that may affect the usability of the records. Previous studies, however, have reported several problems in metadata records which are assumed to be the result of problems with the Dublin Core (DC) semantics.

Park, for example, investigated problems that occurred in 659 metadata records and pointed out that the definitions for some DC elements were ambiguous and overlapped (Park, 2006). In particular, the author cited the DC element pairs <source> and <relation> and <format> and <type>, both of which are often confused in their application. Furthermore, Godby, Smith, and Childress observed several problems in the application of DC elements in 400 metadata records created for a digital library project (Godby, Smith, and Childress, 2003). The authors found that both <format> and <type> contained the names of media types (e.g., photograph, video) and that <description> and <subject> both contained subject headings and textual descriptions. Metadata creators did not appear to distinguish between these two elements supplying values from controlled vocabularies as well as extended free-text descriptions for both. In their analysis of a random sample of 140 records from four digital repositories, Shreeves, Knutson, Stivilia, Palmer, Twidale, and Cole also observed several problems with the application of DC elements - In one collection, the type value of a resource was consistently described in the <source> element, and date values were found in both the <creator> and <contributor> elements. In two other collections, date values were inconsistently formatted, creating confusion regarding the date encoding used (Shreeves et al., 2005).

Moreover, in some of the records Jackson and colleagues analyzed, similar confusions were observed regarding the use of the <date> and <coverage> elements (Jackson et al., 2008). The researchers found several instances where the publication date of a resource was recorded in the <coverage> element. They also discovered many records that had incorrectly used the <format> element to describe applications necessary for accessing the digital object rather than the "file format, physical medium, or dimensions of the resource" as specified in the DC scheme. A survey carried by Park and Childress also showed that information professionals often had difficulty understanding the definitions for <source>, <relation>, <contributor>, <publisher>, <type> and <format> (Park and Childress, 2009).

3   Problem Statement

DCMI claims that the simple and clear semantics of DC, as specified in its scheme, should help metadata creators in easily creating effective metadata records. Researchers, however, claim that the DC scheme lacks clarity and could lead metadata creators in creating records that are not accurate. Given that Dublin Core is one of the most widely used metadata scheme today, (Ma, 2007; Smith-Yoshimura, 2007) and that the number of institutions to adopt the scheme for describing their resources is expected to rise, the following research question is posed:

How do metadata creators perceive the helpfulness of DC semantics (definitions and guidelines) when creating metadata records?

The answer to this question is expected to verify the claims made by previous researchers regarding problems associated with the DC scheme semantics. As noted in previous studies, researchers have criticized the DC scheme semantics without any consideration for its use during the metadata creation process. Ambiguities are often solved when the context is known. In the case of metadata creation, it may be possible that metadata creators do not find any ambiguities with the definitions or guidelines specified by DC when presented with a resource to describe. To this end, an experimental study was set up in which participants were asked to rate the helpfulness of definitions and guidelines while they created metadata records for different resources.

4   Methodology

A total of 120 participants were recruited from Indiana University Bloomington population and randomly assigned to two treatment groups. All participants were asked to use the same online tool (Figure 1) to create metadata records for the same four resources, but, in one group, participants could access DC element definitions only and in the other group, participants could access both DC element definitions and guidelines. Dublin Core definitions and guidelines were obtained from the DCMI[1] website.

---

[1] http://dublincore.org/

The online tool used by participants during the study was designed to contain three windows: a 'resource' window to display the resource, a 'Dublin Core metadata form' window that listed fifteen fields corresponding to the elements of Dublin Core, and a 'Definitions/Guidelines' window that provided the definitions or definitions and guidelines for each metadata element selected in the form.

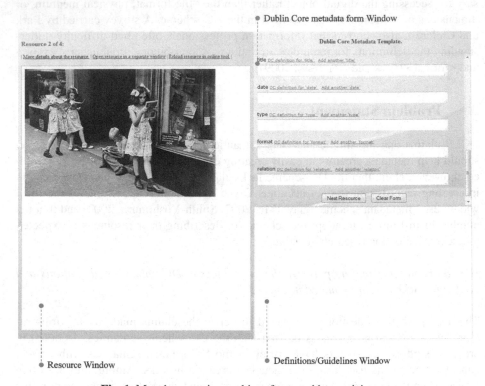

Fig. 1. Metadata creation tool interface used by participants

The four resources used for this study were a web page, an image, a document, and a video. Only one resource at a time was shown to participants. Resources were displayed in the following order: the web page, the image, the document, and the video. The choice of these resources was guided by the actual metadata creation practices at several libraries as indicated by Ma's (2007) survey – her findings showed that images, texts, and videos are common resources for which metadata is created[2]. For each resource, a link that participants could click to obtain some information about the resource displayed was made available in the resource window to ensure that participants had sufficient information to create metadata for the resource.

The 'Dublin Core metadata form' consisted of fifteen fields corresponding to the simple Dublin Core elements. For each field, participants were able to fill in a value

---

[2] The present study is part of a larger study in which data collected for all four resources were subjected to further analysis.

in order to represent the resource shown to them. Each field had a label that corresponded to the name of a Dublin Core element and for each element participants could click on appropriate links to view either the definitions or the definitions and guidelines of the Dublin Core element in the 'Definitions/Guidelines' window. Figure 2 shows the information displayed in the 'Definitions/Guidelines' window for the <title> element when a participant clicks on the link corresponding to the definition for the <title> element. Along with the corresponding definition or guideline, the 'Definitions/Guidelines' window presented participants with a five-point Likert scale that were used to rate the helpfulness of the definition or guideline displayed.

DC definition for 'title'

A name given to the resource.

How helpful is this definition?

Not Helpful At All	Somewhat Unhelpful	Neither Helpful nor Unhelpful	Somewhat Helpful	Very Helpful
○	○	○	○	○

Submit Rating

Fig. 2. Likert-scale used by participants to rate DC definitions and guidelines

The scales had concise annotations which appeared when participants placed their mouse on any of the scales. By having the likert scale annotated with descriptive sentences, the intention was to allow participants to understand the meaning of the labels used. Furthermore, the corresponding annotation for a scale will make it easy to later interpret the actual choice made by participants during data analysis. Table 1 lists the five ratings with corresponding annotations that participants could see.

Table 1. Five-point Likert scale with corresponding annotation

Rating	Rating annotation
Not helpful at all	The definition (or guideline) is incomprehensible and lacks information I need to use the element.
Somewhat unhelpful	The definition (or guideline) is difficult to understand and does not contain enough information I need to use the element.
Neither helpful nor unhelpful	I could have used the element without reading the definition (or guideline).
Somewhat helpful	The definition (or guideline) is clear and contains information I need to use the element.
Very helpful	The definition (or guideline) is very clear and contains all the important information I need to use the element.

To load a new resource and a blank form, participants had to click on a "Next Resource" button in the online tool. Each time a participant moved to a new resource, all values previously entered in the tool were recorded for further analysis.

5   Findings

Tables 2 and 3 list descriptive statistics for the ratings submitted by participants in both groups, i.e., participants ratings when they had access to definitions only and participants ratings when they had access to both definitions and guidelines. Out of the 120 participants, 60 participants had access to both definitions and guidelines and 60 participants could access only definitions. Results from Table 1, therefore, shows the ratings collected from 120 participants whereas results from Table 2 shows results collected from 60 participants. It should also be noted that the participants submitted ratings for the definitions and guidelines only for the first resource, i.e., the web page and therefore the information presented here are ratings collected when participants created records for the web page[3] only. Although this may be considered as a limitation, it was considered redundant to ask participants to supply same information for the other resources as the likely-hood for a participant's perceived helpfulness of the definition or guideline to change during the study was judged low. Results were interpreted according to the annotations listed in Table 1.

5.1   Perceived Helpfulness of Dublin Core Definitions

A majority of participants considered the definitions provided for the Dublin Core elements, except for *identifier* and *language*, to be "somewhat helpful." This can be interpreted to mean that participants found that the definitions provided were clear and contained the information needed to use the element. For the *identifier* element, most participants considered the definition "somewhat unhelpful," which indicates that the definition provided was difficult to understand and did not contain enough information for participants to use the element.

Most participants found that the definition for the *language* element was "very helpful," which can be understood to mean that the definition given was very clear and contained all the important information needed to use the element. It should be noted that for *coverage, description, relation,* and *type* elements, the ratings were negatively skewed toward "unhelpful." This implies that, although the highest number of participants (shown in bold in Table 2) found these definitions "somewhat helpful," the majority of participants found them to be less helpful (i.e., not helpful at all, somewhat unhelpful, and neither helpful nor unhelpful).

---

[3] The web page was a static page consisting mainly of text and some images.

Table 2. Participants' ratings for Dublin Core element definitions

DC Element	Not Helpful at all	Somewhat Unhelpful	Neither Helpful nor Unhelpful	Somewhat Helpful	Very Helpful
contributor	1.7 % (2)	8.3 % (10)	11.7 % (14)	**50.8 %** (61)	27.5 % (33)
coverage	19.2 % (23)	20.8 % (25)	19.2 % (23)	**32.5 %** (39)	8.3 % (10)
creator	1.7 % (2)	6.7 % (8)	10.8 % (13)	**50 %** (60)	30.8 % (37)
date	2.5 % (3)	10.8 % (13)	19.2 % (23)	**43.3 %** (52)	24.2 % (29)
description	14.2 % (17)	22.5 % (27)	25.8 % (31)	**28.3 %** (34)	9.2 % (11)
format	4.2 % (5)	11.7 % (14)	19.2 % (23)	**50 %** (60)	15 % (18)
identifier	20 % (24)	**30 %** (36)	17.5 % (21)	25.8 % (31)	6.7 % (8)
language	2.5 % (3)	6.7 % (8)	22.5 % (27)	30 % (36)	**38.3%** (46)
publisher	1.7 % (2)	5.8 % (7)	10 % (12)	**45 %** (54)	37.5 % (45)
relation	16.7 % (20)	21.7 % (26)	19.2 % (23)	**35 %** (42)	7.5 % (9)
rights	0.8 % (1)	13.3 % (16)	22.5 % (27)	**47.5 %** (57)	15.8 % (19)
source	3.3 % (4)	18.3 % (22)	25 % (30)	**40.8 %** (49)	12.5 % (15)
subject	0 % (0)	8.3 % (10)	15.8 % (19)	**50.8 %** (61)	25 % (30)
title	3.3 % (4)	6.7 % (8)	15.8 % (19)	**38.3 %** (46)	35.8 % (43)
type	5.8 % (7)	19.2 % (23)	19.2 % (23)	**40.8 %** (49)	15 % (18)
Total Respondents:					**120**

Note: Actual number of participants in parentheses. Bold indicate highest percentage of participants. Total number of participants equals 120 because all participants had access to element definitions.

Table 3. Participants' ratings for Dublin Core best practice guidelines

DC Element	Not helpful at all	Somewhat unhelpful	Neither helpful nor unhelpful	Somewhat helpful	Very helpful
contributor	1.7 % (1)	16.7 % (10)	10 % (6)	**50 %** (30)	21.7 % (13)
coverage	0 % (0)	5 % (3)	11.7 % (7)	**56.7 %** (34)	26.7 % (16)
creator	0 % (0)	0 % (0)	5 % (3)	45 % (27)	**50 %** (30)
date	0 % (0)	0 % (0)	1.7 % (1)	28.3 % (17)	**70 %** (42)
description	0 % (0)	0 % (0)	5 % (3)	36.7 % (22)	**58.3 %** (35)
format	0 % (0)	5 % (3)	13.3 % (8)	**58.3 %** (35)	23.3 % (14)
identifier	3.3 % (2)	0 % (0)	5 % (3)	33.3 % (20)	**58.3%** (35)
language	0 % (0)	0 % (0)	3.3 % (2)	40 % (24)	**56.7 %** (34)
publisher	0 % (0)	0 % (0)	1.7 % (1)	**58.3 %** (35)	40 % (24)
relation	10 % (6)	11.7 % (7)	5 % (3)	35 % (21)	**38.3 %** (23)
rights	1.7 % (1)	3.3 % (2)	1.7 % (1)	**48.3 %** (29)	45 % (27)
source	5 % (3)	11.7 % (7)	13.3 % (8)	**50 %** (30)	20 % (12)
subject	0 % (0)	1.7 % (1)	5 % (3)	**55 %** (33)	38.3 % (23)
title	0 % (0)	0 % (0)	1.7 % (1)	46.7 % (28)	**51.7 %** (31)
type	1.7 % (1)	0 % (0)	8.3 % (5)	**51.7 %** (31)	38.3 % (23)
				Total Respondents:	**60**

Note: Actual number of participants in parentheses. Bold indicates highest percent of participants. Total number of participants equals 60 because only half of the total number of participants had access to best practice guidelines.

5.2   Perceived Helpfulness of Dublin Core Guidelines

Responses collected indicated that, in general, participants found that best practice guidelines were helpful (i.e., "somewhat helpful" or "very helpful"). Ratings scores for the helpfulness of best practice guidelines demonstrate a significant shift of perceived helpfulness of the information provided from being "unhelpful" to "helpful" for best practice guidelines compared to ratings assigned elements' definitions.

For instance, a majority of participants found the guidelines provided for the <identifier> element was "very helpful," compared to the majority of participants who found the definition for the same element "somewhat unhelpful." For the <coverage>, <description>, <relation>, and <type> elements, the definition ratings tended toward "unhelpful," but for the guidelines, the rating tendency was toward "very helpful." Compared to the rating scores for the elements definitions, it is, thus, evident that participants found best practice guidelines more helpful than definitions alone in creating metadata records. Table 3 lists the ratings collected from participants for the Dublin Core best practice guidelines supplied during the study.

6   Discussion

Dublin Core is claimed to be easy enough to be used by anyone (Hillman, 2005). Because a scheme's ease of use depends on the ease of use of its elements, it is expected that participants would rate the helpfulness of the Dublin Core elements definitions "very helpful". However, this was not the case. Language was the only element for which the definition was considered "very helpful" by the majority of participants. For most of the other elements, definitions were found to be mostly "somewhat helpful". Ratings collected during the study also revealed that a majority of participants considered that the definition for identifier was "somewhat unhelpful" and for <coverage>, <description>, <relation>, and, <type>, opinions tended toward "unhelpful." In other words, as can be interpreted from the annotation for the label "unhelpful," (see Table 1) the definitions were sometimes considered difficult to understand and did not contain enough information needed to use the element. These findings support observations made by previous researchers regarding problems faced with some Dublin Core elements definitions.

Referring to Table 2, however, it is seen that a relatively high proportion of participants also rated DC definitions for all the elements as "Not helpful at all" or "Somewhat unhelpful". This kind of results further indicates that problems with DC definitions across the full fifteen element set cannot be ignored. In contrast to previous studies which reported problems with some DC element definitions only, this study shows that metadata creators actually have problems understanding the full spectrum of the DC element set. One solution to redress this problem could be to, as suggested by Greenberg, Patuelli, Parsia, and Robertson (2001) and Crystal and Greenberg (2005), provide additional information in the form of guidelines to help understand the application of DC elements.

As observed in Table 3, most participants who used best practice guidelines typically rated the guidelines provided "helpful" or "very helpful." Compared to participants who used definitions, fewer participants considered guidelines as being "Not helpful at all" or "Somewhat unhelpful". Provision of clear guidelines could therefore be a means to assist metadata creators in creating effective records. Because there is still a proportion of participants who could not find the definitions or guidelines helpful, it is likely that further research into the actual problems faced when using DC elements definitions guidelines could indicate directions to take in order to improve the efficiency of DC scheme semantics.

The Dublin Core Metadata Initiative (DCMI) has already started working on an updated version of DC guidelines. To recall, DC guidelines were developed in 1998 and later revised in 2005. Unless these revised guidelines are properly tested by metadata creators before being published, there is a high risk for metadata creators to face similar problems encountered with the current DC guidelines.

7   Conclusions

While previous studies have revealed problems with only some element definitions, this study revealed that when creating metadata records, metadata creators can have difficulty in understanding the meaning of all the definitions for the fifteen DC element set. Given the wide adoption of Dublin Core, there is a pressing need to investigate the clarity of the Dublin Core elements definitions from a linguistic perspective and to find ways to ensure correct application of these elements. Use of guidelines may be one solution, but it does not fully solve the problem. Some participants still found DC guidelines as unhelpful when creating records. It follows that simply having guidelines does not guarantee that metadata creators would be able to apply metadata elements correctly and therefore careful attention need to be equally given to the clarity and helpfulness of guidelines. A clear set of definitions supported by well defined guidelines could be one direction to take to ensure that metadata records created using Dublin Core are complete and accurate. Further investigation to verify this claim, however, is required.

Acknowledgments. The author wishes to express his sincere thanks to Dr. Debora Shaw and Dr. Elin Jacob for their advice and assistance during this study.

References

Crystal, A., Greenberg, J.: Usability of metadata creation application for resource authors. Library & Information Science Research 27(2), 177–189 (2005)

Dalton, J.: Scholarly articles featuring projects using Dublin Core. Journal of Internet Cataloging 7(3), 59–84 (2007)

Godby, C.J., Smith, D., Childress, E.: Two paths to interoperable metadata. Paper Presented at the DC-2003 Supporting Communities of Discourse and Practice-Metadata Research and Applications, Seattle, Washington, September 28-October 2 (2003), http://www.oclc.org/research/publications/ archive/~2003/godby-dc2003.pdf (retrieved April 10, 2010)

Greenberg, J., Pattueli, M., Parsia, B., Robertson, W.: Author-generated Dublin Core metadata for web resources: A baseline study in an organiza-tion. In: Proceedings of the International Conference on Dublin Core and Metadata Application, Tokyo, Japan, October 24-26, pp. 38–45 (2001)

Hillmann, D.: Using Dublin Core (2005),
http://dublincore.org/documents/usageguide/ (retrieved April 12, 2010)

Jackson, A.S., Han, M., Groetsch, K., Mustafoff, M., Cole, T.W.: Dublin Core metadata harvested through OAI-PMH. Journal of Library Metadata 8(1), 5–21 (2008)

Ma, J.: Metadata, Spec kit 298. Association of Research Libraries, Washington, DC (2007)

Palmer, C.L., Zavalina, O.L., Mustafoff, M.: Trends in metadata practices: A longitudinal study of collection federation metadata. In: Proceedings of the 7th ACM/IEEE-CS Joint Conference on Digital Libraries, Vancouver, Canada, pp. 386–395 (2007)

Park, J.: Semantic Interoperability and Metadata Quality: An analysis of metadata item records of digital image collection. Knowledge Organization 33(1), 20–34 (2006)

Park, J., Childress, E.: Dublin Core metadata semantics: an analysis of the perspectives of information professionals. Journal of Information Science 35(6), 727–739 (2009)

Shreeves, S., Knutson, E., Stvilia, B., Palmer, C., Twidale, M., Cole, T.: Is 'quality' metadata 'shareable' metadata? The implications of local metadata practices for federated collections. In: Proceedings of the Twelfth National Conference of the Association of College and Research Libraries, pp. 223–237. Association of College and Research Libraries, Chicago (2005)

Shreeves, S.L., Riley, J., Hagedorn, K.: DLF/NSDL Working Group on OAI PMH Best Practices. Best practices for OAI PMH data provider implementations and shareable metadata. Digital Library Federation, Washington, DC (2007)

Smith-Yoshimura, K.: RLG programs descriptive metadata practices survey results. OCLC Programs and Research, Dublin (2007)

Taylor, A.: The organization of information, 2nd edn. Libraries Unlimited, Westport (2004)

Weibel, S., Koch, T.: The Dublin Core Metadata Initiative: mission, current activities, and future directions. D-Lib Magazine 6(12) (2000),
http://www.dlib.org/dlib/december00/weibel/12weibel.html
(retrieved May 27, 2010)

A Semantic Model for Personal Consent Management

Ozgu Can

Ege University, Department of Computer Engineering,
35100 Bornova-Izmir, Turkey
ozgu.can@ege.edu.tr

Abstract. Data protection and privacy has a significant importance in information sharing mechanisms, especially in domains that handle with sensitive information. The knowledge that can be inferred from this sensitive information may unveil the consumer's personal information. Consumers should control who can access their consent data and for what purposes this data will be used. Therefore, information sharing requires effective policies to protect the personal data and to ensure the consumer's privacy needs. As different consumers have different privacy levels, each consumer should determine one's own consent policy. Besides ensuring personal privacy, information sharing to obtain personal data usage for acceptable reasons should be endorsed. This work proposes a semantic web based personal consent management model. In this model, consumers specify their consent data and create their personal consent policy for their consent data according to their privacy concerns. Thus, personalized consumer privacy for consent management will be ensured and reasonable information sharing for the personal data usage will be supported.

Keywords: Consent Management, Privacy, Semantic Web.

1 Introduction

The remarkable growth in digitization of records brings great advances for consumers. However, sharing personal information brings significant privacy risks for consumers, like *linking attack*. Linking attack is the leakage of a crucial private information by integrating released and publicly available data sets. Therefore, an adversary can track the individuals identity. According to the study of 1990 U.S. Census summary data in [1], 87% of the individuals in the United States are identifiable with their gender, date of birth and 5-digit zip code of their addresses. [2] presents problems and risks of data mining to patient privacy by cross linking the patient data with other publicly available databases, processes such as data mining may associate an individual with specific diagnoses. Thus, consumers must control the access to their personal records and give consent to others who want to access these records. Consent management is a policy that allows a consumer to determine rights for a provider's access control request to one's personal information. On the other hand, the balance between

E. Garoufallou and J. Greenberg (Eds.): MTSR 2013, CCIS 390, pp. 146–151, 2013.

the personal privacy and the quality of service should be ensured. The goal in consent management is stimulating information sharing to improve the quality of the personal data usage for specific acceptable reasons and protecting personal privacy according to personal consent policy. Medical domain is one of the inevitable field to realize the importance of consent management. Patients, who are the subjects of electronic health records (EHRs), have the right to know who is collecting, storing or processing their data and for what purpose this is being done [3]. Health information systems (HIS) must protect patient's consent rights. As each patient may demand different privacy levels for their EHRs, it will not be efficient to use a standard privacy policy for EHRs. Therefore, in this work, a practical personal consent management model is proposed and illustrated for the healthcare domain. In the example model, each patient can specify one's own consent data according to one's personal privacy needs and create personal consent policy. Each access request to one's EHRs are executed according to one's personal consent policy. As a result, the decision of this access request should be a permission or a prohibition.

The goal of the paper is to describe a semantic web based personal consent management model to protect consumer privacy while endorsing reasonable information sharing for personal data usage. In order to achieve this goal, patient information and HIS are chosen as the object and the domain of the sample consent policy, respectively. The paper is organized as follows: Section 2 informs the relevant related work. Section 3 explains the consent management model. Section 4 presents a case study example of the proposed model. Finally, Section 5 expresses the direction of the future work.

2   Related Work

The protection of consumer's user information, especially in health systems, is one of the crucial need for systems to provide consumer's privacy. Recent works can be categorized in two forms that one is for the generalization of published records and the other is controlling access to records. The former work is based on record anonymization to protect user data before publishing it [4] [5] [6]. The latter work is based on access control techniques. [7] proposes a design principle of an electronic consent system and develops a health transaction model. In [8]; threats to the confidentiality, integrity and availability of personal health information are discussed and a security policy model for clinical information systems is given. The approach in [9] uses the domain model, the policy model, the role model, the privilege management model, the authorization model, the access control model and the information distance model for authorization and access control of electronic health record systems. Consentir, a system for patients information and their consent policies are presented in [10]. Consentir supports five different consent policies for patient consent management. Clinical Management of Behavioral Health Services (CMBHS, http://www.dshs.state.tx.us/cmbhs) is a web-based, open source electronic health record. Users of the system are assigned to roles that determines their access level. The system allows patients or their legally authorized representative's (LAR) to determine what data can be seen and by whom. Patients or their LAR can also revoke or modify the terms of their consent. The consent form is then integrated with the patient's record in the Electronic Health Record (EHR) system. In Virtual Lifetime Electronic Record (VLER) Health Community project, patients can control access to their personal health information, including medication lists, lab test results and diagnoses. HIPAAT (http://www.hipaat.com) develops consent management and auditing software for personal health information (PHI) privacy. A trust management system, named as Cassandra, uses electronic health record system as a case study [11]. It is a role based trust management system for access control in a distributed system. The study in [12] focuses on creating and managing of patient consent with the integration of the Composite Privacy Consent Directive Domain Analysis Model of the HL7 and the IHE Basic Patient Privacy Consents (BPPC) profile. [13] describes a framework for enforcing consent policies for healthcare systems based on workflows. Permissions are assigned to subjects who want to access patient's consent. The context of the framework is expressed in terms of workflows.

The proposed consent management model differs from the relevant works in that we combine access control techniques with personalization based on semantic web technologies. In our work, the user manages the access to one's records and controls the privacy of one's data. In order to give the user full control of one's own data, user data is differentiated in two directions: quasi-identifiers and medical data. The main goal in differentiating the user data is to eliminate the risk of linking attack.

3   Consent Management Model

The consent management model consists of the following sets: Subject, User, Role, Organization, Action, Object, Quasi-Identifier, Constraint, Purpose, Policy Objects and Consent Data Policy.

- A *subject* is the owner of data that is going to be accessed.
- *User* is an entity that wants to access to the subject's data and perform actions on this data.
- Each user and subject has a *role* and a set of attributes. For example, users of the health care system can be in a nurse role or a doctor role or a lab technician role.
- An *organization* is an entity where a user is an employee of.
- An *action* indicates operations that a user can perform on an object. For example, updating, viewing or deleting a record. In consent management model, actions are also used by subjects to define operations that they permit or prohibit on their EHRs.
- An *object* is an entity that a user wants to access and perform actions on. An object represents subject's consent data. For example, in a HIS example, objects are medical records of patients' personal health information.

- A *quasi-identifier* is an entity that is determined by a subject to define a privacy requirement value on. Quasi-identifier is a set of attributes in a table which can be linked with external information to re-identify the individuals identity [14]. This set consists of attributes that identify subjects from others uniquely e.g.,age, gender, social security number, zip code and so on.
- A *constraint* is a condition that is used to limit the definitions of an entity related to policy objects.
- *Purpose* states user's intentions on an object.
- *Policy objects* define what actions can a user perform on an object and under what circumstances. Policy object can be a permission or a prohibition. Permission means what an entity can do and prohibition means what an entity can't do.
- *Consent data policy* is the subject's policy definition to finalize the access decision.

The access request has a tuple of $\langle User, Subject, Object, Action, Purpose \rangle$. Consent data policy, which is the respond of the request, is represented as a tuple of $\langle Subject, User, PolicyObject, ConsentData \rangle$. Consent data set is a pair of $\langle Subject, Quasi - Identifiers \rangle$ or $\langle Subject, Object \rangle$. Policy object is formed of $\langle Role, Action, Purpose, Constraint \rangle$. The model is represented with a DL $\mathcal{ALCQ}$ language and has the following atomic concepts and roles:

- atomic concepts are Subject, User, Role, Organization, Action, Object, Quasi-Identifier, Purpose, Policy Objects, Consent Data and Consent DataPolicy.
- the atomic role hasRole links a user and a subject to a role.
- the atomic role isAnEmployee links a users to an organization.
- the atomic roles isOwnerOf and hasOwner are inverse roles and create a link between a subject and an object.
- the atomic role hasRequest links a user to a subject and subject's consent data.
- the atomic role hasConsentPolicy links a subject's consent to a user's request.
- the atomic role hasConsent links subject and consent data to policy objects.
- the atomic role hasConstraint links actions and policy objects to constraints.
- the atomic role hasQuasiIdentifier links a subject to a quasi-identifier.
- the atomic role hasAction links a policy object to an action.

The consent management model rules have the following forms:

$\forall Subject\ hasRole(Subject, Role),\ \ Role \sqsubseteq hasRole.Subject$
$\forall User\ hasRole(User, Role),\ \ Role \sqsubseteq hasRole.User$
$\exists User\ isAnEmployee(User, Organization)$
$Organization \sqsubseteq isAnEmployee.User$
$\forall Object(hasOwner(Object, Subject)) \leftrightarrow \exists Subject(isOwnerOf(Subject, Object))$
$\exists Subject(hasQI(Subject, QuasiIdentifier))$
$\exists Subject(hasConsentData(Subject, ConsentData))$
$\forall PolicyObjects(hasAction(PolicyObjects, Action))$
$CD \equiv S \sqcap (\exists hasQuasiIdentifier.Subject \sqcup \exists isOwnerOf.Subject)$
$U \times S \times O \times A \times P \rightarrow hasRequest.User$
$S \times U \times PO \times CD \rightarrow hasConsentPolicy.Subject$
$R \times A \times P \times T \times \rightarrow PO$
$Permission \equiv \neg Prohibition$ and $Prohibition \equiv \neg Permission$

4   A Case Study

In this section, we illustrate a practical example of the consent management model for electronic health information systems. The example model is illustrated according to the syntax given in the previous section. In the case study, Bob is the doctor of Mary, who has quasi-identifiers and the owner of the `BloodTest` result file:

$hasRole(Bob) \equiv Doctor$
$isAnEmployee(Bob, MedicalCityHospital)$
$isDoctorOf(Bob, Mary) \equiv hasPatient(Bob, Mary)$
$hasRole(Mary) \equiv Patient$
$hasDoctor(Mary, Bob) \equiv isPatientOf(Mary, Bob)$
$isOwnerOf(Mary, BloodTest)$
$hasQuasiIdentifier(Mary, (Name, Gender, DateOfBirth, SocialSecurityNumber))$

Bob makes two requests to publish his patient Mary's quasi-identifiers and `BloodTest` result for his `Research` purpose:

$hasRequest1(Bob) = (Bob, Mary, Publish, QuasiIdentifier, Research)$
$hasRequest2(Bob) = (Bob, Mary, Publish, BloodTest, Research)$

Mary defines two consent data concept that includes her quasi-identifiers and `BloodTest` result, respectively:

$CD1(Mary) = hasConsentData(Mary, QuasiIdentifier)$
$CD2(Mary) = hasConsentData(Mary, BloodTest)$

Mary defines permission for the request to her `BloodTest` result from doctors who are her responsible doctors in order to publish her result for `Research` purpose:

$PermissionDoctor = (Doctor, Publish, Research, DoctorOfPatient(Mary))$

On the other hand, Mary prohibits Bob to publish her quasi-identifiers for his `Research` purpose:

$ProhibitionQI = (Doctor, Publish, Research, DoctorOfPatient(Mary))$

The final responses to Bob's requests will be Mary's consent policies respective to requests:

$hasConsentPolicy1(Mary) = (Mary, Bob, ProhibitionQI, CD1(Mary))$
$hasConsentPolicy2(Mary) = (Mary, Bob, PermissionDoctor, CD2(Mary))$

The first consent policy includes the consent data concept named `CD1(Mary)`. Similarly, the second consent policy includes `CD2(Mary)`. In this manner, Mary can control who can access to her personal records and for what purposes these data can be used. She can categorize her records as consent data and determine access levels according to the request's purpose. Eventually, she allows the usage of her personal data while protecting her privacy.

5   Conclusion

In the proposed consent management model, users can manage who can access which part of their data under what circumstances and for what purposes. Thus, users not only protect their privacy, but also contribute to improve the quality of the personal data usage for specific acceptable reasons. As a future work, the consent policy ontologies of the proposed model will be created and queried to execute and test scenarios of the model. Roles of the consent management model will be represented with Friend-Of-A Friend (FOAF, http://www.foaf-project.org) profiles. A reasoning engine will also be developed to demonstrate the use of consent policy rules.

References

1. Sweeney, L.: Uniqueness of Simple Demographics in the U.S. Population. Technical Report, Carnegie Mellon University (2000)
2. Cooper, T., Collman, J.: Managing Information Security and Privacy in Healthcare Data Mining: State of the Art. Medical Informatics: Knowledge Management and Data Mining in Biomedicine 8, 95–137 (2005)
3. Kluge, E.-H.W.: Informed consent and the security of the electronic health record (EHR): Some policy considerations. International Journal of Medical Informatics 73(3), 229–234 (2004)
4. Sweeney, L.: k-Anonymity: A Model for Protecting Privacy. International Journal on Uncertainty, Fuzziness and Knowledge-based Systems 10(5), 557–570 (2002)
5. Machanavajjhala, A., Gehrke, J., Kifer, D., Venkitasubramaniam, M.: ℓ-Diversity: Privacy Beyond k-Anonymity. In: Proceedings of the 22nd International Conference on Data Engineering (ICDE 2006), p. 24 (2006)
6. Li, N., Li, T., Venkatasubramanian, S.: t-Closeness: Privacy Beyond k-Anonymity and ℓ-Diversity. In: Proc. of Int. Conf. on Data Engineering (ICDE 2007) (2007)
7. Coiera, E., Clarke, R.: e-Consent: The Design and Implementation of Consumer Consent Mechanisms in an Electronic Environment. Journal of the American Medical Informatics Association 11(2), 129–140 (2004)
8. Anderson, R.J.: A Security Policy Model for Clinical Information Systems. In: Proceedings of the 1996 IEEE Symposium on Security and Privacy (1996)
9. Blobel, B.: Authorisation and Access Control for Electronic Health Record Systems. International Journal of Medical Informatics 73(3), 251–257 (2004)
10. Khan, A., Nadi, S.: Consentir: An Electronic Patient Consent Management System. In: 4th Annual Symposium of Health Technology (2010)
11. Becker, M.Y., Sewell, P.: Cassandra: Flexible Trust Management, Applied to Electronic Health Records. In: Proceedings of the 17th IEEE Computer Security Foundations Workshop (CSFW 2004), pp. 139–154 (2004)
12. Ko, Y.-Y., Liou, D.-M.: The Study of Managing the Personal Consent in the Electronic Healthcare Environment. World Academy of Science, Engineering and Technology 65, 314 (2010)
13. Russello, G., Dong, C., Dulay, N.: Consent-based Workflows for Healthcare Management. In: Proceedings of the 2008 IEEE Workshop on Policies for Distributed Systems and Networks (2008)
14. Samarati, P.: Protecting Respondents Identities in Microdata Release. IEEE Transactions on Knowledge and Data Engineering 13(6), 1010–1027 (2001)

Storing Metadata as QR Codes
in Multimedia Streams

Athanasios Zigomitros[1] and Constantinos Patsakis[2]

[1] Department of Informatics, University of Piraeus, Piraeus, Greece & Institute for
the Management of Information Systems, "Athena" Research Center, Greece
azigomit@unipi.gr
[2] Distributed Systems Group, School of Computer Science and Statistics, Trinity
College, College Green, Dublin 2, Ireland
patsakik@scss.tcd.ie

Abstract. With the continuous adoption of the web and the increase of
connection speeds, people are more and more sharing multimedia content. The main problem that is created by this approach is that the
shared content become less and less search-friendly. The information that
is shared, cannot be easily queried, so a big part of the web becomes inac-
cessible. To this end, there is a big shift towards adopting new metadata
standards for image and video that can efficiently help with queries over
image and videos.

In this work we extend our proposed method of embedding metadata
as QR codes in gray scale images, to color video files with a slightly
modified algorithm to make the decoding faster. We then examine the
experimental results regarding the compressed file size, using a lossless
encoding and the distortion of the frames of the video files. Storing the
metadata inside the multimedia stream with QR format has several advantages and possible new uses that are going to be discussed.

Keywords: QR codes, video metadata, LSB.

1 Introduction

Human nature makes us more attracted to image stimuli. Therefore, a huge economic sector is focused on capitalizing image processing. Apart from the press,
which uses still images and plays a significant part in the news, advertisement
and other areas, large amounts of money are invested in video. The biggest part
of the entertainment industry is currently focused on video, whether this is cin-
ema films, or TV shows. However, the displayed information has different target
audience, using different mediums each time to consume it. Hence, there is a
plethora of video file formats available trying to cover the needs of each use-
case. Nevertheless, video is used in many other aspects of our everyday living.
Typical examples are surveillance or traffic cameras, teleconferences etc.

It is quite clear that since a video is a set of images, the amount of stored
information is quite big, which introduces a great difficulty in processing it.

E. Garoufallou and J. Greenberg (Eds.): MTSR 2013, CCIS 390, pp. 152–162, 2013.

But the size of videos is not the actual problem in managing the stored information. One of the biggest challenges in video is data mining, extracting useful information or just specific instances. Contrary to text data, where we usually have efficient methods to search for the occurrences of a string or of a pattern, searching in videos is far more demanding and unfortunately with significantly smaller success rate. Brightness, luminosity, angle of recording, movement, closure, lens distortions are few of the factors that have to be taken into consideration when processing video streams, creating great demands in processing and computing.

Due to the processing cost in terms of resources and time, the collected and processed data must be stored in a convenient format which allows further exploitation. Several approaches have been proposed in the literature [1,2,3], in most cases an external database is used where all this information is stored, as in the case of MPEG-7 [4]. Yet, in other cases, this information is stored inside the file as comments or additional tags. According to the AVI file format specification, the metadata are stored at the start of AVI files. The video filetype MP4 is based on the ISO base media file format known as ISO/IEC 14496-12 (MPEG-4 Part 12) which allows metadata to be stored anywhere in the file, but practically they are stored either at the beginning or at the end of the file, as the raw captured audio/video data is saved continuously. Apparently, in both cases this information can easily be removed or lost over file format changes or editing.

The current article extends the work of [5] and proposes metadata embedding in videos as QR codes in the LSB of each frame. The experimental results illustrate that the use of the proposed method introduces a minimal image distortion, while enabling tracing in some cases of distortion on each frame. Furthermore, it introduces many other new possibilities for novel applications.

2   Related Work

2.1   Storing Metadata

When the applications are based on portability, metadata are embedded in the file, while the approach of a database is used, when the need is for easy reuse, enabling intensive queries on video content, through a central multimedia management system. Compared to the use of databases, embedding metadata in the video files has several additional advantages. It protects the file against loss or unavailability of the central database, while providing a search-engine friendly interface, as the embedded metadata can also be extracted by search engines, making them multimedia aware. This way, they may catalog the multimedia content that is offered by streaming for example sites. Finally, the metadata is not lost when a user downloads and keeps a local copy of the file to their computer.

To allow interoperability several metadata standards have been recommended, with the most well known being, the Qualified Dublin Core (DC), Public Broadcasting Core (PB Core), Extensible Metadata Platform (XMP) and Moving Picture Experts Group 7 (MPEG7).

Dublic Core[1] is a simple standard for describing digital files, using a set of 15 elements. The main goal is the quick search and retrieval of information in digital libraries. The Qualified Dublin Core has 3 additional elements, enables users to add their own qualifiers for the semantic description of the media resulting fine-tunning search results. Metadata in Dublin Core are often stored as name-value pairs within META tags as follows:

```
<META NAME="DC.Title" CONTENT="Metadata - Dublin Core">
<META NAME="DC.Creator.Address" CONTENT="iris@jarmin.com">
<META NAME="DC.Subject" CONTENT="metadata, metatags, Dublin Core,
guidelines, web design, resources, HTML authoring">
<META NAME="DC.Description" CONTENT="A quick guide to Dublin Core
metadata for web designers.">
<META NAME="DC.Date.Created" CONTENT="2000-02-01">
<META NAME="DC.Date.Modified" CONTENT="2000-02-09">
<META NAME="DC.Type" CONTENT="Text.Homepage.Educational">
<META NAME="DC.Format" CONTENT="text/html">
<META NAME="DC.Language" CONTENT="en">
<META NAME="DC.Identifier"
CONTENT="http://www.jarmin.com/meta/dcore.html">
```

The Dublin Core has formally been embedded in ISO 15836, ANSI/NISO Z39.85-2007 and IETF RFC 5013.

Table 1. Dublin Core Elements

Title	Date	Relation
Creator	Type	Coverage
Subject	Format	Rights
Description	Identifier	Audience*
Publisher	Source	Provenance*
Contributor	Language	RightsHolder*

Note: The elements with * are the Qualified Dublin Core additional elements.

Public Broadcasting Core (PB Core)[2] were published in 2005 as a metadata standard for multimedia. This standard has been developed by the public broadcasting community and has been funded by the Corporation for Public Broadcasting to serve the U.S. public broadcasting community. PBCore is mainly based on Dublin Core, introducing several additional elements useful for media. It has been adopted by many users in public media, as well as film archives, academic institutions, and other multimedia collections and archives.

MPEG-7 is also an ISO standard, namely ISO/IEC 15938, but unlike the preceding MPEG standards (MPEG-1,MPEG-2,MPEG-4) which deal with the

---

[1] http://www.dublincore.org/documents/dces
[2] http://www.pbcore.org

coded representation of the multimedia content, the purpose of MPEG-7 is the multimedia metadata structures, used to annotate and describe multimedia content using the XML. MPEG-7 is designed to allow fast and efficient searches on multimedia, based on their content. The MPEG-7 metadata may be physically located with the multimedia files, in the same data stream or on the same storage system as an external file, however the descriptions could also be stored in a remote database.

Adobe has introduced the non-proprietary Extensible Metadata Platform (XMP), which became an ISO standard for metadata, namely ISO 16684-1. XMP is based on Resource Description Framework (RDF) and can be considered as a subclass specific for multimedia files and currently, it is being supported by many vendors. In XMP-enabled applications, information about a projects can be captured during the content-creation process and the embedding is made within the file or into a multimedia content-management system, with the first case being the most widely used. However, since many file formats might not support the XMP standard, the metadata is stored in a separate file. Embedded XMP metadata have been reported by Adobe to remain even if the file is converted to a different format.

One significant problem of all these standards is that by uploading videos on a video sharing website like YouTube, files are transcoded by the platform, stripping them of all stored metadata. Therefore, a huge amount of important information is removed, almost disabling queries over videos. Moreover, by removing metadata, media interaction on the web is becoming less and less usable, so frameworks like Popcorn.js[3] enable developers to create time-based interactive web media.

Addressing to this problem, our work focuses mostly on descriptive metadata and how they can be embedded on the content and not just the file. The distortion of image is necessary but is insignificant and the disadvantage of the limited payload of the QR code can still be enough for various applications. Our goal is not to make the other metadata formats obsolete but to offer an alternative way on how the metadata can be transmitted.

2.2 QR Codes

QR code [6], an abbreviation for Quick Response code, developed by Denso Wave in 1994, is a two dimensional barcode that can store more information compared to the traditional barcode. They have recently become popular because of their use in modern smart phones and mobile devices. One of their big advantages, besides the ability to store more data, QRs have the ability of error correction. Even if they are partially distorted, due to physical distortion of the code, lack of light sources etc, one can still restore the embedded data.

They have a square crossword form, where every small square is called module. According to the data to be stored, the QRs range from 21×21 up to 177×177 modules. Since they can be easily read and correct a big extend of possible

---

[3] http://popcornjs.org/

Table 2. QR code data capacity

Numeric code only	Max. 7,089 characters
Alphanumeric	Max. 4,296 characters
Binary (8 bits)	Max. 2,953 bytes
Kanji/Kana	Max. 1,817 characters

Table 3. Error correction of QR codes

Level L	7% of codewords can be restored.
Level M	15% of codewords can be restored.
Level Q	25% of codewords can be restored.
Level H	30% of codewords can be restored.

errors, modern mobile devices are shipped with special libraries in order to read the encoded messages. Therefore, one may take a photo of a QR that is placed on a magazine or in a museum tag with his smartphone and instantly be redirected to a web page containing additional information. Their capacity, as well as their error correction capabilities are illustrated in Tables 2 and 3.

The watermarking images with QR codes has already drawn the attention of the research community in several works such as [7,8,9,10,11,12,13,14]. Moreover, there is an application of QR code embedding in audio [15]. Even if the idea of embedding metadata in the video content have already proposed it has only been used in a specific domain, that of UAV videos [16,17] and without the use of a 2D barcode. To the best of our knowledge, only one robust watermarking scheme that embeds QR codes in video exist so far [18] but the scope of that work is the copyright protection of the content and not the additional functionality that metadata have to offer.

3 Proposed Method

3.1 Application Scenario

Smooth integration and platform independence is a major issue in software development. The wide range of video formats and players makes co-operation between applications and cross-platform development of content-aware applications very difficult.

Let's assume that we have a media player that is playing a video. The displayed information in many cases would be beneficial input for other running applications and services. It would be very handy for example to be able to extract several metadata from the video, so that the browser displays relevant information about the actors or the place that the video takes place. Even for targeted-advertisement applications, this information is very important, as this would enable them to display content related advertisement.

To allow this information flow, developers could create a buffer, where video players send their metadata, so that other applications can extract them, independently of how this information is stored. It is clear that this creates a problem when we are talking about Operation System-independent development and multi application environments. Moreover, one could block access to this buffer, crippling this feature.

3.2 Core Idea

To this end, we propose embedding the metadata information as part of the video, so that independently of how a user is watching a video, from which combination of application/operating system, this information can be retrieved. One method to achieve this is by embedding the metadata in a watermark-like way in the LSB. The idea is that applications could take a screenshot of the user's desktop, keep the LSB, trace the watermark and extract the information.

It is clear that the aforementioned method can be applied to any operating system and any multimedia player, with trivial overhead. Moreover, by embedding metadata in this form, the metadata are:

– Stored with the file.
– Are always synced with the content.
– Remain after processing the video, which introduce low noise.
– Remain if a video is split or videos are merged.

Since we want to allow the information to be retrieved from a screenshot, where the video can be placed in any part of the screen, there is an obvious need for clear patterns that can easily be traced. Moreover, it would be very beneficial if the pattern could be easily recognized by existing libraries and if it could allow error correction. The criteria above have led us to use QR codes in the LSB as a test-bed, to explore the efficiency, the storage, the performance and distortion of our solution.

3.3 Implementing the Proposed Method

In order to test the proposal to the extremes, we embedded three QR codes in each frame of the videos, one in every color component. With the use of Least Significant Bit (LSB) we alter the bits of every color component to create a binary image of a QR, containing the desired metadata. The payload of the QR depends on the version of the QR, which can also be resized to be smaller in the embedding and in the extraction process to be inversely resized. This scheme is able to retain the metadata in simple transformations and lossless compression of the multimedia stream. Figures 1 and 2 illustrate the embedding process, as along with a frame where information has been embedded with the proposed method.

To embed the metadata, the algorithm reads the movie file properties and then uses the smallest size of height or width, to create a square space in the center of the frame for all the color components where the QR code will be embedded. Then using LSB, the message is embedded in each color component.

Metadata extraction from the multimedia stream process is very straight-forward. If we have access to the actual video file, we load each frame and compute the modulo 2 for every color component, resulting to a binary table. This table is then processed by the QR reader to return the data to the user. Otherwise, an application takes a screenshot of the user's desktop and computes the modulo 2 for every color component, resulting again to a binary table, which is parsed to a QR reader. It is clear that due to the QR pattern, the metadata can be extracted without any problem.

The stored metadata have no limitations on the format and the content to be stored. In the current implementation, vcard format, URLs, geotagging information etc are supported. Depending on the video, users could store movie subtitles. This way, multiple could simultaneously be supported without any synchronization problem.

Fig. 1. A frame with it's embedded QR code

4   Experimental Results

The experiments were conducted using Matlab. The videos that were used can be found at [19]. All 14 video sequences are in the uncompressed YUV4MPEG format and in two different resolutions. Seven Cif video files are 352 by 288 with 300 frames each, while the other seven Qcif files are 176 by 144 with 300 frames each with the same content. The quality measurement of distortion were made using the Matlab package Image quality measures, developed by Athi Narayanan. The metadata that were stored in each QR, were a random 120 character stream

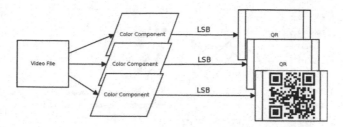

Fig. 2. Embedding process

Table 4. Video quality measurements of cif files

	Mean Sq. Error	PSNR	Normalized cross-correl.	Structural Content	Average Diff.	Max Diff.	Normalized Abs. Error
akiyo	0,5051	51,0974	0,9984	1,0033	0,2189	1	0,0048
bowing	0,4998	51,1433	0,9986	1,0028	0,2012	1	0,0043
coastguard	0,4985	51,1544	0,9985	1,0029	0,2005	1	0,0042
container	0,5018	51,1252	0,9985	1,0029	0,2049	1	0,0035
foreman	0,4985	51,1541	0,9987	1,0026	0,2	1	0,0034
hall__monitor	0,5032	51,1138	0,9985	1,003	0,209	1	0,0038
news	0,4991	51,1486	0,9985	1,003	0,2008	1	0,006
Average	0,5009	51,1338	0,9985	1,0029	0,2050	1	0,0043

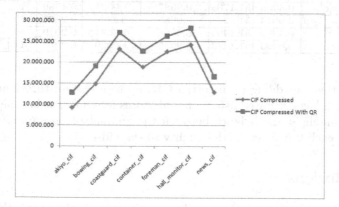

Fig. 3. Filesize difference of original vs QR embedded cif files

in both sizes of the video files (360 characters per frame). We chose YUVsoft codec [20] for compression in order to have a lossless video format [21].

The visual impact of this distortion was not traceable by the human eye, while the PSNR values remained close to optimal the experimental results are illustrated in Figures 3,4 and Tables 4,5. It is clear, that the implementation that was made was targeting to show that even in the extreme cases, the method can still be applied without significant quality cost. A more fine-grained approach would be to store one QR that would be split among the three color components, so that their XOR for example resulted to the needed QR. Additionally, one

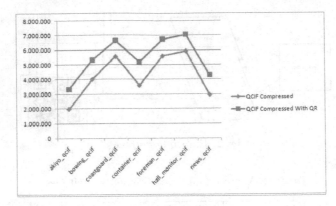

Fig. 4. Filesize difference of original vs QR embedded qcif files

Table 5. Video quality measurements of qcif files

	Mean sq. error	PSNR	Normalized cross-correl.	Structural Content	Average Diff.	Max Diff.	Normalized Abs. error
akiyo_qcif	0,5043	51,1043	0,9984	1,0033	0,2173	1	0,0048
bowing_qcif	0,4978	51,1603	0,9986	1,0028	0,2004	1	0,0043
coastguard_qcif	0,4968	51,1686	0,9985	1,0029	0,1996	1	0,0042
container_qcif	0,4991	51,1487	0,9986	1,0029	0,2022	1	0,0035
foreman_qcif	0,4966	51,1708	0,9987	1,0025	0,1989	1	0,0034
hall_monitor_qcif	0,5014	51,1288	0,9985	1,003	0,2078	1	0,0037
news_qcif	0,4991	51,1493	0,9984	1,0031	0,2019	1	0,006
Average	0,4993	51,1473	0,9985	1,0029	0,2040	1	0,0043

could allow the embedding of distorted QR, up to a certain threshold. Clearly such approach has even less distortion and stores less information, nevertheless it does not highlight the balance between the amount of information that can be stored in each frame versus the quality of the video.

5   Conclusions

Definitely, the proposed solution invokes an obvious disadvantage, that of partially distorting the center of the frame with LSB embedding QRs. Nevertheless, the experiments indicate that the distortion is quite small. On the other hand, the proposed method for embedding metadata has several advantages over currently used methods. The most obvious one is that the metadata are embedded in the video file, more precisely inside the frames. This enables the transfer of metadata in case of file conversion to another lossless video format. Moreover, the metadata are kept even if the video files are split and merged, without synchronization problems.

It should be highlighted that even though we introduce a new approach for storing metadata, we do not propose the use of any metadata standard. We believe that this decision should be left to the developer that adopts such solution.

The only constraint is that the size of metadata which can be stored, obviously depends on the size of the video, in terms of resolution and length.

The proposed method enables easy queries on stored metadata, and their storage follows a well known and standardized industry format, which is noise tolerant. The extraction is so easy that taking a screenshot from any frame, with any application, one may retrieve the stored metadata.

A very important feature is that by embedding information this way, developers can extract the information without the need for cross-platform frameworks, publicly accessible registers etc. Therefore, the solution can be adopted by any application in every operating system, that enables it to take screenshots of user's desktop.

Our future work will focus on extending this embedding process in order to survive possible attacks. Moreover, we are planning to work on certain lossy compression formats and less noisy solutions that can support several image and geometrical transformations, beyond rotation, flipping, which are currently supported.

References

1. Jain, R., Hampapur, A.: Metadata in video databases. SIGMOD Rec. 23(4), 27–33 (1994)
2. Catarci, T., Donderler, M., Saykol, E., Ulusoy, O., Gudukbay, U.: Bilvideo: A video database management system. IEEE MultiMedia 10(1), 66–70 (2003)
3. Kosch, H.: Mpeg-7 and multimedia database systems. ACM SIGMOD Record 31(2), 34–39 (2002)
4. Mpeg 7, http://mpeg.chiariglione.org/standards/mpeg-7 (accessed June 10, 2013)
5. Zigomitros, A., Patsakis, C.: Cross format embedding of metadata in images using QR codes. In: Tsihrintzis, G.A., Virvou, M., Jain, L.C., Howlett, R.J. (eds.) IIMSS 2011. SIST, vol. 11, pp. 113–121. Springer, Heidelberg (2011)
6. QR codes, http://www.qrcode.com/en/ (accessed June 20, 2013)
7. Zhang, S., Yoshino, K.: Dwt-based watermarking using qr code
8. Vongpradhip, S., Rungraungsilp, S.: Qr code using invisible watermarking in frequency domain. In: 2011 9th International Conference on ICT and Knowledge Engineering (ICT & Knowledge Engineering), pp. 47–52. IEEE (2012)
9. Lee, H.-C., Dong, C.-R., Lin, T.-M.: Digital watermarking based on JND model and QR code features. In: Pan, J.-S., Yang, C.-N., Lin, C.-C. (eds.) Advances in Intelligent Systems & Applications. SIST, vol. 21, pp. 141–148. Springer, Heidelberg (2012)
10. Hsu, F.-H., Wu, M.-H., Wang, S.-J.: Dual-watermarking by qr-code applications in image processing. In: 2012 9th International Conference on Ubiquitous Intelligence & Computing and 9th International Conference on Autonomic & Trusted Computing (UIC/ATC), pp. 638–643. IEEE (2012)
11. Xie, R.-S., Wu, K.-S., Xu, G.-P., Ouyang, M.: Research on anti-counterfeiting quick response 2d barcode techniques based on digital watermark. Journal of Shanghai Jiaotong University (Science), 1–5 (2013)
12. Islam, M., Alzahir, S., et al.: A novel qr code guided image stenographic technique. In: 2013 IEEE International Conference on Consumer Electronics (ICCE), pp. 586–587. IEEE (2013)

13. Felix Gunalan, G., Nithya, J.: Qr code hiding using histogram shifting method
14. Chen, J.-H., Chen, C.-H.: Image tamper detection scheme using qr code and dct transform techniques
15. Poomvichid, T., Patirupanusara, P., Ketcham, M.: The qr code for audio watermarking using genetic algorithm
16. Marcinak, M.P., Mobasseri, B.G.: Digital video watermarking for metadata embedding in uav video. In: IEEE Military Communications Conference (MILCOM 2005), vol. 3, pp. 1637–1641. IEEE (2005)
17. Philp, A., Bradley, B., Stach, J., Rodriguez, T.: Real-time application of digital watermarking to embed tactical metadata into full motion video captured from unmanned aerial systems. In: IS&T/SPIE Electronic Imaging, International Society for Optics and Photonics, p. 725410 (2009)
18. Prabakaran, G., Bhavani, R., Ramesh, M.: A robust qr-code video watermarking scheme based on svd and dwt composite domain. In: 2013 International Conference on Pattern Recognition, Informatics and Medical Engineering (PRIME), pp. 251–257. IEEE (2013)
19. Xiph, http://media.xiph.org/video/derf/ (accessed June 28, 2013)
20. YUVsoft codec,
    http://www.yuvsoft.com/download/lossless-codec/index.html (accessed June 13, 2013)
21. Lossless Video Codecs Comparison,
    http://compression.ru/video/codec_comparison/pdf/
    msu_lossless_codecs_comparison_2007_eng.pdf
    (accessed June 21, 2013)

Semantic Mapping in CLARIN Component Metadata

Matej Durco[1] and Menzo Windhouwer[2]

[1] Institute for Corpus Linguistics and Text Technology (ICLTT), Vienna, Austria
matej.durco@assoc.oeaw.ac.at
[2] The Language Archive - DANS, The Hague, The Netherlands
menzo.windhouwer@dans.knaw.nl

Abstract. In recent years, large scale initiatives like CLARIN set out to overcome the notorious heterogeneity of metadata formats in the domain of language resource. The CLARIN Component Metadata Infrastructure established means for flexible resouce descriptions for the domain of language resources. The Data Category Registry ISOcat and the accompanying Relation Registry foster semantic interoperability within the growing heterogeneous collection of metadata records. This paper describes the CMD Infrastructure focusing on the facilities for semantic mapping, and gives also an overview of the current status in the joint component metadata domain.

Keywords: semantic mapping, metadata, research infrastructure.

1 Introduction

The european initiative CLARIN (Common Language Resources and Technology Infrastructure) is a large scale collaborative effort to create, coordinate and make language resources and technology available and readily useable[1]. One cornerstone of this initiative is the Component MetaData Infrastructure (CMDI)[2] a new metadata infrastructure based upon components. These components group together metadata elements and can be created and reused as needed. Components are combined into metadata profiles, which are used to describe specific groups of language resources. This approach allows to fit the metadata closely to the resources. However, this diversity does pose integration problems for the aggregators in the CLARIN joint metadata domain. The CMD Infrastructure solves this by making semantics explicit and shared where possible. Metadata values, elements and components should have a concept link, which refers to a concept in an established concept registry. Multiple metadata elements can share concepts and the semantic mapping thus constructed can be exploited by aggregators. In this paper we describe the CMD Infrastructure and its semantic layer in more detail. The last sections will show and discuss semantic mappings already appearing in the CLARIN joint CMD domain.

E. Garoufallou and J. Greenberg (Eds.): MTSR 2013, CCIS 390, pp. 163–168, 2013.

2   The Component Metadata Infrastructure

The metadata lifecycle of CMD starts with the need of a metadata modeller to create a dedicated metadata profile for a type of resources. The modeller can browse and search the Component Registry (CR) for components and profiles that are suitable or come close. The registry already contains many general components, e.g., for contact persons, language and geographical information. In general many of these can be reused as they are or have to be only slightly adapted, i.e., add or a remove some metadata elements and/or components. Also new components can be created to model the unique aspects of the resources under consideration. All components are combined into one profile. Components, elements and values should be linked to a concept to make its semantics explicit.

All the CLARIN centers offer their CMD records for harvesting in a joint metadata domain. Several aggregators have been build, e.g., the Virtual Language Observatory (VLO) provides a facetted browser for all records [3], while WebLicht allows to chain Web Services described in the records [4]. To overcome the diversity of metadata records, e.g., to find facets, common patterns have to be found. These patterns are based on the explicit, and hopefully shared, semantics of the components and elements.

3   Shared Semantics for CMDI

As stated before any CMD component and element should be linked to a concept. In CMDI the term concept is used very loosly. There is no requirement that the concept is part of a formal ontology, but the main requirement is that resolving the concepts persistent identifier should lead to a good, human readable, definition of the intended semantics. Henceforth concept registries can also have a very diverse nature. Currently there are two main types of concepts: the Dublin Core metadata elements and terms [5] and the ISOcat Data Categories [6]. This way semantics in CMDI are made explicit and can be shared where possible. Aggregators like the VLO can use these concept links to identify which elements can be mapped to a specific facet, i.e., which elements based on domain specific terminology are semantically equivalent. The next section will introduce the ISOcat Data Category Registry.

3.1   The ISOcat Data Category Registry

ISOcat is an implementation of the ISO 12620:2009 standard for Data Category Registries (DCRs). Its an open registry where anyone can create and share Data Categories (DCs). DCs are defined as the "result of the specification of a given data field" [7]. The data model is inspired by ISO 11179 where data elements, which correspond almost one to one with DCs, are considered instances of concepts with additional information on representation, e.g., a data type.

The *Athens Core* group[1] has populated the metadata subset of ISOcat with many DCs inspired by the various metadata frameworks already around at that time, e.g., OLAC, TEI Header and IMDI. Many CMD components and elements are linked to these Athens Core DCs. However, due to the open nature of ISOcat the metadata modeller can create new DCs when needed.

3.2 The RELcat Relation Registry

The current CMD Infrastructure is based on the system components described above. However, due to the use of different concept registries and the open nature of some of these registries, e.g., ISOcat, multiple concepts exist which are essentially the same. Its also envisioned that the requirements of the metadata modeller to capture the fine, e.g., theory specific, semantics of a resource might not always match the more coarser information need of the end users.

In the Relation Registry (RR) RELcat, which is currently under construction, relationships between concepts (possibly from different registries) can be stored [8]. These relationships can be of the 'same as' or 'almost same as' type but also refer to more broader or more specific concepts. In the latter case an ontology or taxonomy can be constructed. To accomodate user specific views on how concepts relate RELcat allows to create user specific relation sets. But its also envisioned that more general, i.e., CLARIN wide, relation sets will be created. In fact there are already such general sets to map Dublin Core elements and terms to ISOcat DCs and vice versa. These generic equivalence relations are used by aggregators, like the VLO. While user specifc sets can be used in search engines to create a broader semantic search to improve the recall.

4 Semantic Mapping in the Joint CMD Domain

In the following section, we give an overview of the current status in the CMD domain with regard to the defined profiles and data categories used, exemplifying on two very common data categories: *Language* and *Name*.

4.1 CMD Profiles

In the CR 124[2] public Profiles and 696 Components are defined. Table 1 shows the development of the CR and DCR population over time.

Next to the 'native' CMD profiles a number of profiles have been created that implement existing metadata formats, like OLAC/DCMI-terms, TEI Header or the META-SHARE schema. The resulting profiles proof the flexibility/expressivity of the CMD metamodel. The individual profiles differ also very much in their structure – next to flat profiles with just one level of components or elements with 5 to 20 fields (*dublincore*, *collection*, the set of *Bamdes*-profiles)

---

[1] The *Athens Core* group was named after the first meeting of a large number of metadata modellers for language resources, which took place in Athens in 2009.
[2] All numbers are as of 2013-06 if not stated otherwise.

there are complex profiles with up to 10 levels (*ExperimentProfile*, profiles for describing Web Services) and a few hundred elements. The biggest single profile is currently the remodelled maximum schema from the META-SHARE project [9] for describing corpora, with 117 components and 337 elements.

Table 1. The development of defined profiles and DCs over time

date	2011-01	2012-06	2013-01	2013-06
Profiles	40	53	87	124
Components	164	298	542	828
Elements	511	893	1505	2399
Distinct data categories	203	266	436	499
Data categories in the Metadata profile	277	712	774	791
Ratio of elements without DCs	24,7%	17,6%	21,5%	26,5%

4.2 Data Categories

In the ISOcat DCR 791 DCss are defined in the Metadata thematic profile, out of which 222 were created by the *Athens Core* group. In the following we describe two show cases – *Language* and *name* – in more detail.

Language: While there are 69 components and 97 elements containing a substring 'language' defined in the CR still only 19 distinct DCs with a 'language' substring are being referenced by CMD components and elements. The most commonly used ones: *languageID* (DC-2482) and *languageName* (DC-2484) are referenced by more than 80 profiles. Additionally, these two DCs are linked to the Dublin Core term *Language* in the RR. Thus a search engine capable of interpreting RR information could offer the user a simple Dublin Core-based search interface, while – by expanding the query – still searching over all available data, and, moreover, on demand offer the user a more finegrained semantic interpretation for the matches based on the originally assigned DCs. Figure 1 depicts the relations between the language data categories and their usage in the profiles. We encounter all types of situations: profiles using only one of the four DCs, most profiles use both *isocat:languageId* and *isocat:languageName* and there are even profiles that refer to both *isocat* and *dublincore* data categories (*data*, *HZSKCorpus*, *ToolService*).

It requires further inspection, if the other less often used 'language' DCs (e.g. *sourceLanguage*, *languageMother*) can be treated as equivalent to the above mentioned ones. They can be expected to share the same value domain (natural languages) and even if they do not describe the language of the resource, they could be considered when one aims at maximizing the recall (i.e., trying to find anything related to a given language). This is actually exactly the scenario the RR was conceived for – allow to define custom relation sets based on specific needs of a project or of a research question.

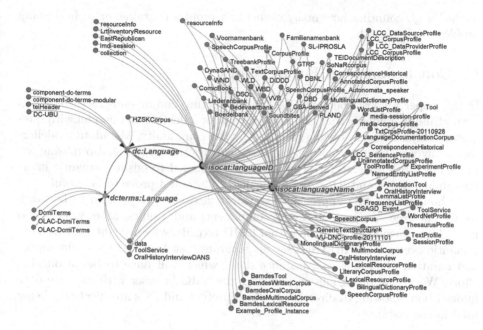

Fig. 1. The four main *Language* DCs and in which profiles they are being used

Name: There are as many as 72 CMD elements with the label `Name`, referring to 12 different DCs. Again the main DC *resourceName* (DC-2544) being used in 74 profiles together with the semantically near *resourceTitle* (DC-2545) used in 69 profiles offer a good coverage over available data.

Some of the DCs referenced by `Name` elements are *author* (DC-4115), *contact full name* (DC-2454), *dcterms:Contributor*, *project name* (DC-2536), *web service name* (DC-4160) and *language name* (DC-2484). This implies, that a naïve search in a `Name` element would yield semantically very heterogeneous results and only applying the semantic information provided by the DCs and/or the context of the element (the enclosing components) allows to disambiguate the meaning.

4.3 SMC Browser

As the data set keeps growing both in numbers and in complexity, the call from the CMD community to provide better ways for exploration gets stronger. One answer to this need is the *SMC browser*[3] a web application being developed by the CMDI team, that lets the metadata modeller explore the information about profiles, components, elements and the usage of DCs as an interactive graph. This allows for example to examine the reuse of components or DCs in different profiles. The graph is accompanied by statistical information about individual

---

[3] http://clarin.aac.ac.at/smc-browser

'nodes', e.g., counting how many elements a profiles contains, or in how many profiles a DC is used.

5 Conclusions and Future Work

In this paper we described the CMD Infrastructure and demonstrated based on current usage numbers that the basic concept of a flexible metamodel with integrated semantic layer is being taken up by the community. Metadata modellers increasingly making use not only of the infrastructure, but are also reusing the modelling work done so far. The provisions designed to ensure semantic interoperability (DCR and RR) are practically in place and prove to be useful.

Although the CMD approach is aimed at flexibility, steps need to be taken to prevent excessive proliferation of components and profiles. More work is also needed on consolidation of the actual CMD records, which might lead to more semantic overlap. CLARIN has set up separate task force for the maintenance and curation of profiles and instance data, which will have to be an ongoing effort. Work is also ongoing on enriching the SMC browser with instance data information, allowing to directly see which profiles and DCs are effectively being used in the instances.

References

1. Váradi, T., Krauwer, S., et al.: Clarin: Common language resources and technology infrastructure. In: Calzolari, N., Choukri, K., et al. (eds.) Proceedings of the Sixth International Conference on Language Resources and Evaluation (LREC), Marrakech. ELRA (May 2008)
2. Broeder, D., Kemps-Snijders, M., et al.: A data category registry- and component-based metadata framework. In: Calzolari, N., Choukri, K., et al. (eds.) LREC, Valletta. ELRA (May 2010)
3. Uytvanck, D.V., Zinn, C., et al.: Virtual language observatory: The portal to the language resources and technology universe. In: Calzolari, N., Choukri, K., et al. (eds.) LREC, Valletta. ELRA (May 2010)
4. Hinrichs, E., Hinrichs, M., Zastrow, T.: Weblicht: Web-based lrt services for German. In: Proceedings of the ACL 2010 System Demonstrations, Uppsala, Sweden, pp. 25–29. Association for Computational Linguistics (July 2010)
5. Powell, A., Nilsson, M., Naeve, A., Johnston, P.: DCMI Abstract Model. Technical report (March 2005)
6. Windhouwer, M., Wright, S.E.: Linking to linguistic data categories in isocat. In: Linked Data in Linguistics, Frankfurt, Germany, pp. 99–107. Springer (2012)
7. ISO 12620: Specification of data categories and management of a data category registry for language resources (2009)
8. Windhouwer, M.: RELcat: A relation registry for isocat data categories. In: Calzolari, N., Choukri, K., et al. (eds.) LREC, Istanbul. ELRA (May 2012)
9. Gavrilidou, M., Labropoulou, P., et al.: The META-SHARE metadata schema for the description of language resources. In: Calzolari, N., Choukri, K., et al. (eds.) LREC, Istanbul. ELRA (May 2012)

Using Metadata Standards to Improve National and IMF DATA[*]

Nalini Umashankar

International Monetary Fund
numashankar@imf.org

Abstract. Metadata standardization leads to greater efficiencies and lower costs in global exchange and internal production of data. Use of metadata standards enhances the accountability of countries for providing quality information about their economy and improves the understanding of data by users. The International Monetary Fund (IMF) experience, as outlined in this paper, demonstrates how metadata standards have resulted in faster, cheaper and more consistent production and dissemination of data.

Keywords: International Monetary Fund, IMF, Metadata standards.

1 Using Metadata to Monitor Data Quality

One of the challenges that we face is to best guide member countries to provide quality information about their economy, while holding them accountable for dissemination of such information. In this regard, the IMF has established the Data Standards Initiatives[1] for guiding the dissemination statistical data and metadata. They comprise the General Data Dissemination System, the Special Data Dissemination Standard (SDDS) and the SDDS Plus. Countries following these standards use the IMF Data Quality Assessment Framework (DQAF). The framework defines five data quality aspects:

1. Integrity
2. Methodological Soundness
3. Accuracy and Reliability
4. Serviceability
5. Accessibility

Countries are required to submit text (metadata) describing their data and dissemination practices to the IMF for posting on an electronic bulletin board. Each country is responsible for the accuracy and timeliness of its metadata. IMF Staff review countries' postings to ensure they provide comprehensive and internationally comparable metadata.

---

[*] The views expressed herein are those of the authors and should not be attributed to the International Monetary Fund (IMF), its Executive Board, or its management.
[1] For more information on Dissemination Standards at the IMF, refer to the following link: http://dsbb.imf.org/

E. Garoufallou and J. Greenberg (Eds.): MTSR 2013, CCIS 390, pp. 169–174, 2013.

The benefits of the Dissemination Standards are that countries are made accountable for providing metadata about their data and users are able to obtain consistent information that facilitates cross- country comparisons as well as a better understanding of the quality of a country's statistics.

The generic DQAF framework serves as an umbrella for these dataset-specific frameworks: National accounts, Consumer prices, Producer prices, Government Finance Statistics and Public Sector Debt Statistics, Monetary Statistics, Balance of Payments and International Investment Position Statistics and External Debt.[2]

1.1   Content of the Framework

The elements and indicators within their respective dimensions are as follows:

1 Prerequisites of Quality: Although it is not a dimension of quality, this group of "pointers to quality" includes elements and indicators that have an overarching role as prerequisites, or institutional preconditions, for quality of statistics. Note that the focus is on the agency, such as a national statistical office, central bank, or a ministry/department. These prerequisites cover the following elements:

1.1   Legal and institutional environments
1.2   Resources available for the statistical program
1.3   Relevance
1.4   Other quality management

2 Assurances of Integrity: This dimension refers to the adherence to the principle of objectivity in the collection, compilation, and dissemination of statistics. The dimension encompasses institutional arrangements that ensure professionalism in statistical policies and practices, transparency, and satisfactory ethical standards. The three elements for this dimension of quality are the following:

2.1   Institutional Integrity
2.2   Transparency
2.3   Ethical standards

3 Methodological Soundness: This dimension specifies that the methodological basis for the production of statistics should be sound and that this can be attained by following internationally accepted standards, guidelines, or good practices. This dimension is necessarily dataset-specific, reflecting different methodologies for different datasets. This dimension has four elements, namely:

3.1   Concepts and definitions
3.2   Scope
3.3   Classification/sectorization
3.4   Basis for recording

---

[2] For further information, refer to the link:
    http://dsbb.imf.org/Pages/DQRS/DQAF.aspx

4   Accuracy and Reliability: This dimension says that statistical outputs should sufficiently portray the reality of the economy. This dimension is also data specific, reflecting the sources used and their processing. The five elements of this dimension cover the following:

4.1   Source data
4.2   Assessment of source data
4.3   Statistical techniques
4.4   Assessment and validation of intermediate data and statistical outputs.
4.5   Revision studies

5   Serviceability: This dimension indicates that statistics are disseminated with an appropriate periodicity in a timely fashion, are consistent internally and with other major datasets, and follow a regular revision policy. The three elements for this dimension are as follows:

5.1   Periodicity and timeliness
5.2   Consistency
5.3   Revision policy and practice

6   Accessibility: This dimension specifies data and metadata to be presented in a clear and understandable manner on an easily available and impartial basis, that metadata are up-to-date and pertinent, and that a prompt and knowledgeable support service is available. This dimension has three elements:

6.1   Data accessibility
6.2   Metadata accessibility
6.3   Assistance to users

2   Using Metadata to Exchange Data

A second challenge is how to make the global exchange of data and metadata faster and cheaper, while reducing the reporting burden of member countries. The Statistical Data and Metadata Exchange (SDMX)[3] standards enable us to meet this challenge. IMF uses SDMX to reduce the work to map metadata structures between agencies, by collaborating internationally to develop common Data Structure Definitions (DSDs), code lists and concept schemes. The IMF increasingly collect and disseminate data using SDMX.

SDMX promises to make global data exchange faster, cheaper, and more consistent, thereby reducing the reporting burden on member countries. For example, the external sector DSD developed by five SDMX sponsoring organizations, under the leadership of the IMF, will allow country authorities to provide one SDMX data file or web service to satisfy the data collection needs of multiple international institutions. Countries will report external sector data using the DSD and standard

---

[3] For more information, click on this link http://www.sdmx.org/

codes (see table 1) to an agency or a registry, and consuming organizations will process data from files that could be shared across processing organizations or pulled from a data providers' web service using information provided to a registry.[4]

Table 1. Coded examples for balance of payments statistics using the external sector DSD V0.2

Title complement	Time series key	Frequency	Reference country or area	Adjustment indicator	Flows and stocks indicator	Accounting entries	Counterpart Area	Reference sector	Functional category	Instrument Assets Classification	Counterpart sector	Maturity	Currency Denomination	Compilation Methodology	Valuation	Unit of Measure
Financial account - Net lending (+) / net borrowing (-)	Q..N.T.FA.N.W1.S1._Z.F._Z._Z._T._Z.	Q	N	T	FA	N	W1	S1	_Z	F	_Z	_Z	T	_Z	N	
Portfolio investment	Q..N.T.FA.N.W1.S1.P.F._Z._Z._T._Z.	Q	N	T	FA	N	W1	S1	P	F	_Z	_Z	T	_Z	N	
Net acquisition of financial assets	Q..N.T.FA.A.W1.S1.P.F._Z._Z._T._Z.	Q	N	T	FA	A	W1	S1	P	F	_Z	_Z	T	_Z	N	
Equity and investment fund shares	Q..N.T.FA.A.W1.S1.P.F5._Z._Z._T._Z.	Q	N	T	FA	A	W1	S1	P	F5	_Z	_Z	T	_Z	N	
Equity securities other than investment fund shares	Q..N.T.FA.A.W1.S1.P.F51._Z._Z._T._Z.	Q	N	T	FA	A	W1	S1	P	F51	_Z	_Z	T	_Z	N	
Listed	Q..N.T.FA.A.W1.S1.P.F511._Z._Z._T._Z.	Q	N	T	FA	A	W1	S1	P	F511	_Z	_Z	T	_Z	N	
Unlisted	Q..N.T.FA.A.W1.S1.P.F512._Z._Z._T._Z.	Q	N	T	FA	A	W1	S1	P	F512	_Z	_Z	T	_Z	N	
Investment fund shares or units	Q..N.T.FA.A.W1.S1.P.F52._Z._Z._T._Z.	Q	N	T	FA	A	W1	S1	P	F52	_Z	_Z	T	_Z	N	
Reinvestment of earnings	Q..N.T.FA.A.W1.S1.P.F52B._Z._Z._T._Z.	Q	N	T	FA	A	W1	S1	P	F52B	_Z	_Z	T	_Z	N	
Money market fund shares or units	Q..N.T.FA.A.W1.S1.P.F521._Z._Z._T._Z.	Q	N	T	FA	A	W1	S1	P	F521	_Z	_Z	T	_Z	N	
Debt securities	Q..N.T.FA.A.W1.S1.P.F3.T._Z._Z.	Q	N	T	FA	A	W1	S1	P	F3	T	_Z	T	_Z	N	
Central bank	Q..N.T.FA.A.W1.S121.P.F3.T._Z._Z.	Q	N	T	FA	A	W1	S121	P	F3	T	_Z	T	_Z	N	
Short-term	Q..N.T.FA.A.W1.S121.P.F3.S._Z._Z.	Q	N	T	FA	A	W1	S121	P	F3	S	_Z	T	_Z	N	
Long-term	Q..N.T.FA.A.W1.S121.P.F3.L._Z._Z.	Q	N	T	FA	A	W1	S121	P	F3	L	_Z	T	_Z	N	
Monetary authorities (where relevant)	Q..N.T.FA.A.W1.S1X.P.F3.T._Z._Z.	Q	N	T	FA	A	W1	S1X	P	F3	T	_Z	T	_Z	N	
Short-term	Q..N.T.FA.A.W1.S1X.P.F3.S._Z._Z.	Q	N	T	FA	A	W1	S1X	P	F3	S	_Z	T	_Z	N	
Long-term	Q..N.T.FA.A.W1.S1X.P.F3.L._Z._Z.	Q	N	T	FA	A	W1	S1X	P	F3	L	_Z	T	_Z	N	
General government	Q..N.T.FA.A.W1.S13.P.F3.T._Z._Z.	Q	N	T	FA	A	W1	S13	P	F3	T	_Z	T	_Z	N	
Short-term	Q..N.T.FA.A.W1.S13.P.F3.S._Z._Z.	Q	N	T	FA	A	W1	S13	P	F3	S	_Z	T	_Z	N	
Long-term	Q..N.T.FA.A.W1.S13.P.F3.L._Z._Z.	Q	N	T	FA	A	W1	S13	P	F3	L	_Z	T	_Z	N	
Net incurrence of liabilities	Q..N.T.FA.L.W1.S1.P.F._Z._Z._T._Z.	Q	N	T	FA	L	W1	S1	P	F	_Z	_Z	T	_Z	N	
Equity and investment fund shares	Q..N.T.FA.L.W1.S1.P.F5._Z._Z._T._Z.	Q	N	T	FA	L	W1	S1	P	F5	_Z	_Z	T	_Z	N	
Equity securities other than investment fund shares	Q..N.T.FA.L.W1.S1.P.F51._Z._Z._T._Z.	Q	N	T	FA	L	W1	S1	P	F51	_Z	_Z	T	_Z	N	
Listed	Q..N.T.FA.L.W1.S1.P.F511._Z._Z._T._Z.	Q	N	T	FA	L	W1	S1	P	F511	_Z	_Z	T	_Z	N	
Unlisted	Q..N.T.FA.L.W1.S1.P.F512._Z._Z._T._Z.	Q	N	T	FA	L	W1	S1	P	F512	_Z	_Z	T	_Z	N	
Investment fund shares or units	Q..N.T.FA.L.W1.S1.P.F52._Z._Z._T._Z.	Q	N	T	FA	L	W1	S1	P	F52	_Z	_Z	T	_Z	N	
Reinvestment of earnings	Q..N.T.FA.L.W1.S1.P.F52B._Z._Z._T._Z.	Q	N	T	FA	L	W1	S1	P	F52B	_Z	_Z	T	_Z	N	
Money market fund shares or units	Q..N.T.FA.L.W1.S1.P.F521._Z._Z._T._Z.	Q	N	T	FA	L	W1	S1	P	F521	_Z	_Z	T	_Z	N	
Debt securities	Q..N.T.FA.L.W1.S1.P.F3.T._Z._Z.	Q	N	T	FA	L	W1	S1	P	F3	T	_Z	T	_Z	N	
Central bank	Q..N.T.FA.L.W1.S121.P.F3.T._Z._Z.	Q	N	T	FA	L	W1	S121	P	F3	T	_Z	T	_Z	N	
Short-term	Q..N.T.FA.L.W1.S121.P.F3.S._Z._Z.	Q	N	T	FA	L	W1	S121	P	F3	S	_Z	T	_Z	N	
Long-term	Q..N.T.FA.L.W1.S121.P.F3.L._Z._Z.	Q	N	T	FA	L	W1	S121	P	F3	L	_Z	T	_Z	N	

3   Using Metadata to Improve Data Consistency

A third challenge is how to improve data consistency by using consistent names and definitions in data production and dissemination systems. The IMF uses master lists for economic concepts and country names to improve data comparisons and make data processes more efficient. The Catalog of Time Series (CTS) provides a hierarchical vocabulary of concepts across economic sectors, and contains names and codes for over 50,000 items. We also maintain standard country names and codes. The Statistics Department manages the master lists in collaboration with other Departments. IMF databases use these master lists in their production systems. Many IMF applications of SDMX use the Catalog of Time Series. Picture 1 below shows examples of the CTS and country codes.

Using master lists ensures the consistent use of names and definitions across databases. Managing these lists centrally allows accuracy and methodology checks to be done once rather than multiple times. Using these lists, with common definitions, in all systems makes it very easy to compare data across countries and economic concepts. The use of these master lists in SDMX leads to faster and cheaper exchange of data and metadata.

---

[4] A registry is a web based application that enables reporting countries to access the DSDs, code lists and report data in SDMX format.

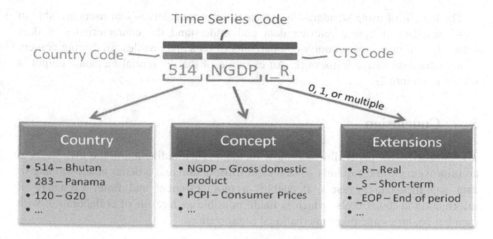

Fig. 1. Example of CTS and Country Codes

4   Using Metadata to Explain Data Characteristics

A fourth challenge is how to improve users' understanding of data and methodology used in compilation of statistics. To this end, IMF published outputs contain explanatory notes, which help users understand the data they see. We store these explanatory notes (which we call "referential metadata)" in a standard format using a DQAF-based schema, allowing us to present these notes in the way most suited to any given output format.

Columns:	Time (10)						2004	2005	2006
Country	Concept	Data Source	Status	Unit	Scale		▽	▽	▽
India	Consumer Prices, All items	International Financial Statistics (IFS)	**Note** ✕					000	106.146
India	Consumer Prices, All items	International Financial Statistics (IFS)	**Geographic coverage** The International Financial Statistics database covers 194 countries and areas.					246	6.146
India	Consumer Prices, All items	International Financial Statistics (IFS)	**Sector coverage** IFS includes data on National					542	128.591
India	Consumer Prices, All items	International Financial Statistics (IFS)	Accounts, Indicators of Economic Activity, Labor Markets, Prices, Government and Public Sector					000	106.146
India	Consumer Prices, All items	International Financial Statistics (IFS)	Finance, Financial Indicators, Balance of Payments, International Investment Position, International					246	6.146

Fig. 2. Illustration of IMF referential metadata content and structure

The benefit of using standards in presentation of metadata is that users are able to view metadata alongside relevant data and understand the characteristics of data better; it facilitates cross country comparisons of data and enables structuring content using a comprehensive framework. An example of the referential metadata output is shown in Picture 2.

5   Conclusion

To summarize, the paper illustrates how metadata standardization in the IMF leads to an improvement in the quality of statistical information and a better understanding of data and metadata by users. It enables a more efficient and faster exchange of information at lower costs, which is made possible as a result of collaboration with member countries and other international organizations.

Leveraging Semantics to Represent and Compute Quantitative Indexes: The RDFIndex Approach*

Jose María Álvarez-Rodríguez[1], José Emilio Labra-Gayo[2], and Patricia Ordoñez de Pablos[2]

[1] South East European Research Center,
54622, Thessaloniki, Greece
jmalvarez@seerc.org

[2] WESO Research Group, Department of Computer Science, University of Oviedo,
33007, Oviedo, Spain
{labra,patriop}@uniovi.es

Abstract. The compilation of key performance indicators (KPIs) in just one value is becoming a challenging task in certain domains to summarize data and information. In this context, policymakers are continuously gathering and analyzing statistical data with the aim of providing objective measures about a specific policy, activity, product or service and making some kind of decision. Nevertheless existing tools and techniques based on traditional processes are preventing a proper use of the new dynamic and data environment avoiding more timely, adaptable and flexible (on-demand) quantitative index creation. On the other hand, semantic-based technologies emerge to provide the adequate building blocks to represent domain-knowledge and process data in a flexible fashion using a common and shared data model. That is why a RDF vocabulary designed on the top of the RDF Data Cube Vocabulary to model quantitative indexes is introduced in this paper. Moreover a Java and SPARQL based processor of this vocabulary is also presented as a tool to exploit the index meta-data structure and automatically perform the computation process to populate new values. Finally some discussion, conclusions and future work are also outlined.

1 Introduction

Public and private bodies are continuously seeking for new analytical tools and methods to assess, rank and compare their performance based on distinct indicators and dimensions with the objective of making some decision or developing a new policy. In this context the creation and use of quantitative indexes is a widely

* This work is part of the FP7 Marie Curie Initial Training Network "RELATE" (cod. 264840) and developed in the context of the Workpackage 4 and more specifically under the project "Quality Management in Service-based Systems and Cloud Applications". It is also supported by the ROCAS project with code TIN2011-27871, a research project partially funded by the Spanish Ministry of Science and Innovation.

E. Garoufallou and J. Greenberg (Eds.): MTSR 2013, CCIS 390, pp. 175–187, 2013.
© Springer International Publishing Switzerland 2013

accepted practice that has been applied to various domains such as Bibliometrics, academic performance and quality (the Impact Factor by Thomson-Reuters, the H-index or the Shanghai and Webometrics rankings), the Web impact (the Webindex by the Webfoundation) or Cloud Computing (the Service Measurement Index by the CSMIC consortium, the Global Cloud Index by Cisco, the CSC index, the VMWare Cloud Index, etc.) or Smart Cities (The European Smart Cities ranking) to name a few (apart from the traditional ones such as the Gross domestic product). Therefore policymakers as well as individuals are continuously evaluating quantitative measures to tackle or improve existing problems in different areas and support their decisions. Nevertheless the sheer mass of data now available in the web is raising a new dynamic and challenging environment in which traditional tools are facing major problems to deal with data-sources diversity, structural issues or complex processes of estimation. According to some efforts such as the "Policy-making 2.0" within the Cross-Over project[1] that *refers to a blend of emerging and fast developing technologies that enable better, more timely and more participated decision-making*, new paradigms and tools are required to take advantage of the existing environment (open data and big data) to design and estimate actions in this dynamic context according to requirements of transparency, standardization, adaptability and extensibility among others with the aim of providing new context-aware and added-value services such as visualization that can help a deepen and broaden understanding of the impact of a policy in a more fast and efficient way. As a consequence common features and requirements can be extracted from the existing situation out:

- Data sources. Data and information is continuously being generated as observations from social networks, public and private institutions, NGOs, services and applications, etc. creating a tangled environment of sources, formats and access protocols with a huge but restricted potential for exploitation. Nevertheless data processing, knowledge inferring, etc. are not mere processes of gathering and analyzing, it is necessary to deal with semantic and syntactic issues, e.g. particular measurements and dimensions or name mismatches, in order to enable a proper data/information re-use and knowledge generation.
- Structure. Quantitative indexes are usually defined (a mathematical model) by experts to aggregate several indicators (in a hierarchy structure) in just one value to provide a measure of the impact or performance of some policy in a certain context. The structure of these indexes are obviously subjected to change over time to collect more information or adjust their composition and relationships (narrower/broader). That is why technology should be able to afford adequate techniques to automatically populate new changes in an efficient way.
- Computation process. This feature refers to the calculation of the index. Observations are gathered from diverse data sources and aligned to the index structure, commonly indicators, that are processed through various mathematical operators to generate a final index value. Nevertheless the computation process is not always described neither open (any minor change

---

[1] http://www.crossover-project.eu/

can imply a long time for validation) implying that cannot be easily replied for third-parties with other purposes, for instance research, preventing one of the most wanted characteristics such as transparency. Furthermore it is necessary to ensure that the computation process is sound and correct.

- Documentation. As the European project Cross-over has stated, new policy-making strategies go ahead of a simple and closed value and it is necessary to bring new ways of exploiting data and information. Moreover the use of the Web as a dissemination channel represents a powerful environment in which information should be available taking into account the multilingual and multicultural character of information. In this context documentation mechanisms must necessarily cover all the aforementioned features to afford a detailed explanation of a quantitative index-based policy to both policy-makers and final users. However existing initiatives usually generates some kind of hand-made report which is not easy to keep up-to-date and deliver to the long-tail of interested third-parties.

On the other hand, the Semantic Web area has experienced during last years a growing commitment from both academia and industrial areas with the objective of elevating the meaning of web information resources through a common and shared data model (graphs) and an underlying semantics based on a logic formalism (ontologies). The Resource Description Framework (RDF), based on a graph model, and the Web Ontology Language (OWL), designed to formalize and model domain knowledge, are a *lingua-franca* to re-use information and data in a knowledge-based environment. Thus data, information and knowledge can be easily shared, exchanged and linked to other databases through the use URIs, more specifically HTTP-URIs.

Obviously semantic web technologies can partially fulfill the features and requirements of this challenging environment for supporting new policy-making strategies. A common and shared data model based on existing standardized semantic web vocabularies and datasets can be used to represent quantitative indexes from both, structural and computational, points of view enabling a right exploitation of meta-data and semantics. That is why the present paper introduces: 1) a high-level model on top of the RDF Data Cube Vocabulary [5], a shared effort to model statistical data in RDF reusing parts (the cube model) of the Statistical Data and Metadata Exchange Vocabulary [4] (SDMX), to represent the structure and computation of quantitative indexes and 2) a Java-SPARQL based processor to exploit the meta-information and compute the new index values.

Finally as a motivating and on-going example, see Table 1, a policy-maker wants to re-use the World Bank data to model and compute a new index, "The Naive World Bank Index". This index uses the topics "Aid Efectiveness" (c_1) and "Health" (c_2) with the aim of comparing the status and health evolution in several countries to decide whether new investments are performed. From these components two indicators have been respectively selected by experts: "Life Expectancy" (in_1) and "Health expenditure, total (%) of GDP" (in_2). Once components and their indicators are defined and data can be retrieved from the

World Bank it is necessary to set how the index and components are computed taking into account that only data about indicators is available. Following a top-down approach the index, i, is calculated through an ordered weighted averaging (OWA) operator using the formula: $\sum_{i=1}^{n} w_i c_i$, where w_i is the weight of the component c_i. On the other hand, both components only aggregates one indicator but the "Aid Efectiveness" must firstly compute the "Life Expectancy" without considering the sex dimension. Making this implies the need of populating the average age by country and year to create a new "derivate" indicator of "Life Expectancy". Apart from that the computation must also consider the observation status and values must be normalized using the $z\text{-}score$ before computing intermediate and final values for each indicator, component and index. Furthermore this index is supposed to change in the future adding new data sources and meta-data, modifying the computation processes (weights) or the structure (new components, indicators and dimensions). Finally, the policy-maker is also interested in applying this index to other scenarios and he also needs a way of explaining in different languages how the index is computed.

Table 1. Example of indicator observations from the WorldBank

Description	Year	Country	Value	Status
Life Expectancy Male	2010	Spain	79	Normal
Life Expectancy Male	2011	Spain	79	Normal
Life Expectancy Female	2010	Spain	85	Normal
Life Expectancy Female	2011	Spain	85	Normal
Life Expectancy Male	2010	Greece	78	Normal
Life Expectancy Male	2011	Greece	79	Normal
Life Expectancy Female	2010	Greece	83	Normal
Life Expectancy Female	2011	Greece	83	Normal
Health expenditure, total (% of GDP)	2010	Spain	74.2	Normal
Health expenditure, total (% of GDP)	2011	Spain	73.6	Normal
Health expenditure, total (% of GDP)	2010	Spain	61.5	Normal
Health expenditure, total (% of GDP)	2011	Spain	61.2	Normal

2   Related Work

Currently one of the mainstreams in the Semantic Web area lies in the application of the Linked Open Data initiative in different domains such as e-Government, e-Procurement, e-Health, Biomedicine, Education, Bibliography or Geography to name a few, with the aim of solving existing problems of integration and interoperability among applications and create a knowledge environment under the Web-based protocols. In this context, the present work is therefore focused in applying semantic web vocabularies and datasets to model quantitative indexes from both structural and computational points of view in a "Policy-Making" context. In order to reach the major objective of building a re-usable Web of Data, the publication of information and data under a common data model (RDF) and formats with a specific formal query language (SPARQL) provides the required building blocks to turn the Web of documents into a real database of data. Research works are focused in two main areas: 1) data production/publishing, with special focus on quality [2], conformance, provenance and trust [12], description of datasets with the Vocabulary of Interlinked Datasets (VoID) and Data Catalog Vocabulary (DCAT) or entity reconciliation [11] processes and 2) data consumption. More specifically, visualization [6], faceted browsing and searching [9], distributed queries, scalable reasoning processes [10] or annotation of web pages [1] among others are key research topics to deploy the Semantic Web and the Linked Data initiative.

In the particular case of statistical data, the RDF Data Cube Vocabulary [5] a W3C Working Draft document, is a shared effort to represent statistical data in RDF reusing parts (the cube model) of the Statistical Data and Metadata Exchange Vocabulary (SDMX) [4], an ISO standard for exchanging and sharing statistical data and meta-data among organizations. The Data Cube vocabulary is a core foundation which supports extension vocabularies to enable publication of other aspects of statistical data flows or other multi-dimensional data sets. Previously, the Statistical Core Vocabulary [8] was the standard in fact to describe statistical information in the Web of Data. Some works are also emerging to mainly publish statistical data following the concepts of the LOD initiative such as [15,14,3,7,13] among others.

All the aforementioned works must be considered in order to re-use existing vocabularies and datasets to address the challenges of creating meta-described quantitative indexes. Mainly semantics allows us to model logical restrictions on data and the computation process while linked data enables the description of indexes in terms of existing concepts and the publication of new data and information under a set of principles to boost their re-use and automatic processing through machine-readable formats and access protocols.

3   Theoretical Modeling of a Quantitative Composite Index

Essentially a quantitative index is comprised of the aggregation of several components. In the same way, a component is also composed of the aggregation of indicators that keep concrete observations. From this initial definition some characteristics and assumptions can be found: 1) although observations can be directly mapped to an index or a component, they are frequently computed applying a bottom-up approach from an indicator to a component and so on. 2) An observation is a real numerical value extracted from some agent out under a precise context. Generally observations only takes one measure and are considered to be raw without any pre-processing. 3) Before aggregating observation values, components and indexes can estimate missing values to finally normalize them in order to get a quantitative value. According to the aforementioned characteristics and assumptions an "observable" element (index, component or indicator) is a dataset of observations under a specific context (dimensions and/or meta-data) that can be directly gathered from external sources or computed by some kind of OWA operator.

Definition 1 (Observation-o). It is a tuple $\{v, m, s\}$, where v is a numerical value for the measure m with an status s that belongs to only one dataset of observations O.

Definition 2 (Dataset-q). It is a tuple $\{O, m, D, A, T\}$ where O is a set of observations for only one measure m that is described under a set of dimensions D and a set of annotations A. Additionally, some attributes can be defined in the set T for structure enrichment.

Definition 3 (Aggregated dataset-aq). It is an aggregation of n datasets q_i (identified by the set Q) which set of observations O is derivate by applying an OWA operator p to the observations O_{q_i}.

As a necessary condition for the computation process, an aggregated dataset aq defined by means of the set of dimensions D_{aq} can be computed iif $\forall q_j \in Q : D_{aq} \subseteq D_{q_j}$. Furthermore the OWA operator p can only aggregate values belonging to the same measure m.

As a consequence of the aforementioned definitions some remarks must be outlined in order to restrict the understanding of a quantitative index (structure and computation):

- The set of dimensions D, annotations A and attributes T for a given dataset Q is always the same with the aim of describing all observations under the same context.
- An index i and a component c are aggregated datasets. Nevertheless this restriction is relaxed if observations can be directly mapped to these elements without any computation process.
- An indicator in can be both dataset or aggregated dataset.
- All elements in definitions must be uniquely identified.
- An aggregated dataset is also a dataset.

Following the on-going example, see Table 1, the modeling of the "The Naive World Bank Index" would be the next one:

- Each row of the table is an observation o_i with a numerical value v, the measure is m_{in} and the status is "Raw".
- Two indicators can be found: $\{$ (in_1, "Life Expectancy"), (in_2, "Health expenditure, total (% of GDP)") $\}$, each indicator contains a set of observations O_{in_i}. The dimensions for each indicator are: D_{in_1} {"Year", "Country", "Sex"} and D_{in_2} {"Year", "Country"}.
- In order to group the "Life Expectancy" without the "Sex" dimension it is necessary to define a new aggregated dataset aq_1 which dimensions D_{aq_1} are {"Year", "Country"} and the OWA operator is the average of values $v \in O_{in_1}$. In this sample the aggregated indicator aq_1 can be assembled due to the indicator "Life Expectancy" accomplishes with the aforementioned necessary conditions: 1) $D_{aq} \subseteq D_{in_1} \wedge D_{aq_1} \subseteq D_{in_2}$ and 2) $m_{aq_1} = m_{in_1} =$ "Life Expectancy".

- In the same way, the set of components: $\{(c_1,\text{"Aid Efectiveness"}), (c_2,\text{"Health"})\}$ are built aggregating the indicators aq_1 and q_2 using as OWA operator the "min" value. In this case "min" or "max" operators can be used due to an observation is uniquely identified in a dataset by a tuple $\{v, m, s\} \cup D$.
- Finally, the index is computed using the general form of an OWA operator $\sum_{i=1}^{n} w_i c_i$ and taking as weights those we select.

As final remark, the computation process is generating new observations, following a bottom-up approach, according to the structure defined in each dataset. Although a logical structure of indexes, components and indicators can be directly established using narrower/broader properties the main advantage of this approach lies in the possibility of expressing new elements by aggregating the existing ones. Nevertheless restrictions about the type of dataset that can be aggregated in each level could be added at any time for other reasons such as validation or to generate a human-readable form of the index.

4   Representation of a Quantitative Composite Index in RDF: The RDFIndex

Since previous section has stated the key definitions to represent quantitative indexes by aggregation, a direct translation built on the top of the RDF Data Cube Vocabulary, SDMX and other semantic web vocabularies is presented in Table 2. Thus all concepts in the index are described reusing existing definitions, taking advantage of previous efforts and pre-established semantics with the aim of being extended in the future to fit new requirements. According to these mappings a definition of the index in the on-going example and some dimensions are presented in Figure 1 and Figure 2.

Since the structure and the computation processes can be built on the top of existing RDF vocabulary it is then possible to make a translation to a generic SPARQL query (includes the basic OWA operator), see Figure 3, in order generate new observations following the bottom-up approach that previous section has outlined.

4.1   A Java-SPARQL Based Interpreter of the RDFIndex

The first implementation of the RDFIndex vocabulary processor[2] is based on traditional language processor techniques such as the use of design patterns (e.g. Composite or Visitor) to separate the exploitation of meta-data from the interpretation. Thus the processor works and provides next functionalities (hereafter load and query an endpoint are completely equivalent due to data is separated from access and storage formats):

- The RDFIndex ontology is loaded to have access to common definitions.

---

[2] https://github.com/chemaar/rdfindex

Table 2. Summary of mappings between the index definition and the RDF Data Cube Vocabulary

Concept	Vocabulary element	Comments
Observation o	qb:Observation	Enrichment through annotations
Numerical value v	xsd:double	Restriction to numerical values
Measure m	qb:MeasureProperty sdmx-measure:obsValue	Restriction to one measure
Status s	sdmx-concept:obsStatus	Defined by the SDMX-RDF vocabulary
Dataset q	qb:dataSet and qb:qb:DataStructureDefinition	Metadata of the qb:dataSet
Dimension $d_i \in D$	qb:DimensionProperty	Context of observations
Annotation $a_i \in A$	owl:AnnotationProperty	Intensive use of Dublin Core
Attribute $at_i \in T$	qb:AttributeProperty	Link to existing datasets such as DB-Pedia
OWA operator p	SPARQL 1.1 aggregation operators	Other extensions depend on the RDF repository
Index, Component and Indicator	skos:Concept	SKOS taxonomy (logical structure)

```
@prefix rdfindex:      <http://purl.org/rdfindex/ontology/> .
@prefix rdfindex-wb:   <http://purl.org/rdfindex/wb/resource/> .
@prefix rdfindex-wbont: <http://purl.org/rdfindex/wb/ontology/> .

rdfindex-wb:TheWorldBankNaiveIndex
   a rdfindex:Index;
   rdfs:label "The_World_Bank_Naive_Index"@en;
   rdfindex:type rdfindex:Quantitative;
   rdfindex:aggregates [
     rdfindex:aggregation-operator rdfindex:OWA;
     rdfindex:part-of [
        rdfindex:dataset rdfindex-wb:AidEffectiveness;
        rdfindex:weight 0.4];
     rdfindex:part-of [rdfindex:dataset rdfindex-wb:Health;
        rdfindex:weight 0.6];
   ];
   #More meta-data properties...
   qb:structure  rdfindex-wb:TheWorldBankNaiveIndexDSD ; .

rdfindex-wb:TheWorldBankNaiveIndexDSD
   a qb:DataStructureDefinition;
   qb:component
   [qb:dimension rdfindex-wbont:ref-area],
   [qb:dimension rdfindex-wbont:ref-year],
   [qb:measure  rdfindex:value],
   [qb:attribute sdmx-attribute:unitMeasure];
   #More meta-data properties...
   .
```

Fig. 1. Example of an index structure in RDF

- The structure of an index described with the aforementioned vocabulary is also loaded to create a kind of Abstract Syntax Tree (AST) containing the defined meta-data.
- Once the meta-data structure is available in the AST it can be managed through three AST walkers that performs: 1) validation (structure and RDF

```
rdfindex-wbont:ref-area a rdf:Property ,
  qb:DimensionProperty;
    rdfs:subPropertyOf sdmx-dimension:ref-area;
    rdfs:range skos:Concept;
    qb:concept sdmx-concept:ref-area .

rdfindex:value a rdf:Property , qb:MeasureProperty;
  rdfs:label "Value_of_an_observation"@en;
  skos:notation "value" ;
  rdfs:subPropertyOf sdmx-measure:obsValue;
  rdfs:range xsd:double .
```

Fig. 2. Example of a dimension and a measure definition in RDF

```
SELECT (d_i ∈ D) [(sum(?w*?measure) as ?newvalue) | OWA(?measure)]
WHERE{
    q rdfindex:aggregates ?parts.
    ?parts rdfindex:part-of ?partof.
    ?partof rdfindex:dataset q_i .
    FILTER(?partof ∈ Q).
    ?observation rdf:type qb:Observation .
    ?part rdfindex:weight ?defaultw.
    OPTIONAL {?partof rdfindex:weight ?aggregationw.}.
    BIND (if( BOUND(?aggregationw), ?aggregationw, ?defaultw) AS ?w)
    ?observation m ?measure .
    ?observation ?dim ?dimRef.
    FILTER (?dim ∈ D).
}GROUP BY (d_i ∈ D)
```

Fig. 3. SPARQL template for building aggregated observations

Data Cube normalization) and 2) SPARQL queries creation and 3) documentation generation (optional).

- In order to promote new observations to the different components and indexes a set of raw observations is also loaded and a new AST walker generates new values, through SPARQL queries (see Figure 4), in a bottom-up approach until reaching the upper-level (index), see Table 3 and Figure 5.

```
prefix rdfindex: <http://purl.org/rdfindex/ontology/>
SELECT ?dim0 ?dim1 ( sum(?w*?measure) as ?newvalue)
WHERE{
    rdfindex-wb:TheWorldBankNaiveIndex
    rdfindex:aggregates ?parts.
    ?parts rdfindex:part-of ?partof.
    ?partof rdfindex:dataset ?part .
    FILTER ((?part =rdfindex-wb:AidEffectiveness) ||
        (?part =rdfindex-wb:Health )).
    ?observation qb:dataSet ?part .
    ?part rdfindex:weight ?defaultw.
    OPTIONAL {?partof rdfindex:weight ?aggregationw.}.
    BIND (if( BOUND(?aggregationw), ?aggregationw, ?defaultw) AS ?w)
    ?observation rdfindex:value ?measure .
    ?observation rdfindex-wbont:ref-area ?dim0.
    ?observation rdfindex-wbont:ref-year ?dim1.
} GROUP BY ?dim0 ?dim1
```

Fig. 4. Example of generated SPARQL query

Finally each new observation also contains a data property to store the hash MD5 of a string comprising (publisher, q, D, v) and separated by $\#$, e.g. "RDFIndex#TheWorldBankNaiveIndex#Spain#2010#0.707", to avoid potential "man-in-the-middle" attacks when the new observations are published. This value are easily generated using the new string functions in SPARQL 1.1 concat and MD5.

Table 3. Example of aggregated observations from the WorldBank

Description	Year	Country	Value	Status
Indicator				
Aggregated Life Expectancy	2010	Spain	82	Estimated
Aggregated Life Expectancy	2011	Spain	82	Estimated
Aggregated Life Expectancy	2010	Greece	80.5	Estimated
Aggregated Life Expectancy	2011	Greece	81	Estimated
Component				
Aid Efectiveness	2010	Spain	0.707	Estimated
Aid Efectiveness	2011	Spain	0.707	Estimated
Aid Efectiveness	2010	Greece	−0.707	Estimated
Aid Efectiveness	2011	Greece	−0.707	Estimated
Health	2010	Spain	0.707	Estimated
Health	2011	Spain	0.707	Estimated
Health	2010	Greece	−0.707	Estimated
Health	2011	Greece	−0.707	Estimated
Index				
The Naive World Bank Index	2010	Spain	0.707	Estimated
The Naive World Bank Index	2011	Spain	0.707	Estimated
The Naive World Bank Index	2010	Greece	−0.707	Estimated
The Naive World Bank Index	2011	Greece	−0.707	Estimated

```
rdfindex-wb:o6808100851579
      a         qb:observation ;
      qb:dataSet rdfindex-wb:TheWorldBankNaiveIndex   ;
      rdfindex-wbont:ref-area dbpedia-res:Spain ;
      rdfindex-wbont:ref-year
  <http://reference.data.gov.uk/id/
  gregorian-interval/2010-01-01T00:00:00/P1Y> ;
      ...
      #rdfs:{label,comment} {literal};
      #dcterms:{issued, date, contributor, author, publisher, identifier}
      # {resource, literal};
      rdfindex:md5-hash "6cdda76088cd161d766809d6a78d35f6";
      sdmx-concept:obsStatus
             sdmx-code:obsStatus-E;
      rdfindex:value "0.707"^^xsd:double .
```

Fig. 5. Partial example of a populated observation for "The World Bank Naive Index"

Table 4. Initial evaluation of semantic technologies for modeling and computing quantitative indexes

Feature	Crucial Step	Main advantages
Data sources	• Collect. • Verify. • Tag (enrichment).	• Common and shared data model, RDF. • Description of data providers (provenance and trust). • A formal query language to query data, SPARQL. • Use of Internet protocols, HTTP. • Data enrichment and validation (domain and range). • Unique identification of entities, concepts, etc. through (HTTP) URIs. • Possibility of publishing new data under the aforementioned characteristics. • Standardization and integration of data sources.
Structure	• Verify. • Tag (enrichment). • Analyze. • Share. • Archive. • Re-use.	• Meta-description of index structure (validation). • Re-use of existing semantic web vocabularies. • Re-use of existing datasets to enrich meta-data. • Context-aware definitions. • Underlying logic formalism. • Orthogonal and flexible.
Computation process	• Verify. • Tag (enrichment). • Apply. • Share. • Archive. • Re-use.	• Meta-description of datasets aggregation. • Validation of composed datasets. • OWA operators support. • Direct translation to SPARQL queries.
Documentation	• Verify. • Apply. • Share. • Archive. • Re-use.	• Multilingual support to describe datasets, etc. • Easy generation with existing tools.
Cross-Domain Features	All	• Separation of concerns and responsibilities: data and meta-data (structure and computation). • Standardization (put in action specs from organisms such as W3C). • Declarative and adaptive approach. • Non-vendor lock-in (format, access and computation). • Integration and Interoperability. • Transparency. • Help to build own indexes. • Align to existing trend (data management: quality and filtering) • Easy integration with third-party services such as visualization. • Contribution to the Web of Data.

5   Discussion and Further Steps

Previous sections have presented the motivation of this work, a vocabulary designed on top of the RDF Data Cube Vocabulary for modeling quantitative indexes and a Java-SPARQL based processor to validate and compute any kind of index. According to the requirements and features of quantitative indexes an initial evaluation is presented in Table 4 to show how the application of semantic technologies can ease indexes management and their computation process to make the most of data[3]: collect, verify, analyze, apply, share, protect, archive and re-use. Furthermore it is relevant to remark that data quality and filtering is currently a big challenge due to the vast amount of data that is continuously being generated. Policy-makers as agents in charge of making decisions must be able to manage this information in a timely and flexible fashion. In this context semantic technologies provides the adequate and standardized building blocks to improve the dynamism and updating capabilities of policy-maker tools. Nevertheless the initial effort to translate existing index definitions and computation processes to this approach can be hard and time-consuming but going beyond of that further updates and tools can perfectly benefit from this effort as other "semantized" domains have already done.

6   Conclusions and Future Work

Data filtering, quality and aggregation is a major challenge in the new data-driven economy. The interest of public and private bodies to manage and exploit information is growing and specific activities such as policy making must take advantage of compiling data and information to make more timely and accurate decisions. In this sense the use of quantitative indexes has been widely accepted as a practice to summarize diverse key performance indicators and establish a numerical value with the aim of comparing different alternatives. Nevertheless traditional techniques and the "infobesity" are preventing a proper use of information and the dynamism of this new environment also requires a high-level of integration and interoperability. In this context the Semantic Web area and, more specifically the Linked Data initiative, provide a standardized stack of technologies for knowledge-based techniques with the aim of boosting data management and exploitation. That is why the application of semantic web principles to model quantitative indexes from both structural and computational points of view can fulfill the requirements of this new data-based environment and leverage semantics to create a real knowledge-based society. The present work has introduced two main contributions: 1) the RDFIndex vocabulary to model and compute quantitative indexes and 2) a Java-SPARQL based processor of the RDFIndex to validate, generate and populate new observations.

Although this first effort has applied semantics to a specific problem new enhancements must be done to cover all potential requirements in the construction of quantitative indexes. In this sense, the presented approach is now being used

---

[3] http://fcw.com/articles/2013/06/11/data-performance-management.aspx

in the modeling of indexes such as the Cloud Index or the Web Index [13]. Furthermore, the proposed representation contains a very interesting property that lies in the possibility of computing indexes and components in a parallel fashion. Other issues such as SPARQL-based validation, performance, provenance and trust, real-time updates, storage or visualization are also on-going work that must be addressed to fit to new data environments.

References

1. Adida, B., Birbeck, M.: RDFa Primer, Bridging the Human and Data Webs. W3C Working Group Note, W3C (2008), http://www.w3.org/TR/xhtml-rdfa-primer/
2. Bizer, C., Cyganiak, R.: Quality-driven information filtering using the WIQA policy framework. Web Semant. 7(1), 1–10 (2009)
3. Bosch, T., Cyganiak, R., Gregory, A., Wackerow, J.: DDI-RDF discovery vocabulary. a metadata vocabulary for documenting research and survey data. In: 6th Workshop on Linked Data on the Web (LDOW 2013) (2013)
4. SDMX consortium. SDMX - Metadata Common Vocabulary. SDMX Consortium (UNECE) 2009, http://bit.ly/1d2U1T8
5. Cyganiak, R., Reynolds, D.: The RDF Data Cube Vocabulary. Working Draft, W3C (2013), http://www.w3.org/TR/vocab-data-cube/
6. Dadzie, A.-S., Rowe, M.: Approaches to visualising Linked Data: A survey. Semantic Web 2(2), 89–124 (2011)
7. Fernández, J.D., Martínez-Prieto, M.A., Gutiérrez, C.: Publishing open statistical data: The spanish census. In: DG.O, pp. 20–25 (2011)
8. Hausenblas, M., Halb, W., Raimond, Y., Feigenbaum, L., Ayers, D.: SCOVO: Using Statistics on the Web of Data. In: Aroyo, L., Traverso, P., Ciravegna, F., Cimiano, P., Heath, T., Hyvönen, E., Mizoguchi, R., Oren, E., Sabou, M., Simperl, E. (eds.) ESWC 2009. LNCS, vol. 5554, pp. 708–722. Springer, Heidelberg (2009)
9. Hogan, A., Harth, A., Umbrich, J., Kinsella, S., Polleres, A., Decker, S.: Searching and Browsing Linked Data with SWSE: The Semantic Web Search Engine. Journal of Web Semantics, JWS (2011) (accepted) (in press)
10. Hogan, A., Pan, J.Z., Polleres, A., Decker, S.: SAOR: Template Rule Optimisations for Distributed Reasoning over 1 Billion Linked Data Triples. In: Patel-Schneider, P.F., Pan, Y., Hitzler, P., Mika, P., Zhang, L., Pan, J.Z., Horrocks, I., Glimm, B. (eds.) ISWC 2010, Part I. LNCS, vol. 6496, pp. 337–353. Springer, Heidelberg (2010)
11. Maali, F., Cyganiak, R.: Re-using Cool URIs: Entity Reconciliation Against LOD Hubs. Library 8 (2011)
12. Moreau, L., Missier, P.: The PROV Data Model and Abstract Syntax Notation. W3C Working Draft, W3C (2011), http://bit.ly/pY9utB
13. Rodríguez, J.M.A., Clement, J., Gayo, J.E.L., Farhan, H., De Pablos, P.O.: Publishing Statistical Data following the Linked Open Data Principles: The Web Index Project, pp. 199–226. IGI Global (2013)
14. Salas, P.E.R., Da Mota, F.M., Breitman, K.K., Casanova, M.A., Martin, M., Auer, S.: Publishing Statistical Data on the Web. Int. J. Semantic Computing 6(4), 373–388 (2012)
15. Zapilko, B., Mathiak, B.: Defining and Executing Assessment Tests on Linked Data for Statistical Analysis. In: COLD (2011)

The Semantics of Negation Detection in Archaeological Grey Literature

Andreas Vlachidis and Douglas Tudhope

University of South Wales, Hypermedia Research Unit, Pontypridd Wales,
CF37 1DL, UK
{andreas.vlachidis,douglas.tuhope}@southwales.ac.uk

Abstract. Archaeological reports contain a great deal of information that conveys facts and findings in different ways. This kind of information is highly relevant to the research and analysis of archaeological evidence but at the same time can be a hindrance for the accurate indexing of documents with respect to positive assertions. The paper presents a method for adapting the biomedicine oriented negation algorithm NegEx to the context of archaeology and discusses the evaluation results of the new modified negation detection module. The performance of the module is compared against a "Gold Standard" and evaluation results are encouraging, delivering overall 89% Precision, 80% Recall and 83% F-Measure scores. The paper addresses limitations and future improvements of the current work and highlights the need for ontological modelling to accommodate negative assertions. It concludes that adaptation of the NegEx algorithm to the archaeology domain is feasible and that rule-based information extraction techniques are capable of identifying a large portion of negated phrases from archaeological grey literature.

Keywords: Negation Detection, Semantic Technologies, Digital Humanities, CIDOC-CRM, Semantic Annotation, Natural Language Processing.

1 Introduction

The latest advances of semantic technologies have opened new innovative ways in which scholars can act and elaborate information via search and browsing software applications that process the "meaning" of words beyond the level of a simple and dry string matching process [1]. Semantic metadata practices enrich information with conceptualisations that enable sophisticated methods for data publishing and pave new ways for information analysis and data integration [2]. The field of negation detection presents a challenging ground for the application of such semantic metadata technologies that ought to be explored and investigated for the delivery of scholarly research solutions that could significantly enhance and advance the ways in which the search of facts and findings is conducted.

Negation is an integral part of any natural language system. It is a linguistic, cognitive and intellectual phenomenon, which enables the users of a language system to communicate erroneous messages, the truth value of a proposition, contradictions, irony

E. Garoufallou and J. Greenberg (Eds.): MTSR 2013, CCIS 390, pp. 188–200, 2013.

and sarcasm [3]. Philosophers, from Plato to Spencer Brown have independently approached negation as a case of heteron (not-being) described as a "positive assertion of the existence of a relevant difference" [4]. Whereas, there is a plethora of studies and theories addressed to the complexity of negation and its characteristics from a philosophical and linguistic point of view, research on automatic detection of negation and representation of its semantics has not been extensive [5].

In recent years, Natural Language Processing (NLP) applications have mainly drawn attention to the automatic detection of negation in biomedical text [6] and in opinion mining and sentiment analysis [7]. The techniques and approaches that are employed to address the issue of negation within NLP vary and cover a wide spectrum of machine learning and ruled-based (regular expressions and syntactic processing) applications. Both machine learning and rule-based approaches have been reported as capable of addressing the task of automatic detection, with the rule-based approaches having an edge and being competitive in the biomedicine domain [8]. However, there is little evidence of research aimed at the study of negation detection in the domain of archaeology, albeit some strong parallels can be drawn between archaeological and biomedicine research questions particularly when dealing with facts and findings [9].

In the scientific research of the biomedicine and the archaeology domain, appreciation and understanding of negated facts is as equally important as the interpretation of positive findings. For example the medical phrase "*The chest X-ray showed no infiltrates*" reveals a significant negated finding which can lead to a correct diagnosis of a cardiac condition. In archaeology "negative results are essential when providing an assessment of the archaeological potential of a specific site" [10], for example the phrase "*No traces of a Roman settlement have been discovered in the area*" can lead to specific conclusions with regards to settlement activity during the Roman period in a particular area. Being able to distinguish such negative assertions in context is highly desirable for the research and analysis of facts and findings especially when those activities are supported by information retrieval systems.

The following sections of this paper discuss the method and evaluation results of the negation detection module of the OPTIMA pipeline [11] for the semantic annotation of archaeological grey literature with respect to the CIDOC CRM ontology. Semantic Annotation refers to specific metadata which are usually generated with respect to a given ontology and are aimed to automate identification of concepts and their relationships in documents [12]. CIDOC CRM is an ISO Standard (ISO 21127:2006) comprehensive semantic framework that makes available semantic definitions and clarifications that promote shared understanding of cultural heritage information [13].

OPTIMA contributed to the Semantic Technologies for Archaeological Research (STAR) project [14], which explored the potential of semantic technologies in query and integration of archaeological digital resources. The output of the pipeline is delivered in the form of semantic indices, expressed as RDF triples that enable semantically defined information retrieval and cross-searching over disparate archaeological digital resources i.e. grey literature and datasets.

The paper highlights the essential role of the negation detection module for the aims of the pipeline and reveals the contribution of the NegEx algorithm [6] in the applied method. The necessary modifications of NegEx are also discussed which led to the adaptation of a biomedicine oriented algorithm to the negation requirements of the archaeology domain. The evaluation results of the negation module of OPTIMA are encouraging, delivering high Precision (89%) and Recall (80%) scores. The performance of the negation module is evaluated with the Gold Standard method of humanly defined annotations. The paper also discusses the issue of the limited support of ontologies, in particular CIDOC-CRM, in modelling and representation of negated findings and concludes with known limitations and future improvements of the work.

2   Method

The negation detection module of the OPTIMA pipeline is primarily developed to support the task of Named Entity Recognition (NER) with respect to the CIDOC-CRM entities *E19.Physical Object*, *E49.Time Appellation*, *E53.Place* and *E57.Material*. NER is a particular subtask of Information Extraction aimed at the recognition and classification of units of information to predefined categories [15]. Since the aim of the semantic annotation pipeline (OPTIMA) is to deliver semantic indices of archaeological grey literature, it is important to be able to exclude from indexing those occurrences of CRM entities that are negated. Thus, the aim of the negation module is to strengthen the precision performance of the pipeline by discarding negated matches that could harm the validity of results at information retrieval level.

2.1   Relevant Work

NegEx [6] is a specific algorithm targeted at the identification of negated findings in medical documents. The algorithm determines whether Unified Medical Language System (UMLS) terms of findings and diseases are negated in the context of medical reports. NegEx is particularly relevant to the scope of the OPTIMA negation module, due to its rule-based design, the use of pattern matching mechanism and the employment of vocabulary listings.

The design of the algorithm is based on the use of offset patterns that utilise a negation related vocabulary. The vocabulary contains terms and phrases that denote negation, which are invoked by a set of rules. The algorithm makes use of two specific patterns; The first pattern [Pre-Neg] identifies negated UMLS terms in phrases which commence with a negation phrase followed by a window of up to 5 tokens before matching an UMLS term, i.e. *<negation phrase> * <UMLS Term>*. The second pattern [Post-Neg] is a reversed version of the above, which matches negated UMLS terms that are up to five tokens prior to a negation phrase, i.e. <UMLS Term> * <negation phrase>.

There are two main parallels for archaeological reports which support the adoption of the NegEx approach by the OPTIMA negation mechanism. Firstly, the use of pattern matching rules and vocabulary terms allows a smooth integration of the algorithm within the requirements and scope of the OPTIMA pipeline for semantic annotation via based rule-based techniques that are supported by knowledge organisation resources (i.e. thesauri and glossaries). Secondly, the good performance of the algorithm in detecting negations about findings in biomedicine context. In archaeological reports, as in medical reports, authors frequently negate facts about findings [10].

2.2   Adapting the NegEx Algorithm in the Archaeological Domain

The process of adaptation of the NegEx in the archaeological domain addressed a range of modifications relating to the coverage and use of negation glossaries as well as adaptations to the scope and application of the negation rules themselves. The main aim of the adaptation exercise was to apply the NegEx approach to the identification of negation phrases involving the four CRM entities (Physical Object, Time Appelation, Place and Material) which are targeted by the NER phase of the OPTIMA pipeline. Modification of the original pattern matching rules to aim at CRM entities instead of UMLS terms is a straightforward task. However, a range of additional adaptation issues required further examination before porting the original algorithm and glossaries in the archaeology domain.

The adaptation strategy considered the following issues which potentially affect application of NegEx to a new domain: i) the size of the negation window which originally had been set to a span of a maximum five word-tokens to fit particularly to the writing style of medical text, ii) coverage and re-usability capacity of existing negation glossaries to support the negation detection task in a new domain, iii) usefulness of the *pseudo-negation* glossary list for limiting the scope of a negation phrase and iv) review on the relevancy of the assumption that medical narrative is "lexically less ambiguous than unrestricted documents" [16] in the context of archaeological reports. In addition, the reported limitation of NegEx at targeting cases of conjunct negated terms was addressed during the adaptation task as discussed in the next section.

2.2.1   Corpus Analysis to Inform the Task of Adaptation

The main aim of the bottom up corpus analysis was to reveal additional vocabulary evidence which could be used by the negation detection mechanism in order to improve adaptation of the algorithm to the context and the writing style of archaeological reports. Therefore, it was decided that a negation window expanding beyond the window limit of five tokens could be exercised for surfacing larger spans.

The first stage of corpus analysis extracted from a volume of 2460 archaeological reports, phrases of a maximum of 10 tokens which contained negation moderators and CRM entity matches. Using the existing NegEx [Pre-Neg] and [Post Neg] glossary listings, the following two separate matching grammars were constructed:

```
({Token.string!="."})[0,5]{PreNeg}({Token.string!="."})[0,5]
({Token.string!="."})[0,5]{PostNeg}({Token.string!="."})[0,5]
```

The grammars are almost identical; they only differ on the listing type which they invoke (i.e. PreNeg or PostNeg). The rules translate as: match a span which expands 5 tokens before a glossary match and 5 tokens after a glossary match excluding full stops (to prevent the rule expanding beyond the limits of a potential sentence). A succeeding matching grammar was invoked for filtering out those phrases that did not contain any of the four CRM entities failing within the scope of OPTIMA.

The second stage implemented a separate pipeline which post-processed the negation phrases delivered by the first stage. The aim of this particular pipeline was to reveal the most commonly occurring Noun and Verb phrases of the negated phrases output. Such commonly appearing noun and verb phrases were then analysed to inform the process of enhancement and adaptation of existing glossaries and negation grammars to the context of archaeology.

In total, 29040 noun phrases and 14794 verb phrases were identified. From them 14686 were unique noun phrases and 2564 were unique verb phrases. Examining the list of the most frequent noun phrases and comparing it with the list of the NegEx lists it became apparent that some of the existing entries were not applicable to the archaeology domain and returned no matches. Such entries are rather particular to the medical domain, for example "suspicious", "decline", "deny" and "unremarkable for". Moreover, frequently occurring negation classifiers of archaeological narrative, such as "unknown", "unclear" and "undated" were not part of the initial NegEx lists. The adaptation exercise created new versions of the [PreNeg] and [PostNeg] lists adapted to the archaeology domain by removing the entries that are particular to the medical domain and by including new entries that are relevant to the archaeology domain.

The analysis of the verb phrases result revealed some very interesting vocabulary patterns. Examining the most commonly occurring verb phrases, a pattern emerged relating to use of passive voice utterances. For example the phrase "should not be considered" occurred 134 times, the phrase "was not excavated" 67 times, the phrase "were not encountered" 39 times, etc. Although, NegEx covered some cases of backward matching via the [Post-Neg] list for phrases where a negation classifier is found at the end of a phrase, the algorithm did not consider extensively the use of passive voice expressions apart from the case "being ruled out".

The intellectual examination of the list of the frequently occurring verb phrases isolated a set of passive voice verbs that could be used to enhance the operation of the negation algorithm. The list of verbs constitutes a specialised vocabulary of 31 entries such as "appear", "associate", "compose", "discover", "encounter", etc., which were composed under a new glossary listing named *Negation-verbs*. The glossary is used by the pattern matching rules discussed in the section below, for identifying negation in phrases, such as *"deposits were not encountered at the machined level"*.

An integral part of the NegEx algorithm is the [Pseudo-Negation] list which is responsible for limiting the scope of a match by identifying false negation triggers. Due to the elaborate and unrestricted report style of archaeological grey literature documents, it was decided to expand the negation window of the algorithm to larger phrases containing a maximum of 10 word tokens instead of 5 that are originally set by NegEx. Thus, the inclusion of the [Pseudo-Negation] operation seemed highly relevant for avoiding matches of positive entity assertions that adjoin with negation phrases.

The general principle of the [Pseudo-Negation] operation was adopted as a means to narrow the scope of a negation window. A new list [Stop-Neg] was created that contained 38 new entries originating from the empirical use of English when separating different clauses in a sentence. The lexical resource Wordnet [17] was employed in the construction of a list containing a range of entries such as "but", "nonetheless", "than", "though" and relevant synonyms from the available synset hierarchies of the Wordnet.

The operation of the [Stop-Neg] list prevents matching beyond the scope of a negation phrase and does not exclude identification of conjunct entities. The original NegEx algorithm reported limitations on accurate matching of long lists of conjunct UMLS terms that expand beyond the word limit (5 tokens) of the negation window [6]. The OPTIMA pipeline is equipped with an Entity Conjunction module which delivers matches of the same CRM entities conjunct with "and", "or", "commas" and other forms of hyphenation. Hence, the negation module can exploit conjunct matches, in order to deliver negation phrases that include a list of entities, as for example the phrase *"no evidence of archaeological features or deposits dating to the Neolithic or Bronze Ages"*. The inclusion of the [Stop-Neg] list in the negation grammars prevents the match of *"post-medieval spread"* as a negated case in the phrase *"absence of evidence after the Roman period, with the exception of the post-medieval spread"* while the first clause of the phrase is identified as a negated match.

2.3   Negation Detection in OPTIMA

The negation detection module of the OPTIMA pipeline incorporates the four glossary listings, [Pre-Neg], [Post-Neg], [Stop-Neg] and [Verb-Neg] with a set of information extraction grammars. A set of three different pattern matching rules is deployed for each of the four different CRM entity types that fall within the scope of the negation module. The arrangement of the negation rules avoids multiple annotation of the same phrase, even if more than one CRM entities are mentioned in a phrase. The description of grammars given below refers to a unified form of a CRM entity which encompasses all four different CRM types for simplicity.

The grammars deliver a single annotation span, which covers all CRM entities involved in a phrase. For example the phrase *"no evidence of Roman pottery"* delivers a single annotation spanning the whole phrase rather than two separate annotations for *"Roman"* and *"pottery"*. Similarly when conjunction of entities is present, the negation span covers all conjunct entities under a single annotation span

The following grammar is targeted at matching cases of negation which commence with a match from the [Pre-Neg] list and end in a CRM entity or a CRM conjunct entity match, for example *"absence of any datable small finds or artefacts"*.

```
{PreNeg}({Token,!StopNeg})[0,10]({CRM}|{CRM_Conjuction})
```

The following grammar matches cases of negation which commence with a CRM entity or a CRM conjunct entity and end with a match from the [Post-Neg] list, for example *"wares such as tea bowl are particularly unlikely to exist"*.

```
({CRM}|{CRM_Conjuction})({Token, !StopNeg})[0,10]{PostNeg}
```

The following grammar is targeted at matching cases of negation which commence with a CRM entity or a CRM conjunct entity and end with a match from the [Verb-Neg] list, for example *"pottery and tile remains were not observed"*.

```
({CRM}|{CRM_Conjuction})({Token,!StopNeg})[0,10]
{Token.string=="not"}({Token})?{VerbNeg}
```

3   Evaluation

The evaluation phase aimed at benchmarking the performance of the negation detection module using standard evaluation methods. Typically the performance of Information Extraction systems is measured in Recall, Precision and F-Measure scores as established by the second Machine Understanding Conference, MUC 2 [18]. The F-Measure score is the harmonious mean of Precision and Recall used to provide a comprehensive view of system's performance. Attempts to improve Recall will usually cause Precision to drop and vice versa. High scoring of F-Measure is desirable since it can be used to benchmark the overall system's accuracy [19].

The evaluation phase has adopted the above measurements including both fully correct and partial matches, as expressed by the following formulae, with N_{key} being the correct answer, and the system delivering $N_{correct}$ responses correctly and $N_{incorrect}$ incorrectly :

$$Recall = \frac{N_{correct} + (Partial_{matches})}{N_{key}} \quad Precision = \frac{N_{correct} + (Partial_{matches})}{N_{correct} + N_{incorrect}} \quad F_1 = 2\frac{Precision * Recall}{Precision + Recall}$$

Partial matches are those having different annotation boundaries than the N_{key} definition, either matching only a part or expanding beyond the limits of a key. Partial matches can be weighted with decimal values ranging from 0 to 1 depending on the importance of such matches in the system's accuracy. The evaluation task treated partial matches as fully correct matches based on the flexible user-centred approach followed during the definition of the $N_{key\,responses}$, which delivered negated phrases that were syntactically complete from a user's point of view. For example, an N_{key} response might be "*No traces of a Roman settlement have been discovered in the area*". However, the negation algorithm is programmed to extract phrases that commence or end with a CRM entity, in this case only the first part is extracted ("*No traces of a Roman settlement*") delivering a partial match. Hence, the match can be treated as fully correct since the N_{key} response is not defined with the algorithm in mind but with what is useful from an end-user point of view.

The set of the N_{key} responses participating in system's evaluation were delivered by the method of manual annotation also known as "Gold Standard" definition, which is typically employed for comparison against system produced annotations. Such manual definitions are usually built by domain experts but their availability is often scarce. In the case of archaeological reports, there was no available gold standard of semantically annotated documents with respect to negated CIDOC-CRM entities. Therefore, the evaluation stage pursued the definition of a gold standard corpus tailored to serve the purposes of the evaluation task.

In total 10 grey literature documents of archaeological excavation and evaluation reports contributed to the gold standard definition. In archaeology, grey literature reports reflect the different stages of a fieldwork project worth recording and disseminating information about. They contain comprehensive explanations, diagrams, summaries and statistics that deliver in depth analysis and discussion usually not possible to be accommodated by traditional publication. The evaluation corpus contained a set of archaeological excavation and evaluation reports, which typically contain rich discussion about the findings and excavation phases over other types of archaeological reports, such as watching briefs and observation reports.

In addition, the selection process included reports from a range of different UK archaeological units aiming to cover different reporting styles and practices. The gold standard overall consisted from 300 pages which contained 144 cases of negation.

3.1   Results

Among the 10 documents that participated in the evaluation task, the negation detection module delivered an overall Recall score 80%, Precision 89% and F-Measure 83% (table 1). The Recall score of individual documents presents a fluctuation ranging from 50% to 100% while fluctuation of Precision scores is smaller ranging from 64% to 100%. The good precision performance of the module is also reflected by the standard deviation score which is 0.11(or 11%) with only one document scoring under 80%. On the other hand, the standard deviation of Recall scores is slightly higher 0.15 (or 15%) with half of the documents scoring under 80%.

Table 1. Performance of Negation Detection Module

Document	Recall	Precision	F-Measure
Aocarcha1-11167	0.74	0.94	0.83
Birmingh2-28160	0.77	1.00	0.87
Essexcou1-10460	0.83	1.00	0.91
Essexcou1-5166	0.76	0.85	0.80
Foundati1-5205	0.87	1.00	0.93
Heritage1-10767	0.50	1.00	0.67
Heritage1-11948	1.00	0.83	0.91
Suffolkc-6115	0.85	0.89	0.87
Wessexar1-25626	0.70	0.64	0.67
Wessexar1-5680	1.00	0.83	0.91
Average	0.80	0.89	0.83

The negation detection module has overall delivered 114 correct and partially correct matches, 14 false positive (falsely identified) matches, while it missed 30 negation answers of the gold standard definition. The number of total false positive matches is half of those matches being missed. This significant difference between the two is also reflected in the Precision and Recall scores where missed matches directly affect recall and false positives precision. Overall, the negation module delivers better precision than recall, indicative of the module's capacity to accurately identify cases of negation while being challenged by the variety in which negation can be expressed in natural language.

4   Discussion

The evaluation results revealed an encouraging performance of the negation detection module which delivered Recall and Precision scores over 80%. Although, the evaluation task had a limited scope and was based on the use of a small scale gold standard definition, it suggests that negation in archaeological text can be addressed with information extraction techniques that use a small set of domain oriented pattern-matching rules. Our results agree with research findings from biomedical text negation [6] reporting that negation phrases typically comply with the Zipf's law regarding the frequency distribution of words in human languages, where a few very common negation patterns can capture a large portion of pertinent negation cases.

According to the evaluation results, use of frequently occurring negation patterns in extraction rules supports the system's precision. The vast majority of automatically identified negation phrases (approximately 9 out of 10) delivered by the negation module were correct. Incorrect cases (false positives) are primarily the result of limitation in the vocabulary used to support the operation of extraction patterns and not due to the incapacity of extraction patterns themselves. For example the phrase "*It is not unusual to find solitary prehistoric cremations*" has a positive meaning which is falsely identified as a negation case. The OPTIMA algorithm, similarly to the NegEx algorithm [6], employs a specialised vocabulary [Stop-Neg], which limits the scope of negation. The original NegEx glossary of pseudo-negation phrases is enhanced with additional terms (drawn from ordinary use of English), through a WordNet Synset expansion technique (section 2.2.1) to include a range of entries such as, "but", nonetheless", "though" and their synonyms. The expanded glossary failed to address fully all the cases of double negatives as for example "not unusual", which has a fairly positive assertion. Possibly use of double negatives is avoided in the restricted context of narrative reports of medical records but in the context of archaeological reports such double negated narratives may occur. Fewer false positive cases relate to the operation of matching patterns as for example the phrase "*non-intrusive survey had accurately predicted the ridge and furrow*" where "*non*" applies only to the immediate noun that follows.

The recall performance of the negation module is reasonable (approximately 8 out of 10) but not as high as precision. The capacity of the algorithm to identify all correct cases of negation in text is challenged by the sometimes creative and indirect writing style of archaeological reports. For example the phrase "*The low quantity and quality of the remains encountered on the site suggests that there is only a minor archaeological implication*" clearly suggests that findings do not have an archaeological interest. However, it is formulated in an indirect style, which does not invoke any negation triggers that could be matched by the module.

Other cases of missed examples concern use of passive voice utterances that do not employ clear negation classifiers but verbs which are loaded with negative sense. For example the phrase "*both these deposits were largely absent*" is missed due to the definition of matching patterns that expect a negation classifier at the beginning of a phrase for example "*Absence of deposits*", or a negation formation at the end of a phrase for example "*deposits were not largely present*". Fewer examples of non-identified cases concern limitations of the NER vocabulary itself. For example the phrase "*there was virtually no artefactual evidence recovered*" is missed because "*artefactual evidence*" is not recognised as a CRM entity.

4.1   Adapting NegEx in Archaeological Grey Literature

The adaptation and redesign process of the NegEx algorithm in the context of negation detection of CRM entities in archaeological grey literature documents has achieved various useful results. The original NegEx algorithm operated within a less ambiguous and more restricted narrative context [6] than the archaeological report narrative. The main challenge of the adaptation process was to address the flexible and sometimes creative writing style of archaeological grey literature documents. Additional work involved review, modification and enhancement of original regular expression rules and glossaries. Based on corpus analysis (section 2.2.1), the adaptation technique gathered valuable information with regards to vocabulary use and writing style, which informed and directed the adaptation process.

A major modification of the original algorithm directly informed from the corpus analysis task, concerned the expansion of the negation window from 5 to 10 tokens, supported by an enhanced [Pseudo-Negation] list with terms and phrases relevant to archaeological narrative. The negation window of the regular expression rules was expanded from 5 to 10 word-tokens to include longer phrases of negation which might appear in archaeological reports. A new matching pattern, not previously included in the original NegEx algorithm due to the direct reporting style of medical reports, was introduced by the adaption task for detecting negation phrases of passive voice expressions. The redesign process has also improved the performance of the original algorithm in the detection of conjunct terms via usage of CRM instances previously identified by the Entity Conjunction module of the NER phase. Moreover, the corpus analysis task has informed modification of the original [Pre-Neg] and [Post-Neg] glossaries with the inclusion of new archaeology related terms and removal of the less applicable original entries.

The evaluation phase revealed valuable feedback with regards to the adaptation effort. Clearly a larger scale corpus analysis supported by archaeology domain-expert input, could reveal new clues in the definition of pattern matching rules capable of addressing the flexible and creative reporting style of archaeological documents. Similarly, a larger evaluation corpus (Gold Standard) including a greater number of manual annotations and documents, would potentially reveal the system's capacity to address the variety and complexity of negation in archaeological grey literature reports. Our experience demonstrates a pathway and implementation technique for porting NegEx to a new domain, which we hope is applicable to other domains but this remains to be tested.

4.2   Method Limitations

The development approach of constructing a negation detection mechanism based on shallow parsing delivered results that suite the aims of semantic indexing. Shallow parsing analyses a sentence or a phrase to its constituent parts but without analysing their role or their internal structure. The negation detection module has managed to identify with reasonable success a vast range of phrases containing one or more CRM entities which were negated via a lexical classifier. Upon successful identification of a negation phrase, all CRM entities of the phrase were discarded from further indexing. This approach did not harm the quality of the indexing due to the vast amount of CRM entities being delivered by the NER phase. On the other hand, this particular approach might be considered as a blanket practice that does not support the aims of a detailed and meticulous text mining effort.

Looking closer at the following example *"No artefacts were retrieved from this deposit"* it is clear that there is absence of artefacts. However, the same absence does not apply to the deposit itself which does exist but under the current configuration is excluded from indexing. Adoption of deep parsing techniques, which analyse the role and structure of the constitute parts of a sentence, could be sufficient to address such cases of detailed negation assignment on the level of subject clause. However, the semantic annotation of such negated cases with respect to ontology classes may prove a challenging task as discussed below.

Consider the above example *"No artefacts were retrieved from this deposit"*. Assignment of the *E19.Physical_Object* class to "artefacts" instance assumes a positive assertion. Similarly an ontological model may define a relationship property between place and physical object. Again this kind of property assumes a positive assertion which does not cover the cases where an object in not in place.

A specific project which addressed the issue of factual argumentation using the CIDOC-CRM ontology is the Integrated Argumentation Model (IAM) [20]. Although, factual argumentation is a broader epistemological issue that concerns falsification or verification of arguments, the aim of IAM to connect such epistemological aspects with instances of a formal ontology could be potentially useful and applicable to the semantics of negation assertion. The project presented benefits to archaeological reasoning for a particular case (the natural mummy Oetzi) but its applicability in the context of semantic annotation of archaeological text remains untested.

Providing a semantic annotation i.e. assigning classes or properties, to textual instances that are negated is not always viable within the scope of an ontology that assumes only positive assignment. A possible answer to this limitation might be addressed with the introduction of a property for declaring the sense of an instance for example *has_sense*, positive or negative. However, introduction of such property will significantly increase the chain of triples defined by a SPARQL query on an application level even for the simplest queries.

An alternative approach could be the introduction of negative print of all ontological classes and properties in order to accommodate negative assertions. Thus, every class or property of an ontological model would have its equivalent contrasting class in the sense of "matter, anti-matter". This particular approach though, would double the size of an ontological model which could lead to issues relating to the maintenance and version control of an ontological model.

5   Conclusions

The paper presented the results of a negation detection module targeted at identifying negated cases of four CIDOC-CRM entities in the context of semantic indexing of archaeological grey literature for information retrieval. The evaluation results demonstrate the capacity of rule-based information extraction techniques to accurately detect a large portion of negation phrases. The employment of three small scale glossaries that support the operation of a few simple pattern matching expressions has proved sufficient to deliver high Recall (80%) and Precision (89%) scores. Current limitations of the method relate to the employment of shallow parsing techniques that do not support deeper analysis of negation phrases, the capacity of glossaries to cover all possible vocabulary variations, and the adequacy of pattern matching rules to address every single case of negation which can be expressed by a creative and sometimes indirect writing style of archaeological reports. However, such limitations do not restrict application of the work in the context of semantic indexing. Future steps include a large scale corpus analysis and evaluation study aimed at expanding glossary coverage and improving the system's performance with regards to archaeological negation narrative. Longer term aims may involve the system's generalisation to the broader field of digital humanities and application of semantic modelling solutions capable of addressing negation at an information retrieval level.

The paper has revealed a method for adapting the NegEx algorithm to the domain of archaeological grey literature. Our experience has shown that porting of NegEx to a new domain is feasible. The method of modification of the original algorithm was driven by a corpus analysis task, which enabled enhancement and adaptation of the original resources to the new domain. This particular method has given promising results for the domain of archaeological reports though its applicability to other domain remains to be tested. The issue of accommodating negative assertions by the current ontological modelling approaches was also highlighted. Negated findings and facts are important for the research and information retrieval in particular domains, such as the medical and the archaeology domain. Semantic technologies can provide a valuable support in modelling and retrieval of such negated findings for enabling new forms of research and information exchange.

Acknowledgments. While we wish to acknowledge support from the ARIADNE project (FP7-INFRASTRUCTURES-2012-1-313193), the views expressed are those of the authors and do not necessarily reflect the views of the European Commission.

References

1. O'Hara, K., Berners-Lee, T., Hall, W., Shadbolt, N.: Use of the Semantic Web in e-Research. The MIT Press, Cambridge (2010)
2. Bizer, C., Heath, T., Berners-Lee, T.: Linked Data - The Story So Far. International Journal on Semantic Web and Information Systems 5(3), 1–22 (2009)
3. Horn, L.R.: A Natural History of Negation. University of Chicago Press, Chicago (1989)
4. Westbury, C.: Just say no: The evolutionary and developmental significance of negation in behavior and natural language. In: 3rd Conference The Evolution of Language, Paris (2000)
5. Blanco, E., Moldovan, D.: Semantic representation of negation using focus detection. In: 49th Annual Meeting of the Association for Computational Linguistics, Portland (2011)
6. Chapman, W.W., Bridewell, W., Hanbury, P., Cooper, G.F., Buchanan, B.G.: A Simple Algorithm for Identifying Negated Findings and Diseases in Discharge Summaries. Journal of Biomedical Informatics 34(5), 301–310 (2001)

7. Maynard, D., Funk, A.: Automatic detection of political opinions in tweets. In: García-Castro, R., Fensel, D., Antoniou, G. (eds.) ESWC 2011. LNCS, vol. 7117, pp. 88–99. Springer, Heidelberg (2012)

8. Goryachev, S., Sordo, M., Zeng, Q.T., Ngo, L.: Implementation and evaluation of four different methods of negation detection. Technical report. Harvard Medical School (2006)

9. Vlachidis, A., Tudhope, D.: A pilot investigation of information extraction in the semantic annotation of archaeological reports. International Journal of Metadata, Semantics and Ontologies 7(3), 222–235 (2012)

10. Falkingham, G.: A whiter shade of grey: A new approach to archaeological grey literature using the XML version of the TEI guidelines. Internet Archaeology 17 (2005),
http://intarch.ac.uk/journal/issue17/falkingham_index.html

11. Vlachidis, A.: Semantic Indexing Via Knowledge Organisation Resources: Applying the CIDOC-CRM to Archaeological. PhD Thesis, University of Glamorgan, UK (2012)

12. Uren, V., Cimiano, P., Iria, J., Handschuh, S., Vargas-Vera, M., Motta, E., Ciravegna, F.: Semantic annotation for knowledge management: Requirements and a survey of the state of the art. Web Semantics: Science, Services and Agents on the WWW 4(1), 14–28 (2006)

13. Crofts, N., Doerr, M., Gill, T., Stead, S., Stiff, M.: Definition of the CIDOC Conceptual Reference Model,
http://cidoc.ics.forth.gr/docs/
cidoc_crm_version_5.0.1_Mar09.pdf

14. Tudhope, D., May, K., Binding, C., Vlachidis, A.: Connecting archaeological data and grey literature via semantic cross search. Internet Archaeology 30 (2011),
http://intarch.ac.uk/journal/issue30/tudhope_index.html

15. Nadeau, D., Sekine, S.: A survey of named entity recognition and classification. Lingvisticae Investigationes 30(1), 3–26 (2007)

16. Ruch, P., Baud, R., Geissbuhler, A., Rassinoux, A.M.: Comparing general and medical texts for information retrieval based on natural language processing: An inquiry into lexical disambiguation. Med-info. 10, 261–265 (2001)

17. Miller, G.A.: WordNet: A Lexical Database for English. Communications of the ACM 38(11), 39–41 (1995)

18. Grishman, R., Sundheim, B.: Message Understanding Conference-6: A brief history. In: 16th International Conference on Computational Linguistics, Copenhagen (1996)

19. Doerr, M., Kritsotaki, A., Boutsika, K.: Factual argumentation-a core model for assertions making. Journal on Computing and Cultural Heritage 3(3), 1–34 (2011)

A Preliminary Approach on Ontology-Based Visual Query Formulation for Big Data

Ahmet Soylu[1], Martin G. Skjæveland[1], Martin Giese[1], Ian Horrocks[2],
Ernesto Jimenez-Ruiz[2], Evgeny Kharlamov[2], and Dmitriy Zheleznyakov[2]

[1] Department of Informatics, University of Oslo, Norway
{ahmets,martige,martingi}@ifi.uio.no
[2] Department of Computer Science, University of Oxford, United Kingdom
{name.surname}@cs.ox.ac.uk

Abstract. Data access in an enterprise setting is a determining factor for
the potential of value creation processes such as sense-making, decision
making, and intelligence analysis. As such, providing friendly data access
tools that directly engage domain experts (i.e., end-users) with data, as
opposed to the situations where database/IT experts are required to extract data from databases, could substantially increase competitiveness
and profitability. However, the ever increasing volume, complexity, velocity, and variety of data, known as the Big Data phenomenon, renders the
end-user data access problem even more challenging. Optique, an ongoing European project with a strong industrial perspective, aims to countervail the Big Data effect, and to enable scalable end-user data access
to traditional relational databases by using an ontology-based approach.
In this paper, we specifically present the preliminary design and development of our ontology-based visual query system and discuss directions for
addressing the Big Data effect.

Keywords: Visual Query Formulation, Ontology-based Data Access,
Big Data, End-user Data Access, Visual Query Systems.

1 Introduction

A tremendous amount of data is being generated every day both on the Web
and in public and private organisations; and, by all accounts, in this increasingly
data-oriented world, any individual or organisation, who posses the necessary
knowledge, skills, and tools to make value out of data at such scales, bears a
considerable advantage in terms of competitiveness and development. Particularly, in an enterprise setting, ability to access and use data in business processes
such as *sense-making* and *intelligence analysis* is key for its *value creation* potential (cf. [1]). Today, however, *data access* still stands as a major bottleneck for
many organisations. This is mostly due to the sharp distinction between employ-
ees who have technical skills and knowledge to extract data (i.e., *database/IT
experts, skilled users* etc.) and those who have domain knowledge and know how
to interpret and use data (i.e., *domain experts, end-users* etc.). The result is

E. Garoufallou and J. Greenberg (Eds.): MTSR 2013, CCIS 390, pp. 201–212, 2013.

a workflow where domain-experts either have to use pre-defined queries embedded in applications or communicate their *information needs* to database-experts. The former scenario is quite limiting, since it is not possible to enumerate every possible information need beforehand, while the latter scenario is hampered by the ambiguity in communication. In such a workflow, the turn-around time from users' initial information needs to receiving the answer can be in the range of weeks, incurring significant costs (cf. [2]).

Approaches that eliminate the man-in-the-middle and allow end-users to directly engage with data and extract it on their own, have been of interest to researchers for many years. As anticipated, for end-users, the accessibility of traditional structured query languages such as *SQL* and *XQuery* fall far short, since such textual languages do require end-users to have a set of technical skills and to *recall* domain concepts and the terminology and syntax of the language being used. For this very reason, *visual query systems and languages* (cf. [3]) have emerged to alleviate the end-user data access problem by providing intuitive visual query formulation tools. A visual system or language follows the *direct-manipulation* idea (cf. [4]), where the domain and query language are represented with a set of visual elements. End-users *recognise* relevant fragments of the domain and language and formulate queries basically by instantly manipulating them. A good deal of research on visual query formulation has been carried out both for *structured* (e.g., relational data) and *semi-structured data* (e.g., XML), such as *QBE* [5] and *Xing* [6]. Early approaches (cf. [3]) successfully establish the fundamentals of research on visual query formulation. However, on the one hand, their success, in practical terms, remains within the confines of abstraction levels they operate on; database schemas, object-oriented models etc. are not meant to capture a domain per se and are not truly natural for end-users. Recent approaches (e.g., [7,8]) close this gap by employing ontologies for visual query formulation, due to their closeness to reality; and the emergence of *ontology-based data access* (OBDA) technologies (cf. [9]) complete the overall picture by making it possible to access data residing on traditional relational databases over ontologies. On the other hand, visual query formulation, still being a considerable challenge in itself, faces inevitable scalability issues both in terms of *query answering* and *query formulation* (aka *query construction*), mainly introduced by the ever increasing *volume, complexity, velocity*, and *variety* of data – the so-called *Big Data* phenomenon (cf. [10,11]).

In this respect, a European project named *Optique*[1] – *Scalable End-user Access to Big Data*, with an industrial perspective, has been undertaken in order to enable end-user data access to traditional relational databases and to countervail the *Big Data effect* characterised by the aforementioned four dimensions. To this end, Optique employs an ontology-based approach for scalable query formulation and evaluation, along with other techniques such as query optimisation and parallelisation. The project involves two industrial partners, namely *Statoil*[2] and

---

[1] http://www.optique-project.eu
[2] http://www.statoil.com

Siemens[3], which provide real-life use cases. In this paper, we specifically present the preliminary design and development of our ontology-based visual query system and discuss directions for addressing the Big Data effect.

The rest of the paper is structured as follows. Section 2 sets the main research context, while Section 3 presents the related work. Section 4 describes our preliminary query formulation system, in terms of its architecture and interface. Finally, a discussion and conclusion are given in Section 5.

2 Background

Visual query formulation is indeed an *end-user development* (EUD) practice (cf. [12]), where the goal is to allow end-users to program without significant programming skills and knowledge. The evaluation criteria are *expressiveness*, i.e., the breadth of a system or language to characterise the domain knowledge and information need, and *usability*, i.e., in terms of *effectiveness, efficiency*, and *user-satisfaction* (cf. [3]). From the usability point of view, the selection of appropriate *visual attributes* (i.e., *perceptual* such as size, texture, and colour), *representation paradigms* (i.e., *cognitive* such as forms and diagrams) and *interaction styles* (e.g., navigation, range selection etc.), that lead end-users to *discern, comprehend*, and *communicate* a maximal amount of information with minimum effort, is of the utmost importance. From the expressiveness point of view, one must identify and support frequently repeating query tasks and necessary domain constructs, that could be easily communicated and realised by end-users through a visual tool. At this point, the difference between *visual query languages* (VQL) and *visual query systems* (VQS) comes into play. A VQL is a language that has a well-defined syntax and formal semantics independent of how queries are constructed, while a VQS is a system of interactions between a user and a computer, with or without an underlying visual language, that generates queries (cf. [13]). A VQS has a natural advantage over a VQL, since users might forget languages, but common knowledge and skills are mostly non-volatile (cf. *syntactic/semantic model* of user behaviour [4]). In any case, there are basically two types of activities, namely *exploration* (aka *understanding the reality of interest*) and *query construction* [3], that have to be supported by a data access system. The goal of the former is to establish an understanding of the domain by means of finding and identifying domain constructs, such as concepts and relationships, and their organisation. The goal of the latter is to formally express the information need. Exploration and construction have adverse (i.e., breadth vs. depth), yet complementary roles; therefore, they have to be addressed and intertwined adequately.

Visual query formulation relies on a domain model to enable end-users to communicate with the system. Experimental research suggests that approaches built on logical models, such as database schemata and object role models, are not as effective as conceptual approaches, where interaction is in terms of real world concepts and hence more natural [14]. In this respect, the use of ontologies

---

[3] http://www.siemens.com

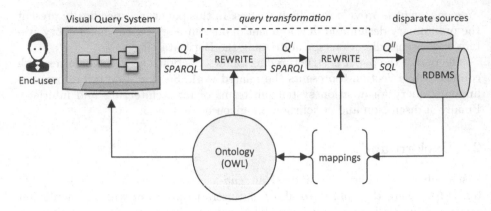

Fig. 1. Ontology-based visual query formulation and OBDA

for query formulation is quite promising, since they are semantically richer and close the gap between the end-user's understating of reality and the system's representation of it. Moreover, ontologies, due to their reasoning power, provide the capability of expressing more with less both in the query formulation stage and the answering stage by relating the whole set of implied information instead of what is explicitly stated and available. However, almost all of the world's enterprise data today resides in relational databases. At this point, the *Semantic Web* [15] and OBDA technologies (e.g., [16,17]) play an essential role by bridging traditional relational data sources and ontologies. An ontology-based VQS falls into the category of *ontology-driven information systems* (cf. [18]). The OBDA approach, over relational databases, is typically built on *mappings* (cf. [19]), to relate the concepts and relations of the ontology to data sources, and *query rewriting* (cf. [17]), to transform queries into complete, correct, and highly optimised queries over possibly disparate data sources (see Fig. 1). As such, an ontology-based VQS employs the visual representations of terms coming from an ontology (e.g., an OWL ontology) for visual query formulation. Once a query is formulated by an end-user, it is extracted in the form of an underlying formal linguistic language (e.g., SPARQL). Then, a query transformation process takes place with two query rewriting phases. The former, by taking constraints coming from the ontology into account, rewrites the query in the same language; while the latter translates query into the language of underlying data sources (e.g., SQL) through mappings defined between ontology and data sources.

Visual query formulation is still an open challenge, yet the Big Data effect has substantially rescaled the problem. Firstly, the volume and complexity dimensions hinder human perception and cognition respectively. A data access system, therefore, has to orient and guide users within the large conceptual space and should provide the right amount of information in intuitive forms. Secondly, the variety dimension necessitate more specific presentations and interaction experiences adapted to data at hand at any moment, while the velocity dimension requires data access systems to address *reactive* scenarios, where data is automatically *detected, assessed,* and *acted upon.* Ontologies have potential to address some of these new challenges; however, in general, a data access system, should support users in various ways (e.g., visualisations, recommendations etc.) and should be integrated and adapted into the *context,* such as *personal, data-related, task-related,* and *organisational* (cf. [20,21]).

3   Related Work

Early approaches to visual query formulation rely on low level models (i.e., database schemas) (cf. [3]), while recent ontology-based approaches mostly target open web data (i.e., *linked data browsers*) (cf. [22]). Data access on the Web is inherently different from traditional database systems, where information needs have to be precisely described with a very weak tolerance for missing or irrelevant results. However, the apparent success of web search makes it a sensible direction to adapt web search approaches to traditional settings. *Faceted search* (cf. [23]) and *Query by Navigation* (QbN) (cf. [24]) are prominent in terms of their suitability for ontology-based query formulation and their inherent compatibility. Faceted search, being an advanced form-based approach, is based on series of orthogonal dimensions, that can be applied in combination to filter the information space; each dimension, called *facet,* corresponds to a taxonomy. In its most common form, each facet option is accompanied with the number of accessible instances upon a possible selection. This is to prevent users from reaching empty result sets. QbN exploits the graph-based organisation of information to allow users to construct queries by traversing the relationships between concepts. Each navigation from one concept to another is indeed a join operation. Actually, end-users are quite familiar with both types of search approaches; faceted search is widely used in commercial websites such as eBay and Amazon for listing and filtering products, while the navigation is the backbone of web browsing. Since, there is a fair share of primary query construction operations, i.e., *select* and *project* for faceted search and *join* for QbN, their combination is promising.

Examples of QbN are *Tabulator* [25], *SEWASIE project* [7], *ViziQuer* [26], and *Visor* [27], and well-known examples of faceted search are *Flamenco* [28], *mSpace* [29], and *Exhibit* [30]. The examples of first category provide weak or no support for select and projection operations; similarly the examples on the latter do not provide sufficient support for joining concepts. The hybrid of QbN and faceted search is available in two forms in the literature. The former is built on *menu-based* QbN; the prominent examples are *Parallax* [31], *Humboldt* [32], and *VisiNav* [33]. The latter is built on *diagram-based* QbN; the prominent examples are *OZONE* [34] and *gFacet* [35]. In menu-based QbN, domain concepts are repented in the form of lists and a user navigates by selecting a concept from the list every time; while, in a diagram-based QbN, concepts are represented as nodes in a graph and a user navigates by expanding and retracting nodes. Moving from once concept to another changes the focus (i.e., *pivoting*) and the user can impose constraints on the active concept by selecting options within each facet. However, the problem with these approaches is their strong focus on web data, which leads them to be highly explorative and instance oriented. That is, firstly, the result of user navigation in the conceptual space is mostly for data browsing purposes; a final query, which encompasses the visited concepts, is not generated. Hence, there is no clear distinction between explorative and constructive user actions and there is a lack of support for *view* (i.e., the active phase of a query task) and *overview* (i.e., the general snapshot of a query task). Secondly, a frequent interaction with the data is required (i.e., *database-intensive*), which is problematic with large scale data sources. The scalability problem is indeed more severe, since no support for tackling with large ontologies is provided.

4   Optique Approach

Our goal, from an architectural perspective, is extensibility and flexibility to ensure scalability and adaptivity to different contexts and needs, and, from a human-interaction perspective, is to minimise both the perceptual and cognitive load on users and to provide intuitive and natural experiences.

4.1   Architecture

The approach we pursue is built on *widget-based user-interface mashups* (i.e., UI mashups), which aggregate a set of applications in a common graphical space, in the form of *widgets*, and allow an interplay between them for achieving common goals (cf. [36]). In our context, widgets are the building blocks of a UI mashup and refer to *portable*, *self-contained*, *full-fledged*, and mostly *client side* applications with lesser functionality and complexity. In a query formulation scenario, a set of widgets could be employed together. For instance, one widget for QbN and one for faceted search could handle query construction synchronously, and one widget could represent query results in a tabular form.

Widgets are managed by a *widget run-time environment*, which provides basic *communication and persistence services* to widgets. The *orchestration* of widgets relies on the requirement that each widget discloses its functionality to the environment through a client side interface and notifies any other widget in the environment (e.g., broadcast, subscription etc.) and/or the widget environment upon each user action. Then, either each widget decides what action to execute in response, by considering the *syntactic* or *semantic signature* of the received event; or the environment decides on widgets to invoke. The core benefits of such an approach are that it becomes easier to deal with the complexity, since the management of functionality and data could be delegated to different widgets; each widget could employ a different representation paradigm that best suits its functionality; widgets could be used alone or together, in different combinations, for different contexts and experiences; and the functionality of the overall interface could be extended by introducing new widgets.

The preliminary architecture for our query formulation system is depicted in Fig. 2. The architecture assumes that each widget has client side and server side components (for complex processing), and that widgets can communicate with

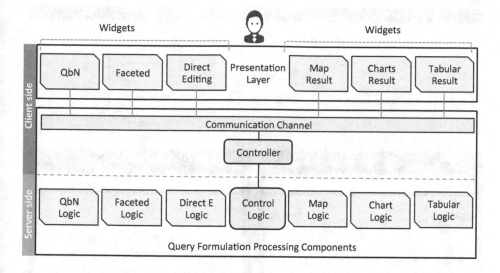

Fig. 2. OptiqueVQS architecture based on widget-based UI mashups

each other and with the environment through a *communication channel*. Communication usually happens through the client side, but a server side communication mechanism could also be realised in order to support remote experiences (i.e., widgets running on distributed devices). There exists an *environment controller* at the client side and a *component control logic* at the server side. The former is responsible for operational tasks such as collecting event notifications from widgets and submitting control commands to them. The latter is responsible for the orchestration logic, that is, it decides how widgets should react to specific events. The widget specification of the W3C[4] and the widget runtime environment proposed in [36] guide our architectural design. Note that the architecture depicted here only concerns the visual query formulation system; the overall Optique architecture which includes other core components, such as for query evaluation, ontology management and evolution, mappings, and distributed query execution, has been discussed in another publication (cf. [37]).

4.2 Interface

The choice of visual representation and interaction paradigm, along with underlying *metaphors, analogies* etc., is of primary importance for the query formulation interface. We have observed that a single representation and interaction paradigm is not sufficient for developing successful query formulation interfaces. Therefore, we strive to combine the best parts of different paradigms (cf. [3]).

---

[4] http://www.w3.org/TR/widgets/

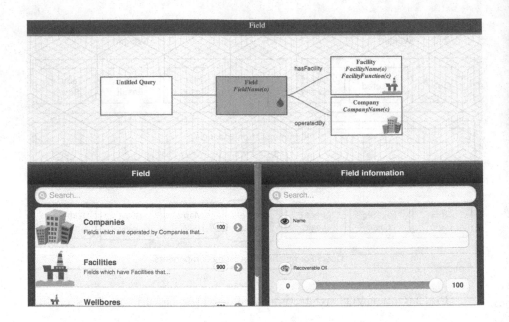

Fig. 3. OptiqueVQS interface – an example query is depicted

We have implemented a preliminary visual query system, *Optique VQS*,[5] which is depicted in Fig. 3. The OptiqueVQS is initially composed of three widgets. The first widget (W1), see the bottom-left part of Fig. 3, employs menu-based representation and QbN interaction paradigms. This widget also supplements domain concepts with meaningful icons and short descriptions. The role of this widget is to allow end-users to navigate concepts through pursuing relationships between them, hence joining relations in a database. Every time a concept is selected, the focus of the interfaces changes to the selected concept (i.e, *pivot operation*). The second widget (W2), see the top part of Fig. 3, follows a diagram-based representation paradigm with QbN; it utilises geometric symbols to depict relationships among schema concepts in a graph. The role of this widget is to provide an overview of the constructed query; it also supports pivoting limited to the concepts involved in a query. Every node appearing in the diagram corresponds to a variable (i.e., of SPARQL) and called *variable-node*. The last widget (W3), see the bottom-right part of Fig. 3, is meant to employ a faceted search approach. However, in the current form, it follows a generic form-based representation paradigm. The role of this widget is to allow end-users to identify attributes that will be included in the result list and to place constraints on the attributes of the active (i.e., focus/pivot) concept. W1 and W3 support view (i.e., the active phase), while W2 supports overview (i.e., the snapshot). Concerning the design rationale behind each individual component,

---

[5] http://sws.ifi.uio.no/project/optique/pubshare/mtsr2013/

Fig. 4. OptiqueVQS interface – the result of an example query is depicted

in terms of representation paradigm, lists (i.e., W1) are good at communicating large amount of information, forms (i.e., W3) are a well-known metaphor for end-users, and a diagram-based approach (i.e., W2) is good at communicating relationships between concepts; and, in terms of interaction paradigm, navigation (i.e., W1 and W2), matching, and range selection (i.e., W3) are known to be intuitive (cf. [3,38]).

In a typical query construction scenario, a user first selects a *kernel concept*, i.e., the starting concept, from W1, which initially lists all available domain concepts. The selected concept immediately becomes the focus concept (coloured in orange), appears in the the graph (i.e., W2), its attributes are displayed by W3, and W1 displays all the concept-relationship pairs pertaining to this concept. The user can select attributes to be included in the result list (i.e., using the "eye" button of each attribute) and/or impose constraints on them through form elements (i.e., W3). Note that W1 does not purely present relationships, but combine relationship and concept pairs (i.e., relationship and range) into one selection; this helps us to reduce the number of navigational levels a user has to pass through. The user can select any available option from the list and this results in a join between two variable-nodes over the specified relationship and moves focus to the selected concept. The user has to follow the same steps to involve new concepts into the query and can always jump to a specific part of the query by clicking on the corresponding variable-node on the graph. An example query is depicted in Fig. 3 for the Statoil use case in energy domain. The query asks for all fields which has a specific facility (e.g., an oil producing platform) and is operated by a specific company (e.g., Statoil).

Regarding the access to result lists, the system will provide several specialised presentation widgets specific to the nature of the data. An example has been depicted in Fig. 4, which shows all fields on a map, colouring those that are operated by Statoil and have an oil producing facility. In this context, it is important that widgets should have the ability to intelligently detect the data type (e.g., items with a geo-spatial extent) and act accordingly, which is not hard to realise in an ontology-driven environment. The data source and widgetised map application used in this example comes from a project providing a semantic gateway to the Norwegian Petroleum Directorate's FactPages dataset [39].

5   Discussion and Conclusion

In this paper, we have introduced a preliminary ontology-based approach on query formulation for Big data. As far as the approach itself is concerned, the multi-paradigm approach that we follow firstly allows us to provide a good balance between view and overview. Secondly, one should be aware that an ontology is more than a class hierarchy and includes complex axioms. In our context, each representation paradigm could handle different kinds of ontology axioms, for instance, a faceted search paradigm is better suited for representing disjointness, a menu-based paradigm with QbN may be a better option for handling cyclic queries, and a diagrammatic representation is better in visualising them.

Concerning the expressiveness, we categorise queries into three levels with respect to their *perceived complexity*. First level corresponds to simple *three-shaped conjunctive queries*, while the second level refers to *cyclic* and *disjunctive queries*. The last level corresponds to queries with *universal quantifiers*, and *negation*. We postulate that most of the end-user queries will be centred around first level. The current interface at the moment addresses the first level queries and basic cycles (i.e., where a concept appears twice). However, we do see possibilities to address second level and third level queries to support advanced users.

At this stage, the current proposal attacks the query formulation challenge itself; our work for addressing the Big Data effect is under progress. Particularly for large ontologies, guiding users among hundreds of concepts, attributes, and relationships is of crucial importance. The possible approaches that we have identified include *adaptations*, that take previous interaction/query logs into account, for pruning the navigational space and to provide recommendations; *heuristics*, that consider what really occurs in data; and *annotations* to rule out unreasonable cases. Such information could be used to rank concepts, relationships, and attributes and then to gradually present them to users.

Acknowledgements. This research is funded by the FP7 of the European Commission under Grant Agreement 318338, "Optique".

References

1. Nunameker, J.F., Briggs, R.O., de Vreede, G.J.: From Information Technology to Value Creation Technology. In: Information Technology and the Future Enterprise: New Models for Managers, pp. 102–124. Prentice-Hall, New York (2001)
2. Giese, M., Calvanese, D., Horrocks, I., Ioannidis, Y., Klappi, H., Koubarakis, M., Lenzerini, M., Möller, R., Özcep, Ö., Rodriguez Muro, M., Rosati, R., Schlatte, R., Soylu, A., Waaler, A.: Scalable End-user Access to Big Data. In: Rajendra, A. (ed.) Big Data Computing. Chapman and Hall/CRC (2013)
3. Catarci, T., Costabile, M.F., Levialdi, S., Batini, C.: Visual query systems for databases: A survey. Journal of Visual Languages and Computing 8(2), 215–260 (1997)

4. Shneiderman, B.: Direct Manipulation: A Step Beyond Programming Languages. Computer 16(8), 57–69 (1983)
5. Zloof, M.M.: Query-by-Example: A data base language. IBM System Journal 16(4), 324–343 (1997)
6. Erwig, M.: Xing: A visual XML query language. Journal of Visual Languages and Computing 14(1), 5–45 (2003)
7. Catarci, T., Dongilli, P., Di Mascio, T., Franconi, E., Santucci, G., Tessaris, S.: An ontology based visual tool for query formulation support. In: 16th European Conference on Artificial Intelligence (ECAI 2004). Frontiers in Artificial Intelligence and Applications, vol. 110, pp. 308–312. IOS Press (2004)
8. Barzdins, G., Liepins, E., Veilande, M., Zviedris, M.: Ontology Enabled Graphical Database Query Tool for End-Users. In: 8th International Baltic Conference on Databases and Information Systems (DB&IS 2008). Frontiers in Artificial Intelligence and Applications, vol. 187, pp. 105–116. IOS Press (2009)
9. Kogalovsky, M.R.: Ontology-Based Data Access Systems. Programming and Computer Software 38(4), 167–182 (2012)
10. Laney, D.: 3D Data Management: Controlling Data Volume, Velocity and Variety. Technical report, META Group (2001)
11. Madden, S.: From Databases to Big Data. IEEE Internet Computing 16(3), 4–6 (2012)
12. Lieberman, H., Paternò, F., Wulf, V. (eds.): End User Development. Human-Computer Interaction Series, vol. 9. Springer (2006)
13. Epstein, R.G.: The TableTalk Query Language. Journal of Visual Languages and Computing 2, 115–141 (1991)
14. Siau, K.L., Chan, H.C., Wei, K.K.: Effects of query complexity and learning on novice user query performance with conceptual and logical database interfaces. IEEE Transactions on Systems, Man and Cybernetics – Part A: Systems and Humans 34(2), 276–281 (2004)
15. Berners-Lee, T., Hendler, J., Lassila, O.: The Semantic Web – A new form of Web content that is meaningful to computers will unleash a revolution of new possibilities. Scientific American 284(5), 34–43 (2001)
16. Rodriguez-Muro, M., Lubyte, L., Calvanese, D.: Realizing ontology based data access: A plug-in for Protégé. In: IEEE 24th International Conference on Data Engineering Workshop (ICDEW 2008), pp. 353–356. IEEE (2008)
17. Rodriguez-Muro, M., Calvanese, D.: Quest, a System for Ontology Based Data Access. In: OWL: Experiences and Directions Workshop 2012 (OWLED 2012). CEUR Workshop Proceedings, vol. 849. CEUR-WS.org (2012)
18. Ruiz, F., Hilera, J.R.: Using Ontologies in Software Engineering and Technology. In: Calero, C., Ruiz, F., Piattini, M. (eds.) Ontologies for Software Engineering and Software Technology, pp. 49–102. Springer (2006)
19. Spanos, D.E., Stavrou, P., Mitrou, N.: Bringing relational databases into the Semantic Web: A survey. Semantic Web 3(2), 169–209 (2012)
20. Coutaz, J., Crowley, J.L., Dobson, S., Garlan, D.: Context is key. Communications of the ACM 48(3), 49–53 (2005)
21. Marchionini, G., White, R.: Find What You Need, Understand What You Find. International Journal of Human-Computer Interaction 23(3), 205–237 (2007)
22. Bizer, C., Heath, T., Berners-Lee, T.: Linked Data – The Story So Far. International Journal on Semantic Web and Information Systems 5(3), 1–22 (2009)
23. Tunkelang, D., Marchionini, G.: Faceted Search. In: Synthesis Lectures on Information Concepts, Retrieval, and Services. Morgan and Claypool Publishers (2009)
24. ter Hofstede, A., Proper, H., van der Weide, T.: Query Formulation as an Information Retrieval Problem. Computer Journal 39(4), 255–274 (1996)

25. Berners-Lee, T., Chen, Y., Chilton, L., Connolly, D., Dhanaraj, R., Hollenbach, J., Lerer, A., Sheets, D.: Tabulator: Exploring and Analyzing linked data on the Semantic Web. In: 3rd International Semantic Web User Interaction Workshop (SWUI 2006) (2006)
26. Zviedris, M., Barzdins, G.: ViziQuer: A Tool to Explore and Query SPARQL Endpoints. In: Antoniou, G., Grobelnik, M., Simperl, E., Parsia, B., Plexousakis, D., De Leenheer, P., Pan, J. (eds.) ESWC 2011, Part II. LNCS, vol. 6644, pp. 441–445. Springer, Heidelberg (2011)
27. Popov, I.O., Schraefel, M.C., Hall, W., Shadbolt, N.: Connecting the Dots: A Multi-pivot Approach to Data Exploration. In: Aroyo, L., Welty, C., Alani, H., Taylor, J., Bernstein, A., Kagal, L., Noy, N., Blomqvist, E. (eds.) ISWC 2011, Part I. LNCS, vol. 7031, pp. 553–568. Springer, Heidelberg (2011)
28. Yee, K.P., Swearingen, K., Li, K., Hearst, M.: Faceted metadata for image search and browsing. In: SIGCHI Conference on Human Factors in Computing Systems (CHI 2003), pp. 401–408. ACM (2003)
29. Schraefel, M.C., Wilson, M., Russell, A., Smith, D.A.: mSpace: Improving information access to multimedia domains with multimodal exploratory search. Communications of the ACM 49(4), 47–49 (2006)
30. Huynh, D.F., Karger, D.R., Miller, R.C.: Exhibit: Lightweight Structured Data Publishing. In: 16th International Conference on World Wide Web (WWW 2007), pp. 737–746. ACM (2007)
31. Huynh, D.F., Karger, D.R.: Parallax and Companion: Set-based Browsing for the Data Web. Available online (2009)
32. Kobilarov, G., Dickinson, I.: Humboldt: Exploring Linked Data. In: Linked Data on the Web Workshop (2008)
33. Harth, A.: VisiNav: A system for visual search and navigation on web data. Journal of Web Semantics 8(4), 348–354 (2010)
34. Suh, B., Bederson, B.B.: OZONE: A Zoomable Interface for Navigating Ontology Information. In: Working Conference on Advanced Visual Interfaces (AVI 2002), pp. 139–143. ACM (2002)
35. Heim, P., Ziegler, J.: Faceted Visual Exploration of Semantic Data. In: Ebert, A., Dix, A., Gershon, N.D., Pohl, M. (eds.) HCIV (INTERACT) 2009. LNCS, vol. 6431, pp. 58–75. Springer, Heidelberg (2011)
36. Soylu, A., Moedritscher, F., Wild, F., De Causmaecker, P., Desmet, P.: Mashups by orchestration and widget-based personal environments: Key challenges, solution strategies, and an application. Program: Electronic Library and Information Systems 46(4), 383–428 (2012)
37. Calvanese, D., Giese, M., Haase, P., Horrocks, I., Hubauer, T., Ioannidis, Y., Jiménez-Ruiz, E., Kharlamov, E., Kllapi, H., Klüwer, J., Koubarakis, M., Lamparter, S., Möller, R., Neuenstadt, C., Nordtveit, T., Özcep, O., Rodriguez Muro, M., Roshchin, M., Ruzzi, M., Savo, F., Schmidt, M., Soylu, A., Waaler, A., Zheleznyakov, D.: The Optique Project: Towards OBDA Systems for Industry (Short Paper). In: OWL Experiences and Directions Workshop (OWLED) (2013)
38. Katifori, A., Halatsis, C., Lepouras, G., Vassilakis, C., Giannopoulou, E.: Ontology visualization methods - A survey. ACM Computing Surveys 39(4), 10:1–10:43 (2007)
39. Skjæveland, M.G., Lian, E.H., Horrocks, I.: Publishing the Norwegian Petroleum Directorate's FactPages as Semantic Web Data. To be published in the Proceedings of the International Semantic Web Conference (ISWC) (2013)

Personalized Vaccination Using Ontology Based Profiling

Ozgu Can, Emine Sezer, Okan Bursa, and Murat Osman Unalir

Ege University, Department of Computer Engineering,
35100 Bornova-Izmir, Turkey
{ozgu.can,emine.unalir,okan.bursa,murat.osman.unalir}@ege.edu.tr

Abstract. Ontology-based knowledge representation and modeling for vaccine domain provides an effective mechanism to improve the quality of healthcare information systems. Vaccination process generally includes different processes like vaccine research and development, production, transportation, administration and tracking of the adverse events that may occur after the administration of vaccine. Moreover, vaccination process may cause some side effects that could cause permanent disability or even be fatal. Therefore, it is important to build and store the vaccine information by developing a vaccine data standardization. In the vaccination process, there are different stakeholders, such as individuals who get the vaccination, health professionals who apply the vaccination, health organizations, vaccine producers, pharmacies and drug warehouses. In this paper, a vaccine data standardization is proposed and a generic user modeling is applied in the context of personalized vaccination for healthcare information systems. Besides, policies are also used to strengthen the proposed personalized vaccination model by defining clinical guidances for individuals. The proposed personalized vaccination system offers a better management of vaccination process and supports the tracking of individual's medical information.

Keywords: Medical Knowledge Management, Semantic Web, Vaccine Ontology, Healthcare, Personalization.

1 Introduction

Healthcare systems around the globe are changing their information systems according to be able to share and reuse the patients' information not only in a department where the information is produced, but also between the departments of an organization and also among the different organizations. Until recently, it was not reasonable to share a patient's data between the departments of the healthcare organizations. In fact, the information obtained from records of a health information system is only the administrative data, such as patient's name, age, insurance information and other personal data. Information about a patient is widely spread out among doctors, clinics, pharmacies, health agencies and hospitals. However, in recent years, information technologies are focused on

E. Garoufallou and J. Greenberg (Eds.): MTSR 2013, CCIS 390, pp. 213–224, 2013.

using and sharing the clinical data in a higher-level structured form of semantic rich information. Thus, sharing personal health information became more prevalent in distributed healthcare environments.

Data standards are the common and consistent way of recording the information. Data, which is modeled by a particular standard, could be transmitted between different systems and it could be processed to have the same meaning in each system, program and institution. The main purpose of data standardization is to provide the common definition of the data. Data standards, generally, allow sending and receiving the data that has the same meaning and the same structure for different computer systems. Today, in the healthcare domain, approximately 2100 different data standards are being used [1]. It can be concluded from this number that each data standard has been developed for a different specific purpose, whereas it is troublesome to share and reuse these data between different systems. On the other hand, the information about a patient is needed to be shared between all principals of healthcare. Therefore, there is a need for a wider communication and interoperability between each stakeholder in the health domain [2]. However, according to other domains, any new application or technology is carried out very carefully to prevent death or permanent disability results. Thus, the adoption of a new technology must meet the highest standards of accuracy and effectiveness [3].

Vaccination is the most effective health event for individuals to improve their own immunity systems and acquire immunity against certain diseases. The administration of vaccine is considered to be the most effective way to improve individual's immune system or prevent her from particular diseases which can result in death or permanent disability. Vaccination process starts with the individuals' birth and continues for her lifelong care plan. Vaccinations are carried out by the departments of each country's health ministries and takes place in distributed environments. Stakeholders of the vaccination domain can be consisted of individuals or their parents (if they are under 18), health professionals, public and private health agencies, vaccine research and development laboratories, vaccine production companies, pharmacies and also schools. All these stakeholders have different responsibilities and take roles in different vaccination processes. In vaccine system, an individual can be a doctor, a patient or medical companies, public and private health agencies. All these stakeholders can make the health care system more complex and difficult to apply to the real world applications. Profiling [4] is a solution to such problems with the help of profile languages like Friend of a Friend (FOAF)(http://www.foaf-project.org) and SIOC (http://sioc-project.org/). A patient has demographic properties like name, surname, blood-type and address. These properties must be gathered inside profiles to distribute to different domains. However, profiling is not as simple as business cards. Links to other profiles based on relationships can also be described inside profiles. Profiles can be expanded with other relationships and other profile definitions [5]. This gives the opportunity to localize user profiles but also keep them universal and sharable.

Policies are generally used to control access to resources. A policy is a declarative rule set that is based on constraints to control the behavior of entities. This declarative rule set defines an information on what an entity can do or cannot do. In vaccine system, we use policies to define a clinical guidance for vaccination. In order to achieve this goal, we create clinical guidance policies based on the vaccination domain by using the user profiles of the health care domain. A brief contribution of this work is as follows:

- developing a data standard to share and reuse vaccination information,
- building an information base for vaccine information systems,
- personalizing vaccine system by:
  - creating user profiles for health domain,
  - warning individuals about allergic reactions before vaccination,
  - tracking allergic reactions that could occur after vaccination,
  - using policies to define a clinical guidance for vaccination.

The paper is organized as follows: Section 2 explains the knowledge representation of the proposed model. The development of vaccine, profile and policy ontologies are clarified in this section. Section 3 expresses the evaluation and validation process of ontologies. Section 4 presents the relevant related work. Finally, Section 5 contributes and outlines the direction of the future work.

2 Knowledge Representation

Knowledge representation will allow for the machines to meaningfully process the available information and provide semantically correct answers to imposed queries [6]. In order to perform the translation of information to knowledge: the information has to be put into context, the concepts have to be explained and defined,relationships between concepts and personal information have to be made explicit [7]. Ontologies are used to represent knowledge in the Semantic Web. Ontology is defined as an explicit specification of a conceptualization [8]. It is the formal representation of the concepts and the relations between these concepts for a specific domain. The new information could be inferred from the old information or defined rules. The main reasons for developing ontology could be summarized as: sharing the common semantics and the structure of the information between computers and people, providing the domain knowledge reusing, making assumptions of a domain explicitly, separating the computational knowledge from the domain knowledge and analyzing the domain knowledge [9].

As several ontology languages have been developed so far, the eXtensible Markup Language (XML) (http://www.w3.org/XML/), XML Schema (XMLS) (http://www.w3.org/XML/Schema), the Resource Description Framework (RDF) (http://www.w3.org/RDF/), RDF Schema (RDFS) (http://www.w3.org/TR/rdf-schema/ and the Web Ontology Language (OWL) (http://www.w3.org/OWL/) are the most common languages that are used to build ontologies in the Semantic Web. In this section, we use OWL to build ontologies which are used to represent vaccine information, personal health profiles and policies that are based on both of

these vaccine and personal information. Ontologies are edited by Protégé 4.3
(http://protege.stanford.edu/), which is an open-source ontology editor
and knowledge-base framework. Developed ontologies can be accessed from
http://efe.ege.edu.tr/~odo/MTSR2013/.

2.1   Vaccine Ontology

In this work, we developed a vaccine ontology (Vaccine_Ontology) to be used in
vaccine information system in order to provide all services that occur in the vaccination process. The main purpose of developing the vaccine ontology is providing
knowledge sharing among the health professionals. There are many other vaccine
ontologies shared among different platforms, we developed our own ontology to
give full support of all different types of diseases. As the knowledge sharing is
important, using this data representation in the vaccine ontology has also the
same level of importance in developing the interoperable electronic healthcare
systems. Vaccine_Ontology has the expressivity of $\mathcal{SROIQ(D)}$ DL (Description
Logic) [10] and consists of 129 concepts, 50 object and 14 data properties. The
core concepts and relations of Vaccine_Ontology are represented in Figure 1.
Vaccine Ontology is developed in OWL 2.0 which supports the compliance with
all OWL and RDF described ontologies and XML Schemas.

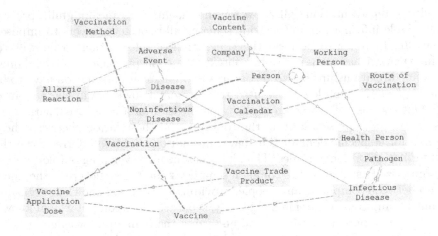

Fig. 1. Vaccine_Ontology concepts

As the primary objectives of this study are interoperability, information sharing and reusability, the vaccine domain is specifically handled with regards to the
usage of stakeholders who are persons and organizations that participate in vaccination process. Stakeholders of the vaccine domain are individuals who are vaccinated - if the individual is not adolescent, the individual's parents-, the health

professionals (nurses and doctors), the ministry of health, private and official
health agencies (e.g. doctor's clinics, hospitals, polyclinics, public health centers),
pharmaceutical warehouses, pharmacies, vaccine manufacturers, vaccine research
and development centers defined as concepts of `Vaccine_Ontology`. The human
stakeholders are represented with `Person` concept, while the others are grouped
under the `Company` concept. In this paper, we will focus on the main concepts of
the `Vaccine_Ontology`: `Vaccination`, `Vaccine` and `VaccineTradeProduct`.

Vaccination is considered to be the most effective health application used
for humans to prevent them from infectious diseases for many years. It is the
administration of a vaccine to stimulate the immune system of an individual
in order to prevent her from infectious diseases that may result in mortality or
morbidity. Vaccination process starts with the birth of an individual and continues for her lifelong care plan. In `Vaccine_Ontology`, `Vaccination` concept
represents this real word event. The object property between `Vaccination` and
`VaccineTradeProduct` is named with `isAdmnistrationOf` which is defined as:

```
<owl:ObjectProperty rdf:about="&ontologies;Vaccine_Ontology.owl#isAdministrationOf">
    <rdfs:domain rdf:resource="&ontologies;Vaccine_Ontology.owl#Vaccination"/>
    <rdfs:range rdf:resource="&ontologies;Vaccine_Ontology.owl#VaccineTradeProduct"/>
    <owl:propertyChainAxiom rdf:parseType="Collection">
        <rdf:Description rdf:about="&ontologies;Vaccine_Ontology.owl#isVaccinationOf"/>
        <rdf:Description rdf:about="&ontologies;Vaccine_Ontology.owl#hasTradeProduct"/>
    </owl:propertyChainAxiom>
</owl:ObjectProperty>
```

The property chain description of `isAdministrationOf` object property is as
follows:

$$isVaccinationOf \ o \ hasTradeProduct \longrightarrow isAdministrationOf$$

This description is used to infer that if *Vaccine A is vaccination of Vaccination B*
and *Vaccine A has a trade product as Vaccine Trade Product C*, then *Vaccination
B is administration of Vaccine Trade Product C*.

The `Vaccine` and `VaccineTradeProducts` concepts are the other two semantically important core concepts of the `Vaccine_Ontology`. `Vaccine` represents
the general vaccines that are administrated to increase the immunity of a particular disease. `BCGVaccine`, `MeaslesVaccine`, `HepBVaccine` (defines Hepatitis B
Vaccine) are example individuals of the `Vaccine`. The `VaccineTradeProduct` is
defined to represent the commercial vaccines which are available on the market.
For example, Hepavax_Gene, Havrix and Prevenar are vaccine trade products for
Hepatitis B Vaccine, Hepatitis A Vaccine and Pnomokok Vaccine, respectively.
Moreover, there are new researches and development activities in the vaccine domain, and a new vaccine product may be placed in to the market. Therefore, in
`Vaccine_Ontology`, the concept of individuals that describe the general vaccines
and the commercial products of these vaccines are separated from each other.
But, they are associated with each other by using the `hasTradeProduct` and
`isTradedProductOf` object properties. These object properties are also inverse
of each other.

Vaccine_Ontology is an ontology that can grow during lifetime with the new instances of concepts. The main goal of developing the Vaccine_Ontology is to use it as an information base for the vaccine information system.

2.2   Profile Ontology

Profiling is a common way to represent personal information. Personalized applications have internal profiling methodologies to create a user's profile. Profiles can be demographical or social information based according to their usage. In a close structured application, like a banking system, profiles can only store limited information about users. However, social networks like Facebook (Facebook, http://www.facebook.com) have much more information about a user, such as their choices, clicks, friends or games. But this information is also restricted to other applications and it is not easy to reach this information from outside. A general profiling method, such as FOAF, defines an open world profile definition which can be accessed by only an URI. In our proposed model, we are extending FOAF with a new profiling methodology which gives the opportunity to describe group profiles, restricted or limited profiles based on demographical or set-based profile properties.

Group profiles are a new way of describing user's roles in daily life like father, doctor or computer game player. All these roles can have different preferences and properties. So, we define group profiles to store person's different preferences. Besides, this methodology gives us the opportunity to assemble people with similar choices and properties. These collections of users are also gathered within this group profile. Figure 2 represents the general view of our architecture.

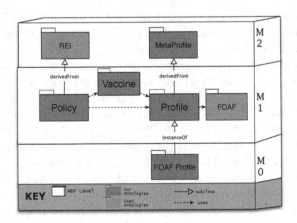

Fig. 2. General view of profiling architecture

Our profiling methodology includes Meta-Object-Facility(MOF)(MOF, http://www.omg.org/spec/MOF/2.4.1/) information levels and it is connected by ontological imports and object level connections. Inside instance level, M0, a person's FOAF profile, which can include its group profiles and demographical information, can be described. At M1 level, we specify tools and definitions to describe the group profiles. M2 level includes only MetaProfile definition which defines set-based profile properties, restrictions and demographical property definitions. Besides, MetaProfile covers the different types of profile properties based on their usage. Behavioral, demographical and social properties and their property restrictions based on demographical and set-based properties are all defined inside MetaProfile. Overall, MetaProfile, Profile and FOAF Profile definitions construct our multi-level profiling architecture to create more complex policies and healthcare definitions.

2.3   Policy Ontology

A policy is a regulation of constraints that defines what is permitted, prohibited or obliged. In this manner, policies enforce rules based upon the requester or the resource that is going to be accessed by the requester and rules express who can or cannot execute which action on which resources. As policies are generally used for access control, we are using policies in order to define restrictions of the vaccine domain ontology. In this work, Rei policy language [11] is used for semantic representation of policies. Rei is based on OWL-Lite and allows users to develop declarative policies over domain specific ontologies. Rei has its own syntax and consists of seven ontologies: **ReiPolicy, ReiMetaPolicy, ReiEntity, ReiDeontic, ReiConstraint, ReiAnalysis,** and **ReiAction.** Rei also includes specifications for speech acts, policy analysis and conflict resolution. Rei policy language endorses four deontic objects: *permission, prohibition, obligation,* and *delegation.* Permission is what an entity can do, prohibition is what an entity can not do, obligation is what an entity should do, and finally dispensation is what an entity need no longer do. The following example represents the definition of a permission deontic object that specifies '*A doctor can read a patient's file*':

```
<deontic:Permission rdf:ID="PermissionReadPatientFile"
       policy:desc="All doctors have the permission to read patient's files">
    <deontic:actor rdf:resource="#var1"/>
    <deontic:action rdf:resource="#readingPatientFile"/>
    <deontic:constraint rdf:resource="#isDoctor"/>
</deontic:Permission>
```

The *Doctor policy* definition of this permission example is represented as:

```
<policy:Policy rdf:ID="DoctorPolicy">
    <policy:actor rdf:resource="#var1"/>
    <policy:action rdf:resource="#reading"/>
    <policy:context rdf:resource ="#PediatricsClinic"/>
    <policy:grants rdf:resource="#grantingPermissionReadPatientFile"/>
</policy:Policy>
```

We specify policies based on the vaccine domain and profiles. Profiles are used as actors of policies rather than using the individual variables that are created in **entity:Variable** class of the **ReiEntity** ontology as the actor of the policy definition. Also, individuals of the vaccine domain are used as objects and actions of policy definitions. Figure 3 represents a policy example that specifies a prohibition indicating *'A person who is pregnant cannot be vaccinated with live attenuated vaccine'*. Live Attenuated Vaccine is a type of vaccine which includes the live pathogen whose virulence is reduced in the laboratory. Live attenuated vaccines should not be given to individuals with weakened or damaged immune systems. So in this prohibition policy example, as pregnancy can be weaken the mother's immune system, `LiveAttenuatedVaccine` and `Pregnant` are individuals of `Vaccine_Ontology` and `Profile` ontology, respectively.

```
<owl:NamedIndividual rdf:about="&vaccinePolicy;Prohibition_vaccinationOfPregnants">
    <rdf:type rdf:resource="&deontic;Prohibition"/>
    <policy:desc>LiveAttenuatedVaccine is prohibited for pregnants</policy:desc>
    <deontic:actor rdf:resource="&profile;Pregnant"/>
    <deontic:constraint rdf:resource="&vaccinePolicy;isLiveAttenuatedVaccine"/>
    <deontic:action rdf:resource="&vaccinePolicy;vacciningPatient"/>
</owl:NamedIndividual>
```

Fig. 3. Prohibition example for `Pregnant` profile

3   Validation of the Ontology Model

As Pellet (`http://clarkparsia.com/pellet/`) supports datatype-ABox reasoning, SWRL support, reasoning debugging and incremental reasoning; we used it to reason ontologies. The defined restrictions are executed and as a result, a consistent ontology ecosystem is built, where profile and policy definitions inside the vaccination domain have become convenient to be executed by queries.

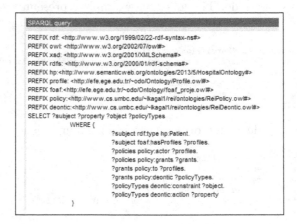

Fig. 4. Query example

We used SPARQL (http://www.w3.org/TR/sparql11-overview/) query language to execute the defined policies. Figure 4 shows the query example that is executed on the defined policies. In this example, we queried policies that are defined for any profile in the vaccination domain. In order to achieve this, first, we found profiles of all patients. Secondly, we queried policies that are related with these profiles. Finally, we listed policies according to their deontic definitions. Figure 5 shows the result of this query. In this result, the prohibition policy defined for pregnant profiles can be seen.

subject	property	object	policyTypes
Alice	vacciningPatient	isLiveAttenuatedVaccine	Prohibition vaccinationOfPregnants

Fig. 5. Query result

4   Related Work

Medical domain has a huge amount of domain knowledge which is described by controlled dictionaries or vocabulary standards. Standards like SNOMED-CT (Systematized Nomenclature of Medicine-Clinical Terms, http://www.ihtsdo.org/snomed-ct/), GALEN (Generalized Architecture for Languages, Encyclopedias and Nomenclatures in Medicine, http://www.openclinical.org/prj_galen.html) [12] and MesH (Medical Subject Headings, http://www.nlm.nih.gov/mesh/) are rich semantic ontologies that are described by formal ontology languages. These high level biomedical ontologies are developed to be used as a terminological vocabulary among biomedical domains. Domain specific ontologies, such as GO (Gene Ontology, http://www.geneontology.org/) [13] and OBR-Prox-Femur Application Ontology [14], are specific ontologies to represent the certain part of the human body. EHRs (Electronic Health Records) that are expressed in these formal terms, could be used for semantic intermediary (e.g. a content, which is defined in an ontology could be defined in another ontology) or inferencing (e.g. determining a statement as a statement of a more general or more specific statement) [15].

In SNOMED-CT, concepts have unique numeric identifiers called ConceptIDs, but these identifiers do not have a hierarchical or implicit meaning. The terms and concepts are connected each other with the predefined relationships. These predefined relationships are grouped in four main relationships: defining, qualifying, historical and additional. All the terms for vaccine and vaccination in SNOMED-CT are described at the concept level and also are very specialized terms. Creating instances by inheriting from these concepts are found nearly impossible. As known, in the software systems the maintenance and support are very important issues for the usage of the system. For example, adding a new instance for a new developed vaccine changes the ontology model of the system and this situation results with high costs but further more it is not a desirable situation for software systems. A vaccine ontology, named VO (Vaccine Ontology), is developed in [16] [17]. VO focuses on vaccine categorization, vaccine components, vaccine quality and vaccine-induced host responses. VO describes vaccines not only administrated to humans but also to animals. The ontology includes nearly about four thousands classes with seventy object properties and four data type properties. However, everything in the domain is described as classes in VO. Therefore, VO has the same problems described for SNOMED-CT.

Most of the healthcare information systems define a patient as a basic profile. However, the concept of a patient is much more complex. A healthcare information system may need a process to create a patient profile based on different health domains[18]. This process narrows all the information about a patient. Although this process may have risks as the calculation persists. A new information about a patient needs an overall calculation. So, this kind of profiling is not suitable for a dynamic system. In [19], profiling is at the ontological level and based on FOAF and SIOC. A patient or a doctor can have interests. Thus, interests, skills and interactions are structured and represented inside user profiles. But, defining an interest and capturing an interest are not the same processes. Capturing an interest is based on domain knowledge and needs a deeper tailoring. In addition, overall representation of a user profile needs to be maintained in a semantically multi-level architecture. There are no restrictions nor definitions to represent interests, skills and interactions inside [19].

The most common policy languages in Semantic Web are KAoS [20], Rei [11], and Ponder [21]. KAoS is a DAML/OWL policy language. It is a collection of policy and domain management services for web services. KAoS distinguishes between *authorizations* and *obligations*. Rei is a policy specification language based on OWL-Lite. It allows users to express and represent the concepts of *permissions*, *prohibitions*, *obligations*, and *dispensations*. Rei uses speech-acts to make the security control decentralized. Speech-acts include *delegation*, *revocation*, *request* and *cancel*. Ponder is a declarative, object-oriented policy language for several types of management policies for distributed systems and also provides techniques for policy administration. Ponder has four basic policy types: *authorizations*, *obligations*, *refrains* and *delegations*. [22] gives a comparison of KAoS, Rei and Ponder policy languages. In [23], profile based policy management is studied in order to make use of semantically rich policies in terms of the personalization scope.

5   Conclusion

Vaccine_Ontology introduced in this paper is developed according to the vaccine and vaccination knowledge in health domain. However, this ontology is not based on any ontology or any standard. The defined concepts in Vaccine_Ontology uses SNOMED-CT terminology. If any concept is found with the same meaning with our ontology, this concept's ConceptID is inserted as a property to the related class. The main idea is building an information base for vaccine information systems. Therefore, if there is an information system using SNOMED-CT vocabulary, this system could exchange health information with the vaccine information system which is based on Vaccine_Ontology. We integrate user profiling method and policies with the Vaccine_Ontology in order to improve the maintenance quality of the vaccine process. The developed ontology in this work is being used for the information base for national vaccination system in Turkey. From the beginning of the developing the model of the vaccine ontology, the aim is using this model as an information base for a software system.

We are now developing the user interface of the vaccine information system by using Java and JSF technologies. Thus, it can be said that Vaccine_Ontology will be a living ontology for the vaccine information system. As a future work, ICD-10 (International Statistical Classification of Diseases and Related Health Problems, http://www.who.int/classifications/icd/en/) codes about vaccination and allergic reactions that can occur after vaccination is going to be added into the Vaccine_Ontology. ICD-10 is developed by WHO and it is a medical standardization to code diseases, signs and symptoms. We will also extend the policy concept as to achieve the management process of the vaccine information system.

Acknowledgment. The medical part of Vaccine_Ontology is supported by Prof. Dr. Fadil VARDAR, works in Department of Pediatric Infectious Diseases, Ege University.

References

1. MN-PHIN Steering Committee: Public Health Data Standards, Improving How Public Health Collects, Exchanges and Uses Data (2006)
2. Lopez, D.M., Blobel, B.G.: A Development Framework for Semantically Interoperable Health Information Systems. International Journal of Medical Informatics 78(2), 83–103 (2009)
3. Della Valle, E., Cerizza, D., Celino, I., Dogac, A., Laleci, G., Kabak, Y., Okcan, A., Gulderen, O., Namli, T., Bicer, V.: The Need for Semantic Web Service in the eHealth. In: W3C Workshop on Frameworks for Semantics in Web Services (2005)
4. Rich, E.: Users are Individuals: Individualizing User Models. International Journal of Man-Machine Studies 18, 199–214 (1983)
5. Goldbeck, J., Rothstein, M.: Linking Social Networks on the Web with FOAF. In: Proceeding AAAI 2008 Proceedings of the 23rd National Conference on Artificial Intelligence, vol. 2, pp. 1138–1143 (2008)
6. Terzi, E., Vakali, A., Hacid, M.-S.: Knowledge Representation, Ontologies, and the Semantic Web. In: Zhou, X., Zhang, Y., Orlowska, M.E. (eds.) APWeb 2003. LNCS, vol. 2642, pp. 382–387. Springer, Heidelberg (2003)
7. Eysenbach, G.: The Semantic Web and healthcare consumers: A new challenge and opportunity on the horizon? International Journal of Healthcare Technology and Management 5, 194–212 (2003)
8. Gruber, T.R.: A translation approach to portable ontology specifications. Journal Knowledge Acquisition - Special Issue: Current Issues in Knowledge Modeling 5(2), 199–220 (1993)

9. Noy, N., McGuinness, D.L.: Ontology Development 101: A Guide to Creating Your First Ontology. Knowledge Systems Lab., Stanford University (2001)
10. OWL Ontology Metrics - OWL at Manchester (2009), http://owl.cs.manchester.ac.uk/metrics/
11. Kagal, L., Finin, T., Joshi, A.: A Policy Language for A Pervasive Computing Environment. In: IEEE 4th International Workshop on Policies for Distributed Systems and Networks, pp. 63–74 (2003)
12. Trombert-Paviot, B., Rodrigues, J.M., Rogers, J.E., Baud, R., Van Der Haring, E., Rassinoux, A.M., Abrial, V., Clavel, L., ve Idir, H.: GALEN: A third generation terminology tool to support a multipurpose national coding system for surgical procedures. Int. Journal of Medical Informatics 59, 71–85 (2000)
13. Harris, M.A., Clark, J., Ireland, A., Lomax, J., Ashburner, M., Foulger, R., et al.: The gene ontology (GO) database and informatics resource. Nucleic Acids Research 32, D258–D261 (2004)
14. Lukovic, V., Milosevic, D., Devedzic, G., Sukic, C., Kudumovic, M., Ristic, B.: OBR-Prox-femur Application Ontology Development and Modeling. HealthMED Journal 2010 4(2), 404–416 (2010)
15. ISO/TS 18308: Health informatics – Requirements for an electronic health record architecture. Tech. speci., TS 18308, International Organization for Standardization, Geneva, Switzerland (2004)
16. He, Y., Cowell, L., Diehl, A., Mobley, H.L., Peters, B., Ruttenberg, A., Scheuermann, R.H., Brinkman, R.R., Courtot, M., Mungall, C.: VO: Vaccine Ontology. In: The 1st International Conference on Biomedical Ontology (ICBO 2009) Nature Precedings, Buffalo, NY, USA (2009)
17. Lin, Y., He, Y.: Ontology representation and analysis of vaccine formulation and administration and their effects on vaccine immune responses. Journal of Biomedical Semantics 3, 17 (2012)
18. Bhatt, M., Rahayu, W., Soni, S.P., Wouters, C.: Ontology driven semantic profiling and retrieval in medical information systems. Web Semantics: Science, Services and Agents on the World Wide Web 7(4), 317–331 (2009)
19. da Silva, J.L.T., Moreto Ribeiro, A., Boff, E., Primo, T., Viccari, R.M.: A Reference Ontology for Profile Representation in Communities of Practice. In: García-Barriocanal, E., Cebeci, Z., Okur, M.C., Öztürk, A. (eds.) MTSR 2011. CCIS, vol. 240, pp. 68–79. Springer, Heidelberg (2011)
20. Uszok, A., Bradshaw, J.M., Jeffers, R.: KAoS: A Policy and Domain Services Framework for Grid Computing and Semantic Web Services. In: Jensen, C., Poslad, S., Dimitrakos, T. (eds.) iTrust 2004. LNCS, vol. 2995, pp. 16–26. Springer, Heidelberg (2004)
21. Dulay, N., Lupu, E., Sloman, M., Damianou, N.: A Policy Deployment Model for The Ponder Language. In: Proceedings of IEEE/IFIP International Symposium on Integrated Network Management (IM 2001), pp. 14–18 (2001)
22. Tonti, G., Bradshaw, J.M., Jeffers, R., Montanari, R., Suri, N., Uszok, A.: Semantic Web Languages for Policy Representation and Reasoning: A Comparison of KAoS, Rei, and Ponder. In: Fensel, D., Sycara, K., Mylopoulos, J. (eds.) ISWC 2003. LNCS, vol. 2870, pp. 419–437. Springer, Heidelberg (2003)
23. Can, O., Bursa, O., Unalir, M.O.: Personalizable Ontology-Based Access Control. Gazi University Journal of Science 23(4), 465–474 (2010)

Big Data for Enhanced Learning Analytics:
A Case for Large-Scale Comparative Assessments

Nikolaos Korfiatis

Big Data Analytics Research Lab, Chair for Database and Information Systems,
Institute for Informatics and Mathematics, Goethe University Frankfurt
Robert-Mayer-Str. 10, 60325, Frankfurt am main, Germany
korfiatis@em.uni-frankfurt.de
http://www.bigdata.uni-frankfurt.de

Abstract. Recent attention on the potentiality of cost-effective infrastructures for capturing and processing large amounts of data, known as *Big Data* has received much attention from researchers and practitioners on the field of analytics. In this paper we discuss on the possible benefits that *Big Data* can bring on TEL by using the case of large scale comparative assessments as an example. Large scale comparative assessments can pose as an intrinsic motivational tool for enhancing the performance of both learners and teachers, as well as becoming a support tool for policy makers. We argue why data from learning processes can be characterized as *Big Data* from the viewpoint of data source heterogeneity (variety) and discuss some architectural issues that can be taken into account on implementing such an infrastructure on the case of comparative assessments.

Keywords: Bigdata, TEL, Learning Analytics, Comparative assessments.

1 Introduction

Current advances in the domain of data analytics refer more and more to the case of Big Data as the foremost pillar of any modern analytics application [1]. While the appearance of the term *Big Data* in the literature spans multiple definitions, a definition of *Big Data* that is appropriate in the context of user activity modeling can be the one provided by the McKinsey research report [2] which defines *Big Data* as "*datasets*" which for practical and policy reasons cannot be "*processed, stored and analyzed*" by traditional data management technologies and require adaptation of workflows, platforms and architectures. On the other hand, research on the field of technology enhanced learning (TEL) highlights the importance of dataset-driven research for evaluating the effectiveness of technological interventions on the learning process. As it is also in the case of traditional data driven evaluation and decision making, data analytics for TEL considers the combination of data from various sources centered on the educational process lifecycle.

The view that we advocate on this position paper is the belief that the definition of *Big Data* itself contains higher level semantics, which under particular application

E. Garoufallou and J. Greenberg (Eds.): MTSR 2013, CCIS 390, pp. 225–233, 2013.
© Springer International Publishing Switzerland 2013

domains (in that case TEL) have different applicability for data infrastructures and research information systems. While someone can argue that the order of magnitude (*volume*) of most datasets generated in TEL is something that can be handled by traditional tools (e.g. a typical database size of 4-5 Gigabytes is not considered problematic for a traditional DBMS), the issue arises when the *variety* of sources where data can be integrated (e.g. log files, assessment scores, essays etc.) comes in consideration. In addition, when these insights are targeted to the stakeholders (learners, teachers and policy makers) by encompassing some type of interactivity (e.g. through visualizations) the case of responsiveness on providing the insights related with the computation time that it takes for such an insight to be calculated is a contributing factor. We frame this factor as *velocity*. We discuss on the interplay between those three factors (*volume, variety, velocity*) by adopting the well-known 3V architectural model of Big Data[3] and introducing an application scenario on the case of large scale comparative assessments, inspired by the recent attention of policy makers on comparative rankings such as the PISA report [4].

Our viewpoint is that big data can greatly enhance TEL and contribute insights on better assessing the results of technological interventions on the learning process. To this end this paper is structured as follows. A discussion of big data architectures is highlighted in Section (2). A subsequent framework is introduced on the application of big data in learner settings on Section (3). The paper concludes on Section (4) with discussion and directions for further research.

2   Big Data on Integrating Insights from Learning Analytics

2.1   Data Source Heterogeneity in TEL

A majority of studies on learning analytics consider the individual as a basic unit of analysis. Nonetheless learners' participation from a data analysis point of view has been addressed as a problem of combining heterogeneous data sources [5]. From that perspective learning analytics considers the following three interconnected stages with reference to modeling the learners' participation in educational activities and in particular namely: (a) User knowledge modeling, (b) User behavior modeling and (c) user experience modeling.

In essence the emphasis is given on two major contributors of different types of data that support users of analytics tools on gaining interesting insights about the learners: (a) *Social Interactions data*: providing the interactions the learner has with the educators and fellow students as well as navigation in the learning platform, and (b) *Social or "attention" metadata*: that determine which aspect of the learning process the learner is actively engaged with. Social interaction data can be considered as a facet of data containing standard user navigation properties, similar to the ones that standard Business Intelligence (BI) tools provide in a corporate environment to an analyst. The latter can be seen in cases such as web usage mining, content navigation extraction etc. and are considered as a mature source for analytics applications since are not difficult to extract from standard application logs (e.g. web server logs for web usage mining). On the other hand attention metadata require an interaction with a learning resource as in the context of a learning object repository, where the learner interacts with a learning object in the context of an activity (e.g. an exercise or an interactive tutorial) and are more difficult to extract due to the fact that in order for them to be generated an interaction has to be recorded. Similar to research issues in other domains such as online communication, the case of "shadow" participation of users, labeled as "lurking" [6], makes the extraction of a relatively large enough data-set from social interaction data quite difficult to achieve.

For example consider the case where a learning repository provides the opportunity to learners to evaluate the quality of learning objects. Published studies concerning participation on online repositories [7] have shown that as in any other case of user generated content, participation of learners on the evaluation of learning objects follows the "Pareto" or 80/20 rule [8]. That provides that roughly 20% of the participants are responsible for the 80% of the "attention metadata" generated by this interaction. The above makes the case of studying learners in a highly vertical set (e.g. in the context of one particular educational domain/activity) inefficient since the quantitative characterization of the learners' activity might contain hidden biases which is not uncommon for quantitative studies. Therefore enhancing learning analytics through the use of big data can allow for metrics from different learning repositories to be aggregated in order to allow for accurate and non-biased quantitative studies.

2.2   Variety on the 3V Architectural Model

As aforementioned Volume, Variety and Velocity constitute an integral aspect of *Big Data* in relation with the different goals that an end user wants to achieve by utilizing large dataset. The interplay of these three distinctive elements has been adapted on the 3V architectural model. The 3V model was first described by Laney [9] on a Gartner Report and considers the three characteristics as a case of interconnected stages [3].

In traditional storage systems the volume (size) defines the amount of data which the system can manage whereas the velocity (speed) defines the speed with which this data is processed. In other words, in OLAP systems the data size can become very large but the data processing speed is slow whereas in OLTP systems the workload size is much smaller, but the data should be processed much faster. The variety (structure) is of no concern in such systems as the data format is known in advance and described very precisely in a pre-defined schema. However, in the age of Big Data the picture is changing and the emerging data variety is starting to transform the system requirements and question the storage efficiency of existing systems.

A particular requirement is that a system from its foundations should be capable of handling increasing data volume, high or dynamically changing velocity and high variety of data formats like the ones that can be combined in different cases of TEL platforms featuring different nature of educational content (e.g. the use of screencasts). In the multitude of different TEL scenarios, the exact significance of each of the 3Vs can vary depending on the requirements and the current TEL platforms should be able to deal with any combination of the 3Vs from a storage perspective.

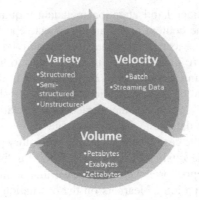

Fig. 1. The 3V architectural model of Big Data (Adopted from [3])

What is interesting with the contribution of the 3Vs as an architectural platform for *Big Data* in TEL is the dynamic changing significance of its elements which depicts in a very abstract way the actual challenge of learning analytics in TEL which depending on the goal and unit of analysis can be different.

3   Utilizing Big Data on Providing Comparative Assessments in TEL

3.1   Case for Support: Collective Effort and Individual-to-Group Comparison

A case of support for comparative assessments as a tool to enhance the motivation of learners and teachers in a TEL scenario can be considered the comparison of individuals to the average or the norm. A particular model that has been applied in cases where users massively participate in a common activity (as in the case of online communities) is the collective effort model. The collective effort model has been introduced in social psychology by Karau and Williams [10] and builds on principles from expectancy theory [11]. According to these principles, an individual needs to feel that his/her effort will lead to a collective level of performance in the context of the group. For example in an online community a participant might start posting and participating in the community activities if he/she believes that he will gain a higher status or visibility in the community. Fig. 2 provides a depiction of the stages of the collective effort model and how it affects individual motivation.

In the middle stage of the process the individual compares his/her effort with the effort of the group. In case he performs lower than the group then an intrinsic effect to contribute more is witnessed. However in the case the performance comparison between the individual and the group outcome is lower, the opposite effect might take place. In that case, it is more likely that the individual effort will be dropped if the comparison of the individual outcome is higher in relation with the group outcome.

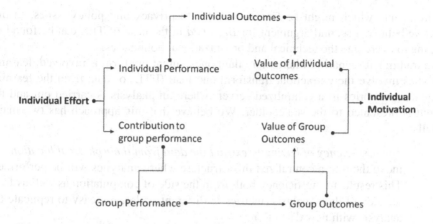

Fig. 2. The collective effort model. Adapted from Karau and Williams [10].

An interesting application of the collective effort model has been undertaken by Ling et al. [2005] where the contributions in terms of individual reviews and ratings were used by the MovieLens recommender system [Miller et al., 2003] in order to provide recommendations to other members of the community.

It is our belief that the collective effort model can provide a theoretical case for support for the use of comparative assessments alongside standardized pedagogy models. Comparative assessments can have a bimodal influence on the case of TEL. For example considering the collective effort model for learners, socio-psychological cues provided by such a comparison can influence intrinsically their participation level. For example a learner that has very good performance in class can think: *"....I am the best in my class, so I don't need to devote more time..."* However after making possible to compare his/her performance with a very large number of other learners, in case he is not on the top this can have a motivational factor as: *I might be the best in my class but when compared with other students from other schools I am not so good.*

Taking this into account we believe that a set of pedagogical approaches adapted on different learner modalities need to be undertaken in order to study how performance comparison metrics can be federated and how these metrics can encapsulate different levels of granularity for individual-to-individual and individual-to-group comparisons (e.g. school level, region level, country level). Nonetheless this scenario also requires a rethinking on the data integration process from different sources. We highlight this case on the section that follows.

3.2   Integrating Data from Different Learning Repositories

As aforementioned in the previous section, a critical stage for encapsulating the intrinsic value of comparative assessments considers the cognitive ability of the individual to evaluate his performance in the context of a common activity with others. However this requires a combination and normalization of data from different environments which might be fragmented due to privacy and policy issues. In that case we believe a second argument for *Big Data* in the case of TEL can be found on helping to overcome the technical and organizational boundaries.

In traditional scenarios where more than one content platform is involved, learning analytics involve the extraction, transform and load (ETL) of data from the learning content repositories to a centralized server, where an analysis is carried out and the output is presented to the stakeholder. We believe that this approach has two major pitfalls:

- *The inefficiency of having to extract the data from their physical location* and move them to a centralized infrastructure where analytics will be performed. This results to inefficiency both from the side of computation as well as from the side of data analysis (metrics in different scales, not easy to replicate the analysis with new data etc.)
- *The organizational and policy implications of having to extract data involving user generated content and activity* which on the one hand are crucial for analysis and comparisons but on the other hand involve open issues in security, privacy and compliance with the legal framework under each provider operates.

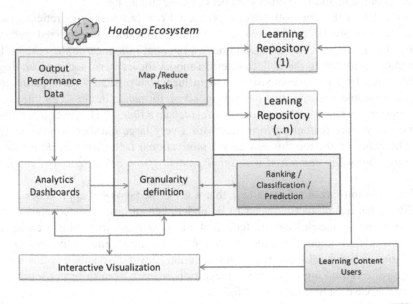

Fig. 3. An example data workflow for providing comparative assessments in TEL with the use of

Fig. 3 provides an example data flow where big data can be utilized for such case. A set of different learning platforms/repositories can be aggregated using the *Big Data* ecosystem in an effective way. The core of such a process considers Apache Hadoop and its ecosystem. This will allow for:

- *Contextualized mapping of the data to be used,* by taking into account the heterogeneity or variety of the learning content residing in different repositories as well
  as the pedagogical strategies involved from the side of evaluation.
- *Computing and aggregating analytics on the physical point where the data reside*
  thus making the computation more efficient and allowing the infrastructure to provide interactive data exploration and visualization workflows in various levels of
  granularity (in day and level of analysis) defined by the user with a pre-
  anonymized procedure in the analytics extraction process.

In particular the Hadoop ecosystem [12] and its flexibility for data analytics is making
a basic implementation of the map/reduce or M/R paradigm introduced by Google
[13]. In a very simple implementation an M/R analytics framework consist of two
separate and distinct tasks: (a) the Map job, which takes a set of data and converts it
into another set, where individual elements are broken down into tuples (key/value
pairs) and (b) the Reduce job which takes the output from a map task as input and
combines those data tuples mostly into a smaller set of tuples by e.g. presenting aggregates. In a learning object repository integration scenario based on this approach a
typical M/R process could consist of:

- *A mapping stage declaring the types of data (interaction data, attention metadata) to be collected from each repository* allowing for contextualized
  modeling based on the architecture and semantics of the learning platform
  (something addressed in the context of linked open data).
- *A reducing stage which allows the reduction of the raw data and aggregation of insights in a centralized output* that can be used for presentation or visualization purposes.

The above constitutes a case for support from a technical/infrastructure viewpoint
where *Big Data* can advance the state of the art in learning analytics. Our view is that
this requires major architectural changes in the support of existing tools and platforms
used in TEL with the integration of the new technologies based on the M/R paradigm.
This will allow for an efficient way of processing large TEL datasets using existing
infrastructures from a cost and organizational point of view [14].

4   Conclusions and Outlook

In this paper we intended to illustrate a case for support for Big Data and the technological ecosystem that accompanies it, with a case study of an educational scenario in
learning analytics and in particular the case for providing comparative assessments.

  While it is generally accepted that research on the field of learning analytics has
advanced our understanding of the effectiveness of using technology tools and platforms for enhancing the educational learning process, it is our inherent belief that *Big
Data* can take this understanding to a next level. Future research could also consider
cases related with user interaction dynamics [15, 16] when interacting in online plat-

forms, comparative evaluation of learning resources [17] as well as evaluating textual feedback through opinion mining [18].

Nonetheless, building such a competence in the current state of development of big data requires better understanding of the use cases and scenarios where big data can be of use in the study of TEL. While we have highlighted the potentiality of big data in the case of providing comparative assessments in order to enhance participation by learners and performance by teachers, we believe that additional pedagogies and motivational paradigms can be redefined in the same way. In that direction we believe that a closer collaboration between data scientists and experts in pedagogies could produce new results in that direction.

References

1. LaValle, S., Lesser, E., Shockley, R., Hopkins, M.S., Kruschwitz, N.: Big data, analytics and the path from insights to value. MIT Sloan Manag. Rev. 52, 21–32 (2011)
2. Manyika, J., Chui, M., Brown, B., Bughin, J., Dobbs, R., Roxburgh, C., Byers, A.H.: Big data: The next frontier for innovation, competition, and productivity. Mckinsey Glob. Inst., 1–137 (2011)
3. Zikopoulos, P., Eaton, C.: Understanding Big Data: Analytics for Enterprise Class Hadoop and Streaming Data (2011)
4. Margaret, W., Ray, A.: PISA Programme for International Student Assessment (PISA) PISA 2000 Technical Report: PISA 2000 Technical Report. OECD Publishing (2003)
5. Bienkowski, M., Feng, M., Means, B.: Enhancing teaching and learning through educational data mining and learning analytics: An issue brief. Washington Dc Office of Educ. Technology. Us Dep. Education, pp. 1–57 (2012)
6. Nonnecke, B., Preece, J.: Why lurkers lurk. In: Proceedings of Americas Conference on Information Systems (AMCIS), pp. 1–10 (2001)
7. Sicilia, M.-A., Ebner, H., Sánchez-Alonso, S., Álvarez, F., Abián, A., García-Barriocanal, E.: Navigating learning resources through linked data: A preliminary report on the redesign of Organic. In: 1st Edunet. Proc. Linked Learn. (2011)
8. Cechinel, C., Sicilia, M.-Á., Sánchez-Alonso, S., García-Barriocanal, E.: Evaluating collaborative filtering inside large learning object repositories. Inf. Process. Manag. 49, 34–50 (2013)
9. Laney, D.: 3D data management: Controlling data volume, velocity and variety. Appl. Deliv. Strat. File. 949 (2001)
10. Karau, S.J., Williams, K.D.: Understanding individual motivation in groups: The collective effort model. Groups Work Theory Res., 113–141 (2001)
11. Christiansen, B.A., Smith, G.T., Roehling, P.V., Goldman, M.S.: Using alcohol expectancies to predict adolescent drinking behavior after one year. J. Consult. Clin. Psychol. 57, 93 (1989)
12. Apache Hadoop, https://hadoop.apache.org/
13. Dean, J., Ghemawat, S.: MapReduce: Simplified data processing on large clusters. Commun. ACM 51, 107–113 (2008)
14. Leo, S., Anedda, P., Gaggero, M., Zanetti, G.: Using virtual clusters to decouple computation and data management in high throughput analysis applications. In: 2010 18th Euromicro International Conference on Parallel, Distributed and Network-Based Processing (PDP), pp. 411–415. IEEE (2010)

15. Wu, P.F., Korfiatis, N.: You Scratch Someone's Back and We'll Scratch Yours: Collective Reciprocity in Social Q&A Communities. J. Am. Soc. Inf. Sci. Technol. (forthcoming, 2013)
16. Korfiatis, N., Sicilia, M.A.: Social Measures and Flexible Navigation on Online Contact Networks. In: Proceedings of the IEEE International Conference on Fuzzy Systems (FUZZ-IEEE), pp. 1–6. Imperial College, London (2007)
17. Papavlasopoulos, S., Poulos, M., Korfiatis, N., Bokos, G.: A non-linear index to evaluate a journal's scientific impact. Inf. Sci. 180, 2156–2175 (2010)
18. Korfiatis, N., García-Bariocanal, E., Sánchez-Alonso, S.: Evaluating content quality and helpfulness of online product reviews: The interplay of review helpfulness vs. review content. Electron. Commer. Res. Appl. 11, 205–217 (2012)

1-5 Stars: Metadata on the Openness Level of Open Data Sets in Europe

Sébastien Martin[1], Muriel Foulonneau[2], and Slim Turki[2]

[1] Paris VIII University
Vincennes-Saint-Denis, France
[2] Public Research Centre Henri Tudor,
29, av. John F. Kennedy
L-1855 Luxembourg, Luxembourg
name.surname@tudor.lu

Abstract. The development of open data requires a better reusability of data. Indeed, the catalogs listing data dispersed in different countries have a crucial role. However, the degree of openness is also a key success factor for open data. In this paper, we study the *PublicData.eu* catalogue, which allows accessing open datasets from European countries and analyse the metadata recorded for each dataset. The objectives are to (i) identify the quality of a sample of metadata properties, which are critical to enable data reuse and to (ii) study the stated level of data openness. The study uses the Tim Berners-Lee's five star evaluation scale.

Keywords: open data, metadata, catalogue, CKAN.

1   Introduction

In the recent years, data openness has been advocated in particular for public administrations, on the one hand to support government action transparency, and on the other hand to ensure the reusability of public data in a variety of services, thus improving services to citizens and companies and fostering innovation (Davies, 2010).

Many initiatives have taken place to open public data. After the leading *data.gov* initiative in the US, many countries in Europe and worldwide have joined the movement. In Europe, the PSI directive (2003/98/EC) on the reuse of public sector information was released in 2003 and has been revised in 2013 to address in particular the publication and reusability of public datasets as open data. The G8 which took place in June 2013 released an Open Data Charter.

While the reuse of public data has a great economic potential (e.g., Vickery, 2012), the level of reuse of the data in a multiplicity of applications and services is still disappointing. Blumer (2013) claims that the low uptake of Linked Open Data in commercial services is mainly due to the type of data published and to governance issues. The integration of open data sets in the semantic environment in which data can be discovered, reused by services and applications, and enriched by other datasets

E. Garoufallou and J. Greenberg (Eds.): MTSR 2013, CCIS 390, pp. 234–245, 2013.

is still a challenge. In Martin et al. (2013), we claim that the reusability of open datasets depends in particular on their easy discovery, their maintenance, and the completeness of associated information, such as licences.

In this paper, we study the *PublicData.eu* catalogue[1], which allows accessing open datasets from European countries and analyse the metadata recorded for each dataset. Our objectives are to (i) identify the quality of a sample of metadata properties, which are critical to enable data reuse and to (ii) study the stated level of data openness.

2 Catalogues and Metadata on Open Data Sets

Many countries in Europe have established local or national portals to provide access to public sector open datasets (Dietrich, 2013). 114 catalogues are recorded on the *datacatalogs.org* website[2]. The European Commission itself has launched the *http://open-data.europa.eu* catalogue late 2012 to provide access to datasets issued by European institutions. Catalogues have been set up to gather datasets across geographic and institutional boundaries. These catalogues include the Open Data catalogue of *DataMarket*[3] and *DataHub*[4]. *PublicData.eu*[5] is a pan-European catalogue launched under the auspices of the *FP7 LOD2* project[6].

There are several software to present and disseminate public data. The *Open Knowledge Foundation* develops and promotes the *CKAN* (*Comprehensive Knowledge Archive Network*)[7] open source software. It allows institutions to record and disseminate their data, including in the RDF format. Reusers can access data through a search engine, navigate through tags associated to datasets. *CKAN* also provides a *RESTful API* to query catalogs and if data formats permit so, to access the datasets. It is used for example by the UK open data catalog, along with Drupal.

The couple *CKAN-DCAT* (*Data Catalog Vocabulary*)[8], according the *Fraunhofer institute* is the most common way of publishing dataset descriptions in Europe, so that it could be considered a de facto standard (Klessmann *et al.*, 2012, p. 445). In this study we analyze the *PublicData.eu* catalogue that aggregates data from *CKAN* open data catalogues all over Europe. It aims to give insight on open data publication in Europe. The *PublicData.eu* catalog currently collects data from 26 sources, has been the first to be published in Europe in 2011. It includes data beyond the European Union, e.g., Serbian datasets. Although not exhaustive, it represents a unique aggregation of European datasets.

---

[1] http://publicdata.eu
[2] http://datacatalogs.org/group/eu-official
[3] http://datamarket.com/data/
[4] http://datahub.io/
[5] http://publicdata.eu/fr/
[6] http://lod2.eu/Welcome.html
[7] http://ckan.org/
[8] http://www.w3.org/TR/vocab-dcat/

3   Methodology

The datasets recorded in catalogues and their reuse conditions are actually extremely diverse. This can represent a challenge for the reuse of datasets. In 2010, Tim Berners-Lee proposed a star system to rate the openness of datasets from:

- 1 star: *"Available on the web (whatever format) but with an open licence, to be Open Data"*,
- 2 stars: *"Available as machine-readable structured data"*,
- 3 stars: as (2) plus *"non-proprietary format"*,
- 4 stars: like (3) plus *"Use open standards from W3C (RDF and SPARQL) to identify things"*, and
- 5 stars: like (4) plus *"Link your data to other people's data to provide context"*.

We therefore propose analyzing the description of datasets from the *PublicData.eu* catalogue following the data openness star system.

3.1   The *PublicData.eu* Dataset

14 477 datasets have the indication of the related EU country. Figure 1 shows the distribution of the datasets across EU countries. The UK is the largest provider of datasets. The distribution of datasets across the other countries reflects to a large extent the dynamics engaged for instance in France and in Spain.

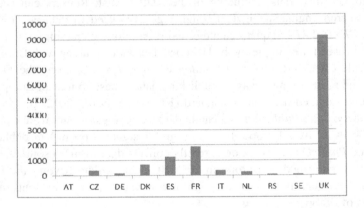

Fig. 1. EU country of the datasets

1 057 datasets indicate the compliance with the INSPIRE directive (infrastructure for spatial information in Europe), i.e., the *INSPIRE* property has value *True*.

For 12 127 datasets, a source catalogue is indicated. Source catalogues include CKAN Austria, CKAN Czech Republik, CKAN Italia, CKAN Serbia, Data Publica in France, Data UK, Dati Piemonte, London Datastore, Offene Daten (Germany), and Open Data Berlin. The wide majority of the records come from the Data UK catalogue. This reflects the EU country coverage of the datasets indicated on Figure 1.

3.2   The Data Collection Mechanism

The descriptions of 17 027 datasets were collected in the course of May 2013 from the *PublicData.eu* portal. They are aggregated from open data catalogues all over Europe. We used the *JSON API* through a script written in Python language. At the end of this process, the data is manipulated as Python tuples, lists and dictionaries, with nested levels of various lengths depending on the complexity of the data and the choices of the suppliers.

From the information gathered in the previous steps, we built a class model that defines all the possible properties that each dataset may have. When a dataset is evaluated from the catalogue, an instance of the dataset class is created, and all properties are populated with a default value. Then this value is replaced, as required, with the value contained in the catalogue. Finally 17 027 instances of the dataset class were recorded in a relational database.

The API allowed identifying the URLs of each dataset, i.e., 17 027. We then connected to the catalogue and retrieved data in JSON format. We found 236 distinct dataset properties. This is partially due to the linguistic diversity that has led some providers to adapt property names in their language, but also to problems of consistency in naming (upper / lower case, spaces / underscore for a single field). It represents a major challenge to understand the content of the *PublicData.eu* catalogue.

Metadata are fulfilled by both the original catalog - in the vast majority of cases – and partially when the records are imported in the *PublicData.eu* catalogue. Metadata added at the level of the *PublicData.eu* catalogue include for instance a reference to the original catalogue (*harvest_catalogue_name* property).

The dataset descriptions from *PublicData.eu* provide a comprehensive insight, if not exhaustive, on the published data and publication practices in Europe. We then analysed the data in order to identify the information made available on data openness and reusability in particular the licensing conditions and the data formats.

4   Licenses

The one star openness level depends upon data licenses. Licensing information can be found in 10 distinct metadata properties, i.e., *licence, License, licence_url, License_details, License_ID, License_summary, License_title, License_uri, License_url,* and *mandate.*

Out of 17 027 datasets, 13 535 have at least 1 license indication, i.e., one of the above mentioned properties no empty and with a meaningful value (i.e., not including "notspecified ", "0" or "n/a" for instance. 12 470 datasets can be considered having some form of open license, i.e., about 73,24% of the total number of datasets.

769 datasets have a Creative Commons license, including 189 with a CC-zero license. 71 use Open Data Commons licenses[9] PDDL and ODBL.

---

[9] http://opendatacommons.org/

However, a significant number of datasets have a national license, such as apie v2[10] to publish information created in particular by French public authorities (1), UK-crown which "covers material created by civil servants, ministers and government departments and agencies"[11] in the UK (534), and the UK Open Government License[12] aimed at facilitating the reuse of UK datasets (Table 1).

Only 128 datasets have an explicitly closed license ("other-closed" license ID). 1 indicates a local author with rights. 25 indicate a GLA license (Greater London Authority Copyright). In addition, 26 datasets are made available with a CADA license[13]. This license was created by the Commission for Access to Administrative Documents in France before the Open Data movement and includes an annual fee for the reuse of administrative data.

Interestingly, a number of datasets have been assigned a software license, such as the Open Software License[14] (1), the Sun Industry Standards Source License[15] (1), LGPL 2 (1), GPL (2), and even for software documentation (GNU Free Documentation License[16]) (2).

Table 1. Licenses indicated for datasets

Creative Commons Attribution	549
Creative Commons Attribution Share-Alike	26
Creative Commons CCZero	189
Creative Commons Non-Commercial (Any)	5
GNU Free Documentation License	2
License Not Specified	252
Open Data Commons Open Database License (ODbL)	67
Open Data Commons Public Domain Dedication and Licence (PDDL)	4
Other (Attribution)	349
Other (Non-Commercial)	6
Other (Not Open)	128
Other (Open)	10
Other (Public Domain)	103
UK Open Government Licence (OGL)	9098

---

[10] https://www.apiefrance.fr/sections/acces_thematique/
reutilisation-des-informations-publiques/des-conditions-
generales-pour-la-reutilisation-des-informations-
publiques/view

[11] http://www.nationalarchives.gov.uk/information-management/
our-services/crown-copyright.htm

[12] http://www.nationalarchives.gov.uk/doc/
open-government-licence/

[13] http://www.cada.fr/IMG/pdf/licence_commerciale_revisee.pdf

[14] http://opensource.org/licenses/OSL-3.0

[15] http://www.openoffice.org/licenses/sissl_license.html

[16] http://www.gnu.org/copyleft/fdl.html

The *license details* property can be used to inform on alterations to the datasets. For instance, a dataset may have been anonymized before it could be published. The dataset *Characteristics of Pupils Living in London*[17] has a license detail property indicating "The Tables are based in part on anonymised individual pupil records from the National Pupil Dataset. [...]." It sometimes indicates access restrictions, e.g., "Dataset available only to ONS approved researchers via the Data Archive" (dataset *Housing Tenure of the Population, Borough*[18]). In other cases it indicates the data source (e.g., "This dataset was generated from a variety of sources with the core attribute data such as Name, Borough and Organization being provided by the London Boroughs" (dataset *Allotment Locations*[19]) or the way in which the data should be interpreted, e.g., "Collection and analysis of satisfaction data is at an early stage and therefore the data should be interpreted with caution." (Dataset *London Happiness Scores, Borough*[20]).

The *license* property sometimes includes a more precise description of the necessary attribution, e.g., "CEH must be acknowledged in any publication that arises from the use of this data" (*Post-Chernobyl soil and vegetation surveys (1986-1987) - map of sample locations*[21]), usage restrictions, e.g., "Should not be used for navigation purposes" (*Protected Wrecks*[22]), or information necessary to understand the data and interpret it accurately, e.g., "Data is captured at various scales (1:10,0,25000, 1250)" (*Conservation Areas* dataset[23]) and "Dataset is complete for Scotland. Care should be taken when using this dataset with lookups to other postcode based geographies. Some postcode unit boundaries have changed since datazones were created therefore exact match of the boundaries are unlikely" (*Data Zones 2001*[24]). In addition to usage and interpretation constraints, certain metadata authors help reuse through dedicated indications, e.g., "Not suitable for applications for which 1:50,000 mapping is too coarse." (*Integrated Hydrological Digital Terrain Model (IHDTM)*[25]).

License related information include therefore a variety of indications beyond the mere license name. Only for a small minority of datasets, the reuse decision can be automated, i.e., when the license identification is sufficiently clear and no additional

---

[17] http://publicdata.eu/api/rest/dataset/
characteristics-of-pupils-living-in-london
[18] http://publicdata.eu/api/rest/dataset/housing-tenure-of-the-
population-borough
[19] http://publicdata.eu/api/rest/dataset/allotment-locations
[20] http://publicdata.eu/api/rest/dataset/
london-happiness-scores-borough
[21] http://publicdata.eu/api/rest/dataset/post-chernobyl-soil-and-
vegetation-surveys-1986-1987-map-of-sample-locations
[22] http://publicdata.eu/api/rest/dataset/protected-wrecks
[23] http://publicdata.eu/api/rest/dataset/
conservation-areas-dataset
[24] http://publicdata.eu/api/rest/dataset/data-zones-2001
[25] http://publicdata.eu/api/rest/dataset/
integrated-hydrological-digital-terrain-model-ihdtm

information is necessary, e.g., the CC0 license. A small number of metadata authors have added information related to the reuse context and suitability.

5   Format

The two star level depends upon the format in which the data is made available. Indeed, the reusability of data is facilitated if data is made available in a machine readable format, with as much expressivity as possible of the related data model. While CSV for instance is a machine readable format, RDF related formats allow embedding the data structure in the dataset and assigning identifiers to resources, thus providing additional information for the reusability of data, by decreasing the risks of ambiguity and misinterpretations.

The data format is provided through various metadata properties, i.e., *content_TYPE, FORMAT, FORMATo_dati, FORMATo_dati__es__numerico, FORMATo_dei_dati, FORMATo_elettronico, FORMATo_elettronico__csv, FORMATo_elettronico__excel, FORMATo_elettronico__pdf, FORMATo_ presentacion, gpx_Format, mimeTYPE, mimeTYPE_inner, ovl_Format,* and *resource_TYPE.* Datasets have only 1 content associated content type, while they can have multiple formats for instance.

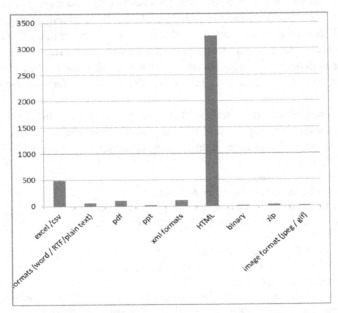

Fig. 2. Distribution of content types

In Figure 2, we grouped the data formats (as recorded in the *content_TYPE* property) in categories, i.e., non XML machine readable data formats (Excel and CSV), image formats (JPEG and GIF), XML formats, including KML, Open XML,

XHTML, and RDF/XML (we included 1 dataset with RDF only which could be available in another RDF serialization such as Turtle), and text formats (Word, RTF or plain text).

Out of 17 027, only 4 051 had a *content_TYPE* property. 4 datasets are available in image formats (JPEG or GIF). 1 dataset has a mime type *application/force-download*, which is a way of forcing the download of files instead of allowing the client to associate an application to open the file (e.g., PDF).

155 datasets are available as CSV files, 329 in Excel format, i.e., in non XML machine readable formats. Only 2,62% of the datasets for which the content type has been recorded (106) are available in XML format, whether XML, XHTML, RDF/XML (we included the one dataset declaring RDF only), KML, and Open XML. Only 0,07% (3 datasets) are available in RDF. Overall, only 590 datasets, i.e., 14,56% of the datasets for which a content type is provided are machine readable and thus comply with the machine readability condition for openness levels of 2 stars and above.

Out of 17 027 datasets, only 11 285 had at least one indication about their format. 8 954 if we consider the *FORMAT* property alone. The *FORMAT* property, which is the most accurately completed, shows the dominant proportion of spreadsheets type's formats, which is fundamental to assess machine-readability, thus the level of openness (Figure 3). In addition, it identifies 56 datasets that are specifically recorded in RDF format. The *FORMAT* property is more often filled than the *content_TYPE* property so that we used it for further analyses.

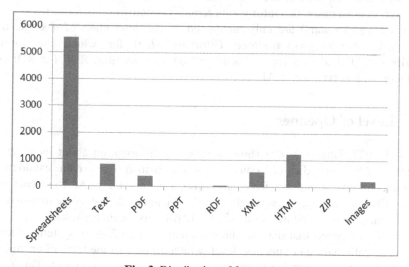

Fig. 3. Distribution of formats

When taking into consideration all properties related to the data format, we found 5 797 datasets. From this observation it is therefore possible to state that 34% of the datasets are available in a machine readable format. Many datasets had a "text/html" *mimeTYPE* property, while their *FORMAT* property was inconsistent. In those cases we ignored the *mimeTYPE* information. We counted datasets whose *FORMAT* was indicated as HTML as non machine readable because HTML does not allow encoding semantics. However, if we would count HTML as machine readable, this would represent 1 221 additional datasets (41% machine readable datasets). In 40% of the cases, the format indicated in one or more of the related fields suggest that the dataset is not available in a machine readable format. In the other cases, this could not be determined from the metadata available. We did not count the datasets for which multiple values were recorded, some of which were machine readable formats and others not.

The three star openness level requires the use of non-proprietary formats. This creates ambiguities. The openness nature of formats can be debated in some cases. Certain formats are proprietary but their specifications are open. In some cases the formats have been open at a certain point of time but additions and further evolutions remain proprietary. Finally in many cases, we could not determine whether the format was or not proprietary because the value of the property was too vague (eg., *hoja de cálculo*). Nevertheless for 49% of the datasets, it was possible to identify a non-proprietary format and for 21% a proprietary format. The use of proprietary formats is therefore a critical issue for improving the level of openness of datasets.

The four star openness level requires the use of open standards from W3C. This includes HTML, XML, and RDF in particular. XML-based formats may however not be developed outside the scope of W3C and be entirely independent from W3C. This is the case for instance of KML. We therefore distinguish between the availability in W3C standards (9,5% of datasets) and the availability in XML based formats (10%). However, in most cases, this information remains unknown.

Linked data (5 stars) are only mentioned in the description of a single dataset (*Brandweer Amsterdam-Amstelland Uitrukberichten*) for which the format is described as "linked data api, rdf json". 58 datasets mention RDF (or RDFa) as a format or content type, i.e., 0,34%.

6   Level of Openness

Out of 17 027 datasets, 6 891 show at least one information about their degree of openness. All these datasets come from the British open data catalogue (the *harvest_catalogue_name* property has value"Data.gov.uk"). At the scale of the British CKAN, the openness is rather well documented, but not exhaustive since *harvest_catalog_name* allows retrieving 8 689 datasets for data.gov.uk.

It should be noted that data.gov.uk considers a -1 to 5 stars system, where 118 datasets actually have a -1 openness level, which means that the level of openness was deemed unscorable according to the *openness_score_reason* property. This property records information related to the level of openness indicated for Data.gov.uk datasets in the *openness_score* property, for instance "open and standardized format", "URL unobtainable", and "The format entered for the resource doesn't match the description from the web server".

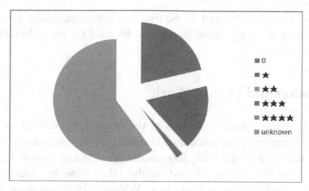

Fig. 4. Distribution of openness levels in UK datasets

Figure 4 shows that for a wide majority of datasets, the level of openness is unknown. This is coherent with the lack of licensing information without which it is impossible to conclude on even a 1 star openness level.

In order to obtain a more complete overview of the openness level of datasets, we had to rely on the description of datasets. From the analyses we conducted on licensing and format properties, it is possible to derive an approximation of the level of openness of the datasets according to the dataset descriptions. The level of openness has to be deduced according to incremental conditions. For instance, the two star level requires both an open license and a machine-readable format.

Looking at the license information recorded by metadata creators, 12 470 datasets have some form of open license, i.e., 73,24% of the datasets should have 1 star or above.

Figure 5 shows the level of openness of the datasets according to the content of the properties we have studied for 1-4 stars. We took into consideration all XML based formats as open W3C formats for this figure but excluded datasets with multiple or uncertain values. The reference to 5 stars indeed should take into consideration linkages which cannot be inferred from dataset metadata.

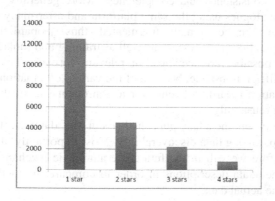

Fig. 5. Level of openness according to the Format and License related properties

Data openness is mainly related to the first level of compliance, i.e., the licensing issue. However data providers have clearly not focused on the publication of data in reusable formats so far.

7   Conclusion and Future Work

Our analysis shows the limited openness of the datasets advertised as open data, as well as the heterogeneity of the associated metadata, thus illustrating the difficulty for reusers, on the one hand to discover datasets, despite the creation of large catalogues of datasets, such as *PublicData.eu*, and on the other hand to effectively reuse the machine readable and contextualized data. While 1 star openness level may be sufficient to ensure the transparency of government action, the ambition to facilitate the reuse of data through the creation of services by third parties is clearly not served below 2 stars.

In certain cases, machine-readability cannot be achieved, typically when the datasets are composed of pictures. Nevertheless data conversion tools and methodologies exist to ensure a better reusability of the data. An open data infrastructure for Europe should include training capabilities as well as tools to facilitate data conversion.

Our results confirm the risks we already pointed out in a previous study (Martin et al., 2013) regarding two major challenges that data providers have to face: the language barrier and the lack of consistency of metadata. These are the main reasons why a metadata property such as license requires taking into account a dozen properties on the *PublicData.eu* catalogue. This directly contributes to the lack of consistency of metadata and reduces the reusability of data.

The revision of the Public Sector Information directive in Europe aimed in particular to address the low use of machine-readable formats by ensuring that public sector information is made available in reusable formats. The DCAT metadata format developed by the W3C[26] can help harmonize the description of open data sets in the future, thus facilitating their discovery. However metadata quality remains an issue, including metadata consistency and completeness. More generally our study shows that even among catalogues using the same platform and after many studies the open data initiatives in Europe remain fragmented thus jeopardizing its impact. Harmonization of practices is necessary as well as training and tools to ensure that as many datasets as possible are available in relevant formats. The licensing issue remains the most difficult obstacle, because of the variety of situations. In this regard, the lack of information regarding license for a significant part of the datasets raises concerns regarding reusability.

Our analyses rely on metadata published about the datasets. It is not always complete, thus jeopardizing data discoverability. Most importantly, it may not always be accurate. Therefore we will in the future use automatic mechanisms to complete and validate the metadata descriptions in order to compare the metadata practice at dataset level and the actual data.

---

[26] http://www.w3.org/TR/vocab-dcat/

Among the obstacles to reusability, we aim to investigate other aspects which became apparent already from our analysis of the dataset metadata, i.e. the governance issues (including the distribution of responsibilities and the update information) and the types of datasets published, essentially through a finer analysis of the keywords assigned to datasets.

Acknowledgement. The authors would like to acknowledge the contribution of the *COST Action IS1004 www.webdatanet.eu.*

References

1. Davies, T.: Open data, democracy and public sector reform: a look at open government data use from data.gov.uk. Practical Participation (web) (2010)
2. Blumauer, A.: The LOD cloud is dead, long live the trusted LOD cloud, http://blog.semantic-web.at/category/linked-data-open-data/ (Blog post June 7, 2013)
3. Dietrich, D.: Europe's Data Catalogues. European Public Sector Information Platform Topic Report No. 2013 / 01 (2013)
4. Martin, S., Foulonneau, M., Turki, S., Ihadjadene, M.: Open Data: Barriers, Risks, and Opportunities. In: European Conference on eGovernment, Como, Italy, June 13-14 (2013)
5. Vickery, G.: Review of recent studies on PSI re-use and related market developments. Report to the European Commission (2012), http://ec.europa.eu/information_society/policy/psi/docs/pdfs/opendata2012/reports/Vickery.docx
6. Klessmann, J., Denker, P., Schieferdecker, I., Sönke, S.: Open Government Data Deutschland. Eine Studie zu Open Government in Deutschland im Auftrag des Bundesministerium des Innern. Berlin, Bundesministerium des Innern (2012)

Metadata Requirements for Repositories in Health Informatics Research: Evidence from the Analysis of Social Media Citations

Dimitris Rousidis[1,2], Emmanouel Garoufallou[2], Panos Balatsoukas[3],
Kostas Paraskeuopoulos[2], Stella Asderi[4], and Damiana Koutsomiha[5]

[1] University of Alcala, Madrid, Spain
[2] Alexander Technological Educational Institute of Thessaloniki, Greece
[3] University of Manchester, UK
[4] American College of Thessaloniki, Greece
[5] American Farm School, Thessaloniki, Greece

Abstract. Social media have transformed the way modern science is communicated. Although several studies have been focused on the use of social media for the dissemination of scientific knowledge and the measurement of the impact of academic output, we know very little about how academics cite social media in their publications. In order to address this gap, a content analysis was performed on a sample of 629 journal articles in medical informatics. The findings showed the presence of 109 citations to social media resources, the majority of which were blogs and wikis. Social media citations were used more frequently to support the literature review section of articles. However, a fair amount of citations was used in order to document various aspects of the methodology section, such as the data collection and analysis process. The paper concludes with the implications of these findings for metadata design for bibliographic databases (like PubMed and Medline).

Keywords: Scholarly communication, Citation Analysis, Digital Library 2.0, Metadata, Search interfaces, Social media, Medical informatics.

1   Introduction

Social media applications (such as blogs, wikis and social networking tools) have transformed the way modern science is communicated on the web. Several authors have highlighted various aspects of this transformation, such as the advancement of research collaboration [1], the improvement of the overall responsiveness and timeliness of scholarly communication [2], and the development of new metrics for measuring scholarly impact [3, 4]. Other authors have examined the way scientists communicate scientific knowledge through the use of social media, such as blogs and Twitter [5, 6, 7, 8, 9].

Despite the fact that there is a large number of studies focused on the examination of the way academic researchers make use of social media resources in order to

E. Garoufallou and J. Greenberg (Eds.): MTSR 2013, CCIS 390, pp. 246–257, 2013.
© Springer International Publishing Switzerland 2013

disseminate scientific knowledge, we know very little about how academic authors use social media resources as citations in their scholarly publications [10]. For example, there are several questions that need to be addressed in this respect, such as: What are the typical characteristics of social media resources that tend to be used as citations in journal articles? What is the format and the content of these citations? What purposes are served by the use of social media citations in academic publications? Seeking answers to these questions could shed light into the modern citation practices of academics and inform the design of new metadata elements for digital libraries in a multi-verse scholarly communication environment. The aim of this study was to examine how researchers in medical informatics used social media resources as citations in their academic publications. In particular the objectives were:

— to develop a methodology for tracing and analyzing the contents of social media citations within journal articles in the field of medical informatics;
— to investigate the use of social media citations within journal articles in terms of the following characteristics: i) the *type* of social media citations (e.g. Facebook, YouTube or Wikipedia); ii) the *format* of social media citations (e.g. textual or multimedia); iii) the *purpose of use* of social media citations within the articles (e.g. to support the literature review section, the methodology section, or the discussion of the results); and iv) the *content of* cited social media resources;
— To discuss some practical implications of this research for the design and use of metadata for bibliographic digital libraries (e.g. PubMed and MEDLINE).

The paper is structured as follows. Firstly, we review the relevant literature in the context of medical informatics and make a case about the need of the present study. The next section outlines the method used in order to address the aim and objectives of this study. Then, we present the results, and finally, we provide some discussion and conclusions.

2 Use of Social Media in Medical Informatics Research

Social media have been primarily used in the medical and health informatics research as a means of health promotion and patient education or support. For example, YouTube videos have been frequently used for the promotion of information related to cancer as well as dietary and nutrition problems [11, 12]; Facebook has been used as a channel for promotion of sexual health issues [13]; and, Twitter has been incorporated in the design of interventions focused on prenatal health education [14]. Also, social gaming interventions have been designed and implemented as a means of engaging people in the self-management of their physical activities and well-being [15].

Despite the fact that social media applications have been extensively used for health promotion and patient engagement or education, only a few researchers have attempted to examine the use of social media for the communication of scientific knowledge related to medical informatics research. Typical examples include studies on the use of Twitter for the communication of academic knowledge during conferences [16], and the analysis of tweets for determining the scholarly impact of academic publications [4]. To our knowledge there is no reported research on the use of social media as citations in academic publications related to medical informatics research. Also, there are quite a few studies attempting to address this issue outside the medical informatics domain. A typical study was conducted by [10] who examined the use of YouTube videos as citations in academic publications. The researchers found that citations to YouTube videos were fewer in the case of medical & health sciences rather than social sciences & humanities. Also, the authors reported that the majority of cited YouTube videos related to Sciences (including Medicine and Health Sciences) were categorized as documentaries, scientific demonstrations, online lectures and educational material. In the case of articles about Arts & Humanities, most citations linked to music videos, while the majority of articles related to Social Sciences contained citations to political and news videos.

Our study differs from the one conducted by [10] because it is not limited to the examination of a single social media type, e.g. YouTube. Instead the aim is to examine different types of social media applications used as citations in scholarly articles. Moreover, the present study goes a step further by attempting to analyze the nature and purpose of social media citations within a single scientific field (i.e. medical informatics). Finally, we attempt to present the utility of the results of our study in the context of metadata design for bibliographic digital libraries. To date, the development of semantics and vocabularies for metadata standards and application profiles has been focused on system-centred approaches. These approaches have been criticized because they do not take into account users' needs and user aspects of the information seeking and scholarly communication behavior [17]. In this study we applied a content analysis technique as a means of analyzing the scholarly behaviour of academics and researchers in relation to the use of social media as citations in peer-reviewed journal articles. Therefore, emerging patterns of social media use (e.g. in terms of types of content and purpose of use) are translated into metadata requirements for bibliographic search result interfaces.

3   Methodology

A total of 629 articles from four leading journals in medical informatics were included in the analysis. The journals used as a source for selected articles were: the *Journal of Biomedical Informatics*, the *International Journal of Medical Informatics*, the *Journal of Medical Internet Research* and finally the *Journal of the American Medical Informatics Association*. The decision to focus on these four journals was made because these represented typical sources of mainstream research in the field of health and medical informatics. All articles that appeared in issues of these four journals during 2012 and 2013 were included in the analysis. Also, articles in early view (i.e. online version of articles before inclusion in an issue) were analyzed (up to March 2013).

In order to address the aim and objectives of this study a two-fold stepwise process was implemented. This involved: firstly, the identification of all articles that contained citations to social media resources; and secondly, the performance of a content analysis for all social media citations used in the identified articles. In order to identify which articles contained references to social media sources an automated method was implemented using a java-based text parsing tool, called *Citation Parser*. The tool scanned articles and created indexes of references made to social media resources. The text parsing tool identified social media citations in a total of 59 articles (9.4%). The Citation Parser showed that the 59 articles contained a total of 109 references to social media resources. These 109 references were subjected to a manual content analysis [18]. In particular, each of the 109 references was analyzed against the following coding categories:

1. *Types of cited social media.* For the needs of this study only citations to the following types of social media tools were subjected to examination: *Facebook, Twitter, Wikipedia, YouTube, Dailymotion, Academia.edu, ScienceStage, Flickr* and *Wordpress*. Also, citations to publicly available blogs and wikis (other than Wikipedia) were included in the analysis. However, in the latter case individually identified resources were broadly categorized as either a blog, or a wiki.
2. *Format of cited social media* (e.g. text, video, photos). Two main types of format were included in the analysis. These were: Text and Multimedia content. In the latter case, contents were coded as videos, photos, codes, graphs, or equations.
3. *Purpose of use of cited social media.* A selection was made between the following coding options: *Social media citations used to support the introduction or the literature review sections*; *Social media citations used to support the methodology and the techniques used for data collection and analysis*; *Social media citations used for the support of the discussion of the results*; and finally, *Other uses of social media citations,* beyond the aforementioned ones.
4. *Content of cited social media.* There were five main options for content. These were: 1. Content focused on specific software / technology, or software development initiatives; 2. Content focused on the methods used for data collection and analysis; 3. Content focused on data reporting (e.g. statistics on the uptake of specific health technologies, raw data sets, or health cost summaries); 4. Content focused on user aspects of medical informatics, including information about patient safety, usability and technology acceptance; 5. Any other type of content not covered by the aforementioned categories.

Two independent researchers applied the aforementioned coding scheme in order to analyze the 109 social media citations identified by the *Citation Parser*. The inter-coder agreement was quite high across the four categories (*Cohen's Kappa* = 0.94). In particular, no discrepancies were observed between the two observers in the case of the first, second and third category of the coding scheme. Eleven citations were coded differently in terms of their content (i.e. the fourth category). In this case, the two independent researchers met and produced a commonly agreed categorization. Post-hoc Poison tests for statistical significance were used in order to identify significant differences, if any, in the occurrence of social media citations across the four categories of the coding scheme. In this case, results are presented as incident rate rations (IRR) with [95% confidence intervals] and two-sided P-values. The remainder of this section describes the *Citation Parser*.

3.1   Citation Parser

The Citation Parser is a text parser – based on Java, MySQL and WampServer technology – that identifies cited social media based on the analysis of the URLs contained in the reference lists of journal articles. Although publicly available tools, like SCOPUS, provide an adequate query facility for searching references within journal articles [10], these tools do not provide a usable interface for managing the URLs retrieved from a given query. The Citation parser allows more flexibility when defining queries through the embedded SQL function. Moreover, the tool provides a very efficient interface for managing retrieved URLs, such as automatic extraction and storage of URL citations to social media; the organisation of URLs related to social media by journal title or type of social media application; and the display of descriptive statistics (such as the number and percentage of articles containing URLs, or the percentage and mean number of URLs related to specific types of social media applications).

The workflow of the tool contains three main functions. These are: 1. parsing of PDF files (i.e. journal articles in a PDF format); 2. creation of a database with all the URLs listed in the reference section of the parsed journal articles; and 3. querying of these URLs for the identification of those related to specific social media applications. A series of pilot tests with different sets of journal articles showed that the Citation Parser could trace the presence of social media citations within article with precision [19] rates ranging between 0.89 and 1.0, thus showing a good level of sensitivity.

4   Analysis

4.1   Types of Cited Social Media

As it is shown in Table 1 the most frequently cited social media sources were those related to blogs and wikis. In particular, references to blogs accounted for a 35% of the citations analyzed in this study. Blogs were followed by citations to wiki-sites (22%) and Wikipedia articles (21%). Among the least cited social media sources were those related to social networking sites (such as Facebook, Twitter and Mendeley) and multimedia sharing communities (like YouTube and Flickr), with Twitter and Academic.edu being the least cited social media (citations to these two types occurred only once).

The results of the Poisson analysis did not show the presence of statistically significant differences in the number of citations between blogs, wiki-sites and Wikipedia articles. However, statistically significant differences were observed between blogs and the remaining types of social media, such as Facebook [IRR=3.4, (1.7 to 7.5), $p = 0.0001$]; Flickr [IRR=6.3 (2.65 to 18.3), $p = 0.0001$]; and YouTube [IRR=7.6 (3.0 to 24.7), $p<0.0001$].

Table 1. Types of cited social media resources

Social media types	Frequencies	%
Blogs	38	35
Wiki-type sites	24	22
Wikipedia	23	21
Facebook	11	10
Flickr	6	5
YouTube	5	5

4.2 Format of Cited Social Media

The format of the majority of cited social media was textual (74%). Multimedia content accounted only for a 19% (i.e. videos = 7%, photos = 5%, codes = 4% and graphs = 3%). The Poisson analysis showed that the difference in the number of citations between textual and multimedia resources was significant at the 0.1 level, IRR = 4.05 (2.5 to 6.9), p = 0.0001. Finally 7% of the citations remained unidentified because it was not possible to access the contents of the cited social media source.

4.3 Use of Cited Social Media Resources within the Article

The most common reason for which authors used references to social media resources was to support the introduction and literature review section of the article (46%, n = 50). In this case citations were used to present:

— trends and usage patterns regarding the uptake of specific health care technologies (usually such information was contained in blogs);
— online demonstrations related to the functionality of specific health technologies (e.g. such citations were linked to blogs and YouTube); and finally,
— detailed definitions associated with various health-related concepts and technologies (Wikipedia and Wiki-articles were the primary sources of such definitions).

Twenty-nine percent (29%, n = 32) of references to social media resources were made in order to support the methodology section, such as the techniques used by the authors for data collection and analysis. It appears that the reason for using social media as citations in the methodology section was to provide readers with the opportunity to access additional material which otherwise would not be possible to include in the actual article either due to page limitations (e.g. lengthy descriptions of specific methods), or because such information was available in a non-textual format (such as videos, high definition images and interactive applications). In this case, the reasons for referencing social media resources were:

— to show how data were collected and how data collection instruments were administered to participants (e.g. this was common in the case of online surveys that involved data collection through the use of Facebook or wiki-sites);

— to present population lists or sample frames (e.g. this involved references to Wikipedia and wiki-sites that contained expanded lists of targeted population); and finally,

— to link to detailed descriptions of methods used for data analysis, such as statistical models and source codes (blogs, Wikipedia and wiki-sites were the most common sources for this type of information).

Finally, references to social media citations occurred less frequently for the support of the discussion of the results (25%, n = 27). In this case, types of cited social media were Wikipedia articles, wiki-sites and blogs. Statistically significant differences in occurrence frequency were observed at the 0.5 level between citations made to support the introduction-literature review section and the discussion of the results [IRR = 1.85 (1.13 to 3.1), p = 0.012]. Non statistically significant differences in the number of cited social media were observed between the Introduction-Literature review and the Methodology sections.

4.4   Content of Cited Social Media

The majority of cited social media included content related to specific types of technologies used in health care (36%) (Table 2). Three types of technologies were covered by cited social media: 1. semantic technologies; 2.social media applications; and 3. clinical decision support tools. *Semantic technologies* included ontologies (e.g. W3C OWL), text mining tools (e.g. Genia tool), clinical vocabularies (e.g. SNOMED-CT) and semantic interoperability standards (e.g. the Health Level 7 standard) (usually this information was contained in wikis and Wikipedia). *Social media applications* contained in cited social media were those related to the promotion of health interventions or health education (e.g. Facebook, wikis, and YouTube). Finally, descriptions and demonstrations of clinical decision support tools were presented both in a visual and textual format through cited social media such as blogs, wikis and the YouTube.

In addition to content related to specific types of technologies, 27% of the cited social media were focused on information related to methods used for data collection and analysis (such as research instruments, sample frames, data-sets and statistical methods). Fewer citations (23%) occurred in the case of social media with contents related to data reporting (such as health cost figures or usage and uptake rates for specific types of technologies). Fourteen percent (14%) of cited social media contained information about user aspects of technology (such as user engagement, models of technology use, usability and technology acceptance). The results of the Poisson analysis showed that the number of social media citations with a content related to user aspects of technology was significantly lower than the number of citations referencing content related to specific types health technologies [IRR = 2.6 (1.4 to 5.1), p = 0.0015], or methods used for data collection and analysis [IRR = 2 (1.04 to 3.9), p = 0.03].

Table 2. Type of content cited using social media resources

Type of content cited	Frequencies	%
Types of health technologies	39	36
Methods for data collection/analysis	30	27
Data reporting	25	23
User aspects of technology	15	14

5   Discussion

The results of this study showed that blogs were the most frequently cited types of social media. Other researchers have shown a similar trend as far as it concerns the frequency of use of blogs by researchers for the communication of scientific information during conferences [9] and knowledge sharing activities [5]. However, in the case of our study, the originality of this finding is related to the nature of cited blogs in academic publications. For example, it appears that blogs were used more frequently in order to support the literature review and introduction section of journal articles rather than the methodology or discussion section. Usually the information contained in the cited blogs was related to the reporting of data about the level of uptake of specific technologies for health promotion and support. Blogs were cited less frequently for the documentation of information related to the methods used for data collection and analysis as well as for the demonstration or description of healthcare interventions.

Also, the findings of this study showed some unique evidence about the use of social media as citations in journal articles, and in particular as far as it concerns the *type of contents* and *type of uses* of cited social media. In terms of *type of uses*, the findings showed that the cited social media were not used merely for data reporting on the uptake of various technologies, or the documentation of information related to specific healthcare technologies. Authors also made use of social media in order to support key aspects of their research, such as the documentation of the data collection and analysis process or the methods used. Although the use of social media for the documentation of methodological aspects of the reported research was identified only in the case of 30 articles (out of 59), this phenomenon has not been reported in the past, especially in recent studies on the information seeking behaviour of academics [20].

Finally, in terms of *type of contents*, this study showed that references made to social media were related to tangible types of content. For example, it appears that authors of academic articles were more interested in using social media with tangible contents, such as descriptions and definitions of specific types of healthcare technologies, online research instruments, raw data-sets, statistical models and source codes.

5.1 Implications for the Design of Metadata for Bibliographic Databases

As well as to the advancement of our knowledge about the use of social media in published scholarly communication (i.e. journal articles), the findings of this study have implications also for the design of metadata for bibliographic databases and digital libraries of published medical and health informatics research, such as *PubMed* and *Medline*. The design of search and search result interfaces for such systems should support a better exploitation of the cited social media material in order to improve the information seeking and relevance judgement behaviour of researchers. Some design implications are presented below:

— *Linked data and the Relation metadata element.* The application of metadata should not be limited to the description of the bibliographic details of the articles. Instead, multiple *Relation* metadata elements should be used in order to document the relationship of an article with tangible content that might be communicated through social media citations. In the case of auto-generated metadata, agents should be trained to automatically index the contents of cited social media resources. For example, the Relation metadata element of Dublin Core [21] could be used in order to connect/relate the bibliographic details of an article with tangible content related to its literature review or the methodology section, such as an online video demonstration about a specific piece of technology, a sample frame used in the data collection process, or raw data sets. In the case of linked data, such relationship statements can be expressed in the form of RDF triples [22].

— *Display of details about tangibility in search results.* Although studies have shown that the criterion of Tangibility is an important predicate of the relevance judgment process [23, 24], metadata presented in search results (such as the title, abstract and keywords) do not provide users with information about the tangibility of the retrieved articles in order to help them assess relevance [25]. There is an opportunity for digital libraries to display more analytical information in their search results about the contents of cited social media in order to inform the tangibility of the relevance judgment process. This analytical information could be presented in the form of additional metadata elements that contain details about different types of tangible social media content associated to the articles presented in a search results list. For example, users should be displayed with information about whether or not a specific article is accompanied or linked to tangible types of content such as, lists of sample frames, online research instruments (e.g. questionnaires), raw data sets, visualizations or simulations of data, mathematical equations, high definition images, or online demonstrations and descriptions of a given piece of health technology.

— *Curation life-cycles for sustainable access to cited social media content.* The preservation and curation of the contents of cited social media is important for the long-term sustainability of the quality and authority of the article itself. Due to the malleable nature of the contents of social media, changes that happen across time may affect the credibility of the initial citation and therefore the validity of the article itself (e.g. an article may cite a blog that no longer exists or a sample frame in a Wikipedia article which has been significantly changed). Although in the case of some Web 2.0 applications changes to the original content can be traced, this can become a challenging issue for more dynamic and socially constructed applications (like Blogs, Twitter, Facebook, or YouTube) where information can be edited without leaving a trace of its original content. Moreover, problems related to the privacy and ownership of information in a socially networked environment can pose significant challenges for the development of curation strategies [26].

— *Faceted search mechanisms at the citation level.* To date, users are able to search within the reference lists of articles using advanced search options (e.g. SCOPUS supports such functionality). However, given the complexity and diversity of modern citations further steps should be made to allow the execution of queries focused on specific types and facets of cited social media. For example, users could be provided with the opportunity to search for references made by one or more authors to a specific video on the YouTube, or a known Wikipedia article. Moreover, users should be able to search for cited Wikis, or Blogs, that correspond to specific *contents* (e.g. specific technologies or user aspects of technology), or *types of uses* (e.g. to support the methodology or the literature review of the reported research process). In this manner, metadata is needed to capture detailed information about the cited social media and support advanced search options for users interested in the identifications of specific facets of this type of cited material [27].

— Although there is no common standard or guidelines for the cataloging of social media resources, the deductive content analysis scheme of this study provides a basic set of metadata elements that could be used for the description of social media. Four main metadata elements can be identified. These are: <type_of_social_media>, <format>, <purpose_of_use> and <content>. Each of the four elements can be decomposed into sub-elements. For example, the <content> metadata element can be decomposed into the following sub-elements: <type_of_technology>, <methods_used>, <data_reported>, <user_aspects>. Similarly, the <purpose_of_use> element can be decomposed into the following three sub-elements: <introduction>, <methodology> and <discussion>.

6   Conclusions

The aim of this study was to examine how academics use social media as citations in their publications. In order to address this aim a content analysis was performed using a sample of 629 journal articles in medical informatics research. The content analysis method involved a two-fold process with an automatic and a manual component. The results of this two-fold process advanced our knowledge about the use of social media as citations in academic publications and progressed our understanding about the role of social media for the communication of tangible contents, especially for the support and documentation of various aspects of the research process, such as the literature review and the methodology. Some implications of these findings for the design of digital libraries were discussed, such as the creation of new metadata elements, the design of preservation life-cycles for dynamic social media contents, and the support for faceted search mechanisms at the citation level.

Despite the usefulness of this exploratory study for understanding the role and the nature of cited social media within scholarly communication, further research is needed to support the generalisability of our findings. For example, future research should examine social media citation practices across different fields. Also, ethnographic studies on the use of social media as citations in academic publications could supplement the results of the content analysis with more in depth information about the motivations and perceptions of researchers and academics. Finally, research is in progress to extend our coding scheme, used for content analysis, in order to support a more in-depth analysis of the contents of social media used as citations in academic publications.

References

1. Procter, R., Williams, R., Stewart, J., Poschen, M., Snee, H., Voss, A., Asgari-Targhi, M.: Adoption and use of web 2.0 in scholarly communications. Philosophical Transactions of the Royal Society 368, 4039–4056 (2010)
2. Priem, J., Piwowar, H.A., Hemminger, B.M.: Altmetrics in the wild: Using social media to explore scholarly impact (2012), http://arxiv.org/html/1203.4745v1 (last accessed March 7, 2013)
3. Priem, J., Costello, K.L.: How and why scholars cite on Twitter. In: Proceedings of the 73rd ASIST Annual Meeting, vol. 47, pp. 1–4 (2010)
4. Eysenbach, G.: Can Tweets Predict Citations? Metrics of Social Impact Based on Twitter and Correlation with Traditional Metrics of Scientific Impact. Journal of Medical Internet Research 13(4) (2011), http://www.jmir.org/2011/4/e123/ (last accessed March 7, 2013)
5. Shema, H., Bar-Ilan, J.: Characteristics of Researchblogging.org science Blogs and Bloggers. Altmetrics 11 (2011)
6. Peters, I., Beutelspacher, L., Maghferat, P., Terliesner, J.: Scientific Bloggers under the Altmetric Microscope. In: Proceedings of the Annual Meeting of the American Society for Information Science and Technology (2012)
7. Groth, P., Gurney, T.: Studying Scientific Discourse on the Web using Bibliometrics: A Chemistry Blogging Case Study (2010), http://journal.webscience.org/308/2/websci10_submission_48.pdf (last accessed March 11, 2013)
8. Weller, K., Dröge, E., Puschmann, C.: Citation Analysis in Twitter. In: Approaches for Defining and Measuring Information Flows within Tweets during Scientific Conferences. Science, pp. 1–12 (2011), http://files.ynada.com/papers/msm2011.pdf (last accessed March 11, 2013)
9. Letierce, J., Passant, A., Breslin, J., Decker, S.: Understanding how Twitter is used to widely spread Scientific Messages. In: Proceedings of the WebSci 2010 Extending the Frontiers of Society OnLine (2010), http://journal.webscience.org/314/2/websci10_submission_79.pdf (last accessed March 11, 2013)
10. Kusha, K., Thelwall, M., Abdoli, M.: The role of online videos in research communication: A content analysis of Youtube videos cited in academic publications. JASIST 63(9), 1710–1721 (2012)

11. Syed – Abdul, S., Fernandez-Luque, L., Jian, W.-S., Li, Y.-C., Crain, S., Hsu, M.-H., Wang, Y.-C., Khandregzen, D., Chuluunbaatar, E., Nguyen, P.A., Liou, D.-M.: Misleading health related information promoted through video-based social media: Anorexia on Youtube. Journal of Medical Internet Research 15(2) (2013), http://www.jmir.org/2013/2/e30/

12. Chou, W.-Y., Hunt, Y., Folkers, A., Augustson, E.: Tweetations for cancer survivorship in the Age of Youtube and Social Media: A narrative analysis. JMIR 13(1) (2011), http://www.jmir.org/2011/1/e7/

13. Pedrana, A., Hellard, M., Gold, J., Ata, N., Chang, S., Howard, S., Asselin, J., Ilic, O., Batrounen, C., Stoone, M.: Queer as F**k: Reaching and engaging gay men in sexual health promotion through social networking sites. JMIR 15(2) (2013), http://www.jmir.org/2013/2/e25/

14. Mackert, M., Kim, E., Guadagno, M., Donovan-Kichen, E.: Using twitter for prenatal health promotion: Encouraging a multivitamin habit among college-aged females. In: Global Telehealth, pp. 93–103. IOS Press (2012)

15. Gotsis, M., Wang, H., Spruijt-Metz, D., Jordan-Marsk, M., Valente, T.: Wellness partners: Design and evaluation of a web-based physical activity diary with social gaming features for Adults. JMIR 2(1) (2013), http://www.researchprotocols.org/2013/1/e10/

16. McKendrick, D., Cumming, G.P., Lee, A.: Tweetations for increased use of twitter at a medical conference: A report and a review of the educational opportunities. JMIR 14(6) (2012), http://www.jmir.org/2012/6/e176/

17. Balatsoukas, P., Garoufallou, E., Morris, A., O'Brien, A., Asderi, S., Siatri, R.: Learners' perceptions on the importance of learning object metadata for relevance judgment. International Journal of Metadata, Semantics and Ontologies 7(4), 283–294 (2012)

18. Krippendorff, K.: Content Analysis: An introduction to its methodology. SAGE, London (2004)

19. Buttcher, S., Clarke, C., Cormack, G.: Information Retrieval: Implementing and evaluating search engines. MIT Press (2010)

20. Niu, X.: National study of information seeking behavior of academic researchers in the United States. JASIST 61(5), 869–890 (2010)

21. Dublin Core Metadata Initiative. Dublin Core Metadata Element Set, Version 1.1 (2012), http://dublincore.org/documents/dces/ (accessed April 23, 2013)

22. Dublin Core Metadata Initiative. User Guide (2011), http://wiki.dublincore.org/index.php/User_Guide (accessed April 23, 2013)

23. Tombros, A., Ruthven, I., Jose, J.: How users assess web-pages for information seeking. JASIST 56(4), 327–344 (2005)

24. Balatsoukas, P., Ruthven, I.: An eye-tracking approach to the analysis of relevance judgements on the web. Journal of the American Society for Information Science and Technology 63(9), 1728–1746 (2012)

25. Balatsoukas, P., Morris, A., O'Brien, A.: An evaluation framework of user interaction with metadata surrogates. Journal of Information Science 35(3), 321–339 (2009)

26. Small, H., Kasianovitz, K., Blanford, R., Celaya, I.: What your Tweets tell us about you: Identity, ownership and privacy of Twitter data. The International Journal of Digital Curation 7(1), 174–197 (2012)

27. Russ, A., Kaisser, M.: Exploratory search on social media. In: Serdyukov, P., Braslavski, P., Kuznetsov, S.O., Kamps, J., Rüger, S., Agichtein, E., Segalovich, I., Yilmaz, E. (eds.) ECIR 2013. LNCS, vol. 7814, pp. 845–848. Springer, Heidelberg (2013)

Semantic Accessibility to E-learning Web Services

Juan Manuel Dodero, Manuel Palomo-Duarte, Iván Ruiz-Rube,
and Ignacio Traverso

Informatics Engineering Department
Universidad de Cádiz
{juanma.dodero,manuel.palomo,ivan.ruiz,ignacio.traverso}@uca.es

Abstract. Semantic web technologies are all the more relevant in modern e-learning environments that are built upon existing web resources, applications and services, which cannot be completely hosted and managed by a centralised web-based system. This paper shows how semantic web and linked data technologies can improve the interoperability between virtual learning environments and external web resources. The ReST architectural principles were applied and a semantically enhanced access interface was defined to enable a richer exploitation of the services provided by external web applications for the aim of the e-learning environment. Following this methodology, several open source web applications have been integrated with a popular course management system, in order to improve web services accesibility from the e-learning system.

1 Introduction

Internet and information technologies are modifying traditional education and learning. The Web has motivated an overall rethinking of our learning processes, as well as the accessibility to and the conception of digital resources that support instructional processes. Monolithic e-learning platforms —namely, Learning Management Systems(LMS) or Virtual Learning Environments (VLE)—, provide holistic environments for the delivery and management of learning experiences, but are failing to keep pace with advances in Internet technologies [7]. New personalized learning environments [26,30] are being constructed on the basis of the myriad of applications and services that emerge in the Web [15]. They are built on top of fundamental Internet technologies such as web services [7,23] and semantic web technologies [4,20,16,9]. What can web services provide for new web-based VLE? Broadly, web services can yield an enhanced support for interoperability and systems integration. Traditional LMS and VLEs, however, have managed solely all learning resources employed and issues occurring in the learning courses.

A learning course is typically bundled as an standardized package or *unit of learning* [22] that contains all learning resources needed to deploy the learning experience [12]. A unit of learning includes the pedagogical structure of the course, according to a explicit description —e.g. based on the IMS Learning Design (LD) specification [17]— of learning activities, resources and roles.

E. Garoufallou and J. Greenberg (Eds.): MTSR 2013, CCIS 390, pp. 258–265, 2013.

It serves to deploy the course in the run-time environment of a given VLE or LMS. External web applications and services, however, cannot be described, packaged and distributed as easily as regular web contents.

When students and teachers execute the activities of a course hosted in a VLE, all the contained web resources, applications and services must be executed and the course elements be properly allocated and deployed [14]. First, an activity structure must be instantiated based on a defined course flow. Second, learning resources must be retrieved and web services allocated. Third, generic user roles have to be populated with the actual VLE users that are enroled in the course. After deploying it, people start interacting with applications and services through a predefined role-based participation in learning activities.

The variety of emergent web applications and service functionalities that can be advantageous for e-learning is unpredictable. Interoperability between the VLE and external web services has proven complicated to approach from the perspective of generalized frameworks and specifications, such as the ELF [29] and OSID. These abstract approaches are based on a function-based style of accessing the service provider through a specific model of the service operation [28]. These service models are often too coupled with the consumer application, i.e. the VLE. In the case of external applications and services, students and teachers can access them by their URIs, as these are often explicited in the structured description of the learning activities. The VLE run-time engine must then configure a pedagogical context for the learning activity with information that is usually not included in the course, such as the actual number and structure of groups that must take part in the experience. For example, if a learning experience that uses a wiki must divide students into n-person teams, it might be required a separate wiki instance per team. The VLE must prepare a number of instances of the wiki service and their specific URIs when deploying the course. It is required some information about the team allocation strategy, which is part of the pedagogical model of the course. In such a simple example, the information needed is only a predefined allocation of users into groups, but in the general case it could be more complex. For instance, there might be the need of dynamic assignment of users to teams, depending on the phase of the learning experience, according to a given collaborative learning pattern [19]. In general, a well-defined educational *information model* can be helpful to deploy and enact the web service ecosystem [2] that supports the learning experiences developed. Unfortunately, such information is not often explicitly shared or linked with the applications and services that actually implement the course.

The overall objective of this paper is to show how semantic technologies can improve the interoperability between the VLE and external web applications. Uncoupled solutions like this can improve the integration of and access to external web resources in a VLE. This general objective is broken down in the following subgoals:

1. To build a web-based learning ecosystem, enriching learning activities and resources in order to enable an adequate educational representation and exploitation of external applications and services.

2. Define an educational information model and a domain-specific model that bind the VLE with the semantics of external web resources that can be employed with an educational purpose.
3. Provide VLE students and teachers with an interface to access and exploit externally hosted web applications and services, in order to uncouple course descriptions from the volatile interfaces of such external resources.

2   Related Work

The IMS Tools Interoperability (TI) specification defines an abstract set of guidelines to integrate third party tools and applications in the context of a VLE. IMS TI requires third party applications to be available and hosted in the VLE. This is unrealistic, however, because most functionalities in the current Web are remotely provided by diverse, unpredictably changeable web applications and services in the *cloud* [11].

A simple solution to web service integration in the VLE is to include their Uniform Resource Identifier (URI) within the packaged course description. This solution assumes that the service URI is priorly known. If the course developer, however, must create and deploy an unknown number of service instances in the eventual learning environments, the exact URI might not be known in advance. The CopperCore Service Integration (CCSI) approach [27] propose using WSDL-based descriptions that generically explain the required web service interface. The CCSI approach considers learning services as a type of coarse-grained functional concept that supports users in the course. Examples of such support services include authorization, authentication, mail, messaging, conferencing, search, activity sequencing and assessment. CCSI builds a run-time service as part of the ELF e-learning framework [29], which provides a framework-based API for interacting with e-learning applications. Although CCSI provides the required functionality, it has been shown to be very time consuming and not suitable for the integration of a large number of different services within a course. The tight coupling between the engine and the service does not allow the efficient creation and deployment of course environments.

Personal Learning Environments (PLE) are mashed-up combinations of *widgets* [30] selected by the VLE user. They provide an alternate way of access to external applications and services. The PLE approach is suitable for informal learning experiences, where the activity flow is mostly unstructured and spontaneous [15]. However, for regular instructional paradigms, based on explicit learning designs that rely on well-defined activity sequences, widget-based access do not provide a fine-grain access control to web services. Besides, widgets must be explicitly programmed against the service interface in order to access them properly.

The Generic Service Integration (GSI) approach [13] defines a layer of indirection between the VLE and the web services that support the learning course. The communication between the VLE run-time and the GSI layer is determined by the API of the service. The GSI layer provides a unified API, whereas a specific adaptation to each service must be performed [14]. The GSI approach is a solution to uncouple web services from the VLE. It presents, however, some dependencies with the service API. If the service API changes or evolves, the GSI layer adaptors have to be extended or updated in order to not affect the VLE layer.

3   ASCETA Semantic Accessibility

The ASCETA R&D project was thought as a practical application of web services and semantic technologies, to facilitate the access to and exploitation of web resources with an educational purpose in VLEs. The aim of ASCETA is to improve the integration of readily available web resources, applications and services in which virtual learning experiences are actually developed.

3.1   Methodology

The research methodology of the project has consisted of two different phases. In phase one, the interaction between the VLE and services follows the principles of a ReST architecture [8] and the VLE operates directly over each service API. Since not all services provide a ReSTful API, specific adapters were developed as needed. In phase two, the style of interaction is modified to introduce RDFa and SA-REST [25] descriptions for externally hosted resources.

The ReST-based integration (phase one) and RDF-driven integration (phase two) of web applications and services are described elsewhere [8,9]. It is based on the following core elements:

1. An RDF(S) extension to existing metadata vocabularies used to define the educational information model and domain-specific model of integrated resources.
2. A module for editing and enriching ReST-based resources with RDFa annotations, which are defined in terms of the former RDF(S) vocabularies.
3. An extension or *plugin* to the VLE to enable the exploitation of RDF-enriched resources and services.

The core elements of semantic integration are the vocabularies and ontologies used to describe the educational information model and the domain-specific model of external resources. The educational metadata schema is provided by the Learning Object Metadata (LOM) standard. Domain-specific vocabularies were reused from schema.org. The educational ontology model is based on binding LOM to schema.org RDF vocabularies, similarly to the Learning Resources Metadata Initiative (LRMI) approach. LOM is used due to its extensive support in existing repositories [21]. As for the domain-specific vocabulary model, schema.org *Creative work* and derived concepts are the choice because of their strong coverage, specific utility for the subject matter of the target learning courses (i.e. Digital Humanities), and simplicity of extension[1].

---

[1] http://schema.org/docs/extension.html

All the software systems and modules that result from the actual implementation of the ASCETA project are delivered as open source software, available through the project web site.

3.2   Pilot Studies

The semantic integration approach has been experimented with a set of general-purpose web applications that have turned out useful in modern virtual learning ecosystems. Preferably, though not exclusively, open source software applications have been selected for testing purposes. Pilot applications have been selected on the basis of its utility in trial learning environments (i.e. Computer Science and Digital Humanities courses), which have used such web applications, though they have hitherto been uncoupled and out of scope of the hosting LMS.

A condition that is fulfilled by the piloting web resources is to offer an open API (either ReSTful or not) to interact remotely with. For web resources that did not provide a ReSTful API, specific ad hoc software wrappers were developed for the sake of uniformity when accessing their operations. In some cases, ReST APIs were developed by the open source community posterior to the phase one of our project. That did not affect our integration approach —rather, it was alleviated of additional development effort. Content Management Systems (CMS) [1] and Task Management Systems (TMS) [3] were selected as open source pilot applications in the Web. These were in turn classified into the following categories:

- *General CMS*: Two different web-based CMS were used, namely Drupal and Ximdex CMS. On the one hand, Drupal provides a module to edit RDFa enriched contents according to schema.org vocabularies. On the other hand, Ximdex CMS implements a component based on Apache Stanbol for the automatic enrichment of web contents with RDFa annotations. Both functionalities are useful for the same intent, i.e. to have a useful set of semantically enriched contents.
- *Special CMS*: An analogous procedure was applied to installations of wiki-oriented and blog-oriented web-based CMS, using MediaWiki and WordPress for such purposes, respectively. In the wiki case, the implementation is based on SemanticMediaWiki [18], a MediaWiki extension widely used to semantically enrich wiki contents [6]. In the blog case, a WordPress plugin was developed to edit RDFa metadata specific annotations to text and video blog contents [24].
- *Project-based TMS*: In this case, a slightly different procedure was applied to enrich descriptions of *project* and *task* resources managed by the TMS. Instead of annotating web contents from outbounds, a linked open data revelation method was applied, based on the reverse engineering of the application source code that implements the object-relational mapping layer of the web application [10]. This method delivers a RDF(S) schema or the application model concepts (i.e. users, projects and issues), maps them to standard vocabularies (e.g. users can be described with FOAF, while projects and

issues are described with DOAP) and finally augments the generated views of the web application with automatic RDFa annotations. This method has been applied to a Redmine project management application service, because currently the implementation of this method only works with Ruby-on-Rails source code.

The user interface provided by the VLE was extended with a plugin to provide access to both ReST-based and RDF-enriched services, as explained in [5].

4 Conclusions

The ASCETA project puts the foundations of a web-based learning ecosystem on the basis of semantically enriched resources that decouple the learning environment from external web applications and services. RDF-based extensions to common web-based CMS have been developed and used for that aim. An educational information model based in LOM and a domain-specific model based on common schema.org vocabularies are used to link activities in the VLE with such external resources. Open source VLEs have been extended and provided with an interface to access and exploit semantically enriched resources.

The architecture of the learning ecosystem applies the ReST principles and uses RDF-based technologies to enrich external applications and services. All the development is based on open source software, having popular web applications such as MediaWiki, WordPress and Drupal readily integrated. A special method of semantic enrichment of open source applications has been tested with Redmine. The latter approach is developed as a Ruby-on-Rails component and it is expected to be extended to other web frameworks such as Django and Spring/JPA. The next step will be to potentiate the analytic capabilities of the learning ecosystem with a purpose of facilitating the assessment of e-learning experiences.

Acknowledgements. This work has been sponsored by a grant from the AS-CETA project (P09-TIC-5230) of the Andalusian Government, Spain.

References

1. Bergstedt, S., Wiegreffe, S., Wittmann, J., Moller, D.: Content management systems and e-learning systems-a symbiosis? In: Proceedings of the 3rd IEEE International Conference on Advanced Learning Technologies, pp. 155–159. IEEE (2003)
2. Briscoe, G., de Wilde, P.: Digital Ecosystems: Evolving Service-Orientated Architectures. In: IEEE Int. Conf. on Bio-Inspired Models of Network, Information and Computing Systems, pp. 1–6. IEEE Computer Society (2006)
3. Cabot, J., Wilson, G.: Tools for Teams: A Survey of Web-Based Software Project Portals. Dr. Dobb's, 1–14 (2009)
4. Clark, K., Parsia, B., Hendler, J.: Will the Semantic Web Change Education? Journal of Interactive Media in Education 2004(3), 1–16 (2004)

5. Cornejo, C.M., Ruiz-Rube, I., Dodero, J.M.: Design of learning activities to access web-based thematic dynamic resources. Design and Evaluation of Digital Content for Education 2 (2011)
6. Cornejo, C.M., Ruiz-Rube, I., Dodero, J.M.: Semantic Management of Digital Contents for the Cultural Domain. In: Recent Trends in Information Reuse and Integration, 1st edn., pp. 211–226. Springer (2011)
7. Dagger, D., Connor, A.O., Lawless, S., Walsh, E., Wade, V.P.: Service-Oriented E-Learning Platforms. From Monolithis Systems to Flexible Services. IEEE Internet Computing 11(3), 28–35 (2007)
8. Dodero, J.M., Ghiglione, E.: ReST-Based Web Access to Learning Design Services. IEEE Transactions on Learning Technologies 1(3), 190–195 (2008)
9. Dodero, J.M., Ghiglione, E., Torres, J.: Engineering the life-cycle of semantic services-enhanced learning systems. International Journal of Software Engineering and Knowledge Engineering 20(4), 499–519 (2010)
10. Dodero, J.M., Ruiz-Rube, I., Palomo-Duarte, M., Vázquez-Murga, J.: Open linked data model revelation and access for analytical web science. In: García-Barriocanal, E., Cebeci, Z., Okur, M.C., Öztürk, A. (eds.) MTSR 2011. CCIS, vol. 240, pp. 105–116. Springer, Heidelberg (2011)
11. Dong, B., Zheng, Q., Yang, J., Li, H., Qiao, M.: An e-learning ecosystem based on cloud computing infrastructure. In: 9th International Conference on Advanced Learning Technologies, pp. 125–127 (2009)
12. Duval, E., Verbert, K.: On the Role of Technical Standards for Learning Technologies. IEEE Transactions on Learning Technologies 1(4), 229–234 (2008)
13. de la Fuente Valentin, L., Miao, Y., Pardo, A., Delgado Kloos, C.: A Supporting Architecture for Generic Service Integration in IMS Learning Design. In: Dillenbourg, P., Specht, M. (eds.) EC-TEL 2008. LNCS, vol. 5192, pp. 467–473. Springer, Heidelberg (2008)
14. de la Fuente, L., Pardo, A., Delgado Kloos, C.: Generic Service Integration in Adaptive Learning Experiences using IMS Learning Design. Computers & Education 57(1), 1160–1170 (2011)
15. García-Peñalvo, F.J., Conde, M.A., Alier, M.: Opening Learning Management Systems to Personal Learning Environments. Journal of Universal Computer Science 17(9), 1222–1240 (2011)
16. Jovanovic, J., Gasevic, D., Torniai, C., Bateman, S., Hatala, M.: The Social Semantic Web in Intelligent Learning Environments: state of the art and future challenges. Interactive Learning Environments 17(4), 273–309 (2009)
17. Koper, R., Tattersall, C.: Learning design: A handbook on modelling and delivering networked education and training. Springer (2005)
18. Krötzsch, M., Vrandečić, D., Völkel, M.: Semantic MediaWiki. In: Cruz, I., Decker, S., Allemang, D., Preist, C., Schwabe, D., Mika, P., Uschold, M., Aroyo, L.M. (eds.) ISWC 2006. LNCS, vol. 4273, pp. 935–942. Springer, Heidelberg (2006)
19. McAndrew, P., Goodyear, P., Dalziel, J.: Patterns, designs and activities: Unifying descriptions of learning structures. International Journal of Learning Technology 2(2), 216–242 (2006)
20. Millard, D.E., Doody, K., Davis, H.C., Gilbert, L., Howard, Y., Tao, F., Wills, G. (Semantic Web) Services for e-Learning. International Journal of Knowledge and Learning 4(2-3), 298–315 (2008)
21. Neven, F., Duval, E.: Reusable learning objects: A survey of lom-based repositories. In: Proceedings of the 10th ACM international conference on Multimedia, pp. 291–294. ACM, New York (2002)

22. Olivier, B., Tattersall, C.: The Learning Design Specification. In: Koper, R., Tattersall, C. (eds.) Learning Design. A Handbook on Modelling and Delivering Networked Education and Training, pp. 21–40. Springer, Berlin (2005)
23. Muñoz Organero, M., Muñoz Merino, P.J., Delgado-Kloos, C.: Personalized Service-Oriented E-Learning Environments. IEEE Internet Computing 14(2), 62–67 (2010)
24. Ruiz-Rube, I., Cornejo, C.M., Dodero, J.M.: Accessing learning resources described in semantically enriched weblogs. International Journal of Metadata, Semantics and Ontologies 6(3-4), 197–206 (2012)
25. Sheth, A.P., Gomadam, K., Lathem, J.: SA-REST: Semantically Interoperable and Easier-to-Use Services and Mashups. IEEE Internet Computing 11(6), 91–94 (2007)
26. Taraghi, B., Ebner, M., Till, G., Mühlburger, H.: Personal Learning Environment-A Conceptual Study. International Journal of Emerging Technologies in Learning 5(1), 25–30 (2010)
27. Vogten, H., Martens, H., Nadolski, R., Tattersall, C., Van Rosmalen, P., Koper, R.: CopperCore Service Integration. Interactive Learning Environments 15(2), 171–180 (2007)
28. Wilde, E., Glushko, R.J.: Document Design Matters. Communications of the ACM 51(10), 43–49 (2008)
29. Wilson, S., Blinco, K., Rehak, D.: Service-Oriented Frameworks: Modelling the infrastructure for the next generation of e-Learning Systems (2004)
30. Wilson, S., Liber, P.O., Johnson, M., Beauvoir, P., Sharples, P.: Personal Learning Environments: Challenging the dominant design of educational systems. Journal of e-Learning and Knowledge Society 3(2), 27–38 (2007)

Exploring the Potential for Mapping Schema.org Microdata and the Web of Linked Data

Alberto Nogales, Miguel-Angel Sicilia, Elena García-Barriocanal,
and Salvador Sánchez-Alonso

Information Engineering Research Unit, Computer Science Department,
University of Alcalá, Ctra. Barcelona km. 33.6,
28871 Alcalá de Henares (Madrid), Spain
{alberto.nogales,msicilia,elena.garciab,salvador.sanchez}@uah.es

Abstract. In recent years the exposure of Linked Open Data (LOD) has become widespread, with an increasing number of datasets available and enabling new opportunities for interlinking. In parallel, microdata in several forms has also proliferated mainly as a means to improve the effectiveness of search engines. Concretely, Schema.org consists of a vocabulary for microdata that enriches the information on pages, helping search engines to provide better results. In this paper we explore the potential of mapping Schema.org and the Web of Linked Data. First, mappings between Schema.org terms and terms in Linked Open Vocabularies (LOV) are extracted. Then we use these mappings to obtain an analysis, aimed at gaining insights about the potential impact of this vocabulary in the Web of Linked Data. The results show that is easier to find a mapping between classes than between properties, but the occurrences of these are many more in LOD.

Keywords: Ontologies, microformats, Schema.org, Linked Data, LOV.

1 Introduction

On June 2, 2011, Bing, Google, and Yahoo! announced the joint effort Schema.org[1]. Schema.org ontologies are intended for the creation of microcontents targeted to improving indexing and search systems (Ronallo, 2012). It consists of a vocabulary allowing webmasters to mark up their pages with microdata, e.g. with a set of tags introduced with HTML5. Microdata allows search engines and other applications to have a better understanding of the contents of a Web site. Therefore, users might benefit by being able to find relevant information on the Web with higher precision, taking benefits of that extra information added to the HTML. The importance of Schema.org can be appreciated in the statistics reported by Mika and Potter (2012). Also, Muhleisen and Bizer (2012) showed that the use of microdata has increased in between the different formats to embed structured data. This may be attributed to microdata being the preferred syntax of the Schema.org initiative.

A different approach to making data and content more accessible for machine consumption is that of Linked Open Data (LOD). LOD consists of the publication of

E. Garoufallou and J. Greenberg (Eds.): MTSR 2013, CCIS 390, pp. 266–276, 2013.

open datasets in Resource Description Framework (RDF)[1] format and setting RDF links to connect different data sources. The publication of these data follows the format according to the Linked Data principles (Bizer, Heath and Berners-Lee, 2009). Its objective is extending the Web with a kind of data commons. Linked Data should not be confused with microformats[2], which are another way to extend the Web that do not follow the same set of principles.

As both Schema.org and LOD are bringing structure and vocabularies to the Web, there is a potential in creating bridges between both. This would enable users to get LOD data about pages that are already marked up with Schema.org vocabularies. For doing so, the first step required is some form of mapping between the classes and properties of Schema.org with the main vocabularies used in the Web of Linked Data. In LOD, there are not mandatory vocabularies, but they get adopted and become popular as the different communities adopt and use them. This requires some form of measure of vocabulary usage metrics in the LOD. Currently, that quantified information about the use of classes and properties in it, is available at the Linked Open Vocabulary (LOV)[3] initiative. LOV is a collection of vocabularies from several fields. Its objective is to provide access methods to these vocabularies, the relations between each other's and how they are linked with the Linked Data Cloud.

In this paper, we report an assessment of the potential of linking microcontent with Linked Open Data through the mapping of Schema.org with Linked Open Vocabularies. This represents a first step towards automated approaches targeted to bridge the Web of Data with a microcontent-enabled Web. Results show that only the fifth part of the vocabularies in LOV provides a class mapping between Schema.org and LOD. Talking about properties just a few of them can be mapped with simple methods. In contrast, we discover that the number of occurrences of the properties in LOD is bigger than the class occurrences. That means that the reach of the properties from Schema.org to LOD is higher than in the classes.

The rest of this paper is structured as follows. Section 2 provides a brief background on Schema.org, the Web of Linked Data and their relation. Then, in Section 3 we describe the data preparation and the methods used for obtaining the mappings. Section 4 is devoted to the analysis of the results obtained, the limitations of the methods used and potential usage scenarios. Finally, conclusions and outlook are provided in Section 5.

2   Background

In 2011, Schema.org started to provide their official dump of their ontology in OWL[4] format. As a vocabulary, it addresses multiple areas and is not domain specific, but we can difference two parts. First, it provides a small set of elements to describe primitive data types like numbers or text, in which we can find classes like Boolean,

---

[1] http://www.w3.org/RDF/
[2] http://www.microformats.org
[3] http://lov.okfn.org
[4] http://www.w3.org/TR/owl-ref/

Date or Number. The rest of the classes and properties are used to describe different fields like Organizations, or entities related to Medicine, Media, etc. Nowadays the schema published at the Web can be found in three formats: one is represented in Microdata, then there is an experimental version in RDFa[5] and finally one in OWL which is not fully-up-to-date.

Schema.org has been used in previous researches. Rosati and Mayernik (2013) described an approach to increase the discoverability and connectivity of resources on the Web in which it is use to mark up HTML web pages. Ambiah and Lukose (2013) used Schema.org in a case study to demonstrate the use of a tool that enriches Web pages automatically. An analysis about visualizing contents in various data forms regardless of the devices used can be found in Pastore (2012). Another approach, to resource description, search optimisation and resource discovery can be found in Hawksey, Barker and Campbell (2013) using Schema.org as embedding metadata. Finally in Li et al (2012) an application to publish media fragments and annotations is described using vocabularies defined in Schema.org.

In this paper we analyze the potential of using Schema.org Microdata to final related resources in the Web of Data. As a link between them, we need to use LOV in order to provide us some statistics of the use of it in LOD. LOV provides users a collection of vocabularies from several fields like librarianship, e-commerce or biology. It also collects information about ontologies that represent vocabularies, detailed information about them, statistics related to LOD or graphical relations between vocabularies. LOV has been reported in several previous researches. Méndez and Greenberg (2012) summarized some advances in Knowledge Organization from the perspective of LOD. Some of these vocabularies have been analyzed by Poveda, Suárez and Gómez (2011) to display the reuse of ontologies in Linked Data. A framework that helps to lift raw data sources to semantic interlinked data sources contains a module based on LOV in Scharffe et al (2012).

However, we are contributing with a new look at the use of LOD and microdata in this paper. On the one hand, none of these previous researches have explored mappings between Schema.org and LOD, so we are providing new insights about which classes and properties of the first one are represented in the second. And on the other hand, we have used some statistics of the occurrences found in LOD to measure the potential impact of using these mappings to get LOD associated to Schema.org microdata.

3   Materials and Methods

As said before, our starting point of the work is to map Schema.org terms with the vocabularies collected by the LOV project. So the first step was to download the vocabularies to work with them. An amount of 238 files were downloaded using Speed Download[6] on May 24th of 2013. Once we had the files, we processed the RDF

---

[5] http://www.w3.org/2006/07/SWD/RDFa/
[6] http://www.yazsoft.com

data. All the files from LOV are in format Notation3[7] (.n3), and to work with them we decided to use RDF.rb[8], which is a pure Ruby library working with RDF data.

The second step is to use these mappings with the information obtained from LODStats[9], Demter, Auer and Martin (2012), which is an approach to generate statistics from RDF datasets. It gives us a comprehensive picture of the current state of the Data Web.

We are interested in establishing the mappings at two levels. One will be a mapping between classes, which has exactly the same name. The other mapping will be done based on the first. Taking in account the mapped classes, we need to match one property from the Schema.org class with another property from a class in LOV mapped in the first step. Table 1 and 2 show an example indicating how the mappings are created for both cases.

Table 1. Mappings for classes

id_mapping	schema_uri	lov_uri
1	http://schema.org/Person	http://xmlns.com/foaf/0.1/Person

Table 2. Mappings for properties

id_mapping	schema_class_uri	schema_prop_uri	lov_prop_uri
1	http://schema.org/Person	http://schema.org/familyName	http://xmlns.com/foaf/0.1/familyName

Our mapping has been made developing a Ruby script using RDF.rb library. We have started comparing classes and properties via string. Also, discriminating case sensitive has not been taking in account. Once we have all these mappings we have used the statistics given by LODStats to know the number of occurrences that any of these elements have in LOD. The results obtained in these steps have been compared with which LogMap, Jimenez et al (2011), has provided us. LogMap is a highly scalable matching ontology, supporting the same formats as OWL-API, which can work with classes, properties and instances. It can be run from the command line, as SEALS packages or by Web-Interface.

4   Analysis and Discussion

In this section we present an analysis about the mappings and the number of occurrences of each. We will first report about the most mapped classes and properties and their impact from Schema.org to LOD.

---

[7] http://www.w3.org/TeamSubmission/n3/
[8] http://rdf.rubyforge.org
[9] http://stats.lod2.eu

4.1   Contrasting Keyphrases

In previous sections we have talked about two kinds of mappings, we also have generated these mappings in two steps. Further, we related the mappings obtained in this first step with the information provided by LODStats. In what follows, we are talking about the top mappings achieved in each step in both ways.

First thing we have done is to establish mappings between the classes of Schema.org and LOV. In total 75 different classes have been mapped which is the 17.5% of the classes in Schema.org. We are comparing these results with the ones obtained using the matching tool called LogMap. Taking in account our results, the top 5 classes according to its occurrences can be examined in table 3, where A stands for results provided by our mapping script and B by the ones by LogMap. Also some vocabularies used for the mappings are presented

Table 3. Top class occurrences in LOV

Class Name	LOV Occurrences (A/B)	Example Vocabularies
Event	16/13	AKT Reference Ontology
Person	11/7	Appearances Ontology
Organization	10/9	BioTop
Country	8/6	Government Data Vocabulary
Language	8/6	LOTED Ontology

In table 4, we have the same information but related with the mapping of the properties. In this case only 12 properties have been mapped, just a percentage of 2.06% referring Schema.org properties. In these mappings, 5 different vocabularies have been used. The comparison with LogMap has found only one concordance because it differences between Data Properties and Object Properties.

Table 4. Top properties occurrences in LOV

Class	Property Name	LOV Occurrences (A/B)	Example Vocabularies
Event	description	5/0	AKT Reference Ontology
VideoObject	duration	4/0	EBU Ontology
PaymentChargeSpecification	valuedAddedTaxIncluded	3/0	GoodRelations Ontology
MediaObject	height	3/0	EBU Ontology
AudioObject	width	3/0	EBU Ontology

Based on the comparisons between our mappings and LogMap, we have found different cases: most of the time the numbers of matchings are the same for each vocabulary, sometimes our matchings have more occurrences, sometimes not and a

Table 5. Comparison with LogMap

Case	Num. of Vocabularies	Percentage
Mapping script	10	13.69 %
LogMap matching	13	17.83 %
Equals	44	60.27 %
File error	6	8.21 %
Total	73	100 %

few times LogMap was not able to work with the file, giving an error. In table 5 you can see this information grouped by cases with the percentages of each.

Analyzing the results obtained there are some important points to be noticed. First of all, some of the matchings provided by LogMap seem to improve results because it discriminates special symbols like "-" used to separate two words like "Government-Organization". In other cases it matches similar words like "Organization" and "Organisation". We also have found a case in which, LogMap seems to use synonyms, matching "School" with "College". In these cases LogMap is improving the results, but there are occasions in which our matching finds more occurrences. We have found a lot of times classes matched by LogMap in which one of the classes contains or is contained by the other class, e.g. "RecyclingCenter" with "Center", in our opinion these matchings can not be considered accurate as they seem to be at different levels in the subsumption hierarchy, however, they provide an interesting perspective to looking for approximate matches in the future.

So that means that the number of vocabularies in which the matching has more occurrences than in ours is less than which table 5 indicates. Taking into account these special cases, the number of matchings in which the number of classes is the same is 50 and in which LogMap is higher are only 7. Therefore the percentages change to 68.49% and 9.58% respectively.

Some statistics to know which are the most used vocabularies in these mappings have been created. You can see the information in table 6.

Table 6. Top LOV occurrences in class mappings

Vocabulary name	LOV abbreviation	Mapping occurrences
GoodRelations	gr	16
VIVO	vivo	10
Places	place	8
vCard	vcard	8
EBUCore	ebucore	7

The first ontology in table 6 is GoodRelations, which is a standardized vocabulary for E-Commerce as it is explained in Hepp (2008). The second ontology that we found in this table is VIVO[10] that is related with the VIVO Project and consists of information in the academic and research domain. The rest of the vocabularies are: the Places Ontology[11] for describing places of geographic interest, the vCard Ontology[12] that promotes the use of vCard for the description of people and organizations and EBUCore[13] which was designed to make users benefit from the flexibility of RDF to adapt the names of Classes and Properties to their respective needs.

If we talk about the mappings of the properties we have table 7 representing the same information. Here we found two vocabularies which are also in the previous table like: EBUCore and GoodRelations. We also found new ones like NEPOMUK Calendaring Ontology, Groza et al (2007) that provides vocabulary for describing calendaring data. Friend of a Friend[14] is devoted to linking people and information using the Web. The only match found by LogMap in properties is using this vocabulary, mapping the class "Organization" with the property "genre". Finally Wildlife Ontology[15] describes biological species

Table 7. Top LOV occurrences in property mappings

Vocabulary name	LOV abbreviation	Mapping occurrences
EBUCore	ebucore	13
NEPOMUK Calendar	ncal	5
Friend of a Friend	foaf	3
GoodRelations	gr	3
Wildlife Ontology	wlo	1

4.2   Impact of the Mappings in LOD

Now we are getting some statistics about how the classes and properties mapped before have repercussion in LOD.

After obtaining the maps, we have contrasted them with the information given by LODStats. Here we have searched the number of occurrences given by LODStats by each Class. Taking that into account, the information about the top classes is shown in table 8.

---

[10] http://vivoweb.org
[11] http://vocab.org/places/
[12] http://www.w3.org/TR/vcard-rdf/
[13] http://www.ebu.ch
[14] http://www.foaf-project.org
[15] http://www.bbc.co.uk/ontologies/wildlife/

Table 8. Top Classes occurrences in LOD

Class Name	LOD Occurrences
Person	3,217,769
Organization	237,655
Event	8,235
City	4,589
Dataset	612

A good remark about table 8 would be to measure which LOV vocabularies have more representation in these occurrences. For example the vocabulary AKT Reference Ontology provides more occurrences than the others, over three millions. Another vocabularies with representation are Friend of a Friend Vocabulary, with two millions more or less, and Semantic Web for Research Communities.

In table 9 we have the same information for properties. In this case we have searched in LODStats using only the name of the properties not taking in account the matchings of the classes.

Table 9. Top Properties occurrences in LOD

Property Name	LOD Occurrences
name	16,656,930
description	8,784,687
height	4,718,986
width	4,718,984
gender	2,848,501

4.3   Limitations

In this section we are reviewing the limitations found through the realization of the experiment. First of all we are talking about the limitations of LOV. As you can see at the webpage some of the vocabularies are not available for two different reasons: sometimes it has an invalid URL or there is a problem of content negotiation and sometimes the .n3 file that contents the information has been never fetched. Also RDF.rb could not process some files. In that way we have not been able to work with all the vocabularies.

If we talk about the limitations of using LODStats. We can see in the website that 1461 datasets have errors with the dumps or with the SPARQL endpoints. So we can not assure that all the information provided is correct.

Finally we have found some limitations with our matching script. On one hand, some vocabularies could not be processed. On the other hand, comparing it with LogMap, we have realized several things. We are not discriminating special symbols like '-', which can be used to separate some words in a class, not being it different. We are not using synonyms, so two words with the same meaning could be matched. Also two words written in different English (American or British), which could have a difference in one letter, are not mapped well.

4.4   Potential Usage

Finally we are exposing an example to demonstrate how the different vocabularies are connected and how we can obtain benefits of the embedded metadata and its interlinkings with the Web of Linked Data.

Let's suppose we start from a concrete Web page, which contains metadata from Schema.org. A list of pages containing it is in the Web Data Commons[16] project, which extracts data from webs with microdata providing statistics. We have searched for a web using Schema.org which tags cities, e.g. www.secondcasa.com. We have looked for information related to "Berlin", obtaining some results.

In the next step we have obtained all the microdata contained for one of the pages from the search. For that we have used the Google Structure Data Testing Tool[17] that allows user to obtain all the microdata contained in a web classifying it by elements, types (giving the metadata form used) and properties. In our example, results throw that there is an element tag with Schema.org, which pertains to "PostalAddress" class and with a property called "addressLocality". The markup HTML contained in the web is below.

```
<span itemprop="address" itemscope
itemtype="http://schema.org/PostalAddress">

<h3>Apartamento de vacaciones<br />Berlin City Schoeneberg</h3>

<span itemprop="streetAddress">Cheruskerstrasse 10 </span><br />

<span itemprop="addressCountry">DE</span>
-<span itemprop="postalCode">10829</span>
<span itemprop="addressLocality">Berlin</span><br />

<span itemprop="addressRegion">Berlín </span> (Alemania)</span></div>
```

[16] http://webdatacommons.org
[17] http://www.google.com/webmasters/tool/richsnippets/

Taking in account what is told before, if we had a matching of the "PostalAddress" class related with the property "addressLocality" through the LOV vocabulary "frapo" (Funding, Research Administration and Project Ontology. Having an endpoint SPARQL over the whole Web of Data. Using a SPARQL sentence, we can recover extra information about Berlin that can be added to the initial webpage. An example of that SPARQL sentence could be:

> *PREFIX frapo: <http://purl.org/cerif/frapo/>. PREFIX.*
>
> *SELECT * WHERE {*
>
> *?s schema:addresLocality "Berlin".*
>
> *}*

5   Conclusions and Outlook

We have released a set of mappings from Schema.org to LOD. In order to get real statistics of the mappings, we have filled the gap between them using LOV. That is a collection of vocabularies referenced in LOD, so we can measure out the real impact of Schema.org in LOD.

We have done two types of mappings. The first is a mapping between the names of the classes. Second one is based on the results of the first, so we are matching the properties from the mapped classes in Schema.org with the equivalents in LOV. As we said before we are mapping Schema.org with LOV, and the results obtained in it with LOD. So our matching is done into two steps.

Finally we have drawn some conclusions with the statistics obtained grouping by classes, properties and vocabularies. We can conclude that we have more mappings between Classes than between Properties. Instead, the impact of the Properties in LOD is bigger, having more occurrences. We have compared these results with other matching tools to know which are the limitations of our mappings.

In future works we are measuring how to take advance of the benefits of Schema.org, the mappings and statistics we have obtained. As we know that Schema.org is used to mark-up WebPages for doing them more readable for search engines.

Acknowledgements. The work leading to these results has received funding from the European Union Seventh Frame-work Programme, in the context of the SemaGrow (ICT-318497), http://www.semagrow.eu/

References

1. Ronallo, J.: HTML5 Microdata and Schema.org. Code4Lib Journal (2012)
2. Mika, P., Potter, T.: Metadata Statistics for a Large Web Corpus. In: Proc. of the Linked Data Workshop (LDOW) at the International World Wide Web Conference (2012)

3. Muhleisen, H., Bizer, C.: Web Data Commons – Extracting Structured Data from Two Large Web Corpora. In: Proc. of the 5th Linked Data on the Web Workshop (LDOW) (2012)
4. Bizer, C., Heath, T., Berners-Lee, T.: Linked Data – The Story So Far. International Journal on Semantic Web and Information Systems (IJSWIS) 5, 1–22 (2009)
5. Rosati, A., Mayernik, M.: Facilitating Data Discovery by Connecting Related Resources. Semantic Web Journal (2013)
6. Ambiah, N., Lukose, D.: Enriching WebPages with Semantic Information. In: Proc. Int'l. Conf. on Dublin Core and Metadata Applications, pp. 1–11 (2012)
7. Pastore, S.: Website Development and Web Standards in the Ubiquitous World: Where Are We Going? Wseas Transactions on Computers (2012)
8. Hawkscy, M., Barker, P., Campbell, L.M.: New Approaches to Describing and Discovering Open Educational Resource. In: Proc. of OER 2013 (2013)
9. Li, Y., Wald, M., Omitola, T., Shadbolt, N., Wills, G.: Synote: Weaving Media Fragments and Linked Data. Linked Data on the Web (2012)
10. Méndez, E., Greenberg, J.: Linked Data for Open Vocabularies and HIVE's Global Framework. El profesional de la Información (2012)
11. Poveda, M., Suárez, M.C., Gómez, A.: The Landscape of Ontology Reuse in Linked Data. In: Proc. of Ontology Engineering in a Data-driven World (OEDW) (2012)
12. Scharffe, et al.: Enabling Linked Data Publication with the Datalift Platform. In: Proc. AAAI Workshop on Semantic Cities (2012)
13. Auer, S., Demter, J., Martin, M., Lehmann, J.: LODStats – An Extensible Framework for High-performance Dataset Analytics. In: ten Teije, A., Völker, J., Handschuh, S., Stuckenschmidt, H., d'Acquin, M., Nikolov, A., Aussenac-Gilles, N., Hernandez, N. (eds.) EKAW 2012. LNCS, vol. 7603, pp. 353–362. Springer, Heidelberg (2012)
14. Jiménez-Ruiz, E., Cuenca Grau, B.: LogMap: Logic-Based and Scalable Ontology Matching. In: Aroyo, L., Welty, C., Alani, H., Taylor, J., Bernstein, A., Kagal, L., Noy, N., Blomqvist, E. (eds.) ISWC 2011, Part I. LNCS, vol. 7031, pp. 273–288. Springer, Heidelberg (2011)
15. Hepp, M.: GoodRelations: An Ontology for Describing Products and Services Offers on the Web. In: Gangemi, A., Euzenat, J. (eds.) EKAW 2008. LNCS (LNAI), vol. 5268, pp. 329–346. Springer, Heidelberg (2008)
16. Groza, T., Handschuh, S., Möller, K.: The NEPOMUK Project – On The Way to The Social Semantic Desktop. In: Proc. I-SEMANTICS, pp. 201–211 (2007)

Semantically Enhanced Interactions between Heterogeneous Data Life-Cycles

Analyzing Educational Lexica in a Virtual Research Environment

Basil Ell[1], Christoph Schindler[2], and Marc Rittberger[2]

[1] Karlsruhe Institute of Technology (KIT),
Karlsruhe, Germany
basil.ell@kit.edu,
[2] German Institute for International Educational Research (DIPF),
Frankfurt am Main, Germany
{schindler,rittberger}@dipf.de

Abstract. This paper highlights how Semantic Web technologies facilitate new socio-technical interactions between researchers and libraries focussing research data in a Virtual Research Environment. Concerning data practices in the fields of social sciences and humanities, the worlds of researchers and librarians have so far been separate. The increased digitization of research data and the ubiquitous use of Web technologies change this situation and offer new capacities for interaction. This is realized as a semantically enhanced Virtual Research Environment, which offers the possibility to align the previously disparate data life-cycles in research and in libraries covering a variety of inter-activities from importing research data via enriching research data and cleansing to exporting and sharing to allow for reuse. Currently, collaborative qualitative and quantitative analyses of a large digital corpus of educational lexica are carried out using this semantic and wiki-based research environment.

Keywords: Virtual Research Environments, Research Infrastructures, Digital Libraries, Semantic Web technologies.

1 Introduction

As more and more digital libraries such as the Europeana[1] or services of the German National Library[2] come to exist and make their content available using Semantic Web standards, new opportunities arise for research projects to exploit these resources. These resources offer new capacities for research, which can be addressed by Virtual Research Environments offering a variety of methods and tools [7,18].

---

[1] http://www.europeana.eu
[2] http://www.dnb.de/EN/Service/DigitaleDienste/
LinkedData/linkeddata_node.html (2013-08-19)

E. Garoufallou and J. Greenberg (Eds.): MTSR 2013, CCIS 390, pp. 277–288, 2013.

In this paper, we describe in detail how Semantic Web technologies can be applied to enable new socio-technical interactions between researchers and libraries based on research data in a Virtual Research Environment. While typically the data life-cycles of digital libraries and of researchers are separated, we exemplify how semantically enhanced Virtual Research Environments offer concrete capacities for interaction between these worlds. Semantic Web technologies offer to these kinds of research environments a possibility for heterogeneous data production, publication, and sharing, supporting a main affordance of data practices in these fields: multiple layers for overlapping and interacting data life-cycles.

An example is given of a concrete research practice, i.e. the qualitative and quantitative analysis of a large digital corpus of educational lexica. The semantically enhanced research environment is built upon Semantic MediaWiki [10]. Additionally, new SMW extensions addressing requirements of research practices are developed. The VRE is created within the project "Semantic MediaWiki for Collaborative Corpora Analysis" (SMW-CorA) in view of concrete needs, taking a participatory and agile design approach based on ongoing requirement elicitation with researchers carrying out their long-term research project within this environment.

The paper is organized as follows: Section 2 gives an overview of the state of the art in the fields of Virtual Research Environments, libraries and the Semantic Web. Afterwards, the design approaches and the support of researchers are described in Section 3, followed by a description of the realized heterogeneous research data life-cycle and its interactions within the semantically enhanced Virtual Research Environment in Section 4. These activities are highlighted in respect of the role of Semantic Technologies in Section 5. The paper concludes with a discussion and an outlook in Section 6.

2   Virtual Research Environments, Digital Libraries, and the Semantic Web

Today, Virtual Research Environments (VREs) aim to enhance research by using the capabilities of networked technologies, distributed resources and computational power.[3] While previously the facilitation of research in the fields of science and technology has been focussed, the World Wide Web is beginning to impact on the fields of humanities and social sciences, addressing and enforcing collaboration of researchers in projects and beyond. Some VREs have started to use Semantic Web technologies in order to enhance research practices. *MyExperiment* is one example, which allows users to create, share and publish workflows of scientists [5]. Accordingly, resources are semantically described and published as RDF data. Furthermore, the VRE *ourSpaces* [6] uses an ontological framework for provenance [12], semantic policy reasoning for access management of resources [17], and a user interface to create metadata. There is still a lack of VREs missing that offer semantically-enhanced interactions on the research data

---

[3] Some VREs are listed at `http://misc.jisc.ac.uk/vre/projects` (2013-08-19)

level. Our VRE SMW-CorA allows users to semantically interact in various ways with research data for which the import process and the formal annotation is described in [16,14,15].[4] In comparison to other VREs, SMW-CorA integrates the research data itself in a semantic environment and enables researchers to carry out research directly on a semantic level: underlying research data as well as data created via research interactions are represented semantically whereas in previous approaches an additional translation process is necessary.

In the domain of Semantic Web, Auer et al. [1] recently described a life-cycle of Linked Data. Beyond the scope of this work by Auer, we would like to emphasize the possible intersections and overlappings of various life-cycles, which we address in a research environment and its interactions with a digital library in a concrete field of humanities and social sciences. The background is that data practices in research and the prospects of data sharing are identified as a conundrum, a problem which has to be addressed for particular research communities and their concrete interactions in research practice [3]. In this paper, the interaction between the library and research data practices is considered in detail where the data and its different life-cycles will be focused.

3   Design and Method

A recent large international survey of social media indicates that Semantic Web technology offers great capacities to enhance research and data practices. The study shows that social media are already used "at all points of the research life-cycle, from identifying research opportunities to disseminating findings at the end" [13]. Nevertheless, the challenge is raised especially in the fields of humanities that requirements should be articulated by the scholars themselves [2] and the solutions should be aligned to specific research communities [3].

Therefore, a specific approach is used for designing concrete capacities of interaction in research practice: a participatory design approach with agile development has been carried out, as required for Virtual Research Environments [4,18]. Apart from researchers, staff members working with a digital library (Research Library for the History of Education, BBF) were involved as active participants in the requirement elicitation and realization process. For establishing ongoing feedback loops we organized several on-site meetings and continued to hold online team meetings in the course of the project. Further, the iterative development, the requirement elicitation as well as the testing of the realized functionalities relied on two researchers in the field of history of education who are carrying out their research in the VRE. After introducing the VRE, in particular the features, the syntaxes of MediaWiki and Semantic MediaWiki to the researchers, they learned to carry out their research within this environment and to explore the data by writing queries while being assisted when necessary by the developers. For two years the two PhD projects manually integrated more than 60 lexica and performed more than 17.700 edits. For the future it is planned to evaluate

---

[4] Further realizations of SMW as a VRE are Docupedia (http://www.docupedia.de), [9] as an archaeological infrastructure, and [11] as an archaeological corpus.

i) the applicability of the VRE to further research projects within the domain of social sciences and humanities, and ii) to assess the usability via cognitive walkthroughs and expert interviews. Recently, we started to realize a VRE for analyzing historical school magazines as a first step towards the assessment of its applicability.

4   The Research Data Life-Cycle and Its Interactions

Data providers may adhere to a data life-cycle model such as the DCC Curation Life-cycle Model [8]. While this model covers actions such as the access to the data by designated users and reusers and the action of receiving data in accordance with documented collecting policies, this model focuses the curator perspective to research data and needed interactions. Given a landscape with multiple data collections maintained by diverse initiatives where overlap exists regarding the digital objects and databases they are centered around, interactions not foreseen by the DCC model can take place. Data consumers e.g. researchers who perform research on data retrieved from a digital library may add new levels of data, enrich it with further information, add missing pieces, create abstractions and aggregations, complement it with new data, add new perspectives or identify and correct errors in the data. The main interactions – described in more detail in subsequent sections – in our realization of a heterogeneous life-cycle model are as follows:

Importing Research Data: Research data such as historical lexica that are hosted by a source such as a digital library and that are relevant for a particular research project carried out within the VRE are imported.

Enriching Research Data: Research data imported into the VRE or created within the VRE are enriched with further information, missing pieces are added, abstractions and aggregations are created, they are complemented with new data, and perspectives are added.

Data Cleansing: Errors in the data are identified and corrected.

Exploring and Analyzing: Unstructured and structured content can be explored; structured content can be qualitatively and quantitatively analyzed.

Export and Sharing: Content can be selected and exported to allow for reuse by third parties.

Note that these interactions need not be executed in any specific sequence. They can be carried out at any time, in parallel, in any order and an arbitrary number of times. Moreover, they are dependent on and enabled by semantic metadata. In the following sections each of these interactions are discussed. Beyond performing interactions with the digital library, the research projects carried out within the VRE may interact due to overlap in lexica relevant to their projects, as well as with life-cycles of data within the Semantic Web in general.

4.1   Importing Research Data

As mentioned above, the research data of the exemplarily realization of the VRE are historical lexica. Lexica that are of interest here are mainly available at the digital library Scripta Paedagogica Online (SPO),[5] hosted by the Research Library for the History of Education (BBF)[6] which has indexed the lexica and rendered them accessible online as image files as part of their library life-cycle. The corpus contains a total amount of nearly 22,000 articles and more than 25 lexica. Each lexicon is bibliographically described as a collected edition in the library database allegro-C and the digital library environment Goobi.[7]

The data consists of images of scanned pages and pertinent metadata. Therein, four levels of entities, their properties and relations are formalized (lexicon, volume, lemma, and image). This collection is accessible via an OAI interface.[8] A custom-made application of the VRE communicates with this interface, creates representations reflecting the levels of entities within the VRE, and imports the scanned images [16]. How this tool creates representations of the data within the VRE can be specified using XSLT (Extensible Stylesheet Language Transformations) documents. The development of a custom import tool is necessary, if the data to be imported are not available via an OAI interface.

Several Semantic Web vocabularies were imported into the VRE to represent the available metadata. These are: FOAF, PRISM, BIBO, SKOS, and DC.[9] Using these well-known vocabularies has benefits since this offers the reusability of exported data by third parties as discussed in Section 4.5.

Additionally to the life-cycle of the digital library the researcher themselves have their own life-cycles of creating and using research data. Thereby they define the scope of relevant lexica in respect to their research question which is iteratively adjusted while getting new insights in the research process. To offer these capacities of integrating lexica which are not digitized and available at the digital library SPO, the *OfflineImport* feature was developed. This feature allows creating pages for lexica, volumes, lemmata, and images given a minimal set of metadata with minimal effort for the researcher. Researchers can annotate the pages of these lexica and perform their analysis in the same way as the automatically integrated lexica. Thus, the data life-cycles of the digital library and the research carried out within the VRE are interacting thus offering feedback in an additional direction: Digital libraries are thus informed about potential consumers of relevant research data, they can set priorities in their digitization activities, and inform the researchers once the requested content has been digitized.[10]

---

[5] The lexica are available at `http://bbf.dipf.de/digitale-bbf/scripta-paedagogica-online/ digitalisierte-nachschlagewerke`

[6] `http://bbf.dipf.de/en`

[7] See `http://www.allegro-c.de/` and `http://www.goobi.org`

[8] An OAI interface implements the Protocol for Metadata Harvesting (OAI-PMH) defined by the Open Archives Initiative (`http://www.openarchives.org/`)

[9] FOAF (Friend of a Friend ontology), PRISM (Publishing Requirements for Industry Standard Metadata), BIBO (The Bibliographic Ontology), SKOS (Simple Knowledge Organization System), and DC (DCMI Metadata Term).

[10] While these interactions are in principle possible and are technologically already realized within our VRE, the processes are yet to be established with the BBF.

4.2   Enriching Research Data

Research data such as the imported lemmata need to be annotated to facilitate analysis. In the social sciences this process of annotating segments of text is referred to as *coding* where annotation facilitates qualitative and quantitative analysis of the content. Since the research data, the historical lexica, are integrated as images from scanned pages, parts of images are annotated instead of parts of texts. Therefore, the *SemanticImageAnnotator* was developed and published as an extension of MediaWiki that allows to select and annotate (either with free annotations or existing thesauri or classification systems) rectangular areas on images.[11,12]

As an example of an annotated part of an image, a section of a lemma of a lexicon can be annotated with i) the type of argument used by the author, such as a moral or ideological argument, ii) the topic that is subject of the argument, and iii) the position taken by the author towards this topic. Furthermore, the affiliation of the author, such as the affiliation to a religious institution, can be stored on the author's page. Thus, by coding and linking the imported and created research data, a semantic network of relevant entities is created by the researchers. Each annotation is stored as an object that links to the image and has semantic properties such as the coordinates on the image, categories, tags, and any other property the researcher wishes to assign. This network can then be subject to qualitative and quantitative analysis (as discussed in Section 4.4) where this network serves the purpose of a surrogate for the underlying research data which is not computer-processable.

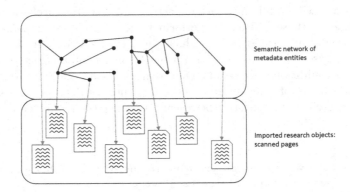

Semantic network of metadata entities

Imported research objects: scanned pages

Fig. 1. The layers of research data and the semantic network

---

[11] This technique can be applied in further use cases of qualitative social sciences and humanities projects where images have to be coded (annotated). Further uses for tool are the annotation of technical diagrams (construction plans, floor plans), pieces of visual art, photos where people and objects are annotated, and the like.

[12] Available at: http://www.mediawiki.org/wiki/ Extension:Semantic_Image_Annotator

This semantic network (depicted in Figure 1) consists of two layers. The bottom layer consists of the imported images which are not computer-processable. The layer above consists of the semantic network where research data are represented as nodes that are linked with further nodes depicting the imported metadata (lexicon, volume, lemma, etc.) as well as entities created within the VRE. Data in both levels can be maintained by multiple life-cycles, thereby establishing interactions between digital libraries, research projects and further initiatives and data sources. When referring to entities during coding, these entities do not need to exist and can be created automatically.

To give an example for an analysis that exploits this network, imagine the following situation: The concept of *Affenliebe* (infatuation) is mentioned in three lemmata L1, L2 and L3 which are authored by three persons P1, P2, and P3 who are affiliated to the institutions I1, I2, and I3, respectively. The term is negatively connotated in L1 and L2 but positively connotated in L3 thus the set of institutions is clustered into two groups regarding the attitude towards this concept: {I1, I2} and {I3}. Furthermore for I3 it is known that, contrary to the institutions I1 and I2, lemmata authored by members of I3 are usually characterized by a religious perspective. This distinction may serve as a basis for explaning the clustering.

Besides linking research data by coding and linking created entities with other created entities, entities can also be linked to entities outside of the VRE. For this purpose we co-developed the *SemanticWebBrowser*[13] extension. On an entity's page, further URIs referring to this entity can be stored. For example, on the page representing an author of a lemma, the author's unique identifier[14] as used by the authority file of the German National Library (DNB) can be stored. At the bottom of each page a fact box displays all property and value pairs, such as Profession: Tutor, that are stored within the local page. The *SemanticWebBrowser* extends this list by external facts – property and value pairs retrieved by retrieving RDF data available at this URI. For example, the property and value pair Date of birth: 1900 could be retrieved from data provided by the DNB. Therefore, researchers can become aware of externally available data and decide for manually importing this data.[15]

4.3 Data Cleansing

Data imported from external sources such as a digital library could contain errors. Further possible sources of error are the import process or the work of other researchers within the VRE. Since these errors can distort results of analyses, researchers need to be able to correct an error or to mark an error and ask for help. Therefore, the researchers can specify in the VRE that they

---

[13] Available at http://www.mediawiki.org/wiki/Extension:Semantic_Web_Browser

[14] For example for Josef Spieler: http://d-nb.info/gnd/117483885/about/rdf

[15] Remaining issues of the beta version of this SMW extension are: 1) to automatically identify additional URIs for an entity, and 2) to enable the users to select which externally available facts to import.

identified and corrected an error, whereby they can describe in a *DataCorrection* element the value they replaced, the reason why it had to be changed and the source this decision is based on. Here, the corrective action can be the removal of a triple (such as *Josef Spieler, date of birth, 1900*) or addition of a triple or both. These corrections are stored as objects carrying semantic properties which offers the possibility for tracing back the changes of structured data within the VRE and between the life-cycles. For example, a list of modifications can automatically be compiled with background information for a source such as a digital library, to inform the original provider of this data about the encountered errors and to publish these corrections so that other consumers can adapt their data as well. This list of modifications and justifications can be exported using the semantic data format RDF. Once confirmed by a data provider, a correction performed within a VRE can be turned into e.g. a SPARQL UPDATE or SQL INSERT command and executed by the provider of the remote data source.

The data correction workflow is depicted in Figure 2. In order to correct the data (which is either imported or created within the VRE), the researcher edits the respective wiki page where the imported data is stored, adds the code `{{DataCorrection}}` and saves the page. This leads to the display of a small box on the page which contains a link to a form where data about the correction can be entered. After editing the correction object, this box displays data entered via the form.

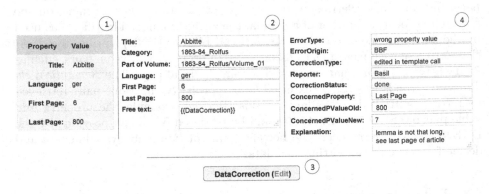

Fig. 2. The data correction feature. The value 800 in (1) is wrong. The page can be edited as shown in (2) and the value can be corrected. When saving the page the DataCorrection box is displayed on the page as shown in (3). The edit button within this box leads to an edit form as shown in (4) where details about the correction can be provided.

At the time of the submission of this paper to the best of our knowledge no ontology exists that allows to represent patches to ontologies. While a Graph Update Ontology[16] exists, this ontology is intended to describe which changes to apply to an ontology automatically. It does not allow specifying the error

---

[16] http://webr3.org/specs/guo/

and to provide evidence or arguments in natural language targeted at the data maintainer, which needs to decide whether to agree and apply each patch. This is a main need of the library to start their quality maintenance activities and requirement for interaction capacities on this level between library and research life-cycles.

4.4 Exploring and Analyzing

For the purpose of exploring the VRE's content, researchers can create and embed queries written in ASK – the query language of SMW – and thus create dynamic views of the content. Examples for these queries are a list of relevant lexica for a certain project that contains a lemma that is annotated with certain terms from a taxonomy or a depiction of dates of birth of lemma authors for a certain lexicon on a timeline. Figure 3 shows an example of a qualitative analysis: the visualization of reference types in annotated lemmata. A lemma can refer to another lemma within the same lexicon (internal reference), to an author (reference to author), and to another publication (reference to literature). For each type of reference each annotation is depicted with a square which is either grey-colored if it does not represent a reference of this type or colored depending on the type of reference it represents.

Fig. 3. Qualitative analysis: visualization of reference types in annotated lemmata

4.5 Export and Sharing

SMW provides facilities to export query results in non-semantic formats such as CSV and JSON, but also to export content as RDF data. Besides sharing information and patches about incorrect data available in external sources as discussed in Section 4.3, results of the researchers' efforts (such as the efforts to enrich and interlink the research data and to create new entities) can be exported as well. Here, the identifiers from imported vocabularies, as described in Section 4.1 are used. For example, if the property *knows* is imported from the FOAF vocabulary, while exporting RDF data for an entity that uses this property then instead of the wiki's own identifier for this property, *foaf:knows* is used which is the identifier of the imported property. This increases the prospects for the exported data to be readily reusable and integrable in other contexts due to the use of well-known vocabularies.

5   Potentials of Semantic Web Technologies

The exemplarily realization of the VRE for the analysis of educational lexica offers several capacities for interactions between the life-cycles of digital libraries and research. On this basis it is possible to summarize the following potentials:

- Import of research data from a digital library is preceded by importing existing vocabularies into the VRE. Research data can then be stored and represented using terms from these standardized vocabularies. The benefits of using these vocabularies are the increased prospects for the data to be readily reusable and integrable in other contexts by third parties. Storing information about equivalent resources residing outside the VRE enables referencing of these entities and display of externally available data.
- The result of the enrichment activities, the semantic network, can be queried and serves as input to qualitative and quantitative analyses. Nevertheless, the layers – where data has been imported from – remain separable but individually semantically addressable. Results of these analyses are dynamic since they depend on the query results as input thus reflecting the current state of the semantic network.
- Annotations created with the *SemanticImageAnnotator* allow to specify which research project an annotation belongs to. This additional information allows separating the annotations of the distinct projects.
- The schema used to represent and link entities can be updated at any time by introducing and using new categories and properties. By using a so far unknown property or category the VRE's ontology is extended thus easily offering a semantic continuum for providing a free degree of formalization in articulation.
- Each object created using the *DataCorrection* feature stores information that enable users to compile lists of correction proposals for each source. Informing the data provider about these errors can benefitial for the provider as well as for other consumers of this data. Patches can be shared with other consumers as well.
- A missing value can be made explicit by using so-called gardening properties. Regarding a missing value for a property P, for the property *missing value for property* the value P can be stored. A gardening page lists all pages where a certain property value is missing. This can guide the enrichment process.

6   Discussion and Outlook

In this paper we describe a semantically enhanced and wiki-based Virtual Research Environment which addresses socio-technical interactions between researchers and digital libraries offering new ways of collaboration throughout their different life-cycles. In detail, we show how these interactions are supported and enhanced through Semantic Web technologies balancing thoroughly and fine-grained the intersections between library, research and the Semantic

Web in general. While the benefits of the utilized Semantic Web technologies are manifold and enable addressing and capturing of heterogeneous data practices, the realization exemplifies the need to adjust the environment to these concrete practices. Different tasks and quality aspects of the life-cycles have thus been implemented. While the realization targets a specific community rooted in the history of education, the supported tasks, the technology and the method developed within the project can be transferred to and be reused in multiple research endeavours since the functionality they provide is not specific to the needs of this particular research. It remains to be evaluated whether in future expansion of our focus these tools are applicable. Concrete examples for transfer and reuse of technical developments are the *SemanticImageAnnotator*, the *SemanticWebBrowser* and the established workflows for data corrections.

Furthermore, designing for concrete research practices and offering a flexibility of the environment needs to take into account that an ongoing support is required until the end of a research project in order to stabilize the endeavor and ensure the scientific output. Currently we are preparing to extend the interaction capacities of the VRE with tools for further types of research data such as videos and interview transcripts. Designing these interaction-aware Virtual Research Environments is one step towards future ecologies of small to large research projects and data providers where data flows between the participants lead to enriched and improved data thus providing benefits in a multitude of collaborations.

Acknowledgements. This project is funded by the German Research Foundation (DFG) entitled: Entwicklung einer Virtuellen Forschungsumgebung für die Historische Bildungsforschung mit Semantischer Wiki-Technologie - Semantic MediaWiki for Collaborative Corpora Analysis (RI 803/10-2, STU 170/21-2) in the domain of Scientific Library Services and Information Systems (LIS). It is realized in a co-operation between the German Institute for International Educational Research (DIPF), the Karlsruhe Institute of Technology (KIT), the Library for Research on Educational History (BBF), and historical educational researchers mainly of the Georg-August-University Göttingen. We are grateful that Rudi Studer, Denny Vrandečić, Elena Simperl, Cornelia Veja, Klaus-Peter Horn, Anne Hild, Anna Stisser, Benedikt Kämpgen, Martin Wünsch, Sabine Liebmann, Stefan Cramme, and Gwen Schulte have actively supported our endeavor.

References

1. Auer, S., et al.: Managing the Life-Cycle of Linked Data with the LOD2 Stack. In: Cudré-Mauroux, P., et al. (eds.) ISWC 2012, Part II. LNCS, vol. 7650, pp. 1–16. Springer, Heidelberg (2012)
2. Borgman, C.L.: The Digital Future is Now: A Call to Action for the Humanities. Digital Humanities Quarterly 3(4) (2010)
3. Borgman, C.L.: The conundrum of sharing research data. Journal of the American Society for Information Science and Technology 63(6), 1059–1078 (2012)

4. Carusi, A., Reimer, T.: Virtual Research Environment collaborative landscape study. JISC, Bristol (2010)
5. De Roure, D., Goble, C., Stevens, R.: The design and realisation of the Virtual Research Environment for social sharing of workflows. Future Generation Computer Systems 25(5), 561–567 (2009)
6. Edwards, P., Pignotti, E., Eckhardt, A., Ponnamperuma, K., Mellish, C., Bouttaz, T.: ourSpaces – Design and Deployment of a Semantic Virtual Research Environment. In: Cudré-Mauroux, P., et al. (eds.) ISWC 2012, Part II. LNCS, vol. 7650, pp. 50–65. Springer, Heidelberg (2012)
7. Fraser, M.: Virtual research environments: Overview and activity. Ariadne 44, 31–40 (2005)
8. Higgins, S.: The dcc curation lifecycle model. In: Larsen, R.L., Paepcke, A., Borbinha, J.L., Naaman, M. (eds.) JCDL, p. 453. ACM (2008)
9. Huvila, I.: Being Formal and Flexible: Semantic Wiki as an Archaeological e-Science Infrastructure. In: Revive the Past: Proceeding of the 39th Conference on Computer Applications and Quantitative Methods in Archaeology, Beijing, April 12-16, 2011, pp. 186–197 (2012)
10. Krötzsch, M., Vrandečić, D., Völkel, M.: Semantic MediaWiki. In: Cruz, I., Decker, S., Allemang, D., Preist, C., Schwabe, D., Mika, P., Uschold, M., Aroyo, L.M. (eds.) ISWC 2006. LNCS, vol. 4273, pp. 935–942. Springer, Heidelberg (2006)
11. Leclercq, E., Savonnet, M.: Access and annotation of archaelogical corpus via a semantic wiki. In: Fifth Workshop on Semantic Wikis-Linking Data and People (Semwiki) (2010)
12. Moreau, L., Freire, J., Futrelle, J., McGrath, R.E., Myers, J., Paulson, P.: The open provenance model: An overview. In: Freire, J., Koop, D., Moreau, L. (eds.) IPAW 2008. LNCS, vol. 5272, pp. 323–326. Springer, Heidelberg (2008)
13. Rowlands, I., Nicholas, D., Russell, B., Canty, N., Watkinson, A.: Social media use in the research workflow. Learned Publishing 24(3), 183–195 (2011)
14. Schindler, C., Ell, B.: Semantic MediaWiki for Collaborative Corpora Analysis: Analyzing Educational Reference Books in a Virtual Research Environment. Peer-Reviewed Abstract (2012); ECER 2012
15. Schindler, C., Ell, B.: Kollaborative Analyse von historischen Netzwerken: Virtuelle Forschungsumgebung für die Historische Bildungsforschung. In: Hans-Ulrich Grunder, A.H.U.P.M. (ed.) Netzwerke in bildungshistorischer Perspektive, Verlag Julius Klinkhardt, Bad Heilbrunn, Bad Heilbrunn (Oktober 2013)
16. Schindler, C., Veja, C., Rittberger, M., Vrandečić, D.: How to teach digital library data to swim into research. In: Proceedings of the 7th International Conference on Semantic Systems, pp. 142–149. ACM, New York (2011)
17. Şensoy, M., Norman, T., Vasconcelos, W., Sycara, K.: OWL-POLAR: Semantic policies for agent reasoning. In: Patel-Schneider, P.F., Pan, Y., Hitzler, P., Mika, P., Zhang, L., Pan, J.Z., Horrocks, I., Glimm, B. (eds.) ISWC 2010, Part I. LNCS, vol. 6496, pp. 679–695. Springer, Heidelberg (2010)
18. Voss, A., Procter, R.: Virtual research environments in scholarly work and communications. Library Hi Tech 27(2), 174–190 (2009)

Integrating Heterogeneous and Distributed Information about Marine Species through a Top Level Ontology

Yannis Tzitzikas[1,2], Carlo Allocca[1], Chryssoula Bekiari[1],
Yannis Marketakis[1], Pavlos Fafalios[1,2], Martin Doerr[1], Nikos Minadakis[1],
Theodore Patkos[1], and Leonardo Candela[3]

[1] Institute of Computer Science, FORTH-ICS, Greece
[2] Computer Science Department, University of Crete, Greece
[3] Consiglio Nazionale delle Ricerche, CNR-ISTI, Pisa, Italy
{tzitzik,carlo,bekiari,marketak,fafalios,martin,minadakn,patkos}@ics.forth.gr,leonardo.candela@isti.cnr.it

Abstract. One of the main characteristics of biodiversity data is its cross-disciplinary feature and the extremely broad range of data types, structures, and semantic concepts which encompasses. Moreover, biodiversity data, especially in the marine domain, is widely distributed, with few well-established repositories or standard protocols for their archiving, access, and retrieval. Our research aims at providing models and methods that allow integrating such information either for publishing it, browsing it, or querying it. For providing a valid and reliable knowledge ground for enabling semantic interoperability of marine data, in this paper we motivate a top level ontology, called `MarineTLO` that we have designed for this purpose, and discuss its use for creating `MarineTLO`-based warehouses in the context of a research infrastructure.

1 Introduction

Biodiversity data, especially in marine domain, is widely distributed, with few well-established repositories or standard protocols for their archiving and retrieval. Currently, the various laboratories have in place databases for keeping their raw data, while ontologies are primarily used for metadata that describe these raw data. One of the challenges in the iMarine project[1] is how users could experience a coherent source of facts about marine entities, rather than a bag of contributed contents. Considering the current setting, where each iMarine source has its own model, queries like *"Given the scientific name of a species, find its predators with the related taxon-rank classification and with the different codes that the organizations use to refer to them"*, cannot be formulated (and consequently nor answered) by any individual source. To formulate such queries we need an expressive conceptual model, while for answering them we also have to assemble pieces of information stored in different sources. For example, Figure 1

---

[1] iMarine, FP7 Research Infrastructures, 2011-2014.

E. Garoufallou and J. Greenberg (Eds.): MTSR 2013, CCIS 390, pp. 289–301, 2013.

illustrates information about the species `Thunnus albacares` which are stored in different sources (here FLOD, ECOSCOPE and WoRMS, more about these sources in the next section). These pieces of information are complementary, and if assembled properly, advanced browsing, querying and reasoning can be provided.

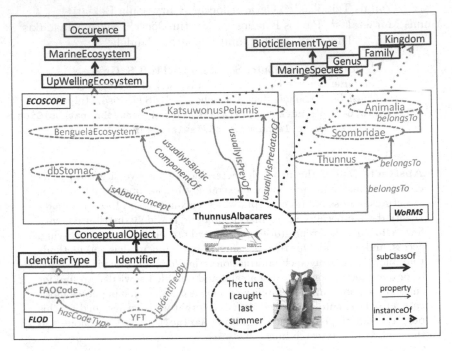

Fig. 1. Integrated information about `Thunnus albacares` from three sources

We believe, therefore, that a unified and coherent model for better accessing/reasoning upon and across different marine data sources is a critical and, at the same time, challenging objective, in order to provide a valid and reliable knowledge ground for enabling semantic interoperability of marine data, services, applications and systems. In a nutshell, the key contributions of our work are: (a) we identify use cases motivating the need for having harmonized integrated information, (b) we introduce a generic core model, called `MarineTLO`, for schema integration, (c) we describe the mappings between this model and three main sources of marine information for building integrated warehouses, (d) we comparatively evaluate two different triplestores for the problem at hand, and (e) we report results regarding the ability of the `MarineTLO`-based warehouse to answer queries which are not answered by the underlying sources. To the best of our knowledge, there is not any other such warehouse. The rest of this paper is organized as follows. Section 2 discusses motivating application scenarios, Section 3 describes the proposed approach, and finally Section 4 concludes and identifies directions for future work and research.

2 Requirements and Motivating Scenarios

Here we describe the main underlying sources (§2.1), and then (§2.2) four motivating scenarios as came up by the organizations participating to iMarine.

2.1 Main Underlying Sources

• **Fisheries Linked Open Data (FLOD) RDF Dataset.** FLOD (created and maintained by FAO), is dedicated to create a dense network of relationships among the entities of the Fishery domains, and to programmatically serve them to semantic and traditional application environments[2]. The FLOD content is exposed either via a public SPARQL endpoint[3] (suitable for semantic applications) or via a JAVA API to be embedded in consumers' application code. Currently the FLOD network includes entities and relationships from the domains of Marine Species, Water Areas, Land Areas, Exclusive Economic Zones, and serves software applications in the domain of statistics, and GIS.

• **ECOSCOPE Knowledge Base.** IRD[4] offers a public SPARQL endpoint[5] for its knowledge base containing geographical data, pictures and information about marine ecosystems (specifically data about fishes, sharks, related persons, countries and organizations, harbours, vessels, etc.).

• **WoRMS.** The World Register of Marine Species[6] currently contains more than 200 thousands species, around 380 thousands species names including synonyms, and 470 thousands taxa (infraspecies to kingdoms).

2.2 Motivating Scenarios

The availability of a top-level ontology for the marine domain would be useful in various scenarios.

For Publishing Linked Data. There is a trend towards publishing Linked Data, consequently a rising issue concerns the structure that is beneficial to use during such publishing. The semantic structure that will be presented can be used by the involved organizations for anticipating future needs for information integration, and thus alleviating the required effort for (post) integration.

Fact Sheets. FactSheetGenerator[7] is an application provided by IRD aiming at providing factual knowledge about the marine domain by mashing-up relevant knowledge distributed across several data sources. Figure 2 shows the results of the current FactSheetGenerator when searching for the species Thunnus albacares. Currently the results are based only on ECOSCOPE, and related

---

[2] Information from: http://www.fao.org/fishery/topic/18046/en
[3] http://www.fao.org/figis/flod/endpoint/sparql
[4] Institut de recherche pour le developpement (IRD), France (http://www.ird.fr/)
[5] http://ecoscopebc.mpl.ird.fr/joseki/ecoscope
[6] http://www.marinespecies.org/
[7] http://www.ecoscopebc.ird.fr/

knowledge stored in other sources (e.g. about commercial codes or taxonomic information) cannot be exploited. The approach that we will present in this paper can be exploited for advancing this application, i.e. for providing more complete semantic descriptions.

Fig. 2. `Thunnus albacares` in FactSheetGenerator

For Semantic Post-processing of the Results of Keyword Search Queries. Another big challenge nowadays is how to integrate structured data with unstructured data (documents and text). The availability of harmonized structured knowledge about the marine domain can be exploited for a *semantic post-processing* of the search results (over dedicated or general purpose search systems). Specifically the work done in the context of iMarine so far, described in [3,4], proposed a method to enrich the classical (mainly keyword based) searching with *entity mining* that is performed at *query time*. In particular, the results of entity mining (entities grouped in categories) complement the query answers with information which can be further exploited by the user in a faceted and session-based interaction scheme [10]. This means that instead of annotating and building indexes for the documents (or web pages), the annotation can be done at *query time* and using the desired entities of interest. These works show that the application of entity mining over the *snippets* of the top hits of the answers can be performed at real-time, and indicated how semantic repositories can be exploited for specifying the entities of interest and for providing further information about the identified entities.

The current application within iMarine of this "semantic post-processing" service uses FLOD. Figure 3 shows a screendump of the results for the query `tuna` over a deployment as a portlet where the underlying system is *gcubeSearch* and the triplestore is FLOD. The approach presented in this paper can improve this service from various perspectives: more entities can be identified in the results, the system will be able to provide more complete information about the identified entities, etc.

For Enabling Complex Query Services over Integrated Data. `MarineTLO` can be used as the schema for setting up integrated repositories that offer more

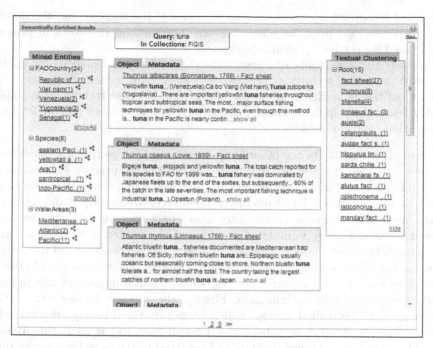

Fig. 3. Examples of semantic post-processing of search results within gcube as portlet

complex query services which cannot be supported by the individual underlying sources. In general there are two main approaches for such repositories: the *materialized* integration approach (or *warehouse* approach), and the *virtual* integration (or *mediator*) approach.

Materialized Approach. The *materialized approach* relies on a central repository (RDF triplestore in our case) where all data are to be stored. *Mappings* (in the broad sense) are exploited to *extract* information from data sources, to *transform* it to the target model and then to *store* it at the central repository. Over such a repository more complex queries can be answered.

It is good practice not to modify extracted information after its transformation except for the use of common identifiers. Rather, any need for updating individual information is covered by requesting source providers to make updated sources available. There are some important issues that should be taken into account for designing and maintaining a data warehouse. Firstly (design phase) the information from each source that is going to be used should be selected. Specific views over the sources should be chosen in order to be materialized. Next (maintenance phase) issues should be tackled concerning the warehouse initial population by the source data and the update of the data when sources are refreshed. The notion of *graph spaces* of RDF triplestores can alleviate this problem. The great advantage of materialized integration is its flexibility in transformation logic, decoupling of the release management of the integrated resource from the management cycles of the sources, and the decoupling of access load from the source servers. The method that we will present can be used for setting up such repositories.

Moreover the availability of a materialized repository is beneficial for applying entity matching techniques (e.g. see [9]) since more information about the domain entities is available, while the application of these techniques is significantly faster than applying them without having a repository (i.e. by fetching information from the network).

Virtual Approach. On the other hand, the *virtual integration* approach does not rely on a central repository but leaves the data in the original sources. *Mappings* (in the broad sense) are exploited to enable *query translation* from one model to another. Then data from disparate sources are *combined* and returned to the user. The mediator (a.k.a. integrator) performs the following actions. First it receives a query formulated in terms of the unified model/schema and decomposes the query into *sub-queries*. These queries are addressed to specific data sources. This decomposition is based on the mappings generated between the unified model and the source models, which play an important role in sub-queries' execution plan optimization. Finally, the sub-queries are sent to the wrappers of the individual sources, which transform them into queries over the sources. The results of these sub-queries are sent back to the mediator. At this point the answers are merged into one and returned to the user. Besides the possibility of asking queries, the mediator has no control over the individual sources. The great advantage (but in some cases disadvantage) of virtual integration is the real-time reflection of source updates in integrated access. As regards system's complexity (complexity of query rewriting and of execution planning), this depends on the structural complexity of the global view and the differences between this view and that of the underlying models. The higher complexity of the system (and the quality of service demands on the sources) is only justified if immediate access to updates is indeed required.

3   MarineTLO-Based Integration

At first (§3.1) we describe MarineTLO, then (§3.2) we describe a discovery service (called SDS), and the process for creating MarineTLO-based descriptions, and finally (§3.3) the process for creating MarineTLO-based warehouses.

3.1   The Ontology MarineTLO

MarineTLO is not supposed to be the single ontology covering the entirety of what exists. It aims at being a *global core model* that *i)* covers with suitable abstractions the domains under consideration to enable the most fundamental queries, *ii)* can be extended to any level of detail on demand, and *iii)* data originating from distinct sources can be adequately mapped and integrated, as it happened for others and related domains [5],[2]. Figure 4 drafts the intended architecture of knowledge models.

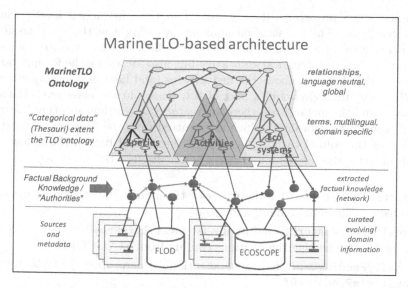

Fig. 4. `MarineTLO`-based architecture

Note that the adoption of a single and coherent core conceptual model has various benefits: *(a)* reduced effort for improving and evolving it since the focus is given on one model, rather than many [8], and *(b)* reduced effort for constructing mappings since this approach avoids the inevitable combinatorial explosion and complexities that results from pair-wise mappings between individual metadata formats and/or ontologies [2].

Since the marine domain is complex, and multiple views or projections should be supported for inference, the `MarineTLO` makes use of (i) categorical and cross-categorical relations as logical derivation of classes and properties of Ecoscope and FLOD, (ii) categories of classes (metaclasses) which support certain type of inference about classes in an analogous way as classes support certain types of inference about instances and enable the assignment of attribute values to a class. Also attention has been given to the design of `MarineTLO` for preserving *monotonicity*. Since the primary role of `MarineTLO`, is the meaningful integration of information in an Open World, it aims to be monotonic in the sense of Domain Theory. That is, the existing constructs and the deductions made from them should remain valid and well-formed, even as new constructs are added to the `MarineTLO`. A particular consequence of this principle is that no class is declared as complement of sibling concept under a common direct superclass.

Outcome. The current full version of `MarineTLO` contains 55 classes and 37 properties (its documentation is web accessible[8]). For the needs of the intended applications and the main underlying sources (i.e. FLOD, ECOSCOPE, WoRMS), only a subset of the full version is used and is further specialized. With the name "`MarineTLO`", we hereafter refer to this subset. Its current version (1.0) contains

---

[8] `www.ics.forth.gr/isl/MarineTLO/documentation`

47 classes and 8 properties. It is organized in two abstraction levels: schema and metaschema. The metaschema aims at providing a method for classifying the schema level in meaningful abstractions, which can be exploited not only for expressing cross-categorical knowledge but also for aiding the formulation of generic queries. Figure 5 shows the metaclasses (and how they are organized in a subClassOf hierarchy), and a part of the classes in the class level. Between the classes and the metaclasses, there are *instanceOf* relationships (implemented as RDF typeOf relationships) which are omitted from the diagram. A short description of the role of each of the eight properties of MarineTLO follows (for reasons of space their domain and range is not discussed):

- belongsTo: it is used for the needs of taxonomic classification (species to genuses, genuses to families, and so on).
- usuallyIsPredatorOf (and its inverse usuallyIsPreyOf): they are superproperties for hosting the relations coming from ECOSCOPE.
- usuallyFeedingOn: it is a generalization (superproperty) of the relation usuallyIsPredatorOf.

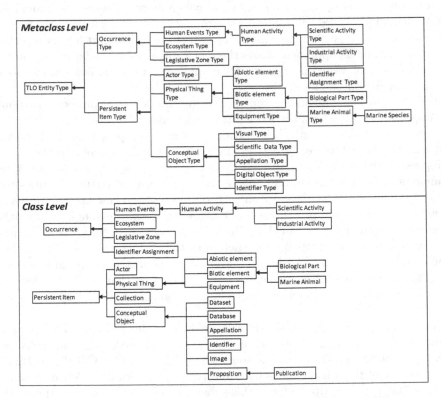

Fig. 5. The metaclasses and part of the classes of MarineTLO

- `hasIdentifierType`: it is used to link a species (e.g. `Thunnus Albacares`) with the types of codes of this species that are provided by various authorities (e.g. codes from FAO, IRD, WoRMS, etc).
- `isReferencedBy`: it allows stating that an information object (e.g. a picture) refers to a species.
- `usuallyIsComponentOf`: it is used to define the biotic constituent parts of a type of ecosystem (e.g. that `ThunnusAlbacares` is usually part of upwelling ecosystems).

The example shown in Figure 1 illustrates how pieces of information that come from different sources and concern one particular species, namely `Thunnus albacares`, are assembled. The labels of the frames indicate the used sources.

3.2 The Species Discovery Service (SDS) and Its Use for Producing MarineTLO-Based Descriptions

The *Species Discovery Service*, for short SDS, under evolution in the context of iMarine and part of the gCube infrastructure [1], aims at offering an uniform access over different biodiversity repositories. It is a *plugin-based mediator service* for key biodiversity data sources that provides users with seamless access to both nomenclature data and species occurrences from the major information systems including GBIF and OBIS for occurrence data, Catalogue of Life, OBIS, Interim Register of Marine and Nonmarine Genera (IRMNG), ITIS, NCBI, and WoRMS for nomenclature data. We have implemented a tool that uses SDS API and transforms the fetched information into descriptions structured according to the `MarineTLO`. Its functionality is performed in two phases: the first takes as input a list of scientific names to be retrieved and the data sources that will be searched and submits the query to SDS. The output is a Darwin Core Archive (DwC-A) file, containing the classifications of the given input. During the second phase the tool parses the DwC-A archives and produces the descriptions according to `MarineTLO` through the used mappings. All the scientific names in the archive are classified under certain `MarineTLO` classes and the associations (w.r.t. their classification) are also added.

3.3 On Constructing `MarineTLO`-Based Warehouses

We have been investigating the materialized (warehouse) approach described in section 2.2. Specifically we coded the `MarineTLO` ontology using OWL 2 [7] and set up a repository using two different triples stores which are described in the next section. Apart from `MarineTLO`, the repository contains the entire FLOD, the entire ECOSCOPE, and a part of WoRMS derived by running the process just described for 95 species, and the required mappings (between `MarineTLO` and FLOD, ECOSCOPE and WoRMS) which are described next.

Used Triplestores. We have comparatively evaluated two different triplestores: OWLIM-Lite and Virtuoso. The first has been designed for medium data volumes (below 100 million statements). It contains a persistence layer, however reasoning and query evaluation are being performed entirely in main memory. On the other hand *OpenLink Virtuoso* supports *backward chaining* reasoning, meaning that it does not materialize all inferred facts, but computes them at query level. Its reasoner covers the related entailment rules of `rdfs:subClassOf` and `rdfs:subPropertyOf`. Practically this means that transitive relations (i.e. *subClassof, subPropertyOf*, etc.) are not physically stored in the knowledge base, but they are added to the result set at query answering.

Mappings. In general what we call *mapping* comprises: extensions to the metaschema, extensions to the schema, `rdfs:subClassOf` and `rdf:subPropertyOf` relationships between the elements of `MarineTLO` and the schema at hand, plus some inference rules. Below we sketch the defined mappings. For instance, the *ECOSCOPE2TLO mapping* consists of `subClassOf` and `subPropertyOf` like those shown in Figure 6. The *WORMS2TLO mapping* contains analogous relationships. However, in FLOD any resource is an instance of `CodedEntity`, and for distinguishing a vessel (e.g. `vessel_289`) from a species (e.g. `thunnus_albacares`) we need to do one step further and look at its code. For instance, we can distinguish *FAOSpecies* as follows: $FAOSpecies = \{ x \mid CodedEntity(x) \text{ and } (\exists y \; isClassifiedByCode(x,y) \text{ and } SpeciesCode(y)) \}$. The required mapping can be defined using `owl:Restriction`. This is supported by OWLIM, but it is not supported by Virtuoso. For the latter we can express this mapping through a SPARQL INSERT query.

```
(tlo:EcoscopeSpecies, rdfs:subClassOf, tlo:TLOSpecies)
(ecoscope:fish, rdfs:subClassOf, tlo:EcoscopeSpecies)
(ecoscope:is_Predator_Of, rdfs:subPropertyOf,
tlo:usuallyisPredatorOf) (ecoscope:is_Prey_Of,  rdfs:subPropertyOf,
tlo:usuallyisPreyOf) (ecoscope:bioticComponentOf,
rdfs:subPropertyOf, tlo:usuallyisComponentOf)
(ecoscope:used_data_source, rdfs:subPropertyOf, tlo:isReferencedBy)
```

Fig. 6. Mapping ECOSCOPE2TLO

Comparison of the Two Repositories

Number of Triples and Loading Times. Table 1 shows the sizes in triples of the contents of the OWLIM and Virtuoso repositories. The first contains in total 10.8 millions triples. This number includes the inferred triples, since this repository materialized them. The creation of the repository from scratch (by loading the corresponding files) takes around 30 minutes. The time is short because the used edition of OWLIM loads everything in main memory. In Virtuoso the number of triples is significantly lower, because the inferred triples are not stored. The creation here takes 4h and 20 minutes[9]. The execution of the INSERT query (needed

---

[9] Experiments done using a QuadCore linux machine with 4GB RAM.

Table 1. MarineTLO-based warehouses using OWLIM and Virtuoso

KB part	triples in OWLIM	triples in Virtuoso
MarineTLO	277	58
FLOD	9,092,087	2,148,128
ECOSCOPE	170,980	84,184
WoRMS	70,174	9.552
FLOD2TLO mapping	180	15
ECOSCOPE2TLO mapping	205	11
WORMS2TLO mapping	180	8
TOTAL	10,822,758	2,241,956

for FLOD), created about 32,000 triples, i.e. the FLOD-originated triples from 2,148,128 increased to 2,180,678.

Query Performance. To test query performance, we used queries provided by the iMarine partners (more below). The average time in OWLIM was ranging from 62ms to 8.8 seconds, while in Virtuoso from 31ms to 3.4 seconds. We observe that Virtuoso is faster despite the fact that OWLIM keeps everything in main memory, while Virtuoso does not necessarily do so. In general performance depends on the capabilities of the adopted triplestore used (for a comparative analysis see [6]).

Evaluation. For evaluating the stucturing of MarineTLO, and the process used for creating the MarineTLO-based repository, we had to investigate whether they offer the required abstractions for (a) adequately modeling the domain, (b) hosting information coming from different sources, and (c) allowing answering useful queries which cannot be answered by the individual underlying sources. For the latter, we formed a collection of *competence queries* in collaboration with the involved partners and their priorities. Table 2 shows *some* indicative and fundamental ones. The columns at the right show which of them are answerable by the underlying sources (fully or partially). The real competence queries include queries that combine more than one of the listed queries, e.g. *"I want the biotic types and the identifiers of the predators or competitors of the x species"*. Such queries cannot be answered by any particular source, and this is the concrete evidence of the benefits offered by the integrated model.

Table 2. Basic Queries

Query		Ability to answer by		
For the scientific name of a species, find:		FLOD	Ecoscope	WoRMS
i	its identifier in the involved sources (e.g. FLOD codes, ECOSCOPE codes, WoRMS Id)	partial	partial	partial
ii	its WoRMS classification			full
iii	its references/images/db		full	
iv	its biotic type		partial	full
v	its predators		full	
vi	its competitors		full	

3.4   Lessons Learned and Next Steps

In future (until April 2014) we plan to continue along the same lines and evolve `MarineTLO` by considering more sources and more competence queries, and enhancing the configurability of the workflow used for producing `MarineTLO`-based wareshouses. Another task that we do in parallel is the inspection of the repository for detecting the missing connections that are required for satisfying the needs of the competence queries. We currently use matching tools like `SILK`[10] for creating the missing relationships. The `MarineTLO`-based warehouse is under constant evolution. Today it contains information about 18,500 marine species. Apart from the three main sources, it currently includes information from `dbpedia` and a SPARQL endpoint is publicly available[11] and it is used by various search services[12]. From this activity we have observed that the data fetched from the sources are in many cases problematic (consistency problems, duplicates, wrong values), and placing them together in a warehouse makes easier the identification of such errors. Moreover, the availability of the warehouse enables defining `sameAs` connections by exploiting transitively induced equivalences.

4   Concluding Remarks

To tackle the need for having integrated sets of facts about marine species, and thus to assist research about species and biodiversity, we have described a top-level ontology for that domain. It provides a unified and coherent core model for schema mapping which enables formulating and answering queries which cannot be answered by any individual source. We have identified and described particular use cases and applications that exploit this ontology, and have focused on the mappings that are required for building integrated warehouses. We discussed the realization of the mappings depending on the reasoning capabilities of the selected triplestore and we evaluated the warehouse as regards its completeness and its ability to answer queries which are not answered by the underlying sources.

Acknowledgement. This work was partially supported by the ongoing project *iMarine* (FP7 Research Infrastructures, 2011-2014).

References

1. Candela, L., Castelli, D., Pagano, P.: Managing big data through hybrid data infrastructures. ERCIM News (89), 37–38 (2012)
2. Doerr, M., Hunter, J., Lagoze, C.: Towards a core ontology for information integration. Journal of Digital Information 4 (2003)

---

[10] `http://wifo5-03.informatik.uni-mannheim.de/bizer/silk/`
[11] `http://virtuoso.i-marine.d4science.org:8890/fct`   also browsable through `http://62.217.127.213:8890/fct/`
[12] Including `http://62.217.127.118/x-search-fao/`

3. Fafalios, P., Kitsos, I., Marketakis, Y., Baldassarre, C., Salampasis, M., Tzitzikas, Y.: Web searching with entity mining at query time. In: Salampasis, M., Larsen, B. (eds.) IRFC 2012. LNCS, vol. 7356, pp. 73–88. Springer, Heidelberg (2012)
4. Fafalios, P., Tzitzikas, Y.: X-ENS: Semantic Enrichment of Web Search Results at Real-Time. In: Procs of SIGIR 2013 (2013)
5. Gangemi, A., Fisseha, F., Pettman, I., Keizer, J.: Building an integrated formal ontology for semantic interoperability in the fishery domain. In: Procs. of ISWC 2002 (2002)
6. Haslhofer, B., Momeni Roochi, E., Schandl, B., Zander, S.: Europeana RDF store report (2011)
7. Hitzler, P., Krtzsch, M., Parsia, B., Patel-Schneider, P.F., Rudolph, S.: OWL 2 Web Ontology Language Primer. In: W3C Recommendation, World Wide Web Consortium (October 2009)
8. Ibrahim, L., Pyster, A.: A single model for process improvement. IT Professional 6(3) (May 2004)
9. Noessner, J., Niepert, M., Meilicke, C., Stuckenschmidt, H.: Leveraging terminological structure for object reconciliation. In: Aroyo, L., Antoniou, G., Hyvönen, E., ten Teije, A., Stuckenschmidt, H., Cabral, L., Tudorache, T. (eds.) ESWC 2010, Part II. LNCS, vol. 6089, pp. 334–348. Springer, Heidelberg (2010)
10. Sacco, G.M., Tzitzikas, Y.: Dynamic Taxonomies and Faceted Search: Theory, Practice, and Experience, vol. 25. Springer (2009)

A Semantic Approach for the Annotation of Figures: Application to High-Energy Physics[*]

Piotr Praczyk[1,2] and Javier Nogueras-Iso[2]

[1] CERN, Geneva, Switzerland
[2] Computer Science and Systems Engineering Dept., Universidad de Zaragoza, Spain

Abstract. Figures play an important role in the process of understanding a scholarly publication, providing overviews of large amounts of data or ideas that are difficult to present using only the text. This work presents a system allowing to describe and to search for scientific figures in the High Energy Physics (HEP) domain. It proposes an application HEP Figures Ontology (HFO), based on existing ontologies, for the annotation of scientific figures in a semantic triplestore. Finally, this work studies the searching functionalities provided by triplestores based on the HFO model, and compares them with traditional digital library systems.

1 Introduction

Figures play a very important role in the process of scholarly publishing. Representing data in a graphical manner allows to show patterns in large datasets and to make complicated ideas easier to understand. In recent years, digital libraries have shifted their focus towards a more complete description of publishing artefacts. Formerly, only publications were considered as first-class citizens of the publishing ecosystem. Now, the increasing number of efforts is made to give access to figures, tables and datasets being part of the publications.

Focused on the specific High-Energy Physics (HEP) domain and the development of INSPIRE [1] (the digital library of the entire domain of HEP), in previous works we proposed an approach for the automatic extraction of figures from scholarly publications encoded in PDF format [2], the integration of datasets coming from the HepData [3] site with bibliographic records of the publications [4], and the necessary infrastructure inside a digital library system (Invenio) to allow the storage of additional non-paper objects together with non-MARC meta-data about them [5].

However, this previous work was not sufficient to provide a complete retrieval system allowing to search and access to all scholarly artefacts. One of the missing pieces was to have all the different publishing artefacts gathered in a single place and annotated in a uniform manner. The structure of relations between those objects can reflect both the scientific process behind their creation and the relation on a more conceptual level. A possible strategy for establishing a

---

[*] This work has been partially supported by the Spanish Government through the project TIN2012-37826-C02-01.

E. Garoufallou and J. Greenberg (Eds.): MTSR 2013, CCIS 390, pp. 302–314, 2013.

common vocabulary for the annotation of artefacts and creating links between them is the adoption of Semantic Web technologies, which allow the description of resources in terms of a well-defined meaning thanks to a shared reference to ontologies available on the Web.

Semantic technologies have been successfully applied to increase the visibility and discovery in other related domains such as general analysis of statistical data [6] or accessibility of bibliographic databases [7]. Following this strategy, the objective of this work is to propose a semantic approach for the annotation of the different artefacts involved in the scholarly publications of HEP research. We propose an application ontology, called HEP Figures Ontology (HFO), which is based on existing domain ontologies. Additionally, we also study the searching functionalities provided by a semantic triplestore based on this HFO model and compare its performance with a traditional digital library system.

2 Related Work

There are formal vocabularies allowing to describe concepts of High-Energy Physics (HEP) such as the HEP taxonomy [8], which is an SKOS-based vocabulary for the classification of INSPIRE publications, or the compilation of properties of elementary HEP particles published by the Particle Data Group[1]. However, according to our knowledge, there are no ontologies for the description of figures in this specific domain. Therefore, this section reviews some works that intersect partially with our interest in defining a model for the description of figures in this domain.

HepData[2] [4] is an example of a project gathering and allowing access to the data behind publications, in particular behind tables and figures. The data stored on HepData servers comes either from authors of the described publications or from a manual analysis of the figure content. HepData stores information about over 7000 manually selected scholarly publications. Most of the data corpus consists of results of Monte Carlo (MC) simulations encoded in the form of histograms. This is reflected in the structure of the underlying data model, which is too specific for our purpose of describing figures not only focused on MC simulations.

Making use of semantic technologies, Cyber-Share [9] aims at providing a platform facilitating the documentation of the entire scientific process. For each research project supported by CyberShare, unformatted sources are processed to generate RDF annotations. Additionally, OWL ontologies are generated automatically using the vocabulary and properties found in RDF annotations. Although the proposed workflow and some technologies could be reused in the context of INSPIRE, the ontologies generated by CyberShare are specific for each research project annotations. However, our aim is to define an application ontology for the common description of figures.

---

[1] http://pdg.lbl.gov/2012/html/what_is_pdg.html
[2] http://hepdata.cedar.ac.uk/

Dumontier et al. [6] created an ontology for describing statistical graphs. The objectives of their work varied from ours. Their principal objective was to build a system allowing access to scholarly graphs by people with sight disabilities. The emphasis of their work was placed on the description of the structure of statistical graphs, considering the visual design decisions taken by the creator. Their approach allows also to describe the data encoded in a graph. The second of their objectives was to perform searching for particular data values encoded in the graphs. The database used for experiments was constructed from the original spreadsheets used to create graphs, allowing the datasets to be described in terms of absolute numerical values. However, within INSPIRE we are in a different situation because we cannot obtain access to the original sources of all the data and data series associated to figures cannot be described in terms of numerical values.

An interesting work by Samadian et al. [10] provides insight into the process of semantically annotating the results of medical examinations. Their techniques can be generalised and reused in the context of INSPIRE and HEP in general. The authors describe a complex information system storing a number of simple medical measurements (gathered over time in different places and under different conditions). The gathered observations are used to derive more complex knowledge.

Part of the described vocabulary can also be used when annotating figures. The SIO ontology[3] (Semantic Science Integrated Ontology) contains concepts of different types of figures. This description is however too simplistic to be used in our scenario. The work discusses also the semantic annotation of different types of units, which is much more complete than the one needed for HEP data associated with figures.

3   HEP Figures Ontology (HFO)

The HEP Figures Ontology (HFO) consists of several modules. The central module provides a framework for the description of the meaning and the structure of figures (and their associated scholarly objects) in the most abstract possible way. Additionally, in the case of describing specific figures such as plots, there are two other modules for the descriptions of coordinate systems, and data lines and areas. Last, there is another module devoted to the description of carrier properties of figures. By the carrier properties we understand all the metadata that connects logical elements of a figure with their positions on the canvas of the encoding graphical file. These modules are explained in the following subsections. The ontology is accessible on-line in OWL format[4].

3.1   Central Concepts in HFO

Figure 1 depicts the taxonomy of some of the most important artefacts of scholarly publishing, which lies at the heart of HFO. Figures and tables form the

---

[3] http://semanticscience.org

[4] https://github.com/ppiotr/InvenioSemantics/
blob/master/files/inveniomodel.owl

centre of interest of HFO and, as such, they are classified in a much higher detail than publications or data. The taxonomy of different types of figures has been constructed by reviewing a corpus of available HEP publications and identifying the most common types.

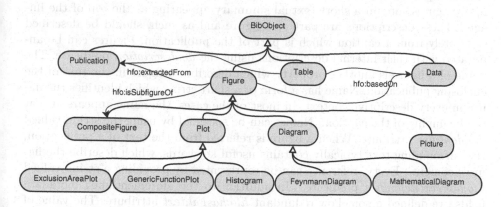

Fig. 1. The central part of HFO

Figures can be divided into two principal categories (plots and diagrams) corresponding to two general purposes they are expected to serve. Plots tend to show the quantitative information by presenting numerical datasets in a way which facilitates their interpretation. Diagrams tend to provide a qualitative description, showing ideas and logical connections between them. Both those categories are present in our ontology as specialisations of the Figure class. Both plots and tables share an important characteristic of presenting numerical data in a structured manner. As such, they can be seen as graphical representations of a certain dataset. With the advent of data preservation initiatives, digital libraries started treating not only publications, but also datasets as objects of the first category. When describing figures and tables, we can create links to appropriate publications from which those objects have been extracted. Similarly, if possible, we establish a connection between a plot and a dataset. It is worth noting, that we can have many distinct plots representing the same dataset.

Creating a comprehensible taxonomy of all possible types of graphics was not our goal. Authors of scholarly publications typically follow a set of common practices for creating figures. People tend to create representations similar to those which they have already seen. However, there are no strict rules limiting what can and what cannot be considered a figure. The hierarchical structure of concepts in HFO allows to provide the most accurate description by instantiating (a possibly non-leaf) concept. Sometimes many plots or other graphics form a single figure. HFO describes such situations by specifying a special type of a figure (CompositeFigure), which should be interpreted as a container for figures.

Besides the specification of the type, the top-level description of figures consists of other attributes. To achieve this level of description, we use some of the properties from the Dublin Core ontology together with specially defined HFO predicates. The most visible of the annotation properties is the caption of a figure. Captions summarise the content of a figure and thus contain relevant keywords which can be used in the implementation of figure search. When annotating figures with their captions, HFO uses the Dublin Core *title* field. Many figures contain a short textual summary appearing at the top of the image. These descriptions are part of a figure and as such, should be described separately from a caption which is part of the publication. Figures can be annotated with their internal descriptions using the *dc:description* predicate. The name of a figure is another property which describes a figure in the text of the enclosing publication. Name has a form of a short string which identifies the figure in every descriptive context. In most of the cases, the name appears also at the beginning of the caption. Names can be specified by using the string-valued *dc:identifier* attribute. When a figure is referred from the text of a publication, the surrounding text typically contains useful keywords, which describe the figure's content. Every reference can be represented by providing a string-valued *hfo:hasTextReference* predicate. In addition to the aforementioned metadata fields, we defined a somehow redundant *hfo:hasFulltext* attribute. The value of this attribute has to be a string literal and it should consist of a space-delimited list of words appearing inside a figure. The order of the words is not significant.

Besides the typical description summarised before, figures are annotated with the HEP concepts represented by the figure, e.g. the name given to a specific type of simulation or an elementary particle. Typically, these attributes would be the same for a figure and for the publication from which the figure originates. In particular, entities of various types in HFO are linked with concepts from the HEP taxonomy [8] using the *dc:subject* property.

Figure 2 shows an image extracted from a publication stored in INSPIRE[5], which we used as an example of annotation along this paper. The same figure shows the top-level annotation. The figure is connected with the publication from which it has been extracted using the *hfo:extractedFrom* property. The presented properties describe the figure as a part of a publication rather than as an independent entity.

3.2   Description of Coordinate Systems

Typically, there is a single coordinate system appearing within a single plot. However, sometimes we might encounter exceptions from this rule. A plot containing multiple coordinate systems is different from a figure containing multiple plots. Usually coordinate systems contain two axes, but three-dimensional plots are not unusual. Figure 3 shows the most important elements used to describe axes. A figure can be connected using the *hfo:contains* relation with a coordinate system which in turn can contain axes. Axes contain axis ticks and can be described by axis labels.

---

[5] http://inspirehep.net/record/1238420

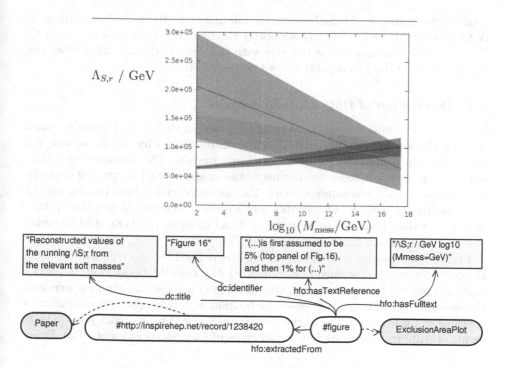

Fig. 2. The figure used as an example with figure-level annotation

Axis ticks serve as a reference during the interpretation of the data. They link positions on axes with concrete numerical values. In a plot, ticks are represented by small lines intersecting axes. HFO describes ticks as having only one coordinate - distance from the origin of the coordinates system. Ticks can be of two different types: major and minor. Typically, major ticks are assigned a label encoding the corresponding numerical value. Minor ticks typically do not have labels. Their corresponding numerical values can be derived in a non-ambiguous manner from their location relative to nearest annotated ticks. HFO represents both types of ticks using special classes inheriting from *AxisTick*. *AxisTick* instances must have an *hfo:atPosition* attribute, which indicates the location of a tick relative to the axis. The position is represented as a floating-point literal indicating the fraction of the total length of an axis. The tick is located at the specified distance from the axis origin.

At the level of general description, axis labels and tick labels could be represented as string literals. However, the carrier description adds more attributes to those objects. HFO encodes axis and tick labels with individuals of a specialised type, which can be linked with the corresponding tick or label using the *hfo:hasLabel* predicate. The text representation of a label can be linked with the label entity using the Dublin Core *title* attribute. Typically, axes express a measurement of a certain quantity or particle using a specified unit. Units and particles are linked with axes using *hfo:isDescribedBy*. The *hfo:contains* relation can transport *hfo:isDescribedBy* relations into the container entities. If A *hfo:contains* B and B *hfo:isDescribedBy* C, then also A *hfo:isDescribedBy* C. Figure 4 shows annotation of the axis with the described unit. HFO ruses the constructs from the Measurable Units Ontology (MUO).

3.3   Description of Data Lines and Areas

Before we delve into the details of the description of the data of plots, we must describe the basic design decisions which we have made. First of all, we describe only plots which map real numbers into real numbers. This assumption is consistent with a two-dimensional nature of the medium used to present plots (a sheet of paper or a computer screen). The second decision involves the way of representing the data. HFO describes plot's content in terms of graphical primitives rather than trying to be more general and describe mathematical formulae behind a plot (which might not exist).

Figure 5 provides an overview of the entities defined for describing data series. Every data series is described in a framework of a coordinates system. In particular, it is related to a pair of axes. One of them is marked as argument axis and the second as the value axis. Besides the relation with two axes, every *DataSeries* contains a number of entities of the *DataSeriesElement* type, which encode fragments of graphics. There are four major types of *DataSeries* elements: DataPoint

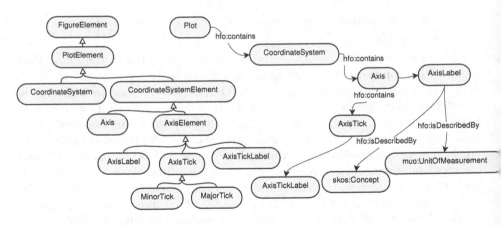

Fig. 3. The taxonomy of figure elements and a graph of relations between concepts

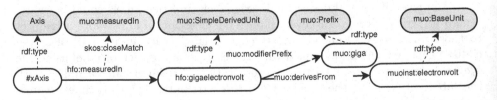

Fig. 4. Relation between an axis and the corresponding unit

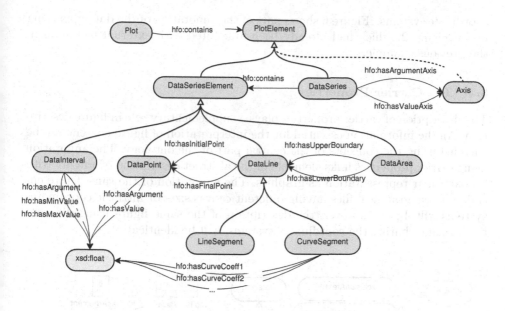

Fig. 5. The most important entities describing data of a plot

type to describe a single point in the 2-dimensional real space; *DataInterval* type to describe mappings between a single real value to an interval of real values; *DataLine* type to describe continuous line segments connecting two data points; and *DataArea* type to describe 2-Dimensional areas. The domain of a mapping containing a *DataLine* contains the closed interval in real numbers spanned by two domain points of both ends. There are two types of *DataLines*: straight line intervals and curves. On the other hand, *DataAreas* are limited by 2 *DataLines*. By being allowed to mix different types of *DataSeriesElements*, users of the ontology are provided with high flexibility of describing different types of data series (discrete, continuous, single-valued, multi-valued).

Describing geometrical shapes requires providing the coordinates of their points. In the case of semantic description of figures, we wanted to describe data lines in the most general possible way, abstracting from the concrete encoding of the graphs as files. The most obvious approach would involve using the axes and values on them. However, in the case of our main application domain (HEP figures automatically extracted from publications), this approach would lead to difficulties. We cannot assume that the description of a particular axis will not change as a result of a future re-extraction of a document or a manual correction of an extraction error. For this reason we decided to use the features of the axes which were least likely to change, namely the location of the axis line itself. We encode all the points using the fraction of the axis length as a reference value, i.e. the point where axes intersects has (0, 0) coordinates. The end of the x-axis is encoded as (1,0) and so on. Most of the data points and shapes located in the area of a plot have both their coordinates in the range between -1 and 1, however it is possible to encounter shapes exceeding the boundary of coordinate systems. Figure 6 shows part of the annotation of the data appearing inside Figure 2, which had already been annotated with external metadata in the previous example.

3.4   The Carrier Properties

The description of carrier properties plays a supplementary role in figure description. All the information essential for the interpretation of figure content can be encoded using the concepts of the central part of the ontology. The annotation using carrier properties links elements of the abstract description of a figure with its particular representation as graphics. The annotation of the same figure encoded in two graphical files having different canvas sizes or intrinsic coordinates systems will differ. However, the description of the same figure using different file formats, sharing the coordinates systems, will be identical.

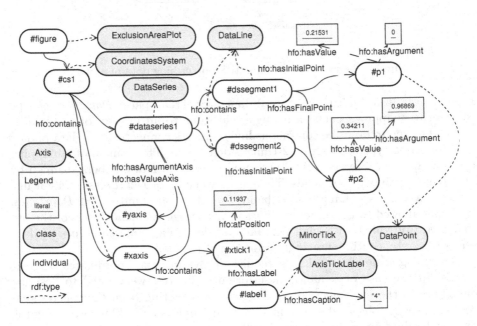

Fig. 6. Part of the annotation of an example figure

Many entities from the central ontology are represented in the original graphics as a sum of certain number of graphical entities. For example, inside the graphical file axes are represented by lines, legends and captions can be enclosed in rectangles. Those graphical primitives can be described using subclasses of the graphical entity class present in Semanticscience Integrated Ontology[6]. As the carrier description is dependent on the intrinsic coordinates system of the

---

[6] http://semanticscience.org

representation as a file, those graphical primitives can be described in the same coordinates system. The link between concepts from the central ontology and the graphical primitives can be established using the *hfo:isRepresentedBy* property (see an example in Figure 7).

The carrier description should be used only with those elements of a figure whose meaning does not reveal their position in the original medium. It should be avoided in the places where position is encoded in an indirect manner. For example, data lines are encoded using the coordinates in an abstract coordinates system. The carrier description provides a link between the abstract coordinates system and the canvas coordinates system. This link can be used to translate the coordinates of data into the canvas system.

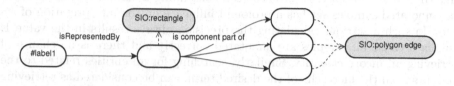

Fig. 7. An example of the carrier description of a tick label

4   Testing the Infrastructure for Figure Searching in INSPIRE

In this section we test the retrieval of figures using the semantic search. We compare the performance of semantic searching with the present traditional INSPIRE-like text-based search functionality based on exact matching.

Before being able to perform any experiments concerning searching for figures, we needed to prepare a database of semantic descriptions and populate it with sample figures and their description.We randomly selected a set of 76 publications stored in INSPIRE. All those articles were subsequently processed in the automatic extraction process (see more details in [2]), which produced the metadata of figures together with their vector graphics representations. We manually reviewed all the extracted results, rejecting a few which were extracted incorrectly. Subsequently, we transformed the metadata of the set of previously obtained results into HFO-compliant annotations and uploaded them on a knowledge base. After all the preliminary processing, out of 76 processed publications, 59 contained at least one figure or table. In total, we gathered the annotation of 517 figures and tables.

The standard way of accessing the data encoded in the form of semantic triples is SPARQL. Once the knowledge base was created, we developed a search component to facilitate the translation of user queries into SPARQL queries. In our present work we restrict our attention to retrieving only entire figures rather than their constituent parts (e.g. data series). Listing 1.1 shows a SPARQL query searching for figures. This query exploits the structure of concepts in HFO and in HEP taxonomy instead of using exact matching.

```
PREFIX dc: <http://purl.org/dc/elements/1.1/>
PREFIX hep: <http://cern.ch/thesauri/HEPontology.rdf#>
SELECT ?subject WHERE { ?subject hfo:contains* ?s1.
   ?s1 dc:subject ?concept. ?concept skos:broader* hep:hadron }
```

Listing 1.1. Hierarchy-aware version of the query

We used the previously created knowledge base to evaluate the impact of replacing standard exact-match queries with hierarchy-aware searches. The execution of present test had the objective of measuring the quality of searching within a correctly extracted knowledge base. We interfered with the extraction process by eliminating the misextracted figures. As a consequence, we assume that the knowledge base is 100% correct. Assuming a complete correctness of the annotated samples set has a profound influence on the interpretation of results. In such a setting, calculating the precision always results in the value 1. This is because all samples are annotated correctly and there is no chance of retrieving an incorrect entity. Similarly, searching for all entities related to the concepts from the hierarchy of the desired term, can be considered as retrieving all the correct answers and no incorrect. This allows to define the recall of the exact matching query as the number of returned results divided by the number of results retrieved using the extended query.

In the example query, we are searching for figures annotated with a concept of hadron. Hadrons are a wide class of particles, which share the common property of being constructed from quarks. There are many different types of hadrons (e.g. mesons, protons, antiprotons). All of these are relevant when searching for hadrons. The first query, simulating the search which could be achieved using exact indexing of INSPIRE, returns 4 results. The modified query, exploiting the dependencies between concepts, finds 10 results. This means that the recall of the exact query is in this case equal to 0.4. Similarly, searching for leptons returned 28 and 37 results. This corresponds to the recall of 0.76 for the first query. The recall of the exact match query can vary from 0 in the case of searching for a general term, which is not directly used in any annotation to 1 for the case of searching for the most specific term of the taxonomy. Table 1 summarises the results we have obtained by executing the evaluation over different sets of HEP concepts. The results presented in the table represent arithmetic averages of recalls for all the concepts for which at least one result has been found by the more general query. We performed the experiment of comparing the number of returned results for all the HEP terms used to annotate at least one figure. These results include all the specific concepts which we have used for the annotation and ignore the existence of the concepts which would not give any results during the exact matching, while yielding results when executing the general query.

We repeated the experiment with all the used concepts which could be further specified using the HEP taxonomy. The result was lower. The last row of the table represents results which we have obtained when computing the recall using all the concepts from the entire HEP ontology. In all the analysed cases, the

Table 1. Difference of recall between exact-match and semantic queries

Query	Exact-match (INSPIRE)	Semantic prototype
All used HEP concepts	0.984	1
All used concepts having a specialisation	0.915	1
All the concepts from the HEP ontology	0.848	1

usage of a more complex query, which can be executed thanks to the usage of a RDF database, increases the accuracy of retrieved results.

5   Conclusions and Future Work

In this work we have presented the ontology allowing a detailed description of figures of HEP. HFO ontology will enable INSPIRE to store the semantic description of scientific graphs and to implement searching functionalities. However, the direct searching is only one of the possible Applications of HFO. At present we are working on a similarity measure allowing to compare figures using their semantics. Such a similarity measure will allow INSPIRE to detect figures which are similar at the semantic level. This in turn will allow to develop better tools allowing to navigate the content of the digital library. Using the developed similarity measure will also allow to compute clusters of similar figures and detect those which describe, for example, the same phenomena or use the same units.

HFO can also be used to establish a common vocabulary between different systems which process figures, increasing the semantic interoperability between systems and advancing the vision of Semantic Web. Many figure types present in HFO and typical for HEP appear also in other disciplines. Other types could be added in a compatible manner. Also small modifications of HFO (e.g. replacement of the HEP taxonomy with a different topic-specific taxonomy) could enable the usage of HFO in the context of different areas of knowledge like biology or chemistry. Finally, additional work must be done in order to provide the annotation of diagrams and to provide the complete automatic annotation of figures.

References

1. Holtkamp, A., Mele, S., Simko, T., Smith, T.: INSPIRE: Realizing the dream of a global digital library in High-Energy Physics. In: 3rd Workshop Conference: Towards a Digital Mathematics Library, Paris, France, July 07-08, pp. 83–92 (2010)
2. Praczyk, P.A., Nogueras-Iso, J., Mele, S.: Automatic extraction of figures from scientific publications in high-energy physics. Accepted for Publication in: Information Technology and Libraries (2013)
3. Buckley, A., Whalley, M.: HepData reloaded: reinventing the HEP data archive. arXiv:1006.0517v2 (2010)
4. Praczyk, P., Nogueras-Iso, J., Dallmeier-Tiessen, S., Whalley, M.: Integrating scholarly publications and research data – preparing for open science, a case study from high-energy physics with special emphasis on (Meta)data models. In: Dodero, J.M., Palomo-Duarte, M., Karampiperis, P. (eds.) MTSR 2012. CCIS, vol. 343, pp. 146–157. Springer, Heidelberg (2012)

5. Praczyk, P.A., Nogueras-Iso, J., Kaplun, S., Simko, T.: A Storage Model for Supporting Figures and Other Artefacts in Scientific Libraries: The Case Study of Invenio. In: Proc. of 4th Workshop on Very Large Digital Libraries (VLDL 2011), Berlin, Germany (2011)
6. Dumontier, M., Ferres, L., Villanueva-Rosales, N.: Modeling and querying graphical representations of statistical data. Web Semantics: Science, Services and Agents on the World Wide Web 8(2-3), 241–254 (2010)
7. Lacasta, J., Nogueras-Iso, J., Teller, J., Falquet, G.: Transformation of a keyword indexed collection into a semantic repository: applicability to the urban domain. In: Gradmann, S., Borri, F., Meghini, C., Schuldt, H. (eds.) TPDL 2011. LNCS, vol. 6966, pp. 372–383. Springer, Heidelberg (2011)
8. Pepe, A., Yeomans, J.: Protocols for scholarly communication. In: 5th Conference on Library and Information Services in Astronomy, Cambridge, MA, USA (2006)
9. Gándara, A., Villanueva-Rosales, N.: Documenting and sharing scientific research over the semantic web. In: Proceedings of the 12th International Conference on Knowledge Management and Knowledge Technologies, i-KNOW 2012, pp. 18:1–18:8. ACM, New York (2012)
10. Samadian, S., McManus, B., Wilkinson, M.D.: Extending and encoding existing biological terminologies and datasets for use in the reasoned semantic web. J Biomed. Semantics 3(1), 6 (2012)

Towards a Stepwise Method for Unifying and Reconciling Corporate Names in Public Contracts Metadata: The CORFU Technique

Jose María Álvarez-Rodríguez[1], Patricia Ordoñez de Pablos[2],
Michail Vafopoulos[3], and José Emilio Labra-Gayo[2]

[1] South East European Research Center,
54622, Thessaloniki, Greece
jmalvarez@seerc.org
[2] WESO Research Group, Department of Computer Science,
University of Oviedo 33007, Oviedo, Spain
{patriop,labra}@uniovi.es
[3] Multimedia Technology Laboratory,
National Technical University of Athens, 15773, Athens, Greece
vafopoulos@medialab.ntua.gr

Abstract. The present paper introduces a technique to deal with coporate names heterogeneities in the context of public procurement metadata. Public bodies are currently facing a big challenge trying to improve both the performance and the transparency of administrative processes. The e-Government and Open Linked Data initiatives have emerged as efforts to tackle existing interoperability and integration issues among ICT-based systems but the creation of a real transparent environment requires much more than the simple publication of data and information in specific open formats; data and information quality is the next major step in the pubic sector. More specifically in the e-Procurement domain there is a vast amount of valuable metadata that is already available via the Internet protocols and formats and can be used for the creation of new added-value services. Nevertheless the simple extraction of statistics or creation of reports can imply extra tasks with regards to clean, prepare and reconcile data. On the other hand, transparency has become a major objective in public administractions and, in the case of public procurement, one of the most interesting services lies in tracking rewarded contracts (mainly type, location, and supplier). Although it seems a basic kind of reporting service the truth is that its generation can turn into a complex task due to a lack of standardization in supplier names or the use of different descriptors for the type of contract. In this paper, a stepwise method based on natural language processing and semantics to address the unfication of corporate names is defined and implemented. Moreover a research study to evaluate the precision and recall of the proposed technique, using as use case the public dataset of rewarded public contracts in Australia during the period 2004-2012, is also presented. Finally some discussion, conclusions and future work are also outlined.

E. Garoufallou and J. Greenberg (Eds.): MTSR 2013, CCIS 390, pp. 315–329, 2013.
© Springer International Publishing Switzerland 2013

1   Introduction

Public bodies are continuously publishing procurement opportunities in which valuable metadata is available. Depending on the stage of the process new data arises such as the supplier name that has been rewarded with the public contract. In this context the extraction of statistics on how many contracts have been rewarded to the same company is a relevant indicator to evaluate the transparency of the whole process. Although companies that want to tender for a public contract must be officially registered and have an unique identification number, the truth is that in most of rewarded contracts the supplier is only identified by a name or a string literal typed by a civil-servant. In this sense there is not usually a connection between the official company registry and the process of rewarding contracts implying different naming problems and data inconsistencies that are spread to next stages preventing future activities such as reporting.

In the case of the type of contract and location, there are already standardized product scheme classifications [20,22] that are currently used with different objectives such as statistics, tagging or information retrieval. Geolocated information can be also found in different common datasets and nomenclatures such as the Nomenclature of territorial units for statistics in the European Union, the Geonames dataset, the GeoLinkedData initiative or the traditional list of countries and ISO-codes. However corporate, organization, firm, company or institution names (hereafter these names will be used to refer to the same entity) and structure are not yet standardized at global scope and only some classifications of economic activities or company identifiers can be found such as the TARIC (On-line customs tariff database). Thus the simple task of grouping contracts by a supplier is not a mere process of searching by the same literal. Technical issues such as hyphenation, use of abbreviations or acronyms an transliteration are common problems that must be addressed in order to provide a final corporate name. Existing works in the field of Name Entity Recognition [18] (NER) or name entity disambiguation [7] have already addressed these issues. Nevertheless the problem that is being tackled in these approaches lies in the identification of organization names in a raw text while in the e-Procurement sector the string literal identifying a supplier is already known.

In the particular case of the Australian e-Procurement domain, the supplier name seems to be introduced by typing a string literal without any assistance or auto-complete method. Obviously a variety of errors and variants for the same company, see Table 4 in the Appendix I, can be found such as misspelling errors [19], name and acronym mismatches [26] or context-aware data that is already known when the dataset is processed, e.g. country or year. Furthermore it is also well-known that a large company can be divided into several divisions or departments but from a statistical point of view grouping data by a supplier name should take into account all rewarded contracts regardless the structure of the company.

On the other hand the application of semantic technologies and the Linking Open Data initiative (hereafter LOD) in several fields like e-Government (e.g. the Open Government Data effort) tries to improve the knowledge about a specific area providing common data models and formats to share information and data between agents. More specifically, in the European e-Procurement context [3] there is an increasing commitment to boost the use of electronic communications and transactions processing by government institutions and other public sector organizations in order to provide added-value services [21] with special focus on SMEs. More specifically the LOD initiative seeks for creating a public and open data repository in which one the principles of this initiative that lies in the unique identification or resources through URIs can become real. Thus entity reconciliation techniques [1,12] coming from the ontology mapping and alignment areas or algorithms based on Natural Language Processing (hereafter NLP) have been designed to link similar resources already available in different vocabularies, datasets or databases such as DBPedia or Freebase. Nevertheless the issue of unifying supplier names as a human would do faces new problems that have been tackled in other research works [4] to efficiently extract statistics of performance in bibliographic databases. The main objective is not just a mere reconciliation process to link to existing resources but to create a unique name or link (n string literals $\rightarrow$ 1 company $\rightarrow$ 1 URI). For instance in the case of the ongoing example the string literals "Oracle" and "Oracle University" could be respectively aligned to the entity <Oracle_Corporation> and <Oracle_University> but the problem of grouping by a unique (*Big*) name, identifier or resource still remains. That is why a context-aware method based on NLP techniques combined with semantics has been designed, customized and implemented trying to exploit the naming convention of a specific dataset with the aim of grouping n string literals $\rightarrow$ 1 company and, thus, easing the next natural process of entity reconciliation.

2   Related Work

According to the previous section, some relevant works can be found and grouped by the topics covered in this paper:

- Natural Language Processing and Computational Linguistics. In these research areas common works dealing with the aforementioned data heterogeneities such as misspelling errors [19,9] and name/acronym mismatches [26], in the lexical, syntactic and semantic levels can be found. These approaches can be applied to solve general problems and usually follow a traditional approach of text normalization, lexical analysis, pos-tagging word according to a grammar and semantic analysis to filter or provide some kind of service such as information/knowledge extraction, reporting, sentiment analysis or opinion mining. Well-established APIs such as NLTK for Python, Lingpipe, OpenNLP or Gate for Java, WEKA (a data mining library with

NLP capabilities), the Apache Lucene and Solr search engines provide the proper building blocks to build natural-language based applications. Recent times have seen how the analysis of social networks such as Twitter [10], the extraction of clinical terms [25] for electronic health records, the creation of bibliometrics [4] or the identification of gene names [8,5] to name a few have tackled the problem of entity recognition and extraction from raw sources. Other supervised techniques [17] have also be used to train data mining-based algorithms with the aim of creation classifiers.

- Semantic Web. More specifically in the LOD initiative the use of entity reconciliation techniques to uniquely identify resources is being currently explored. Thus an entity reconciliation process can be briefly defined as the method for looking and mapping [6] two different concepts or entities under a certain threshold. There are a lot of works presenting solutions about concept mapping, entity reconciliation, etc. most of them are focused on the previous NLP techniques [12,1] (if two concepts have similar literal descriptions then they should be similar) and others (ontology-based) that also exploit the semantic information (hierarchy, number and type of relations) to establish a potential mapping (if two concepts share similar properties and similar super classes then these concepts should be similar). Apart from that there are also machine learning techniques to deal with these mismatches in descriptions using statistical approaches. Recent times, this process has been widely studied and applied to the field of linking entities in the LOD realm, for instance using the DBPedia [13]. Although there is no way of automatically creating a mapping with a 100% of confidence (without human validation) a mapping under a certain percentage of confidence can be enough for most of user-based services such as visualization. However, in case of using these techniques as previous step of a reasoning or a formal verification process this ambiguity can lead to infer incorrect facts and must be avoided without a previous human validation.

On the other hand the use of semantics is also being applied to model organizational structures. In this case the notion of *corporate* is presented in several vocabularies and ontologies as Dave Reynolds (Epimorphics Ltd) reports[1]. Currently the main effort is focused in the designed of the Organizations Vocabulary (a W3C Working Draft) in which the structure and relationships of companies are being modeled. This proposal is especially relevant in the next aspects: 1) to unify existing models to provide a common specification; 2) to apply semantic web technologies and the Linked Data approach to enrich and publish the relevant corporate information; 3) to provide access to the information via standard protocols and 4)to offer new services that can exploit this information to trace the evolution and behavior of the organization over time.

---

[1] http://www.epimorphics.com/web/wiki/organization-ontology-survey

- Corporate Databases. Although corporate information such as identifier, name, economic activity, contact person, address or financial status is usually publicly available in the official government registries the access to this valuable information can be tedious due to different formats, query languages, etc. That is why other companies have emerged trying to index and exploit these public repositories; selling reporting services that contain an aggregated version of the corporate information. Taking as an example the Spanish realm, the Spanish Chambers of Commerce, "Empresia.es" or "Axesor.es" manage a database of companies and individual entrepreneurs. This situation can be also transpose to the international scope, for instance Forbes keeps a list of the most representative companies in different sectors. The underlying problems lies in the lack of unique identification, same company data in more than a source, name standardization, etc. and, as a consequence, difficulty of tracking company activity. In order to tackled these problems some initiatives applying the LOD principles such as the Orgpedia [2] and the CrocTail [15] (part of the "Corporate Research Project") efforts in United States or "The Open Database Of The Corporate World" [23] have scrapped and published the information of companies creating a large database containing $(54,080,317$ of companies in May 2012) with high-valuable information like the company identifier. Apart from that, reconciliation services have also been provided but the problem of mapping (n string literals $\rightarrow 1$ company $\rightarrow 1$ URI, as a human would do and the previous section has presented) still remains. Finally public web sites and major social networks such as Google Places, Google Maps, Foursquare, Linkedin Companies, Facebook or Tuenti provide APIs and information managed by the own companies that is supposed to be specially relevant to enrich existing corporate data once a company is uniquely identified.

3   The CORFU Approach

According to [4,16] institutional name variations can be classified into two different groups: 1) Non-acceptable variations (affect to the meaning) due to misspelling or translation errors and 2) acceptable variations (do not affect to the meaning) that correspond to different syntax forms such as abbreviations, use of acronyms or contextual information like country, sub-organization, etc. In order to address these potential variations the CORFU (Company, ORganization and Firm name Unifier) approach seeks for providing a stepwise method to unify corporate names using NLP and semantics based techniques as a previous step to perform an entity reconciliation process. The execution of CORFU comprises several common but customized steps in natural language processing applications such as 1) text normalization; 2) filtering; 3) comparison and clusterization and 4) linking to an existing information resource. The CORFU unifier make an intensive use of the Python NLTK API and other packages for querying REST services or string comparison. Finally and due to the fact that the corporate name can change in each step the initial raw name must be saved as well as contextual information such as dates, acronyms or locations. Thus common contextual information can be added to create the final unified name.

1. Normalize raw text and remove duplicates. This step is comprised of: 1) remove strange characters and punctuation marks but keeping those that are part of a word avoiding potential changes in abbreviations or acronyms; 2) lowercase the raw text (although some semantics can be lost previous works and empirical tests show that this is the best approach); 3) remove duplicates and 4) lemmatize the corporate name. The implementation of this step to clean the corporate name has been performed using a combination of the aforementioned API and the Unix scripting tools AWK and SED.

2. Filter the basic set of common stopwords in English. A common practice in NLP relies in the construction of stopwords sets that can filter some non-relevant words. Nevertheless the use of this technique must consider two key-points: 1) there is a common set of stopwords for any language than can be often used as a filter and 2) depending on the context the set of stopwords should change to avoid filtering relevant words. In this particular case, a common and minimal set of stopwords in English provided by NLTK has been used. Thus the normalized corporate name is transformed into a new set of words.

3. Dictionary-based expansion of common acronyms and filtering. A dictionary of common acronyms in corporate names such as "PTY", "LTD" or "PL" and their variants has been created by hand in order to be able to extract and filter acronyms.

4. Filter the expanded set of most common words in the dataset. Taking into account the aforementioned step this stage is based on the construction of a customized stopwords set for corporate names that is also expanded with Wordnet (ver. 3.0) synonyms with the aim of exploiting semantic relationships. In order to create this set two strategies have been followed and applied: 1) create the set of words by hand (accurate but very time-consuming) and 2) extract automatically the set of "most common words" from the working dataset and make a hand-validation (less accurate and time-consuming).

5. Identification of contextual information and filtering. Mainly corporate names can contain nationalities or place names that, in most of cases, only add noise to the real corporate name. In this case, the use of external services such as Geonames, Google Places or Google Maps can ease the identification of these words and their filtering. In order to tackle this situation the REST web service of Geonames has been selected due to its capabilities to align text with locations.

6. Spell checking (optional). This stage seeks for providing a method for fixing misspelling errors. It is based on the well-known speller [19] of Peter Norvig that uses a train dataset for creating a classifier. Although the accuracy of this algorithm is pretty good for relevant words in corporate names, the empirical and unit tests with a working dataset have demonstrated that misspelled non-relevant words is more efficient and accurate using a stopwords set/dictionary (this set has been built with words that are not in the set of "most common words", step 2, and exist in the Wordnet database). Furthermore some spelling corrections are not completely adequate for corporate names due to words could change and, therefore, a non-acceptable variant of the name could be accidentally included. That is why this stage is marked as optional and must be configured and performed with extreme care.

7. Pos-tagging parts of speech according to a grammar and filtering the non-relevant ones. The objective of this stage lies in "classifying words into their parts of speech and labeling them accordingly is known as part-of-speech tagging" [11]. In order to perform this task both a lemmatizer based on Wordnet and a grammar for corporate names ("NN"-nouns and "JJ"-adjectives connected with articles and prepositions) have been designed. Once words are tagged next step consists in filtering non-relevant categories in corporate names keeping nouns and adjectives using a walker function in the generated tree.

$$CorporateName = \begin{cases} <NBAR>:<NN.*|JJ>*<NN.*> \\ <NP>:<NBAR> \\ <NP>:<NBAR><IN><NBAR> \end{cases}$$

Fig. 1. Grammar for regular expression-based chunker in Python NLTK

8. Cluster corporate names. This task is in charge of grouping names by similarity applying a string comparison function. Thus if the clustering is applied n times any name will be grouped by "the most probably/used name" according to a threshold generated by the comparison function. This first version of CORFU has used the WRatio function to compare strings (available in the Levenshtein Python package) and a custom clustering implementation.

9. Validate and reconcile the generated corporate name via an existing reconcile service (optional). This last step has been included with the objective of linking the final corporate name with an existing information resource and adding new alternative labels. The OpenCorporates and DBPedia reconciliation services have been used in order to retrieve an URI to new corporate name. As a consequence the CORFU unifier is partially supporting one of the main principles of the LOD initiative such as unique identification.

Table 1. Example step-by-step of the CORFU technique

Step	Name	Example
0	Load corporate names	• "Accenture Australia Holding P/L" • "Oracle (Corp) Aust Pty Ltd"
1	Normalize raw text and remove duplicates	• "Accenture Australia Holding PL" • "Oracle Corp Aust Pty Ltd"
2	Filter the basic set of common stop-words in English	• "Accenture Australia Holding PL" • "Oracle Corp Aust Pty Ltd"
3	Dictionary-based expansion of common acronyms and filtering	• "Accenture Australia Holding Proprietary Company Limited" • "Oracle Corporation Aust Proprietary Company Limited"
4	Filter the expanded set of most common words in the dataset	• "Accenture Australia Holding" • "Oracle Aust"
5	Identification of contextual information and filtering	• "Accenture Australia Holding" • "Oracle Aust"
6	Spell checking (optional)	• "Accenture Holding" • "Oracle"
7	Pos-tagging parts of speech according to a grammar and filtering the non-relevant ones	• "Accenture" • "Oracle"
8	Cluster corporate names	• "Accenture" • "Oracle"
9	Validate and reconcile the generated corporate name via an existing reconcile service (optional)	• ("Accenture", dbpedia-res:Accenture) • ("Oracle", dbpedia-res:Oracle_Corporation)

4   Use Case: Unifying Supplier Names in the Australian e-Procurement Domain

As previous sections have introduced there is an increasing interest and commitment in public bodies to create a real transparent public administration. In this sense public administrations are continuously releasing relevant data in different domains such as tourism, health or public procurement with the aim of easing the implementation of new added-value services and improve their efficiency and transparency. In the particular case of public procurement, main and large administrations have already made publicly available the information with regards to public procurement processes. In this case of study the information of Australia is used to test the CORFU unifier. It is comprised of a dataset of more than 400K supplier names during the period 2004-2012. In order to be able to extract good statistics from this dataset the unification of names must be applied to. That is why the CORFU stepwise method has been customized to deal with the heterogeneities of this large dataset as Table 2 summarizes.

5   Evaluation

5.1   Research Design

Since the CORFU approach has been designed and implemented [2] it is necessary to establish a method to assess quantitatively the quality of the results. The steps to carry out this experiment are: 1) Configure the CORFU technique, see Table 2; 2) Execute the algorithm taking as a parameter the file containing the whole dataset of company names; 3) Validate (manually) the dump of unified names; 4) Calculate the measures of precision, see Eq. 1, recall, see Eq. 2, and the F1 score (the harmonic mean of precision and recall), see Eq. 3 according to the values of tp (true positive), fp (false positive), tn (true negative) and fn (false negative). In particular, this evaluation considers the precision of the algorithm as "the number of supplier names that have been correctly unified under the same name" while recall is "the number of supplier names that have not been correctly classified under a proper name". More specifically, tp is "the number of corporate names properly unified", fp is "the number of corporate names wrongly unified", tn is "the number of corporate names properly non-unified" and fn is "the number of corporate names wrongly non-unified".

$$Precision = \frac{tp}{tp + fp} \qquad (1) \qquad\qquad Recall = \frac{tp}{tp + fn} \qquad (2)$$

$$F1 = 2 \cdot \frac{Precision \cdot Recall}{Precision + Recall} \qquad\qquad (3)$$

---

[2] https://github.com/chemaar/corfu

Table 2. Customization of the CORFU technique for Australian supplier names

Step	Name	Customization
1	Normalize raw text and remove dupli-cates	Default
2	Filter the basic set of common stop-words in English	Default
3	Filter the expanded set of most com-mon words in the dataset	Two stopwords sets: 355 words (manu-ally) and words with more than $n = 50$ apparitions (automatically)
4	Dictionary-based expansion of common acronyms and filtering	Set of 50 acronyms variations (manu-ally)
5	Identification of contextual information and filtering	Use of Geonames REST service
6	Spell checking (optional)	Train dataset of 128457 words provided by Peter Norvig's spell-checker [19].
7	Pos-tagging parts of speech according to a grammar and filtering the non-relevant ones	Default
8	Cluster corporate names	Default
9	Validate and reconcile the generated corporate name via an existing recon-cile service (optional)	Python client and Google Refine

5.2   Sample

In order to validate the CORFU approach the dataset of supplier names in Australia in the period 2004-2012 containing 430188 full names and 77526 unique names has been selected. The experiment has been carried out executing the aforementioned steps in the whole dataset to finally generate a dump containing for each supplier the raw name and the unified name. These mappings has been validated by hand to quantify the typical measures of precision and recall.

5.3   Results and Discussion

According to the results presented in Table 3, the precision and recall of the CORFU technique are consider acceptable for the whole dataset due to $77526 - 40278 = 37248$, a 48% of the supplier names, has been unified with a precision of 0.762 and a recall of 0.311 (best values must be close to 1). The precision is pretty enough but the recall presents a low value because some corporate names were not unified under a proper name; some of the filters must therefore be improved in terms of accuracy.

In order to improve the results for relevant companies, the experiment has also been performed and evaluated for the first 100 companies in the Forbes list,

Table 3. Results of applying the CORFU approach to the Australian supplier names

Total number of companies	Unique names	CORFU unified names	% of unified names	Precision	Recall	F1 score
430188	77526	40277	48%	0.762	0.311	0.441
430188	299 in 77526	68	100%	0.926	0.926	0.926

actually 68 companies were found in the dataset. In this case, results show a better performance in terms of precision, 0.926, and recall, 0.926, and all these supplier names, 299 in the whole dataset, were unified by a common correct name. The explanation of this result can be found due to some of the parameters of the CORFU technique were specially selected for unifying these names because of their relevance in world economic activities.

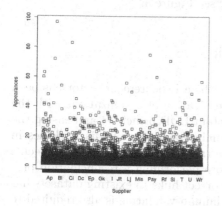

Fig. 2. Full view of supplier and number of appearances in the sample dataset

Fig. 3. Bubble Cloud of the first 100 Forbes companies and number of appearances in the sample dataset

On the other hand, it is important to emphasize that the last step of linking these names with existing web information resources using the reconciliation service of OpenCorporates or DBPedia in Google Refine can generate $37248 * 0.762 = 28383$ correct links (36.61%) instead of the initial 8%. Thus the initial problem of linking (n string literals $\rightarrow$ 1 company $\rightarrow$ 1 URI) has been substantially improved. Finally, the frequency distribution of supplier and number of appearances is depicted on Figures 2 and 3 with the objective of presenting how the cloud of points (appearances) that initially were only one per supplier has emerged due to the unification of names, for instance in the case of "Oracle" 75 apparitions can now be shown. On the other hand and due to the unique identification of supplier names, new RDF instances are generated, see

```
:o1  a  org:Organization ;
  skos:prefLabel
    ''Oracle'';
  skos:altLabel
    ''Oracle Corporation '',
    ''Oracle (Corp)
      Aust Pty Ltd'',
    ...;
  skos:closeMatch
    dbpedia-res:
      Oracle_ Corporation ;
  ...
```

```
SELECT  str (? label )
  (COUNT(? org )  as  ?pCount)
WHERE{
  ?ppn  : rewarded-to ?org  .
  ?org  rdf:type  org:Organization.
  ?org  skos:prefLabel ?label .
  ...
}
GROUP BY  str (? label )
ORDER BY  desc (?pCount)
```

Fig. 4. Partial example of a RDF organization instance

Fig. 5. Example of a SPARQL query for counting supplier names

Figure 4, and can be querying via SPARQL to make summary reports of the number of rewarding contracts by company, see Figure 5.

6   Conclusions and Future Work

A technique for unifying corporate names in the e-Procurement sector has been presented as a step towards the unique identification of organizations with the aim of accomplishing one of the most important LOD principles and easing the execution of reconciliation processes. The main conclusion of this work lies in the design of a stepwise method to prepare raw corporate names in a specific context, e.g. Australia supplier names, before performing a reconciliation process. Although the percentage of potential correct links to existing datasets has been dramatically improved it is clear that human-validation is also required to ensure the correct unification of names. As a consequence the main application of CORFU can be found when reporting or tracking activity of organizations are required. However this first effort has implied, on the one hand, the validation of the stepwise method and, on the other hand, the creation of a sample dataset that can serve as input for more advanced algorithms based on machine learning techniques such as classifiers. From public bodies point of view this technique also enables a greater transparency providing a simple way to unify corporate names and boosting the comparison of rewarded contracts.

Finally, future actions in this work consist in the extension of the stopwords sets for corporate names, a better acronym detection and expansion algorithm, other techniques to make string comparisons and group names such as $n-grams$ or the creation of a new final step to enhance the current implementation with a classifier that can automatically learn new classes of corporate names. Furthermore the technique must be reported to the Web economics [24] domain and the international "Public Spending" [14] initiative, as supporting tool, to be applied over other datasets to correlate and exploit metadata of public contracts.

References

1. Araujo, S., Hidders, J., Schwabe, D., De Vries, A.P.: SERIMI Resource Description Similarity, RDF Instance Matching and Interlinking. In: WebDB 2012 (2011)
2. Erickson, J.: TWC RPI's OrgPedia Technology Demonstrator (May 2013), http://tw.rpi.edu/orgpedia/
3. Directorate-General for Informatics European Commission. The eProcurement Map. a map of activities having an impact on the development of european interoperable eprocurement solutions (August 2011), http://www.epractice.eu/en/library/5319079
4. Galvez, C., Moya-Anegón, F.: The unification of institutional addresses applying parametrized finite-state graphs (P-FSG). Scientometrics 69(2), 323–345 (2006)
5. Galvez, C., Moya-Anegón, F.: A Dictionary-Based Approach to Normalizing Gene Names in One Domain of Knowledge from the Biomedical Literature. Journal of Documentation 68(1), 5–30 (2012)
6. Isele, R., Jentzsch, A., Bizer, C.: Silk Server - Adding missing Links while consuming Linked Data. In: COLD (2010)
7. Klein, D., Smarr, J., Nguyen, H., Manning, C.D.: Named entity recognition with character-level models. In: Proceedings of the Seventh Conference on Natural Language Learning at HLT-NAACL 2003, CONLL 2003, vol. 4, pp. 180–183. Association for Computational Linguistics, Stroudsburg (2003)
8. Krauthammer, M., Nenadic, G.: Term identification in the biomedical literature. J. of Biomedical Informatics 37(6), 512–526 (2004)
9. Stanford Natural Language Processing Lecture. Spelling Correction and the Noisy Channel. The Spelling Correction Task (March 2013), http://www.stanford.edu/class/cs124/lec/spelling.pdf
10. Li, C., Weng, J., He, Q., Yao, Y., Datta, A., Sun, A., Lee, B.-S.: TwiNER: Named entity recognition in targeted twitter stream. In: Proc. of the 35th International ACM SIGIR, SIGIR 2012, pp. 721–730. ACM, New York (2012)
11. Loper, E., Bird, S.: NLTK: The Natural Language Toolkit. In: Proceedings of the ACL Workshop on Effective Tools and Methodologies for Teaching Natural Language Processing and Computational Linguistics, pp. 62–69. Association for Computational Linguistics, Somerset (2002), http://arXiv.org/abs/cs/0205028
12. Maali, F., Cyganiak, R., Peristeras, V.: Re-using Cool URIs: Entity Reconciliation Against LOD Hubs. In: Bizer, C., Heath, T., Berners-Lee, T., Hausenblas, M. (eds.) LDOW, CEUR Workshop Proceedings. CEUR-WS.org (2011)
13. Mendes, P.N., Jakob, M., García-Silva, A., Bizer, C.: DBpedia spotlight: shedding light on the web of documents. In: Proc. of the 7th International Conference on Semantic Systems, I-Semantics 2011, pp. 1–8. ACM, New York (2011)
14. Vafolopoulos, M.M.M., Xidias, G., et al.: Publicspending. gr: Interconnecting and visualizing Greek public expenditure following Linked Open Data directives (July 2012)
15. Michalec, G., Bender-deMoll, S.: Browser and API for CorpWatch (May 2013), http://croctail.corpwatch.org/
16. Morillo, F., Aparicio, J., González-Albo, B., Moreno, L.: Towards the automation of address identification. Scientometrics 94(1), 207–224 (2013)
17. Nadeau, D.: Semi-Supervised Named Entity Recognition: Learning to Recognize 100 Entity Types with Little Supervision. PhD thesis, School of Information Technology and Engineering, University of Ottawa, Ottawa, Canada (2007)

18. Nadeau, D., Sekine, S.: A survey of named entity recognition and classification. Lingvisticae Investigationes 30(1), 3–26 (2007)
19. Norvig, P.: How to Write a Spelling Corrector (March 2013), http://norvig.com/spell-correct.html
20. Rodríguez, J.M.Á., Gayo, J.E.L., Silva, F.A.C., Alor-Hernández, G., Sánchez, C., Luna, J.A.G.: Towards a Pan-European E-Procurement Platform to Aggregate, Publish and Search Public Procurement Notices Powered by Linked Open Data: the Moldeas Approach. International Journal of Software Engineering and Knowledge Engineering 22(3), 365–384 (2012)
21. Rodríguez, J.M.A., Gayo, J.E.L., De Pablos, P.O.: Enabling the Matchmaking of Organizations and Public Procurement Notices by Means of Linked Open Data. Cases on Open-Linked Data and Semantic Web Applications 1(1), 105–131 (2013)
22. Rodríguez, J.M.A., Paredes, L.P., Azcona, E.R., González, A.R., Gayo, J.E.L., De Pablos, P.O.: Enhancing the Access to Public Procurement Notices by Promoting Product Scheme Classifications to the Linked Open Data Initiative. Cases on Open-Linked Data and Semantic Web Applications 1(1), 1–27 (2013)
23. Taggart, C., McKinnon, R.: The Open Database of The Corporate World (May 2013), http://opencorporates.com/
24. Vafolopoulos, M.: The Web economy: goods, users, models and policies. Foundations and Trends® in Web Science, vol. 1. Now Publishers Inc. (2012)
25. Wang, Y.: Annotating and recognising named entities in clinical notes. In: Proceedings of the ACL-IJCNLP 2009 Student Research Workshop, ACLstudent 2009, pp. 18–26. Association for Computational Linguistics, Stroudsburg (2009)
26. Yeates, S.: Automatic Extraction of Acronyms from Text. In: University of Waikato, pp. 117–124 (1999)

Appendix I

Table 4. Examples of supplier names in the Australian rewarded contracts dataset

Raw Supplier Name	Target (potential) Supplier Name and URI
"Accenture" "Accenture Aust Holdings" "Accenture Aust Holdings" "Accenture Aust Holdings Pty Ltd" "Accenture Australia Holding P/L" "Accenture Australia Limited" ... "Accenture Australia Ltd"	"Accenture" http://live.dbpedia.org/resource/Accenture
"Microsoft Australia" "Microsoft Australia Pty Ltd" ... "Microsoft Enterprise Services"	"Microsoft" http://live.dbpedia.org/resource/Microsoft
"Oracle (Corp) Aust Pty Ltd" "Oracle Corp (Aust) Pty Ltd" "Oracle Corp Aust Pty Ltd" "Oracle Corp. Australia Pty.Ltd." "Oracle Corporate Aust Pty Ltd" "Oracle Corporation" "Oracle Risk Consultants" "ORACLE SYSTEMS (AUSTRALIA) PTY LTD" ... "Oracle University"	"Oracle" http://live.dbpedia.org/resource/Oracle_Corporation
"PRICEWATERHOUSECOOPERS(PWC)" "PricewaterhouseCoopers Securities Ltd" "PricewaterhouseCoopers Services LLP" "Pricewaterhousecoopers Services Pty Ltd" "PriceWaterhouseCoopers (T/A: PriceWaterhouseCoopers Legal)" ... "Pricewaterhouse (PWC)"	"PricewaterhouseCoopers" http://dbpedia.org/resource/PricewaterhouseCoopers
...	...

Merging Controlled Vocabularies through Semantic Alignment Based on Linked Data

Ioannis Papadakis and Konstantinos Kyprianos

Ionian University, Dept. of Archives and Library Science
Ioannou Theotoki 72, Corfu, 49100, Greece
papadakis@ionio.gr, k.kyprianos@gmail.com

Abstract. In this paper, a methodology is presented that aids in finding equivalent terms between semantically similar controlled vocabularies. It is based both on lexical similarities discovery and semantic alignment through external LOD datasets. The proposed methodology has been deployed for the identification of equivalent terms within two datasets consisting of subject headings, namely Dione and NYT and facilitated through the employment of the LOD datasets of DBpedia and WordNet. The effectiveness of the methodology is assessed through a comparative evaluation between the deployment of the methodology presented in this paper and the deployment of a lexical similarities-based algorithm presented in previous work.

Keywords: controlled vocabularies, semantic alignment, linked data.

1   Introduction

Controlled vocabularies such as subject headings and thesauri are described as carefully predefined lists of words and phrases that are employed to organize knowledge [9]. They are widely used from libraries and other memory institutions in order to capture the meaning of their collections and resources. Thus, controlled vocabularies could be seen as the cornerstone of the resulting information search and retrieval tools that facilitate access to such resources.

The time and effort that specialized personnel consistently devotes to the development of such knowledge, underpins the quality of retrieval services that are provided by each organization separately. However, when it comes down to interoperability across services that refer to different organizations, things are not quite the same.

The fact that different institutions capture concepts in different ways, has led to the creation of semantically similar yet syntactically and linguistically heterogeneous controlled vocabularies with overlapping parts [5]. Consequently, information search and retrieval across multiple organizations has become a difficult and tedious task.

In an effort to overcome such issues and bring together semantically similar yet different controlled vocabularies, various matching tools and methodologies have been developed [10, 13]. They focus on the identification of semantically similar terms that may exist between different vocabularies. The most popular approaches in

E. Garoufallou and J. Greenberg (Eds.): MTSR 2013, CCIS 390, pp. 330–341, 2013.
© Springer International Publishing Switzerland 2013

the pursuit of such similarity are: a) *lexical similarity*, which compares terms according to the order of their characters [4] and b) *semantic alignment*, which is based on semantic techniques to identify similar terms between two structured vocabularies.

In this paper, a methodology is proposed that aims in bringing together semantically similar yet different controlled vocabularies through the semantic alignment of the underlying terms. The semantic alignment comes to reality through the employment of Linked Open Data – LOD technologies for the identification of semantically equivalent terms across controlled vocabularies.

The remainder of this paper is structured as follows. In the next section, related work about controlled vocabulary matching is presented. In section 3, a methodology is proposed that is capable of bringing together semantically equivalent terms from two controlled vocabularies with the employment of external LOD datasets. Then, the deployment of the proposed approach in an institutional repository and the corresponding results are presented. A short comparative evaluation follows and finally, section 5 concludes the paper and points directions for future work.

2   Related Work

During the past few years, a significant number of systems and methodologies have been introduced[1] for the alignment of semantically similar controlled vocabularies. Along these lines, undergoing research is mainly focused in *element-level* similarity establishment.

2.1   Element-Level Matching

Element-level matching techniques compute correspondences by analyzing entities or instances of those entities in isolation, ignoring their relations with other entities or their instances [10]. When it comes down to thesauri and/or subject headings alignment, it seems that lexical similarity is the most common approach [3]. Lexical similarity includes a number of techniques that take under consideration edit-distance (the degree of similarity is based on the number of insertions, deletions and substitutions that are needed to transform one term to another), prefix and suffix variations, n-grams etc. to measure similarities between the corresponding terms [11].

The advent of the LOD movement [12] motivated a significant number of thesauri and subject headings providers (i.e. LCSH[2], RAMEAU[3], BnF [14], STW[4], GEMET[5],

---

[1] Ontology Matching. Available at: `http://ontologymatching.org/index.html` Date accessed: 28/02/2013

[2] Library of Congress Subject Headings – LCSH. Available at: `http://id.loc.gov/` Date accessed: 03/03/2013

[3] RAMEAU linked data service. Available at: `http://data.bnf.fr/` Date accessed: 02/03/2013

[4] STW Thesaurus. Available at: `http://zbw.eu/beta/econ-ws/about` Date accessed: 02/03/2013

AGROVOC[6], etc.) to make use of the aforementioned techniques in order to identify similarities between the underlying terms[7]. Such similarities are commonly expressed through Simple Knowledge Organization System – SKOS[8] terminology and made publicly available through linked data technologies[9]. Along these lines, BLOOMS+ [8] employs LOD datasets to align the ontologies that underpin the underlying controlled vocabularies. BLOOMS+ uses Wikipedia to construct a set of category hierarchy trees for each class in the source and target ontologies. BLOOMS+ then determines which classes to align by computing the similarity between source and target classes based on their category hierarchy trees. Similarity is computed according to a sequential architecture of three matches: exact match, partial match and semantic broadcast. The first two are based on lexical similarity and the latter one is based on the propagation of previously calculated similarities [7].

In the following section, an element-level matching methodology is proposed that brings together terms from two semantically similar controlled vocabularies. The proposed methodology introduces a semantic alignment process that is based on linguistic LOD datasets such as WordNet[10] and DBpedia[11]. At this point, it should be mentioned that the proposed approach does not require any kind of structure for the compared datasets (e.g. the existence of a schema or ontology).

3   Proposed Approach

In this paper, a methodology is introduced that is capable of bringing together semantically equivalent terms from two controlled vocabularies with the employment of external LOD datasets. As mentioned earlier in this paper, the proposed approach performs semantic alignment that does not rely in the inherent structure of the corresponding vocabularies. Instead, it takes advantage of external linguistic datasets that are readily available on the lod-cloud[12]. Such datasets contain explicitly defined, linguistic relations (i.e. synonyms, hyponyms, meronyms, holonyms, etc.) among their terms.

---

[5]GEMET Thesaurus. Available at: `http://eionet.europa.eu/gemet` Date accessed: 28/02/2013

[6] AGROVOC Thesaurus. Available at: `http://aims.fao.org/` Date accessed: 28/02/2013

[7] According to the LOD principles, *"participation in the LOD cloud requires the existence of links to external resources, so that people/agents can go from one datastore to another"* Available at: `www.w3.org/DesignIssues/LinkedData.html` Date accessed: 25/03/2013

[8] SKOS. Available at: `http://www.w3.org/2004/02/skos/` Date accessed: 21/03/2013

[9] Bizer, C., Cyganiak, R., & Heath, T.: How to publish linked data on the web. (2007) Available at: `http://wifo5-03.informatik.uni-mannheim.de/bizer/pub/LinkedDataTutorial/` Date accessed: 22/03/2013

[10] WordNet: a lexical database for English. Available at: `http://wordnet.princeton.edu/` Date accessed: 28/02/2013

[11] DBpedia. Available at: `http://dbpedia.org` Date accessed: 28/02/2013

[12] The lod-cloud. Available at: `http://lod-cloud.net` Date accessed: 22/03/2013

Given a controlled vocabulary S acting as a source and a controlled vocabulary T acting as a target, the goal of the approach is to discover equivalent terms in S and T. In order to achieve this, the following process is proposed:

Initially, each term of S is matched against the terms of an external linguistic dataset L. The terms of S that have lexical similarities with one or more terms of L, formulate set S'. Consequently, the terms of L that are associated with one or more terms of S formulate set L'. Each term of S' is connected through a *isLexicalEquivalent* relation to one or more terms of L' (solid line in Fig. 1). 'isLexicalEquivalent' is defined as a symmetric and transitive relation. This initial step employs lexical similarity methodologies that are commonly met in element-level matching, as described in sect. 2.1.

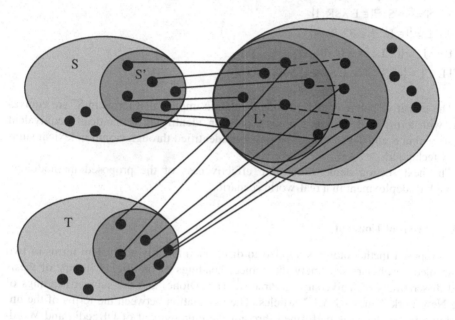

Fig. 1. Proposed methodology

Then, it is examined to see if terms in L' and the rest of the L are associated through an explicitly defined, equivalence relation. The terms of L that are equivalent with some or all the terms of L', constitute the set L''. Each term of L'' is associated through a *isSemanticEquivalent* relation to one or more terms of L' (dashed line in Fig. 1). This step employs semantic matching methodologies that are commonly available in LOD datasets (more details will be given in the following sections).

The terms within the union of sets L' and L'' are matched against the terms of T. The terms of T that have lexical similarities with one or more terms of L' and L'', formulate the set T'. Each term of T' is associated through a 'isLexicalEquivalent' relation to one or more terms of L' and L''.

Essentially, *isLexicalEquivalent* and *isSemanticEquivalent* are specializations of the *isEquivalent* relation. The former refers to terms that are found equivalent through lexical similarity techniques, whereas the latter refers to terms that are found equivalent through semantic alignment.

Formal Definitions

1. **S** is the set of terms in *Source* dataset
2. **T** is the set of terms in *Target* dataset
3. **L** is the set of terms in the *Linguistic* dataset
4. **R** is the *isEquivalent* relation between terms of two datasets
5. $\mathbf{R_L}$ is the *isLexicalEquivalent* relation between terms of two datasets
6. $\mathbf{R_S}$ is the *isSemanticEquivalent* relation between terms of two datasets
7. $xRy - \{(x,y): xR_L y \lor xR_S y\}$
8. $S' = \{s \in S : \exists l \in L \land sR_L l\}$
9. $L' = \{l \in L : \exists s \in S \land lR_L s\}$
10. $L'' = \{l \in L : \exists x \in L' \land lR_S x\}$
11. $T' = \{t \in T : \exists x \in L' \land y \in L'' \land tR_L x \lor tR_L y\}$

The transitive nature of 'isEquivalent' relation implies that terms in S' are equivalent with terms in T'. Such a process aims in identifying semantically equivalent terms within S and T that cannot be possibly identified through common lexical similarity techniques.

The next section demonstrates the effectiveness of the proposed methodology through its deployment in a real-world scenario.

3.1   Proof of Concept

The proposed methodology is applied to discover implicitly equivalent terms of two controlled vocabularies, namely the subject headings of the digital library of thesis and dissertations of University of Piraeus[13] (i.e. Dione) and the subject headings of the New York Times – NYT[14] articles. The association between the terms of the underlying vocabularies is performed through the employment of DBpedia and WordNet LOD datasets.

Dione consists of 3,323 bilingual (English-Greek) subject headings describing theses and dissertations on several disciplines (e.g. economics, business, banking, informatics etc.) within a DSpace installation. NYT provides approximately 10,000 subject headings that describe the underlying articles. Both vocabularies are published as LOD[15, 16].

---

[13] University of Piraeus digital library (Dione). Available at:
http://digilib.lib.unipi.gr/dspace/? Date accessed: 28/03/2013

[14] New York Times. Available at: http://www.nytimes.com/ Date accessed: 28/03/2013

[15] Neel SPARQL endpoint. Available at: http://neel.cs.unipi.gr/endpoint/ Date accessed: 28/02/2013

[16] NYT Linked Open Data. Available at: http://data.nytimes.com Date accessed: 28/02/2013

DBpedia [6] extracts structured information from Wikipedia and makes it available on the web as linked data. The current version (as of February 2013) contains more than 3.5 million entities and covers many domains. Each entity is identified through a global unique URI and is accessible through DBpedia's SPARQL endpoint[17]. The intrinsic nature of DBpedia (i.e. encyclopedia) and its wide approval renders DBpedia as a linguistic dataset suitable for the needs of this research.

WordNet is a large lexical database of the English language that is available as linked data. It consists of a set of synsets (e.g. synonyms). Each synset denotes a distinct concept and contains terms that are interlinked through conceptual-semantic relations. WordNet can also be accessed through a SPARQL endpoint[18].

As it will be shown later in this paper, both of the aforementioned LOD datasets contain equivalence relations among their terms (i.e. 'wikiPageRedirects' and 'containsWordsense' for DBpedia and WordNet respectively) that are necessary for the deployment of the proposed methodology.

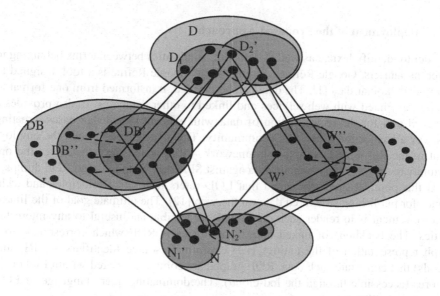

Fig. 2. Proposed methodology deployment

Fig. 2 illustrates the deployment of the proposed methodology presented in fig. 1 that leads to the identification of the implicitly equivalent subject headings of Dione and NYT through the employment of DBpedia and WordNet. Following the formalization of sect. 3, a number of mappings are defined:

---

[17] DBpedia's SPARQL endpoint. Available at: http://dbpedia.org/sparql/ Date accessed: 04/03/2013

[18] WordNet SPARQL endpoint. Available at:
http://wordnet.rkbexplorer.com/sparql/ Date accessed: 04/03/2013

1. let the *source dataset S* be **D** (i.e. Dione)
2. let the *target dataset T* be **N** (i.e. NYT)
3. let the *linguistic datasetA L* be **DB** (i.e. DBpedia) and
4. let the *linguistic datasetB L* be **W** (i.e.WordNet)
5. D_1' corresponds to S', assuming that the linguistic dataset L is DB. In a similar manner, D_2' corresponds to S', assuming that the linguistic dataset L is W.
6. **DB'** and **DB''** correspond to L' and L'' respectively, assuming that the linguistic dataset L is DB. In a similar manner, **W'** and **W''** correspond to L' and L'' respectively, assuming that the linguistic dataset L is W.
7. N_1' corresponds to T', assuming that the linguistic dataset L is DB. In a similar manner, N_2' corresponds to T' assuming that the linguistic dataset L is W.

In the following section the deployment details of the aforementioned methodology are presented.

3.2   Deployment of the Proposed Approach

In order to identify lexical as well as semantic similarities between terms belonging to different datasets, Google Refine[19] is employed. Google Refine is a tool designed to manipulate tabular data [1]. The data can be cleaned, transformed from one format to another, extended with web services and linked to other databases. It also provides a powerful tool for the reconciliation of data with existent knowledge bases, creating this way a connection to the LOD community. This is achieved through the employment of the Resource Description Framework – RDF extension[20] that gives the opportunity to end-users to reconcile data against SPARQL endpoints and RDF dumps.

At this point, it should be noted that LOD refers to a set of principles and techniques for publishing structured data on the web [12]. The ultimate goal of the linked data movement is to render such data highly accessible and useful to any interested parties. The backbone of linked data technologies is RDF which corresponds to a graph representation of the entities (i.e. Uniform Resource Identifiers – URIs and literals) that constitute such data. RDF graphs are commonly stored within LOD triplestores (accessible through the lod-cloud). The dominating query language of LOD triplestores is SPARQL[21].

More specifically, the implementation of the proposed methodology is based on the following six steps:

1. Subject headings from Dione are imported to Google Refine.
2. DBpedia and WordNet endpoints are registered in Google Refine as SPARQL reconciliation services.

---

[19] Google Refine. Available at: https://code.google.com/p/google-refine/ Date accessed: 28/02/2013

[20] RDF Refine - a Google Refine extension for exporting RDF. Available at: http://refine.deri.ie/ Date accessed: 28/02/2013

[21] SPARQL Query Language for RDF. Available at: http://www.w3.org/TR/ rdf-SPARQL-query/ Date accessed: 20/06/2013

3. The subject headings of Dione are matched against DBpedia's and WordNet's reconciliation services. The first matching process (i.e. matching between Dione and DBpedia datasets) results in a subset of DBpedia whereas the second matching process (i.e. matching between Dione and WordNet datasets) results in a subset of WordNet.
4. The terms in the sets of the previous step (i.e. subsets of DBpedia and Word-Net) are enriched with semantically equivalent terms deriving from the rest of DBpedia and WordNet.
5. Subject headings from NYT are imported to Google Refine.
6. The subject headings of NYT are matched against the terms deriving from steps 3 and 4.

Next, a detailed description of each step is provided.

Step 1: The list of subject headings from Dione is imported to Google Refine as a single-column spreadsheet. Thus, set D as defined in sect. 3.1 contains 3,323 terms.
Step 2: Google Refine's functionality can be extended to handle RDF data through the RDF extension. Such an extension allows the registration of the SPARQL endpoints of DBpedia[22] and WordNet[23] as reconciliation services.
Step 3: Google Refine introduces *reconciliation service* as a service capable of finding lexical similarities between terms belonging to different datasets. In the event of typed terms, Google Refine initiates an interactive procedure that allows the limitation of comparisons to specific types of terms, thus dramatically reducing the overall duration of the process. Since Dione's subject headings are imported as a single-column spreadsheet (i.e. untyped terms), Google Refine considers them to belong to a single, anonymous type. On the contrary, DBpedia and WordNet contain typed terms. Thus, reconciliation between Dione's and DBpedia's/WordNet's terms is limited to the 'skos:Concept' type.

Upon completion of the reconciliation process, the end-user may examine the suggestions provided by Google Refine, and accordingly accept or discard the suggested matches. In the proposed approach, the end-user is a well-trained subject librarian that performs, also, a manual qualitative evaluation of the suggestions. Such a process results in the discovery of 1,574, 1-1 lexically equivalent terms between Dione and DBpedia/WordNet. More specifically, DB' and D_1' consist of 1,119 terms each and W' and D_2' consist of 455 terms each.

The success rate of the reconciliation process differs significantly on the basis of the number of words that constitute a subject heading. Indeed, as the number of words increases, the reconciliation success rate decreases. A subject heading consisting of one to two words has the best success rate. Reconciliation success rate drops dramatically for subject headings consisting of more than three words and/or subdivisions. This is attributed to the fact that neither DBpedia nor WordNet contain terms with subdivisions.

---

[22] DBpedia SPARQL endpoint. Available at: `http://dbpedia.org/sparql` Date accessed: 28/02/2013
[23] WordNet SPARQL endpoint. Available at: `http://wordnet.rkbexplorer.com/sparql/` Date accessed: 28/02/2013

Table 1. Reconciliation success rate

Dione	DBpedia	WordNet
One-word Subject Headings	331 (29%)	297 (65%)
Two-words Subject Headings	658 (59%)	128 (28%)
Subject Headings with 3+ words	130 (12%)	30 (7%)
Subject Headings with Subdivisions	0	0
Sum	**1,119**	**455**

Step 4: The enrichment of the aforementioned sets with semantically equivalent terms from DBpedia and WordNet is achieved through the employment of Google Refine's "Add column By Fetching URL" function. More specifically, Google Refine provides the opportunity to create sets containing terms that are semantically related according to a specific property. For the needs of the proposed approach, "dbpedia-owl:wikiPageRedirects" and "wordnet:containsWordsense" are selected from DBpedia and WordNet respectively. Thus, DB" consists of 5,700 terms and W" contains 986 terms.

Step 5: The list of subject headings from NYT is imported to Google Refine as RDF dump files[24]. Thus, set N contains 10,000 terms.

Step 6: Finally, the lexically equivalent terms deriving from step 3 and the semantically equivalent terms deriving from step 4 are reconciled against NYT subject headings, to discover possible lexical similarities. Such a process results in the following 1-1 matches:

1. N_1' consists of 163 terms and N_2' consists of 117 terms.
2. DB' consists of 86 terms and DB" consists of 77 terms.
3. W' consists of 72 terms and W" consists of 45 terms.

In the following section, a comparative evaluation between a traditional lexical similarity methodology and the proposed one is presented.

4   Comparative Evaluation

The ultimate goal of the methodology introduced in this paper is to discover equivalent terms between semantically similar datasets. In order to assess the effectiveness of the proposed approach, it was decided to compare the results of the deployment of the proposed approach with the results of the deployment of an approach that is based on the discovery of just lexical similarities. Such a decision is justified from the fact

---

[24] NYT Linked Open Data. Available at: http://data.nytimes.com/ Date accessed: 28/02/2013

that the absence of schema in the NYT dataset makes it impossible to apply any ontology-based alignment approach.

In a previous work [2], a lexical similarities-based methodology (introduced in [3]) was deployed in order to discover equivalent terms between the subject headings of Dione and NYT. The deployment of the two methodologies (i.e. the work in [2] and the proposed methodology) on the same datasets facilitates a comparative evaluation between them, based on the corresponding deployment results.

According to [2], the lexical similarities-based algorithm resulted in the identification of a list of 207 pairs of equivalent terms (namely listA) between Dione and NYT datasets, whereas the proposed methodology resulted in the identification of (see sect. 3.2, step 6) a list of 280 pairs of equivalent terms (namely listB). A comparison between the two lists[25] reveals that their intersection consists of 180 common pairs, 27 pairs available only in listA and 100 only available in listB (see fig. 3). Twenty two of the 180 common pairs appear in listB as the product of semantic alignment, whereas the rest of the 158 pairs appear in listB as the product of lexical similarities matching.

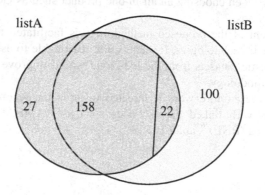

Fig. 3. Comparative evaluation results

The results of the comparative evaluation as presented in fig. 3 reveal that Google Refine performs slightly poorer as compared to the lexical similarities-based algorithm presented in [3] (i.e. 207 vs. 158 successful matches). Thus, it seems that although Google Refine makes it possible for non-expert users to apply complex lexical similarity techniques to their data, such ease of use does not come without a price.

On the other hand, the semantic alignment methodology based on DBpedia and WordNet datasets significantly increased the number of successful matches between Dione and NYT. More specifically, as it is shown in fig. 3, 100 new pairs of equivalent terms are discovered.

---

[25] ListA is available at: `https://docs.google.com/spreadsheet/ccc?key=0AuzgNdHCG27DdDRrMU1XMTVRcjJPZEg0cWowMDJxc3c#gid=0` and ListB is available at:
`https://docs.google.com/spreadsheet/ccc?key=0AuzgNdHCG27DdFZjRDNNLVRMRWg2TkJWZGFZN1BENXc#gid=0`

5   Conclusions and Future Work

In this paper, a methodology is presented that is capable of finding equivalent terms between semantically similar controlled vocabularies. It is based both on lexical similarities discovery and semantic alignment through external LOD datasets. The methodology is deployed to the subject headings of Dione and NYT with the help of the LOD datasets of DBpedia and WordNet.

The effectiveness of the methodology is assessed through a comparative evaluation between the deployment of the methodology presented in this paper and the deployment of a lexical similarities-based algorithm presented in a previous work. The results of the comparative evaluation are very promising. As shown in this paper, the advent of widely available tools such as Google Refine renders the deployment of the proposed methodology as a straightforward process that can be applied to other cases aiming in discovering equivalent terms in different yet semantically similar datasets. However, it must be noted that there is a trade-off between accuracy and out-of-the-box functionality when choosing an all-in-one product such as Google Refine instead of dedicated solutions.

The deployment of the proposed methodology is facilitated through the employment of linked data technologies. It seems quite reasonable to assume that the use of even more linguistic datasets from the lod-cloud would improve the effectiveness of the proposed methodology.

Along these lines, future work is targeted towards the reconciliation of Dione's subject headings with linked data services such as RAMEAU, SWD, Biblioteca National de Espana (BNE)[26] and LIBRIS[27].

References

1. Maali, F., Cyganiak, R., Peristeras, V.: Re-using cool URIs: Entity reconciliation against LOD hubs. In: Proceedings of the Linked Data on the Web Workshop, vol. 3 (2011)
2. Kyprianos, K., Papadakis, I.: Providing LOD-based functionality in digital libraries. In: Dodero, J.M., Palomo-Duarte, M., Karampiperis, P. (eds.) MTSR 2012. CCIS, vol. 343, pp. 13–24. Springer, Heidelberg (2012)
3. Papadakis, I., Kyprianos, K.: Merging Controlled Vocabularies for More Efficient Subject-based Search. International Journal of Knowledge Management 7(3), 76–90 (2011)
4. Kwak, J., Yong, H.: Ontology matching based on hypernym, hyponym, holonym, and meronym sets in WordNet. International Journal of Web & Semantic Technology 1(2), 1–14 (2010)
5. Lin, F., Sandkuhl, K.: A survey of exploiting WordNet in Ontology Matching. In: Bramer, M. (ed.) Artificial Intelligence in Theory and Practice II. IFIP, vol. 276, pp. 341–350. Springer, Boston (2008)

---

[26] Biblioteca de Espana. Available at: `http://datos.bne.es/sparql/` Date accessed: 02/03/2013

[27] LIBRIS. Available at: `http://libris.kb.se/` Date accessed: 02/03/2013

6. Bizer, C., Lehmann, J., Kobilarov, G., Auer, S., Becker, C., Cyganiak, R., Hellmann, S.: DBpedia – A Crystallization Point for the Web of Data. Journal of Web Semantics: Science, Services and Agents on the World Wide Web 7, 154–165 (2009)
7. Pesquita, C., Stroe, C., Cruz, I.F., Couto, F.M.: BLOOMS on AgreementMaker: Results for OAEI 2010. Ontology Matching, 137-145 (2010)
8. Jain, P., Yeh, P., Verma, K., Vasquez, R., Damova, M., Hitzler, P., Sheth, A.: Contextual ontology alignment of lod with an upper ontology: A case study with proton. The Semantic Web: Research and Applications, 80-92 (2011)
9. Harping, P.: Introduction to controlled vocabularies: terminology for art, architecture and other cultural works. Getty Research Institute, Los Angeles (2010)
10. Euzenat, J., Shvaiko, P.: Ontology matching. Springer, Haidelberg (2007)
11. Farooq, A., Arshad, M.J., Shah, A.: A layered approach for similarity measurement between ontologies. Journal of American Science 6(12), 69–77 (2010)
12. Bizer, C., Heath, T., Berners-Lee, T.: Linked data-the story so far. International Journal on Semantic Web and Information Systems (IJSWIS) 5(3), 1–22 (2009)
13. Ivanova, T., Terzieva, V.: Ontology Mapping Tools, Methods and Approaches–Analytical Survey (2010), http://www.bg-openaire.eu/jspui/handle/10867/93 (date accessed: June 15, 2013)
14. Simon, A., Wenz, R., Michel, V., Di Mascio, A.: Publishing bibliographic records on the web of data: opportunities for the BnF (French National Library). In: Cimiano, P., Corcho, O., Presutti, V., Hollink, L., Rudolph, S. (eds.) ESWC 2013. LNCS, vol. 7882, pp. 563–577. Springer, Heidelberg (2013),
http://eswc-conferences.org/sites/default/files/
papers2013/simon.pdf

Transient and Persistent RDF Views over Relational Databases in the Context of Digital Repositories

Nikolaos Konstantinou[1], Dimitrios-Emmanuel Spanos[1], and Nikolas Mitrou[2]

[1] Hellenic Academic Libraries Link
Iroon Polytechniou 9, Zografou, 15780, Athens, Greece
[2] School of Electrical and Computer Engineering, National Technical University of Athens
Iroon Polytechniou 9, Zografou, 15780, Athens, Greece
{Nkons,dspanos}@cn.ntua.gr, mitrou@cs.ntua.gr

Abstract. As far as digital repositories are concerned, numerous benefits emerge from the disposal of their contents as Linked Open Data (LOD). This leads more and more repositories towards this direction. However, several factors need to be taken into account in doing so, among which is whether the transition needs to be materialized in real-time or in asynchronous time intervals. In this paper we provide the problem framework in the context of digital repositories, we discuss the benefits and drawbacks of both approaches and draw our conclusions after evaluating a set of performance measurements. Overall, we argue that in contexts with infrequent data updates, as is the case with digital repositories, persistent RDF views are more efficient than real-time SPARQL-to-SQL rewriting systems in terms of query response times, especially when expensive SQL queries are involved.

Keywords: Linked Open Data, RDF Views, Bibliographic information, Digital Repositories, R2RML, Mapping.

1 Introduction

The Linked Open Data (LOD) movement is constantly gaining worldwide acceptance, emerging as one of the most prominent initiatives of the Web 3.0 era. As it can be observed, in many aspects of public information, a shift toward openness is taking place. The value of exposing data as LOD is being recognized in the cultural heritage domain (europeana.eu, clarosnet.org), governance (data.gov.uk), even in the news world (guardian.co.uk/data).

The technological building blocks that contribute to this shift have reached to a maturity level, able to sustain production environments available to public access. This is made available using technologies such as HTTP, XML, RDF and SPARQL, all internationally accepted W3C standards. Having these as technological background, the LOD vision is largely being materialized, slowly but steadily, by bringing existing data into the Semantic Web.

E. Garoufallou and J. Greenberg (Eds.): MTSR 2013, CCIS 390, pp. 342–354, 2013.
© Springer International Publishing Switzerland 2013

As to what drives the changes towards this direction, we can observe numerous benefits, both for the publishers, as well as for the target audience, or consumers:

- Ease of *synthesis* with external data sources, in the form of integration (beyond OAI-PMH), fusion, and mashups. The end user (or developer) can perform searches and retrieve results spanning various repositories, from a single SPARQL endpoint. Also, it is made possible to download parts or the whole data in order to combine it with other data and process it according to his/her needs.
- Semantic *enrichment*. Term and definition ambiguity is eliminated, allowing data to be uniquely understood and consumed both by humans as well as by software agents.
- *Inference*. It is possible to infer implicit facts based on explicitly stated ones. These new facts can then be added to the graph, thus augmenting the initial knowledge base.
- *Reusability*. Third party applications can be built on top of the datasets, as the data can be reused in third-party systems. This can be materialized, either by including the information in their datasets, or by real-time querying the published resources.
- *Intelligence* in the queries. Taking into advantage ontology hierarchy and concept interrelations, results can be obtained that exceed the keyword capabilities. In the same manner, Google uses the Freebase ontology[1] in order to return intelligent results which are more related to the users' queries.
- Digital repository *content can be linked*, and made part of the broader context of the Web. Instead of being an isolated dataset targeting a special group of people, library data can better fulfill their purpose by being part of the information users can discover and reuse on the Web.
- Richer *expressiveness* in describing and querying available information. Both the terminology that can be used to describe the dataset, as well as the queries that can be posed against it, with the use of semantic web technologies can be more complex and more expressive, allowing for a richer set of capabilities.

In order to offer solutions towards creating LOD, the methodological approaches that enable it can largely be regarded as falling into one of the following two approaches: in the first approach, *"transient"* RDF views are offered on top of the data, in the sense that the RDF graph is not materialized; instead, queries on the RDF graph are answered with data originating from the actual dataset, in a manner similar to the concept of SQL views. The second approach involves *"persistent"* RDF views, meaning that the data is exported (or dumped, as it is often called) asynchronously in RDF graphs. In the *"persistent"* approach, the idea is similar to the materialized view: data is exported in an RDF graph leaving the source unaltered.

It is interesting to mention, since adopting RDF as a dataset format to work upon entails so many benefits, a valid question would be, why not redesign new systems to operate fully using RDF graphs as their data backend? First of all, technologies such as relational databases have matured in the latest years far more than semantic technologies, offering a richer capability set. Furthermore, current established

---

[1] Freebase API: `https://developers.google.com/freebase/`

practices utilize technologies that have been successfully tested through time and have proven effective in preserving digital information and assuring its unaltered endurance in time. Therefore, such mature and reliable technologies cannot be abolished without at least allowing for a period of time to run both technologies alongside. This would allow for any problems to be accentuated and be solved before jumping to new technologies. In the case of LOD generation, potential risks are more associated with lack of expertise by the personnel that needs to be trained in order to adopt and operate the new technologies, and less associated with the maturity of the related technologies themselves.

Next, we discuss about available approaches regarding how to operate an institutional repository, whose operation typically involves a number of persons, an established methodology, and an infrastructure that is optimized towards serving its goals. With this in mind, instead of fully migrating to newer technologies, we rather suggest operating them side-by-side, as an additional content distributing channel, over the same source dataset, comprising digital repository contents.

All the above lead to the conclusion that in order to expose digital repository contents as LOD, several policy-related choices have to be made, since several alternative approaches exist in the literature, without any one-size-fits-all approach [1]. One of the most important factors to be considered is discussed in this paper: Should RDF provisions take place in real-time or should database contents be dumped into RDF at time intervals? Or, as explained before, should the RDF view over the contents be *transient* or *persistent*?

Both approaches constitute viable approaches, each with its specific characteristics, benefits and drawbacks. However, each case requires specific handling, in the sense that there are no one-solution-fits-all approaches. In this paper we analyze the pros and cons of each method as far as the institutional digital repository domain is concerned, taking into account the particularities it presents. Performance measurements are conducted concerning the exporting and querying times in variable initial datasets and settings, and respective measurements are presented and discussed.

The paper is structured as follows. Section 2 overviews related approaches that can be found in the bibliography. Section 3 presents the environment in which the measurements took place, the results, and an in-depth analysis and discussion. Section 4 concludes the paper with our most important conclusions and directions future work could take.

2   Related Work

The problem of generating RDF content from existing data sources has been investigated extensively and has gradually become a common task for data providers who wish to make their data available as RDF and reap the associated benefits discussed in Section 1. The data sources that a provider may have at her disposal will normally range from unstructured, free-text documents to semi-structured spreadsheets and structured databases.

The latter ones represent one of the most popular sources of data, with widespread adoption and a mature theoretical and practical background. Likewise, the problem of mapping relational database contents to an RDF graph has attracted a fair amount of attention and several solutions for carrying out this task are available. Such solutions and tools – often coined by the term RDB2RDF tools – present considerable variance and can be classified to distinct categories, according to a number of criteria [2]. One such criterion is the access paradigm of the generated RDF graph, according to which RDB2RDF methods can be classified to *massive dump* and *query-driven* ones. The former ones, also known as batch transformation or Extract-Transform-Load (ETL) approaches, generate a new RDF graph from a relational database instance (e.g. [3, 4]) and store it in physical form in some external storage medium. This external medium is often a database especially customized for the management and retrieval of RDF data, which is referred to as a *triple store*. The RDF graph generated by such approaches is said to be *materialized*. Triple stores do not provide any means to transform, or maintain any kind of mappings between the relational database contents and the resulting triples, leaving the synchronization methodology up to the user. On the contrary, query-driven approaches provide access to an RDF graph that is implied and does not exist in physical form. In this case, the RDF graph is *virtual* and is only considered when some appropriate request is made, usually in the shape of a semantic query.

This distinction of tools and approaches can also be viewed under the prism of the *data synchronization* criterion, according to which methods are distinguished depending on whether the generated RDF graph always reflects the current database contents or not. Transient views, as they have been defined in Section 1, have no need of a synchronization scheme, since the accordance among the RDF graph and the underlying database is always guaranteed. Another advantage of transient views stems from the fact that they do not need any additional storage for the RDF graph produced, given that the latter is *implied* and not materialized at all.

These two advantages highlight the superiority of transient views over persistent ones. It comes as no surprise that a lot of research effort focused, over the previous years, in efficient algorithms that translate SPARQL queries over the RDF graph in semantically equivalent SQL ones that are executed over the underlying relational database instance [5, 6]. Although, on first thought, the online query translation approach might seem inefficient, some evaluation experiments, such as the ones in [7], in fact show that some SPARQL-to-SQL rewriting engines (e.g. D2RQ [8] or Virtuoso RDF Views [9, 10]) outperform triple stores in the query answering task, achieving lower responses. This is due to the maturity and optimizations strategies of relational database systems that already outperform triple stores by factors up to one hundred [7]. Therefore, as long as the SPARQL-to-SQL translation does not introduce a large delay, the transient view access paradigm will still outperform triple stores. Still however, this is not an undisputed claim, as other works have shown that such rewriting engines perform more poorly than triple stores [11].

We investigate the performance of both persistent and transient views in a digital repository context and argue that in contexts with infrequent data updates, a static approach might be more suitable than a dynamic rewriting RDB2RDF system.

3   Evaluation

This section analyzes the performance evaluation experiments that were conducted. The experimental setup is described, as well as the obtained results and conclusions that can be drawn.

3.1   Experiments Setup

In order to measure the performance of the proposed approach, three separate DSpace installations were created. Using a random generator, these installations were populated with 1k, 10k, and 100k items, respectively. The metadata that was assigned originates from the Dublin Core (DC) vocabulary, as used in "vanilla" DSpace installations. Each randomly generated item was set to contain between 5 and 30 metadata fields, with random text values ranging from 2 to 50 text characters. Moreover, a number of users were inserted to each of these repositories, populating them with 1k, 10k, and 100k users respectively. As a result, we had three repositories, one with 1k items and 1k users, 10k items and 10k users, 100k items and 100k users.

Technically, DSpace 3.1 was used, backed by a PostgreSQL 9.2 RDBMS, on a Windows 7, 64-bit machine, running on a 2.10GHz Intel Core Duo, with 4 GB RAM. In the same infrastructure, both the D2RQ experimental R2RML version 4 (available online at download.d2rq.org) and the OpenLink Virtuoso server, open-source version 6.16, x64 were installed and configured.

In the transient view case, queries were performed using D2RQ and an R2RML [12] mapping file over the DSpace database. In the persistent view case, queries were performed after exporting the DSpace database as an RDF graph, using D2RQ and R2RML Parser (a tool that was introduced in [3]) with the same R2RML mapping file, and subsequently loading the RDF dump in the Virtuoso instance.

While the Virtuoso Universal Server supports R2RML mappings, the feature of viewing an external database as an RDF graph is available only in its commercial release, which was not available at the time of the tests. Therefore, it was not possible to test Virtuoso's R2RML views over the PostgreSQL DSpace schema. Instead, in order to measure Virtuoso's transient view performance, we had to dump the PostgreSQL database contents and load them into Virtuoso.

It is interesting to note that, in order to create and populate the experimental repositories with dummy data, bulk SQL insertions needed to be performed in the database. This is an operation that requires caution, since, unless care is taken, the required time could be unacceptable. Technically, this involved removing database table indexes and re-creating them at the end of the insertions.

Regarding Virtuoso, we noted that in order to execute complex queries on Virtuoso, using R2RML-based transient views, the program memory used (MaxMemPoolSize variable) had to be increased from 400M (default value) to 800M. We also noted that database caching, for some measurements, influences greatly the results while in other cases it seems to not have any impact at all. For instance, the SPARQL query Q2c (see Appendix II) on graph 1c using D2RQ, took 0.89 seconds, while subsequent calls took 0.33, 0.35, and 0.36 seconds, respectively.

However, the time that was required to dump database contents into graph 2s using D2RQ, seems to be slightly, if at all, affected by caching, as it took 96.79s, 95.17s, 96.47s, and 93.89s, at consecutive executions. In either case, in this paper the measurements contain the average of several measurements, without counting the first one.

Table 1 below gathers the results regarding the time that was needed to export database contents as RDF graphs in (a) simple and (b) more complex mappings that will next be analyzed.

Table 1. Time taken to export database contents as RDF in cases of (a) simple mappings on the DSpace eperson table, and (b) more complex mappings containing many JOIN statements among many tables

Users	triples	D2RQ	R2RML Parser	Items	triples	D2RQ	R2RML Parser
1k	3,004	14.52	3.30	1k	16,482	3.15	0.914
10k	30,004	95.58	6.79	10k	159,840	28.96	7.732
100k	300,004	906.26	25.06	100k	1,592,790	290.92	80.442

(a)   (b)

The first conclusion that can be read off these experimental measurements is the fact that dumping the contents of the DSpace database to an RDF graph takes much longer using D2RQ than using R2RML Parser. Therefore, when real-time access to the data is required, D2RQ is preferred, but in cases when dumps at time intervals suffice, the R2RML Parser tool is preferred. Of course, dumping the data into RDF, requires some time afterwards in order to load the graphs into Virtuoso, but as it is shown next, it is a small sacrifice considering the speed that it gives to queries.

3.2   Results Regarding Simple Mappings

In order to measure behavior in simple settings, the mapping definition that was used targeted only the users that are stored in the DSpace installation (tables eperson, epersongroup, and epersongroup2eperson, the last one holding information about the many-to-many relationships among persons and groups). An excerpt of the mapping file is presented in Appendix I.

Table 1(a) shows the time it took to export the results into an RDF graph. After exporting the RDF graphs, three test cases were considered:

a. Transient views, using D2RQ over PostgreSQL, and an R2RML mapping
b. Persistent RDF views, using Virtuoso, over an RDF dump of the database according to the R2RML mapping
c. Transient views, using Virtuoso over its relational database backend, and an R2RML mapping.

In case *b*, the RDF graphs were loaded in the Virtuoso instance. The required time was *0.53*, *2.16*, and *19.12* seconds, respectively. In order to measure SPARQL performance, the queries presented in Appendix II were devised.

Table 2 below sums up the measurement results. As it can be observed from the query response times, in cases *a* and *c*, the most demanding query was Q2s, taking more than 1h to compute over graph 3s (containing 100k users). This behavior is due to the numerous (6) triple patterns in the graph pattern. Query Q1s also appeared to be demanding, taking 398.74 seconds to compute over graph 3s. However, none of these delays was observed in case *b* (persistent RDF view), in which the most demanding query was Q1s, taking 2.31 seconds to compute over graph 3s.

Table 2. Query response times, in seconds, in simple mapping settings

	Graph 1s			Graph 2s			Graph 3s		
Q1s	6.18	0.1	0.56	44.75	0.31	0.88	398.74	2.31	3.8
Q2s	11.48	0.07	2310	11.76	0.08	3522	11.91	0.12	4358
Q3s	3.18	0.04	0.22	11.44	0.04	0.68	57.08	0.04	1.28
	a	*b*	*c*	*a*	*b*	*c*	*a*	*b*	*c*

3.3   Results Regarding Complex Mappings

The second set of measurements was performed as follows: After populating the DSpace repositories with 1k, 10k, and 100k items, respectively, a mapping file was created, aiming at offering a view over the metadata values in the repository. This mapping file tends to become very complex since each mapping declaration can comprise results from 5 joined tables, a fact that is due to the highly normalized DSpace schema. Appendix I shows an excerpt of the mapping file, specifically the part that targets at the dc.contributor.advisor values.

Table 1(b) holds the time in seconds that was required to export the database contents as an RDF graph, using D2RQ, and R2RML Parser, over the same mapping file and relational database backend.

Subsequently, the resulting graphs were inserted in a Virtuoso instance. This process took *1.87*, *11.04*, and *201.03* seconds, respectively. Next, the three SPARQL queries that are presented in Appendix II were devised, in order to measure performance. Table 3 below concentrates the measurement results.

Table 3. Query response times, in seconds, in complex mappings

	Graph 1c		Graph 2c		Graph 3c	
Q1c	125.34	0.27	1100.58	1.77	13921.64	11.18
Q2c	0.34	0.048	0.35	0.05	1.04	0.05
Q3c	144.01	0.13	1338.84	2.19	>6h	10.19
	D2RQ	*Virtuoso*	*D2RQ*	*Virtuoso*	*D2RQ*	*Virtuoso*

It must be noted that these queries in this experiment were evaluated in real-time against the D2RQ installation (transient views), and against the RDF graph dumps that were inserted in the Virtuoso instance (persistent). Although Virtuoso supports R2RML, it was not possible in this case to evaluate the queries against its R2RML implementation since it does not yet support the R2RML `rr:sqlQuery` construct that allows for arbitrary SQL queries to be posed against the database.

Overall, in the results table we can observe that Q3c was the most resource-hungry. Taking more than 20 minutes to compute over graph 2c, it was left overnight to compute over graph 3c, and was stopped since this amount of time was considered unacceptable, considering that the same query over the same graph in the persistent RDF view approach took 10.19 seconds to compute. Query Q2c was the fastest to compute at all times since it was not supposed to return any results. Query Q1c was more interesting since its graph pattern containing 6 triple patterns took approximately 3.87 hours for D2RQ to compute on graph 3c (containing 100k items), and 11.18 seconds for Virtuoso.

3.4   Discussion

Among the most important evaluation results are the ones visualized in Figure 1 below. From Figure 1(a), we can deduce that for queries Q1s and Q3s, query execution times increase as the size of the underlying graph increases, while query Q2s execution time remains more or less the same since it does not return any results. In Figure 1(b), in order to be objective in the measurements regarding Virtuoso performance, we added to the Q1c response time the time that was needed in order to dump into RDF the relational database contents, using R2RML Parser, and to subsequently load the RDF dump into Virtuoso. Also in this case, the execution time increases as the graph size increases, a fact that also holds for dumping the RDF using R2RML Parser, loading the dump into Virtuoso, and query Q1c answering over graphs 1c, 2c, and 3c in Virtuoso.

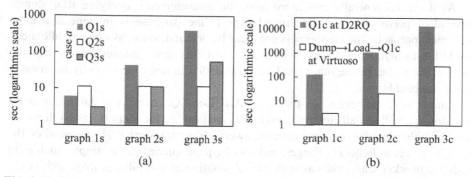

Fig. 1. In 1(a), we depict a query response time visualization in the simple mapping case a, while in 1(b) we visualize query Q1c execution time over D2RQ (transient RDF view) and over Virtuoso (persistent RDF view, after dumping the database contents using R2RML Parser, and loading the RDF dump into Virtuoso) in the complex mapping setting

Overall, as it can be deduced from the experiment outcomes, in the case of digital repositories, real-time SPARQL-to-SQL conversions are not the optimal approach, despite the presence of database indexes that would presumably increase performance compared to plain RDF graphs. The round-trips to the database pose a burden that cannot be alleviated by relational database indexing techniques. RDF dumps perform much faster, especially in the cases of SPARQL queries that involve many triple patterns that are subsequently translated to numerous JOIN statements, which are usually expensive. Therefore, despite the advantages transient views demonstrate in the general case, in the case of digital repositories the additional computational burden they impose causes persistent views to be more preferable.

Regarding the initial time, required to export the database in an RDF graph, the R2RML parser concluded its export in much less time than D2RQ. Of course, this required the extra step of loading the RDF dump into Virtuoso, as illustrated and explained in Figure 1(b).

Overall, using Virtuoso with R2RML views enabled seems to be performing well; this solution however, comes at the expense of the following: R2RML transient views are only offered over Virtuoso's relational database backend, in the open-source version. Connection to external data sources is available only in the commercial Virtuoso edition. Moreover, no arbitrary SQL queries are supported as logical tables in the R2RML mapping file, thus diminishing mapping potential and capabilities.

4   Conclusions and Future Work

In this paper we present and evaluate an approach for exposing digital library information as LOD. After introducing the problem framework and examining several of the approaches that exist in the literature, we perform a set of measurements over two distinct approaches, and evaluate the measurement results. The first case concerns on-the-fly, transient RDF views over the relational database contents while the other case concerns querying asynchronous exports, i.e. persistent RDF dumps.

As it can be generally concluded from the measurements, querying RDF dumps instead of performing real-time round trips to the database is in general a more efficient approach. The answer was not clear beforehand, since, as one would expect. SPARQL-to-SQL translators can take into account indexes and database optimizations, but on the other hand, this translation in real-time is costly in terms of computational burden.

Simple as it may seem, on-the-fly SPARQL-to-SQL query translations is not a solution that will suit all environments and is not justified for every occasion. It would be advisable to prefer real-time query answering over transient RDF views when the data is subject to frequent changes, and less frequent queries (for example, such as in social networks). Cases such as institutional repositories and bibliographic archives in general are not typically updated to a significant amount daily, and selection queries over their contents are far more frequent than the updates.

The cost of not having real-time results may not be as critical, considering that RDF updates could take place in a manner similar to maintaining search indexes, typically used to enable full-text search in web applications. The trade-off in data freshness is largely remedied by the improvement in the query answering mechanism.

Also noteworthy is the fact that still, exporting data as RDF covers half of the requirements that have to be met before publishing repository data: the second half of the problem concerns its bibliographic dimension. Widespread ontologies have to be used where applicable in order to offer meaningful, semantically enriched descriptions of the DSpace repository data. Moreover, linking the data to third party datasets is an aspect that is not hereby discussed, as it is out of the scope of the paper. Overall, this paper's contribution is a methodology that offers an insight in the initial problems associated with the effort required to publish digital repository data as (Linked) Open Data, and the results one could expect.

Future steps that could be followed in order to expand this work include considering more mapping tools supporting R2RML (such as Ultrawrap (capsenta.com)), in order to evaluate dump times and query times. Additionally, more institutional repository solutions (such as Eprints (eprints.org)) or triple stores (such as Sesame (openrdf.org)) could be considered for inclusion in the measurements.

Acknowledgements. This work was partially funded by the Hellenic Academic E-Books project (http://www.kallipos.gr).

References

1. Villazon-Terrazas, B., Vila-Suero, D., Garijo, D., Vilches-Blazquez, L.M., Poveda-Villalon, M., Mora, J., Corcho, O., Gomez-Perez, A.: Publishing Linked Data - There is no One-Size-Fits-All Formula. In: Proceedings of the European Data Forum (2012)
2. Spanos, D.-E., Stavrou, P., Mitrou, N.: Bringing relational databases into the semantic web: A survey. Semantic Web Journal 3(2), 169–209 (2012)
3. Konstantinou, N., Spanos, D.-E., Houssos, N., Mitrou, N.: Exposing Scholarly Information as Linked Open Data: RDFizing DSpace contents. The Electronic Library (in press, 2013)
4. Auer, S., Dietzold, S., Lehmann, J., Hellmann, S., Aumueller, D.: Triplify – Light-Weight Linked Data Publication from Relational Databases. In: Proceedings of the 18th International Conference on World Wide Web (WWW 2009), New York, NY, USA, pp. 621–630 (2009)
5. Chebotko, A., Lu, S., Fotouhi, F.: Semantics Preserving SPARQL-to-SQL Translation. Data & Knowledge Engineering 68(10), 973–1000 (2009)
6. Cyganiak, R.: A Relational Algebra for SPARQL. Technical Report HPL 2005-170 (2005)
7. Bizer, C., Schultz, A.: The Berlin SPARQL Benchmark. International Journal On Semantic Web and Information Systems 5(2), 1–24 (2009)
8. Bizer, C., Cyganiak, R.: D2R Server - Publishing Relational Databases on the Semantic Web. In: Proceedings of the 5th International Semantic Web Conference (2006)
9. Erling, O., Mikhailov, I.: RDF support in the Virtuoso DBMS. In: Pellegrini, T., Auer, S., Tochtermann, K., Schaffert, S. (eds.) Networked Knowledge - Networked Media. SCI, vol. 221, pp. 7–24. Springer, Heidelberg (2009)
10. Blakeley, C.: Virtuoso RDF Views Getting Started Guide (2007), http://www.openlinksw.co.uk/virtuoso/Whitepapers/pdf/ Virtuoso_SQL_to_RDF_Mapping.pdf (accessed July 2, 2013)

11. Gray, A.J.G., Gray, N., Ounis, I.: Can RDB2RDF Tools Feasibily Expose Large Science Archives for Data Integration? In: Aroyo, L., et al. (eds.) ESWC 2009. LNCS, vol. 5554, pp. 491–505. Springer, Heidelberg (2009)
12. Das, S., Sundara, S., Cyganiak, R.: R2RML: RDB to RDF Mapping Language. W3C Recommendation (2012), http://www.w3.org/TR/r2rml/ (accessed August 29, 2013)

Appendix I – Mapping File Excerpts

Next, we provide the most important excerpts from the R2RML mapping files used during the experiments. In the simple mapping case, the declarations are as follows:

```
map:persons-groups
    rr:logicalTable [ rr:tableName '"epersongroup2eperson"'; ];
    rr:subjectMap [ rr:template
'http://data.example.org/repository/group/{"eperson_group_id"}';
];
    rr:predicateObjectMap [
        rr:predicate foaf:member;
        rr:objectMap [ rr:template
'http://data.example.org/repository/person/{"eperson_id"}';
                        rr:termType rr:IRI; ] ].
```

In the complex mapping case, the SQL queries get more complicated, as in the excerpt that follows:

```
map:dc-contributor-advisor
    rr:logicalTable <#dc-contributor-advisor-view>;
    rr:subjectMap [ rr:template
'http://data.example.org/repository/item/{"handle"}';
    ];
    rr:predicateObjectMap [
        rr:predicate dc:contributor;
        rr:objectMap [ rr:column '"text_value"' ]; ].

<#dc-contributor-advisor-view>
    rr:sqlQuery """
    SELECT h.handle AS handle, mv.text_value AS text_value
    FROM handle AS h, item AS i, metadatavalue AS mv,
metadataschemaregistry AS msr, metadatafieldregistry AS mfr
WHERE
    i.in_archive=TRUE AND
    h.resource_id=i.item_id AND
    h.resource_type_id=2 AND
    msr.metadata_schema_id=mfr.metadata_schema_id AND
    mfr.metadata_field_id=mv.metadata_field_id AND
```

```
mv.text_value is not null AND
i.item_id=mv.item_id AND
msr.namespace='http://dublincore.org/documents/dcmi-terms/'
AND
mfr.element='contributor' AND
mfr.qualifier='advisor'
""".
```

Appendix II – SPARQL Queries

Appendix II concentrates the SPARQL queries that were executed against the mapping results, in order to conduct the measurements presented in Tables 1, 2 and 3.

Table 4. On the left, we provide the SPARQL queries Q1s, Q2s, and Q3s that were executed against simple mappings, and on the right the SPARQL queries Q1c, Q2c, and Q3c that were executed against more complex mappings

Q1s	Q1c

`SELECT DISTINCT ?eperson ?name`
`WHERE {`
`  ?eperson rdf:type`
`foaf:Person.`
`?eperson foaf:name ?name.`
`FILTER (?name != "mlo vqlbcbk"`
`)}`
`ORDER BY ?eperson`
`LIMIT 500`
	`SELECT DISTINCT ?item ?title`
	`?creator`
	`WHERE {`
	`  ?item dcterms:title ?title.`
	`  ?item dcterms:creator ?creator.`
	`  ?item dcterms:identifier ?id .`
	`  ?item dcterms:type ?type.`
	`  ?item dcterms:subject ?subj.`
	`  ?item dcterms:date ?date.`
	`FILTER (?date != "2008-06-`
	`20T00:00:00" )}`
	`ORDER BY ?creator`
	`LIMIT 100`

Q2s	**Q2c**

`SELECT DISTINCT ?eperson1`
`?groupname1 ?eperson2`
`?groupname2`
`WHERE {`
`?eperson1 rdf:type`
`foaf:Person.`
`?eperson2 rdf:type`
`foaf:Person.`
`?group1 foaf:member ?eperson1.`
`?group2 foaf:member ?eperson2.`
`?group1 rdf:type foaf:Group.`
`?group2 rdf:type foaf:Group.`
`OPTIONAL {`
`?group1 foaf:name ?groupname1.`
`?group2 foaf:name ?groupname2.`
`} } LIMIT 500`
	`SELECT DISTINCT ?item1 ?item2`
	`?creator1 ?type1 ?type2`
	`WHERE {`
	`?item1 dcterms:title "example".`
	`?item1 dcterms:creator ?creator1.`
	`?item1 dcterms:identifier ?id1.`
	`?item2 dcterms:title "example".`
	`?item2 dcterms:creator ?creator1.`
	`?item2 dcterms:identifier ?id2.`
	`OPTIONAL{`
	`?item1 dcterms:type ?type1.`
	`?item2 dcterms:type ?type2. } }`
	`ORDER BY ?creator1`
	`LIMIT 100`

Q3s
SELECT DISTINCT ?eperson WHERE { ?group foaf:member ?eperson. ?group foaf:name "Administrator". ?eperson foaf:name "john smith" } ORDER BY ?eperson

Q3c
SELECT DISTINCT ?item ?title ?creator WHERE { ?item dcterms:title ?title. ?item dcterms:creator ?creator. ?item dcterms:identifier ?id OPTIONAL{ ?item dcterms:type ?type } OPTIONAL{ ?item dcterms:subject ?subj } OPTIONAL{ ?item dcterms:date ?date. FILTER (?date > "2008-06- 20T00:00:00"^^<http://www.w3.org/200 1/XMLSchema#dateTime>) } } ORDER BY ?creator

Document Mark-Up for Different Users and Purposes

David King and David R. Morse

Department of Computing and Communications,
The Open University, Milton Keynes, MK7 6AA, UK
{david.king,david.morse}@open.ac.uk

Abstract. Semantic enhancement of texts aids their use by researchers. However, mark-up of large bodies of text is slow and requires precious expert resources. The task could be automated if there were marked-up texts to train and test mark-up tools. This paper looks at the re-purposing of texts originally marked-up to support taxonomists to provide computer scientists with training and test data for their mark-up tools. The re-purposing highlighted some key differences in the requirements of taxonomists and computer scientists and their approaches to mark-up.

Keywords: mark-up, XML annotation, stand-off annotation, biodiversity.

1   Introduction

To assess global challenges surrounding issues such as climate change and invasive species requires a baseline of historical data. One source of historical data is the Biologia Centrali-Americana (BCA). The BCA was privately issued in installments between 1879 and 1915 by F. Ducane Godman and Osbert Salvin of The Natural History Museum, London. As described in its prospectus "The work consists of 63 volumes containing 1,677 plates (of which more than 900 are coloured) depicting 18,587 subjects. The total number of species described is 50,263 of which 19,263 are described for the first time." This record of Central America's plants and animals can usefully be compared to contemporary species distributions. The BCA is available in scanned form from the Biodiversity Heritage Library [1, 2]. It has recently been re-keyed and manually marked-up by the INOTAXA [3, 4] project to help taxonomists search the contents of its 63 volumes. Curation of the marked-up volumes is continuing pending their public availability.

The manual annotation of large-scale works like the BCA is time consuming and demands expert review to curate the results. The task could benefit from automation, but attempts to automate the process face the problem of not having suitable corpora against which to develop and test the required text-mining tools.

One project, ViBRANT [5], seeks to use INOTAXA's re-keyed data to produce a corpus to support the development of text-mining tools for biodiversity documents. However, the apparently straightforward task of re-purposing INOTAXA's mark-up has highlighted several issues because of the different audience requirement of the mark-up.

E. Garoufallou and J. Greenberg (Eds.): MTSR 2013, CCIS 390, pp. 355–360, 2013.

In this short paper we will describe the different needs of scientists in biodiversity and computing, how this affects the mark-up made to the documents, and how this in turn affects the re-working of annotations to meet the differing requirements.

2   Taxonomists' Requirements

XML is intended to bring structure to unstructured text and can be applied to scientific biodiversity documents [6, 7, 8]. As the prevailing mark-up technology, it was adopted by taxonomists, often in collaboration with colleagues from their supporting library services, to result in three leading XML schemas today [9]. All are applied directly to the source text so that the XML mark-up is inline with the original text.

TaxonX [10] is a lightweight mark-up focused on taxon treatments (description of species). It was created by an interdisciplinary group as part of Plazi [11] with the goal of modeling taxon treatments to provide a basis for data mining and extraction.

taXMLit [12] is a detailed mark-up focused on data curation, extraction and analysis. This schema was developed from TEI [13] as part of the INOTAXA project with the ambitious goal of covering all document and data content types. Hence, it offers very flexible possibilities for data mining though tagging a wide range of components within taxonomic papers.

TaxPub [14] is an extension of the National Library of Medicine DTD focused on layout and taxon names [15]. The schema was developed by Plazi in collaboration with U.S. National Center for Biotechnology Information [16]. Whereas TaxonX and taXMLit are mark-up XML schemas developed primarily to encode historical taxonomic literature, TaxPub aims to facilitate mark-up of new, born digital taxonomic publications as part of the publication process [17].

Each schema has its own strengths and weaknesses arising from the priorities of the taxonomists who developed them. TaxonX primarily models treatments, which are key data for taxonomists, but only records other data at a generic level. In contrast, the extensive tag sets of taXMLit and TaxPub permit detailed mark-up of all content elements. In practical terms, TaxonX requires the user to investigate documents at a treatment level, whereas the other two schemas enable other forms of enquiry to be accomplished as easily, such as searching by habitat. However, this flexibility is at the cost of complexity in mark-up and time required to produce it.

Achieving the full potential of XML marked-up documents requires supporting queries tailored to the schema's specific elements. These can be incorporated into a portal for ease of human use, as well as being built into web services. For TaxonX the portal is Plazi and for taXMLit the portal is INOTAXA [3]. TaxPub is not used this way, but as an enhanced archive format. TaxonX publications can be archived in PubMed Central [18] for subsequent retrieval.

The portals are also necessary for general work with the marked-up documents, because the portals can remove the inline mark-up that otherwise makes the text difficult for humans to read.

The subtly different purpose can make it difficult to convert marked-up documents across these schemas [19]. For example, taXMLit provides for divides location into three levels (locality, country and continent) whereas TaxonX and TaxPub have only 'location' as one entity to cover all levels. Hence, it is possible to convert from taXMLit to the others automatically, but it may not be possible to do the reverse. However, all three XML schemas permit the addition of data that is not in the source document. In the location example, it is unlikely that the source text explicitly mentions all three tiers of location, but this enhancement can be provided in the XML mark-up. The choice of how to enhance a source document is one of the key differences between taxonomists' view of the text and computer scientists'.

3   Computer Scientists' Requirements

Computer scientists prefer to preserve the original text intact. This allows further analysis on the text without the complications of having to allow for changes caused by the presence of inline mark-up. This approach makes reuse of the text easier too. It also permits the application of several layers of annotation covering different purposes to the text.

To meet these needs computer scientists prefer to use stand-off mark-up, in which the mark-up is held in a separate file to the source text. This does raise document management issues, such as version control across files that are avoided if both text and mark-up are in the one document. Arguably, data scientists should be able to handle such issues though.

At one time much work in this domain used XML-based stand-off annotation, following the ISO Linguistic Annotation Framework [20]. Of late however, there is a move towards a lighter weight form of annotation, exemplified in the biodiversity domain by the brat stand-off format [21] and accompanying mark-up tool [22].

Concerns such as multiple views of the document, are generally of little concern to the taxonomic community because they are focused on one use of the document, even if they do have different working practices to achieve that one use. In contrast, the authors, who are data scientists, have been looking to apply other forms of analysis to the text to determine if additional cues for accurate information extraction are available. As the original text is unaltered, it is relatively easy to apply a second layer of analysis over the existing taxonomic mark-up and search for significant overlapping patterns. This multiple application of different annotations would be far more difficult if working with inline XML.

4   Working Differences in Practice – Some Examples

Figure 1 shows part of a page from the BCA's first volume about birds. It is a conventional discussion piece on a species.

Taxonomists need to know the provenance of the species being discussed. Hence the mark-up includes more than just the taxon name in the text. Typically it will contain additional information such as the name of the authority (the person who first identified the species). An example of this form of enhanced mark-up, using a simplified version of taXMLit, is shown in figure 2. [Note the overloaded use of TEI's rend attribute which includes font rendering and taxonomic rank information.] In this example, the species Vireolanius melitophrys was first described by Du Bus, and that is recorded in the mark up of the taxon name. The mark-up is embedded in the text.

Computer scientists are interested in taxonomic names for information extraction. The originating authority is of no concern. Figure 3 shows the brat stand-off annotation format. This format gives the location of each species name in the document's page, expressed in terms of a character offset from the beginning of the page.

VIREOLANIUS.

Vireolanius, Bonaparte, Consp. Av. i. p. 330 (1850) (ex Du Bus); Baird, Rev. Am. B. i. p. 395.

This genus, with the next, form a distinct section of the Vireonidæ, by reason of their stout beaks and their more robust build. They approach the Shrikes (Laniidæ); and, indeed, we think it not at all improbable that their more immediate relationship with the African genus *Laniarius,* which they strongly resemble in many points of coloration, will some day have to be reconsidered; but to do so here would lead us into a discussion far beyond the limits of the present work. We may remark, however, that Swainson placed the species he described in the genus *Malaconotus,* calling it *M. leucotis,* and in the same genus he placed several species now considered to belong to *Laniarius.*

From *Cyclorhis Vireolanius* is hardly to be distinguished structurally; but, as Prof. Baird remarks, the beak is not quite so strongly curved and not so deep at the base.

Cyclorhis, however, is very homogeneous as now restricted, and to include *Vireolanius* in it would be to introduce an aberrant element. Moreover we feel sure that the alliance is not so close as appears at first sight, though the differences are not to be satisfactorily stated at present.

Vireolanius contains four species, one of which, *V. melitophrys,* is restricted to the highlands of Mexico and Guatemala. *V. pulchellus, V. eximius,* and *V. leucotis* are probably all lowland species, and are distributed, the first throughout Central America, the second in Colombia, and the last in Guiana and Upper Amazonia.

Fig. 1. Part of a page scan from the BCA

```
<div type="taxon synonymy">
 <p elementid="BCA-aves-v3p1-2240">
  <hi rend="genus">
   <hi rend="italic">Vireolanius</hi>
  </hi>
  <hi rend="species">
   <hi rend="italic">melitophrys</hi>
  </hi>,
  <bibl rend="primary">
  <author>Du Bus</author>,
  <title>Esq. Orn.</title>
```

Fig. 2. A taxonomist's view of the taxon name

```
T25 genus 1647 1658 Vireolanius
T26 specificepithet 1659 1670 melitophrys
```

Fig. 3. A Computer Scientist's view of the taxon name

Hence, when re-purposing the INOTAXA marked-up documents to provide gold standard data for training and testing text-mining tools, some marked-up information is lost. This is also important when attempting to provide meaningful text-mined texts for taxonomists to use, if possible the text-mining tool needs to collocate the authority name in the text to add it to the taxon name mark-up.

A second discrepancy is apparent on this sample page. The genus name *Laniarus* is not marked-up in the INOTAXA supplied XML because it is an African species to which the Central American bird, that is the object of the discussion, is being compared. This work is concerned with documenting Central American residents only; hence, the African bird is not marked-up. In contrast, to train and test a text-mining tool that can accurately identify taxonomic names, all such names must be marked up; the geographical location of the species is irrelevant for this task. Therefore, the INOTAXA supplied data could not be automatically converted to a text-mining training set in stand-off format, but had to be manually curated too, looking for omissions such as this.

5   Conclusion

The two groups of scientists have different purposes for the mark-up. Taxonomists see mark-up as a means to exploit the documents' contents. Computer scientists see mark-up as part of a process to explore the documents. For taxonomists ease of document management outweighs concerns about future reuse, the opposite is true for computer scientists. Hence, the different preferences for inline and stand-off mark-up.

The same text, and even apparently the same type of entities within a text, can be interpreted differently for there can be subdivisions that are applicable to only one discipline. Taxonomists further complicate the issue by including data that is not present in the source text in their mark-up. Highlighting again the fundamental difference that taxonomists want the mark-up to support their work exploiting the documents, indeed going beyond the documents, whereas computer scientists are content to study the documents as artifacts in their own right. These differences in requirements open up interesting problems when converting from one mark-up regime to the other, as elements need to be discarded or added appropriately; a challenge to inform our continuing research within ViBRANT.

Acknowledgements. The ViBRANT project for funding this work. ViBRANT is funded by the European Union 7th Framework Programme within the Research Infrastructures group. The INOTAXA project for generously making their materials available for this work.

References

1. Biodiversity Heritage Library, http://www.biodiversitylibrary.org/
2. BHL Book of the Week: BiologiaCentrali-Americana,
   http://blog.biodiversitylibrary.org/2012/09/
   biologia-centrali-americana-hispanic.html

3. INOTAXA, INtegrated Open TAXonomic Access, http://www.inotaxa.org/
4. Weitzman, A.L., Lyal, C.H.C.: INOTAXA — INtegrated Open TAXonomic Access and the " BiologiaCentrali-Americana". In: Proceedings Of The Contributed Papers Sessions Biomedical And Life Sciences Division, SLA, p. 8 (2006), http://units.sla.org/division/dbio/Baltimore/index.html
5. ViBRANT, Virtual Biodiversity Research and Access Network for Taxonomy, http://vbrant.eu/
6. Murray-Rust, P., Rzepa, H.S.: Scientific publications in XML - towards a global knowledge base. Data Science 1, 84–98 (2002)
7. Cui, H.: Approaches to Semantic Mark-up for Natural Heritage Literature. In: Proceedings of the iConference 2008 (2008), http://ischools.org/conference08/pc/PA5-2_iconf08.doc
8. Parr, C.S., Lyal, C.H.C.: Use cases for online taxonomic literature from taxonomists, conservationists, and others. In: Proceedings of TDWG Annual Conference (2007), http://www.tdwg.org/proceedings/article/view/269
9. Penev, L., Lyal, C.H.C., Weitzman, A., Morse, D., King, D., Sautter, G., Georgiev, T., Morris, R.A., Catapano, T., Agosti, D.: XML schemas and mark-up practices of taxonomic literature. In: Smith, V., Penev, L. (eds.) e-Infrastructures for Data Publishing in Biodiversity Science, vol. 150, pp. 89–116. ZooKeys (2011)
10. TaxonX, http://www.taxonx.org/
11. PLAZI, http://www.plazi.org/
12. Weitzman, A.L., Lyal, C.H.C.: An XML schema for taxonomic literature – taXMLit - (2004), http://www.sil.si.edu/digitalcollections/bca/documentation/taXMLitv1-3Intro.pdf
13. TEI, Text Encoding Initiative, http://www.tei-c.org/index.xml
14. TaxPub, http://sourceforge.net/projects/
15. Catapano, T.: TaxPub: An extension of the NLM/NCBI Journal Publishing DTD for taxonomic descriptions. Proceedings of the Journal Article Tag Suite Conference (2010), http://www.ncbi.nlm.nih.gov/books/NBK47081/#ref2
16. US National Center for Biotechnology Information, http://www.ncbi.nlm.nih.gov/
17. Penev, L., Agosti, D., Georgiev, T., Catapano, T., Miller, J., Blagoderov, V., Roberts, D., Smith, V., Brake, I., Ryrcroft, S., Scott, B., Johnson, N., Morris, R., Sautter, G., Chavan, V., Robertson, T., Remsen, D., Stoev, P., Parr, C., Knapp, S., Kress, W., Thompson, C., Erwin, T.: Semantic tagging of and semantic enhancements to systematics papers: ZooKeys working examples. ZooKeys 50, 1–16 (2010), doi:10.3897/zookeys.50.538
18. PubMedCentral, http://www.ncbi.nlm.nih.gov/pmc/
19. Willis, A., King, D., Morse, D., Dil, A., Lyal, C., Roberts, D.: From XML to XML: The Why and How of Making the Biodiversity Literature Accessible to Researchers. In: Proceedings of the Seventh conference on International Language Resources and Evaluation (LREC 2010), European Language Resources Association (ELRA), Valletta (2010), http://www.lrec-conf.org/proceedings/lrec2010/pdf/787_Paper.pdf
20. Ide, N., Romary, L.: International standard for a linguistic annotation framework. Journal of Natural Language Engineering 10(3-4), 211–225 (2004)
21. brat standoff format, http://brat.nlplab.org/standoff.html
22. brat rapid annotation tool, http://brat.nlplab.org/

Federating Natural History Museums in Natural Europe

Konstantinos Makris[1], Giannis Skevakis[1], Varvara Kalokyri[1], Polyxeni Arapi[1],
Stavros Christodoulakis[1], John Stoitsis[2], Nikos Manolis[2], and Sarah Leon Rojas[3]

[1] Laboratory of Distributed Multimedia Information Systems and Applications,
Technical University of Crete (TUC/MUSIC), 73100 Chania, Greece
{makris,skevakis,vkalokyri,xenia,stavros}@ced.tuc.gr
[2] Greek Research and Technology Network (GRNET) 56,
Mesogion Av. 11527, Athens, Greece
{Stoitsis,manolisn23}@gmail.com
[3] Fraunhofer Institute for Applied Information Technology FIT,
Schloss Birlinghoven, 53754 Sankt Augustin, Germany
sarah.leon.rojas@fit.fraunhofer.de

Abstract. An impressive abundance of high quality scientific content about Earth's biodiversity and natural history available in Natural History Museums (NHMs) around Europe remains largely unexploited due to a number of barriers, such as: the lack of interconnection and interoperability between the management systems used by museums, the lack of centralized access through a European point of reference like Europeana, and the inadequacy of the current metadata and content organization. To cope with these problems, the Natural Europe project offers a coordinated solution at European level. Cultural heritage content is collected from six Natural History Museums around Europe into a federation of European Natural History Digital Libraries that is directly connected with Europeana.eu. This paper presents the Natural Europe Cultural Digital Libraries Federation infrastructure consisting of: (a) The Natural Europe Cultural Environment (NECE), i.e. the infrastructure and toolset deployed on each NHM allowing their curators to publish, semantically describe, manage and disseminate the Cultural Heritage Objects (CHOs) they contribute to the project, and (b) the Natural Europe Cultural Heritage Infrastructure (NECHI) interconnecting NHM digital libraries and further exposing their metadata records to Europeana.eu.

Keywords: digital curation, preservation metadata, metadata aggregation, digital libraries, interoperability, Europeana.

1 Introduction

Countless cultural and biodiversity treasures are deposited in Natural History Museums across Europe, many hidden away beyond easy access. Bringing them to light requires solutions able to overcome a number of barriers such as: the lack of interconnection and interoperability between the management systems used by museums, the lack of centralized access through a European point of reference like Europeana, as well as the inadequacy of current content organization and the metadata used.

E. Garoufallou and J. Greenberg (Eds.): MTSR 2013, CCIS 390, pp. 361–372, 2013.
© Springer International Publishing Switzerland 2013

The Natural Europe project [15] offers a coordinated solution at European level that aims to overcome those barriers improving the availability and relevance of environmental cultural content for education and life-long learning use, in a multilingual and multicultural context. Cultural heritage content related to natural history, natural sciences, and nature/environment preservation, is collected from six Natural History Museums around Europe into a federation of European Natural History Digital Libraries that is directly connected with Europeana.

Needed to deal with a number of strong requirements for metadata management, and establish interoperability with cultural heritage, biodiversity and learning repositories, the Natural Europe project offers appropriate tools and services that allow the participating NHMs to: (a) uniformly describe and semantically annotate their content according to international standards and specifications, as well as (b) interconnect their digital libraries and expose their Cultural Heritage Object (CHO) metadata records to Europeana.eu.

This paper presents the Natural Europe Cultural Digital Libraries Federation infrastructure along with its tools and services consisting of: (a) The Natural Europe Cultural Environment (NECE), i.e. the infrastructure and toolset deployed on each NHM allowing their curators to publish, semantically describe, manage and disseminate the CHOs that they contribute to the project, and (b) the Natural Europe Cultural Heritage Infrastructure (NECHI) interconnecting NHM digital libraries and further exposing their metadata records to Europeana.eu.

2   The Natural Europe Cultural Digital Libraries Federation

In the context of Natural Europe, the participating NHMs provide metadata descriptions about a large number of Natural History related CHOs. These descriptions are semantically enriched with Natural Europe shared knowledge (shared vocabularies, taxonomies, etc.) using project provided annotation tools and services. The enhanced metadata are aggregated by the project, harvested by Europeana to become available through its portal and exploited for educational purposes.

The architecture of the Natural Europe Cultural Digital Libraries Federation, presented in Fig. 1, consists of the following main components (further described in the next sections):

- The *Natural Europe Cultural Environment (NECE)*, referring to the toolset deployed at each participating NHM, consisting of the Multimedia Authoring Tool (MMAT) and its underlying repository (CHO Repository). It facilitates the complete metadata management lifecycle: ingestion, maintenance, curation, and dissemination of CHO metadata. NECE also specifies how legacy metadata are migrated into Natural Europe.
- The *Natural Europe Cultural Heritage Infrastructure (NECHI)*, interconnecting NHM digital libraries and further exposing their metadata records to Europeana.eu. Moreover, NECHI provides services for searching and accessing all museums' CHOs from a single point.
- *Search Widgets* for Natural Europe and Europeana cultural material search, supporting simple, faceted or connected search (on Natural Europe and Europeana).

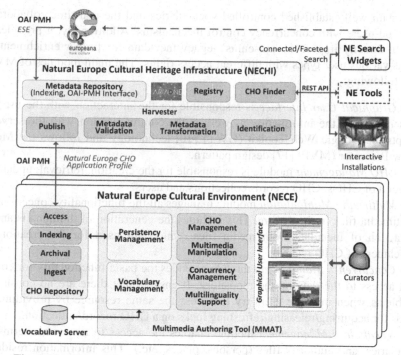

Fig. 1. The Natural Europe Cultural Digital Libraries Federation Architecture

3 Natural Europe Cultural Environment (NECE)

The Natural Europe Cultural Environment (NECE) [12], as presented in Fig. 1, refers to the toolset deployed at each participating NHM, which consists of the Multimedia Authoring Tool (MMAT) and the CHO Repository. These tools support the complete metadata management life-cycle: ingestion, maintenance, curation and dissemination of CHO metadata. The systems comprising NECE support a rich metadata element set, the Natural Europe CHO Application Profile. A brief description of the MMAT and the CHO Repository is presented in Sections 3.1 and 3.2, while Section 3.3 presents the Natural Europe CHO Application Profile.

3.1 Multimedia Authoring Tool (MMAT)

MMAT is a multilingual web-based management system for museums, archives and digital collections, which facilitates the authoring and metadata enrichment of Cultural Heritage Objects[1]. It supports the Natural Europe CHO Application Profile, as well as a variety of the most popular multimedia formats. The main features of MMAT include the publication of multimedia objects, the semantic linkage of the described

---

[1] A demo version of MMAT is available at:
http://natural-europe.tuc.gr/music/mmat

objects with well-established controlled vocabularies and the real-time collaboration among end-users with concurrency control mechanisms. Additionally, it provides the means to directly import the museums' legacy metadata for further enrichment and supports various user types with different access rights. The main modules of MMAT are the following:

- The *Graphical User Interface* is responsible for the interaction with the user, the presentation of the information as well as the communication with the server. It adopts the Google Web Toolkit (GWT) [10] technology and follows the Model-View-Presenter (MVP) [17] design pattern.
- The *CHO Management* module is responsible for the creation, retrieval, update and deletion of CHOs, CHO records/collections and users.
- The *Multimedia Manipulation* module manages all the functionality concerning the multimedia files in the system. This includes the generation of thumbnails and the extraction of metadata from media files, which are used for the creation and enrichment of CHO records.
- The *Concurrency Management* module provides the basic functionality for concurrent access to the data on the repository. It ensures that there are no consistency problems when multiple users try to access the same resource by providing methods for acquiring/releasing/refreshing locks on a CHO record/collection.
- The *Vocabulary Management* module enables the access to taxonomic terms, vocabularies, and authority files (persons, places, etc.). This information resides on the Vocabulary Server, providing indexing and search capabilities.
- The *Persistency Management* module manages the submission/retrieval of information packages to/from the CHO Repository.

3.2   CHO Repository

The CHO Repository is responsible for the ingestion, maintenance and dissemination of both content and metadata. It adopts the OAIS Reference Model [11] and accommodates modules for the ingestion, archival, indexing, and access of information packages, i.e., CHOs, CHO records/collections, and user information.

The *Ingest Module* receives, validates, processes and finally transfers the information packages submitted by the MMAT to the Archival Module in order to be stored/updated/deleted to the CHO Repository.

The *Archival* and *Indexing Modules* serve information package storage and retrieval requests submitted by the Ingest and Access Modules respectively. They maintain (preserve and index) content and metadata by employing an eXist XML database and an Apache SOLR Indexer.

The *Access Module* exposes a number of services to the MMAT and the Natural Europe Harvester in order to retrieve information stored in the CHO Repository. As regards to the MMAT, the module provides functionality for applying access control policies and performing fast search/retrieval operations by exploiting indices maintained by the Indexing module. Concerning the Natural Europe Harvester, the module offers an OAI-PMH interface, allowing NHMs to expose their metadata to NECHI and subsequently to Europeana.

3.3   Natural Europe CHO Application Profile

The Natural Europe CHO Application Profile [14] is a superset of the Europeana Semantic Elements (ESE) [8] metadata format. It has been developed through an iterative process involving the NHMs' domain experts and the technical partners of the project, driven by the needs and requirements of the stakeholders and the application domain of the project.

The Natural Europe CHO Application Profile consists of the following parts:

- The *Cultural Heritage Object (CHO) information* that provides metadata information about the analog resource or born digital object (specimen, exhibit, cast, painting, documentary, etc.). It is composed of the following sub-categories:
  - The *Basic information*, which deals with general descriptive information (mostly scientific) about a Cultural Heritage Object.
  - The *Species information*, that is applicable to describe information related to the species of a described specimen (animals, plants, minerals, rocks, etc.) in the context of Natural Europe.
  - The *Geographical information*, which contains metadata for the location in which a specimen has been collected.
- The *Digital Object information*, that provides metadata information about a digital (photo, video, etc.) or digitized resource (scanned image, photo, etc.) in the context of Natural Europe. It is composed of the following sub-categories:
  - The *Basic information*, that deals with general descriptive information about a digital or digitized resource.
  - The *Content information*, which is related to the physical characteristics and technical information exclusive to a digital or digitized resource (URL, Content Type, Format, Extent, etc.).
  - The *Rights information*, which describes the intellectual property rights and the accessibility to a digital or digitized resource.
- The *Meta-metadata information*, that provides metadata information for a CHO record. These include the creator of the record in the Multimedia Authoring Tool, the different languages that appear in the metadata, etc. Additionally, it describes the history of the record during its evolution in the MMAT, including the operations and entities that affected it.
- The *Collection information*, that provides metadata information for logical groupings of contributed CHOs within a museum.

Fig. 2 presents a simplified example of a CHO record taken from the Natural History Museum of Crete (NHMC), described using the Natural Europe CHO Application Profile.

```
<record xmlns="http://www.natural-europe.eu/nhm/aip/">
    <objectUri>http://nhmc.natural-europe.eu/12dda2d5</objectUri>
    <contextUri>http://www.nhmc.uoc.gr/museum/40319</contextUri>
    <contentType>IMAGE</contentType>
    <licenseUri>http://creativecommons.org/licenses/by-nc-nd/3.0</licenseUri>
    <scientificName xml:lang="la">Canis lupus</scientificName>
    <classification xml:lang="la" annotation="FAMILIA">Canidae</classification>
    <classification xml:lang="la" annotation="ORDO">Carnivora</classification>
    <classification xml:lang="la" annotation="CLASSIS">Mammalia</classification>
    <classification xml:lang="la" annotation="REGNUM">Animalia</classification>
    <commonName xml:lang="el">Λύκος</commonName>
    <commonName xml:lang="en">Wolf</commonName>
    <title xml:lang="en">Wolf, Canis lupus</title>
    <title xml:lang="el">Λύκος, Canis lupus</title>
    <creator xml:lang="en" annotation="Photographer">Trichas, A.</creator>
    <creator xml:lang="el" annotation="Φωτογράφος">Τριχάς, Α.</creator>
    <subject xml:lang="en">Mammals</subject>
    <subject xml:lang="el">Θηλαστικά</subject>
    <description xml:lang="en">Photo of wolves in forest diorama in the Paranesti NHM.</description>
    <description xml:lang="el">Φωτογραφία λύκων σε διόραμα δάσους στο ΜΦΙ στο Παρανέστι.</description>
    <contributor xml:lang="en" annotation="Curator">Lymberakis P.</contributor>
    <contributor xml:lang="el" annotation="Συγγραφέας μεταδεδομένων">Λυμπεράκης, Π.</contributor>
    <type xml:lang="en">Preserved specimen</type>
    <type xml:lang="el">Συντηρημένο δείγμα</type>
    <format>image/jpeg</format>
    <identifier>nhmc.image.40319</identifier>
    <rights annotation="Rights Reserved - Free Access">Natural History Museum of Crete ©</rights>
    <alternative xml:lang="en">Photo of Canis lupus</alternative>
    <alternative xml:lang="el">Φωτογραφία ενός Canis lupus</alternative>
    <extent>500 x 323 pixels</extent>
    <spatial xml:lang="en" annotation="Country">Greece</spatial>
    <spatial xml:lang="el" annotation="Χώρα">Ελλάδα</spatial>
    <geolocation latitude="35.296227084320144" longitude="23.91901402771254"/>
</record>
```

Fig. 2. A CHO record conforming to the Natural Europe CHO Application Profile

4 Natural Europe Cultural Heritage Infrastructure (NECHI)

The Natural Europe Cultural Heritage Infrastructure for metadata aggregation (presented in Fig. 1) has been based on the ARIADNE technologies and services [2]. ARIADNE is a standards-based technology infrastructure that allows the publication and management of digital learning resources in an open and scalable way. The components of the ARIADNE infrastructure have been appropriately configured in order to support the aggregation of NHMs CHO metadata based on Natural Europe CHO Application Profile. These are presented in the following sections.

4.1 Natural Europe Harvester

The Natural Europe Harvester is based on an ARIADNE Harvester instance, which has been deployed and configured to manage the harvesting of the metadata records provided by Natural Europe content providers. The Natural Europe Harvester uses OAI-PMH for harvesting the metadata from the OAI-PMH targets and publishes them to a central repository through the publish service. The Natural Europe harvester integrates the following services:

- **Publish Service.** For the publishing of the harvested metadata into a central repository, the Simple Publishing Interface (SPI) specification [20] has been used. The SPI provides a simple lightweight protocol for publishing data and metadata to a repository. In the context of Natural Europe, the 'source' is the Natural Europe harvester and the 'target' is the metadata repository that acts as an adapter to the publishing API.
- **Transformation service.** The transformation service converts metadata from the Natural Europe CHO Application Profile format to Europeana/ESE specification format in order to allow the aggregated CHO records of the participating Natural History Museums to be accessed by the Europeana.eu.
- **Identification service.** Provides persistent digital identifiers to resources in the ARIADNE infrastructure. The HANDLE system is used as the backend service to create globally unique, persistent and independent identifiers. This system allows the assignment, management and resolution of persistent identifiers in a distributed environment.
- **Metadata validation service.** Provides syntactic and semantic validation of metadata instances against predefined application profiles, in this case based on Natural Europe CHO Application Profile. The validation service combines different validation techniques including XSD schema, Schematron rules, and validation of vcards present in the metadata with a separate vcard parser or validator. With the validation service one single metadata record or all records exposed through OAI can be validated against the appropriate scheme. Reports are automatically generated.

4.2 Metadata Repository

The Metadata Repository, based on the ARIADNE Next Repository software, features both a metadata and file store where CHOs and metadata instances are persistently managed in an open and scalable architecture. Through several open standards and specifications it supports stable querying, publishing and harvesting of CHOs. It provides a flexible building block that can be adapted to different situations and that enables interoperability with external components (e.g., the harvester component).

The Repository supports indexing to enable efficient and fast search on top of large metadata collections using Apache Lucene. This text search engine library allows indexing all elements of the applied metadata scheme during their insertion in the repository enabling fast search on top of them. The Apache SOLR framework is being used to provide powerful, efficient and facetted search algorithms.

The Metadata Repository also offers an OAI-PMH target service in order to allow the metadata exposure. In the context of Natural Europe, this service is used by the Europeana.eu in order to access the aggregated metadata records of the participating Natural History Museums that have been transformed to ESE.

4.3 Registry Service

The ARIADNE Registry Service has been deployed and configured to hold information about the repositories that are included in the Natural Europe Cultural Federation.

The end user can review all the participating repositories and get information about them, e.g. their OAI-PMH target. Moreover, all the metadata related to a registered repository can be inspected, allowing the user to find information like the metadata formats supported by a repository.

4.4   Cultural Heritage Objects Finder

In order to let users search cultural material and browse the results, the ARIADNE Finder has been deployed and configured appropriately. The finder hides the protocols and standards that are used in the middle layer. It can also be exploited by any repository that supports REST-based APIs with JSON binding of LOM. The Natural Europe instance of the finder has been coupled on the Metadata Repository.

In order to enable efficient and fast search on top of large collections, the finder web tool takes advantage of the indexing services used in the backend Repository. Queries are submitted in JSONP format and results can be returned in both JSON and XML formats. All formulated queries are interpreted as conjunction of disjunctions.

For each repository (NECHI and Europeana) a search widget was implemented. The decision to have separate search widgets was based on the fact that, unlike the Natural Europe service, the Europeana search does not support faceted search through its web API. Two widgets have been implemented for each service: A standalone widget embeddable to any web page[2], and one embedded in the ROLE PLE (1.1)[3] [18] that can be used as a plugin in Moodle. The widgets can support three types of search:

- **Simple search**: The simple search queries the service corresponding to the widget for a given keyword or key phrase. For each result a summary is displayed.
- **Connected search**: The ROLE widgets allow the user to perform a joint search in both repositories: Europeana and Natural Europe. This functionality uses the IWC of the ROLE.
- **Faceted search**: As already stated, the faceted search functionality is only available in the Natural Europe widget and allows the filtering of the search results using facets (type, data provider, license, etc.).

5   Natural Europe Metadata Life-Cycle

The metadata life-cycle as defined by the Natural Europe Cultural Federation architecture comprises the metadata management and exploitation, and can be described in two steps.

During the first step, the curators of the NHMs prepare and manage the CHOs that they will contribute to the project using the tools and services provided by the NECE infrastructure. This step is divided in four phases:

---

[2] http://bit.ly/12ddc6T
[3] Europeana Search: http://bit.ly/181Z84Q, Natural Europe Search: http://bit.ly/181YZOT

- In the **pre-ingestion phase** each NHM selects the CHO records/collections that will be contributed to the project and ensures that they will be appropriately migrated into Natural Europe.
- In the **ingestion phase** any existing CHOs and CHO descriptions are imported to the Natural Europe environment. The latter are further enriched through a semantic annotation process. Using MMAT (**Fig. 3**) museum curators can inspect, modify, or reject the imported descriptions.
- The **maintenance phase** refers to the storage and management of CHOs and CHO metadata using MMAT and the CHO Repository.
- The **dissemination phase** refers to the controlled provision of the maintained metadata to 3rd party systems and client applications, e.g. NECHI.

In the second step, the contributed CHOs from all the NHMs are harvested by the Natural Europe Harvester in NECHI. The collected metadata are indexed, validated, given persistent identifiers, and transformed to ESE. Subsequently, the metadata are disseminated to Europeana. Moreover, they are also exposed (through the Cultural Heritage Objects Finder) to 3rd party systems and Natural Europe applications, in order to be exploited for educational purposes. Finally, the participating NHMs or any other organization is able to embed the Natural Europe Search Widgets (**Fig. 3**) in its website in order to promote cultural heritage.

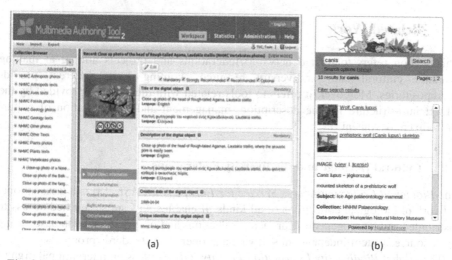

(a)   (b)

Fig. 3. (a) The Multimedia Authoring Tool in use. (b) The Natural Europe Search Widget.

6 Deployment and Use

By today (3rd year of the project), a large number of CHOs have been published by each NHM using MMAT, exposed to the Natural Europe Cultural Federation and disseminated to Europeana, as presented in Table 1. Till the end of the project the total number of CHOs (last column) for each NHM will be reached.

Table 1. Number of CHOs published and to be published by each NHM

Museum	CHOs		
	Published	Remaining	TOTAL
Natural History Museum of Crete (**NHMC**)	2611	1399	**4010**
National Museum of Natural History – University of Lisbon (**MNHNL**)	1708	902	**2610**
Jura-Museum Eichstätt (**JME**)	1172	478	**1650**
Arctic Center (**AC**)	302	178	**480**
Hungarian Natural History Museum (**HNHM**)	3134	1076	**4210**
Estonian Museum of Natural History (**TNHM**)	1923	0	**1923**
TOTAL	**10850**	**4033**	**14883**

As far as MMAT is concerned, improvements of the user-interface and the search functionalities have been made after continuous feedback from museum partners in a number of tool releases. Heuristic evaluation of the MMAT was performed, while extensive usability studies have been and will be performed in a number of curator workshops organized by the participating NHMs [12], [19].

A cloud infrastructure is being supported over GRNET VIMA infrastructure and cloud versions of Natural Europe tools have been created. This way new NHMs can easily join Natural Europe and use its tools without any effort from their side.

7   Related Work

This section refers to related networks/federations and projects aiming at making available cultural and biodiversity resources coming from different providers/repositories. Moreover, it refers to tools related with the services provided by the NECE infrastructure for the description, management and dissemination of cultural/biodiversity content.

7.1   Cultural Heritage and Biodiversity Federations

The *Biological Collection Access Service for Europe (BioCASE)* [3] is a transnational network of biological collections of all kinds. It enables widespread unified access to distributed and heterogeneous European collections and observational databases using open-source, system-independent software and open data standards/protocols.

The *Global Biodiversity Information Facility (GBIF)* [9] is an international organization that focuses on making scientific data on biodiversity available via the Internet using web services. The data are provided by many institutions from around the world; GBIF's information architecture makes these data accessible and searchable through a single portal.

The *Opening Up the Natural History Heritage for Europeana (OpenUp!)* project [16] mobilizes the multimedia information using the existing information networks in the biodiversity research domain and links them to the Europeana.eu. Access is based on the established technical infrastructure of BioCASE that also feeds into GBIF.

Natural Europe has established close relations with BioCASE and OpenUp. In the context of Natural Europe, a framework for the connection of the Natural Europe NHMs' CHO repositories (federated nodes) to the BioCASE network has been developed and implemented (presented in [12]), exploiting mappings between the Natural Europe CHO Application Profile and the ABCD schema [1].

7.2 Tools for Description and Management of Cultural Content

CollectiveAccess [5] is a web-based multilingual cataloguing tool for museums, archives and digital collections. It allows integration of external data sources and repositories for cataloguing and supports the most popular media formats. Although it supports a variety of metadata standards (Dublin Core, PBCore, SPECTRUM, etc.), direct support for the ESE specification is not provided. Moreover, CollectiveAccess does not implement any harvesting protocol, thus is not possible to publish content to Europeana's web portal. Finally, the current version of CollectiveAccess lacks any importing mechanism, crucial in the case of museums having already described their cultural content with metadata in legacy or internal (museum specific) formats.

Collection Space [4] is a web-based application for the description and management of museum collection information. Collection Space does not support the ESE specification and its metadata dissemination mechanisms are limited (REST-API). Moreover, they do not support any harvesting protocol.

Custodea [6] is a system mainly intended for historical and cultural institutions that need to deal with digitization. It covers harvesting of digital content and representations, data transformation, creation and storage of metadata, vocabulary management, publishing and provision of data for Europeana and other institutions. However, the front-end application is desktop-based, which greatly complicates the collaboration of museum curators.

8   Conclusion and Future Work

We presented the architecture and deployment of the infrastructure used in the Natural Europe project, allowing curators to publish, semantically describe, and manage the museums' CHOs, as well as disseminating them to Europeana. This infrastructure consists of (a) the Natural Europe Cultural Environment (NECE), and (b) the Natural Europe Cultural Heritage Infrastructure (NECHI). It is currently used by six European NHMs participating in the Natural Europe project, where a large number of CHOs have already been published. A long term vision of the project is to attract more NHMs to join this effort. Technically, with the cloud infrastructure and the cloud versions of the Natural Europe tools this can be easily supported without effort from the NHM side.

A semantically rich cultural heritage infrastructure for NHMs is currently being developed, as a proof of concept that will give a Semantic Web perspective to the Natural Europe cultural content and will further support EDM [7].

Acknowledgements. This work has been carried out in the scope of the Natural Europe Project (Grant Agreement 250579) funded by EU ICT Policy Support Programme.

References

1. ABCD Schema, http://wiki.tdwg.org/ABCD/
2. ARIADNE, http://www.ariadne-eu.org/content/services
3. BioCASE, http://www.biocase.org/
4. CollectionSpace, http://www.collectionspace.org
5. CollectiveAccess, http://www.collectiveaccess.org/
6. Custodea, http://www.custodea.com/en/home
7. Europeana Data Model Definition V.5.2.3,
   http://pro.europeana.eu/documents/900548/
   bb6b51df-ad11-4a78-8d8a-44cc41810f22
8. Europeana Semantic Elements Specification V.3.4.1,
   http://pro.europeana.eu/documents/900548/
   dc80802e-6efb-4127-a98e-c27c95396d57
9. Global Biodiversity Information Facility (GBIF), http://www.gbif.org/
10. Google Web Toolkit (GWT), http://www.gwtproject.org/
11. ISO 14721:2012 Open Archival Information System (OAIS) Reference Model,
    http://www.iso.org/iso/iso_catalogue/catalogue_tc/
    catalogue_detail.htm?csnumber=57284
12. Makris, K., Skevakis, G., Kalokyri, V., Arapi, P., Christodoulakis, S.: Metadata Management and Interoperability Support for Natural History Museums. In: Aalberg, T., Papatheodorou, C., Dobreva, M., Tsakonas, G., Farrugia, C.J. (eds.) TPDL 2013. LNCS, vol. 8092, pp. 120–131. Springer, Heidelberg (2013)
13. Makris, K., Skevakis, G., Kalokyri, V., Gioldasis, N., Kazasis, F.G., Christodoulakis, S.: Bringing Environmental Culture Content into the Europeana.eu Portal: The Natural Europe Digital Libraries Federation Infrastructure. In: García-Barriocanal, E., Cebeci, Z., Okur, M.C., Öztürk, A. (eds.) MTSR 2011. CCIS, vol. 240, pp. 400–411. Springer, Heidelberg (2011)
14. Natural Europe Cultural Heritage Object Application Profile,
    http://wiki.natural-europe.eu/index.php?title=Natural_
    Europe_Cultural_Heritage_Object_Application_Profile
15. Natural Europe Project, http://www.natural-europe.eu
16. OpenUp! project, http://open-up.eu/
17. Potel, M.: MVP: Model-View-Presenter. The Taligent Programming Model for C++ and Java (1996)
18. ROLE project, http://www.role-project.eu/
19. Sattler, S., Bogner, F.: D6.2 Integrated Pilot Evaluation Report. Natural Europe (Project Ref. No 250579, Area CIP-ICT-PSP.2009.2.5 – Digital Libraries) (2013)
20. Ternier, S., Massart, D.V.: A Simple Publishing Interface for Learning Object Repositories. In: World Conference on Education Multimedia, Hypermedia and Telecommunications, pp. 1840–1845. AACE (2008)

Toward Common Ontologies of Facets of the Archival Access Portal

Tarvo Kärberg[1,2]

[1] University of Tartu, Tartu, Estonia
karberg@ut.ee
[2] National Archives of Estonia, Tartu, Estonia
Tarvo.Karberg@ra.ee

Abstract. This article discusses the importance of providing flexible access to archived content and gives an overview of development of the new multi-faceted archival access portal of the National Archives of Estonia (NAE). The article describes how the development and implementation of total five taxonomies and classifications as facets for refining the search were carried out, what issues were encountered, and which solutions were chosen.

This case study reflects the journey toward common ontologies of archival access portal facets. Some key recommendations and questions for the subsequent project will be given at the end of this article.

Keywords: archival access, taxonomy, ontology, facets.

1   Introduction

The National Archives of Estonia (NAE) – as many other memory institutions – has realized that multifaceted access to preserved knowledge, including flexible search and navigation, is a goal of increasing importance in addition to active preservation. "Webification" is not an easy task, especially with multimedia content and few metadata descriptions [1]. Reaching the goal is in order to pay more attention to the descriptive information accompanying archived content. Descriptive information is defined in the OAIS model as the set of information, consisting primarily of Package Descriptions, which is provided to Data Management to support the finding, ordering, and retrieval of OAIS information holdings by Consumers [2]. But the main complexity in designing a public archival access portal for Consumers lies in the fact that there are usually no standardized Consumers, and reaching to widely designated community's needs is not a trivial task. Different users have their own personal basis of knowledge and interests, so they need different starting points for flexible searches. With OAIS, during the Search Session which tends to be iterative (first identifying broad criteria and then refining the criteria on the basis of previous search results), the Consumer will use the OAIS Finding Aids to identify and investigate potential holdings of interest [2]. OAIS does not define precisely how the Consumer/user discovers the materials of potential interest through the Finding Aid or how a Finding Aid should

E. Garoufallou and J. Greenberg (Eds.): MTSR 2013, CCIS 390, pp. 373–383, 2013.

look in practice. Still, OAIS additionally states that when candidate objects of interest are identified, more sophisticated Finding Aids such as browse image viewers or animation may be used to further refine a Result Set [2]. In classical, text-based searches, the vocabulary of keywords for refining the search is hidden somewhere in the background of databases, so for the user it can be difficult to know the "right" keywords which will ensure the desired search results.

Furthermore, when the public archives have developed several systems for content-specific descriptions they usually need to be searched separately because those databases contain many different metadata elements, and accompanying all these into the general access portal search algorithm will significantly slow down the speed of the search and reduce the positive access experience.

This was one of the reasons why NAE made an in-depth analysis for a new archival access portal which concentrates largely on end-user needs and novel access techniques in 2012. According to the analysis, the archival access portal should have predefined facets enabling users to adapt applications faster, as facets show the vocabulary used and give results with less user effort. In faceted exploration, the user always sees all remaining search options within the search process and can select them step-by-step in order to refine the query [3].

As NAE has many small databases which contain specific metadata about different types (photos, maps, audio-video, etc.) of archival content, an efficient way should be found to accompany those systems in searches through the facets as well. Furthermore, facets should be composed from classifications already available in those systems as much as possible.

We decided to implement five facets: place names, person and corporate names, periods/timeframes, topics/original keywords and subject areas/domains.

Two major issues were raised:

- How can specific databases be included in the general search without interfering in their existence?

  The continual existence of specific databases was demanded as those systems are actual cornerstones to archival access. They provide functionalities for describing specific content, holding it in one concrete place and containing advanced search options for finding the content through some specific metadata elements.
- How to cope with different classifications used in the content-specific systems?

  Content-specific systems are developed at different times and therefore contain significantly different classifications.

2   Case Study

As the (general) access information system contained archival classifications (e.g. fond, series) and general descriptions (e.g. appraisal, arrangement) and several specific information systems contained content-specific descriptions, we realized that the best way to providing fast and efficient access across different levels is to develop services which synchronize some main descriptions (e.g. title, dates) from the content-specific systems to the general access system. For that purpose the metadata schemas of content-specific systems and general access system were compared and most common elements (e.g. photo title = archival unit title; parchment title = archival unit title) mapped. Very trivial criteria were used – content independent metadata elements were synchronized to the general system.This means that, for example, a photo which is in a specific database and has the metadata elements title "Singing Chorus" and dimensions "3814x2731" can be found in the general archival access portal by searching the word in the title, but not through the dimensions, as it was not populated in the main archival access portal. When the user wanted to search using content-specific elements, it could be done only through the search of the specific database. If new descriptions are added to the specific content databases they will again populate the updates to the general systems via asynchronous services. Searching specific content through general elements in the main archival access system is a big step forward providing more successful results, but it can be still improved by accompanying some specific metadata elements to general facets. For example, we have the metadata element "Photographer" in the photo description database. This element is not populated to the main archival access system as it is a content-specific element; however, it can be treated as one of the values for the "Person" facet. This means that we can provide more dimensions to the search and raise the level of positive finding experience when the relevant content from the lower level systems comes out in the main access portal in multiple ways.

By analyzing keywords and classifications in specific databases we realized that they are in significantly different formats and granularities. Some of them are lists, some are trees, and some are just simple text elements without any order. In validating the values we encountered several issues, such as person names that were not consistently inputted in the same format. There were names that were inputted as one metadata element in one system, but in the other as two, and in some systems even as three separate metadata elements. Furthermore, different input techniques in one metadata field have been practiced through different time periods. For example, some person names were inputted into one metadata field using different name orders and symbols: Jane Doe; Smith John; and Doe, John.

We discussed the choices for describing the classifications as ontologies, but finally decided that as the scope of the project is tightly limited, classifications are spread all over the systems, and keywords are categorized poorly or not at all, it is not reasonable to create different types of relationships between categories at this stage. We decided to solve the situation in two stages: to compose facets as taxonomies in the first project and turn taxonomies into ontologies later within the scope of the other project. As the first project is currently in the final phase, the second stage project has been initiated. One of the outcomes will be open vocabularies which will be delivered by the open data principles and described according to semantic models.

Even so, the taxonomies composed within the scope of the first project were not only straight classification hierarchies as explained in the following pages.

2.1   Periods

A work group of archival professionals was gathered to define periods. As the overall timeframe of fonds was known, the work group could take the oldest (dated in 13th century) and latest (current time) record in the national archives as the start/end point and the public authorities in charge throughout time (e.g. Polish, Swedish and Danish period, Russian period) as the backbone of defining timeframes. So, on the one hand it became a chronological order, but on the other hand an administrative classification.

The archival professionals came up with 12 categories starting from medieval time (keskaeg) and concluding with the Republic of Estonia (Eesti Vabariik). The main challenge lied in the fact that the experts needed to agree on exact dates which could be counted as start and end dates of periods. By defining some periods a compromise agreement to start from January 1st and end on December 31th was made (row 4, Table 1).

The constructed time periods were quite unique, as they contained the textual representation of the period already in the title (e.g 1918-1940: Eesti Vabariik) of the classification element, explicitly showing the user which years the period will contain (Table 1).

Table 1. Periods

No.	Title of the period (Estonian)	From	To
1	13. sajand -1561: Keskaeg	01.01.1200	03.06.1561
2	1561-1710: Poola, Rootsi ja Taani aeg	04.06.1561	28.09.1710
3	1710-1783: Vene aeg	29.09.1710	31.12.1782
4	1783-1796: Vene aeg: asehaldusaeg	01.01.1783	31.12.1795
5	1796-1917: Vene aeg	01.01.1796	28.02.1917
6	1917-1918: Ajutine valitsus	01.03.1917	20.11.1917
7	1918: Saksa okupatsioon	21.11.1917	28.11.1918
8	1918-1940: Eesti Vabariik	29.11.1918	20.06.1940
9	1940-1941: Eesti NSV	21.06.1940	05.07.1941
10	1941-1944: Saksa okupatsioon	06.07.1941	01.09.1944
11	1944-1991: Eesti NSV	02.09.1944	08.05.1990
12	1991-: Eesti Vabariik	09.05.1990	31.12.4000

The values (from, to) are used in the background for automated linking with the archival content. This facet will use the date limits of the archival fond to narrow down the search, thus the period facet will automatically cover all the descriptions in the archival access portal as being related which each archival fond. This is the simplest facet compared to the other four, but gives at least the same or even more effort as others that have an impact on all fonds.

The period names are currently in Estonian, but are planned to be translated into English to give foreign Customers a better understanding of which period facet they are using or can use.

2.2   Places/Administrative Units

The work to define administrative units/districts (e.g. urban municipalities, parishes) began before the development of the new archival access system, because it was seen as an important component of the maps' information system at the NAE. It soon found use in the photo information system as well.

The taxonomy of administrative units consists of five trees, of which four are Estonian place name groups organized by time (before 1917, 1917–1950, 1950–1991, after 1991) and one tree is reserved for foreign countries divided by continents (Table 2).

Table 2. Administrative units

No.	Unit name in Estonian	Unit name in English
1	Eesti (kuni 1917)	Estonia (since 1917)
2	Eesti (1917-1950)	Estonia (1917–1950)
3	Eesti (1950-1991)	Estonia (1950–1991)
4	Eesti (alates 1991)	Estonia (from 1991)
5	Välisriigid	Foreign countries
	Aafrika maailmajagu	Africa
	Aasia maailmajagu	Asia
	Ameerika maailmajagu	America
	Euroopa maailmajagu	Europe
	Okeaania maailmajagu	Oceania

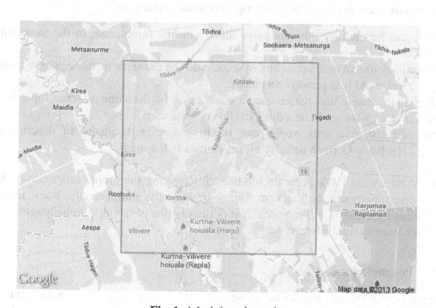

Fig. 1. Administrative units

Administrative units are not pure classical trees, as they have other metadata beside the name as well. Administrative units are equipped with location coordinates, which allow for using map components to show rectangles or polygons of the place location on the map. As the administrative unit borders were in some cases not precisely known or there were some overlapping with neighbor units it was decided to show only rectangles on the map as they will give sufficient initial information for the end-users where the administrative units approximately are located.

The lowest level of the administrative units was linked with the descriptions from the manor database, so the metadata (e.g., name, date relations, comments) and approximate location of the manor on Google maps (Figure 1) can now be seen.

With the help of the administrative units the user can easily browse the archival content through the desired period. Administrative units can be used for search formulation in three ways.

Firstly, the user can type some letters in the search box and the system recommends the place name(s) containing the inputted symbols. Secondly, the user can select the desired place name from the hierarchy of administrative units when browsing the trees. Thirdly, the user can mark a region on the map and the search will be performed taking into consideration which region is marked and whether the option "overlap with" or "are within the box I have drawn" is selected. By choosing "overlap with," all administrative units are found which have some intersection with the marked region. By choosing "are within the box I have drawn," all administrative units are found which fit entirely in the marked region. If the user uses administrative units as facets to refine the search, then only the tree form can be used.

The main issue regarding the administrative units is the fact that they are very difficult to link accordingly to some descriptions automatically, as

- there can be multiple administrative units with the same name in the same time period;
- the administrative unit names can in some cases be the same as some people names (e.g., Jüri could be a person or a place);
- the administrative unit names can in some cases be the same as some topic facet values (e.g., Käru could be a thing (trolley) or a place);
- the administrative unit names can be in a foreign language in descriptions (e.g., Habbat in German actually means Habaja in Estonian).

Thus, there are no 100% accurate solutions for creating the proper relationships between descriptions and the Estonian administrative units automatically. Some human controlling expertise is still required. It is definitely one of the global challenges what deserves attention in the future work.

2.3   People/Organizations

Originally, persons and organizations were spread throughout many archival databases across NAE, such as photographers and persons on photos in the photo database, creators in the cartographical/map system, performers and authors in the audio-video database, archival creators as persons in the archival descriptions system, and non-archival creator organizations in the archival descriptions system. These were all collected together and the most necessary improvements were performed (e.g., dividing a "Name" element into two separate elements: "First Name" and "Surname") as the authority files were inconsistent. In some systems the names were accompanied with occupation or comments. They were all identified as separate metadata elements. The "slicing" and "matching" were done both automatically and manually. The initial processing was carried out by algorithms, but the finalizing confirmation was performed by skilled archivists. The algorithm's mission was to predict whether the name contains the accompanying description or not and place the found strings to separate fields. Algorithm searched special symbols (white-space, comma, semi-colon) and interpreted them as separators. As the names were described in various formats (e.g. First Name, Surname; Surname, First Name, First Name Surname, affiliation) even in the range of one repository the algorithm sometimes failed to distinguish all strings correctly and human intervention was needed. Archivists' mission was to carry out any corrections and finalize the values of person names.

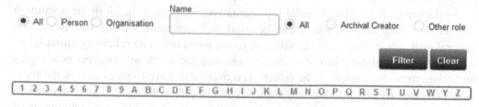

Fig. 2. Persons and organizations

The descriptions of persons and organizations were all placed into ISAAR (CPF) [4] descriptions format and provided with characteristics such as "Person," "Organization," "Archival Creator," and "Other" (Figure 2). For machine-readability the ISAAR (CPF) was technically solved with SOAP (Simple Object Access Protocol) service which produces a XML output which can be transformed with the help of XSLT (Extensible Stylesheet Language Transformations) to various formats (e.g. EAC-CPF).

A person can thereby easily advance as an archival creator or vice versa – the archival creator can be seen as a person. Thus, one item can act in two ways: The user can browse the person trough the archival agencies or by refining the previously performed search. This adds an additional dimension to the classification and reduces the dependence of search success on the user's knowledge.

2.4   Topics

We agreed that it was not effective to implement the thesaurus (approximately 55,000 keywords) which was available for the Estonian libraries, as our goal was to have a minimal set of topics defined and not to have duplications with some of our other taxonomies. It could have been possible to filter a subset of the general thesaurus, but then it would not have produced the relations. The main principle we followed was that we don't need to create or provide a massive thesaurus if it is not really linked with the content. Having a thesaurus is not just the value in itself. Thus, the current topics are based on keywords which were initially collected mainly from other in-house systems and then organized and processed by a group of archival professionals. The outcome of their work was almost 2000 keywords containing, for example, record types (e.g., contract, legal act), things (e.g., balloon, road), non-administrative places (e.g., market, farm), concepts (migration, coastal protection), roles (medical attendant, diver), activities (rewarding, demining) and more. The main principle for organizers was not to duplicate the subject areas and other taxonomies, as this could then produce too many results and not actually help to narrow the search. Therefore the topics do not contain for example place names, periods or persons.

One relatively simple algorithm which compared topics used in the lower level systems with the new hierarchy of topics was constructed. This algorithm created new relations between descriptions and topics using a keywords comparison. The implementation of that algorithm was carried out in MSExcel by formula which compares cells on two separate sheets and writes down the identification code of the item if it finds identical strings.

As the topics list is already quite representative, we hope to use it in the upcoming project as a "tag library" which can be used and complemented by the users. The general principle is that the NAE will give to the users only one relatively small set of topics which are already linked to the content and the users will suggest new topics and relations to the content in the future. The users will have chances to link the topic with descriptions and provide new topics to the topics collection. The exact procedures for that will be agreed in the next project, as well for obtaining annotations of the resources in a structured way, if possible.

2.5   Subject Areas

A work group of archival professionals was gathered to define subject areas similarly with defining the time periods. The work lasted from 2012 to the first half of 2013, producing around 300 organized results. These subject areas are all some do-mains/fields (e.g. national defense and military, court, college, religion and church, parties and political unions), which can have sub-domains. For example, a domain "unions" can have sub-domains such as "trade unions", "youth unions", "sport un-ions" and many more. Relationships between the subject areas and descriptions were created only on the archival creators' level, as domains are quite general and best describe the organization or person whose activities have created the archival fond. On the lower level, topics can be used to describe the actual content more precisely. The first linking to archival creators was primarily performed manually by the archivists. This linking is an ongoing project and more links will definitely be produced during the archivists' daily work.

The main difference between subject areas and topics is in the principle that subject areas are general topics which are composed by the archival specialists. They are created by experts who have good understanding of the content. Subject areas will show the belonging of the entire fond and not only some item like topics.

2.6 Using Facets

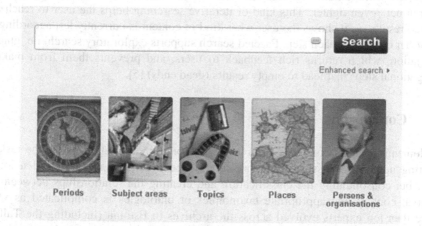

Periods   Subject areas   Topics   Places   Persons & organisations

Fig. 3. Simple search with five facets

Those defined facets are used on the first page of the simple search (Figure 3) as a starting point for browsing if the user does not know what to type in the search form.

This means that the user does not need to enter symbols in the search box, but he or she can click on one of the images and start browsing by just clicking, not typing. This allows the archival access portal to be used as a selection-based search system in which the user can invoke a search query by using only the mouse or by touching the screen of the tablet. This approach may lower search barriers, especially when the user has not mastered computer use.

Search criteria	Help
Found 129 results for search where: Search term = car	☒

Search	Help
car	Search

▸ Enhanced search
▸ New search

Browse   Help

▾ Persons & organisations
▾ Subject areas

Frontpage ▸ Search results

Search results for "car"

Results per page: 10 ▾   Results 1 - 10 / 129   << < 1 2 3 4 5 6 7 8 9 10 > >>

#	Level	Finding data	Title	Amount	Period	Storage	Actions
1	File	ERA.32.2.13743	Paul Pentsoni kaebus Rakvere-Paide Rahukogu määruse peale 23. veebr. 1928 Carl Tambergi poolt kohtupristav Anderfeldti tegevuse kohta esitatud kaebuse asjus	-	-	ERA.M6	
2	File	ERA.14.15.1502	Rambach, Luise-Therese-Caroline Aleksandn tr	-	11.10.1921 - 14.07.1922	ERA.M1	
3	File	ERA.14.15.2077	Rose, Carl-Erik	-	30.01.1940 - 30.04.1940	ERA.M1	
4	File	ERA.1.7.338	Caritas	Pages: 38	Since 1932-04-12	ERA.M6	

Fig. 4. Search results and refining options

The real power of facets will show their potential in narrowing the search by providing a selection of available facets (Figure 4). As only these facets which can currently be used (in Figure 4 "Persons & Organizations", "Subject areas") are displayed, it is quite easy to narrow the results there. When the facet name is clicked the sub-categories with the number of linked values will be revealed and the user can pull the "search net" even tighter. This kind of iterative searching helps the user to reach the desired results, as it shows the user what kind of content is currently left according to his or her choices at each step. Faceted search supports exploratory search, i.e. guided navigation, which returns rich feedback to users, and prevents them from making navigational steps that lead to empty results (dead ends) [5].

3   Conclusions

Implementing facets confronts archivists with some great challenges, as the task of creating necessary classifications particularly needs detailed research and a lot of time, but consolidating the classification and creating the relationships between the archival content and appropriate taxonomies or ontologies is complicated as well. More than ten experts evolved across the archives in Estonia (including the Tallinn City Archives) in creating facets and links – the main contribution took more than a year and it is sure that there will be much further work on the development of new vocabularies and relations. In the NAE five different facets were created. Creating facet values required quite a lot of manual work from the work group consisting of archival professionals, as the archival descriptions tend to be too general (metadata does not contain appropriate characteristics) or misleading (difficult to distinguish automatically between some classification values) for the automated processing algo-rithms. There are many situations when the human experts could only decide or confirm what the exact value should be and to what content it should be linked. Sometimes even reading the content would be required to identify the right classification.

All facets are now consolidated together in the archival information system, [1]and they can be managed (modified, updated, complemented) in the same place as well. All lower level systems will be triggered to update their classifications values when changes are performed. Archivists have reached the understanding that the facets and the links between the descriptions and classifications are not final, as the formation process of archival taxonomies and ontologies are dynamic in time and could never be fully completed along with the linking.

Therefore it is important to have and to use common guidelines and best practices for encoding different metadata schemas and implementing specific organized inter-pretation of knowledge structures (e.g. thesaurus).

As the next project is going to concentrate on the creation of ontologies and open vocabularies through open data principles, there are some key recommendations and questions which need to be solved for the upcoming project:

- The constructed taxonomies are halfway to becoming ontologies, but the agreement on exact RDF-OWL format is still vital to providing machine-processable ontologies.

---

[1] The archival information system is in the final phase of development. As the URL is a subject to change it is not presented in this article.

- All created ontologies should be open, so that other memory institutions can use them according to the open data principles.
- It is important to create procedures for changing or adding new ontology elements over time, as ontologies are dynamic resources.
  How to cope with ontologies and classifications used in agencies when transferring records to the archive?
- Which rules should be followed when allowing users to tag the archival content? How can the folksonomy be treated as ontology when users can determine suitable annotations relatively freely?
- As a major part of the facet values are in Estonian, they could be translated into other languages or linked with some ontology which is in foreign languages.

As the success rate of automated algorithms for linking descriptions to facet vocabularies is not high enough, human intervention is needed in the near future as well. By continuing the semi-automated linking work the NAE will try to use the help of users. A perspective idea is to compile packages of the generated new relations and allow users to make corrections and suggestions through crowdsourcing principles.

References

1. Sluijs, K., Houben, G.J.: Relating user tags to ontological information. In: Proceedings of the 5th International Workshop on Ubiquitous User Modeling (2008)
2. CCSDS: Reference Model for an Open Archival Information System (OAIS), Consultative Committee for Space Data Systems. Magenta Book (2012),
   http://public.ccsds.org/publications/archive/650x0m2.pdf
3. Brunk, S., Heim, P.: tFacet: Hierarchical Faceted Exploration of Semantic Data Using Well-Known Interaction Concepts. In: Proceedings of the International Workshop on Data-Centric Interactions on the Web (2011)
4. ISAAR (CPF): International Standard Archival Authority Record for Corporate Bodies, Persons and Families, 2nd edn. (2004),
   http://www.ica.org/download.php?id=1648
5. Ferré, S., Hermann, A., Ducassé, M.: Semantic Faceted Search: Safe and Expressive Navigation in RDF Graphs. Research report (2011) ISSN: 2102-6327

A Meta - model Agreement for Architectural Heritage

Michail Agathos and Sarantos Kapidakis

Ionian University, Department of Archives and Library Science
Laboratory on Digital Libraries and Electronic Publishing, Ioanni Theotoki 72, 49100, Corfu
{agathos,sarantos}@ionio.gr

Abstract. This work presents the formulation of a conceptual model for archi-tectural heritage, a meta-model, which attempts to encompass the common as-pects of diachronic architectural theories for architecture composition. The model incorporates definitions of some of the essential theories that represent the underlying conceptualization of the information contained in an architectur-al work and its aim is to create a particular understanding that can be used to design and build monument inventories. A practical application of the above model is the derivation of ARMOS (Architecture Metadata Object Schema), a metadata schema underlying this model, consistent with the recording prin-ciples of ICOMOS for monuments, aiming at reducing semantic heterogeneity in the description of architectural works, especially historic buildings.

Keywords: Architecture, Architectural Heritage, Architectural Theory, Con-ceptual Modeling, FRBR, Immovable Monuments, Metadata Standards, Meta-Models, Monument Inventories, ICOMOS, Semantic Interoperability.

1 Introduction

Monument inventories are the initials and most basic forms of documentation that list the built heritage and describe their basic attributes, in their majority, host records of historical buildings, which form a rich store of information about the past, some of it unique. Despite the recognition of their necessity and significance of these records, structural and semantic heterogeneities that exist between the various metadata sche-mas used to describe immovable monuments, stored in autonomous monument inven-tories, are very difficult to resolve.

Introducing a conceptual model is a way of achieving interoperability. Like other memory institutions (museums, libraries), monument inventories need a model which will represent the underlying semantics of the built heritage, in order to facilitate the integration, mediation, and interchange of architectural heritage information. The formulation of the ARMOS meta-model presented in this study, has a twofold intend: To recommend a basic level of functionality for monument inventories, capturing the main entities as their attributes, that are typically reflected in monument records and proposing a set of attributes for these entities, as well as common metadata require-ments for such records. A second objective is to modify the traditional and static con-ception of the history of architecture, reflected in monuments, which considers immovable monuments as finished and irremovable objects, exploring and

E. Garoufallou and J. Greenberg (Eds.): MTSR 2013, CCIS 390, pp. 384–395, 2013.
© Springer International Publishing Switzerland 2013

introducing the relationships that coexist among them. In exchange, this new movable perspective of continuous transformation will allow us to understand the built heritage in a better way [1]. The meta - model of ARMOS incorporates as entities (and relationships), basic architecture theories, promoting a way of looking at the built environment, which cannot only help us to recognize and discover basic types of monuments but also enhance our ability to see the differences as well as similarities among architectural works.

2   Enabling Interoperability for Works of Architecture

Achieving uniform access in multiple autonomous and heterogeneous monument inventories requires dealing with the problem of metadata interoperability. Having inspected in previous works [2-3], a large number of metadata schemas used to describe immovable monuments, from local and national monument inventories, we can conclude that metadata schemas used for these types of resources, present various structural and semantic heterogeneities.

Structural heterogeneities caused mainly by the distinct structural properties of the various metadata schemas. According to categorization of Haslhofer and Klas [4] '*Naming conflicts*' is one kind of structural heterogeneity, as distinct metadata models for monuments assign different names to elements representing the same real world concept. '*Domain Coverage conflict's* is another kind of heterogeneity, that occur in monument records due to the fact that real and important world concepts reflected in one schema are left out in other, although both schemas were designed for the same semantic domain.

Semantic heterogeneities on the other, occurring because of conflicts in the intended meaning of metadata elements or in the content values in distinct interpretation contexts. In the domain of architectural heritage '*Terminological Mismatches*' is a frequent conflict, as different domain concepts are mapped to model elements with the same names. Moreover in the various schemas that we have studied, different scaling systems are used to measure content values (*Scaling/Unit Conflicts*).

In order to resolve the above heterogeneities, techniques such as metadata standardization or mapping are powerful. Ideally, a uniform metadata standard approach for historical buildings would ensure maximum interoperability for the encoding of information, but the diversity of the built heritage and the differences in national inventorisation traditions, and policies are such that the production of an international standard or recommendation would be neither feasible nor desirable. In such a situation, the application of a global conceptual model, a common meta-model, is a way of achieving interoperability. At this case the various metadata schemas must align their metadata elements with the more general elements defined in the global model, which formalizes the notions in a certain domain [4].

3   Searching for an Effective Conceptual Model for the Built Heritage

Just as we know that there isn't a "one-size-fits-all" metadata schema or set of controlled vocabularies suitable for all types of resources, neither is there a single conceptual model [4]. In reality it is hard to find a model that will cover all possible ontological requirements of all systems in an integration context. The domain needs solutions for explicit representation of these structures in ways that meet the requirements of the environment where this information is created, maintained and used.

In the area of cultural heritage institutions, museums and libraries, have achieved to formalize the conceptualization reflected in their records, through two successful global conceptual models: ICOM CIDOC (International Council of Museums), developed an object-oriented conceptual model intended to facilitate the integration, mediation and interchange of heterogeneous cultural heritage knowledge produced by museums in order to document their collections, referred to as CIDOC CRM (issued as ISO standard 21127 in 2006) [5]. In the case of the immovable monuments, CIDOC CRM has many areas of potential application: The event-centric documentation of the model provides a more accurate view of the past or current life history of a cultural object [6]. CARARE schema intended for harvesting monument records is CIDOC-CRM compliant. It focuses on both the objects and their digital representation, it is a descriptive schema (not for extended descriptions) and therefore it is not so analytical in handling information concerning management purposes [7]. The meta-model of ARMOS, presented bellow, incorporates as entities, upper level concepts, which are rich in theory and well understood from the community. The modeling process of ARMOS takes into account that an effective conceptual modeling requires that the abstraction is an appropriate simplification (Zeigler, 1976). Thus, even if the upper level concepts presented in ARMOS could be expressed through a subset of CIDOC CRM, the extensive and complex semantics of the CIDOC as the complexity of its structure could lead to varying interpretations (with complex ontological facets) as well as inconsistent alignments between the model itself and the various metadata schemes used from the community of architectural heritage. Moreover, the model of ARMOS introduces relationships, which are missing from CIDOC-CRM.

In the area of libraries, Functional Requirements for Bibliographic Records, referred to as FRBR, designed in 1998 by International Federation of Library Associations (IFLA). It is a conceptual model based on the entity-attribute-relationship model of analysis, aiming to capture and represent the underlying semantics of bibliographic information and to facilitate the integration, mediation of this type of information. According to Baca and Clarke [8], for many types of works of art, architecture, and material culture the conceptual model of the FRBR Group 1 entities (Work-Expression-Manifestation-Item) does not apply. This is due to the very definition of what a work is for FRBR, and what a work means in the realm of unique cultural objects. Moreover FRBR capture a useful conceptualization of literary works (attributes - relationships), which differs considerably by the descriptive needs of works of architecture. Nevertheless, influenced from FRBR, the conceptualization presented bellow - specifically the notion of *Architectural Composition* in architectural works - gave us the ability to keep in our model only the holistic approach of FRBR to retrieval and access, using domain independent entities (See section 6).

Although monument inventories fall under the common umbrella of cultural heritage institutions, the application of the above models in the case of architectural heritage has several significant points of divergence. Historical background, constructional attributes, typological and morphological features represent building information. To depict such sophisticated information, it is important to recognize all different categories of the data, their attributes and their relationships and to represent them in an integrated conceptual model.

4   Work to Work Relationships in Architectural Records

Unlike other material of our culture (sculptures, paintings, vessels etc), architectural works such as historical buildings are complex works, consisting of multiple parts, which could be considered as works in their own right (a building has interior and exterior spaces, may be part of a larger complex of buildings etc). This complexity presents certain challenges, one of which is to investigate the relationships among them.

4.1   Intrinsic Relationships

According to CCO[1], a common cataloguing practice is to conceptually subdivide an architectural structure into multiple components, making several records for one building, including, for example, a record for the building as a whole, and additional records for each significant element (such as a chapel, portal, dome, and so on) and finally linking records together through whole-part relationships. The relationship between the whole and the parts, (e.g. monastery – church) is also known as larger entity component or parent-child relationships. An intrinsic (direct) relationship is considered as an essential relationship between two works, as a part cannot be fully understood without its whole - the part inherits much of its information from the whole and this type of relationship should always be recorded.

4.2   Extrinsic Relationships

The built environment often involves architectural complexes in which each building is significant in itself still all are related in some manner [9]. Two or more individual architectural works may have an informative invisible relationship that could be considered as an extrinsic relationship. In the context of CCO, an extrinsic relationship is not essential; although doing so may be informative, the cataloger does not need to identify the extrinsic relationship during the cataloguing process. Instead, for the documentation of the built heritage, these extrinsic relationships must be identified and recorded, allowing us to understand continuities, similarities, and variations of our architectural heritage. This has been supported by the fact that an architectural

---

[1] Cataloguing Cultural Objects, A guide to Describing Cultural Works and their Images.

structure is best understood in the context of similar structures, such as books in the context of the series (although this is an intrinsic relationship).

Extrinsic relationships are generally temporal, conceptual, or spatial. A Temporal relationship may include architectural works for which, a typological and morphological examination have shown that one building is a predecessor or successor of the other. A conceptual extrinsic relationship can link structures, which could be considered as a source of inspiration, influence or variation to one another.

An extrinsic relationship can also be the result of a spatial association, such as two or more architectural works intended to be seen together, in order to be studied or understood better. Spatial features can be described both quantitatively and qualitatively. A quantitative description of the location of the features implies the description of the exact coordinates of the location (i.e. its geo-referenced geometric shape) [10]. On the other hand, a qualitative description of the location of the geographic features can be expressed in terms of its spatial relations with other geographic features (e.g. if a building belongs to a sequence of architectural entities, or the position of the building in its plot). Qualitative spatial relationships are representing space at a level of abstraction that hides unnecessary details.

The understanding and recording of the various invisible relations between individual architectural works enhance our ability to see the differences as well as similarities among these structures by recognizing these connections, allowing us to "wander" through the evolution of architecture.

5   Formulating a Meta – Model for Architectural Works

A domain model is a conceptual model identifying the entities we want to describe, the relationships between them and the necessary attributes to effectively describe the entities. It acts as a communication tool and should be understood by technical and non- technical audiences [11]. More specifically, a meta- model is the schema used by an application to understand a metadata expression given the nature of terms and how they combine to form a metadata description, thus making it possible for a single standard, though expressed in several different formats, to still be understood in a uniform way by users and applications. ARMOS metadata schema, which is presented in the next section, is a valid instance of this model.

In order to understand the above architectural theories sufficiently, we have worked closely with the architectural community[2]. To the extend of our knowledge, there are so far no relevant modeling approaches for such upper - level architectural concepts proposed in literature.

The model takes the form of a lightweight entity-relationship conveying the following semantics:

Architectural Composition: constitutes the core concept of the overall model. The substance of *Composition* is concepts - the conceptual content that underlies all the

---

[2] Concepts of Group 1 incorporated in ARMOS meta- model have been discussed in detail with faculty members of University of Kent – School of Architecture as well as with members of Corfu Architect Association.

architectural design ideas. As in the case of the notion "F1 Work" in FRBRoo[3], this entity comprises the births of original ideas. *Architectural Composition* is the organization of the whole out of its parts, the conception of single elements, the interrelating of these elements, and the relating of them to the total form. Architectural composition is the beginning of the existence of a structure (e.g. of a building) and is realized through *Typology* that acts as a first externalization of these architectural ideas. Defining *Composition* as an entity provides us with a grouping capability. The entity is directly related with an agent (e.g. the architectural work of Corfiot Architect Ioannis Chronis), with a place (e.g. Architecture of the Ionian Islands) or with a period (e.g. the international architecture style in the 1920s and 1930s).

Typology: is the intellectual architectural content that an architectural composition takes each time it is "realized." Space and mass are the raw materials of typology; from them the architect creates an ordered expression through the process of composition. In typological science, the term typology can be understood as a term purely used to classify individuals within a group. In the field of architecture, typology is considered as a rigorous method for analysis, organization, and classification of a variety of structures into representative classes (Schneekloth & Franck, 1994). Typology is a comparative classification of dominant architectural solutions with objective and rational criteria. This classification method is considered critical for reducing the infinite variety of detailed buildings to more structured and abstract categories of relevant and representative designs. On the context of ARMOS the notion of Typology, according to the architectural theory, is divided into three levels: The class level (e.g. educational building), the type level (e.g. high school) and the group level (e.g. two storey's L shaped). Defining *Typology* as an entity in the model gives us a means of reflecting the distinctions in intellectual architectural content that may exist between one realization and another of the same architectural idea (see the example bellow).

Acomp: *Architectural Composition:* Church Architecture (13th century).
   t_1: Typology: Single-naved basilica.
   t_2: Typology: Double-naved basilica.

Patterns: in architecture, it is the capturing of architectural design ideas as archetypal and reusable descriptions (visual or textual) grouping objects by certain inherent structural similarities. Typology depicted in patterns, which in turn are embodied in architectural works. In the context of this model the idea of patterns incorporates the idea of type as a formal structure and as inherent similarities. The notion of type underlies all logical inferences that help one to classify the phenomena, to put them in groups based on their similarities, as well as to make distinctions between them. Raphael Moneo conceives type as a concept that describes a group of objects characterized by the same "formal structure" [12]. A *pattern* may have a visual representation - an image - or/and a textual description like the example bellow:

---

[3] FRBRoo: Functional Requirements for Bibliographic Records Object Oriented Model.

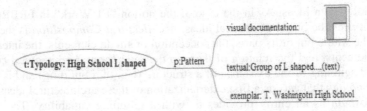

Fig. 1. Analysis of the notion of *Pattern* on the context of ARMOS

Morphology: The entity encompasses all the design and construction features (materials and techniques) applied to design ideas. Morphology is the physical embodiment of a specific typology of an architectural composition. It refers to features such as the relation between openings and solids, the expression of materials such as texture and own color and the functional applied ornamentation. Morphology does not refer so much to the decoration of a building (this is style or the rhythm) as to the elements of its general composition such as facades, plans, walls, windows, balconies etc. When the production process involves changes in the physical embodiment of a specific typology the resulting product is considered a new Morphology (see the example bellow).

Acomp: Architectural Composition: Church Architecture (13th century).
   t: Typology: Single-naved basilica[4].
     m_1*: Morphology:* Single – naved Basilica with a dome.
     m_2*: Morphology:* Single – naved Basilica with wooden roof.

Exemplar(s): The entity exemplifies a single morphology. It is one or more physical objects (architectural works) in which the various morphological features have been embodied. However, variations may occur from one architectural work to another. This enables us to draw relationships between individual works with various extrinsic relationships, discussed in the previous section (such as: *similar, influenced, variation, preceding, succeeding*) allowing us to understand continuities, similarities, and variations among buildings. In the example bellow the Basilica of Saint Anthony of Padua exemplifies a specific morphology: the "Single – naved Basilica with a dome"

Acomp: Architectural Composition: Church Architecture (13th century).
   t: Typology: Single-naved basilica
     m: Morphology: Single – naved Basilica with a dome
       ex: Basilica of Saint Anthony of Padua

Documentation: this entity encompasses all the analytical and interpretive documentation (visual or textual / digital or not digital), which accompany an architectural work and produced during the design and construction phases, ranging from paintings and prints to photographs, archaeological and architectural plans, sections and drawings, models, reports etc. Products of Documentation, in the context of this model, considered as separate and distinct related works.

---

[4] For brevity, each entity is accompanies by its initial letter, *t* for Typology and so on.

Administrative Sets: The entity represents various administrative subsets of information related to an architectural work, used from authorities or individuals for its management. According to institutional purposes, administrative metadata provide information to local authorities to help manage these structures for purposes of protection, restoration, conservation or planning. In the context of ARMOS each administrative subset contains a different set of attributes reflecting distinct administrative functions (e.g. Physical Condition Set -Legal Protection/Nomination Set).

Agent: The entity encompasses individuals, group of individuals or organizations that are treated as entities only to the extent that they are involved in the conceptualization of an architectural idea or in the creation of an architectural work (e.g., as architect, engineer, artists, decorator, construction company e.t.c.).

Place: The entity encompasses a comprehensive range of locations associated with an architectural idea or architectural work: terrestrial, historical and contemporary, geographic features and geo-political jurisdictions.

Period: The entity encompasses single dates, historical periods or a range of dates, for a wide range of activities associated with the conception of an idea or the production of an architectural work.

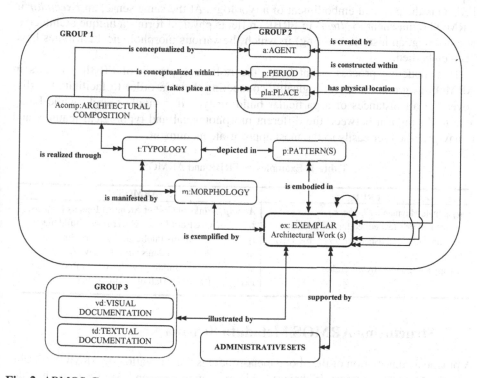

Fig. 2. ARMOS Conceptual Model: The above figure depicts a model for architectural composition that has maximal expressivity in the architectural knowledge domain using a minimal set of the above concepts

6   ARMOS and FRBR: A Common Logic

Historically, one goal of cataloguing is to make it possible to distinguish one version of an object or work from another [13]. This is successfully implemented in FRBR due to its innovation to cluster publications and other items around the notion of a common conceptual origin - the 'Work' - in order to support information retrieval. It distinguishes four levels of abstraction (Work - Expression - Manifestation - Item) from ideational content to the physical thing in hand [14].

As in the case of "Work" in FRBR, in ARMOS the notion of *'Architectural Composition'* is an abstract entity. There is no single material object one can point to as the *"Composition"*. We recognize an architectural concept through individual typological or morphological attributes of the concept, but the concept itself exists only in the commonality of content between and among the various typological expressions. *'Typology'* in ARMOS (*'Expression'* for FRBR), as a first externalization of an architectural concept, reflects intellectual content. The boundaries of what constitutes a new architectural concept in ARMOS, differ considerably of those of FRBR (which provides precise and helpful boundaries for the notion of *'Expression'*) and must not be confused. On the context of the ARMOS the various building typologies are considered simply as different expressions of the same architectural concept and not as separate works. The entity defined as Morphology (equivalent to *'Manifestation'* in FRBR) is the physical embodiment of a typology. At the same sense, an *Exemplar* in ARMOS (equivalent to *'Item'* in FRBR) reflects physical form - a unique architectural work (e.g. an historic building) in which the various morphological attributes have been embodied.

This modeling process - that keeps the holistic approach of FRBR - allows in ARMOS to group buildings logically, connecting them in order to facilitate the discovery of all instances of a particular building type in a single search, while being able to distinguish between the different morphological and typological features and to navigate the user easily to the most appropriate monument.

Table 1. Examples of FRBR and ARMOS

FRBR	ARMOS	
w_1 Ronald Hayman's *Playback*	$Acomp_1$	Works of Corfiot Architect Ioannis Chronis.
e_1 the author's text edited for publication	t_1	One Roof Public Government Buildings.
m_1 the book published in 1973 by Davis-Poynter	t_2	Two Roofs Public Government Buildings.
	m_1	Public Buildings with stone walls.
i_1 copy autographed by the author	m_2	Public Buildings with wooden Roof.
	ex_1	The Town Hall of Corfu.

7   Structuring ARMOS Metadata Schema

A practical contribution of the above meta-model is the derivation of ARMOS (Architecture Metadata Object Schema), which acting as an Application Profile, aiming at the description and administration of immovable monuments (especially historic buildings). The ARMOS bridge the gap of the absence of a data content standard for in depth cataloguing for historical buildings. Application profiling of metadata specifications in its simplest form supports the process of selection of a set of metadata elements from an element vocabulary, possibly extending the base element vocabulary as defined in the specification, using locally defined elements, and choosing a set of useful value vocabularies for use with these elements [15-16].

The basic metadata elements of the profile[5] (attributes of each entity of the above model) were derived from a logical analysis of the data that are typically reflected in monument records. The principal sources used in the analysis included a gathering of existing metadata elements hosted in various heterogeneous schemas by local and national monument inventories[6], used to describe different types of immovable monuments [2-3], [17]. The analysis also takes into account a later study in which mature and official metadata standards (MIDAS, CDWA, CDWA Lite, VRA CORE 4.0, CDI) evaluated with quantitative measures for their effectiveness in describing architectural works [3]. Finally, the proposed element vocabulary of ARMOS conforms to principles of International Council on Monuments and Sites for the recording of monuments, groups of buildings and sites[7] including all the recommendations for a basic level record of a monument [18].

The above circumstances and the fact that most of the examined mature metadata standards, have been designed for general collection description of material of our culture, resulted in a profile which was created by extending Core Data Index to Historic Buildings and Monuments (CDI) and by taking elements from various mature metadata specifications designed for extended descriptions, especially from CDWA (Categories of Description of Works of Arts). CDWA is a data content standard designed for describing unique works of art, architecture, and material of our culture providing an extensive set of descriptive metadata elements and guidelines. CDI on the other provides the ARMOS with descriptive metadata with commonly understood semantics. Moreover, in order to eliminate the absence of important elements for the description of these resources (requirements unmatched by other schemas), ARMOS is supplemented by 'new' elements, locally defined, for which a namespace was created[8].

Data elements of the schema are grouped into categories corresponding to the entities of the model. The schema presented as a hierarchy, including aggregate data elements and simple data elements. ARMOS use a hierarchical structure of elements-within-elements, similarly to the LOM abstract model, so we could say that ARMOS

---

[5] The details of each element and guidelines for adding content will be available from http://dlib.ionio.gr/standards/armos. At this time an hierarchical index of the proposed elements is available (showing the attributes of each entity of the conceptual model).

[6] For this study, we analyzed the serialization of data of 50 monument inventories in Greece recorded in a study in 2011 (keeping in total 900,000 records), as well as the serialization of 11 national monument inventories recorded by UNESCO in 1984 .

[7] As these were ratified by the 11th ICOMOS General Assebly in Sofia, October 1996.

[8] Namespace: armos - http://dlib.ionio.gr/standards/armos

belongs to the IEEE LOM family of specifications. Each element can be either a container element, thus containing other elements, or a leaf element, which holds a value of a certain data type. The top-level elements are called categories. ARMOS harmonisation profile provides not only a set of data elements, but also a default pattern for the use of those data elements, a "base" application profile to which other application profiles should also conform.

8   Testing and Improvements

All metadata terms of the proposed schema are identified with URIs. In this sense a normalized documentation will be prepared in which the above elements will be described as precisely as possible (*Principle of Appropriate Identification* such in the case of DCAPs – Duplin Core Application Profiles), including enough description in order to be of optimal usefulness for the intended audience of the schema (*Principle of Readability*). Moreover the schema specifies a small set of vocabularies that should be used to provide values for the various metadata elements in order to resolve scaling/unit conflicts. In order to evaluate the overall effectiveness, identifying areas in the schema requiring attention and revisions, ARMOS have been tested with concrete examples of historic building of the Old Town of Corfu (Greece), inscribed in the UNESCO World Heritage List in 2007. A complete example of an historic building is available at: http://dlib.ionio.gr/standards/armos.

9   Conclusion

Metadata schemas relevant to historic buildings have not been achieved until now the milestone of formal standardization. However in open environments, like in the case of monument inventories, having no central standardization authority, interoperability techniques such as those presented above, provide powerful solutions. The production of ARMOS conceptual model presented in this study, move us away from the traditional flat metadata descriptions of historic buildings, often including isolating and disconnecting information in text-based record forms, along with pre-established entry fields in order to facilitate queries, into a fresh perspective on the structure and relationship of these records. Furthermore the derivation of ARMOS metadata schema that is consistent with the semantic web recommendations will help to achieve greater interoperability on the metadata practices and descriptions for these types of resources, providing the community with a profile which guides data structure, data values, and data content.

References

1. Casanova, et al.: Evolutionary Processes, Morphology and Typology of Historical Architecture as a Line of Research: a Tool for Conservation. In: 16th International Conference on Urban Planning, May 18-20, Development and Information Society, Essen (2011), http://www.corp.at/archive/CORP2011_209.pdf (accessed May 10, 2013)

2. Agathos, M., Kapidakis, S.: Discovering Current Practices for Records of Historic Buildings and Mapping them to Standards. In: First Workshop on Digital Information Management, Corfu, Greece, March 30-31, pp. 61–75 (2011), http://hdl.handle.net/10760/15847
3. Agathos, M., Kapidakis, S.: Describing Immovable Monuments with Metadata Standards. Int. J. Metadata, Semantics and Ontologies 7(3), 162–170 (2012)
4. Haslhofer, B., Klas, W.: A survey of techniques for achieving metadata interoperability. ACM Comput. Surv. 42(2) (2010)
5. Crofts, N., Doerr, M., Gill, T., Stead, S., Stiff, M.: The CIDOC Conceptual Reference Model: Resources: Version 5.0.4 of the Definition of the CIDOC Conceptual Reference Model (2011)
6. Doerr, M., Kritsotaki, A.: Documenting events in metadata. In: Proceedings of CIPA-VAST Conference, Nicosia, Cyprus, pp. 56–59 (2006)
7. Papatheodorou, C., Dallas, C., Ertmann-Christiansen, C., Fernie, K., Gavrilis, D., Masci, M.E., Constantopoulos, P., Angelis, S.: A New Architecture and Approach to Asset Representation for Europeana Aggregation: The CARARE Way. In: García-Barriocanal, E., Cebeci, Z., Okur, M.C., Öztürk, A. (eds.) MTSR 2011. CCIS, vol. 240, pp. 412–423. Springer, Heidelberg (2011)
8. Baca, M., Clarke, S.: FRBR and Works of Art, Architecture, and Material Culture. In: Taylor, A.G. (ed.) Understanding FRBR: What It is and How It will Affect Our Retrieval Tools, pp. 103–110. Libraries Unlimited, Westport (2007)
9. Baca, M., et al.: Cataloging Cultural Objects: A Guide to Describing Cultural Works and Their Images. American Library Association, Chicago (2006)
10. Hart, A.: D 2.3 Modelling and Processing Contextual Aspects of Data. Report, Planet Data, Network of Excellence (2012), http://wiki.planet-data.eu/uploads/7/7e/D2.3_draft.pdf
11. Diamantopoulos, N., Sgouropoulou, C., Kastrantas, K., Manouselis, N.: Developing a Metadata Application Profile for Sharing Agricultural Scientific and Scholarly Research Resources. In: García-Barriocanal, E., Cebeci, Z., Okur, M.C., Öztürk, A., et al. (eds.) MTSR 2011. CCIS, vol. 240, pp. 453–466. Springer, Heidelberg (2011)
12. Moneo, R.: On Typology. Oppositions: A Journal for Ideas and Criticism in Architecture 13(1) (1978)
13. Baca, M. (ed.): Introduction to Metadata. Getty Publications, Los Angeles (2008)
14. Le Boeuf, P.: A strange model named FRBRoo. Cataloging & Classification Quarterly 50(5-7), 422–438 (2012)
15. Nilsson, M., Baker, T., Johnston, P.: The Singapore Framework for Dublin Core Application Profiles (2008), http://dublincore.org/documents/singapore-framework/
16. Nilsson, M.: Harmonization of Metadata Standards. Deliverable of the PROLEARN IST-507310 European Project (2008)
17. Sykes, M.H.: Manual on Systems of Inventorying Immovable Cultural Property. Unesco, Paris (1984)
18. ICOMOS.: Principles for the Recording of Monuments, Groups of Buildings and Sites, Sofia (1996), http://www.icomos.org/charters/archives-e.pdf

Highlights of Library Data Models in the Era of Linked Open Data

Sofia Zapounidou[1], Michalis Sfakakis[1], and Christos Papatheodorou[1,2]

[1] Department of Archives and Library Science, Ionian University, Corfu, Greece
[2] Digital Curation Unit, IMIS, "Athena" Research Center, Athens, Greece
{l12zapo,sfakakis,papatheodor}@ionio.gr

Abstract. Semantic Web technologies and Linked data form a new reference framework for libraries. The library community aims to integrate its data with the Semantic Web and as a result new library data models have been developed. In this context, significant research effort focuses on the alignment between the library models with relevant models developed by other communities in the cultural heritage domain. However there exist several issues concerning the interoperability between all these data models. This paper seeks to contribute in the interoperability of four models, namely FRBR, FRBRoo, EDM and BIBFRAME. It highlights the commonalities and the divergences between them by using a case bibliographic record and by exploring how this record is represented by each one of them.

Keywords: semantic web, library data models, linked data, FRBR, FRBRoo, EDM, BIBFRAME.

1 Introduction

Libraries develop and preserve rich metadata for their holdings. Exchange of these metadata between libraries is made through specific bibliographic standards. The most well known is the MARC (MAchine Readable Cataloguing) data structure standard [1], developed in the 1960s and widely used since then by libraries worldwide. Despite its success and its many updates since its first development, MARC faces the challenges to enable provision and use of library data by third party applications, as well as to adapt its framework to the current trends of the metadata models [2].

The insufficiencies of current bibliographic data representation standards have been well studied by experts and library-related international organizations [3–8]. As a result, there is a growing interest in establishing meaningful representation and communication of bibliographic data in the environment of the web of data, which has already appeared exploiting Semantic Web technologies that enable the publication and consumption of structured data. These technologies known as *Linked Data* [9] provide a new reference framework for libraries aspiring to integrate their data into the Semantic Web [2], thus providing very rich datasets that may be used, exploited and extended by other libraries or communities. Some pilot efforts have

E. Garoufallou and J. Greenberg (Eds.): MTSR 2013, CCIS 390, pp. 396–407, 2013.

already been undertaken by the library community to redefine the bibliographic universe in accordance with the new reference framework described above. These different interpretations are expressed almost simultaneously and may cause interoperability problems, making integration of library data into the Semantic Web not a simple task. Library institutions and stakeholders, library data, and library processes need to be defined explicitly according to the requirements and benefits of the new data publishing framework [2].

The aim of this paper is to contribute in the interoperability of such approaches. Therefore, it tries to compare bibliographic data models developed by different initiatives in the library community with the aim of discovering the common ground between them. For this purpose four data models are explored: FRBR, FRBRoo, Europeana Data Model (EDM) and BIBFRAME model. Since libraries mainly collect monographs, this paper examines the way monographs could be conceptually modeled by the mentioned models. The monograph chosen as a case study to be investigated is a well-known literary work, 'Don Quixote de la Mancha'. It consists of two separate works: the first one was published in 1605 with the title 'El ingenioso hidalgo don Quixote de la Mancha' and the second one was published in 1615 with the title 'Segunda parte del ingenioso cauallero don Quixote de la Mancha'. The monograph selected is an English translation of both parts incorporated in one single volume. The description of the monograph was found in the bima0000074081MARC21 record downloaded as a MARCXML file from the National Library of Spain Catalog. For the mentioned models and the given monograph the paper investigates the following research questions:

— Is there any consensus on their conceptual modeling view in the case of monographs?
— Can the different point of views converge and how?
— Can bibliographic data following such models, be integrated?

The next section of the paper provides a short description of the followed approach. A short description of the mentioned data models along with a brief representation of the monograph chosen is provided in section 3. In section 4 a comparison is presented aiming to highlight the main characteristics of each model and its expressiveness in revealing the semantics of the information provided by the bibliographic records that share similar characteristics with the monograph in hand. Finally, the lessons learnt are summarized in the conclusions section.

2   Overview of the Approach

In order to highlight the commonalities and divergences at conceptual level between the used models, it was decided at the beginning of this investigation to use a real representation of a well known monograph. Therefore, the 'Don Quixote de la Mancha' bibliographic record was selected as an appropriate case to start representing the most fundamental aspects of the models, while it could be utilized for more complicated representations by the examined models. This record was selected because it represents a multipart monograph published in a single volume. Additionally, the parts of this work have also been published as independent volumes. Therefore, this case provides the ability to build more complex instances of the models and to assess their expressiveness. Moreover, this record was used as a case study from a Europeana Task Force group [10] and therefore we can verify its core representations for the FRBR and FRBRoo models, while for the representation of the BIBFRAME model we used the representation produced from the bibframe.org [11] tools.

Table 1 presents a labeled version of the MARC record containing the most significant metadata of the monograph required to populate the most characteristic and respective classes of the models. For this purpose, all the mentioned models were studied in terms of elucidating the semantics of their classes and relationships. Then, the classes of each of them that can model the 'Don Quixote de la Mancha' record were identified and a graphical representation for each model for the monograph on hand was sketched. These graphical representations accompany the models' descriptions found in the next section. All graphical representations were afterwards compared to reveal both common ground and differentiations regarding the conceptual modeling approaches adopted by the models under investigation. For readability purposes, it should be stated that the graphical representations are simplified and thus some straightforward entities were deliberately omitted, such as authors, contributors etc as well as complete URIs required by the RDF language.

Table 1. Labeled version of the bima0000074081 MARCXML record

Personal name / Author	Cervantes Saavedra, Miguel de (1547-1616)
Uniform title	[Don Quijote de la Mancha. Inglés]
Title	The history of the most renowned Don Quixote of Mancha [Texto impreso]: and his trusty squire Sancho Pancha [sic] / now made English according to the humour of our modern language and adorned with seueral copper plates by J.P.
Publisher/Date	London : printed by Thomas Hodgkin and sold by William Whitwood ..., 1687
Physical description	[16], 616, [3] p., [7] h. de lám.; Fol.
Contents	Partes primera y segunda
Title note	Las iniciales J.P. corresponden al traductor, J. Philips, como consta en la dedicatoria
Added author	Hodgkin, Thomas (s. XVII), imp.; Whitwood, William, ed.; Phillips, John (1631-1706), tr.

3   Library Data Models: Representation of the Case Study

3.1   Functional Requirements for Bibliographic Records –(FRBR)

Functional Requirements for Bibliographic Records [6] is the result of a long-term study initiated by one of the resolutions adopted by the 1990 Stockholm Seminar on

Bibliographic Records. That resolution asked for a clear delineation of "the functions performed by the bibliographic record with respect to various media, various applications, and various user needs" [12].

The FRBR study presented a conceptual entity-relationship model that defined key bibliographic entities, their attributes and the relationships between them. The bibliographic entities were grouped into three groups: Group 1 entities refer to intellectual or artistic products (*Work, Expression, Manifestation, Item*), Group 2 entities refer to people (*Person*) and/or corporate bodies (*Corporate Body*) that create, publish or preserve the Group 1 entities, Group 3 entities are used as topics in the Group 1 entities (*Concept, Object, Event, and Place*).

In Group1 entities (*Work, Expression, Manifestation, Item*, also known as WEMI) are defined from the abstract to the concrete level. *Work* and *Expression* reflect the content, while *Manifestation* and *Item* reflect the physical form of the content. *Work* refers to the intellectual or artistic creation, *Expression* refers to the realization of the intellectual or artistic creation, *Manifestation* refers to the physical embodiment of an expression of a work, *Item* refers to a single copy of a given manifestation.

Each entity is defined by a set of attributes. For instance a *Manifestation* is described by 38 attributes, such as title of the manifestation, statement of responsibility, edition/issue designation, place of publication /distribution, date of publication/distribution, fabricator/manufacturer, etc. It should be noticed that most descriptions in library catalogues correspond to the Manifestation entities of the model, while library holdings correspond to Item entities.

The entities of the model are inter-linked by a set of relationships. The entities *Work* and *Expression* are correlated with the relationship *is realized through*. Moreover, the relationship *is created* correlates a *Work* with the entities of Group 2 (*Person, Corporate Body*). The entities *Expression* and *Manifestation* are interlinked though the relationship *is embodied in*, while the entities *Manifestation* and *Item* are correlated through the relationship *is exemplified by*. *Expression* is correlated with the entities of Group 2 through the relationship *is realized by*, while *Manifestation* and *Item* are correlated with the same group of entities via the relationships *is produced* and *is owned by* respectively. Furthermore, the entities of Group 3 are correlated with the entities of the Groups 1 and 2 through the relationship *has as subject*.

Even though the FRBR study defined the entities in each group, it focused on Group 1 entities. The entities in the other two groups involved authority data and were further analyzed in two subsequent reports, namely Functional Requirements for Authority Data – FRAD [13] and Functional Requirements for Subject Authority Data – FRSAD [14]. All these models are also known as the FRBR family of models. Gordon Dunsire expressed the FRBR family of models in RDF and made these RDF vocabularies available through the Open Metadata Registry (http://metadataregistry.org/).

Figure 1 depicts briefly the instances of the four entities derived from the MARC21 record in question: the instance of the *Work* is 'Don Quixote de la Mancha', its *Expression* in an English translation by J.Philips, a *Manifestation* of the English translation published in 1687 by William Whitwood and printed by Thomas Hodgkin and an *Item* of this Manifestation, which in this case is a digitized copy.

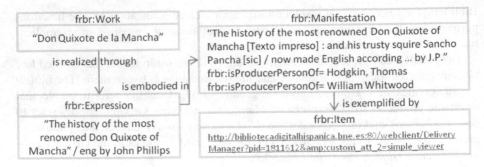

Fig. 1. A monograph represented by FRBR

3.2   Functional Requirements for Bibliographic Records Object-Oriented version (FRBRoo)

The object-oriented version of FRBR, known as FRBRoo, is a harmonization of the CIDOC-CRM and the FRBR models. CIDOC CRM [15] is a reference model which represents conceptually the cultural heritage domain and consists of a hierarchy of 86 entities (or classes) and 137 properties. It ensures semantic integration between different cultural metadata schemas and aims to eliminate their possible semantic heterogeneities. The aim of the harmonization of the two models was the development of an ontology that would enable the representation of bibliographic information, thus facilitating "the integration, mediation, and interchange of bibliographic and museum information" [16]. To address this aim, FRBRoo includes concepts from both FRBR family of models and CIDOC-CRM: FRBR Group 1 entities were further analyzed and refined; temporal entities, events and time processes were included; creation and production processes were also modeled.

As far the Group 1 entities are concerned, various interpretations of *Work* have been incorporated into FRBRoo, e.g. *F14 Individual Work, F19 Publication Work, F16 Container Work* that may respectively correspond to one single work, a work prepared for publication with the publisher's contributions, and an aggregate work. Dimensions of time and place were also expressed in the model to support the description of intellectual creation and physical production processes.

FRBRoo may support uniformly static or dynamic views of the bibliographic universe. It may support the description of bibliographic products independently from their creation, modification and publication processes just as the FRBR family of models does. It also enables more dynamic descriptions by taking into account the dimension of time, and by modeling both creation and production processes and their intellectual or artistic products. FRBRoo results into being a dynamic flexible model that provides cataloguing agencies the means to describe their holdings according to their cataloguing policies, to their view (static or dynamic may it be) of their collections.

Figure 2 provides a representation of the monograph in hand according to FRBRoo. Five classes are utilized for this purpose. The class *F15 Complex Work* having as instance the 'Don Quixote de la Mancha', the class *F22 Self-Contained*

Expression having as instance the English translation by John Phillips, the class *F24 Publication Expression* that incorporates the printer's and the publisher's information, the class *F3 Manifestation Product Type* that carries the title of the *F24 Publication Expression* as appeared in the title page. Finally, the class *F5 Item* has as instance a URI to the digitized copy of the monograph.

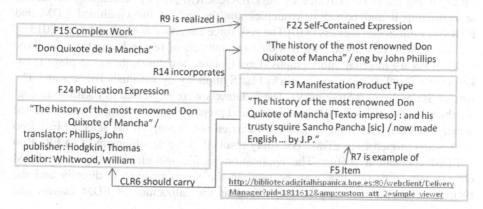

Fig. 2. A monograph represented by FRBRoo

3.3   Europeana Data Model (EDM)

Europeana (http://www.europeana.eu/) is an aggregation portal providing access to born-digital or digitized cultural heritage content provided by memory institutions all over Europe. Descriptions over Europeana are made with a basic data model called Europeana Semantic Elements [17], which uses 12 elements in addition to the 15 elements of the Dublin Core Metadata Element Set. The Europeana Data Model (EDM) has been created to offer an advanced data model that may better express the semantics of the cultural heritage descriptions provided by different communities. No community – driven standard was used as a basis for its development and the Semantic Web framework was taken into account [18].

For each provider, EDM distinguishes between real provided cultural heritage objects (e.g. painting), their digital representations (e.g. digital image of painting), and their descriptions (e.g. metadata about painting). EDM has three core classes, namely *edm:ProvidedCHO* (for provided Cultural Heritage Object), *edm:WebResource* (for the *edm:ProvidedCHO* digital representations) and *ore:Aggregation* (for the aggregation of the activities made by the provider of the *edm:ProvidedCHO*).

Alignment of EDM with library metadata is a work in progress. In 2012, two reports have been published [19, 20], both taking into consideration the FRBR model, seeking to express FRBR entities with EDM classes, and focusing on specific library materials (monographs, multi-volume works and serials). The latest report was the revised D5.1. alignment report [20] which suggested that all FRBR Group 1 entities (*Work, Expression, Manifestation, Item*) will be expressed by the *edm:ProvidedCHO* class and "the distinction between them will lie only in the metadata used and in the

relationships expressed"[20]. In this report, the need of further investigation was recognized, suggesting at the same time the integration of FRBRoo entities in EDM using FRBRoo terms.

As a result the EDM – FRBRoo Application Profile Task Force was launched in
July 2012. The scope of this taskforce was to build upon the existing mapping of
FRBRoo and the EDM provided by the CIDOC CRM [15] by "extending, correcting
or restricting it and providing examples for the use of the combined EDM and
FRBRoo name-space clusters" [10].The task force ended its work on 30 April 2013.

The Task Force worked with real datasets and sets of research questions for three
types of library material: monographs (Don Quixote test case), theatrical plays (Sha-
kespeare's Hamlct) and musical works (1st Symphony by Johannes Brahms and The
Rite of Spring by Igor Stravinsky). These datasets were expressed in FRBRoo to enable the selection of basic FRBRoo classes and properties conforming to a set of stated
principles. Then a mapping process was carried out to map all the selected FRBRoo
classes and properties to EDM. The study resulted in the development of an FRBRoo
– EDM application profile. The application profile includes two sets: the EDM
classes and properties that may be used in the mapping process directly and the
FRBRoo concepts that may be considered as specializations of EDM classes and
properties.

Figure 3 presents the representation of the Don Quixote monograph as implemented by EDM, while Figure 4 provides the representation of the monograph as
implemented by the EDM – FRBRoo Application Profile.

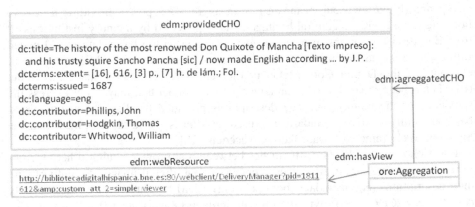

Fig. 3. A monograph represented by EDM

As mentioned the Europeana Data Model holds data at the manifestation level of
FRBR. Thus, the monograph in hand is represented by two entities: the
edm:providedCHO that holds all information about the monograph entitled 'The history of the most renowned Don Quixote of Mancha' and published in 1687 by William Whitwood. The other entity is the *edm:webResource* that links to the digitized
copy of the monograph.

The EDM – FRBRoo application profile within the scope of "allow(ing) a better
representation of the FRBR Group 1 entities" [21] maps EDM classes to FRBRoo

(Figure 4). Thus, the monograph in question is modeled as follows: an instance of the class *edm:InformationResource* represents the instance of the FRBR *Work* 'Don Quixote de la Mancha'. A second instance of the class *edm:InformationResource* is mapped to the FRBR *Expression* class. The class *edm:providedCHO* is mapped to the class *F24 Publication Expression* of FRBRoo and, finally, the class *edm:webResource* represents the digital copy, which actually carries the information from the publication expression.

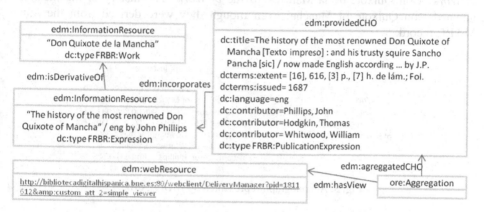

Fig. 4. A monograph represented by EDM - FRBRoo

3.4   Bibliographic Framework Initiative Data Model (BIBFRAME Model)

In October 2011, Library of Congress announced the launch of a new programme regarding the creation of a new Bibliographic Framework. This framework aims to accommodate many bibliographic formats and data models and the only prerequisite stated is the use of Linked Data technologies and the Resource Description Framework [22]. On May 22, 2012 the Library of Congress announced its cooperation with Eric Miller's Zepheira Group for the development of a bibliographic data model [23]. The draft model was presented on November 2012 and a BIBFRAME mailing list was created for the exchange of ideas and further development of the model.

The BIBFRAME model main classes are: *Creative Work, Instance, Authority and Annotation* [24]. The class *Creative Work* reflects the "conceptual essence of the cataloguing item" [24] and seems to be semantically closer to the FRBR *Work* and *Expression* entities. The class *Instance* reflects "an individual, material embodiment of the Work" and seems to be alike to the FRBR *Manifestation* entity. The class *Authority* is rather straight-forward; this class is used to identify *People, Places, and Organizations* involved in the creation or publication of a *Work*. For the expression of topics, BIBFRAME *Authority* simply works as a linking mechanism to LC Subject Headings published as linked data at the ID.LOC.GOV site [25]. The class *Annotation* expresses comments made about a BIBFRAME *Work, Instance, Authority*. Examples of BIBFRAME annotations are: library holdings, cover arts, sample texts, reviews, etc. The BIBFRAME model is still under development.

The MARC 21 record of the Don Quixote monograph (bima0000074081.xml file) was submitted to the transformation service available at the official BIBFRAME.org website [11]. The transformation service derived two instances of *bf:Work* and one *bf:Instance*. The first Work is 'Don Quixote de la Mancha', the second Work is 'The history of the most renowned Don Quixote of Mancha' and its instance published in 1687. The relationship between the second Work and its instance are depicted briefly in Figure 5. Note that the BIBFRAME transformation service did not relate the *bf:Work* 'Don Quixote de la Mancha' to the *bf:Work* 'The history of the most renowned Don Quixote of Mancha' even though they were derived from the same MARC record.

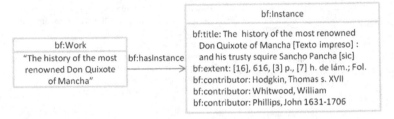

Fig. 5. A monograph represented by BIBFRAME

4   Discussion

Modeling the English translation of the 'Don Quixote de la Mancha' under each model's semantics revealed some common ground and some significant differences as well. All models recognize that there is a given number of entities (classes), and that each of them is associated with specific characteristics (attributes). Furthermore, the classes are correlated through a set of relationships that enrich the semantics of each model. Moreover, they all have been somehow expressed in a Semantic Web framework with the re-use of existing or development of new element sets and vocabularies. FRBR has been expressed in RDF by Gordon Dunsire, FRBRoo, EDM and BIBIFRAME are all developed in RDF. Thus, the exact semantics of each model's entity and the semantic differences between them may be identified in detail.

All models make a distinction between content and its carrier. The abstraction levels firstly defined in the FRBR model are recognized by the other three models (FRBRoo, EDM, BIBFRAME) as an important asset for the library community that must be taken into consideration. FRBRoo and EDM associate their entities to the FRBR Group 1 entities. BIBFRAME aims to accommodate FRBR Group 1 entities in the near future. Additionally, there seems to be more common ground between FRBR and FRBRoo models and between EDM and BIBFRAME models. FRBR and FRBRoo models are similar to each other following the basic FRBR four levels of abstraction (*Work, Expression, Manifestation, Item*). EDM and BIBFRAME are more similar to each other adopting a two-level approach: *edm:providedCHO* and *edm:webResource* in EDM, *Creative Work* and *Instance* in BIBFRAME.

A main difference is that each model recognizes a different number of abstraction layers. FRBR and FRBRoo model intellectual or artistic creations and their physical embodiments with four classes (also known as WEMI hierarchy), while EDM and BIBFRAME use only two levels. FRBR and FRBRoo go beyond existing bibliographic standards, while the current Europeana Data Model and the BIBFRAME model seem to build upon the semantics of MARC21. In EDM all information concerning WEMI are added to the *edm:providedCHO* [20] and BIBFRAME has been initiated as an "... effort to translate MARC 21 to a Linked Data model" [24].

Another difference is that information about contributors, namely translator J.Phillips, publisher W. Whitwood and printer T. Hodgkin, is represented in different entities in each model. In FRBR and FRBRoo the translator's contribution determines the creation of an *frbr:Expression*, while in EDM and BIBFRAME model the translator's contribution is described in a lower level of each model's hierarchy: in *edm:providedCHO* and *bf:Instance* respectively. FRBR includes the information about the printer and the publisher in *frbr:Manifestation*, while FRBRoo contextualizes them through a new class, *F24 Publication Expression*. In the other two models the semantics of these pieces of information are not discriminated and are given in *edm:providedCHO* and *bf:Instance* respectively.

These differences reflect the models' disparate creation contexts and the different modeling approach they follow. FRBR was created to express intellectual creations in a library setting. It was developed according to the entity-relationship model and its "Group 1 entities represent the different aspects of user interests in the products of intellectual or artistic endeavour"[12]. As a result, four levels have been identified to enable search, identification, selection, and obtaining library materials. A user, for example, may search for a work entitled 'Don Quixote de la Mancha' (*Work*), search this Work only in its English versions (*Expression*), search a specific publication where contributions of interest to the user have been made (*Manifestation*) and then obtain a physical or digital copy (*Item*). FRBRoo follows the CIDOC CRM logic which describes the history of objects over time and results in capturing the history of a library object starting from its conception and ending with its last ownership status. FRBRoo extends FRBR following an object-oriented approach and includes CIDOC CRM entities. The aim was to "model processes starting from initial idea to the item a user holds" [16]. The FRBR Group 1 entities were further analyzed and more classes that qualify *Works, Expressions, Manifestations* were identified.

EDM has been developed as a simple data model that providers can easily use to make their digitized resources available through the Europeana portal. It is a generic model that "adopts an open, cross-domain Semantic Web-based framework" [18] and may uniformly accommodate standards from the libraries, archives and museums communities. Its two levels of abstraction, *edm:providedCHO* and *edm:webResource* are mapped to the FRBR *Manifestation* and *Item* entities respectively. The recently developed EDM-FRBRoo mapping proved that only a subset of the semantically rich FRBRoo classes is needed to describe the Europeana content. As a result the new application profile is closer to FRBR and FRBRoo models [10].

BIBFRAME is a linked data model developed with the aim of providing a simplified model to "which various content models can be mapped" [24] and at the present initial stage focuses on integrating data from MARC21 and RDA records into the Semantic Web. Regarding its dual approach and the relationship with FRBR, it is stated that "the origin of the Work/Instance aspects of the BIBFRAME can reflect the FRBR relationships in terms of a graph rather than as hierarchical relationships, after applying a reductionist technique" [24].

5   Conclusions

This first investigation revealed common ground and divergences among the four tested models. The comparison of the FRBR, FRBRoo, EDM and BIBFRAME models performed on the MARC21 record 'Don Quixote de la Mancha' has revealed that interoperability is not an impossible task to undertake especially when certain levels of interoperability are considered. As far as the technical aspect of interoperability is considered, it could be concluded that it is achievable because all models are developed in RDF. Semantic interoperability is not a straightforward issue but it has been shown that there is a consensus regarding conceptual modeling as far as the distinction of content and its carrier is concerned.

Each model has its own classes and properties defining its own semantics. Thus, it may be assumed that a mapping between the models may be possible. The successful EDM-FRBRoo mapping advocates in favor of this assumption. Taken into consideration that the EDM-FRBRoo mapping was accomplished in a very specific context, that of Europeana, any mapping between the four models should be made with a specific context in mind. This specific context is a matter of achieving organizational interoperability in the library domain. Consensus among the library community regarding the representation of collections and materials may and should be built. This is the prerequisite for developing application profiles and cataloguing guidelines that could be usable and implementable in new advanced library systems.

Further investigations should be performed using a larger set of bibliographic records that comprise more cases of bibliographic descriptions. Then, considerably evaluation results will improve the quality of the mappings between the data models and contribute in the semantic interoperability between them.

References

1. Library of Congress: MARC Standards, http://www.loc.gov/marc/
2. W3C Library Linked Data Incubator Group: Library Linked Data Incubator Group Final Report: W3C Incubator Group Report. Report, W3C (October 25, 2011)
3. Heaney, M.: Object-oriented cataloging. Information Technology and Libraries 14, 135 (1995)
4. Ridley, M.: Beyond MARC. In: Weihs, J. (ed.) International Conference on the Principles and Future Development of AACR Toronto, Canada, October 23-25. Canadian Library Association, Library Association Publishing, American Library Association, Ottawa, London, Chicago (1998)

5. Howarth, L.C.: Content versus Carrier. In: Weihs, J. (ed.) International Conference on the Principles and Future Development of AACR Toronto, Canada, October 23-25, pp. 148–157. Canadian Library Association, Library Association Publishing, American Library Association, Ottawa, London, Chicago (1998)

6. IFLA Study Group on the Functional Requirements for Bibliographic Records: Functional Requirements for Bibliographic Records Final Report. Saur, München (1998)

7. Tennant, R.: A Bibliographic Metadata Infrastructure for the 21st Century. Library Hi Tech. 22, 175–181 (2004)

8. Calhoun, K.: The changing nature of the catalog and its integration with other discovery tools. Report, Library of Congress (2006)

9. W3C: Linked data, http://www.w3.org/standards/semanticweb/data

10. Task Force EDM FRBRoo, http://pro.europeana.eu/web/network/europeana-tech/-/wiki/Main/Task+Force+EDM+FRBRoo

11. Library of Congress, Zepheira Inc.: BIBFRAME.org, http://bibframe.org/

12. IFLA Study Group on the Functional Requirements for Bibliographic Records: Functional Requirements for Bibliographic Records. Final Report, IFLA (2009)

13. International Federation of Library Associations and Institutions: Functional Requirements for Authority Data: A conceptual model. K.G.Saur, München (2009)

14. IFLA Working Group on the Functional Requirements for Subject Authority Records: Functional Requirements for Subject Authority Data (FRSAD): A Conceptual Model. Report, IFLA (2010)

15. Bœuf, P., Le, D.M., Ore, C.E., Stead, S.: Definition of the CIDOC Conceptual Reference Model, version 5.1 (draft). ICOM/CIDOC CRM Special Interest Group (2013)

16. Bekiari, C., Doerr, M., Bœuf, P., Le, R.P.: FRBR object-oriented definition and mapping from FRBRER, FRAD and FRSAD (version 2.0). International Working Group on FRBR and CIDOC CRM Harmonisation (2013)

17. Europeana Project: Europeana Semantic Elements Specification Version 3.4.1. Europeana (2012)

18. Isaac, A.: Europeana data model primer. Europeana Project (2011)

19. Europeana Project: Definition of the Europeana Data Model elements Version 5.2.3. Europeana Project (2012)

20. Angjeli, A., Bayerische, M., Chambers, S., Charles, V., Clayphan, R., Deliot, C., Eriksson, J., Freire, N., Huber, A., Jahnke, A., Pedrosa, G., Phillips, V., Pollecutt, N., Robson, G., Seidler, W., Rühle, S.: D5.1 Report on the alignment of library metadata with the European Data Model (EDM) Version 2.0. Report, Europeana Project (2012)

21. Doerr, M., Gradmann, S., Leboeuf, P., Aalberg, T., Bailly, R., Olensky, M.: Final Report on EDM – FRBRoo Application Profile Task Force. Report, Europeana Project (2013)

22. Library of Congress: A Bibliographic Framework for the Digital Age. Report, Library of Congress (2011)

23. Library of Congress: The Library of Congress Announces Modeling Initiative (May 22, 2012), http://www.loc.gov/bibframe/news/bibframe-052212.html

24. Miller, E., Ogbuji, U., Mueller, V., MacDougall, K.: Bibliographic Framework as a Web of Data: Linked Data Model and Supporting Services. Report, Library of Congress (2012)

25. BIBFRAME.org: On BIBFRAME Authority (May 22, 2013), http://bibframe.org/documentation/bibframe-authority/

agriOpenLink: Towards Adaptive Agricultural Processes Enabled by Open Interfaces, Linked Data and Services

Slobodanka Dana Kathrin Tomic[1], Anna Fensel[1], Christian Aschauer[2],
Klemens Gregor Schulmeister[2], Thomas Riegler[3], Franz Handler[3],
Marcel Otte[4], and Wolfgang Auer[4]

[1] The Telecommunications Research Center Vienna (FTW), Vienna, Austria
`{tomic,fensel}@ftw.at`
[2] University of Natural Resources and Life Sciences, Division of Agricultural Engineering
(BOKU), Vienna, Austria
`{christian.aschauer,klemens.schulmeister}@boku.ac.at`
[3] Josephinum Research (JR), Wieselburg, Austria
`{thomas.riegler,franz.handler}@josephinum.at`
[4] MKW Electronics GesmbH (MKWE) Weibern, Austria
`{marcel.otte,wolfgang.auer}@mkw.at`

Abstract. Today, users involved in agricultural production processes increasingly rely on advanced agricultural machines and specialized applications utilizing the latest advances in information and communication technology (ICT). Robots and machines host numerous specialized sensors and measurement devices and generate large amounts of data that combined with data coming from external sources, could provide a basis for better process understanding and process optimization. One serious roadblock to this vision is a lack of interoperability between the equipment of different vendors; another pitfall of current solutions is that the process knowledge is not modelled in a standardized machine readable form. On the other hand, such process model can be flexibly used to support process-specific integration of machines, and enable context-sensitive automatic process optimization. This paper presents an approach and preliminary results regarding architecture for adaptive optimization of agricultural processes via open interfaces, linked data and semantic services that is being developed within the project agriOpenLink; its goal is to provide a novel methodology and tools for semantic proces orchestraion and dynamic context-based adaptation, significantly reducing the effort needed to create new ICT-controlled agricultural applications involving machines and users.

Keywords: Semantic Services, Semantic Processes, Ontology, Open Interfaces.

1 Introduction

Precision farming is a new paradigm in agricultural production motivated by the need to optimize the use of production resources, and to reduce costs and environmental impacts of production. It is a synonym for in-house robotics, field robotics and

E. Garoufallou and J. Greenberg (Eds.): MTSR 2013, CCIS 390, pp. 408–413, 2013.

intelligent agricultural machines, and their ability to detect their context, e.g. a location, and perform highly localized actions within a production process in a timely manner.

While the precision farming market is growing, the awareness that *interoperable* equipment can bring large benefits, is still low. The *interoperable* equipment can be seamlessly plugged-in within the system, and have their data easily collected and flexibly interlinked with other available data, aiding to flexible creation and control of agricultural process. The vision of flexible plug-and-play of devices or processes is currently far from being reached. The approach of the *agriOpenLink* initiative, which we present in this paper, is to contribute open interfaces and open process models for agriculture, offering methodology and tools for automated creation of new processes over plug-and-play process infrastructure. We extensively use service and semantic technology: the system functions map into dynamically combinable semantic services enabling the system to flexibly grow as new devices and services are plugged in. An ultimate goal is to offer efficient technology to the developers of applications for agriculture, and to stimulate creation of new applications.

The paper is structured as follows. The challenges are described in Section 2. Section 3 presents the approach within the context of related work. Section 4 outlines the architecture of the semantic process management, and Section 5 concludes the paper.

2   Problem Description

Two severe obstacles must be surmounted to reach the full benefits of the precision farming vision: closed data interfaces and closed process implementations.

Closed Data Interfaces: One major trend we are witnessing today in the precision farming market is an emergence of process applications which use integrated equipment of a single vendor, and generate data that cannot be used for integration with other systems. Contrary to this practice, *agriOpenLink* aims at integration of the heterogeneous equipment of different vendors, by means of a simple extensible open source library (Data Interface API), which may establish itself as a de facto standard.

Closed Process Implementation: Although emerging applications instrument specific agricultural processes and offer user-friendly interaction over portable devices and the Internet, the process optimization model is hidden within specific application code. The process knowledge is not formally captured and the process implementations are closed; hence different processes cannot exchange internal data or impact each other. Accordingly, they cannot flexibly react on external context, and there is no support for dynamic creation of new processes based on combination of existing ones. To address this problem *agriOpenLink* makes use of **service and semantic** paradigms. Semantic technology offers means to interlink data and services based on their semantic meaning and use this interlinked structure as a base for reasoning, and triggering of control actions. It is an aim of *agriOpenLink* to establish formal machine readable semantic models of several agriculture processes and to develop a semantic service based process platform - agriOpenLink Process Tool-box - to support flexible process creation, monitoring and optimization, as well as flexible creation of new processes as new atomic functions and new equipment are made available.

3   agriOpenLink Approach

In this section we describe taken approach in the context of the relevant related work.

Open Data and Ontologies for Agriculture: In this field there is already a significant body of knowledge, and a strong semantic community behind it. Semantic approaches in agriculture aim at solving lexical interoperability, data interoperability, knowledge model interoperability and object interoperability [1]. An organization with a significant role in designing ontologies for agriculture is Food and Agriculture Organization of the United Nations (FAO; http://aims.fao.org). FAO is developing agriculture management information standards such as AGROVOC thesaurus, Agris and openAgris. Further research work focuses on agricultural ontologies and information systems approaches, e.g., as presented in [2]. *agriOpenLink* aims at using existing semantic models, while innovation is in the production process modelling.

Interface Data Models for Agriculture: Currently, several initiatives develop standards for the data interfaces for agricultural applications. One example is ISO Standard ISOagriNET [3], a standard for the communication between agricultural equipment in the livestock farming. Its level of adoption is relatively low and an open source implementation of the standard is not available. For grassland management and crop farming the XML based markup language agroXML (http://www.agroxml.org) is state of the art. For the data exchange between machines and personal computers (e.g. farm computer) the ISO-XML Standard is the current standard. agroRDF is an accompanying semantic model that is at the moment still under heavy development. It is built using Resource Description Framework (RDF) of W3C. ISO11783 also called ISOBUS, specifies the interfaces and data network for control and communication on agricultural machines like tractors. This standard is well established and there are commercial and open source implementations available. *agriOpenLink* aims at developing and open source realization of the interface data model (*agriOpenLink* Data Interface API) and the process for extending it based on semantic schema paradigm.

Semantic Services: Semantic services are atoms of process functionality that can be flexibly linked together. Service-oriented architectures (SOA) today have significant limitations because of the heavyweight WS-* specifications stack and lack of semantics in descriptions of service. Web APIs based on so-called REST (Representational State Transfer) principles provide a lightweight, increasingly popular alternative and allow for accessing data and functionality in an automated manner. Semantic Web Services add ontology and rule-based service descriptions [4], e.g. OWL-S ontology applies to SOAP (Simple Object Access Protocol) services represented with WSDL (Web Service Description Language). The Web Services Modeling Ontology (WSMO) [5] is a broader scoped extension. WSML (Web Service Modeling Language) [6] includes the ability to define rules. SAWSDL (Semantic Annotations for WSDL and XML Schema) is the only W3C recommendation in the area of Semantic Web Services. It enables referencing from WSDL service schema into arbitrary ontological models. The WSMO-Lite [7] service ontology fills the SAWSDL annotations with concrete semantic service descriptions. Semantically enabled RESTful services

[8] leverage the advantages coming from the combination of Linked Data and service technologies [9]. *agriOpenLink* develops methods for exposing agricultural process data as Linked Data, and services as Linked Services and appropriate ontologies. The project applies the principles of WSMO as the semantic service framework with the most elaborated mediation part, and uses SPARQL *(*SPARQL Protocol And RDF Query Language*)* query in service discovery and matching.

Agriculture Process Modelling and Optimization: Theoretical mathematical analysis of agricultural processes is commonly based on model simulator tools. Some examples include APSIM (Agricultural Production Systems Simulator) [10] and IBSAL (Integrated Biomass Supply Analysis and Logistics Model [11]. Often used for applications in the agricultural sector is GASP IV a FORTRAN-based simulation language which provides the framework for modelling systems involving both continuous and discrete phenomena [12]. *agriOpenLink* uses existing simulation and optimization process models to establish their mapping into ontology for extensible adaptive processes. The aim is to enable developers to build process models and model and instrument their context-based optimization.

Semantic Process Composition and Enablers for Service Activation: Composing processes by flexibly chaining services significantly reduces development costs and increases operational agility. Service composition paradigm addresses dynamic user needs and dynamic changes in service functionality. Service composition technologies try to separate processes and rules [13]. Among them, the hybrid service composition based on WSMO framework may be the most flexible one: while stable parts of a composition are specified using processes, the parts likely to change are specified using rules. Enablers for dynamic composition and activation of services are notification services and access control. Currently prevailing notification services lack standard mechanisms for the semantics of the notifications. Some emerging approaches like sparqlPuSH [14] combine the power of semantic representations with a pull/push notification system. Access control manages who gets access to what data or data producing services in which context and with which degree of detail e.g. by specifying privacy policies. The *agriOpenLink* process creation approach extends the hybrid service composition approach based on WSMO with capabilities to modify the processes and rules independently and reuse rules and decision logic. The goal is to link together the rules, processes and context sources during the composition process, and to take advantage of reasoning on linked data where a monitoring service subscribes to particular conditions/rules on data, as well as of filtering rules based on graph patterns as simple as SPARQL queries.

4   agriOpenLink Semantic Process Management Architecture

The key aspects of our approach related to process creation and control are depicted in Figure 1. The functionality of the process infrastructure is mapped into semantic services, which dynamically register, hence are discovered and dynamically invoked. Service developers implement and deploy services, and on the other hand, annotate and publish service descriptions in the semantic service repository. Data coming from the agricultural platforms (with *agriOpenLink* Data Interface) is subject to analytics and is stored into the knowledgebase. Application developers create process-based applications using goal-oriented process and service models. Invocation of concrete services is based on service ranking; process of ranking and filtering utilizes dynamic requirements, ranking algorithms and SPARQL queries.

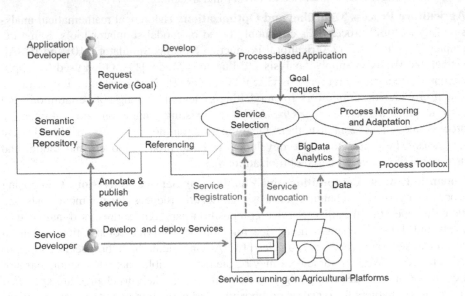

Fig. 1. Semantic Process Management Architcture

With this approach we aim at: *extensibility and re-configurability* by assuring inte-roperability of data and of process models; *notification-based monitoring* of the con-text built by linking measurements and status data, providing the input for process optimization and service selection; *real-time optimization* by configuration of policies acting on the context for fast immediate process adaptations; pro-active *optimization recommendations* based on analysis of the potential for process optimization.

5   Conclusions

In this paper we present an approach of an industrial research initiative *agriOpenLink* that develops methodology and designs tools for creating applications for control and optimization of farming processes. *agriOpenLink* common inter-disciplinary metho-dology spans mathematical process modelling, process ontology definition, interface data model realization, design of the infrastructure for semantics-enabled dynamic process control, and finally testing tools with users. This approach addresses many stakeholders in the agricultural sector: at the interface level the development of an open source interface standard may have high multiplication effect by involving many relevant data producers; at the system level the improvement of process modelling and optimization methodology and its implementation based on semantic services technology requires focused coordination of ICT and process expertise. In this process it is our goal to reach a broad community of users - the developers creating smart farming applications - who may join our efforts in establishing *agriOpenLink* open interface and process solution.

Acknowledgments. This work is supported within the project *agriOpenLink* partially funded by the Austrian Research Promotion Agency (FFG) within the program "Future ICT". The Telecommunications Research Center Vienna (FTW) is supported by the Austrian government and the City of Vienna within the competence center program COMET.

References

1. Roussey, C., et al.: Ontologies in Agriculture. Ingénierie des Systèmes D'Information 16(3), 55–84 (2011)
2. Goumopoulos, C., et al.: An Ontology-Driven System Architecture for Precision Agriculture Applications. International Journal of Metadata, Semantics and Ontologies (IJMSO), 72–84 (2009)
3. ISO17532: Stationary equipment for agriculture - Data communications network for livestock farming. Beuth Verlag, Genf.
4. Fensel, D., et al.: Enabling Semantic Web Services: The Web Service Modeling Ontology. Springer (2006)
5. Roman, D., et al.: Web Service Modeling Ontology. Applied Ontology 1(1), 77–106 (2005)
6. de Bruijn, J., Lausen, H., Polleres, A., Fensel, D.: The web service modeling language WSML: An overview. In: Sure, Y., Domingue, J. (eds.) ESWC 2006. LNCS, vol. 4011, pp. 590–604. Springer, Heidelberg (2006)
7. Vitvar, T., Kopecký, J., Viskova, J., Fensel, D.: WSMO-Lite Annotations for Web Services. In: Bechhofer, S., Hauswirth, M., Hoffmann, J., Koubarakis, M. (eds.) ESWC 2008. LNCS, vol. 5021, pp. 674–689. Springer, Heidelberg (2008)
8. Verborgh, R., et al.: Efficient Runtime Service Discovery and Consumption with Hyperlinked RESTdesc. In: 7th International Conference on Next Generation Web Services Practices (2011)
9. Pedrinaci, C., et al.: Services and the Web of Data: An Unexploited Symbiosis. In: AAAI Spring Symposium (March 2010)
10. McCown, et al.: APSIM: A novel software system for model development, model testing and simulation in agricultural systems research. Agricultural Systems 50(3), 255–271 (1996)
11. Ebadian, M., et al.: A new simulation model for multi-agricultural biomass logistics system in bioenergy production. Biosystems Engineering 110(3), 280–290 (2011)
12. Alan, A.: A combined continuous - discrete FORTRAN-based simulation language. School of Industrial Engineering Purdue University Lafayette
13. Feldkamp, D., Singh, N.: Making BPEL flexible. Technical Report SS-08-01, Association for the Advancement of Artificial Intelligence (2008)
14. Passant, A., et al.: sparqlPuSH: Proactive notification of data updates in RDF stores using PubSubHubbub. In: 6th Workshop on Scripting and Development for the Semantic Web, Crete, Greece (May 2010)

Issues in Harvesting Resources from Agricultural Repositories

Devika P. Madalli

Documentation Research and Training Center (DRTC)
Indian Statistical Institute (ISI), India

Abstract. Harvesters facilitate aggregating metadata from various repositories and other sources such as journals and enable a centralized access to full text and objects. While harvesting can be fairly simple and straight forward, it is not without its challenges. This paper intends to highlight some of the issues in harvesting metadata in agricultural domains. It suggests some possible solutions with instances from Demeter, a *pkp* based harvester compared with DSpace based harvesting facility implemented at Indian Statistical Institute. Also described is Tharvest, a thematic harvester model for agricultural resources from generic repositories.

1 Introduction

Metadata harvesting mainly depends upon the use of standards by data providers. Yet for various reasons repository managers, while populating the collections, often do not follow global standards for metadata. In some cases they adopt a standard such as Dublin Core [www.dublincore.org], AGRIS but make some deviations to comply with local needs. Repositories use non-standard terminology for names of elements. For instance – use of the term 'contributor' instead of element 'author', even when there is a provision for using 'collaborator' where the 'contribution' can be specified. It is due to such arbitrary variations that data cannot be harvested in a straight forward way. There are also other issues such as those with syntax of the baseURL itself. In such cases we are faced with the question of interoperability. We discuss in the following sections some issues in harvesting and also illustrate two services *Demeter* and *Indus* implemented at Indian Statistical Institute that harvest agricultural metadata. Also described is the step in Tharvest, a thematic harvesting facility for agricultural resources from generic repositories.

2 Harvesters

Harvesters facilitate centralized access, browse and search facilities to resources that maybe part of different collections. Harvesting is based upon the OAI-PMH standard and protocol for interoperability of repositories as prescribed in [1]. According the standard two important providers are *data providers* and *service providers*.

E. Garoufallou and J. Greenberg (Eds.): MTSR 2013, CCIS 390, pp. 414–422, 2013.

Data providers are basically repository initiators/owners. They usually collect and organize resources in repositories. The requisite to be interoperable is that the data providers must be compliant with the OAI-PMH standard. Service providers collect resources from such data providers in order to facilitate centralized access and search to resources exposed by the providers. They also facilitate access to full text or full resource wherever the data providers offer Open Access resources. Service providers can in turn be data providers and thus act as links to meta aggregators.

One of the popular harvester software is the Open Harvester System of Public Knowledge Project *(http://pkp.sfu.ca/harvester)*. DSpace, *(*www.dspace.org), a popular Open Source software for hosting and managing repositories also facilitates harvesting metadata records. We describe here two services implemented at Indian Statistical Institute based on the above two harvesters. Indus is a DSpace based harvester that covers repositories in Asia collecting records in agricultural domain and Demeter is a pkp*(pkp.sfu.ca/harvester)* harvester based aggregator covering 22 data providers.

3   Indus

*Indus (*http://drtc.isibang.ac.in/indus*)* is an aggregator for agricultural information resources in Asia. At present it has strength of about 35000 records from 8 Asian countries in 89 sets. It deploys the DSpace harvesting facility. Indus covers both repositories and journals in agriculture and related domains. For open access repositories full text is available and for some material with restricted access, resources for which metadata level access is provided are also included.

Fig. 1. INDUS: an aggregator for Agriculture resources

Collections in Agricultural domain are sourced from OpenDOAR, Grainger and Open Archives sites. For journals the main source is the pkp harvester official site, DOAJ site and also the OJS (Open Journal System) lists. In addition to these, resources are identified from generic repositories such as SodhGanga, where there are only a few agriculture related sets. We also conducted a Google based search to collect journals in agriculture and related domains that are not listed in OJS and DOAJ sites.

4   Demeter

*pkp*is a popular harvester used commonly to aggregate metadata from different sources. Demeter (at Indian Statistical Institute) is based on the PKP harvester. At present Demeter is implemented as a test bed. Preliminary study of performance of Demeter against Indus is ongoing. As per observations, there are some shared features and strengths in both the harvesters and some differences that we point out in the following sections.

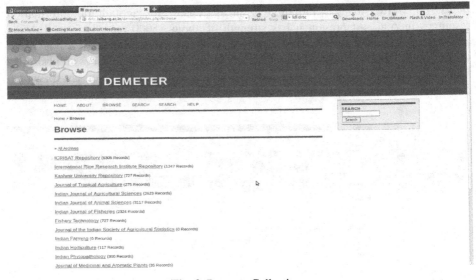

Fig. 2. Demeter Collections

5   Comparison of pkp and DSpace Based Harvesting

As described above, at the Documentation Research and Training Center, Indian Statistical Institute, we have implemented both pkp for Demeter and DSpace based harvesting for Indus. Mainly they are implemented as service providers but they can both be data providers also. Though Dublin Core is used as default it is possible to crosswalk data between other metadata formats in both these systems. Tabulated below are key differences in the two systems.

Table 1. Comparison of Demeter and Indus

Feature	Indus	Demeter
Organization	Hierarchical organization as in thesauri is possible	Organization is a flat linear arrangement by data providers
Browse facility	Browse facility provided by 'Author', 'Title', 'Date' and 'Subject'	Browse simply brings the list of data providers and when each is clicked, it again flatly lists records in a chronological order as populated
Search facility	Field level search possible. In addition search features such as proximity search, fuzzy search and boosting terms possible	Simple and advanced level searching by different elements
RSS feeds	RSS Feeds and Atom provided	No RSS feeds and Atom feeds
ORE Support	ORE support provided	No ORE support
Email alerts	Email alerts can be configured for alerting new additions	No email alerts

Thematic Harvesting from Generic Repositories

In the process of developing Indus and Demeter, several sources were searched to identify agriculture and related domain resources. It was noted that there were general focus repositories within which some sets were related to agriculture. In some other cases such as in some ETD repositories, the organization was not by themes or domain and disciplines but by dates. In such cases the challenge is that of harvesting thematically by key terms in order to comprehensively include agricultural resources. We observed that most of the repository and interoperability work has been undertaken among partners, institute and projects that deal with agriculture domains. In such cases harvesting resources is straightforward. Some attempts have also been noticed in thematic harvesting but they involve in manual verification that may be both time consuming and subject to arbitrariness owing to human intervention and decision making.

6   Related Work

Studying literature and Internet based reports, it is noted that there is very little work ongoing towards for domain specific harvesting or thematic harvesting in agriculture and related domains from generic repositories.

Most of the work in repository building is anchored in the agriculture domain itself. For instance Project Harvest that focuses on information resources in agricultural journals for development of the e-journal repository [2] [http://www.library.cornell.edu/harvest/proposal.htm]. Similarly EC project VOA3R (http://voa3r.cc.uah.es/) deals with agriculture and aquaculture. Abian and Cano describe a system for managing learning resources in agriculture especially in domain of agro-ecology and organic agriculture [3]. It is straightforward to harvest records from such projects provided they are OAI complint data providers. However, the question arises how we cull out agriculture related records from generic repositories such as university repositories or institutional repositories which may not be organized by disciplines and topics of resources may be in diverse domains.

In an experience report by Simek etal. [4] a comparative analytical study of different agricultural repositories is presented where different workflows and metadata schema were followed. Projections are given regarding the compliance or deviation from the standard Dublin core elements so that based on common minimum shared elements harvesting can be achieved. The works rather closest to the present effort are Avano [5] and High North Research Documents [HNRD] [6] (http://highnorth.uit.no) that harvest thematically from generic repositories based on OAI sets. Avano and HNRD use keyword research system and deploy manual verification to ascertain the suitability of the resources to added. In contrast to this, we propose in our model a step for verification with an AGROVOC lookup tool that verifies terms from agricultural and related domains that are indexed from the 'title', 'keyword' and 'abstract' fields. Details are discussed the sections that follow.

Proposed Model for Thematic Harvesting

With present technologies for harvesting, it is possible to achieve thematic harvesting by 'sets' in OAI PMH. For example for Indus, the command *http://drtc.isibang.ac.in/indus/ oai/request?verb=ListSets,* lists 89 sets as shown below.

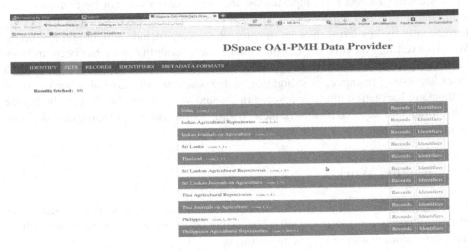

Fig. 3. Retrieval by *Sets*

Indus only deals with agriculture and related areas. It also functions as a data provider. It is possible using appropriate OAI command to harvest by specific sets under the domain 'Agriculture' in Indus. For example, if one wants to harvest only Indian Agricultural Repositories from Indus then the ListSets above displays 'Identifiers' against the Indian Agricultural repositories using which the relevant sets only could be harvested.

Harvesting by Date

Harvesting by date is relevant in cases where the aggregator is simply adding records by particular year or month or after a particular date. For example, in ETD (Electronic Theses and Dissertations) we could source by the datestamp for each year the theses were granted by a university. This may also be relevant to trace research output per year of an institute or university as represented by publication date in their institutional repository.

Harvesting by Domain

Consider a university repository where resources from all departments are uploaded. It may be an ETD repository organized sometimes by different departments and sometimes simply by years. One example is provided below. In one of the ETD repositories, resources related to agriculture are under keywords as shown below and on closer examination these belong to many collections or sets including 'Economics', 'Marketing' among others.

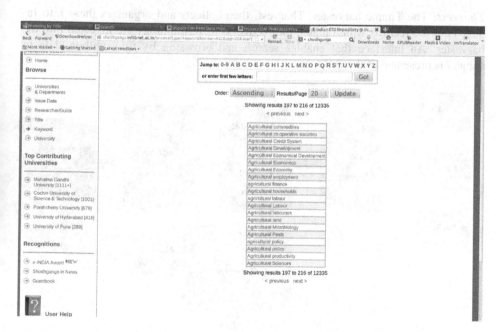

Fig. 4. Scattered Agriculture related resources in a repository

Proposed is a model for identifying agriculture related resources from generic repositories and re-harvesting selectively to provide access to such aggregated collections in agriculture.

Data Collection: We collect the sets from generic repositories such as open access university repositories. Resources from harvested sets are also targeted. We mostly use directories such as DOAJ, OpenDOAR and OpenArchives to source data providers that are OAI-PMH compliant. In addition we conducted random Google based searches to check repositories that may contain agriculture related resources. These are included in the input sets.

Indexing: All such sourced sets are indexed using Apache Solr. Solr is an indexing and search platform with a powerful retrieval mechanism *(http://lucene.apache.org/solr/#intro)*. For our thematic harvester we use full-text indexing so that all words of the keywords, title and abstract fields are indexed.

AGROVOC Lookup: In order to ascertain whether a certain record belongs to agriculture domain or not we adapt an AGROVOC lookup tool. Agrovoc(*http://aims.fao.org/standards/agrovoc/about)*, is a structured thesaurus of terminology in agriculture and related domains and is used a default standard for vocabulary control in agricultural systems world wide [7]. The indexed terms are compared with the terminology to find matches. The records of the matched terms are collected into an interim database.

Tharvest: The Theme harvester, Tharvest, then collects and organizes these into Indus. Thus the records which match the AGROVOC terminology are ingested into the harvester. An interface that enables search and browsing by title, author, date or subject is presented to the end users.

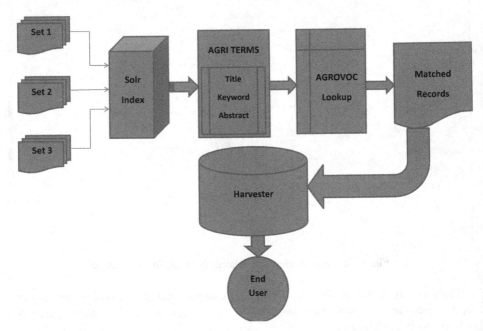

Fig. 5. Tharvest: Thematic harvest for 'Agriculture'

We followed the steps described above in developing Tharvest using AGROVOC for verifying records belonging to agriculture related domains automatically. However, in the process several issues were thrown up and some of these are highlighted below.

7   Issues in Harvesting

Harvesting depends mainly on two factors; compliance with OAI PMH standard and the metadata standard/s used by repositories though there are also several other factors that affect harvesting. Some of the salient issues are:

Linking: Linking mechanism in harvested records is based on URIs. Hence the standard of URI itself comes into focus. It is observed that URIs is not a problem with OJS (Open Journal System) based journals as also with ePrints (a repository software – http://eprints.org) based repositories. These use data providers' address directly in the URI. Whereas DSpace uses CNRI handles for persistent IDs for data providers who are registered with CNRI service. However, a significant number of repositories that use DSpace have not registered with CNRI and simply use the default format, http://handle.net/123..9.html which leads nowhere. In such cases only metadata can be seen since the URI will not link to the actual full resource.

BaseURLs: It is difficult to trace the baseURLs of repositories unless they are registered with one the of the directory services such as OpenDOAR or Grainger. We are left to guess based upon whether the data provider is using something like DSpace or ePrints and what could be the baseURLs. If some cases the guess maybe correct but in others the implementers change the content or syntax for the baseURLs. It then becomes impossible to access such repositories for harvesting. The irony is that though OAI-PMH is standard for the interoperability there is no strict standard imposed for the syntax and content of baseURLs.

Other Issues
Some other issues are generic and not any platform specific and mostly to do with metadata.

In qualified Dublin Core there is a way to specify for vocabulary used, what is the standard. But if plain Dublin Core is harvested it becomes difficult to associate the terminology with the standard. Further there is the issue of poor quality metadata. Many authors uploading resources are not aware of the metadata standards and they provide very minimal metadata and also may use non-standard vocabulary. It becomes the purview of the repository managers to implement metadata quality check by appointing metadata editors before committing resources to repositories.

8   Conclusion

Tharvest is a model for harvesting thematically from generic repository. At present the system is a test bed and successfully tried to harvest resources related to agriculture from three generic repositories. The next step will be the full-fledged implementation and populating it with more records. In the end the harvested records will be populated into Indus. In the steps following its implementation it is intended to run evaluation for performance and also for comparing the success rate of the procedure of using AGROVOC based lookup tool for identifying agriculture related resources versus manual checks as adopted by other systems. The experience with building Tharvest brought forth several issues as discussed above and these are broadly applicable to thematic harvesting in any other domain.

References

1. Lagoze, H.: The Santa Fe Convention of the Open Archives Initiative. D-Lib Magazine 6(2) (2000, 2009)
2. Project Harvest,
   http://www.library.cornell.edu/harvest/proposal.htm
3. Abian, A., Cano, R.: Harvesting Learning Resources on Organic Agriculture and Agroecology to Semantic Repositories. University of Alcala (2008)
4. Simek, P., Adamides, G., LeHenaff, D., Rasmussen, I.A., Sicilia, M.A., Waksman, G.: Contrasting metadata quality processes and coverage in agriculture-related repositories:An experience report. In: WCCA 2011, Prague, pp. 511–517 (2011)
5. Merceur, F.: Avano, assessment of one year management of a thematic OAI-PMH harvester. In: 33rd IAMSLIC Annual Conference Changes on the Horizon, USA (2007)
6. Odu, O., Longva, L.: High North Research Documents: A new thematic and global service reusing all open sources. In: Open Repositories, University Library of Tromsø, Norway (2012)
7. Sini, M., Lauser, B., Salokhe, G., Keizer, J., Katz, S.: The AGROVOC Concept Server: Rationale, goals and usage. Library Review, 200–212 (2008)

Preliminary Work towards Publishing Vocabularies for Germplasm and Soil Data as Linked Data

Valeria Pesce[1], Guntram Geser[2], Caterina Caracciolo[1], Johannes Keizer[1], and Giovanni L'Abate[3]

[1] Food and Agriculture Organization of the United Nations, Rome, Italy
{Valeria.Pesce,Caterina.Caracciolo,Johannes.Keizer}@fao.org
[2] Salzburg Research, Salzburg, Austria
guntram.geser@salzburgresearch.at
[3] Consiglio per la Ricerca e la sperimentazione in Agricoltura,
Centro di Ricerca per l'AgroBiologia e la Pedologia (CRA-ABP), Firenze, Italy
giovanni.labate@entecra.it

Abstract. The agINFRA project focuses on the production of interoperable data in agriculture, starting from the vocabularies and Knowledge Organization Systems (KOSs) used to describe and classify them. In this paper we report on our first steps in the direction of publishing agricultural Linked Open Data (LOD), focusing in particular on germplasm data and soil data, which are still widely missing from the LOD landscape, seemingly because information managers in this field are still not very familiar with LOD practices.

Keywords: Agriculture, germplasm, soil, Knowledge Organization Systems, metadata sets, vocabularies, RDF, Linked Data, classifications.

1   Introduction

agINFRA (www.aginfra.eu) is a co-funded FP7 programme aiming to provide tools and methodologies for creating large networks of agricultural data using grid- and cloud-based technology. One of the outputs of the project will be the publication of the data managed by project partners as Linked Open Data (LOD), to achieve full data interoperability. Project partners contribute various "data sets"[1], all of which come with some sort of metadata associated, for the purpose of correct data storage and retrieval.

Two fundamental things play a crucial role in data interoperability:

a) The metadata elements needed to describe each individual piece of information in the data sets, and

---

[1] There is no agreed definition of what a "data set" is. For this paper, a broad definition should be assumed: see the definition by the W3C Government Linked Data Working Group: A collection of data, published or curated by a single source, and available for access or download in one or more formats". http://www.w3.org/TR/vocab-dcat/#class--dataset

E. Garoufallou and J. Greenberg (Eds.): MTSR 2013, CCIS 390, pp. 423–429, 2013.

b) The sets of values for (some of) the metadata elements of above, usually called "controlled vocabularies", or "authority data".

While the former are often referred to as metadata sets, metadata element sets or vocabularies, the latter are often called controlled vocabularies, authority data, value vocabularies or Knowledge Organization Systems (KOSs). However, they both are commonly referred to as "vocabularies" (cf. [1], [2]). In this paper, we say vocabularies and KOSs, respectively.

Independently of the terminology adopted, both types of vocabularies are crucial, and necessary to understand the data. Therefore the first step planned in the agINFRA project was the identification and publication (when necessary) of the vocabularies and KOSs used by the various data owners to describe and classify their data.

The types of resources covered by agINFRA are: bibliographic resources, educational resources, germplasm data, soil data. The analysis performed within the project revealed that these types of resources have different features. On the one hand, bibliographic and educational resources are described by rather homogeneous metadata sets, and also the use of KOSs is rather consistent. On the other hand, for germplasm and soil information, there is quite an important amount of data available, but so far little work has been devoted for its inclusion in the Linked Data cloud. This is why in this paper we focus on germplasm and soil data.

2   Vocabularies and KOSs for Germplasm Data and Soil Data

By "germplasm" one means the collection of genetic resources for an organism. In the case of plants, it can be a seed or any plant part that can be turned into a whole plant. Germaplasm is collected both to develop new hybrids/varieties/cultivars, and for conservation purposes. In all cases, various pieces of information need to be stored, including the taxonomic name adopted for it and the authority for the species name, its common/commercial names when existing, identifier for the germplasm and for the institution collecting it, the geographical area of origin (e.g. latitude, longitude, altitude), and of course the date of acquisition. Often, the data set also keep track of pedigree, phenotype, chromosomal constitution, breeding institution, biological status of accession, the type of germplasm storage and so on.

As for "soil", there is a wide variety of definitions and interpretations of it, and each database on soil will store different information depending on the type of perspective adopted. For example, agronomists, environmental researchers, geologist, engineers, or water experts typically use different notions of characterizing depths, history, chemical composition and morphological aspects and classifications, as well as sampling methodologies and geographical reference systems. For this reason it is especially important that metadata standards for all these aspects are established and used, and that the possibility for their integration is carefully explored and exploited. For both germplasm and soil data, some metadata standards and KOSs already exist, but few data sets already use them.

Germplasm Data. The set of Multi-crop Passport Descriptors (MCPD) is widely used for information exchange among crop conservation and research institutions worldwide. Its first version (V.1) dates back to 2006, while V.2 was published in 2012 [3]. MCPD is also used by the national germplasm inventories in Europe to provide information to the EURISCO catalogue[2] (with six additional descriptors for the specific purposes of EURISCO). The EURISCO catalogue also includes the germplasm collections of the Italian Agricultural Research Council (CRA). The Crop Germplasm Research Information System (CGRIS)[3] of the Chinese Academy of Agricultural Sciences (CAAS) uses its own set of passport descriptors which represents the de facto standard in China and will be mapped to the MCPD.

Importantly, the MCPD does not include descriptors for Characterization and Evaluation (C&E) measurements of plant traits/scores, which is the most important information for plant researchers and breeders. An initial set of C&E descriptors [4] for the utilization of 22 crops have been developed by Bioversity International[4] together with CGIAR and other research centers. C&E measurement data determine the values of germaplasm, such as resistance to specific pathotypes, grain yield, and protein content. Therefore, they are critical for selecting relevant germplasm. However, as assessed by the EPGRIS3 project, C&E data is difficult to standardize and integrate in central databases [5]. A major recent achievement therefore is the Darwin Core extension for genebanks (DwC-germplasm) which is represented in RDF/SKOS. The extension has been derived from the MCPD standard and includes basic descriptors for C&E measurements [6] as suggested by EPGRIS3.

The traditional wealth of checklists of plant names and taxonomies is recently being further developed into the form of ontologies. See for example the Plant Ontology, explicitly referenced in the DwC-germplasm vocabulary, the Trait Ontology and the Phenotypic Quality Ontology. They all provide important controlled vocabularies for the domain at hand.

Soil Data. Most of soil-related data is still stored in databases, the description of which is often called "metadata", for example by the U.S. National Soil Information System (NASIS) [7]. The international Working Group on Soil Information Standards[5] (WG-SIS) aim to develop, promote and maintain internationally recognized and adopted standards for the exchange and collation of consistent harmonized soils data and information worldwide. Widely used metadata standards for soil are ISO 19115 and ISO 19119, which covers geographic information and services, and it is applied to catalog and fully describe datasets, including individual geographic features and feature properties. ISO 19139 provides the XML schema implementation, including the extensions for imagery and gridded data. Users of the Content Standard

---

[2] http://eurisco.ecpgr.org/
[3] http://icgr.caas.net.cn/cgris_english.html
[4] http://www.bioversityinternational.org/
[5] http://www.soilinformationstandards.org/

for Digital Geospatial Metadata[6] (CSDGM) have been recommended by the U.S. Federal Geographic Data Committee (FGDC) transitioning to the ISO standards [8].

The main international KOSs for talking about soil are the Soil Taxonomy [9] and the World Reference Base for Soil Resources [10]. An important recent achievement is the Multilingual Soil Thesaurus[7] (SoilThes) that has been developed in the eContentplus project GS SOIL [11]. SoilThes was created as an extension of the General Multilingual Environmental Thesaurus (GEMET)[8] and contains the concepts of the World Reference Base, the soil vocabulary of ISO 11074[9] and additional soil-specific concepts. GEMET is the official thesaurus for the Infrastructure for Spatial Information in the European Comminity (INSPIRE) directive[10], within which draft guidelines for data specification on soil are under development [12]. Another ISO Standard related to soil data is ISO 28258: Soil quality Digital exchange of soil-related data. In relation to XML schema implementation, the Centre for Geospatial Science in the University of Nottingham has developed SoTerML [13] (Soil and Terrain Markup Language), a markup language to be used to store and exchange soil and terrain related data. SoTerML extends of GeoSciML for SOTER model compliant with ISO/TC190/SC 1 N140 "Recording and Exchange of Soil-Related Data". SoTerML development is being done within the e-SOTER Platform. GEOSS plans a global Earth Observation System and, within this framework, the e-SOTER project[11] addresses the need for a global soil and terrain database.

A recent initiative to harmonize different Soil schemas is the Soil-ML project [14], a soil equivalent of the Geoscience Markup Language (GeoSciML) Definitions for application schema "ISO 28258 Definitions".[12]

3   Vocabularies for Germplasm and Soil Data as Linked Data

For germplasm-related vocabularies, some of the most relevant work has been mentioned above: the Darwin Core extension for genebanks (DwC-germplasm) is already represented in RDF/SKOS. A lot of activity around semantic technologies is also going on around the major plant /trait /gene ontologies, the Plant Ontology (explicitly referenced in the DwC-germplasm), the Gene Ontology, the Trait Ontology [15] and the Phenotypic Quality Ontology [16]. They give an overview of the interlinking between these ontologies and their availability as OWL and as web services.

A very interesting project is the iPlant Semantic Web Program[13], focused on "next-generation" data and service integration: the program has implemented the SSWAP

---

[6] http://www.fgdc.gov/metadata/csdgm/

[7] https://secure.umweltbundesamt.at/soil/en/about.html

[8] GEMET, http://www.eionet.europa.eu/gemet/

[9] ISO 11074:2005 Soil quality - Vocabulary,
    http://www.iso.org/iso/catalogue_detail.htm?csnumber=38529

[10] INSPIRE: http://inspire.jrc.ec.europa.eu/

[11] http://www.isric.org/specification/SoTerML.xsd

[12] See http://schema.isric.org/sml/4.0/UML_Model/
    Soil%20Overview.pdf for a graphical overview of the schema.

service[14], based on the SSWAP protocol[15]. Three major information resources (Gramene, SoyBase and the Legume Information System) use SSWAP to semantically describe selected data and web services. Moreover, the Gene Ontology and Plant Ontology will be soon incorporated into SoyBase: "This will further facilitate cross-species genetic and genomic comparisons by providing another level of semantic equivalence between taxa." [16]

As far as soil-related vocabularies are concerned, GEMET has been published as SKOS and mapped to AGROVOC; also SoilThes has been published as SKOS and is linked to GEMET. For the spatial aspect, soil data can rely on many advanced RDF standards, mainly in the framework of the EU INSPIRE Directive.

The methodology adopted by agINFRA for the publication of vocabularies as LOD aims at reusing existing resources as much as possible. According to the methodology agreed in the project, the first step consists in analyzing the datasets available and the metadata sets and KOS used (presented in this paper). The table below summarizes the germplasm and soil data sets considered so far in agINFRA, together with the metadata sets and KOS used.

Table 1. Germplasm and soil datasets in agINFRA, with adopted metadata sets and KOSs

Type of resource	Collection name	Metadata set used	KOS used
Germplasm	**CRA Germplasm (Italy)**	Multi-crop Passport Descriptors (MCPD) V.2	(Options see discussion below)
	CGRIS (China)	Own set of germplasm descriptors	
Soil datasets and maps	**Italian Soil Information System (ISIS)**	ISO 19115/19139[16]	US Soil Taxonomy, World Reference Base for Soil Resources

Then, we can distinguish the following cases:

1) The data set already uses some standard vocabularies published as LOD. Then the LOD publication is straightforward.

2) The data set uses some local vocabularies, with the same intended meaning as some standard vocabulary. Then, if the data owners agree on replacing them with those standard vocabularies, we are back to case 1.

---

[13] iPlant: http://www.iplantcollaborative.org/discover/semantic-web

[14] SSWAP: http://sswap.info/

[15] Simple Semantic Web Architecture and Protocol (SSWAP): an OWL implementation that offers the ability to describe data and services in a semantically meaningful way.

[16] ISO 19115/19139: Geographic information – Metadata, and XML schema implementation, http://www.iso.org/iso/home/store/catalogue_tc/catalogue_tc_browse.htm?commid=54904&published=on&includesc=true

3) The data set uses some local vocabularies, with the same intended meaning as some standard vocabulary. But the data owners need to keep the local ones. Then, agINFRA will introduce a set of mapping between the local and standard vocabularies.

4) The data set uses some local vocabularies, with no overlap with any standard vocabularies. Then agINFRA will publish them as LOD under the project namespace.

4   Conclusions

The study of current germplasm and soil data management practices revealed that experts in these two areas are actually looking forward to the adoption of LOD technologies to improve the interoperability of their data. The publication of additional germplasm and soil-related vocabularies will be a big step forward and will represent one of the novel contributions that agINFRA makes to the agricultural data management community.

We foresee that publishing both types of vocabularies as Linked Data will amplify their power by making them machine-readable, easily re-usable and linked or potentially linkable to other vocabularies.

Acknowledgements. The research leading to these results has received funding from the European Union Seventh Framework Programme (*FP7/2007-2013*) under *grant agreement* n° *283770*. We would like to thank Fang Wei, from the Institute of Crop Science, Chinese Academy of Agricultural Sciences, Beijing, China, for his advice on the germplasm and soil related information in this paper. We would also like to thanks Vassilis Protonotarios, from the University of Alcala, Spain, for his contribution to an earlier version of this work.

References

1. Méndez, E., Greenberg, J.: Linked Data for Open Vocabularies and HIVE's Global Framework. El Profesional de la Información 21, 236–244 (2012),
   http://www.elprofesionaldelainformacion.com/
   contenidos/2012/mayo/03_eng.pdf
2. Isaac, A., Waites, W., Young, J., Zeng, M.: Library Linked Data Incubator Group: Datasets, Value Vocabularies, and Metadata Element Sets. W3C Incubator Group Report (2011),
   http://www.w3.org/2005/Incubator/
   lld/XGR-lld-vocabdataset-20111025/
3. Alercia, A., Diulgheroff, S., Mackay, M.: FAO/Bioversity Multi-Crop Passport Descriptors V.2, MCPD V.2 (2012),
   http://eurisco.ecpgr.org/fileadmin/
   www.eurisco.org/documents/MCPD_V2_2012_Final_PDFversion.pdf
4. Bioversity International: Key access and utilization descriptors for crop genetic resources (2011),
   http://www.bioversityinternational.org/index.php?id=3737

5. van Hintum, T.: Inclusion of C&E data in EURISCO - analysis and options. EPGRIS-3 Proposal, Wageningen (2009), http://edepot.wur.nl/186143
6. Endresen, D., Knüpffer, H.: The Darwin Core Extension for Genebanks opens up new opportunities for sharing germplsam data sets. Biodiversity Informatics 8, 12–29 (2012), https://journals.ku.edu/index.php/jbi/article/viewFile/4095/4064
7. U.S. Department of Agriculture, NRCS: NASIS-Related Metadata, http://soils.usda.gov/technical/nasis/documents/metadata
8. Federal Geographic Standard Committee (FGDC): Geospatial Metadata Standards (2012), http://www.fgdc.gov/metadata/geospatial-metadata-standards
9. U.S. Department of Agriculture, Natural Resources Conservation Service: Soil Taxonomy - A Basic System of Soil Classification for Making and Interpreting Soil Surveys (1999), http://soils.usda.gov/technical/classification/taxonomy
10. IUSS Working Group: World reference base for soil resources, 2nd edn. World Soil Resources Reports No. 103. FAO, Rome (2006), http://www.fao.org/ag/agl/agll/wrb/doc/wrb2006final.pdf
11. GS SOIL: Establishment of a multilingual soil-specific thesaurus. Deliverable 3.5. Prepared by Schentz, H., et al. (May 31, 2012), http://www.gssoil-portal.eu/Best_Practice/GS_SOIL_D3.5_Soil_Specific_Thesaurus_final.pdf
12. INSPIRE Thematic Working Group Soil: D2.8.III.3 INSPIRE Data Specification on Soil – Draft Technical Guidelines (2013), http://inspire.jrc.ec.europa.eu/documents/Data_Specifications/INSPIRE_DataSpecification_SO_v3.0rc3.pdf
13. Pourabdollah, A., Leibovici, D.G., Simms, D.M., Tempel, P., Hallett, S.H., Jack-son, M.J.: Towards a standard for soil and terrain data exchange: SoTerML, Computers & Geosciences, vol. 45, pp. 270–283 (August 2012), http://dx.doi.org/10.1016/j.cageo.2011.11.026, http://www.sciencedirect.com/science/article/pii/S0098300411004195
14. Montanarella, L., Wilson, P., Cox, S., McBratney, A.B., Ahamed, S., McMillan, B., Jaquier, D., Fortner, F.: Developing SoilML as a Global Standard for the Col-lation and Transfer of Soil Data and Information. Geophysical Research Abstracts. In: Proceedings EGU General Assembly 2010, vol. 12. Copernicus (2010)
15. Arnaud, E., Cooper, L., Shrestha, R., Menda, N., Nelson, R.T., Matteis, L., Sko-fic, M., Bastow, R., Jaiswal, P., Mueller, L., McLaren, G.: Towards a Reference Plant Trait Ontology for Modeling Knowledge of Plant Traits and Phenotypes (2012), http://wiki.plantontology.org/images/6/6e/Ref_TO_KEOD_2012.pdf
16. Cooper, L., Walls, R.L., Elser, J., Gandolfo, M.A., Stevenson, D.W., Smith, B., Preece, J., Athreya, B., Mungali, C.J., Rensing, S., Hiss, M., Lang, D., Reski, R., Berardini, T.Z., Li, D., Huala, E., Schaeffer, M., Menda, N., Arnaud, E., Shrestha, R., Yamazaki, Y., Jaiswal, P.: The Plant Ontology as a Tool for Comparative Plant Anatomy and Genomic Analyses (2013), http://pcp.oxfordjournals.org/content/54/2/e1.short
17. Nelson, R.T., Avraham, S., Shoemaker, R.C., May, G.D., Ware, D., Gessler, D.D.G.: Applications and methods utilizing the Simple Semantic Web Architecture and Protocol (SSWAP) for bioinformatics resource discovery and disparate data and service integration (2010), http://www.biodatamining.org/content/3/1/3#B13

Ontology-Based Representation of Scientific Laws on Beef Production and Consumption

Piotr Kulicki[1], Robert Trypuz[1], Rafał Trójczak[1],
Jerzy Wierzbicki[2], and Alicja Woźniak[2]

[1] The John Paul II Catholic University of Lublin, Faculty of Philosophy
Al. Racławickie 14, 20-950 Lublin, Poland
{kulicki,trypuz}@kul.pl
[2] Polish Beef Association
ul. Kruczkowskiego 3, 00-380 Warszawa, Poland
jerzy.wierzbicki@pzpbm.pl

Abstract. We present an ontology called *Science* designed for representing scientific laws and rejected hypotheses from scientific papers and experimental results in the area of beef production and consumption. The ontology is designed on the basis of 1) classifications of scientific laws presented in the works of Polish philosophers of science and nature: K. Ajdukiewicz and W. Krajewski and 2) the analysis of empirical material from the project database of articles. *Science* imports *OntoBeef* ontology of the subject domain. Both ontologies, i.e. *Science* and *Onto-Beef*, are based on **DOLCE**. It is shown how to represent scientific laws in the ontologies and how to generate new scientific laws from the old ones coded in the *Science*.

Keywords: ontology, scientific law, livestock, beef.

1 Introduction

Each science researches some specific piece of reality. It commits to the existence of categories of beings in its domain of interest and creates vocabulary enabling to express scientific laws concerning these beings. Ontologies are valuable tools for specifying the meaning of words in such vocabularies.

The most important of scientific activities are observations and experiments which are directed towards discovering and formulating scientific laws. According to Krajewski [7] scientific law is a constant relationship between things (not classes of things), and more precisely, between the qualities possessed by the objects or between events in which the objects participate. We believe that an explicit ontological representation of scientific laws can be useful for browsing the content of scientific papers and for discovering new knowledge.

In this paper, our domain of interest is *beef production and consumption*, being, in fact, an overlap of many sciences, such as cattle feeding and farming, sensory analysis, evaluation of material of animal origin, chemical research, technology and chemistry of meat, marketing and consumer research, economics of

E. Garoufallou and J. Greenberg (Eds.): MTSR 2013, CCIS 390, pp. 430–439, 2013.

consumption and development of green areas. Since 2011 we have been exploring the domain taking part in an interdisciplinary project ProOptiBeef[1]. Within the project, an OWL domain ontology called *OntoBeef* was created.

This paper describes an ontology-based representation of scientific laws within the domain of beef production and consumption by using *OntoBeef* categories.

It is already known that in food and agricultural science ontology serves not only as *lingua franca* for researchers in the area but it is also used as a powerful tool for scientific information especially for efficient and user friendly search support [13,8,12] and expert systems [9]. In the research presented in this paper we are aiming at an ontology based expert system in which knowledge from literature is expressed in terms of ontology to facilitate search and to enable gaining new knowledge.

2   Previous Works

OntoBeef and its applications have been presented in [8,12]. It is an OWL ontology consisting currently of 2349 classes, 96 object properties and 12892 axioms[2]. It is more structured than well known agricultural thesauri such as AGROVOC [2]. Compared to other agricultural ontologies such as ATO, VT, ATOL [6,11,4,5] it focuses on concepts related to beef, but in the same time covers a wider spectrum of phenomena.

OntoBeef is based on an OWL version of DOLCE [10] as a foundational ontology. Let us mention here four top classes of DOLCE important for this paper. DOLCE distinguishes: 1) endurants (i.e. entities 'wholly' present at any time of their existence", e.g., Bovinae), 2) perdurants ('i.e. 'entities that 'happen in time', e.g., Feeding), 3) qualities (i.e. entities that can be perceived or measured, e.g., Tenderness) and 4) regions (i.e. quality spaces providing values used for measuring qualities, e.g., pH).

So far *OntoBeef* has been used as the basis for two applications. The first one is a Java desktop application named Oxpecker (see [8, section V]). It facilitates the access to the database of descriptions of scientific articles, which were collected in the project. The database contains descriptions of around 2800 articles. It collects information about the structure of papers (title, author(s), abstract, etc.) and some content data such as definitions of terms, scientific laws and rejected hypotheses. Oxpecker uses the annotation of articles by IRIs of *OntoBeef* classes to find articles which best match the user's query. The other *OntoBeef*-driven application is a web application which at the beginning served as a thesaurus[3]. It enabled us to search for categories and had a Linked Open Data connections to four external ontologies. Recently the application got some functionalities of Oxpecker and for each *OntoBeef* class it provides the scientific laws which govern its instances. The last of these functionalities is the main subject of this paper and is extensively described below.

---

[1] http://www.prooptibeef.pl/
[2] http://onto.beef.org.pl/ontobeef/owl/Domain.owl
[3] http://onto.beef.org.pl/ontobeef/

3 Science Ontology

Most of the papers, collected in DB of articles created in ProOptiBeef, have proved and disproved statements attached. The statements were extracted from the articles by a group of experts who analyzed the papers within ProOptiBeef project. *OntoBeef* was applied to represent them. For this purpose we have created a new ontology, we called it *Science*[4], which imports *OntoBeef* and uses its classes to express scientific laws.

Currently *Science* provides the taxonomy of scientific laws and its ontological characterization. It does not contain many aspects important for complete characterization of scientific laws; for instance representation of methods, observations, material samples and experimental results is missing in it. We plan to develop richer ontology of science in future works.

The types of scientific laws, we adopted in the project, were taken from the works of Polish philosophers of science and nature: Ajdukiewicz and Krajewski [1,7]. They represent standard, classical views on science which we find appropriate for our task as confluent with the usual practice in the kind of science we deal with. The distinctions proposed by them were analyzed in terms of their use in ontological modeling and reasoning. Then we have chosen the types of laws which are present in our domain of interest and specified their meaning. Some types of laws introduced in [7] (like, for instance, structural laws[5]) have not been taken into account. We would like to note that our specification of meaning of 'ordering law' is slightly different from the original one presented in [1,7]—the difference we shall explain while describing this type of law bellow. We also provided some additional distinctions for example between methodological and objective laws.

Figure 1 depicts the final taxonomy of scientific laws. Below we shall present some examples of laws chosen from our *Science* ontology (so far we have coded 56 scientific laws). For each type of laws we shall present its natural language description (as given by domain experts) and its ontological formalization in RDF or Description Logic.

Let us start with the top distinction between *methodological* and *objective* laws. *Methodological (or Meta-) laws* concern primarily scientific methods which can be used to obtain some knowledge about qualities of things. Qualities of things are concerned secondarily here. An example of meta-law is:

Example 1 (Meta-law)

t1: *Near infra red spectroscopy can be applied for prediction of beef tenderness.*

We represent it in *Science* as below. Let us note that `science` and `domain` are prefixes in the RFD models of *Science* and *OntoBeef*, respectively.

---

[4] http://onto.beef.org.pl/ontobeef/owl/Science.owl
[5] Structural ordering laws state that there is an order of elements in space or in time, e.g. "if a plant has a root and a shoot, then the first one is lower than the second" [7].

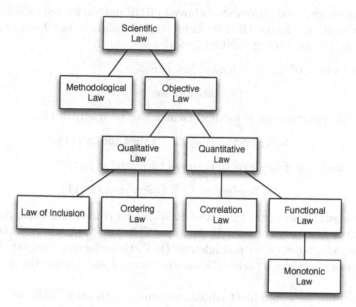

Fig. 1. Taxonomy of scientific laws

```
<owl:NamedIndividual rdf:about="&science;t1">
 <rdf:type rdf:resource="&science;Meta_Law"/>
 <skos:prefLabel xml:lang="en">t1</skos:prefLab>
 <thesisContent xml:lang="en">
    Near infra red spectroscopy can be applied for prediction of beef tenderness.
 </thesisContent>
</owl:NamedIndividual>

<owl:Class rdf:about="&domain;2072">
 <skos:prefLabel xml:lang="en">NIR spectroscopy</skos:prefLab>
 <rdfs:subClassOf>
  <owl:Restriction>
   <owl:onProperty rdf:resource="&science;isMethodIn"/>
   <owl:hasValue rdf:resource="&science;t1"/>
  </owl:Restriction>
  </rdfs:subClassOf>
</owl:Class>

<owl:Class rdf:about="&domain;2213">
 <skos:prefLabel xml:lang="en">beef tenderness</skos:prefLab>
 <rdfs:subClassOf>
  <owl:Restriction>
   <owl:onProperty rdf:resource="&science;isSubjectIn"/>
   <owl:hasValue rdf:resource="&science;t1"/>
  </owl:Restriction>
 </rdfs:subClassOf>
</owl:Class>
```

The same information represented above in RDF model, for readability reason, we shall present in shorter DL-like form (the translation has been performed automatically by the Protégé editor) as follows:

– t1 is an instant of methodological law class:

$$t1 : \text{methodological law}$$

– Each NIR spectroscopy is method (which can be used) in t1:

$$\text{NIR spectroscopy} \sqsubseteq \exists \, \texttt{isMethodIn} \, \{t1\}$$

– Each concrete beef tenderness is subject (of study) in t1:

$$\text{beef tenderness} \sqsubseteq \exists \, \texttt{isSubjectIn} \, \{t1\}$$

Note that `owl:Restriction` part of RDF model containing value restriction `owl:hasValue` is now expressed by formula '$\exists$ `Role` $\{t1\}$', where `Role` stands for some object property, with singleton '$\{t1\}$'. Henceforward, where it will be self-explanatory, we shall prefer the shorter way of expressing the ontological statements.

Another thing we would like to draw the reader's attention is the way we treat scientific laws. Following Krajewski we believe that scientific laws say something primarily about concrete objects (individuals) rather then classes or notions. That is why, while modeling meta-law t1 (and other laws we analyze as the following examples), we stated that 'each concrete beef tenderness is subject (of study) in t1', instead of possible reified, skos-like approach, in which we could have write that 'beef tenderness (as a reified class or a notion) is subject (of study) in t1'.

In spite of the philosophical justification we also have technical reasons to prefer that way of modeling over the reifying classes. Now we can use the *OntoBeef* ontology, which contains multiple relation between its notions and can be used for other purposes, directly in the representation of scientific laws. It makes it possible, among others, to include the presentation of scientific laws in our thesaurus web application in a direct manner.

Objective laws concern primarily objects, not research methodologies. They are divided into *qualitative* and *quantitative* laws. *Qualitative laws* concern primarily endurants or perdurants, while *quantitative* ones concern primarily dependencies between qualities possessed by endurants or perdurants. More precisely, qualitative laws focus on values the qualities have in some quality spaces. Quantitative laws are then divided into *correlation* and *functional* laws.

Correlation law states a correlation between values of qualities, but it is unknown how they are related, i.e. how they influence each other. For this type of law we just state that two (or more) qualities are parameters in it (see example below).

Example 2 (Correlation law)

t2: *There exists a correlation between thermal shortening of meet under thermal treatment and beef thermal loss.*

Its modeling in *Science* is:

- t2 : correlation law
- thermal shortening ⊑ ∃ isParameterIn {t2}
- beef thermal loss ⊑ ∃ isParameterIn {t2}

Functional laws state that a value of one (dependent) quality $C1$ is a function of a value of the other (independent) quality $C2$ (see example below).

Example 3 (Functional law)

t3: *Beef slaughtering season has influence on beef fat acids profile.*

- t3 : functional law
- beef slaughtering season ⊑ ∃ isIndependentParameterIn {t3}
- beef fat acids profile ⊑ ∃ isDependentParameterIn {t3}

If the function is known to be monotonic, function law is a *monotonic* law. Type of monotonicity is expressed by **hasMonotonicTypeRel** object property. It ranges a class with two values, namely: **positive** and **negative**. Let us consider an example below.

Example 4 (Monotonic law)

t4: *Beef tenderness improves with longer aging time.*

Knowledge that t4 is an instance of a class of monotonic law and has positive monotonic type we express in RDF model as follows:

```
<owl:NamedIndividual rdf:about="&science;t4">
  <rdf:type rdf:resource="&science;Monotonic_Law"/>
   <hasMonotonicTypeRel rdf:resource="&science;positive"/>
</owl:NamedIndividual>
```

Then we express the part of characterization a monotonic law inherits from the functional one:

- beef aging time ⊑ ∃ isIndependentParameterIn {t4}
- beef tenderness ⊑ ∃ isDependentParameterIn {t4}

Now let us with to qualitative laws. Among them there are laws of *inclusion* and *ordering* laws. *Laws of inclusion* establishes a subsumption relation between classes of endurants or perdurants.

Example 5 (Inclusion law)

t5: *Bovine serum albumin is the main beef allergen.*

- t5 : inclusive law
- bovine serum albumin ⊑ ∃ isInstantOfSubclassIn {t5}
- beef allergen ⊑ ∃ isInstantOfSuperclassIn {t5}

One may wonder why we use object properties: 'isInstantOfSubclassIn' and 'isInstantOfSuperclassIn ' instead of simply connect classes by 'rdfs:subClassOf'. Our intention behind this ontological choice was to separate a taxonomy of our ontology, which is established after meaning negotiation with our domain experts from a taxonomical knowledge coming from scientific laws. After the experts accept the inclusion law, it becomes a part of ontology and two classes before bound to it are connected by rdfs:subClassOf.

Ordering laws establish an order within a class C of endurants or perdurants. The class is divided into two subclasses $C1$ and $C2$ by a given differentiation factor F – $C1$ is a class of objects C without F and $C2$ is a class of object C with F. It is worth noting that in our modeling of ordering laws, classes $C1$ and $C2$ are not explicitly mentioned. Then it is stated that all objects from class $C1$ have greater (or smaller) values of quality Q then all elements of $C2$. Ordering laws, like monotonic laws, have positive or negative monotonicity. Ordering laws, unlike monotonic laws, do not use number scale to measure quality. Let us consider the following law:

Example 6 (Ordering law)

t6: *Addition of antioxidant to ground beef improves its oxidative stability.*

We formalize this example as follows:

- t6 : ordering law
- ground beef $\sqsubseteq \exists$ isContextIn {t6}
- oxidative stability $\sqsubseteq \exists$ isQualityIn {t6}
- antioxidant $\sqsubseteq \exists$ isDifferentiationFactorIn {t6}
- hasMonotonicTypeRel(t6, positive)

The modeling should be understood as follows: all instances of 'ground beef with addition of antioxidant' have greater values of quality 'oxidative stability' then all instances of 'ground beef without antioxidant'. In short: adding antioxidant to ground beef has a positive impact to its oxidative stability.

We have mentioned above that our understanding an 'ordering law' differs from the original one presented in [1,7]. In our specification of ordering laws, they establish an order between instances of one class of objects with and without differentiation factor. In general ordering laws may establish an order between object of different kind (e.g. we can compare hardness of glass and diamond).

4   Gaining New Knowledge

We use OWL-API application to deduce new scientific laws on the basis of ones already coded in *Science* ontology. Since we present ongoing research, we shall point out only two of possibly many ways of obtaining new knowledge from our ontology.

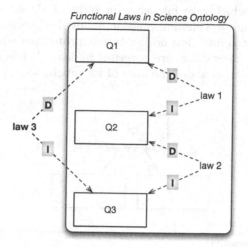

Fig. 2. Application finds a new function law 3 taking into account two already existing in the ontology laws 1 and 2. Dashed arrow with "**D**" ("**I**") is a relation "treats as (in)dependent quality".

The first type of reasoning is illustrated in figure 2. It concerns functional laws. Having two laws in the ontology, e.g. law 1 treating Q1 as dependent quality and Q2 as independent one, and having law 2 treating Q2 as dependent quality and Q3 as independent one, the reasoning system generates a new scientific law (law 3) treating Q1 as dependent quality and Q3 as independent one.

Example 7 (New laws). From two theses present in *Science*:

- rate of glycolysis $\sqsubseteq \exists$ isIndependentParameterIn {t7}
- beef aging time $\sqsubseteq \exists$ isDependentParameterIn {t7}

and

- beef aging time $\sqsubseteq \exists$ isIndependentParameterIn {t4}
- beef tenderness $\sqsubseteq \exists$ isDependentParameterIn {t4}

our application infers a law:

- rate of glycolysis $\sqsubseteq \exists$ isIndependentParameterIn {t-new}
- beef tenderness $\sqsubseteq \exists$ isDependentParameterIn {t-new}

New laws found by the application are intended to be verified by the domain experts and if accepted, will be added to the list of laws.

The second type of reasoning is a 'reverse inheritance' of scientific laws. It is illustrated in figure 3. Let us consider class C1 with two children C2 and C3 and assume that C1 is not governed by any scientific law in our ontology, whereas C2 and C3 are governed by scientific laws: 1 and 2 respectively. In this situation our system signalizes that although there is no law governing all instances of

C1, there are laws which take into account some of them. System points out the subclass of C1 and provides information about the laws governing them. For instance, "sensory attribute" has no law in our prototype, whereas its subclass "beef tenderness" or "beef color" are governed by laws. While browsing "sensory attribute" system informs about the laws of its subclasses.

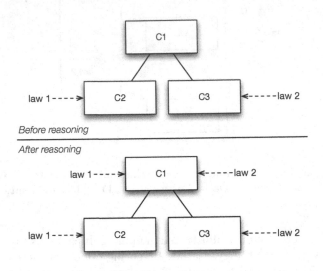

Fig. 3. Application signalizes existence of laws considering subclasses of given class

5   Conclusions and Further Work

We presented an ontology of scientific laws appropriate for agricultural and food science and the way in which the results of research from scientific papers can be represented in it. Ontological representation enables efficient and precise search within the set of represented scientific laws. It also leads to new knowledge obtained by connecting laws from articles and ontology.

Further works include ontological connection of scientific laws with the database of scientific papers and with a repository of experimental results, which is developed within ProOptiBeef project. Another direction is to study mutual support and conflicts between theses expressed in the papers from the database. We plan to apply there the ontology of beliefs presented in [3].

We are also planning to enhanced *Science* ontology by representation of methods, observations, material samples and experimental results.

Acknowledgments. Research was realized within the Project no. WND-POIG. 01.03.01-00-204/09 Optimizing of Beef Production in Poland According to "from Fork to Farm" Strategy co-financed by the European Regional Development Fund under the Innovative Economy Operational Programme 2007 – 2013.

We would like to also thank Paweł Garbacz for his help in creation of science ontology and the anonymous referees for useful comments on the earlier version of the paper.

References

1. Ajdukiewicz, K.: Pragmatic Logic. Reidel, Dordrecht (1974)
2. Caracciolo, C., Stellato, A., Morshed, A., Johannsen, G., Rajbhandari, S., Jaques, Y., Keizer, J.: The agrovoc linked dataset. Semantic Web 4(3), 341–348 (2013)
3. Garbacz, P., Lechniak, M., Kulicki, P., Trypuz, R.: Do you still want to vote for your favorite politician? Ask Ontobella! In: FOMI, pp. 102–113 (2009)
4. Golik, W., et al.: ATOL: The Multi-species Livestock Trait Ontology. In: Dodero, J.M., Palomo-Duarte, M., Karampiperis, P. (eds.) MTSR 2012. CCIS, vol. 343, pp. 289–300. Springer, Heidelberg (2012)
5. Hocquette, J.F., Capel, C., David, V., Guéméné, D., Bidanel, J., Ponsart, C., Gastinel, P.L., Le Bail, P.Y., Monget, P., Mormede, P., Barbezant, M., Guillou, F., Peyraud, J.L.: Objectives and applications of phenotyping network setup for livestock. Animal Science Journal 83(7), 517–528 (2012)
6. Hughes, L.M., Bao, J., Hu, Z.-L., Honavar, V., Reecy, J.M.: Animal trait ontology: The importance and usefulness of a unified trait vocabulary for animal species. Journal of Animal Science 86(6), 1485–1491 (2008)
7. Krajewski, W.: Prawa nauki - przegląd zagadnień metodologicznych. Książka i Wiedza (1982)
8. Kulicki, P., Trypuz, R., Wierzbicki, J.: Towards beef production and consumption ontology and its application. In: Proceedings of FedCSIS, pp. 483–488 (2012)
9. Maliappis, M.T.: Applying an agricultural ontology to web-based applications. International Journal of Metadata, Semantics and Ontologies 4, 133–140 (2009)
10. Masolo, C., Borgo, S., Gangemini, A., Guarino, N., Oltramari, A., Schneider, L.: The WonderWeb Library of Fundational Ontologies and the DOLCE ontology. WonderWeb Deliverable D18, Final Report (vr. 1.0. 31-12-2003). Technical report, ISTC-CNR (2003)
11. Park, C.A., Bello, S.M., Smith, C.L., Hu, Z.-L., Munzenmaier, D.H., Nigam, R., Smith, J.R., Shimoyama, M., Eppig, J.T., Reecy, J.M.: The vertebrate trait ontology: A controlled vocabulary for the annotation of trait data across species. Journal of Biomedical Semantics 4(13) (2013)
12. Trójczak, R., Trypuz, R., Gradzki, P., Wierzbicki, J., Wozniak, A.: Evaluation of beef production and consumption ontology and presentation of its actual and potential applications. In: Proceedings of FedCSIS (2013)
13. Vila, K., Ferrández, A.: Developing an ontology for improving question answering in the agricultural domain. In: Sartori, F., Sicilia, M.Á., Manouselis, N. (eds.) MTSR 2009. CCIS, vol. 46, pp. 245–256. Springer, Heidelberg (2009)

Semantic Shared Spaces for Task Allocation in a Robotic Fleet for Precision Agriculture

Domagoj Drenjanac[1], Lukas Klausner[2], Eva Kühn[2],
and Slobodanka Dana Kathrin Tomic[1]

[1] The Telecommunications Research Center Vienna (FTW), Vienna, Austria
{drenjanac,tomic}@ftw.at
[2] Institute of Computer Languages, Vienna University of Technology, Vienna, Austria
eva@complang.tuwien.ac.at, lukas@palu.at

Abstract. Task allocation is a fundamental problem in multi-robot systems where heterogeneous robots cooperate to perform a complex mission. A general requirement in a task allocation algorithm is to find an optimal set of robots to execute a certain task. This paper describes how coordination capabilities of the space-based middleware are extended with the semantic model of robot capabilities to improve the process of selection in terms of flexibility, scalability and reduced communication overhead during task allocation. We developed a framework that translates resources into a newly defined semantic model and performs automatic reasoning to assist the task allocation. We conducted performance tests in a specific precision agriculture use case based on the robotic fleet for weed control elaborated within European Project RHEA-Robot Fleets for Highly Effective Agriculture and Forestry Management.

Keywords: Task Allocation, Space-Based Computing, Semantics, Robotic Fleet.

1 Introduction

Today cooperating robots are commonly used in controlled and structured environments, such as factories, where they are managed from a central place that supervises mission execution. Due to the advances in the perception and locomotion technology there is a great potential to use multiple cooperating robots in heterogeneous and unstructured environments. This however imposes new requirements on communication and coordination of actions in teams, and the well-established centralized coordination approach needs to either be enhanced or replaced with a distributed approach.

Task allocation is a fundamental problem in multi-robot systems where the core requirement is to find an optimal set of heterogeneous robots that have to cooperate in order to execute a complex mission [1]. Critical enabler for distributed task allocation is an efficient coordination. The shared space-based coordination model defines a centralized tuple space as a shared message repository exploiting generative communication among processes. This work extends coordination capabilities of the space-based middleware XVSM (eXtensible Virtual Shared Memory) [2], [3], particular its

E. Garoufallou and J. Greenberg (Eds.): MTSR 2013, CCIS 390, pp. 440–446, 2013.

Java-based implementation MozartSpaces. XVSM is based on a Linda [4] tuple space model. Our framework, Semantic MozartSpaces [5] introduces a new data model based on RDF and SPARQL where RDF is used to construct nested blank nodes in a triple store and SPARQL facilitates query and update interactions with the triple store.

The remainder of this paper is structured as follows: Section 2 introduces motivating use-case while section 3 summarizes related work. Section 4 presents developed approach, section 5 evaluates the framework, and finally section 6 concludes the paper and presents future work.

2   Precision Farming as a Motivating Scenario

Precise management of agricultural land is aimed to diminish the use of chemical inputs and improve crop quality, humans' safety, and reduce production costs by using a fleet of heterogeneous robots equipped with advanced sensors and actuators.

Precision farming scenario introduced in the RHEA project [6] provides motivation for presented work. The scenario starts with the field inspection facilitated by two aerial mobile units equipped with high-resolution cameras taking the field photos to elicit growth stage of a crop and the diffusion of the weed. After that, the centralized fleet management system assists the system operator in choosing a suitable strategy for field treatment taking into account weed infestation map and available field robots, their implements and sensors. The selection of the treatment strategy takes into account many parameters, e.g., the type of tasks to be performed, the number and features of available robots and field information. The treatment strategy can be applied in two use cases: (1) when a weed infestation map is known in advance and all tasks are defined before a mission starts (e.g., spraying in a wheat field), and (2) when there is no weed infestation map and weed patches (tasks) are identified (using a camera mounted on a tractor) during a mission execution (corn field).

3   Related Work

The use of semantics in task and resource modeling in robotics systems is an emergent research field. In [7] authors explore a novel usage of semantic information for an improvement of a task planning in complex scenarios, e.g., robots operating in unstructured environments with a great number of objects. In [8] authors study joint collaboration of Web Service paradigm and ontology for a service discovery, composition and a task allocation. In their solution all entities expose their functionalities as Web Services allowing their discovery and composition. Our work differs from the reviewed work as we use semantic approach for both the resource and task modeling. Rational for using semantic is twofold: (1) it provides the basis for policy-based automatic mapping between task requirements and available resources and thus makes the whole process more flexible and (2) it provides a general task description language that most of the reviewed frameworks lack.

Several research projects as well as commercial products have adopted the space-based model to construct robust coordination platforms. Linda made the shared space-based coordination model popular, where the tuple space consists of tuples that can be concurrently accessed by several processes. Semantic Tuple Spaces [9] (sTuples) use a web ontology language OWL for describing and matching resources. Semantic Web Spaces [10] are based on a Linda-inspired coordination model integrated with core semantic technologies such as RDF and it is utilized for coordination between agents sharing semantic data. Our work is based on an open source implementation of the Space Container [11] approach called MozartSpaces. The comparative advantage of the MozartsSpaces over the other space-based implementations is that it structures the space into containers that store entries (tuples) using different coordination patterns. Our semantic extension of the MozartSpaces borrows some concepts from the Semantic Tuple Centres [12], which treats a semantic tuple as an object of an application domain. However, while Sematic Tuple Centres has its own data format for exchanging semantic tuples and queries, we use Turtle and SPARQL. In contrast, in our solution tuples do not have a mandatory public reference.

4   Semantic Extension for MozartSpaces

This section gives an architecture overview of the Semantic MozartSpaces. The core part of the architecture is the data model that exposes a mapping process between MozartSpaces and semantic entries. The basic concept is a container hosted in a single runtime instance of the space where a container is addressable by its URL and therefore can be accessed as any other resource on the Internet. A container hosts different entries where the value of an entry is an object with several properties.

Fig. 1 illustrates the usage of the Semantic MozartSpaces. On client-side the instances of Java classes (e.g., class Task) are created and the resource mapper, a component that maps a Java object to nested blank nodes, translates them into their Turtle representations (nested blank nodes), and writes them into the container. When the entry is written in the container, it is assigned an internal ID. This ID is used to generate a URI that identifies the entry. Vice versa, at client-side the nested blank node can be taken from the container and translated into the Java class instance.

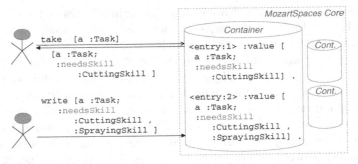

Fig. 1. Take and write semantic entries from Semantic MozartSpaces

The advantage of Semantic MozartSpaces is that SPARQL queries can be used for entry selection (take operation in Fig. 1). Additionally, such queries enable the

context that can be added at client-side, or it can be achieved via a pre-aspect of the container (server-side). Context entries can be used as a parameter for SPARQL queries, so that more general and flexible queries are supported, e.g., in our use case a context entry can describe the state of a robot.

5   Experimental Environment and Results

The described implementation has been tested to acquire initial efficiency measurements, i.e., to determine the expected performances and scalability of the Semantic MozartSpaces and to identify potential optimization areas. A simple experimental setup resembles the RHEA scenario: we simulate a user that generates tasks for the mission. The tasks require some skills, e.g., a spraying, a flaming or a cutting skill or their combination. Robots (executors) select tasks for execution based on matching between their skills and task requirements. We evaluated performance of the spaces in two scenarios: (1) when tasks are simultaneously produced and executed and (2) when first all tasks are produced and then executed. After that, we tested system scalability by adding more executors, from 3 to 14, for the same number of tasks, and evaluated system performances. One simplification of the evaluation scenario as compared to the real world is related to the task duration which is 2500 ms (correspond to approximately 4 meters trajectory of a robot moving at 6km/h).

Fig. 2 shows how the number of executors and tasks influences execution time in the scenario where tasks are simultaneously produced and executed. The results show that the execution time increases when the number of tasks increases. Conversely, it decreases when new executors are added. Execution time decreases by approximately 30% when two executors are added, 5 in total, and is decreased by additional 40% when 3 more executors are added, 8 in total. Adding 6 more executors, reduces the execution time by approximately additional 40%. 14 executors perform 5 times faster than 3 executors (they finish 600 tasks in 130 s and 3 executors in 650 s).

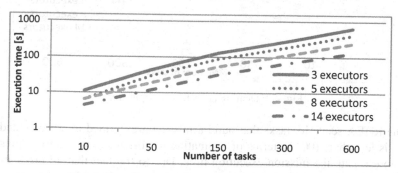

Fig. 2. Simultaneously producing and executing tasks

In the scenario where the tasks are first produced and then executed, specific amount of a time is needed to generate a desired number of tasks. Fig. 3 shows how the production time behaves when a number of produced tasks increases. The production time slowly increases, stays around 1 s, when the number of tasks is less than 100 and increases faster when the number of produced tasks is higher than 100, e.g., it is around 1 s for 5 tasks, and around 5 s for 600 tasks.

Fig. 4 shows how the number of executors and tasks influences execution time in the scenario where tasks are first produced and then executed. Execution times, when multiple executors are deployed, converge when there are more than 300 tasks. E.g., 8 executors perform 50 tasks in 18 s and 600 in 410 s where 14 perform 50 tasks in 10 s and 600 in 380 s. We detected that 14 executors don't outperform 8 executors, especially when there are more than 300 tasks. This is due to complex scheduling mechanisms in the MozartSpaces and Jena. Moreover, the scenario where tasks are produced and then executed scales worse than the one where tasks are simultaneously produced and executed. E.g., in the later scenario 14 executors perform 600 tasks in 130 s, and in the former in 380 s.

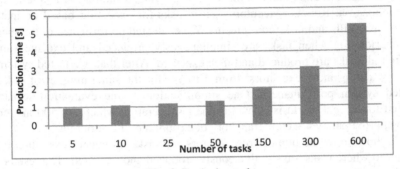

Fig. 3. Producing tasks

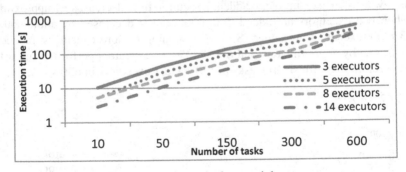

Fig. 4. Executing tasks from a triple store

In the RHEA scenario, tasks that build a mission are defined in advance and their number is less than 100. In terms of estimating performance, we can use presented results to estimate the mission execution time. Due to the fact that all tasks are produced in advance, we choose simulation results from Fig. 3 and Fig. 4 to predict the execution time. First, we estimate a time to produce 100 tasks to 1,5 s (Fig. 3) and then use Fig. 4 to select the optimal number of executors. Logical choice would be to select 14 executors since they have lowest execution time. However, for real robots utilized in RHEA it is expensive to add new units. Therefore, we choose to execute the mission using 3 available executors where the time to complete the mission is around 90 s (corresponds to 150 m trajectory), in total 91,5 s (1,5 s for production and the rest for execution). It is worth to notice that the execution time depends on a time that executor needs to perform a task, 2500 ms. Extending the awareness of the robots in the RHEA scenario adds flexibility in task selection; however quantification of this benefit requires more elaborate task model which is out of the scope of this paper and is part of our future work.

6   Conclusion and Future Work

The integration of the space-based paradigm with underlying semantics provided a robust and scalable middleware for a task allocation in multi-robot systems. Developed data model automatically translates annotated java classes, i.e., tasks and resources, to RDF nested blank nodes and stores them to underlying triple store. Furthermore, we have demonstrated how the framework behaves in the RHEA scenario where a set of robots execute specific tasks and how the execution time depends on an insertion of new resources. To conclude, simulations we did can serve as a starting point for predicting mission duration in various scenarios.

Future work will mainly focus on modeling a more elaborate task model that we expect to simplify coordination and task allocation issues in more complex scenarios. Tasks will define location parameters that correspond to geographical representation of an area in a field where a task has to be performed. Additionally, we will study how geographical distribution of a central task repository influences mission duration, communication and coordination patterns between robots.

References

1. Brahmi, Z., Gammoudi, M.M.: Semantic shared space-based complex tasks allocation method for massive MAS. In: Proc. of 2nd Int. Conf. on Computer Science and Information Tech., Beijing (2009)
2. Craß, S.: A formal model of the Extensible Virtual Shared Memory (XVSM) and its implementation in Haskell:Design and specification. Vienna University of Technology (2010)
3. Craß, S., Kühn, E., Salzer, G.: Algebraic Foundation of a Data Model for an Extensible Space-Based Collaboration Protocol. In: 13th Int. Database Engineering and Application Sym., Calabria, Italy (2009)
4. Gelernter, D.: Generative Communication in Linda. ACM Computing Survey (1985)
5. Klausner, L.: Semantic XVSM – design and implementation. Master Thesis, Vienna University of Technology (in progress)
6. RHEA project, http://www.rhea-project.eu/
7. Galindo, C., Fernandez-Madrigal, J.A., Gonzalez, J., Saffiotti, A.: Using Semantic Information for Improving Efficiency of Robot Task Planning. In: Proc. of ICRA Workshop on Semantic Information in Robotics, Rome, Italy (2007)
8. Mokarizadeh, S., Grosso, A., Matskin, M., Kungas, P., Haseeb, A.: Applying Semantic Web Service Composition for Action Planning in Multi-Robot Systems. In: 4th Int. Conf. on Internet and Web Application Services, Venice, Italy (2009)

9. Khushraj, D., Lassila, O., Finin, T.: sTuples: Semantic Tuple Spaces. In: Proc. of 1st Int. Conf. on Mobile and Ubiquitous Systems: Networking and Service, Boston, USA (2004)

10. Nixon, L., Simperl, E.P.B., Antonechko, O., Tolksdorf, R.: Towards Semantic Tuplespace Computing: The Semantic Web Spaces System. In: Symposium on Applied Computing, Seoul, Korea (2007)

11. Kühn, E., Mordinyi, R., Keszthelyi, L., Schreiber, C.: Introducing the Concept of Customizable Structured Spaces for Agent Coordination in the Production Automation Domain. In: Proc. 8th Int. Conf. Autonomous AgentsMultiagent Systems, Budapest, Hungary (2009)

12. Nardini, E., Omicini, A., Viroli, M.: Semantic tuple centres. J. Sci. Comput. Program. 78 (2013)

Author Index

Agathos, Michail 384
Allocca, Carlo 289
Álvarez-Rodríguez, Jose María 175, 315
Arapi, Polyxeni 361
Aschauer, Christian 408
Asderi, Stella 246
Auer, Wolfgang 408

Balatsoukas, Panos 246
Bardi, Alessia 35
Bekiari, Chryssoula 289
Belmonte, Javier 60
Blumer, Eliane 60
Bountris, Effie 22
Bursa, Okan 213

Can, Ozgu 146, 213
Candela, Leonardo 289
Caracciolo, Caterina 423
Christodoulakis, Stavros 361
Christodoulou, Yannis 22
Chuttur, Mohammad Yasser 135
Conway, Mike C. 14, 87

de Torcy, Antoine 87
Dodero, Juan Manuel 258
Doerr, Martin 289
Douza, Maria 22
Drenjanac, Domagoj 440
Durco, Matej 163

Ell, Basil 277

Fafalios, Pavlos 289
Fensel, Anna 408
Foulonneau, Muriel 234

García-Barriocanal, Elena 266
Garoufallou, Emmanouel 1, 246
Geser, Guntram 423
Giese, Martin 201
Greenberg, Jane 1, 14

Handler, Franz 408
Horrocks, Ian 201

Jimenez-Ruiz, Ernesto 201

Kalokyri, Varvara 361
Kalou, Aikaterini K. 48
Kapidakis, Sarantos 384
Karagiannidis, Charalampos 111
Karampiperis, Pythagoras 75
Kärberg, Tarvo 373
Keizer, Johannes 423
Kharlamov, Evgeny 201
King, David 355
Klausner, Lukas 440
Konstantinou, Nikolaos 342
Korfiatis, Nikolaos 225
Koukourikos, Antonis 75
Koutsomiha, Damiana 246
Koutsomitropoulos, Dimitrios A. 48
Kühn, Eva 440
Kulicki, Piotr 430
Kyprianos, Konstantinos 330

L'Abate, Giovanni 423
Labra-Gayo, José Emilio 175, 315
La Bruzzo, Sandro 35
Lagoze, Carl 123

Madalli, Devika P. 414
Makris, Konstantinos 361
Manghi, Paolo 35
Manolis, Nikos 361
Manouselis, Nikos 99, 111
Marketakis, Yannis 289
Martin, Sébastien 234
Minadakis, Nikos 289
Mitrou, Nikolas 342
Moore, Reagan 14
Morse, David R. 355

Nogales, Alberto 266
Nogueras-Iso, Javier 302

Ordoñez de Pablos, Patricia 175, 315
Otte, Marcel 408

Palavitsinis, Nikos   111
Palomo-Duarte, Manuel   258
Papadakis, Ioannis   330
Papatheodorou, Christos   396
Paraskeuopoulos, Kostas   246
Patkos, Theodore   289
Patsakis, Constantinos   152
Pesce, Valeria   423
Praczyk, Piotr   302

Rajabi, Enayat   67
Ricci, Fabio   60
Riegler, Thomas   408
Rittberger, Marc   277
Rojas, Sarah Leon   361
Rousidis, Dimitris   246
Ruiz-Rube, Iván   258
Russell, Terrell G.   87

Salampasis, Michail   6
Sánchez-Alonso, Salvador   67, 266
Savrami, Katia   22
Schindler, Christoph   277
Schneider, René   60
Schulmeister, Klemens Gregor   408
Sezer, Emine   213
Sfakakis, Michalis   396
Sicilia, Miguel-Angel   67, 266
Skevakis, Giannis   361
Skjæveland, Martin G.   201
Solomou, Georgia D.   48
Soylu, Ahmet   201
Spanos, Dimitrios-Emmanuel   342

Stoitsis, Giannis   75
Stoitsis, John   361

Tomic, Slobodanka Dana Kathrin   408,
    440
Traverso, Ignacio   258
Trójczak, Rafał   430
Trypuz, Robert   430
Tsiflidou, Effie   99
Tudhope, Douglas   188
Turki, Slim   234
Tzitzikas, Yannis   289

Umashankar, Nalini   169
Unalir, Murat Osman   213

Vafopoulos, Michail   315
Vilhuber, Lars   123
Vlachidis, Andreas   188

Ward, Jewel H.   87
Whitton, Mary   14
Wierzbicki, Jerzy   430
Willliams, Jeremy   123
Windhouwer, Menzo   163
Woźniak, Alicja   430

Xu, Hao   87

Yannopoulos, Angelos   22

Zapounidou, Sofia   396
Zhang, Le   14
Zheleznyakov, Dmitriy   201
Zigomitros, Athanasios   152